THE TACTICS OF PSYCHOTHERAPY

THE TACTICS
OF
PSYCHOTHERAPY

The Application of Psychoanalytic
Theory to Psychotherapy

WILLIAM F. MURPHY, M.D.

INTERNATIONAL UNIVERSITIES PRESS, INC.
New York   New York

Manufactured in the United States of America

CONTENTS

PREFACE

Psychoanalytically based psychotherapies are made up of a primary analytic element and a secondary element of educational retraining therapy. The analytic portion is exploratory in nature and concerned mainly with undoing repressions and making the unconscious roots of the patient's problems conscious. The educational part is more concerned with manifest situational problems. This book is concerned with the sector psychotherapy of F. Deutsch, which places a minimal accent upon the educational aspects. It is therefore, a psychotherapy that most closely resembles psychoanalysis and makes a maximum use of the enormous clinical experience embodied in present day psychoanalytic theories. Psychoanalytic therapy is designed mainly for the neuroses. That the psychoanalytic approach can be used at all with other cases is due to the presence of a neurotic element in practically all cases. It is this element that is amenable to influence. Psychotic elements can be treated by psychotherapy only indirectly.

Most methods of teaching psychotherapy stress the necessity for learning how to listen. Although this is important, a passive attitude to the listening process is often endowed with a magic therapeutic efficacy that it does not possess. Therapists should be taught how to be active in their approach to therapy while they are taught how to listen. The two processes are not mutually exclusive. Chaotic masses of verbalized feelings need to be organized and integrated. The good therapist must actively aid the patient to do this. He must also help the patient to recognize and express as well as accept and control his feelings, and understand them in terms of their origin and meaning. This is best done by the type of word feedback used in sector psychotherapy, where certain affect-laden words of the patient are persistently explored and re-echoed. In this manner the unconscious feeling states that hide behind common verbal imagery can be developed, made conscious and more amenable to control. This is a necessary prelude to the resolution of the contradictory feelings always found in the neurotic patient.

vii

A therapist is like a guide conducting a tourist through a large and populous country with a rich historical past and a complex culture. He must know the history and topography of the land thoroughly and be able to organize the trip according to the available time, age and interests of the tourist. Short-term psychotherapy is like a quick dash through the main cities, museums and chief places of interest. In contrast to psychoanalysis, the country is less thoroughly explored and only a smattering of the language of the inhabitants is learned. The works of Freud and condensations of the psychoanalytic literature, such as Fenichel's outline, are like useful guidebooks. The plans for the "trip" can often be developed around the material in the first few interviews. When the itinerary is not well planned and executed with some degree of precision, confusion, fatigue and boredom tend to complicate the therapeutic picture. A plan for any journey must also be flexible and allow for unforeseen circumstances.

Some teachers have hesitated to teach psychoanalysis to psychiatrists in any but the most superficial sense. They discourage the reading and application of psychoanalytic theory because of the ease with which such material can be misused or misunderstood without the benefit of a personal analysis. Sector psychotherapy offers the psychiatrist who is forced to do without formal psychoanalytic training an opportunity to become better acquainted with some of the clinical know-how and truths of psychoanalysis. It enables the research worker to examine evidence which will show him in a convincing manner the rationality of psychoanalytic constructs. It also makes the medical student and resident therapist aware that psychoanalysis is practical and clinically oriented.

Guidance is a necessary part of all therapeutic interview techniques and is done almost exclusively by means of verbal communication. Some therapists have tended to stress the influence of nonverbal cues. No one will deny their importance. An awareness of these, confidence in his method of therapy, tact, kindliness, serenity, patience, a large fund of humor and empathic understanding, and above all a love of the truth and a strong intellectual curiosity about all kinds of people—these qualities are all valuable for a therapist and helpful in getting, keeping and aiding patients. However, for teaching purposes, they are secondary to verbal communication techniques. It is doubtful if these qualities can be taught. Such character traits are developed early in life and vary from day to day. If they are present, a good teacher may develop or intensify them, but if a therapist is truly deficient in any of these areas, only psychoanalysis can possibly alter the picture. Many therapists are barred from such help, however, because it is unavailable or ineffective for one reason or another. It is probably unnecessary for a gifted few. Verbal communication techniques can be easily taught and relatively easily mastered. As in learning a new language, this book can only instruct the beginner in fundamentals. Fluency and ease will come with practice and inherent talent.

A psychotherapist is called upon to reconstruct the lives of his patients to a greater or lesser degree. Every symptom is based on one or more character traits and no symptom will be abandoned for long without a modification of these traits. To change character it is necessary to change an individual's perception of himself and the world inside and outside of himself. To paraphrase Edel (1961), the patient must be made to revise his own history and see himself more objectively than he has ever done before. It is necessary to take the enormous amount of verbal material that is offered and emphasize unnoticed details, remove and replace accents, enlarge minor areas of interest and shrink others, even major ones. The therapist works always through cooperation with the healthy and objective portions of the patient's personality. Such portions are presumably always present. To achieve a lasting change the therapist must have a large measure of objectivity himself. A main task of the therapist is to reduce a fragmentation of the patient's psyche in terms of the past and present, self-concerns and bodily concerns, and feelings for things and for persons. The tendency to develop dissociation and fragmentation of the personality and object relationships exists from the beginning of ego development and is the chief adversary of the synthesizing and integrating ego tendencies with which the therapist must ally himself. The mechanisms of displacement, denial and repression are the chief means by which fragmentation and dissociation of the ego are maintained. Every therapist must become familiar with the way these mechanisms operate in the interview situation. These verbatim recordings are evidence that modern dynamic psychotherapy is a derivative of clinical psychoanalysis. Only psychoanalysis has come close to organizing and making understandable the type of case material ordinarily obtained from patients. Organization is not the same as explanation but is a necessary prerequisite. Sector psychotherapy is based upon everyday experience with interviews such as these. What appears to be true today can never be based upon permanent facts. There is a changeable element that varies from decade to decade. Like all science, psychotherapy is subject to fashion and changes in emphasis. Professedly it should be founded on observation alone without undue influence by fashion, politics, religion, philosophy or imagination, but this is only an ideal. It is hoped that other schools of psychiatry will be encouraged to publish complete records of their interviews with patients so that alternative explanations, theories and emphases can be examined. In this manner the practice of psychotherapy might be aided or developed along rational lines.

Sector psychotherapy as a method of exploration combined with treatment is safe. It does not disturb a precarious emotional equilibrium, precipitate psychoses, etc. Much nonsense has been written concerning psychiatrogenic illnesses precipitated by treatment. Many who consider psychotherapy as unable to alter a mental disturbance for the better are more than willing to credit it with the blame for any adverse developments. Many articles on psychotherapy stress the harmful effects of "deep analysis" without the slightest idea of what "deep" means or respect for the complex mechanisms of defense of even the most feeble ego. A therapist's influence, like the voice of reason, is always faint. Any influence, whether negative or positive, must be repeated many times before it takes effect. When the therapist has been well trained, the positive influences will always far outweigh the negative.

Symptom removal practically always produces anxiety, depression, or both, since symptoms defend the patient from these feelings. No character analysis can be effective without the production of anxiety and depression as well as somatic and other types of symptoms. The therapist looks upon these symptoms as a sign of progress and learns to direct the patient's energies toward other and more adequate solutions of the ever-present problems concerning wishes that must be curtailed or modified by inner or outer circumstances. In the long run the neurotic patient must learn how to mourn, forgive, forget, renounce and try again. Injured pride or narcissism is the therapist's most common obstacle, rather than instinctual needs and moral inhibitions.

The large measure of uncertainty and the inherently tentative nature of our knowledge of psychopathological processes have led many therapists into an uncritical acceptance of psychoanalytic theory and technical procedures. This is owing less to conviction than to the fact that there are few if any alternative theories of personality structure available that have such an enormous clinical background of observable facts to support them. A study of these examples of sector therapy should be of help in placing such faith on a firmer footing.

The greatest potential value of a good working theory of psychopathology lies in the possibility of rational progress and a systematic growth in knowledge. A critical appraisal of pooled clinical experience in the light of such a theory is only possible when the reporting of the evidence is objective. Modern recording techniques permit this type of objectivity to a far greater extent than mere case reports where conscious and unconscious bias can be expected and suspected. Recordings have a healthy reality about them that permits constructive criticism. All interviews are full of "stuff" that willy-nilly can be or is developed or manipulated, and a recording exposes the way this is done as no other method can. Psychotherapists are inherent manipulators and the technique of psychotherapy can best be taught by showing in detail how manipulation is accomplished and why it is necessary. In psychotherapy all calculation and manipulation should be subservient to one end, which is to help the patient in his struggle with his past unsolved conflicts. This is embodied in and expressed in terms of a present struggle with himself and the environment around him. The therapist has to help the patient organize various aspects of his self-relationships in the service of human relationships so that he can experience the creative power of love and minimize the destructive power of hate. The well-trained and experienced therapist has few illusions about what love really is and realizes that his task is so to reconcile a patient with himself and the disappointing past that his efforts in the present to obtain self-love can succeed. Obtaining a reasonable amount of love from others is usually a by-product of this accomplishment. Only when a person can take the experience of involvement with himself seriously can he become seriously involved with others.

Psychotherapy, regardless of accents and fashions in theory, works principally with abstract patterns of relationship. Modern physicists have acknowledged that the constituents into which matter has been analyzed are only hypothetical interactions. We are compelled to recognize that the concepts of mental health and disease are also best understood in terms of hypothetical interactions. Psychoanalysis has done the best job so far in organizing, naming and describing these interactions. It appears that most of the great discoveries have been made and the principal task now is the application of these psychoanalytic findings to psychotherapy in such a manner that it will be available for therapeutic purposes to nonanalysts. This implies that for a while there will be a greater need for psychoanalytic technical knowledge applicable to psychotherapy than for theory that has no direct clinical use. Therapists who have not been psychoanalyzed themselves will give their loyalty to a technique only when they are able to apply it themselves and obtain conviction through the experience that it works. Sector psychotherapy works to the extent that it strengthens the ego of the patient through the reintegration of repressed and dissociated material. It also helps the therapist by giving him an ever-increasing general understanding of patients' unconscious needs, hopes and fears.

In addition to the novice and resident, there is a rapidly growing number of graduate psychiatrists who have already had extensive experience in psychotherapy and who wish to improve their technique. All therapists need to acquire a practical understanding of how unconscious thoughts and feelings and ego defense mechanisms operate. They also need practice in detecting important patterns of behavior in terms of symptom development and use in order to develop an ability to appraise realistically what can and cannot be done for patients. Both the novice and the experienced therapist can learn how to construct and use psychoanalytic concepts only through repeated experience with their sophisticated use by others.

Therapists of all dynamic schools subscribe to a belief in the importance of the unconscious in determining symptom and destiny but too often recognize its manifestations only when they are obvious. The unconscious is revealed continually in the everyday interview situation as well as in dreams, fantasies and slips of speech. It is necessary for a therapist to learn how to listen at many levels even if the practical use of the material disclosed is contraindicated. This book has been written in the belief that listening with the "third ear" can be learned and developed by practice.

In spite of the large number of articles and books that have been written about psychotherapy, there have been few that have conveyed explicitly the verbal techniques employed by the therapist with his patients. A detailed presentation and theoretical discussion of the technique of the clinical interview was published by Dr. Felix Deutsch in collaboration with the present author (1955). Since then, additional teaching experience has demonstrated that there are many tactical areas concerning theory and technique of the interview in a psychotherapeutic context that need to be re-emphasized, amplified, discussed and illustrated. The student therapist needs to be taught how to obtain information by reading between the lines of what a person says and how to recognize the difference between what a patient says and what he means. In many teaching centers too little attention has been paid to teaching the technique of psychotherapy and too much has been made of therapeutic generalities. The evaluation of individual technique and day-to-day work with patients has been relatively neglected owing principally to a shortage in teaching personnel and inherent difficulties in teaching psychotherapy. Although this condition has been remedied in many teaching centers, much remains to be done. Without the ability to evaluate his own treatment procedures critically, a graduate psychiatrist, no matter how able, cannot obtain worth-while satisfaction from the results of his labors and keep up with what is expected of him by his patients. The student therapist should also be taught that a sound technique does not preclude naturalness and humanity and that the finest degree of rationality, scientific investigation and judgment can be used in the context of a warm, human relationship. The most disturbing feature of present-day teaching of psychotherapy is its fragmentation. This is especially true of therapy supervision, where a student is allowed to go it alone and then report to a supervisor who receives an idealized summary of what has gone on between the therapist and patient. Although the blind spots and personal biases of the therapist can be readily detected by a competent supervisor, they can seldom be modified. The development of unobtrusive tape recorders now allows the therapist to listen to his patients more observantly and the supervisor to hear what is going on in a manner that was never before possible. The recording of interviews places a stress on technique which is invaluable for beginners who are all too prone to repeat idiosyncratic mistakes until they become classified as valuable personal experience. Taping for teaching purposes needs to be done only occasionally. It is not a substitute for good supervision. It is especially important in the case of the initial interview, which so often contains the key to the structure of the case and the entire psychotherapeutic plan and outlook. Recording allows freedom from note taking. Both procedures have definite disadvantages and abuses but are useful for the student and the research worker. Just as the therapist deals mainly with the fantasies of his patients, the supervisor deals to a degree with the fantasies of his students about their patients. Recordings in any case can help to establish a more objective approach to treatment procedures and demonstrate that what is heard determines theory as well as vice versa.

The student who has studied *The Clinical Interview* will find his understanding of the case material in this book considerably enhanced. An effort has been made to present cases of graded complexity with a stress upon anxiety states in hysterical personalities, as such cases are more commonly encountered and more easily comprehended than many others. Above all, an effort has been made to illustrate the importance of the role of loss and pathological mourning in the etiology of mental illness. All of the cases were seen in a clinic where the fee was established by other personnel. The recording was done openly and occasioned no comment. Anxiety about recording is ordinarily experienced more by the therapist than the patient. When comments are made, it has been the author's policy simply to state that the taping was being done in place of taking notes and that he believed everything the patient had to say was important. The great majority of patients have agreed with this point of view. The only alterations that have been made in the material have been minor changes in names, places and dates in order to protect the patients' anonymity. These recordings have been transcribed primarily for teaching psychotherapy. Due to the nature of the case material and the need to emphasize basic considerations some degree of repetition of comments has been unavoidable.

This book reflects the teaching of Dr. Felix Deutsch, to whom it is gratefully dedicated. The author also would like to thank the many residents who over the years have listened to this material and participated in the seminars where it was used, Miss Suzette H. Annin for her invaluable editorial services and my wife Dr. Ruth M. Murphy, for her help with the final form of the manuscript.

WILLIAM F. MURPHY, M.D.

THE TACTICS OF PSYCHOTHERAPY

I

ACTIVITY IN THE ASSOCIATIVE APPROACH

A Phobia Concerning Visiting

The technique of modern individual psychotherapy is based mainly upon theoretical principles derived from psychoanalysis. These are for the most part strategic in nature. Their general nature makes their application difficult for the ordinary therapist who is unskilled in the catch-as-catch-can tactics that are part of the usual psychotherapeutic interviews. Such tactical knowledge is seldom present intuitively and is usually acquired through trial and error. It is especially difficult to come by if the psychotherapist has not been analyzed or treated in psychotherapy and, therefore, has no model to follow other than his idealized fantasies of an analyst or psychotherapist. This fantasy may or may not be enriched by a study of the literature on psychoanalytic or psychotherapeutic techniques, but even here the principles are extremely general in nature. Information is seldom given to show how the clinical material was acquired and, above all, how the deductions derived from it were made. The ability to apply psychoanalytic principles to the psychotherapeutic situation is not easily acquired. While the psychoanalyst's personal analysis forms the foundation of his techniques, controlled analyses of patients, seminars, a detailed study of psychoanalytic literature and a continual self-analysis help him to avoid the many pitfalls that lie in wait for even the most wary beginner. Without a personal analysis, cynicism and other resistances of a general as well as a personal nature allow the theoretical principles of psychoanalysis to be ignored, misapplied and distorted out of recognition. They are usually ignored either by an exaggeration of the importance of the manifest situational factors and the patient's "pat" story, or by too much dependence upon intellectual argument and rational explanation to change a patient's irrational convictions. They are misapplied and distorted mainly through lack of experience and personal bias. Uncorrected experience is often dangerous because one can make the same mistake repeatedly and confuse the results with such concepts as experience, inevitability and normal reaction. Nowadays two exactly opposite errors in psychotherapy are very common. In one the therapist bombards the patient with "insight" without the type of preparation that produces conviction. In the other the therapist continually plays a passive role and allows the patient to become overwhelmed by a chaotic mass of material which is left in an unorganized and semiconscious state.

At the present state of psychiatric residency training, the majority of psychiatrists who plunge into psychotherapy have to be guided by the kind of intuition which comes from empathizing with the patient. This has made difficult the entire task of training psychiatrists who wish to become psychoanalysts, as they have to be retrained and induced to give up the cheaply won transient successes that can come from abusing certain transference states, i.e., giving the patient love while they wait for the patient to reciprocate by getting better. While such a procedure is very welcome to the majority of neurotic patients, it effectively masks the expression of important conscious and unconscious aggressive elements that are vital to our and their understanding of the past and the development of their symptoms. Many of the mistakes of beginners are due to an unwise imitation of psychoanalysts, and a confusion in the methods, goals and techniques used in psychoanalysis and psychotherapy.

While no student therapist can hope for detailed instructions on what to say in each unique interview situation, there are certain specific responses of a tactical nature that can best be taught by example rather than by the type of discussion of case material that takes place in the usual recorded session. Good tape recordings of the teacher's own performance in the psychotherapeutic situation are an ideal medium for this purpose. These can furnish the beginning therapist with a model available for discussion. Tested verbal devices can be demonstrated and reasonably well separated from mistakes and the individual idiosyncrasies of the teacher's personal style. The transcription of these tape recordings allows the student who cannot attend seminars to study at his leisure the technical principles of the interview situation and the development of the material. While subtle nuances conveyed by the voice and sight of the patient and doctor are lost in the spoken or printed word, enough information remains to make this method of teaching worth while. To accomplish this task as adequately as possible, interviews must be picked that are interesting and instructive enough to hold the reader's attention. The treatment process itself should be standardized and any deviations from it explained adequately. Such a method of treatment should also be logical and simplified to the extent that the student can see what the therapist is endeavoring to do, the reasons for doing it, and how it was accomplished or why it failed. The method of treatment that best meets these specifications is the sector therapy of F. Deutsch, which is a development of the associative anamnesis method of interviewing. This method is actually a refinement of the minimal interference techniques commonly associated with the psychoanalytic approach to psychotherapy, but adapted to the exigencies of the ordinary psychotherapeutic situation in a logical manner that is available for study, testing and analysis in terms of its rationale.

It has often, and correctly, been claimed that psychiatry is the least scientific of all the medical specialties due to the lack of follow-up studies, controls and other evaluation procedures. We will consider the enormous difficulties of evaluation procedures in this field in more detail later. However, the basis of any evaluation procedure is an accurate reporting of the data from which inferences are made as well as the inferences themselves. Here again verbal material is not the only data in a therapeutic interview, but the reporting of it is a step in the right direction. Sector therapy is the first and only type of psychoanalytically oriented psychotherapy where a large number of tape recorded transcriptions of interviews have been published. These have been annotated in detail. While others have published recorded interviews, these have been few in number, incomplete and with no detailed explanation of technique. A special feature that makes sector therapy valuable is that the patient does not learn to produce the kind of material he thinks the therapist wants. Any treatment process is one of mutual evaluation. Often, with other techniques, if the patient feels the therapist is interested in sexual or aggressive material or personal relationships, he will produce this kind of material both in dreams and manifest activities. Different schools of psychological thought have seldom had difficulty in finding cases to prove their theories. Some have even presented fragments of recordings. It is only when the complete activities of both therapist and patient in the entire interview are recorded that we can comprehend the necessity for controlled activity as well as minimal interference, and the value of the tactical principles which have evolved in the sector-therapy method of treatment.

The original associative approach to interviewing techniques appears to have developed from the direct application of the psychoanalytic technique by teachers to the vis-à-vis therapy situation, with modifications made according to the personality of the interviewer and his previous analytic experiences and the exigencies of the interview situation. The theory and rationale of the associative anamnesis was developed by F. Deutsch over a period of many years, along with that of sector psychotherapy.

The basic technique of the associative anamnesis type of interviewing has been described adequately and in detail elsewhere. A brief resumé of the highlights of this technique will be made for the purpose of review. It will be accompanied by a more extensive discussion of some aspects of the theoretical principles behind the technique which experience teaches are difficult for many to grasp. Most technical principles can be understood better within the framework of an actual interview situation, and all of the principles to be mentioned in the following resumé will be illustrated and discussed in detail later.

Before the interview begins, the psychiatrist usually knows the name, age, sex and source of referral of the patient. This is all that is necessary. Other basic data can be obtained either during the interview or after it is finished. The rules governing the use of minimal interference and the associative type of interview can easily be parodied or reduced to an absurdity by the anxious or compulsive type of psychiatrist who tends to hide his aggression and feels he is at the mercy of the patient's willingness to speak. In 1946 when I began to teach the associative anamnesis at Cushing Veterans Administration Hospital, the basic rule concerning noninterference with the patient's productions was often so rigidly adhered to that the elements of the technique were obvious and some patients parodied the doctors. One would ask, "Have you been to mess yet?" and the other would repeat archly, "Mess?" Also, during case presentations, when a resident was asked about an elementary fact, such as the marital status of the patient, he might reply, "He didn't say." In any case, there is no rule which says that questions cannot be asked before, during or after the interview. In the majority of cases, these questions can be structured and timed so that they fit readily into the context of the interview. It is important, however, that, after every digression introduced by the therapist, we return to where we left the patient. This does not allow us to understand immediately the unconscious connections that determine the shift in material, but it prepares us for it later on. We have to learn how patients avoid and conceal material, and not only what is connected with what but how it is done. Later we will understand why. The associative technique is based upon the fact that when the patient is allowed to talk freely without too many interruptions he tells us *more* than he would if he were asked questions. He is allowed to volunteer any information that has meaning in the sense that this is considered revealing and/or concealing. Actually, the beginner in psychotherapy must learn to read between the lines, as in this manner much that is relevant to the meaning, origin and use of the symptom will be revealed. How this is done is best demonstrated by example. The freedom to talk without too much interference allows deeply buried emotional material to develop and become conscious. People take time to develop trust, and memories take time to become mobilized. They are attached to complex emotional states that must be encouraged to ripen and then be sustained and simplified by a judicious guidance of the material. Noninterference, however, is a relative term. It does not mean that the psychiatrist cannot be active and that he is entirely dependent upon a patient's willingness to speak. Many patients need continual encouragement. When the initial interview is over, we should have some idea of the patient's situation in the present as regards his home, work and family, and in the past as regards his childhood home, parents and siblings. We should also have as much information as possible concerning the time of origin and development of his presenting complaints. This is in accord with the theory that the patient's symptoms and behavior are always regarded as repetitive and as an enlarged and revised edition of a previous pattern, usually going back to childhood. The initial interview is so important that most of this book will be given over to illustrations of the various principles used in its construction or, at times, ignored for the sake of expediency. It is important to know when to ignore rules. Psychotherapy is not the same as psychoanalysis. Much of the clinical material in this book will be devoted to an illustration of activity in the therapeutic interview. The activity begins during the initial interview and continues until the end of therapy. It is based at first upon general tactics and strategic principles and later upon the specific nature of the patient and his difficulties, when and at the level at which they are understood.

When an internist knows the diagnosis of a disease, he can look up the treatment specific for this disease and then treat complications, if any, as they arise. The psychotherapist can use present-day psychiatric nomenclature and therapeutic texts only to a very limited extent. Actually the initial interview is what will outline the treatment.

The rules governing the use of the associative anamnesis type of interviewing are deceptively simple:

The patient is asked about his presenting difficulty and then allowed to talk freely. When he stops, one or more of his own words are repeated questioningly, sometimes with the addition of the phrases, "What do you mean?" or "What makes you think so?" or "How do you know this?" The use of these phrases in quantity marks the good therapist as well as the scientific approach. The word repeated is usually one that will lead in the direction of the most information concerning the patient's difficulty. The selection of the proper word or phrase becomes of increasing importance as the interview develops because of the increasing complexity of the multiple-choice problem. In the initial stages of the interview, the therapist's chief role is that of a listener who is attempting to trace in time and in detail the origin of the patient's complaints. Therefore, the words chosen will be those which will lead to the greatest amount of information in the area most vital for our understanding of the difficulty that has brought him to us. This area may not be obviously related to the symptoms, especially in the early stages of an interview. The patient in essence is allowed to associate to his own speech, which is manipulated by the therapist. In this manner, not only is he led into certain areas but the material is isolated and obtained in terms of his own words and thoughts. Noninterference can be a vice as well as a virtue. It does *not* produce free associations. Unless the therapist takes conscious advantage of the material that is produced, he stands the danger of leading the patient into areas that are dominated mainly by the therapist's own concepts, prejudices and unconscious problems. Fortunately, most patients, whose own problems are usually pressing, tend automatically to stay on the right track. This is the main reason why minimal interference works as well as it does. To communicate at all with a patient is to introduce ourselves into his fantasy life. It is always surprising when listening to a recorded interview to note how active minimal activity can and usually does become. Our main interest in our activities as therapists should be derived from our conscious recognition and intelligent control of them. Ordinarily we do not interrupt a patient. In the case of garrulous patients who tend to overwhelm the therapist with material, we can pick up a word or phrase at any time if we wish, preferably when they stop momentarily to draw a breath, as this makes the conversational relationship appear more natural. Every effort should be made to disguise the fact that a technique is being used.

One of the most common mistakes in this area is that made by the therapist who tries to give a patient the impression that he understands everything. This may be easily sensed by the patient, who will then hide much more than he had originally intended. Other patients react to this "understanding" with such high expectations that they are easily disappointed and disillusioned when a magic "cure" does not quickly arrive. One must be especially on the lookout for medical and psychiatric terms and inquire into their meaning. This must be done with tact as, for instance, "I realize you know about such things now, but what did this term mean to you then?" This is especially important in cases of psychosomatic disease and with patients who have received treatment by other therapists.

In cases where the initial complaint refers to a bodily condition, the patient will sooner or later mention some person. The nature of the relationship to this person ordinarily should be expanded as much as possible by showing interest in words referring to him, since this person will usually be found to play an important role in the origin and maintenance of the patient's pattern of difficulties. Usually such a person will be connected with or stand for other figures of great importance in the patient's past. Such combinations as the boss in the present and the father in the past, or the wife and the mother, are of common occurrence. There are important exceptions to this rule which will be discussed later.

Every important relationship pattern in the present can be considered as a distorted repetition of a similar one in the past. The neurotic patient's problem is inseparably bound up with his past fantasy life. Because the past is less contaminated by reality and more subject to the pressure and distorting effects of the unconscious fantasies of the patient, it is more important for our understanding of the patient's fantasies and the symptoms that represent them in the present. Because the past is easier to understand, the patient is encouraged to return there. This is best accomplished by picking up such cue words as "never," "always," or "used to." Such words refer to a pattern of behavior over the years with roots in the past. When they are not forthcoming, they can be created by suggesting a generalization concerning a series of specific details. If this is accepted, an inquiry can be made about the origin of the pattern of behavior. Once a patient has been returned to the past, an attempt is made to keep him there and enlarge his memories of it. The patient's emotional state determines not only the present verbal material but also usually determines the amount and the type of memory recall. This means that the recalled past will usually have obvious connections with the material concerning the present.

Questions asked by the patient are usually a trap or an evasion. They must be treated as associative material and should not or cannot be answered, at least until the motive for their being asked and the reasons why the patient cannot answer them himself are known. If the therapist is forced to answer a question, he must make sure that the answer does not place him in an untenable position and that the patient understands the answer. For example, a typical question might run, "What do you think is causing these headaches?" or "Do you really think I am crazy?" We can be sure the patient has asked such questions a thousand times before. Cheap reassurances or opinions of any kind will soon lose their effect and eventually create distrust. Attempts to be honest, as by saying, "I don't know yet," may alarm or anger many patients. The best reply is, "*You* must have thought a lot about this. Of course, you don't know whether you are right or wrong. But what are *your* ideas?" In this manner we obtain information about the patient's fantasies, which are what he lives by. Another danger in answering questions is that the reply of the patient can easily be "What do you mean?" or "How do you know?" I have listened to embarrassing tape recordings in which a patient has done an excellent associative anamnesis upon a therapist who felt he had to play the role of someone who knows all and can answer any problem. The pitfalls in communication in this area are difficult to exaggerate and can best be dealt with by examples in verbatim interviews.

The therapist should accustom himself to bear periods of silence. The burden of the interview, if any, should be placed on the patient, who is often too glad to spare himself anxiety by attempting to force the doctor to ask questions or expand his own ideas. However, most of the time it is not necessary to wait more than a few minutes before taking up a word or phrase of the patient's in a questioning manner. With some patients who are very anxious and reticent, the therapist can create the illusion of participating actively without saying anything in particular, stopping as soon as the patient relaxes and evidences a willingness to talk. In any case it is unnecessary and useless, as a rule, to try to "outsit" a patient.

The time elements are of major importance. The dates of the occurrences of symptoms and major events in the patient's life should be asked for repeatedly and kept in mind. It is usually best to ignore inconsistencies in ages and dates until a later part of the interview, or a later interview; these are often a sign of unconscious distortion and give us a valuable clue to the time of occurrence of some of the major problems in a patient's life. If the inconsistency is mentioned, it must be done in the manner of one puzzled and unaware of any importance of the material, and any correction should be readily accepted. This allows the patient to save face, avoid feeling trapped and realign his memories with the minimum of discomfort while he gives us the maximum of information. The time axis is one of the principal aids of the therapist in helping the patient to increase his perception of reality. An awareness of the chronological development of a problem goes along with insight concerning its origin and expectations about its future course; this is a help in mastering associated and complicating anxieties. Such an awareness of time relationships should be woven into each interview until it becomes a part of the patient's response to his problems. Just as a patient is induced to split his personality artificially into an observing, controlling, verbally oriented adult portion and an emotional, experiencing and childlike portion, so must a therapist split his observing ego into one part which is oriented toward past temporal and chronological developmental factors and another part which pays attention to dynamic and associative ramifications of the material in the present. Keeping track of dates and ages is one way of accomplishing this. They often cannot be taken literally, but numbers and ages that recur have important symbolic and screening values. At times, simply bringing together material isolated in the interview but connected by a date or age will produce important new material and a certain awareness in the patient that is effective later in producing meaningful insights.

As a rule, a therapist remains passive and does not show the patient that he understands the meaning of the material that is presented until the time is ripe for a confrontation. It is often difficult to determine this time. As a patient continues to talk, certain truths and consequences become apparent to him as well as to the therapist. These may be brought out by a juxtaposition of two or more of his own statements from different parts of the interview. Many words used by a patient have two or more meanings. Sometimes a word with an unconscious meaning will be used in a different context by the therapist so that its "real" meaning can no longer be evaded by the patient. The interview that follows will illustrate this maneuver, which is called confrontation. It is done in a questioning manner. It allows the patient to make his own interpretations and leads to a greater willingness to accept any insights obtained in this manner. Any attempt in this direction should be made hesitantly and in a fashion that allows the patient to retract or disavow the material if he is too much disturbed by it. Even so, such a disavowal will often call for explanations which can be as revealing to the patient as to the therapist. It is best for the patient and doctor to discover things together. The matter of face-saving cannot be emphasized too much. This means that when a patient obtains insight he should be made to feel that it is his own hard-won accomplishment and not that he is a fool not to have known these things already and that the smart therapist knew it all along. All of this is connected with our efforts to get a patient to tolerate as well as to control the infantile part of himself that he often despises, resents and denies. In some cases the infantile part is in such control that he is glad to have the therapist play the role of the seer and magician. Such a role may be gratifying to a therapist but it is difficult to sustain and with the first failure all the patient's awe and worship will turn to unreasoning contempt.

Passing comments are listened to with great attention as they are usually a giveaway concerning important and hidden meanings as well as various displacements of emotion. Such comments may be picked up but this must be done with caution and a readiness to abandon them if they appear too loaded with emotion.

A positive transference state is induced as rapidly as possible by means of imitating the patient as well as using his own words. If he sits primly or slouches, we tend to do the same. A prim patient will often react angrily to the therapist who lounges easily in his chair and will feel that he isn't interested. If the situation is reversed, the patient may well feel the therapist disapproves of him. Used with *care,* this type of behavior produces the reaction, "I like him because he is like me and speaks my language." It is better, of course, to behave in a manner modeled upon the patient's ideal of a therapist after this is ascertained. This must *not* be overdone. The primary purpose is the establishment of an initial good contact until one becomes aware of what the patient needs. The impression that one makes upon a patient is dependent mainly upon the patient's readiness to fit the appearance and mannerisms of the therapist, as well as the interviewing situation itself in its broadest sense, into his own life's patterns of relationship. This produces what are called transference states. These are transient in nature and should not be mistaken for or compared with a transference neurosis, which is a condition that develops usually in psychoanalysis and is more intense, inclusive and pervasive. It differs qualitatively and quantitatively from the transference states that usually occur during psychotherapy and will be discussed in more detail in Chapter VII. It should be obvious that any role playing on the part of the therapist is limited to what is natural and normal for him. Such limits vary considerably with different therapists and cannot be modified easily, if at all.

It is also obvious that the problem of selecting and collecting verbal material for development and expansion is not only one of multiple choice but is to a large extent a function of the therapist's knowledge, experience, and that descriptively elusive quality known as common sense. Psychiatric common sense is based upon an awareness of the laws of the unconscious and the defense mechanisms of the ego, as well as the demands of reality. Therefore, it is only to be expected that clinical experience and training will make a difference in the ease with which a meaningful and revealing interview is developed. For all this, many therapists are able from the beginning to do excellent work. This means they can give a patient much more than the relief obtained from simply verbalizing his conflicts. This relief is considerable, especially if the therapist is so skilled that he directs the patient into the areas where the material is ripe for verbalization. Some areas are only decoys, screens, cover-ups and evasions. Others are so crammed with affect that they are too dangerous. The very process of verbalization means putting indefinite, ambivalent and unknown feelings into a reality-oriented format with a subject, predicate, modifiers, etc. However, verbalization is not enough. If the areas that are developed are ripe for discussion, affect will appear which may or may not be intense; i.e., abreactions will occur. However, abreaction is not enough. If the therapist is able, gradually the patient will begin to see his symptoms as the logical end result of a way of life or characteristic mode of reaction based upon past experiences and the revival of old gestalts by day-to-day experiences. Such dynamic and genetic insight will enable him to see himself in perspective and reduce the immediacy of his demands upon himself and the world around him. However, dynamic insight is not enough and neither is insight into the historical or genetic development of his problems. All patients tend to weave their therapists into their fantasy life by distorting what they experience to suit their needs. In turn they are modified by the very act of doing this. The modification is dependent upon conscious and unconscious perceptions and is in direct proportion to the discrepancy experienced or the manner in which the therapist does *not* act the role assigned to him. The refusal to be seduced into playing a role is the simplest and best type of so-called corrective experience. This may be a harsh, punitive or distant role as well as a tender, loving one. Transference reactions on the part of the patient may be hidden or displaced onto other persons, things, or even images of themselves or parts of their bodies. Sometimes these more or less isolated transference reactions may develop to the point where they are out in the open, highly organized and the chief concern of the patient. This is called a transference neurosis. In such a case, therapy has become psychoanalysis no matter what we call it. Naturally, the more the psychotherapeutic procedure resembles analysis in number of hours and behavior on the part of the therapist, the more this is likely to occur in some patients. Handling a transference neurosis without training poses the same type of difficulties as are found in any other area where treatment procedures and prognosis are dependent upon ability plus training. Unfortunately, in the field of psychotherapy the end results are so difficult to evaluate that mediocrity, stupidity and even outright negligence can easily be hidden or plausibly explained.

Occasionally someone approaches us with the request for advice concerning the problem of "a friend" and we have little difficulty in recognizing this indirect way of discussing his own problems as a *conscious*, face-saving device. *Unconscious*, indirect communications of this sort are very common and we soon become aware that most patients are always hiding themselves in the disguise of others. All the characters one meets in the usual associative anamnesis should be thought of as part aspects of the patient's personality, façades, alter-ego figures, or representatives of important persons from his past. Few mistakes will be made if they are considered as such. Also, when a patient discusses a novel or the latest play, he stresses the elements that apply to his own problems, ambitions, and attitudes toward life. This knowledge is useful; many patients who cannot talk about themselves will readily, if unknowingly, reveal themselves through the use they make of other persons. Some patients can talk about themselves in a revealing fashion only in the guise of others. At times we can deliberately induce a patient to talk about other persons to reduce his anxieties as well as to learn his secrets. The same applies to his readings in psychiatric literature. In psychoanalysis, the idea once prevailed that reading about analysis made for complications. This is rather doubtful and the tendency nowadays is to analyze rather than to forbid such behavior.

The fantasy life of the patient, both conscious and unconscious, is the chief concern of the psychotherapist. So-called reality problems, like questions, are evasions of the real issue, which is why the patient cannot solve reality problems himself. The chief reasons for this somewhat hard attitude are based upon experience as well as theory. Attempts to modify psychoneurotic symptoms by medication, changing the environment, giving advice, deconditioning, etc., are not intrinsically wrong but usually the results are disappointing *unless* the unconscious and conscious factors that give the environment meaning are known and understood. Of special importance are the hidden infantile ambivalent attitudes which lead to perpetual demands and longings that cannot be gratified because they clash with adult ambitions and ideals and because of the ease with which past disappointments are revived. Situational factors are extremely important in one sense. The vicissitudes of the present call forth various roles on the part of the patient. These are roles that have been played repetitively and, although they may appear to vary considerably, they tend to show definite structural patterns based upon past experiences. Another and more complex way of stating this is that a person's patterns of relationship with *objects, persons, himself* and his *body image* tend to be similar and to be repeated many times over the years with only minor variations. In this respect, a patient is the author, audience and director of a play. While he is versatile enough to take any of the main roles convincingly, he needs other persons to complete the cast. While everyone does this to some extent, the psychoneurotic play is out of touch with the reality situation. This is what gives the behavior of the various types of psychiatric patients the appearance of being irrational. The initial interview should show this clearly to the therapist, and in fortunate cases some of the perspective that is acquired can be communicated to the patient. In some rare cases, this will lead to deep insight. It may even act like a seed crystal in a supersaturated solution and start a process that will initiate far-reaching changes in the patient's characteristic modes of response.

Let us now listen to an initial interview which will illustrate some of the things that have been discussed.

Before we begin, let us remember that the value of this method of interviewing is based upon the continuity and interrelationships of the material produced. The interview is considered as a unit which provides rational insights and inferences. Part of the therapeutic effect of this type of interviewing is based upon the fact that both patient and therapist share the insights produced, although certainly to a different degree. In all the interviews that follow, the important or key words will be in italics. Many of these will be words that the therapist feels are highly charged emotionally. They have become entangled with many ideas and feeling tones and are like complicated knots in a rope that have to be patiently teased apart. They need to be explained and dwelt upon until their various meanings are clear to the patient. The emotional charge they carry will be considerably reduced in intensity by the abreaction that accompanies this process. Other words in italics will be those that are important for the reader to remember as he "listens" to the interview.

The concept of *feedback* is important here. When emotionally charged words are fed back to a patient, they develop and intensify the memories associated with the word and aid in the evocation of complex feeling patterns that are a necessary part of the process of remembering.

Note particularly how the therapist attempts to speak the patient's language and uses his insight into the nature of the patient's unconscious only *indirectly*.

The patient was a thirty-two-year-old mother of two children who was handicapped by a moderately severe anxiety hysteria. She was a thin woman of medium height and unexceptional appearance, neatly and appropriately dressed. She had short curly brown hair, attractive eyes and a pleasant smile. The doctor greeted her with a handshake, motioning her into a chair, and then sat down, smiled, and began.

"Could you tell me something about the difficulty you mentioned over the phone?"

She sighed.

"It's always so hard to explain just the way I feel. Well, I'd just be sitting here and, uh, all of a sudden I'd get a very frightened feeling, like I *wasn't myself* or other people weren't *real* and, uh, I try to say to myself it's *foolish*. And, uh, a little while later it wears off a little bit but I still feel *nervous* all day long and I hate to be *alone*. My *husband* works nights. My *father* would be upstairs and sometimes I'd call him down just to feel as though *somebody was around me*. And, uh, I might be driving the car in traffic and then all of a sudden I'd say to myself, what if I had to get out of the car? Who would take the car from here out of the traffic? If I see a *policeman* near me I'd say to myself, well, he'll come in the car and take the car home and I'll be all right. I keep saying to myself it's *silly* to feel like that and I'd try to work myself out of the feeling. But it's very hard to do sometimes. I might be *nervous* for three or four days afterwards and just keep thinking *foolish things* all the time."

She obviously needed someone to protect her from some kind of fantasied event. The first person and protectors mentioned in connection with her trouble were her husband and father. Their role in the origin of her troubles was probably important but there was more important fantasy material immediately available. The clue lay in the words "foolish things" so the therapist took this up.

"What do you mean, like what?"

"Like, uh, I've *always* had the feeling of being *buried alive*."

This not only showed the length of the problem but allowed one to inquire about the past. Returning to the past usually takes precedence over other material. "Buried alive" probably referred to certain regressive fantasies and could be investigated later. It often refers to an inability to "live" and may hide deep feelings of depression.

"Always? You mean even when you were a little girl?"

"Well, only since I've been getting these feelings. I've been doing this now for about *thirteen* years."

A definite number like this can be as overdetermined as any emotionally charged word. There are ways of testing this statement.

"How old are you now?"

"Thirty-two."

"You mean then since you were around nineteen or twenty?"

"No, a little younger than that, probably longer than thirteen years."

Why did she say thirteen? Numbers often have a symbolic value as well as an actual meaning. Did something traumatic happen when she was thirteen? This question would have to wait.

"How old would you say?"

"Well, right after I quit school. I must have been sixteen or seventeen."

As part of the effort to get into the past, the therapist took the younger age.

"Sixteen?"

"Yes. And I noticed the first day it started on me because I was working and, uh, the day before that I heard that some *boy* had *dropped dead* in school. Then the next day when I went to work I was just sitting there at the machine when I thought of him."

What killed the boy and who was he? In terms of the unconscious, he was an aspect of herself and also someone in the outer world like a brother or a symbol of something of importance that had been lost.

"You knew him?"

She said that she didn't know him but for a long time had been obsessed by the thought of his death. Before sixteen she felt "wonderful" and could go anywhere by herself. The boy had a "heart attack" and had dropped dead. She had gone to a doctor and found her heart was all right. Ever since this time she had "just kept thinking foolish things." The therapist developed this theme. Foolish things referred to dreams of being buried alive, waking and hearing someone calling her name, and anxiety attacks whenever she went visiting. She liked to visit her thirty-year-old sister but would get panicky going there and coming back. There was thus a double anxiety—going there and back home too. At home her father, mother and three brothers lived upstairs. The brothers' ages were thirty-five, twenty and eighteen. Two younger siblings had died. A two-month-old brother had died nine years ago when she was twenty-three. An eleven-year-old sister had died of cancer about six months before the brother's death. He had died from chronic *"heart trouble."* He was a "change of life" baby, born "kind of *mongoloid.*" This child was probably related to the boy who dropped dead. This was an obvious area for development, but she appeared reluctant to discuss it and quickly began to talk about an episode when she was nine. Her grandmother had died. She and her brother had gone to the funeral parlor, had seen another body and had run out. These "little things" haunted her. Other "little" or "foolish" things related to how when one person *died on the street,* she felt she would be next, or the third—"things go in threes."

The eleven-year-old sister, who died of cancer when the patient was twenty-two, had never lived with the family. Her mother was sick at the time the child was born. The baby had been taken by a friend and did not return after her mother got better. She had wondered why. She was ten when this sister was born. Mother's sickness was erysipelas, which meant she couldn't walk and had to go to a *mental* hospital for a rest. She blamed herself for the baby sister being farmed out. She wasn't old enough to take care of it, although she was the oldest girl. Her grandmother died shortly afterwards from old age. At one time she had fallen downstairs. Father didn't want to live in that house any more because it was "bad luck." Something was always happening there and someone being hurt. It was as if some bad, aggressive presence haunted the place. Around the time of grandmother's death her cousin, Margie, who was five years older than she, had a baby a few months after a forced marriage. The baby was born the day grandmother died. Margie had lived with her since she was a child.

At times she became so anxious that she depersonalized. She felt as if she "wasn't a person," or alive, or walking around. She would hear herself talking and feel she had to think of words to say so she could hear herself say them. She would wonder if her name was really Maryanne, and would ask herself, "Who's Maryanne?" She did not feel she was really grown up; i.e., "I don't feel as though I'm adult. I don't feel grown up. I feel as though, like I've been downtown and a little baby would say 'Hi' to me or something, and I, no, I'd see a cute little baby and I'd say 'Hi' or something, and the woman would say, 'Well, say Hi to the lady,' and I'd say to myself, 'I'm a lady?' It's strange to think of someone calling me a lady or a woman." She then said she had been getting increasingly nervous ever since she had seen a television play in which a dead person came to life. She felt she had to find out what was doing this to her. Something was driving her. She had begun to get hazy feelings. She would be looking at things and they would not "penetrate through." The interview then continued as follows.

"Are you thinking of anything else?"

"I don't realize I am. I might be but it never enters my head. It seems funny that I'd be *good* as gold and all of a sudden just like that it would come on me. I don't know whether it was in the back of my mind."

This seemed to imply that the hidden thoughts were *bad.*

"You think you might be thinking about something *bad?*"

"I might be, yes."

"Why, what makes you think so?"

"I don't realize that I am but, uh, I'd just be standing there and all of a sudden *my stomach* would jump and I'd get a *hot flash* and I'd get frightened as anything. And I don't know why I should be. I'd be talking to friends or out in a night club or something and I'd be sitting there and all of a sudden it would just come on me!"

Now was the time to explore her fantasies more directly. The therapist suspected that her ideas were more definite than she had been willing to admit before.

"Well, what do *you* think about these attacks? You must have done a lot of thinking about these things."

"Oh yes, I have!"

"Well, what have you thought? Do you have some ideas? Of course you don't know whether they are right or not."

"No, I don't!"

"But you've had some ideas?"

"Yes."

"What *are* your ideas?"

"Well, uh, I don't know what it is; my idea is that it goes back to my childhood some place. Whether I have a *guilt complex* and that it's bothering me now, or whether it's just being scared of dying."

The simplest way to fit this material together so far was that she felt guilt over something or someone dead or dying, and fear of dying herself in retaliation for the wish. The words "guilt complex" were very interesting but the opportunity to get back into the past was too valuable to neglect.

"What do you mean back to your childhood? How far back do you mean?"

"Well, there was never actually a lot of affection or love in the family and we always—my father worked nights and we used to just about *go our own way*. My mother would be out and I would be *stuck with the kids* all the time after I was old enough to take care of my brothers."

Mother being out or going away was like mother dying and she becoming the little mother. Did she wish or fear this? Was she angry with mother for leaving her? Did she hate the sisters or brothers? Her husband was also away nights.

"What kids do you mean?"

"Well, my younger brothers, the eighteen- and twenty-year-old ones. I was about *twelve*."

"When you started taking care of the children?"

"When David was born, I was about twelve, and right away I had the responsibility of watching him because my mother was a beano player."

She laughed and continued.

"She likes beano. She's a *gambler at heart*. And every time my father would go to work she would *take off* and go play beano, when it was legal in Massachusetts. Now she goes up to New Hampshire in a chartered bus."

"And when you say back to your childhood, you mean how old?"

"Oh, I don't know, maybe eight or *nine*."

The therapist knew already that nine was an important age, but her feelings must have begun earlier.

"Eight or nine? You mean when you started to take care of the baby or before?"

"I remember once I was only about *six* or *seven,* I must have been about six, and maybe even *five* because I went *downtown* and this woman came up to me, she was a policewoman, and she said, 'Are you lost?' And I said, 'No, I'm not lost, I *know my way downtown and back home again.*' And she said, 'Well, I'll buy you some of that *candy* if you tell me if you're really lost or not.' And I said, 'Gee, all right, I'm *lost.*' So she took me down to the police station and they got hold of my mother and they found out where I lived, and all the time I was there I kept telling them 'I'm not lost. I know my way home.' And they got the cruiser and they took me home and after that my mother tied me in the yard. So whether *that* has any bearing on my thinking *I'm lost in life* or not I don't know. Sometimes I wonder if that had any effect."

This story had all the value of a screen memory; i.e., it betrayed the pattern but the elements were different. It meant that for a price she would do or say things. Being lost meant being bad. She probably had known her way around in more ways than one. She could hardly develop a "guilt complex" over this adventure. Why was she tied up? Was mother afraid of her "going to town?"

"You mean you had been downtown before?"

"Yes, I knew my way down."

"You mean like mother, you had gone with her?"

"Oh, yes, I'd gone with her, so this one day I went down by myself!"

Was she proving she could be like a mother?

"Did you use to go out a lot when you were five or six?"

"No, not too much."

"Now and then?"

"Just down to the store and back. Never any place else really."

"Just you, not your sister?"

"Oh yes, there was always, well my sister wasn't, yes my sister was born then. I was about six and she was four. We all went together. There was my brother, my sister and I. For quite a few years and, uh, we used to go down to the store."

"And mother would stay home then?"

"No, I think she came."

"She didn't go out and play beano then?"

"No, no."

"You were all too small?"

"Yes, she stayed home more or less then."

"She was good to you then?"

"Oh yes, she's always been good."

"Not very affectionate?"

"Not affectionate, as far as I can remember. I know my father used to sit in the rocking chair and rock us when we were small. He often used to sing 'Danny Boy' to us and songs like that."

"He was the affectionate one?"

"Yes, he was more affectionate than my mother."

"Much more?"

"Not too much more, no."

She really had wanted to be a better mother herself. This may have produced a premature type of independence that hid dependent longings and fears and could also have reinforced the normal oedipal longings, hates and inadequacy feelings. This was all screened by problems concerning "going to town" and "visiting."

"Do you think you missed that?"

"I think it's possible."

"What makes you think that?"

"I'm not affectionate now myself."

"How do you mean?"

"Well, I make an awful lot of the kids when they are *babies*. My daughter is *eight years old now*, but I don't make too much of her and my husband tells me I'm wrong, that I should show her more affection, but I feel as though I'm taking my *angry feelings* out on her, too."

This sounded as if she were angry at her daughter in the way she felt mother was angry at her. Did she feel her badness made mother angry? Was this the source of her guilt? Why did she want to go to town? Where? At one level, to the candy store probably, but was there a more genital and less oral level?

"How do you mean?"

"Oh, I don't know. I'm always telling her not to talk to any *strangers* and not to get into *anybody's car* and she says, 'No, I'd never do that'."

This was the opportunity that the therapist had been waiting for. Her daughter was probably a version of herself at eight or nine. The business about the stranger was obviously some kind of seduction fantasy.

"Why? Are you afraid?"

"I'm afraid somebody might try to *pick her up* or *something*. She's so friendly."

"To do what?"

"Well, take her away some place, in other words *hurt* her. I don't know whether—"

Her voice died away.

"You've heard of such things?"

"Oh yes."

"What do you mean? What have you heard?"

"Oh, well, I've, you mean now or when I was younger?"

"When you were younger?"

"Well, I did, I did, uh, I went with *this* girl who used to go up to this old man's house. I was only about *seven* at the time and, uh, I'd wait outside for *her* until she'd come out."

Now the therapist could explore this story in detail. The older girl was probably another alter-ego image.

"How old was she?"

"Oh, she was about eleven or twelve, maybe thirteen."

"How old was the old man?"

"Oh, he was, old to me then."

"That's what I mean."

She laughed.

"He was *really* old."

"Really old?"

"Yes. Well, he must have been in his forties anyway, or fifties."

"You saw him?"

"I'd see him *on the street* and *everything* and she used to say, 'Well, want to come up with me?' And I'd say 'No.'"

"She'd go up to his house?"

"Yes."

"He didn't hurt her?"

"Not that I know of."

"What did he do?"

"I don't know, I never went up there with her."

"Well, I mean you had ideas."

"Oh, yes. I think they were *fooling around* or *something*."

"What do you mean? I mean you can talk freely here."

"This subject always embarrasses me. Well, *touch her* and *everything*. I don't know whether he actually went to the *very extreme point* and *all that*, but I know that she would *undress* and *everything*. She used to come down and tell me how nice it was."

"She'd undress and they would touch each other's sexual parts, you mean?"

"Yes."

"Play with each other?"

"Mmm, that's it."

"And he might have had intercourse, you think?"

"It's possible but I don't know. I'm not sure of that point."

At that age she actually wasn't sure what intercourse meant and was more interested in touching and looking and *fooling around* (foolish things).

"And she told you it was nice?"

"Yes, and she said, 'You should come up with me,' and I kept saying 'No, I don't want to go up there.' "

It sounded like a dialogue between two parts of herself.

"So you remember all that. I mean you understood what was going on?"

"Oh, yes!"

"At six or seven?"

"I think I was that young. Maybe, well it was while I was living at that bad house and I moved from that house when I was eleven. And it was before that."

The bad house was the cause of deaths and accidents and probably equated with her bad self. The therapist attempted to link up some of the material.

"That was the time you wandered downtown?"

"Yes, it was a couple of years after that because we moved from one house to another in the same section and we were in the other house, I remember, before that started."

The therapist realized this material was premature.

"And you were afraid that, you mean that what happened to this girl might happen—"

She interrupted.

"I don't want my daughter to be like that!"

Now was the time to play devil's advocate.

"What do you mean? I thought he didn't hurt her."

"I don't think he actually hurt her, but I don't ever want, well, I'm *confused*."

"You said she liked it."

"Yes, but I don't ever want my daughter to get acquainted with any man like that, who would *touch* her or anything. You know, just give her a *nickel* or something to, uh, just *touch her*."

The therapist remembered the policewoman and the candy.

"You've heard of that?"

"Yes."

Now it was obvious that she must have participated in fantasy or fact in some similar incident.

"You remember?"

"Uh-huh."

Her voice became faint.

"What do you mean?"

"Well."

She gave a long sigh.

"I guess I might as well come right out and tell you the whole truth. It's so embarrassing though. It wasn't me who went up to the old man's house. It was *my cousin* that used to go up there, but there was this *other man* that had a *daughter* that was, oh, *mongoloid* or, she wasn't, she, *I think she was a mongoloid*. She was *old for her years*. Her face was small with a pug nose. I guess she must have been *part mongoloid* because she never went to school or anything. And, uh, he was a couple of houses up from where we lived and there was a grapevine in the back yard and he would tell me to come up and see him and that he would give me a *nickel* or a *dime*."

This was an enormous step forward. Her mother and this man both had a mongoloid child. Unconsciously he was *father* and the mongoloid child who died was her defective bad self who was old for her years like her cousin. Both were little "prostitutes." "Old for her years" means advanced, not retarded!

"How old were you then?"

"Oh, I don't think I was any more than eight, eight or nine, because it was the time we lived up near the park and, uh, I used to go up, never, uh, I never did anything *sexual*. It was just *touching*, in other words, and he just *touched* me and that was all. I mean I never did anything, *as far as I can recall*, anything *bad. Real bad!*"

"What do you mean by real bad?"

"Well, *intercourse* in other words. I never did that, but I did go up for the *nickels* or the *dime*."

The child's attitude then was the opposite of the adult's attitude now. Masturbatory touching, and "fooling around" were *good* and intercourse *bad* (dirty).

"And he just touched you?"

"That's all."

"Did you touch him?"

"I can't remember whether I really did that or not."

The therapist attempted to lighten the burden of her guilt.

"But then you were so young; it was just in fun."

"Just for *money*!"

"You didn't mind, did you?"

"No! I wonder if that has any bearing on my *cold feelings* today, or my fears for my daughter, but that always stuck in my mind. I never told my husband anything like that."

She had now introduced a new area of relationship and had developed some superficial insight through the linking of material.

"What do you mean, cold feelings?"

"Well, I'm not very warm towards him. To me *sex* is very *dirty*, to me now."

Obviously she would prefer to talk about the present rather than the past.

"You mean it wasn't dirty then?"

"It didn't seem to be too bad then."

"When did it start to get dirty?"

"Well, since I've been married, I think."

For many girls who have not solved their oedipal problems, marriage simply means a restoration of the infantile family with all its incestuous and masturbatory prohibitions of sexual intimacy.

"Since you've been married?"

"Yes, I never liked it!"

"You don't like to have him *touch* you?"

"No! I love him and everything but, uh, I don't know whether my mind goes back to the time when I was a kid or not."

"You mean that now it's almost the same."

"As if I have to do it. It's a chore like to me. It's *strange*."

It sounded as if her infantile sexual experiences had an alien or compulsive masturbatory component. This strange feeling was a near relative of the ones she had complained about earlier.

"But didn't you ever? I mean how long did you go to this man?"

"Well, while we lived, when we lived up there in that house, up until I was probably thirteen."

"From about eight or nine to around thirteen?"

"Thirteen or fourteen, yes."

"You'd go up and he'd give you a nickel or a dime and you'd sort of touch each other."

"Mmm. In fact I even went to his house while *his wife* was there and when his wife wasn't looking—"

She giggled.

"He would just give me a *touch*, you know."

"Touch?"

"And I'd get my *nickel*."

"You didn't mind it then?"

"I don't know whether I minded it or not but it was the money involved that I liked because I never, *we never had much money* and the nickel or the dime looked big, so I did it for money."

Money had already become a substitute for love. The therapist decided to take up the past deprivations later. Money was also an excuse for touching.

"So you were, in a sense, like a little bad girl?"

"Yes."

"Who does it for money, eh?"

"Yes."

"You've thought of that?"

"Yes. I know that today I think, gee, how could I have ever done anything like that."

"But you know children do those things?"

"I know, that's why I'm always drumming it into my daughter's head!"

"And then there was your cousin?"

"She had to get married!"

"She had to get married? She liked it?"

"Yes."

She gave a slight laugh and continued.

"But I'm not warm-blooded. I'm very cold."

"But how about after thirteen? When you moved, then you didn't have any older boy friend?"

"No, no, after I moved from there, well, I *went up to his house a couple of times* and then he moved from where he was living and I never saw him after that. But I never did anything bad after I was fourteen. I know for a fact because then I started in my menstruation."

Was this when she began going *visiting*? Was this a development of the going to town story?

"Didn't you miss it?"

"No, it never bothered me."

The question remained, did she turn to masturbation?

"Did you want to touch it yourself?"

"No, I don't think so. Even today it's just something that I've never been able to do."

"So then around the time when you were eight or nine and you were going up to, what will we call him?"

"Uh, I think his last name was N."

"Well, we'll call him Mr. N. When you were going up to his house, wasn't this around the time grandmother died?"

"Mmm, yes."

"And the baby was born?"

"Mmm, yes. Right around that time."

"And your cousin had to get married?"

"Mmm, yes."

"And let's see. You went into the funeral parlor?"

"Yes."

This was a way of testing the relationship of these separate items which were probably causally connected in her unconscious.

"All these things were happening around the same time."

"When I was young, yes. Whether they stuck in my mind, I don't know."

"I wondered if you thought that, as you got a little older, whether you wondered if you were a bad girl?"

"I know, uh, sometimes when I think of the things I did when I was younger, I, I could shoot myself!"

"What do you mean?"

"Well, like going up to this house. I wasn't even going to say anything about it but I figured if I wanted to get any help I'd better buckle down and tell just about everything I can remember. And, uh, it never actually bothered me much when I was younger. In fact I used to go up there even when he wouldn't tell me to!"

"You mean go up there because you enjoyed it, not just for the money?"

"I can't actually remember whether I really enjoyed it or not. I *might have.*"

"You mean anyway you wanted to go?"

"Yes!"

"That's what I mean because you said you went there even when he wouldn't ask you to come."

"Yes, I had nothing to do and his wife would come to the door and I'd just say I wanted to play with *their daughter,* you know, come up to see their daughter."

This type of deception might apply to her going visiting in the present at an unconscious level.

"And they believed you?"

"Yes, that I was coming up to see *her.*"

Now was the time to give her insight through confrontation.

"You went *visiting?*"

"Yes, I just went visiting."

It was better for her to accept this before becoming aware of the import.

"You liked to go visiting?"

"Yes, it isn't vivid in my mind whether I enjoyed it or not."

This was a signal to go easy.

"But I don't understand. What do you mean, whether you liked it? You felt two ways because you said you'd like to shoot yourself."

"Well, going up there to that house."

"You mean having this fellow pay you and being like your cousin?"

"Yes!"

"Only you didn't do as much as your cousin."

"No, I don't recall doing, going to the extreme."

"Just masturbating?"

"Yes, I don't ever remember him ever, uh, asking me to do the worst."

She laughed in an embarrassed manner.

"Just with your hands?"

"Yes, that's about all that there was, and then there was a boy who lived across the street from us. Everytime I used to go in, like, you know, like playmates, he was a couple of years older than I am and, uh, I remember him trying to be fresh all the time, but I never uh, I don't ever recall doing anything like that."

"Just with the older man?"

"Well, when I was eight or nine I guess he must have been in his forties, late forties."

"He would seem old anyway to a little girl?"

"Yes, today he's probably, he was about *my father's age* at the time, I guess."

"About your father's age?"

The inference was obvious. This had to be handled with delicacy, as one would handle dreams of the naïve.

"Yes, in his forties, early forties, middle forties."

"Do you think of those things now when you go visiting?"

"Oh, no! No, I don't think I do. "

The therapist switched the subject before she became too much aware of the import.

"But you said you used to like to go there, and then after you got married it all changed?"

"Oh yes, it, uh, it changed but even to this day I feel as though I am still being a bad girl. In other words, even with my own husband, we're just normal, actually normal like a man and wife, but I feel as though it isn't nice to do."

When and how did such a strong feeling of guilt develop? The real crisis must have centered around the death of the baby, the sickness and loss of the mother, the death of the grandmother, and the cousin's pregnancy. It was highly likely that a nickel stood not only for love but also for a baby relationship, as she had to take care of the brothers at this time. At thirteen to fourteen the oedipal wishes had been dangerously intensified by what amounted to a prepuberty seduction and a whole series of unfortunate reality events, all with traumatic effects leading to massive suppression and repression of sexuality.

"How old were you when you got married?"

"Twenty-one."

"How about from thirteen when you began to menstruate up until twenty-one?"

"No!"

"No other experiences?"

"No, I used to go out with boys and they'd try to get fresh and everything, but I never let them get anywhere, after I got to be thirteen or fourteen."

"How come?"

"I don't know. I just said to myself probably that I'm not going to do that any more."

"You mean you felt so guilty about it?"

"Yes, probably I had guilt feelings, uh."

She frowned and looked tense and unhappy.

The therapist changed the subject once more.

"How's your cousin?"

"Well, she got married at fifteen."

"How come she got pregnant?"

"Well, she got, uh, she went roller skating and she met this boy. He was a couple of years older than she, well, practically her own age. That's who she married."

"She was sort of wild?"

"Yes, she was fifteen but she was a lot older in many ways and very matured for fifteen. She acted much older than that."

"She liked to do more than touch?"

"Yes."

"She told you about it?"

"Oh, yes. She used to take me over there. I never went up there!"

"That wasn't the same when you had your affair?"

"No."

"So in a sense then around eight or nine when you had an affair with this man you were sort of copying her, eh?"

"Yes, I think so, more or less."

"Then, as you said, even as a little girl of five or six, you went downtown. Were you looking then?"

"Oh, no, no! I just took a walk down there!"

"But you remember at five or six then that is when you first started to hear about the old man."

"Yes."

"But it was when you got to be eight or nine that you did these things?"

"Yes, I don't know how it came about but all of a sudden I was going up to that house all the time."

Now another attempt could be made to link the past and the present.

"Do you ever think about it now?"

"Well, I have a, I think it's in my *self-conscious,* I mean in my subconscious mind."

She made a long pause.

"But if my husband ever wants to—"

She hesitated.

"Play around and touch you?"

"Yes."

She laughed.

"Then I feel as though I just can't any more."

"You still think about this old man?"

"Yes! I feel as though I'm being bad again and I can't seem to let myself go and relax with my husband. He has that complaint all the time."

She laughed again.

"He's always saying, you're so cold-blooded, like a cold dish."

"You weren't cold back in the past?"

"No, I don't think so."

"You had some *feeling* down there?"

"Yes!"

"Do you remember?"

"I have, uh, I have feelings now but to go about it, the first thing to, it's just getting started."

"I see what you mean. You mean that you don't want anything to do with it. You feel that you shouldn't do it, that it is bad."

"Yes."

"But after you get started, it's okay?"

"Well, yes. I relax a little bit and I have normal feelings and everything, but I never bother my husband. I've never gone after it."

"He has to make all the approaches?"

"He has to make all the actions. I don't do anything!"

"But after you get started, everything is all right?"

"Yes, but I have to keep thinking that this is all right now."

"You keep telling yourself, but you are not sure?"

"Yes. I keep saying to myself this is all right, there's no *harm* in this. It's quite normal. I've gone out with couples and joked about sex!"

"And yet at the same time when you go visiting you get these strange feelings?"

"Yes, even in the house."

This gave away the secret. Father was upstairs. Visiting was connected with the old man who represented the father of her childhood, and coming home with the father of today. More to the point, it involved doing harm.

"As if your mind is far away?"

"Yes, I get them in the house too. My husband would be, we'd be sitting down looking at TV and all of a sudden I'd feel nervous and scared about something and I'd go out and take a couple of aspirins, thinking it would relax my nerves, and still I can't seem to *put my finger* on what I am thinking at the time. Whether it could be, like I say, from my childhood or a *guilt complex*, I don't know."

The old man had been a partner in her acting out a masturbatory oedipal fantasy with its forbidden sexual and aggressive components.

"What do you mean, guilt complex?"

"Well, guilty of doing things like that."

"What things like that did you do? Were you *touching* yourself?"

"No, no, I never did *much*."

"When you were little?"

"No, I don't think I can recall."

"What do you mean by things like that?"

"Well, going up to the man's house and doing bad things. Today it affects me so that I still think they're bad."

There had to be other reasons for her problems, as she was so much concerned with death.

"So you think that this is one of the reasons?"

"Well, I thought that it was a guilt complex or something, way in the back of my mind. I know all these things that happened and today they are affecting me or whether it was going into the funeral parlor and seeing my grandmother and having a fright like that. My brother went in the other room and I was scared and I had to follow him in. I didn't want to be in the room alone."

"What did you see?"

"There was *another woman* in the room, or a *man,* in the other room, and then we walked out and went to school. I don't know whether that has anything to do with it and, like you say, the other, and I don't know. I feel very mixed up, but I don't see why I should get things like a *hot flash* and turning *white* and being *scared.*"

Did she feel responsible for grandmother's death? Was the other woman mother? The man was an afterthought.

"Tell me, when your grandmother died and the baby was born defective and your mother went away, did you think that was because you were a bad girl that these things were happening?"

"I recall saying to myself, I wish my grandmother would die but I don't know whether saying something like that and then having her die like that made me feel as though I had wished it on her."

"As you say, you were afraid there was something bad in that house."

"Well, it was my *father's* house, it was bad luck."

"But you wondered whether it was you?"

"Yes, and he just moved out of there after my grandmother died."

"When you said you wished grandmother would die, why did you want her to die?"

"I don't know. My mother never got along with her and she was kind of like a bossy mother-in-law, I guess. My mother was unhappy with her around."

"She was father's mother?"

"Yes, she was kind of a picky woman. In fact, I remember one time I had to sit at the kitchen table all day long because I didn't eat my oatmeal in the morning, well not all day really."

"Mother wasn't around?"

"I think that was when she was sick."

"With the erysipelas in Medfield?"

"Yes. I remember she made me sit there until I ate every drop of that oatmeal before she would let me out."

"That's when you hated her?"

"Yes."

"After that she died because you said she died after the birth of the baby that made mother get sick and go away."

"Mm. Oh, no! My grandmother wasn't dead when my mother was up in Medfield."

"No, but your mother was up in Medfield and that's when you were at home and grandmother was making you eat the oatmeal and stay by the table."

"Yes."

"And it was shortly after that that she died?"

"Yes, and I remember going up to the hospital with my grandmother, my father and sister and brother in the car, and my mother was standing at the car crying because she wanted to come home, saying there was nothing wrong with her and my grandmother saying, 'No, she can't come.' And my mother would say, 'I'll meet you down at the gate and take me home.' My grandmother kept saying, 'No, you can't, you can't do that, she's supposed to be here.' "

"You must have hated her?"

"I think that's why I hated her."

"She kept your mother away from you?"

"Yes. And even today I, I can't talk to my mother civil like. I'm always yelling at her. I don't know, she's not the type of mother I would like, in other words. She hasn't had any teeth in her mouth for, oh, ten years. She curls her hair and is neat in appearance but, uh, I can't talk to her civil. I keep telling her to get some teeth and she gets out of bed at eleven o'clock and then sits down and watches the one o'clock movie on TV and I'd go up there and say, 'Gee Ma, why don't you wash the venetian blinds over the sink. It's right in front of your eyes while you're doing the dishes.' And she would say, 'Well, why don't you leave me alone. I'll do my work and you do yours.' And then I'd go downstairs and say to myself, why do I yell like that, I don't want to, because *if anything ever happened to her I'd feel bad.*"

"So you mean that when you yell like that you feel a little anxious?"

"I feel mad at myself for doing it."

"Yes, but when you get so mad you must feel anxious because look what happened to grandma. You got mad at her."

"Yes."

"Do you ever feel sometimes or be afraid that if you got angry it might come true? Do you get these thoughts?"

"Well, yes, I have the thought that if my mother died I would have to go up there and clean the house for my father, while he was working, cook his meals for him. Then I'd say, gee, don't think of anything like that, because I wouldn't want it to actually happen."

"He'd be all alone then?"

"Yes, I'd have to actually take care of him."

"And you'd have to go *visit* him?"

"Yes!"

She laughed.

This meant she had accepted and could tolerate the insight already imparted. The therapist laughed too, to ease the burden.

"You've had enough *visiting*, huh?"

"Yes, I guess I *did*, but I'd figure out, well, my father will come down here and live, or we'll move upstairs where there's more room and I'd make plans if anything ever happened to my mother, and then I'd say, *stop saying things like that* to yourself. That's the last thing in the world I'd ever want. I wouldn't want to wish anything like that, so I'd just stop thinking about it."

Actually, there were three trends to her thinking. The infantile oedipal portion of her ego wanted the hated, disappointing mother to go away, the adult ego realized that there would be no gain now, and the superego threatened her with a fate similar to the mother.

"How long have you felt this way?"

"About my mother? Oh, that's, that's only after I got married because I used to do this work around the house, *myself* and my sister and I used to clean the house every Saturday and there wasn't actually anything to get mad about, but she was always *money, money*; money was always her main object all the time. She'd bleed anybody if they got a dollar in their pocket. She'd want it."

There was tremendous rage at this greedy, passive, sexy mother. She felt envious and full of anger because of a frustrated mother-daughter relationship. The part she hated in mother was really a part of herself and her cousin, but she had developed a reaction against it. She had also been doing the duties of mother at home before her marriage; a rivalry?

"So all she did was take life easy and have babies?"

"Yes, she never *cared* for them though."

"Did your mother have the trouble with father that you have with your husband?"

"She's, he's *always* said that she was *cold*, too."

"She was cold too?"

"That's what he *always* says, like father *always* said."

"You mean sexually?"

"Yes."

"He confides in you?"

"Well, uh, just recently now, in fact I never knew until a year ago that they *had* to get married. He came out and told me one time."

"You mean mother was like your cousin?"

"Yes!"

"She ran around?"

"Well, I don't think she ran around *so much* because they were from the country and there wasn't much to do there, I guess. That's where they met. He boarded at her house while he was doing a job and they met that way and I imagine, as far as I know he's the only one she ever went with."

"She never went with anyone else?"

"As far as I know, I'm not sure."

The therapist laughed as if it were not a serious matter.

"You're not sure about that, eh?"

"I don't know."

"Why, what do you mean?"

"I don't know what she did when she was young. I just remember one time my father came in, he had a couple of beers, and he was mad about the house being a mess. The dishes were in the sink and he said this wouldn't have happened if he didn't have to get married, or words to that effect, and, gee, it hit me. I thought don't tell me that they had to get married. And to this day he always says he's going to *leave that house,* but he never leaves. He can't bring himself to leave."

"Leave her?"

"Yes, he's said that now the last fifteen years, he wasn't going to put up with it any longer."

"Since you were a girl? That would be since you were around sixteen?"

"Oh, I don't, they're *always* bickering. They're *always,* I've never seen them loving!"

"You mean that mother and father have threatened to break up?"

"Well not really."

It was apparent that her wishes had run in this direction and her fears as well. The punishment for being messy and bad was being left.

"You were afraid?"

"Uh, yes. I don't think it was that long ago actually."

"You said fifteen years."

"Well, *after I got married* he started talking like that. I don't think I ever heard that when I was younger but I've never seen any outward affection."

"And you began to wonder about what would happen if mother died or if they separated?"

"Mmm. He used to come in the house and he'd, he'd yell every time he came in, and if she was out he'd tell me about it."

"Did you know where she was going?"

"Oh, yes, beano!"

"Are you sure she was going to beano? Did you ever think she was going visiting?"

"No, I don't think I ever thought that. No, I don't think I ever did. *Maybe when I was younger, it might have popped into my head* but I never think to this day that she would ever go out on my father or anything. She's not the type."

"She was the type that got pregnant?"

"Yes! After, uh, when I was about fourteen or fifteen I finally said to myself that's never going to happen to me. It kind of stuck in my head that nobody was ever going to say that I had to get married!"

"You mean like mother?"

"Well, I didn't know at the time."

"Then it was like your cousin?"

"Like my cousin, yes!"

"But your cousin was just like a mother to you, too."

"Yes, oh yes, she was just like a mother to me."

"How do you mean?"

"Yes. She always lived with us and if I got an earache or anything I'd wait until she came home to put oil in my ear, and when she got married I always went over to her house and stayed there. I hardly ever went home."

"You visited her?"

"Well, not now. She's moved to California now."

"When did she move?"

"Oh, a couple of years ago."

What made her wait until now to come into treatment? Was it the loss of this good mother figure? Did she miss visiting her or Mr. N. or both?

"A couple of years?"

"Yes. About two years ago she moved out there. In fact, *her daughter came back in August* because she doesn't like it out there. She's *living with us now.* She's twenty-two. But every time I wanted to know anything, in fact I explained to her what I was doing with the old man just to tell somebody, to find out if it was all right, you know? And I explained to her and she says, 'Well, as long as you don't go to extremes, I don't see any harm in it.' "

Did she fantasy the girl might "touch" her husband or father?

"She meant as long as you didn't have intercourse, anything went?"

"Yes, so I just took it for granted, well, she says it was all right."

"When did you go to her?"

"Oh, when I was younger, just before she got married."

"When was that?"

"She was married at fifteen. I was some five years younger."

"You were ten or eleven then?"

"I was then. She's five years older."

"You were ten?"

"And I explained to her and she said it was all right. 'Don't ever let him really have intercourse or anything. Don't go that far, but the other is all right,' so I thought it was all right, seeing she was older."

"But you now wonder whether these things had something to do with your feeling guilty and upset because you said now you could shoot yourself?"

"Yes, and picking on my daughter all the time, that's what gets me the maddest."

"You mean picking on her because you don't want her to be like that, in spite of what your cousin said?"

"Yes, whether I'm taking my guilt out on her or not. I'm always yelling!"

"Don't go near the old men?"

"Yes, don't ever let, don't ever go near a car even if they offer you a dollar or anything, don't EVER go near a car."

"What are you afraid will happen to her, the same as happened to you?"

"Yes, in a way I'm wondering if she will."

"But after all, you didn't do so bad!"

She laughed.

"I don't know whether I did or not."

"I mean why are you so afraid?"

"Well, to me it's very dirty and I don't want my daughter to do anything like that. It would just about kill me to think that she ever went out and did anything like that."

"And you say it started becoming dirty when you started to menstruate?"

"After that I never went near anybody at all."

"You were ashamed of menstruating?"

"Well I figured after that, that if anybody ever, if you ever did go to the extreme that I would get pregnant or something, and I didn't want that to happen."

Now it began to appear more clearly. The affair with the man was a phallic masturbatory touching. She didn't want to become like the dirty, castrated, bad, neglecting mother. But why the *car*? She was omitting some details.

"You mean you didn't want to have babies and be like mother who didn't wash the blinds and had no teeth?"

"After I was menstruating, I didn't want to do anything like that again. And after we moved, I got away from him anyway. I wasn't near him anyway after that."

"But you went back?"

"To his house a couple of times, and then he moved."

"But what you mean is you were sort of afraid that if you stuck around with him after you began to menstruate that the temptation, that the older you got there was more temptation for the worst to happen?"

"Yes, it's true!"

"To see what it was like to really have intercourse?"

"Yes."

"You began to get afraid of yourself?"

"Yes, I didn't want that to happen."

"But I mean part of you said, hey, I want to try it out and see what it's like, and another part said, don't you do it, you'll get a baby."

"Yes, that's true."

"Do you remember?"

"That always stuck in my mind that I was going to get pregnant if I ever did that."

The punishment of becoming a woman and having the baby was castration at a body-image level or loss (death) of the little boy part of her, and loss of respect and love at a social level.

"So you mean that there was a strong temptation and that you really had to put up quite a fight?"

"Mmm. I think so. Not with *him* but with *boys* that I went out with."

This showed the difference between her phallic tomboy relationship with the fatherly man and her more feminine relationship with boys.

"You thought, look what happened to cousin?"

"Yes, and even after I was eighteen or nineteen I'd go out with fellows and naturally they'd try to fool around and I'd say, no! I just said, no, no, sir!"

"You mean you were afraid to have a baby?"

"Oh, yes. I always was afraid of getting caught like that and not being married."

"Why?"

"Oh, I couldn't live the shame down!"

"Like mother, you mean, or who? Your cousin?"

"No, I didn't know about mother then. My cousin!"

"But your cousin didn't do so badly?"

"No."

"How come you were so ashamed?"

"It always stuck in my head that I was never going to do anything like that."

At this time she must have been starting to develop a social conscience.

"You mean that some people talked about your cousin?"

"Oh, yes. Everybody talked about her."

"Who?"

"Oh, neighbors."

"They said she was bad?"

"Yes, they always said she was bad, that she always ran around. She didn't have a mother's care."

"And they said she did these bad things?"

"Yes."

"So you mean there were two kinds of thoughts that you had—one is the thought that you got from the neighbors about what a bad girl your cousin was, and part of you said, hey, I know her, she's nice and I love her?"

"Yes, I always thought a lot of her."

"So you got *confused*?"

"Yes."

"Over which way to feel?"

"That's true, yes."

"Like you are now, in a way. Part of you says it's perfectly all right to do it and the other part says, oh no, it's dirty, you shouldn't."

"Yes."

"Hard to tell whether *you're* right or the *neighbors* are right."

Here the therapist was attempting to modify the strictness of the superego.

"That's true, I don't know whether, I know it's right in my mind but it still seems to be wrong. And yet it's perfectly legal, a man and wife, it's just normal. I KNOW that but I can't seem to believe it completely and to—"

"Convince yourself?"

"Yes, convince myself."

"You can't forget?"

"No, I can't seem to forget those things."

What she could not forgive or forget was that she still longed for the pleasure she denied herself and felt furious at mother and cousin, self and child. The inadequate, ambivalent mother relationship was everywhere behind the oedipal one. Being touched had made up for the lack of a tender physical relationship with her parents. In this sense, it screened anxious, guilty, depressive and aggressively destructive feelings.

"That's the whole answer, huh?"

"Yes."

"The old man was a nice person and your cousin too?"

"Oh yes, he wasn't mean or anything."

"So it's really confusing. Here was this nice guy who wasn't mean to you and gave you money and just wanted to touch you, and then your cousin who was a nice girl, a better mother than your mother?"

"Yes."

"And then all these neighbors, whom you sort of respected, said these things about your cousin and you knew what they would say about the man!"

"Mmm. I always thought a lot of my cousin. In fact, she and I were closer than my other sister and her."

"So you must still be confused then when you go *visiting*. And you're afraid of your daughter being this way, like you were?"

"Yes, I often think of whether she would tend to do things like I did. Gee, to me I'd, I'd actually *kill her* if I thought that she would."

"Really?"

"Well, no, I don't know whether I'd kill her but I'd give her a a beating. I'd really beat her if I ever found out *she* was *visiting* like that."

Here she had picked up the word "visiting" in a new sense. The goal was reached. She had developed insight to a limited degree.

"You mean you feel that if mother had taken better care of you—?"

"Mmm. Yes, and explained things to me. In fact she never even explained menstruating. My cousin had to explain that to me."

"So you mean if she had taken better care of you, you wouldn't have done these things? You wouldn't have had to go visiting?"

"I don't think so."

"Then you would not have thought of these things like you do now and you would get along better with your husband?"

"Possibly, I don't know whether—"

"Because as you say you don't get as much fun from it as you wish you did."

"I'm not relaxed."

"That's what I mean. You don't feel that you get as much fun as you would like to?"

"Mmm. I'd like to go to my husband once in a while but I feel embarrassed to do it."

"Like you went to the old man when it was fun?"

"Yes."

"Where you really enjoyed it?"

"Yes. My husband says 'Why don't you ever come to me,' and I say 'I can't, I don't know why, I just can't.' I can't turn around and put my arm around him and let him know that I really want to."

"How do you, do you have any trouble doing that to your daughter also?"

"Doing what?"

"Putting your arms around her?"

"Yes! Now that she, right after my son was born, uh, you see before that I used to, oh, make an awful lot of her. Then after my son was born I went to my son to give him all the affection, and I *dropped* her, which is wrong."

"Did that ever happen to you?"

"It's possible because I was the second girl and my father made an awful lot of my sister. That was his baby. My sister was after me."

"So you mean he used to make a lot of you and then he dropped you for your sister?"

"It could have happened. I know that everything she wanted he'd give her, and if I wanted anything it was always, just wait."

"Well, let's see. Today is Monday. Can you see me Wednesday at the same time?"

"Yes indeed. Do you think I can be helped?"

"Yes, I think so."

When this young woman began her story, it became apparent that she had two sets of problems. One revolved about the theme of death, anger, going away, punishment, shooting herself, killing or beating her daughter. The other centered about sex and money, candy and visiting. *Visiting* and *going away* were bridge words that connected the two sets of problems and we could say that the entire sector focused upon the theme of visiting and its pleasure-pain, reward and punishment aspects.

In this case leaving home and visiting were connected with the old man, and staying home with a more direct relationship with father. Father and the old man were connected by similar age and the theme of the mongoloid child. The meaning of this theme was inadequately developed but it probably meant defective, bad and easily killed, and represented her bad self.

It would seem that part of her was always longing for the pleasant sexual contacts she had with the old man. This "touching" relationship appears to have been a masturbatory substitute for an inadequate sensual and tender relationship with her mother and father. The oedipal overtones were obvious. She was left by mother to take care of the babies and felt inadequate and abandoned and must have turned to father with an intensity that made her an easy and willing victim of the "old man." The preoedipal longings were less obvious but also centered on the word *touching*. We can reasonably suspect that she acted out on the old man an early masturbatory fantasy. We are not sure exactly what was touched but we can be fairly sure it was the phallus (clitoris). In this respect she was more a phallic tomboy than her motherly cousin who did other things with *her* old man. The pubertal struggle between her fundamentally incestuous sexual drives and her guilt feelings was never adequately settled, as her relationship with her cousin allowed a dissociation or split to develop in her ego and superego, which in itself was a development of an earlier confusion and split in her attitude towards both her parents and grandmother. Mother was away doing her own brand of visiting and father was the more motherly one. This had led to ambivalence toward herself, her child and her husband as well as her parents and beloved cousin. Another way of stating the problem would be in terms of a confusion in her identifications and relationships with her primary objects. In her mind's eye, she was plagued by other sights and sensations—memories of things past. A part of her did not function in the present reality. She and the old man acted like children together. She felt she had not grown up. All neurotics have unfinished business back in the past. A defective relationship cried out to be completed. She suffered from a deficiency disease, a sort of rickets of the mind, but the "funnel breast" or the "bow legs" were not visible. Around sixteen a boy dropped dead. Whom did this boy represent? The baby *she* resented who had died? Was he the tomboy part of herself? What sensitized her toward giving this part up? From thirteen to sixteen the more developed feminine part and the little tomboy part struggled for control. The boy's heart death was a warning that not only might her parents really break up but that she too could die in the sense that an irreparable loss might occur (castration). From then on the little tomboy was locked up insecurely in her unconscious. He broke out in disguise again and again and when she married. The normal sexual foreplay with her husband acted as a threat, inasmuch as it was a body-image representative of the forbidden tomboy, aggressive, sexy, bad part of her that led to death, abandonment and loss. This part of her was always laden with guilt displaced onto the bad house. The house ordinarily stands for the mother, so we can say that she may have identified with the negative aspects of her mother who was sexually passive, went visiting and was a gambler interested in money. In one sense we could see she was acting like a little prostitute, but her problems were not nearly as severe as those of the adult with this type of disorder. Another aspect refers to the mother who, when she had the baby, lost her legs and mind and teeth—she could not walk and was put away. This was a disguised castration threat. It had come from making babies, being sloppy and lazy. Wanting to go "visiting" and gambling were equivalent to visiting and touching for money, signifying compulsive greediness and coldness. She thus found herself identifying with the hateful negative characteristics of her mother and ended up full of unconscious death wishes and passive aggressive sexual fantasies, like so many other phobic patients. The deaths of her grandmother and siblings had been traumatic, like the seduction and her visit to the undertaker. She was trauma prone. In the present she really longed for a masturbatory type of touching which was *repressed*. The longing had returned to haunt her and disrupt her sexual and tender relations with her husband.

The therapeutic problem consisted mainly of ventilating as completely as possible the ambivalent relationship between the mother and daughter that drove the patient with greater than usual intensity toward her father and cousin. This was fundamental, for it was due to this attitude and the deficiencies in the mother-daughter relationship that the little girl's oedipal relationship developed the pathological intensity which sent her visiting. She was not only driven toward father but also toward her cousin who acted as a second mother. She had identified easily with this cousin, who was not only an alter-ego figure but obviously had her own oedipal problems, as she had lost her own mother and had gone "visiting" with *her* "father."

We could also look at her problem in terms of an incomplete mourning reaction. Actually, she had a psychotic mother who neglected her children and was away much of the time. Chronic episodes of indifference, coldness and absence can summate and have all the effects of a more sudden and complete loss. They result in pathological mourning marked by repressed grief, hate and yearning, as well as a partial withdrawal and regression. The latter is characterized by a chronic cynicism or lack of trust of others, inhibition of feelings, and autistic and masturbatory fantasies which may or may not be acted out. These fantasies are a poor substitute for reality. They are often unconscious or semiconscious and attempt to undo or compensate for the past sorrows and defects in psychosexual and social development or maturation. The patient said she did her touching for money and used the excuse that there was little money at home. She really meant love from mother. Money and sexual touching were both substitutes for a missing tender sensual relationship with the mother. Problems relating to her self-image and to her mercenary feelings of greediness and guilt were implied. She accused her mother of such qualities. Another factor which was implicit in her therapy was the exploration of her masturbatory daydreams or fantasies. Once these were brought out in the open they could theoretically be discarded. There would be a danger here as there are many aggressive and depressive feelings being repressed and tied up with the memories of the cousin and the old man and her infantile past in general. As her ego enlarged its boundaries of conscious awareness, her symptoms would tend to improve. However, she could become more and more angry at her parents and possibly at her husband. She might demand that he make more money or find him unsatisfactory as a lover. The impression she gave at this time, however, was that this would probably not happen and that she would probably become a more tender and tolerant person toward both her child and her husband and less interested in the family upstairs. All in all, the prognosis at this time could reasonably be considered a good one.

In fact, her therapy on a twice-a-week basis lasted for a year, with a complete remission of her symptoms during the latter half of her treatment, accompanied by some changes in her personality in the direction of maturity. She became less shy and more positive in her relationships with women, took an active role in the local Parent Teachers Association, and encouraged her husband to obtain a better job away from this city and her parents. At the time she left therapy she was fully determined and able to achieve her long-standing ambition of having a home of her own. On the negative side, she remained somewhat inhibited in her sex life in regard to foreplay, tenderness and spontaneity. She gave up her parents but never became openly reconciled to or forgiving of her mother's behavior. The father became the focal point of her anger on many occasions during her therapy. At the close of it, she actually rejected both her parents. The greatest improvement in her libidinal relationships was with her children. She developed a close and warmly affectionate relationship with her daughter, which she declared was the most satisfactory aspect of her therapy. This remark hinted that a partial solution of the basic mother-daughter problem had occurred.

Hysterical and phobic patients are governed predominantly by their feelings. Our principal problem with them is one of undoing repressions and displacements. Expiation of guilt feelings is a common problem. It should be carefully noted how all the patient's productions are treated at a fantasy level. The therapist must leave reality problems to the patient, his lawyer, religious counselor, social worker or physician. Attempts to advise or play the loving friend are usually wrong, especially during the initial interview.

II

PSYCHOTHERAPY AND PATHOLOGICAL MOURNING

A Phobia Concerning Shaking

From the point of view of analytical psychotherapy, the most important clinical cause of psychopathology lies in the inability of a child to master the loss of the relationship to a love object. Losses can be acute, subacute or chronic, and are usually occasioned by death, abandonment, illness or chronic neglect. There are other causes more or less related to neglect, such as lack of opportunity to relate, inability of parents to respond, etc. The most important love objects are naturally the parents, especially the mother. Siblings, parental substitutes, pets, beloved possessions and familiar surroundings play a lesser but important role. The effects of the loss are primarily determined by constitutional and temporal factors and the availability of satisfactory replacements. Constitutional elements have to be ignored. The time of greatest susceptibility lies roughly between three and six months, when the child begins to develop important discriminatory powers, and around six or seven years, with the full development of the instinctual patterns of relationship. Object relationships at this time can be considered of special importance. The normal reaction to loss is a mixture of sadness, yearning, anger, guilt and withdrawal. This reaction is called mourning. It ends with a detachment of interest from the lost object and an attachment to a new object after a period of suspicion and testing. During mourning, and especially during the period of detachment, many characteristics of the lost object are taken over (incorporated) and become a permanent part of the mourner's personality and character traits. An awareness

44

of the possibility of loss and replacement when mourning is satisfactorily concluded usually leads to a heightened awareness of reality in terms of caution, foresight, reconciliation, and a distrust of magic, wishful thinking and feelings of omnipotence and invulnerability.

Pathological mourning is characterized by repression of affects, denial of loss, and an inability to express and complete the mourning reaction. The repression and denial are often partial, and the various affective components of mourning are handled differently in each case. Identifications with the lost object are often poorly integrated or assimilated. Ego splitting and disunity occur. An internal disharmony is projected onto and acted out on the environment. It is also acted out in the internal world of relationships to the self.

Repressed affects and denied patterns of relationship are displaced to many areas which will be considered in detail in the next chapter. The pathology and complications of the withdrawal process are of special importance. The withdrawal and detachment from persons, things and feelings are often massive. Autistic fantasies associated with masturbatory activities, fetishistic preoccupations and hypochondriacal concerns may become an open or secret way of life and a partial barrier to maturation. Pathological mourning and withdrawal are always associated with regression and pathological narcissism, which will be considered in more detail in Chapter XIV. As each level of maturation depends upon those preceding it, the effects of pathological mourning are cumulative. Denial and repression can only be maintained by the expenditure of psychic energy. When the demands of the environment upon psychic energy finally become too much to handle, a "last straw" or external event usually precipitates an anxiety attack. This is a warning of an impending ego collapse in the form of a depression, dissociative process or regression to a more infantile level where less energy is needed. The periods of greatest danger and stress are those that involve a qualitative or quantitative increase in intimate personal relationships and intense feelings. These intimacies resurrect the old dangers of love dependency, rejection, hurt and hate. Psychoanalytic psychotherapy is concerned principally with the undoing of denied losses and repressed affects, as well as the integration of dissociated ego elements. It strives to complete a delayed mourning process, restore hope, and encourage a resumption of growth in which the patient can renounce the past, forgive, forget and replace the lost objects. In another sense, it untangles, simplifies, orders and masters a complex mass of projected and introjected relationships and associated affects.

Bowlby (1963) has discussed the clinical implications of pathological mourning in an exceptionally lucid manner and has demonstrated convincingly that unconscious angry yearnings to recover a lost object (or relationship) are the basic problem in many clinical syndromes. He distinguishes four main variations of adult pathological mourning.

(1) A persistent *unconscious* yearning to recover the lost object. (2) Intense and persistent anger and reproach expressed toward the object and/or the self. (3) Caring for some other bereaved person or vicarious figure, often amounting to a compulsion. (4) A partial denial that the object is permanently lost, leading to an ego split or dissociative process. These variants exist together in a multitude of combinations and are the basis of many clinical conditions. Another variation is a distortion of the identification with the lost object. This identification is a partial one, leading to a struggle due to a failure to solve the ambivalent relationship to the lost object. It will be illustrated later by many cases. The role of guilt in connection with loss is important whether based on real deeds or conscious or unconscious wishes. Guilt due to anger and reproach displaced onto the self has been mentioned. Displacement makes such reproaches ineffective. Inability to express anger leads to an inability to express love, and in effect prevents a resolution of mourning, including a reversal of the detachment and withdrawal components. Bowlby prefers the term *detachment,* as he feels ego defensive, countercathectic aspects are obvious in many cases, and unconscious, strong feelings for the original lost object persist. Anna Freud (1960) prefers the term *withdrawal,* referring to the withdrawal of libido from the lost object (and outer world) and its investment in the self- (and body) images. In my opinion, both processes take place. In this book, detachment will also refer to intellectual isolation elements and a loss of spontaneity and recognition of one's true feelings, and withdrawal will also refer to a giving up of meaningful contact with others. Bowlby emphasizes an old contention of many analysts that the intensity of the reaction to a loss (or trauma) is often predicated on previous losses, separations, rejections and other narcissistic injuries. These can summate. The relationship of loss to trauma will be discussed later (Chapter V). When there is a denial of *loss,* the patient *consciously* believes the object is recoverable. When the *yearning* component is repressed, he believes the same *unconsciously.* In either case, grief is only experienced in part, as loss is only partially admitted. It has often been observed that care for a vicarious figure is especially common in girls and that when siblings suffer a parent loss together, one then mothers or

fathers the other. There are many variations of this theme. All the cases in this book will illustrate various aspects of pathological mourning. There are many varieties of loss. A failure to solve problems of the oedipal stage can be discussed in terms of unresolved mourning. This falls in line with ideas that earlier losses (traumas) are responsible for the failure to solve the problems of the losses that occur during the oedipal period.

The best and most obvious example of pathological mourning will be shown in Chapter XVI. An important element of pathological mourning is present in all the neuroses. Its final shape is usually expressed in terms of the oedipus complex. While anger, guilt and yearning are prominent, detachment and withdrawal are often minimal.

We have listened to the opening interview with a young phobic woman whose pathological mourning for a lost mother relationship involved an unsolved oedipal fixation, the acting out of a masturbatory fantasy, and an ego split that kept her from a happy married life. Let us consider a similar type of case concerning a young man. Anxious, phobic and hysterical patients are common and among the more interesting. In the patient we will now interview, guilt feelings play a principal role in the development of his problem. We will also see how oedipal problems can manifest themselves in a different form in a young man, and that masturabatory fantasies are not necessarily expressed by genital touching, as in the first case.

A young naval lieutenant came to the psychiatrist because he was dissatisfied with the psychiatric treatment he had been receiving from the Navy. An appointment had been arranged by his Navy therapist. He had been in treatment for a month and had left because he felt he could be cured of his difficulties more readily by an older man. He was a pleasant-faced, attractive young man with a ready smile and a soft voice. He appeared slightly tense but relaxed quickly as he talked. The therapist motioned him to be seated and then began.

"Would you sit here, please. I don't know very much about you. Your doctor told me something about your case and he told you that I was going to see you, didn't he?"

"Yes."

"Could you start right from the beginning, if you don't mind, and tell me how you happened to come here."

"Well, I'll do the best I can, Doctor. Well actually I've been troubled with a certain amount of *nervous disorder* ever since, say, the age of *fourteen* or so, roughly, uh, I always had a good deal of *tremors* in my *hand* and *what not*."

The therapist noticed this possible giveaway at once. When a man complains he had trouble with his hands at fourteen, it usually means that a masturbatory problem was present. This can have many variations. Fourteen was repeated primarily to fix it in the therapist's mind and secondarily to enlarge the area of memories around this time. As in so many cases, many words are offered and practically any of them will lead to the same goal, which is the enlargement of memories around the time when the symptom began. The onset is extremely important, and must be returned to again and again throughout therapy with increasing clarity about the origin and meaning of the symptom. *Fourteen* was the most practical word. *Nervous disorder* could be saved for further use. To use *hands, tremors* or *what not* would be tactically bad at this point and would probably lead to irritation and simple restatement.

"Why do you pick fourteen?"

"Because roughly that's about the time I can first remember having the *tremors.*"

"What happened?"

"Uh, one thing I can just remember starting to take on *tremors.* I would say they first began probably with—"

He paused, frowned and continued.

"I can remember in general science class in high school, my first year in high school, of doing a demonstration experiment with the class. You know, they do these little deals and my hands *noticeably* trembled while trying to, whatever the heck the thing was, *fool with a test tube or something,* and, uh, I can remember being very conscious of it and realizing that *everyone else* in the room had *noticed* it also. And, uh, I can also remember in high school starting, I took a course in mechanical drawing after, right after a gymnasium class and after exercising in the gymnasium going through the parallel bars, or something like that, trying to do the fine work with the drawing, I *noticed* that my hands were *trembling* a good deal."

Noticing it, looking at himself and the fantasy of the entire class noticing it gave away certain as yet poorly defined exhibitionistic tendencies and guilt feelings. Fooling with a test tube or something at fourteen was possibly symbolic of a masturbatory problem.

"You *noticed* that?"

"Yes, yes, I became *aware* of it. I guess that you *notice* the insignificant comment, *comments* that I was very conscious of in front of my friends."

The therapist was interested in what sensitized him to these "comments." These had to be treated as a fantasy which must be explored. Any connection they had retained with reality was useless to us from the point of view of therapy.

"What kind of *comments*?"

"Oh, I wouldn't say anything particularly, that would particularly place itself in my memory, just the fact that they pointed to the obvious *tremors*."

"So is that your trouble, your tremors?"

The patient's refusal to be drawn out must have annoyed the therapist. This was probably sensed by the patient, who tried to convert the interview into a question-answer anamnesis. This would destroy the emotional linkages and associative immediacy of the responses, although it might reduce the anxiety that lack of structuring produces in some patients. The therapist immediately recovered and apologized. A better response might have been, "How do you mean?"

"The beginning of my *nervous symptoms* in my life? Uh, I just want to give you the background. This thing existed to a greater or lesser extent in me for some time. Oh, the immediate circumstances surrounding my coming here, is that what you'd like?"

"Oh, go right ahead. You are doing fine!"

"Uh, well, like I say, I had these *things* all through high school and college."

"You mean the *tremors*?"

"*Tremors*, yes. They always bothered me. I always felt quite conscious about it, but usually they weren't too severe and, after all, a young man doesn't particularly very often get himself in a position where people would *notice* whether his hands were trembling or not. And so I lived with *it*, let's put it that way. It was *part of me* and I lived with *it*. In college though, I guess it was in my junior year in college, I took a course in analytical chemistry and biometric analysis where you work with ten-thousandths of a milligram weight on an analytical balance and have to take them up with tweezers. You probably have taken these courses yourself. Uh, you understand, Doctor?"

He laughed uneasily and continued.

"It was impossible, Doctor, for me to get in there."

He laughed again, and shook his head.

"And pick up those damn weights and get them off the pan. You know that's very fine and close, delicate work. And with the fact I was taking several other chemistry courses which required lab work, my tremors mounted with the increased tension put upon them by attempting to control them, and I got in a pretty bad way there. In fact, a similar thing happened to me in college to what happened to me when I wound up here, which I'll get to a little later. I got a *terrific* case of the *shakes*. I just couldn't, couldn't bring myself under *control* at anytime whatsoever. In fact, there was one night I just went tearing out and got drunk in order to *control my tremors,* which didn't help me."

He was like a man who had become panicky but who denied his fears, observed himself shaking and said the *shaking* made him uneasy. It was now becoming more probable that *tremors* and *shakes* had become the symbolic representatives of phallic masturbatory fantasies which he could not control. He literally felt exposed. As will be seen, the shakes also represented a punishment as well as a gratification. They were not simply the *effect* of the punishment fantasies *accompanying* the masturbatory ones.

"Why, what happened?"

"Well, outside of numbing my nerves with a little alcohol—"

"No, I mean to give you the shakes, how did you happen to get this terrific case?"

"They just seemed to build up, Doctor. I can't tie it up with any particular incident. Uh, I had found out, however, during the number of years I had these things that my *not smoking* would have almost an instantaneous effect on them. I could almost control my tremors one hundred per cent by *ceasing to smoke!* So, then, in my junior year in college, I sort of had this kind of *severe attack.* To escape from it one night I went out and got drunk and on the next day I was offered a cigarette, and that was the end of that!"

The problem of control was displaced to *smoking.* Stopping represented an expiatory act which controlled his guilt.

"What do you mean?"

"I just quit smoking! I quit smoking!"

"What do you mean by a terrific attack?"

Here, *terrific shakes* was condensed with *severe attack.*

"Uh, well, I couldn't do anything, Doctor, I, all I did was *shake.*"

"In your junior year?"

This was to pin down the time.

"Junior year at college, yes."

"How old were you then?"

"I would be a little over twenty."

"And all you could do was *shake*?"

"Yes, sir,"

"You mean in the class?"

The element of exhibitionism was an important component in arousing feelings of guilt and shame.

"Oh, yes, but when I realized, I didn't go to class for a day or so."

There was now a good chance that he was suffering from a form of masturbatory anxiety and guilt and was finding it difficult either to remember or talk about. He had displaced the guilt feelings onto another vice—smoking. Perhaps by talking about where he stayed one could find out what he did. In connection with shaking, there is a delicate euphemism for masturbation used in the Navy, "to shake the dew off the lily."

"You stayed in your room?"

"Uh."

He made a long pause.

"Well, I told you one night I went out and got drunk, the rest of the time I spent at various places. I guess there wasn't too much time involved."

"What do you mean, various places? Where were you living during your junior year?"

"I had a, the college I went to didn't have any boarding facilities. I had a room, a private room on the outside. I used to live there."

"You mean you stayed home then, in your room?"

"Yes."

"And *shook?*"

"I'd say I *shook* no matter where I went, Doctor. I don't recall particularly where I went."

At this point such a recall may have been too painful or possibly wasn't important.

"That must have been very embarrassing. Do you remember?"

"Oh, yes, I remember."

"What do you remember about it?"

"Well, it actually started in the summer before my junior year began. I was in school. I was going to summer school at the time. I was only taking two courses a day. One course was offered in the morning for two hours, and the other in the evening for two hours. The only session they had running was an evening session. It wasn't the analytical chemistry course, although actually that came just a month or two later, but the same problem would have evolved right there. I was associated with the chemistry because I always thought to myself I never could have done this if I had *continued smoking*, but, uh, I, well I'd *always* had my tremors at this time."

The usual attempt to go into the more easily understood past could now be made.

"What do you mean, always?"

"Well, I told you, ever since the time I was *fourteen* years old I had them perpetually."

"Not before?"

"No sir, *as far as I know*. And, uh, well, the tremors just seemed to be getting worse, progressively worse, One night as I was going to school they just got, I don't know, pretty bad, and by the time I got out of class that night I was a wreck. I *had been trying to give up smoking*."

"Smoking?"

"Yes. It was a course in *ethics*. I was taking thermodynamics in the morning. I was just filling in my time taking an *ethics* class at night to make it worth while attending the summer session. Uh, since my nerves had been getting bad I tried to *not smoke*, and I'd try in fact right through the day, but the rest of the day I'd start *smoking* again, you know, a *habit*. So I was placing so much importance on it all, as soon as I'd *smoke* I'd get *bad tremors*. Well I suppose this day sometime during the day I had *smoked*. And my *tremors* mounted as the day went on. By the time I got out of that course in the evening, I just went out and got *drunk,* because by going out and getting drunk I could get to the point where I could light a cigarette without taking one hand and grab the other one and direct it to the cigarette. Is that very clear?"

A *bad habit* was making him more and more anxious. It was in an *ethics* class that his anxiety became intolerable. The word *habit* was a general one so an approach could be made to other bad habits besides smoking.

"As you say, *bad habits* are hard to break."

"Well then again, *smoking*, I don't consider it a bad habit. It's not like being an *alcoholic*. So anyway, I, in this one night I had to, I felt compelled to alleviate myself of the shakes by going out and getting *drunk*."

"Another bad habit?"

"Yes, certainly! But, uh, I had basic intelligence enough to realize that this was probably the solution to the problem of my nerves, and so the next day I gave up smoking, and I gave it up and meant it. I completely gave up smoking and, as I say, that one circumstance does improve my nerves a very great deal, and it did then."

"Gave up your bad habit, huh?"

"I gave up the habit of smoking."

The therapist smiled.

"Were there other ones? What other bad habits did you have?"

"I thought you were going to make reference to drinking."

"No others?"

"No, *not particularly.*"

"What do you mean, not particularly?"

"Well, I wouldn't want to put myself up as a mountain of morals but I've been known to go out with girls and pet them and *what not* at this age."

Now things were getting warm. There are many ways to masturbate.

"By at this age, you mean when you were twenty?"

"Yes."

"By petting and what not do you mean doing something else when you were out with girls?"

"I don't think most boys at twenty, I don't think they'd do much else hardly!"

He was obviously not ready to go any further.

"Anyway, you didn't do anything else?"

"Yes, that's right."

This was an equivocal remark.

"Then you went out with girls?"

"I was going out with girls since I was about *fourteen.*"

This was when his "anxiety" had begun.

"Since you were *fourteen?*"

"Oh, roughly, maybe even before, I don't know. Maybe we had mixed parties when I was in grade school so that *pulls it* down to about twelve."

"So you didn't need anything else then, huh?"

"Need what else? Do you mean masturbation?"

He paused. The therapist waited. After a while he continued.

"I never did masturbate then, Doctor."

A discussion of masturbation now might be premature and too intellectual.

"You went out instead and petted?"

"Yes! Actually I think, in fact I went over these things in my life and I find it hard to believe, but it never occurred to me to masturbate in my younger days. I never felt inclined that way."

"Really! How do you mean? How come?"

"Well, that's a difficult question to answer."

"Of course, but I mean you have ideas."

"How come? It just didn't occur to me as the thing to do. If something doesn't occur to you, you don't ask yourself why it doesn't, do you?"

"Occasionally I should think your curiosity, you knew about such a thing?"

"Uh, remotely, only remotely, doctor."

"How do you mean?"

"Uh, I had heard the word. In fact, it never occurred to me very much for anybody to take it out on themselves that way."

The aggressive, defiant and primitive aspects of the act were being stressed.

"You mean you had been taught differently. Is that what you mean?"

"No, they never really taught me anything. I acquired most of my knowledge of the facts of life by a process of osmosis or from my brother, just plain conversation with young boys of that age."

Here he could be given a rest while the structure of his family was explored.

"You have a brother?"

He said that he was the youngest of five and had two brothers and two sisters. He was now twenty-five, and the oldest sibling was a girl of thirty-two. After this, the therapist returned to the sexual theme.

"And so you knew very little about sex?"

"Well, it just hadn't occurred to me in my youth to masturbate. I never thought about masturbating or was tempted to masturbate. That was the end of that."

"You just went ahead and necked?"

"Yes."

"I can understand because, even though no one told you, you said you were interested in a course of *ethics,* so I wondered if you just took that or if you were interested in ethical problems or questions."

"I would have had to take the course eventually, anyway, and since I happened to be around there that summer I took it. Let's see. One thing that was, well let's say, relatively, I consider it somewhat of an *unbalance* in my sexual life around that period was that in going out with girls and *necking* and, uh, well, very rarely *necking,* but if I started *petting* girls at all then I would very frequently, in fact damn near always *lose my seed* and it was a fact which always *disturbed* me somewhat."

This was the missing clue to a variation on the theme of masturbation.

"How do you mean? How should it disturb you?"

"Well, uh, just by basically being uncomfortable among other reasons. I didn't consider it, I suppose I also considered it somewhat *abnormal.*"

He had probably started to say "I didn't consider it abnormal." This is an excellent illustration of the rule that there are no negatives in the unconscious.

"How do you mean abnormal?"

"I mean I didn't figure this was happening to other people, other boys my age, and I think it is basic enough to disturb anyone, a child at that age."

The therapist made it more personal.

"Surely, to think they are abnormal. You thought you were abnormal?"

He replied after a long pause.

"I don't think I ever quite put it in terms of *abnormality,* perhaps *overpassionate.* I don't know. Maybe I was dumb or something. It didn't occur to me to think of myself as abnormal."

Now he wanted to retract a word with the anxiety-laden connotations of being a passive mother's boy, queer, homosexual.

"But you used that word, so I wondered what you mean."

"Only in so far as to my knowledge that this wasn't happening to other boys that age."

"How did you know?"

"That's a good question. I didn't imagine it was happening to the other boys of that age."

"That's what I mean. You just felt like, I bet, other boys aren't doing this."

"Yes, I figured this didn't happen to other boys. I don't recall ever having asked any, however, if it happened to them or not. I was aware from the facts of life that this was supposed to happen during sexual union and I sure as hell wasn't having sexual union and here it was happening to me."

"So how could you explain it? What did you think?"

He paused again and then continued.

"Well, I wouldn't exactly say I ever explained it. I just *accepted* it and tried to *avoid* it for one thing. It happened when I was petting girls which was contrary to my *religious* belief, and therefore something which I tried to *avoid,* and so I'd probably say I tried to *avoid it* rather than explain it."

There was a conflict between accepting and avoiding. The therapist had to remember to keep away from reality and treat everything as fantasy. In psychotherapy "religious" must be thought of as pertaining to the parental teachings of an early era when they were considered all-powerful. As such, it is legitimate grist for the mill. Of course, the reality of religion, which is a matter of faith, has nothing to do with psychotherapy per se. His last statement showed that his avoidance was probably a phobic avoidance of a masturbatory fantasy displaced to petting and smoking.

"You were religious?"

"Yes."

"And you mean you were taught not to?"

The therapist was using this route to get into the past.

"Yes, you are not supposed to go out and pet. *Little* boys aren't supposed to go petting with little girls, etc. So, I guess I was, up to about this time in college. So I gave up the smoking and my nerves were considerably improved, very much improved."

He revealed that from a psychosexual point of view he was a little boy. It was noticeable how easily he switched (displaced) from petting to smoking.

"When you stopped your bad habit of smoking?"

"When I stopped smoking! Smoking I don't consider a bad habit. In fact I like to smoke, Doctor."

He was getting braver.

"I thought you called it that."

He paused.

"Maybe I did. Perhaps I did. I probably did. Anyway my nerves improved considerably in college."

"When you stopped?"

"When I stopped. I stopped, it was the middle of July or in August, something like that and, I, uh, well, I stopped smoking, as I said. Finally Lent rolled around and I *even stopped drinking* for Lent."

"And petting?"

"*I was perpetually trying to stop that,* Doctor."

This was the key to his shaking problem.

"How do you mean?"

"Well, like I told you before, it is something contrary to my principles and I therefore attempted all my life and according to my religious beliefs to avoid it."

"You were pretty religious?"

"Yes, I was."

Now another attempt could be made to learn more about his background.

"Where did you get it?"

"My mother is very religious."

"Mother?"

"Yes. My father is now too, I think, but always in a different way than my mother."

"How do you mean?"

"Well, my father is, uh, well let's say my mother is a very emotional woman. She's, she feels things more than she thinks them. She feels passionate in a religious way. I mean it's something she was brought up with. I don't think she ever stopped to sit down and consider really why she believed it. It is just so much the fact that she does believe it. I'm not doing her justice. I'm just trying to paint a rough picture. My father is more the, uh, well he's an extremely intelligent man, not that my mother isn't intelligent, but my father is an intelligent man who is blasé, realistic and unexcitable. I shouldn't say that because up until a few years ago my father was a very excitable type. He used to fly off the handle a lot, whereas now he is very, very calm."

In describing parents or siblings, patients are usually describing facets of themselves.

"Fly off the handle! About what?"

"Well, he used to be quite excitable about most anything from a bum report card to anything."

"You mean when you were a kid?"

"Yes. It was just that my father had quite a temper. His wrath was pretty generally held in awe."

His language had a somewhat Biblical flavor, showing the identification of father with God.

"By you?"

"By myself, and I think by the rest of the children in the family too. Not without justification was his wrath held in awe."

He then went on to describe father's rages and how he was "cuffed around." There was always "tension" in the air. It took so little to make father "explode." He raged and shouted at mother. It went on far into the night. He would listen to it when he was a little boy lying in bed and get very anxious. He and mother were religious when he was little, but this theme made him dry up, pause, and ask, "So where were we?"

The therapist returned again to the sexual problem.

"You said you were fighting very hard to keep from going out and necking, and perpetually losing the struggle."

"Yes, I got up to Lent where I gave up *drinking* too."

"Too, along with—?"

"Smoking. I had already given up smoking."

"Oh, yes. Just kept the petting, huh?"

He laughed uneasily.

"We went through that already!"

"*That*, you wouldn't give up even for Lent, huh?"

"Well, that didn't really occur to me! Uh, so Easter Sunday, after I didn't smoke and I didn't drink, I was pursuing my *usual* resolve, but anyway I sat down and kind of jokingly said to myself that this would never do, you know, for me to have no minor vices. I sat down and I mixed up a cocktail and got hold of a cigarette."

"When was this?"

"Easter Sunday, my junior year in college. It is significant because that is when I started smoking and drinking. I had the cocktail and cigarette. I don't think there was a cocktail or a cigarette I had in my entire life that I enjoyed as thoroughly. It was just a moment supreme, you know, just with a cocktail and a cigarette. And I enjoyed them so much and they had no effect whatsoever on my nerves! My hands were as calm as could be, so I figured, well, what the hell! This doesn't seem to bother me, so very moderately I pursued the habit. I was always inclined to be a somewhat heavy smoker. I was up to a pack a day in the course of a month or two, but my nerves were all right. My senior year in college they started going again, in the beginning of my senior year. By the end, by the time college was done, I had pretty much my old nerves back."

Now it could be assumed that the "petting" was the main problem.

"Why do you think that was so?"

"Well, I had, uh—"

He paused and appeared sad and then continued.

"I had certain frustrations during my senior year of college, you know. I fell in love with a girl. It was a completely unsuccessful operation as far as her falling in love with me was concerned."

"How do you mean that? What was wrong?"

He paused.

"Well, it was just a question of—if I actually knew the answer to that I would have corrected it and be happily married by now."

"Of course, but you had ideas. What you mean is you don't know whether you were right or wrong, but you must have had ideas."

"Well, do you want me to tell you about the entire thing?"

"Just as you please. What were your ideas?"

"Well, one of my ideas, my sexual relations with women and the manner in which I pursued them have somewhat altered since. I am trying to think of whether I should try and express myself in the light of that or not."

"Just as you wish."

"I've come up with a couple of conclusions as regards—"

He paused again for a few minutes.

"Well, this girl's name is Mary. She had formerly been the girl of my *best friend* and they split up and so the field was left *wide open* for me. I had known her for some time when she was going out with him and, well, the thought heretofore had *never* crossed my mind that Mary was my girl. She was Jack's girl and that was the end of it, you know, and we were great friends. We double dated all the time but that's all, you know, friends. However, when Mary and Jack broke up, it left the field wide open for anybody who was interested. I used to see a lot of Mary because she lives right down by me and I used to drive her back and forth from school when she went to college, so pretty soon I was going out with Mary, but, uh, well I guess I was *still a little conscience-bound by her being Jack's girl, although she wasn't.* I suppose the big reason for my lack of success with Mary was because I didn't, uh, I *was too inclined to set her up on a pedestal* rather than treat her like a woman."

The best friend was his father through a series of displacements. He was talking about an oedipal type of love object, which is either elevated to a pedestal like the virgin mother or made into a prositute. Splitting the mother into an all-good, sexless object and bad prostitute allowed him to evade conflict with her and the dreaded wrath of father. The longing for the sexual, bad mother was retained in disguised masturbatory fantasies and was evoked by sensual feelings in his penis when he petted. It was accompanied by the dread of castration and abandonment. He was like an adolescent boy.

"How do you mean?"

He paused again before continuing.

"Uh, well, uh, although I had a physical desire for Mary I don't think I expressed it to her by the manner in which I pursued her. I don't make things clear to you, huh?"

This meant he wasn't clear about it himself because the feelings were irrational and contradictory.

"You mean you didn't pet with her like you did with the others?"

"I suppose it would amount to that. I kind of, I suppose, passed up the opportunity to neck with Mary when it came along because I idolized her so much. That would be fairly accurate. It's *not too clear to me either,* Doctor. I mean the *whole* business."

It was highly probable that this was a disguised reference to the dreaded "hole" of the woman, as castration anxiety colored his feelings to such a large extent and he was fixated psychosexually at an oedipal phallic level. Of course, *none* of this deep material was directly useful in this interview and seldom, for that matter, in the entire course of therapy. The work had to be done with near derivatives until the patient was "ripe" for these discoveries. In the meantime, a knowledge of the inner structure of his problems helped the therapist to structure the interview and organize the material.

"You mean why you did?"

"Yes, why you do some of the things I've done, I suppose."

"But as you said you felt that petting was wrong and you idolized her and you didn't want to do what you considered wrong with *her.*"

"Yes, I suppose, I, uh, well, all I wanted to do was marry Mary and build a sweet little nest in the west and let the rest of the world go by, or something like that. It never quite worked out."

He must have behaved like a little boy with a woman too mature to endure it very long.

"And you think it was because you were that way?"

"I think so because there are a *couple of repeated instances* in my life where that same thing has happened."

"By the same thing, you mean you idolized them?"

"Yes."

"And wouldn't neck with them?"

"Yes, and once the opportunity had come and gone I realized it all too late. I'd kind of *scared* the *girl* off by then, I guess, it being too obvious or something, I don't know. Well, I guess she didn't contribute very much to, the *whole* affair didn't contribute very much to the peace and quiet of my nerves during my senior year in college. As a matter of fact, during my senior year in college, I did next to no studying, and I had worked pretty hard for the first three years of college. My senior year in college I spent damn near every evening out drinking beer and very few nights with the books. I majored in chemistry in college, and as I said I had worked hard for three years. I didn't have too many courses to take in my senior year anyway and I had done pretty well in my science courses. I had a good background. so that I, with a little cramming at the very end, I was able to squeeze a C out of everything with the exception of a course in French which,

unfortunately, I needed to make up the two-year language require-
ment, so I unfortunately flunked this course in French and even
though I had more credits than were required for graduation and
even though it was the only course I ever flunked in the four years
I was in college, I didn't graduate with my class from college, which
didn't exactly contribute to my peace of mind, either."

Not graduating increased his feelings of not acting his age and being
an inadequate boy. This feeling was also part of the oedipus complex.
From the point of view of the ego, his narcissism was severely damaged.
He had also turned away from heterosexuality and drank beer with
the boys. There were also pregenital failures like just "squeezing out"
a C. The narcissistic damage was most important here.

"When was this?"

"This was in June 1950."

"In '50?"

"That was kind of the popping blow so that my nerves started
back where they pretty much were. They had been building up along
that path for six months or so but by June 1950 I was back pretty
much with my good old set of nerves."

"And by your nerves, you mean tremors?"

"Well, the Korean War broke out right after I didn't graduate
from college and a few months later I wound up coming into the
Navy. I did twenty-two months in the Navy as an enlisted man and
then I finally got commissioned, and, uh, I wound up as an officer.
All this time I carried around quite a set of nerves with me, you
know, my *good old set of nerves,* but they were something I was
usually able to keep fairly well under control and they are not too
obvious. To me they always seemed obvious but I have ascertained
to my *satisfaction* that they weren't too obvious to other people. I
managed to get by *pretty good* until—"

He made a long pause.

"Well, until we went on a round-the-world cruise about this time
last year. I was in French Indo-China and the night before we left
Saigon I went out and got pretty drunk, I figure very, very drunk,
which was not too uncommon a habit while on this trip. Many times
we all rolled home. I possibly rolled maybe a little harder than the
other people. Next day, well, I was all right for a day. My *nerves*
were *pretty bad,* you know, and I had a hell of a time trying to, well
by the time I got to eat dinner that night I had a hell of a time just
sitting at the table eating dinner, and I tried to sit and watch the
movie in the ward room after dinner and I couldn't do it. Then I

started to get this *closed-in feeling* and I was convinced then that I was going to *die* of a *heart attack* at any minute."

The reference to the "good old set of nerves" and "getting by pretty good" referred to his satisfaction over retaining his secret defiant masturbatory substitutes. The ambivalence was obvious. Something had led to an acute claustrophobic attack and overwhelming castration anxiety displaced onto the heart. Why should he think of such things?

"You have heard of such things?"

"No, well I suppose, people drop dead from heart attacks every day, don't they?"

"I mean how do you know?"

"Well, my father developed a little heart trouble in the last year or two but nothing so serious that he has been in any way threatened with dropping dead."

Now it could be understood why father had turned *religious,* which to him meant giving up phallic masturbatory wishes directed at the mother. This was also a manifestation of the wish to castrate or kill father and the denial of all this dangerous and abhorrent material.

"He has heart trouble?"

"He's about over it now."

"What happened?"

"Well, he complained of a few little pains around his heart or something. He had a cardiogram taken. I think it has something to do with *cholesterol* accumulating in his arteries or in his veins or *something, cutting out* the supply of blood to and from his *heart,* but then my knowledge of the *whole thing* is somewhat scanty. But anyway he retired and by pursuing the thing with a lot of rest and strict compliance with the orders of his doctor he is just about completely recovered from it."

His accumulated badness led to castration and becoming like a woman.

"And you thought you had heart trouble?"

"Well, this particular day I did, yes. I was in real rough shape. It's hard to put it in words exactly the way I felt but it was pretty rough."

"Did you think it was from too much drinking?"

"Well, the drinking surer than hell didn't help any."

"*Smoking*?"

"Smoking probably did much more trouble, much more harm than drinking did."

"But not *necking*?"

"*Well,* there we'd have to go into quite a discourse. Uh—"

He paused.

"I, uh—"

He paused again.

"My views on necking had somewhat changed. They *hadn't really altered* I suppose, but certainly my activity with the opposite sex had taken on a new stride by this time."

He was obviously acting now in a counterphobic manner but he had not really changed. He had probably gone to prostitutes for which Saigon was famous in the Navy, but the prostitute mother was only the other side of the all-pure mother.

"When was that? You mean in Saigon?"

"Well, not particularly in Saigon but, uh, I had been intimate with women by this time."

"When did it happen? When did you begin?"

"Oh, roughly, say a year and a half ago."

"So it was nothing new?"

"But *actively* about a year ago and, uh, no, it was nothing particularly new, but I had been in various places in Japan, you know. To put it in the vernacular I had gotten laid several times in Japan, during our stay there, and that night in Saigon I was in a similar situation, but I found the whole thing somewhat revolting and shoved off."

The danger referred to by "actively" was that of being out of control.

"You mean extra-special? Something was different, you mean?"

"No, nothing was extra-special, different. It's just that I never, uh, uh, I *never really felt particularly satisfied.* Let's put it this way, in all of these instances my animal nature was satisfied but my—"

He paused.

"Your ethical nature—?"

"My ethical nature or intellectual nature was not satisfied and I, well in other words I just found the whole thing somewhat revolting and *particularly* at this time."

"Particularly at this time, how do you mean?"

"Well, in this instance in Saigon."

"Why particularly?"

"I don't know, it's just like you reached down to the bottom of the barrel, you know. You get to the end of a dead-end street."

Even here the imagery was related to the claustrophobic feelings. From the aspect of the id, it referred to the dangerous regressive intravaginal and intrauterine fantasies of a phallicized body image. From the aspect of the ego, he saw himself as unlike other men in being unable to enjoy normal sexual relationships with nonprostitutes. His narcissistic pride was hurt. From the aspect of his superego, he was not living up to his ideals and would be castrated, as a punishment for acting out "masturbatory" fantasies.

"Did you feel you had reached the end of a dead-end street?"

"Yes. I didn't want any more of this. I didn't want any part of it."

"How do you mean?"

"Fed up! What the hell am I doing here in the first place, so I got the hell out. But anyway, and this acted up, and the next day I had no more of a hangover than anybody would expect to have who had been out drinking most of the night. However, as the day wore on and evening came around I got this terrific *closed-in feeling* and my nerves were going like a bat out of hell. I couldn't sit still or anything. I saw the chief pharmacist's mate and got phenobarbital but that didn't help me. He gave me a shot of brandy. That helped a little and the thing of it was I couldn't get my mind off *myself* or off the consciousness of every breath I drew and all the time thinking maybe it was going to be my last one, and I suddenly started fearing the *wrath of God* and thinking I was going to *drop dead.*"

He used the word "wrath" now in a different context. God was the Father Almighty and at the same time he identified with him. He must have wished father ill or dead and the punishment now fitted the crime. Father was also the one who damned things, which meant punished.

"Because of—?"

"Thrown into eternal damnation."

"Because of what you had done, you mean?"

"Not *specifically* what I had done the night before."

This meant that indirectly it *was* connected with the act.

"But you mean *everything?*"

"I suppose. I don't know. I didn't bother to give the matter much consideration."

"You mean you were in the same position, the same way as mother. You were a *feeling person* and not a *thinking one,* and you felt you would be cast down and damned?"

This was the beginning of an attempt by the therapist to split the patient's ego into a feeling part connected with the past and a thinking part allied with the therapist and his attitude.

"Well, I suppose roughly that's about it. Anyhow, I finally got to sleep and was a little better the next day but not a hell of a lot. Well, it worked out. I got to Singapore and I soothed my conscience a good deal by going out to confession."

Here he could make his peace with a symbolic father.

"When did this happen?"

"This was in August."

"When did you come home?"

"The end of November. I gave you only the first instance of this thing. I finally came to Boston and was still feeling bad and turned myself in to sick bay. I was working with a nice guy but he didn't seem to know what to do. Anyway I decided I needed more than phenobarbital and thought I'd get some real treatment on my own. I knew a fellow who had a somewhat similar trouble who was cured after a year with one of you people, and I decided I'd try anything to get over this. What do you think?"

"I think your nerves can be helped considerably if you really want it."

"I do, Doctor. Something has to be done."

"Well, that's all we'll have time for today. I'll see you Thursday at 2:30 p.m."

"Okay, thanks. See you then."

This anxious young man noticed his trembling hands and felt ashamed and abnormal. Everything turned about the problem of controlling himself. Unlike the first case, he never could accept sexual wishes or openly defy his parents or their internalized representatives. Instead he petted, but achieved the same result. His superego noticed this and accused him of not controlling himself. He compromised by displacing his guilt onto smoking. Giving up this "bad habit" allayed his guilt and anxiety temporarily. He was mother's baby, timid and religious, but another part was blasé, realistic and violent like father. He tried to effect a compromise. This led to a tremor. More important, it led to *noticing* the tremor, which took on symbolic values through displacement and was magnified by the process. Falling in love posed such a problem that the tremors became a terrific attack of shakes. Why? The analyst would say that his attitude towards Mary was that of a little oedipal phallic boy who could not reconcile himself to have a pure relationship with a mother who had a sexual relationship with father. He felt too little, left out, dissatisfied and depressed. He wanted to get rid of father and be mother's one and only baby again, but he ended up by projecting unsettled remnants of the infantile conflict onto reality and lost his friend's girl, lost his class and almost lost father. It was as if his superego could blame everything on his aggressive and sexual oedipal wishes. The return of the repressed oedipal longings and guilt feelings mean that he never resolved these problems but only denied and repressed them. Actually, they were tied up with his inability to break away from his parents enough to defy them temporarily and masturbate, and then master it consciously, like most adolescents. The tremors thus represented his intense ambivalence toward sex and parents, id and superego. The anxiety was in one sense a warning which heralded the approach of a depression over his many losses. In this case, the main loss was that of the infantile relationship with the mother with the accompanying deflation of his infantile narcissism. From the point of view of the superego, he feared castration by father, a fear that was displaced to the heart and cloaked by religious imagery. From a conscious point of view, he simply feared abandonment and loss of love. His "narcissistic mortifications" (Eidelberg, 1957) have been described. These in the main referred to feelings of being unlike other boys or brothers.

The first patient allowed the instincts a freer rein and became terrified of losing control in a somewhat different manner from the second, who looked upon his sexual preoccupations as more alien. In both, the accent was on repression and displacement. The therapeutic problem in the second case was somewhat more difficult, as the superego was more severe and the possibility of reality id, ego and superego satisfactions more limited. The principal job would be that of mitigating an overly severe and aggressive superego while bringing to consciousness his timidity and need to disguise his attitudes and desires toward women in the present and mother in the past. His sibling relationships would enter in to intensify his feelings of inadequacy, as he was the baby of the group. Exposing in detail his disguised masturbatory petting fantasies would be vital to his treatment, as the knowledge gained would force him to give up the two extremes in his sexual behavior. His "religiosity" would be used by him for a while to evade the issues, but little by little he could be brought to see the difference between religion and religiosity or the way he distorted religious beliefs to serve his own needs. There is no reasonable basis for a quarrel between religion and clinical psychotherapy. The real unknown factor was the extent of his aggressive feelings toward the father and how much of his tension was due to the introjection of the "tense" relationship father had toward mother in their household.

This was undoubtedly mixed with a longing for a tender or "good" relationship with him and could fatefully influence his attitude toward the therapist and necessitate working through a long series of sadomasochistic sexual fantasies, and it would be difficult to deal simultaneously with the terrified, shy mother part and the aggressive raging father part of his ego. However, his desire to come to the older man for therapy was a good omen.

During his treatment, the pattern emerged of a shy boy ambivalently attached to a mother who was overly religious and forever warning him about sin, which to him meant sex (masturbation or petting). She had been very anxious about his health when he was four to six and had often taken him into her bed because of nightmares about "bogey men" in his closet and mild night terrors occasioned by listening to his heart beating and being fearful it would stop. These fears were a displacement from urinary and masturbatory problems concerning castration. He had wet his bed frequently as a small boy of four and five and, when older, was very concerned over wet dreams. Very early in his development he blamed his mother for letting him be a sissy and had tried to turn to his father whom he secretly admired very much, but they had never been close. He did feel that father really was concerned about him being a man more than mother was and despaired of ever being as successful in business or as a man. He was very much impressed by his mother's subservience to father. A whole series of sadomasochistic fantasies were associated with his idea of heterosexual relationships, especially on a physical level. Later it developed that his shyness had really begun around four when he went to school. At this time he had suffered from a school phobia. Concurrently he had played exhibitionistic games with girls and boys in the neighborhood and he had "discovered" the difference in the sexes. This had led to his bed wetting, which had been no problem since he was two years old. The most important themes in all the material were those of castration anxiety and exhibitionism.

From the point of view of pathological mourning, the loss was probably based upon the ambivalent attitude of an overprotective mother plus the lack of a good relationship with the father. This had increased his dependence upon and ambivalence toward mother. He had solved his problems by a partial withdrawal expressed by masturbatory fantasies about an all-good mother, and a dread of physical intimacy. His guilt, anxiety about being cut off (castrated— abandoned by God), angry disgust, repressed death wishes—all these affects were aroused by his losses, repressed and shaped, patterned or given their final form in terms of the typical oedipal situation.

He was seen three times a week for eight months and was symptom free at the time that a transfer to another naval station interrupted his therapy. Two years later a Christmas card announced he was married and the father of a child. No difficulties were mentioned.

III

THE NATURE OF THE
PATIENT TREATED
A Phobia Concerning Blushing

The great majority of patients who need psychiatric treatment cannot be treated by psychoanalysis without modification of the technique to such an extent that it is debatable whether it can be called psychoanalysis. For many patients analysts deliberately use a psychotherapy based upon psychoanalytic insights. Sector therapy is only one such psychotherapy. Here the activity of the therapist is designed to evade the difficulties that make the classical technique inappropriate. The majority of psychoanalysts improvise their own kind of psychotherapy, playing each case by ear. This has made the entire field of psychoanalytically based psychotherapy a chaotic one, and the border between psychotherapy and psychoanalysis hazy and wavering. While we have a fairly good idea of what goes on in classical psychoanalysis, no one has the slightest idea of what goes on in psychotherapy, everyone being a law unto himself. There is much to be said for the "intuitive" approach in the case of anyone with the training and experience of the graduate psychoanalyst, but it is confusing to the regular psychiatrist.

There are many difficulties that make patients unanalyzable. Some patients, for example, are unwilling or unable either to free associate or to develop a transference neurosis that can be worked with and modified. Some are unable or unwilling to use hard-won insights. The associative process itself is subject to many disturbances. Many obsessive-compulsive and depressive patients present the therapist with a schedule of reality events and rigidly cling to this type of material.

They recite event after event, can only think concretely, and appear unable to make or accept any changes in their verbal routine. Hysterics, phobics and schizophrenics frequently appear to associate very well but are either too passive, anxious or blocked in their cognitive functions to achieve a synthesis of material into new and stable patterns. For these patients a therapist must actively attempt to make up for the missing functions in the interview situation. This will be discussed further when it is being specifically illustrated. Many borderline psychotic patients, psychotics in remission, psychopaths, psychosomatic cases and many types of chronic neurotics with and without acting-out tendencies are unable to tolerate the feelings involved in a transference neurosis. For these patients a genuine attachment activates past memories of old hurts that lead to a partial withdrawal and mobilizes fantasies and impulses at deeply regressed levels. An acute psychotic episode or a deeper withdrawal from relationships with persons can be precipitated. For some, any deep attachment poses a tremendous threat to their narcissism and produces withdrawal or panic states. Often, this type of patient will flood the analytic hours with narcissistic reveries and tolerate no interference with their productions. Others may be totally silent either lying down or sitting up, and others will talk about themselves in only the most indirect or abstract manner. Sector psychotherapy is ideal for these patients as transference manifestations are handled indirectly, often through artificially induced displacements, and at the most are only referred to in passing or when the entire therapeutic structure is threatened by a collapse.

A large number of patients would be ideal candidates for psychoanalysis but are unable to pay for it at a frequency of four or five times a week. Others are unable to take off from work the requisite number of hours during the week. Some are so old or so handicapped by illness, lack of intelligence or situational factors that the analyst may feel that the time and expense of an analysis are prohibitive. For many, no psychoanalysts are available. Next to psychoanalysis, sector psychotherapy offers the ideal approach to these patients' problems as they can be treated by it in a manner that will not complicate an analysis in the future. Often with these patients circumstances change or the results of therapy are dramatic enough to make the patient or therapist realize that psychoanalysis is worth a bigger sacrifice than the patient was at first willing to make in money and time.

Regardless of all rules, patients are so different in their capacities to tolerate and use insight that no blanket rule allows us to judge whether or not a psychoanalysis will be worth the time and money spent on it. The overidealization of psychoanalysis has permitted many to believe that this procedure is a sort of superpsychotherapy which can handle the most difficult type of case. This is mainly because most psychoanalysts are better psychotherapists than most non-analysts due to selection, training and experience. Moreover, few psychoanalysts bother to explain that much of their work is psychotherapy. Some make no distinction at all between psychotherapy and psychoanalysis. The clear-cut and valid distinctions between the two will be discussed in detail in Chapter VII. For the present, it can be stated that psychoanalysis remains chiefly a dynamic approach which attempts to *reduce* pathological fixations and charges of affect. Most psychotherapies are designed to enhance repression and ego *defenses* in general. Actually, sector psychotherapy uses both processes. In any case, all therapies have limits of application.

In sector psychotherapy, as in psychoanalysis, we intensify a natural split in the ego between the present observing, thinking and feeling "I" portion and various past images of the self. There are many variations of this type of split. Sometimes it is called the real feeling self versus the phony or pseudo self, or it may be called the adult self versus the infantile self. In sector psychotherapy, we idealize the "really" mature adult self and ascribe to the infantile self all unacceptable characteristics. The infantile part we treat is usually the part fixated at a certain psychosexual level and mainly responsible for a patient's symptoms. It is necessary to tolerate it and control it and learn to sympathize with it, but neither to condemn nor condone it. In the interview situation the infantile part is often called by the nickname the patient went by as a child. If possible, a name is used that the patient dislikes considerably, as this aids the splitting process in the beginning. Sometimes the name is allowed to grow up and change, for example, from little Teddy to Ted, with its shift from infantile passive disliked elements to more mature, active, acceptable ones. This form of splitting has its drawbacks in some patients, especially schizoid personalities, and in compulsive obsessionals who already use this maneuver to an extreme degree. They isolate their reasoning self from their basic feeling self. However, there are ways of coping with these difficulties, best shown by actual examples. The "I" and the self are two of the most important and natural aspects of the ego. This is an easily recognized split in every person's life. Neither of these terms is synonymous with the ego, which is a psychoanalytic construct embracing psychic activities which include the "I" and the self and other controlling, organizing and directing aspects which are, for the most part, unconscious.

The ego begins in the first few months of life as an integrating, steering and controlling organization. This concept is, of course, arbitrary, if useful, and rather ill-defined. Ego precursors are present in a rudimentary form from the moment of conception and, in a sense, are related to physiological areas known as organizers. The need for a resolution of and response to multiple sensory perceptions represents the stimulus that originally and eventually leads to ego development. The coalescence of sensory perceptions that takes place when two or more sensory organs are simultaneously stimulated eventually gives rise to ego nuclei that will later join into a more or less unified ego. The mouth, snout, eye and skin ego is a good example of such a nucleus. Ego nuclei are present from the beginning of life. As new organs and combinations of organs become available, they are added on and the resultant phenomenon is changed in the direction of increasing complexity. At first the ego is a sensorimotor ego. By the time the myelinization of the nervous system has been completed, the ego is a unified structure of considerable complexity. Conscious awareness at one or more levels is an integral part of such an ego. When the ego is said to begin at a certain time, this means the ego at a certain arbitrarily chosen level of development. The adult ego is an integrate of all previous ego states, any one of which, under certain regressive conditions, can predominate or reappear. In the interview situation, as we push a patient back into the past, we induce him to regress just as if he were under hypnosis. Patients who once lisped or stuttered may do so again. Others revive gestures and mannerisms which have not been present for many years. To a large extent the ego remains a body ego. Feeling tones associated mainly with the body are always of primary importance in the interview situation. In the infant, the inner and outer worlds, the body and the self and the universe around it are one. Perception is diffuse and protopathic. An inevitable awareness of separation and differentiation develops as the "I" and the "non-I" parts of the inner and outer worlds separate. From then on, frustration and loss in the outer world march hand in hand with a heightened or epicritic awareness of the difference between wishes and the past, and outside possibilities of gratification and the present. This is called reality awareness.

Insight is usually associated with loss of illusions and the necessity for postponement, mourning and renunciation, with compromise and dissatisfaction, and with anxiety and depression. Of course, this is not the entire story; if it were, insight would never be tolerated. The acquisition of it is fortunately also associated with rewards in the form of superego approval, ego pleasures in mastery and integration, and the expectation of future satisfaction of instinctual sexual and aggressive needs, especially such pregenital derivatives as curiosity and accumulation of knowledge. There is also the anticipation of other future rewards. The anxiety and depression that accompany insight are mentioned only to stress the fact that any recovery process ultimately involves exposing the patient to the painful aspects of reality which he has been denying and unable to integrate. One of the chief jobs of the therapist is to regulate the dosage of insight so that the anticipation of future rewards outweighs the pain attached to the acquiring of it. Otherwise, we lose our patient, one way or another. In sector psychotherapy this regulation is usually done automatically by the patient, especially in the beginning. The signs and signals of too much activity on the part of the therapist will be illustrated in some of the interviews that follow.

The "I" is differentiated out of the initial primitive awareness of the body ego. It is, to a large degree, connected with the seeing function of the eye and sensations in the skin, especially around the mouth, lips, and tongue. Seeing, tasting, perceiving and sampling are fundamentally attributes of the body ego. Through a conditioning or associative process, seeing becomes the forerunner of a new type of introjective awareness. The protopathic or primitive awareness of body organs and rhythms is overlaid by an oral, visual layer centered on the mother's face, breast and skin. This is the nucleus of the "I." New systems centered on other organ sensations, and of increasing complexity, will be added. Systems centered on complex personal relationships with others will develop into the various "selves." The "self" is in this sense a precipitate of experience with others. It is synonymous with a role or is an integrate of the roles taken in relationship with others. It develops simultaneously along with personal relationships and the awareness of patterns of relationship between the "I" and others in the outside world. Awareness of the self by the "I" begins around the fifteenth month. By the time a patient is able to say "I like (or dislike) myself," he is discussing a complex intrapsychic problem.

We have to intensify the natural split between the "I" and the "self" in order to sharpen the perception of three types of reality—the reality of thought, the reality of feeling, and the reality of fantasy.

Fantasy reality is what our patients live by and is our main concern in therapy. The ideal therapeutic interview integrates all three types of *inner* reality perceptions so that they can work in harmony with the reality of the *external* world. To achieve this the therapist must often be active and introduce questions about one or more missing relationships between the "I" part of the ego and the body image, the various self-images, things and persons.

The "I" portion of the ego relates itself both consciously and unconsciously to an internal and an external world, i.e., inside and outside. The internal world, for the purposes of psychotherapy, consists principally of the *body image* and the *self-image*.

The *body image* is an integrate of all previous body images. It has conscious and unconscious aspects. Our conscious concept of our body tends to lag somewhat behind our chronological age. There is also an idealized good and bad body image. Our conception of our bodily organs varies tremendously in accord with our actual knowledge and fantasy life. When we ask a patient who has had an appendectomy what that meant to him, he may reply, pointing to his scar, "the part that is inside here that sticks up like this," and his erect finger suggests that what he means is confused with a phallic image, or he may say, "it hangs down like a bunch of grapes," which leads to further exploration of his conceptions.

Images of the self have been mentioned. They are idealized in a good or bad sense and change fairly rapidly. There is also an integrated over-all self-image.

The external world consists principally of *things* and *persons*. The four categories—things, persons, self and body—that make up the inner and outer worlds are all we encounter clinically. Therefore, we do not need to talk in terms of introjects, etc., at present. All objects in either world can be perceived in part or in toto; all are integrates of previous concepts, and as a rule displacements of patterns of relationship from one category to another occur easily. A part can represent a whole and vice versa. Thus, an adolescent's "hot rod" can represent his phallus. His entire body can represent his phallus. A friend can represent himself or part of himself or his parents or sibling, etc.

It is important to remember that in dealing with the neurotic, dynamic psychotherapy always emphasizes the unconscious. All manifest material is regarded as a screen which covers unconscious displacements. We can and do talk with patients, especially psychotics and borderline characters, about "reality," but we shall consider this activity later.

The "I" portion of the ego tends to perceive "reality" in terms of patterns which are complex and highly organized structures. It is important in therapy that these patterns be made conscious. The patterns are abstract, but in each of the four spheres of relationship they use concrete objects.

A pattern can be recognized as existent in a temporal and sequential sense. We acted thus in the *past* and now in a similar fashion in the *present*. In psychotherapy our main interest lies first in the similarity of these patterns. A girl who had lost her father and turned to her three brothers at an oedipal level revealed that she had three lovers and had married one of them. She collected things with an obvious phallic symbolism in threes; e.g., she had three violins, etc. The recognition of the three-pattern was accompanied by much emotion (abreaction) and convinced her of the reality of certain unconscious needs and wishes. This type of displacement will be illustrated in the case material that follows. Integrated awareness implies that the chances are increased for an improvement in conscious control of behavior and reality adaptation in both a social and an individual sense. It also implies the necessity for reconciling contradictory elements in the various spheres that have been mentioned. These contradictory elements are qualitative and will be considered in more detail in the next chapter.

In terms of the pathological mourning that is an antecedent of neurosis, integration implies a conscious awareness of loss, renunciation, reconciliation and turning toward new objects. Unconscious yearning, hates, guilts and griefs are expressed in a masturbatory fantasy. This is a vital part of the withdrawal process and frequently acted out (in disguise). Analysis of this fantasy is necessary to accomplish integration, acceptance and control of the above-mentioned affects.

In the interview situation it is necessary to keep asking oneself the question: "How does this obvious and manifest material contain a pattern that applies to other areas that are unconscious and at present more important?" It usually does. The function of the therapist is to seek out and expose the unconscious in a manner that is acceptable and convincing to the patient. Any neighbor can give advice about the manifest content—and such advice ordinarily will have little effect.

The patterns of relationship in the various spheres differ in appearance because of the limitations imposed by the nature of the objects used in their expression and development. Let us consider the following case for examples of this.

The patient was a young man in his early thirties who had telephoned for an appointment. He was embarrassed and uneasy and talked eagerly and fast.

"Well, how can I help you?"

"I know you're busy, Doctor, and I shouldn't be taking up your time because, uh, but, uh, I wanted to ask you something and was *afraid*. Uh, the story briefly is this. I'm married and have two children and another one coming and am very happily married. In fact, I'm *mad* about my wife and have become more and more since I married her. Well, about seven years ago, after I got out of the service—a couple of months—I was on a subway car on the way to town. I was hanging on one of the hangers up above. *Nobody* was looking at me. *Nobody* was talking to me and all of a sudden my face *flushed* intensely and it went away. So, a couple of days later it happened again and then I started to thinking about it more and as I talked to people I said wouldn't it be *stupid* if it happened now for no apparent reason, and it would happen. So, about the time I met my *wife* and it started really getting the best of me then because I was flushing in front of her and the people we were meeting."

The main problem here, as in so many interviews, was to slow down the production of material, thin it out, and answer the obvious questions. What was he *afraid* of? Why did he have to reassure the therapist about his marriage? The double meaning of "mad" was a possible clue, but it was too early to take advantage of this naïve giveaway. *Nobody* usually means someone important. *Flushing* was obviously the key word here and connected with being looked at and talked to by *nobody*.

"Flushing?"

"That's right, Doctor, yes."

"What do you mean?"

"Getting *red*, or just my *face* was *heating up, flushing*. Ah, as I say so, with no reason. I mean, and, er, I mean I could be *talking* with somebody and in an ordinary conversation and it would happen. So ah, I went down to a clinic and I saw the doctor down there and, uh I told him the story, and I saw him for about a year and a half, during which time I went with my wife."

Once more he associated the symptom with his wife, so the therapist tested and reinforced the association.

"So you thought of *flushing* when you met your *wife*?"

"No, a couple of months before."

The problem now arose: What set it off and how did the wife get involved?

"A couple of months before you met her?"

"Before I met her. I was just riding on the subway car and it happened. I don't know why, I wasn't thinking of *anything*. *Nobody looked* at me. *Nobody said* anything to me. It just happened. But, uh, when I met her, uh, *it actually started* a little more because, well, I mean she was a *girl* and I hadn't been out with many girls in my life."

There are no negatives in the unconscious; i.e., he was thinking of *something*. He also confirmed the connection of the symptom with the wife. He was ripe at the time he met her. There was an obvious link to the past in the last sentence.

"Really! How come?"

"Well, I mean, it's all my childhood, I think, this is responsible. I mean just that."

This was a re-emphasis of the invitation to get into the past, so much so that it was a little suspect, although worthwhile using nevertheless.

"What do you mean?"

"Well, I mean, I, uh, I was never, I always wanted to play baseball or football, although I never did, and if I got in the game I would *strike out*, and so I *quit*. I mean I was always, I never had any confidence in myself. I was self-conscious."

This meant he was looking at and talking to a part of himself. The therapist could have asked again what he meant, but instead tried to reinforce his journey into the past. It could be guessed that he was referring to girls and the game of love.

"You mean even when you were a little fellow?"

"Well, I mean ever since I can remember, probably in the fourth grade. I tried to pal around with some kids and I guess they more or less, they didn't want me to."

"When you were ten years old?"

This pinned down the time element.

"I'd say starting in about the fifth grade."

"Ten or eleven?"

"Yes. I mean you might say that I was a *sissy* to a certain extent."

A sissy is a sister, a girl. At the age of fixation in cases of phobia, a little boy's idea of a girl is based mainly on an anatomical defect.

"A sissy?"

"Only in so far as I, I, I, couldn't play ball with them, you know, because if I got the bat in my hand I figured I was going to strike out. I told myself before I even got up, so I would, you know, and I mean I wanted to play ball. I wanted to do, you know, what they did and as far as sports went I never could."

The bat and ball symbolized the anatomical area where he felt defective.

"How come?"

"Well, my father was the type of guy that you never could talk to him about anything. I mean he was a wonderful father. He gave me everything he could and he always treated me well, but I could never go to him with a problem, you know, talk to him as a father or some other fellow to tell your troubles to. He never knew that anything like that existed. I mean it's just, I went to my *mother* if anything was on my mind. I never went to my father."

He was a mother's boy because his father too was defective in his eyes.

"You were close to your *mother*?"

"In that respect, not too."

He was nervous about this so the therapist gave him a rest and found out vital information.

"How many others were in the family?"

"No, no one else."

"Just you?"

"Yes."

"And you felt you were a sissy?"

"Yes. I mean, in that respect. I mean I couldn't *fight*. I'd avoid a fight. I couldn't engage in any kind of sports because I just couldn't. Ah, I was in the Boy Scouts, and a gang of fellows that you'd want to pal around with, that are considered to be the tops—regular boys—I mean they used to treat me as though I were a sissy, you know."

"They thought you were too close to *mother*?"

"Yes, uh, I guess you could put it that way."

"Mamma's boy!"

"That's right, yes."

He began to flush. There was a danger of his becoming angry at the therapist which was outweighed by the need to arouse the feelings connected with his difficulty. The "madness" could be easily deflected.

"*They* thought?"

"Yes."

"What did *mother* think about it?"

"I never told anybody."

"Never talked about it to mother?"

"No, I never said anything at all. Then I never went with a, I never kissed a girl till I was about eighteen years old. Never knew the facts of life or *anything like that.*"

Anything like that could cover a wide range. If he didn't know the facts, he did have many fantasies which took their place. The therapist was on watch for this type of expression which underlines the need to explore the material further.

"What do you mean?"

"Ah, I never knew anything about *childbirth* until I was probably about eighteen. Never knew how it took place till I was eighteen years old. So, uh, having gone out with very few girls I met my wife and, uh, she was giving me a definite impression. I thought that she was *carrying the torch for somebody,* all the time that I was, up until the year after I met her when I gave her a diamond and, uh, then there were some songs that she said she liked which were always reminiscent. And all this time I kept saying there's *another guy* that you went with that she was carrying the torch for and, uh, I'd better *equal myself to him.* I've got to get over this *foolish* flushing, reddening of the face. The result is it kept building up."

Now flushing was connected with inadequacy feelings and *another guy,* as well as mother. His wife was the present representative of the past mother. She carried someone else's torch. What a wonderful symbol! The little boy felt foolish and stupid. He had to equal himself to an image of part of father that existed *before* father proved inadequate.

"How old were you when you met your wife?"

"Uh, twenty-three, Doctor. I had three years in the service."

"So, you found out about the facts of life around, you say, eighteen?"

He must have known them a great deal earlier but had to repress the knowledge as for some reason it was painful. This kind of repression occurs frequently in hysterical types.

"Yes, sir."

"How did it happen?"

"I don't actually remember. I just picked it up here and there. I mean I always wondered what the story was, I mean all the things the kids would tease me about 'cause I was *stupid* about something like that. They wouldn't tell me what the story was. A couple of them took me up in a parking place one day and they picked up a condom on the end of a stick. I didn't know what it was. They were waving it at me and I just stood there and they were all laughing and they seemed to say, he doesn't know what it is. It's a big joke."

"How old were you then?"

"Oh, I'd say fifteen, I guess."

"Fifteen?"

"I guess. The doctor did a lot for me. He more or less convinced me that life was worth living. I mean, I could live with *the thing*. And when I saw him I even didn't care whether I woke up in the morning. I mean it had me in such a state of *depression*."

The inadequate thing he was depressed about was betrayed by flushing. At the most important level to him, it referred to his phallus.

"Flushing, you mean?"

"That's right."

"Flushing made you depressed?"

"Well, it made me feel as though, like I say, I mean, he asked me whether I'd rather flush or have my left arm *missing*. I told him I'd rather have my left arm *missing*, which is still the way I feel. I needed a doctor's advice to get *rid* of this trouble. I'd try to find out how seriously it bothered me. So he carried me through for, up until the time I got married. He put me on my feet enough so that I could get married. I did get married, for which I'm thankful. I mean, he did a lot for me. But my wife is *an only child*. Her father had died twelve years before we met. Her mother had devoted her life to bringing her up and had entwined herself around her like a grapevine."

He was so ashamed of this part that offended him he would like to pluck it out. His need for a father to protect him was obvious and now it could be seen that he had picked a wife who was exactly like himself—an alter ego—a mother's girl—someone he would have been like if his inadequate phallus were missing.

"Really?"

"So I met, so we got married."

"How do you mean?"

"Well, her whole life was her daughter!"

"She was a mother's girl?"

"Well, her mother made her!"

"How do you mean?"

"So I got married and, uh, can't make out sexually, no sexual relations! My wife is freezing up all the time! I have to live with my mother-in-law; that's the condition of the marriage! So my mother in-law is in one room and we're in the next room. For one and a half years no sexual intercourse!"

"One and a half years?"

"One and a half years!"

"How did it happen?"

"After the baby was born. I don't know how the baby was conceived. I probably had a penetration of an inch when the conception took place."

"What do you mean? You mean your wife wouldn't let you penetrate?"

The concept of penetration was too aggressive for the sissy part of "them." It was laden with sadomasochistic fantasies.

"She wanted to but she just couldn't. I don't know. I took her to a woman doctor who examined her and in front of me she told her to grow up."

His voice became shaky and he clenched his left fist.

"What did she mean?"

"That there was nothing wrong with her! She just had to relax and, uh, she'd tighten up, she'd get so tight and nervous that I couldn't penetrate at all, and then I just couldn't perform the relationship. Another thing, during this time her mother was putting me through the *tortures of hell*, raising hell, and we couldn't even go to a show once in two weeks because she was left home all alone, and all this ridiculous stuff."

His voice now became very shaky.

"So that a tension was always existing there and things were just getting worse instead of better."

He sighed.

"So it's been going on now for about seven years and I've got to the point now where—"

He blocked. He wanted to rebel against the mother but the sissy part needed her and was afraid of her. Tortures (torches) of hell was a nice play on words, but to use such a phrase now in any other sense would only antagonize the patient.

"You mean you're still with the mother?"

"Six months ago I got my own house and asked her if she wanted to come, so she came bag and baggage."

"You mean you bought a house and the mother-in-law moved in with you?"

The therapist looked incredulous. It was better to get him eventually to raise the question why himself.

"That's right! But it's not as bad as what it used to be because it's my house and she can't raise hell about the ice chest and this and that and *the kids* doing this and that, and that's some relief, although she's still there."

More vital information could now be obtained and an indirect approach to his past could be made. It was also better not to let him waste all his anger on the mother-in-law, who nearly always represents the bad part of the internalized image of mother.

"You have kids?"

"Two children."

"How old are they?"

"Uh, five and a half and three and another one on the way."

"So I take it that with these three children your wife accepted this *thing*?"

"Definitely. Once we did it *the thing* was all right."

This was obvious but worth emphasizing.

"You did what?"

"Once we did have the relationship it was all right after that, but it was just trying to get it done the first time."

"You mean it took a year and a half?"

"That's right, before I had *full* penetration, or even *half* penetration."

He measured penetration like a phallic boy whose concept of manhood is based upon the size and length of the penis.

"Then it was all right?"

"After that, I guess. So now over a period of all these years *this thing* has built up. It increased itself to the point where I can be *flushed* from the time I get up in the morning, practically, until the time I go to bed at night. Uh, if I'm home eating supper at night with my wife and my mother-in-law I'm anxious to get over supper so I can get away from the table because my face is flushed. Or if we're watching television it's flushed. The intensity varies with the circumstances."

Now it could be seen that *the thing* had another meaning. The interest invested in the phallus or body part was also attached to the aggressive penetrating part of the sexual act. He had become ashamed of the raging frustrated little boy part that wanted to but did not dare to "stand up" to mother. His entire body image was that of an inadequate big angry phallus which he had to hide. In this sense the bigness was a reaction formation. The sissy part was still afraid of the mother, and at the same time longed for her love. Apparently he was still wrestling with the problem of his guilt and frustration-laden infantile sexual strivings toward his mother.

"How do you mean?"

"Well, if we went out visiting to a friend's house, uh, I like people, I always have liked them, I like to sit with them, so we go up to a friend's house, we go in the parlor, we sit down, start talking. If the lights in the parlor are not too bright, I'm a little more calm, I'm not too bad. If the lights are all bright in the room then my face is like a beacon light. All night long it remains that way. Uh, we go out to have coffee, we sit around the table, then it intensifies even worse and I feel like I'm just going to *blow right up*. The perspiration starts on my forehead and I just wish I was any place but where I am, so I blow up."

He felt exposed, inadequate, belittled, aroused, frustrated and furious—all in one. He was an enormous angry phallus—a big prick!

"How do you mean?"

"Well, I mean it's *so hot*. I just get so hot, so intense when I'm sitting around the table having coffee, and if there's more than one cup, if there's three or four, I mean, by the time I get out of that house at the end of the night, I'm ready for a week's recuperation. Er, I mean, it just takes an awful lot out of me to go out for that night visiting because I'm so aware of *this thing* and it's *ridiculous*! I mean *the whole thing is ridiculous*, but uh, I mean, the result is that I'm in a state of *nervous tension* practically all the time. It just keeps going on all the time."

This was a double-entendre. The "hole thing" was even more inadequate. His wife was a caricature of himself. This was what he was threatened with being like, i.e., *castrated.* He felt he already was in one sense and others could see it when they looked at him and when he talked. This was another reason he had to be all phallus. He was like a certain joke that ends with "Mr. Morecock, meet Mr. Allcock."

"Like your wife was when you were having relations?"

"Before we had relations she was probably uh, she was quite upset about *sex*."

"What do you mean?"

"Well, she was crying a few times. She wanted to do it. She didn't know why she couldn't."

"Before?"

"Before we actually did have them, she was quite upset that we weren't having them properly. But uh, like I say, I mean, no matter—"

He blocked again. The therapist shifted the line of thought.

"What do you feel made her so tense? Do you feel it was something to do with the way she was attached to *mother*?"

"Well, I think that she was, *as you say*, she was too close, too close to her mother. And the fact that we were right room to room, uh, living there. We couldn't move in the bed without the squeak going into the other room."

"As you say" meant he wanted to retreat. Intercourse was reminiscent of guilty masturbatory fantasies.

"You mean she was afraid of mother overhearing you having intercourse?"

"Probably. Although we did go away for a weekend and tried it, tried it out that way, but— Then of course the first night I should have *taken it easy*; I tried to have relations the first night with her and got her kind of *scared* that night, which didn't help it out any."

He laughed.

"Scared?"

"Well, I mean she took two hours to get ready for bed and then came to bed with all kinds of cold cream on and, uh, as soon as I started she didn't think it was right that I should touch her and, er, I mean—"

He had probably been "scared" of his anger. The picture was a little clearer now. Childhood masturbation in one sense is an attempt to give to oneself good sensual feelings that compensate for those not obtained from the parents. It is full of defiance and longing fantasies. His wife's attitude was a reminder of the frustrating cold mother whom he hated. From another angle she expressed what he thought himself, as, like her, he had not grown up.

"What did she mean?"

It was easier to let him talk about *her* fears.

He laughed.

"Well, I started to touch her breast and she said, 'Well I don't know whether you should do this,' and then immediately I tried to get into the act. Before I knew it I had a pre-ejaculation *myself*, so I laid her down on her back. Then she became very *excited*, very *scared*. I suppose I should have let it ride for a few nights without attempting it because of what might, you know, the *consequences*. She was pretty *scared* about it. I guess I was too."

The inadequate, angry, frightened phallus wouldn't work.

"Scared?"

"I guess so."

"Scared of what?"

"I don't know. Probably *her* mother had given *her* some story. As far as I can see, we were all brought up in a cloak of *darkness* as far as sex is concerned. There are a lot of people around my age that were never told anything, brought up to—"

He was blocked again by the intensity of his feelings.

"You mean others too?"

"I mean in *my own case*. I mean, I think maybe that's part of *my* trouble. Sexually I think I'm probably *doing something wrong* when I have relationships with my wife."

Suddenly he had become braver. This type of insight was valuable but transient. It had to be pinned down, emphasized and amplified. It was effective because he had done it himself at a *level* he was prepared for.

"What makes you think so?"

"I don't *know*, I—"

He wanted to retract this small fragment because of painful thoughts attached to it. He was encouraged to talk at a different level.

"I mean why do you *think* it is that?"

"Well, I just look back and try to figure out. I figure that something started it. *I don't know*, uh, if I had sat down at home and said to myself, well, wouldn't it be awful now if I started *flushing*, but it started out without even thinking about it."

To a therapist, obviously flushing was connected with doing something wrong.

"Before you met your wife?"

"Yes, I mean I wasn't thinking of blushing, *nobody* was *embarrassing* me. *Nobody* was *saying* anything to me. *Nobody* was even *looking* at me. And then all of a sudden I *flushed*. So I figured there must be something in the background there."

In his own way, he realized there were unconscious thoughts. The therapist tried to reduce the anxiety by slowing down and amplifying his train of thoughts.

"And you think that this was due to the fact that you knew nothing about sex and were *frightened* about it, or what?"

"Well, I think that it might be that just that I was brought up without ever being told that it was part of life, that it was a *good* thing, and *all this and that*. I mean, I was more or less sheltered from knowing anything about it."

"Well, how did that happen?"

He laughed.

"Well, nobody ever told me."

"You mean mother—?"

"My mother never told me."

"Never told you—?"

"Nothing!"

"And you—"

"In fact I had a *wet dream* one night when I was a kid and didn't know what happened. I thought I *wet my pants* and, er, I mean I was *scared stiff* that she would find the sheet the next morning and think that I was *wetting* the *bed*. I didn't know what had happened!"

Where has he gotten that idea? With a fixation at a phallic level, fantasies about controlling the urinary stream are important. This is why it is called at times phallic urethral. It might well be called phallic urinary.

"Why, did you wet the bed?"

"I had a wet dream."

"Did you ever wet the bed?"

"No, not much, but I mean things like that—you're brought up under those conditions, you don't know what sex is. Then when you —well, you know!"

He wanted to blame it on mother. Actually he himself equated urinating and sexual relations.

"How did it happen? Was mother so prudish, or what?"

The therapist had as yet been unable to learn much about his past.

"Yes, she's that type, very much."

"What do you mean?"

"Well, I mean, as I look back I wonder how my father made out, you know, got along."

He laughed.

"Probably many's the time that he wished that he'd, or he wanted a relationship and it never did happen to him. I *don't know*."

This "I don't know" simply showed that he had done a lot of fantasying about it, which had remained uncorrected by reality. He had *looked* in fantasy and felt guilty and aroused.

"They didn't have relationships?"

"No, I, I say as I look back, I think that she's probably the type who didn't care for it too much."

"It" referred mainly to the phallus and its product. He was talking about his mother at more than one level. Sex was overshadowed by toilet morals.

"Why, what makes you think that? Didn't they sleep together?"

"Oh, yes, but it's just that, as *you say*, prudish."

He picked up the therapist's word, showing that the transference state was positive. He was also disclaiming responsibility for the statement and showing his need for support by father.

"She was?"

"Yes."

"In what way did she show it?"

"Well, I mean, you know, she would never discuss sex or didn't want to talk about that. It was *foolish*."

"She said it was foolish?"

Foolish was like silly and stupid.

"Well, anything along that line would be, you know, I mean she'd cut you off."

This referred to his phallic pride which had to be encouraged. His father had been inadequate to do it.

"You mean you tried sometimes?"

"Well, when something was mentioned about it, I mean, er, I don't know. She's, she's really, she's definitely that way. I mean just a couple of years ago she had an adopted cousin of mine, her sister died at childbirth and she took the *girl* and brought her up."

A new person appeared, a representative of the girl part of himself, so the therapist investigated this important new twist to the material. Had he envied and wanted to become like this girl to get mother's love, as well as to get rid of the hated inadequate phallus of childhood?

"How old is she?"

"She's thirteen."

"Thirteen?"

"Fifteen. Fifteen."

"Fifteen? When did she adopt her?"

"Oh, when she was about, er, just *after I got out of the service*. She'd had her all that time."

"You went in the service when you were how old?"

"I was about twenty."

"Twenty?"

"Nineteen or twenty."

"And she adopted her around that time, and so how long were you in the service?"

"Three years."

"Three years! So when you were twenty-three you came home?"

His symptom had begun when he came home and found the girl

there. This may have been a factor that pushed him into treatment and marriage.

"That's right. So, uh, this, I went over there one day about three years ago and I looked in the desk, my sister's desk, and there was a box of rubbers. So I opened it up and there were some little coins in there, so I went out to my mother and says, 'What's this doing in here, Ma?' She said, 'What do you mean what's this doing. It's *Mary's box*. She's keeping things in it.' I said, 'You know what came in this box?' She says, 'No.' So I told her. So she threw the box out but she never even knew what came in the box!"

He laughed.

"At least she wouldn't admit it."

In fantasy he had to keep mother pure. *He* wouldn't admit things to himself. The thought of father with her was too galling. The symbolism of the box and the things kept in it was apparent but useless at this stage.

"She didn't know what rubbers were?"

"That's right. So I figure how my father ever made out, I don't know."

This was more evidence that he didn't want father to "make out." There were also important attitudes to investigate.

"They weren't very affectionate?"

"Never a display of any as far as I'm concerned. I never remember seeing any display of affection between them. In fact, I could never visualize the two of them having relationships, myself, after I did find out what the score was."

"When was that?"

"I guess I was around eighteen or so. I don't remember how I actually found out the facts of life. I got in the Army. I guess I was still learning a few things."

He was like Mary. He would not admit knowledge that made him feel inadequate, lonely, bad and depressed.

"When you were eighteen, you say! How did it happen?"

"Uh, how did I find out? I can't remember, to tell the truth."

This statement usually makes a therapist aware that there is a denial of a lie.

"You mean by finding out the facts of life, what do you mean? You mean you never had relations with a girl?"

"That's right. I never had relations with anybody prior to marriage."

"Oh, I see. Not while you were in the Army?"

"No."

"So you were still finding out when you were in the Army?"

"That's right. In fact, someone recommended a book when I got married, *Ideal Marriage*. I was twenty-three years old then. I read that book and I found out *things* in there then that I never even knew!"

"What do you mean?"

"Well, I mean, er, there was a chapter, 'The Genital Kiss.' That's something that I, er, had I been asked about that I'd say it was *perversion*. I mean, I would never, that thought *never* even entered my mind. Uh, I'd probably go through twenty years of marriage and would never even know that anything like that ever existed. I mean, er, maybe I'd find out myself—"

The therapist wondered why he picked this act out. "Never" probably meant hardly ever, but most likely meant he was especially attracted to this area and also repelled. The genital kiss was a *phallic* representative of the breast-mouth sucking act. He was a mother's boy, a sissy. The analyst would say that his phallic fixation had oral underpinnings or that a defect in his oral relation with his mother was displaced to a phallic relationship, where it became intensified and fixated owing to its inappropriateness. The orality also was hinted at in his connecting *flushing* with *drinking* the coffee. It is not only that the hot coffee heated him. The therapist did not forget that the fantasy and associative elements outweighed reality elements in the production of his neurosis. There were other reasons for his phallic fixation, mainly his need to deny that creatures like mother and women could do without such an important thing. His attitude of anxiety about his marital relations, like that of his wife, was based on anxiety over the possible loss of the penis. As *looking* was so important, it was possible that as a little boy the sight of the "castrated" female genital was a trauma. His emphasis on the genital kiss had also served to deny his feelings of inadequacy in being dirty and unable to control his penis in terms of masturbation and ejaculation. The question now arose, "Did the little girl part of him have perverse fellatio longings?" This was a dangerous area, to be handled with great caution in order to prevent possible homosexual anxieties.

"You mean that you'd heard of it because you heard of it as a perversion, you said. How did you know it was a perversion if you hadn't heard of it?"

"Well, I mean, er, I figured that something like that would be a perversion."

"You mean from what you'd heard?"

"Yes, I mean, like fellows you take for *queers*. Two queers get together, or it boils down to about the *same thing*. Not the same thing, with the opposite sex. It's a little different, but, *I don't know*. I get to the stage now where as I said, uh, I mean, I just go through day after day and I'm in this state, this, my face is in a heated, is heated, and the intensity is always varied. I mean I'm continually embarrassing my wife whenever we go out, er, if I hear of her being asked out for the night to some place where there are three or four couples, uh, if I can do anything to get out of that I'm going to get out of it because, I mean, to me that's a night of *horror*, not a night of enjoyment at all. It's ridiculous. I mean, I just sit there and, uh, get myself worked up from the time I get there until I get home. There's no *enjoyment* involved there, although I just would like to let myself go and have a good time but I, this redness in the face is just holding me back all the time. I don't know, uh—"

There was *horror* at the thought of being *queer* or castrated. And now the therapist could see another reason for the rage; i.e., his inadequate penis prevented enjoyment of intercourse in the present and its counterpart with mother in the past. He hated to see other couples getting what he wasn't getting. The rage and excitement appeared associated with an oral version of a primal scene.

"You mean redness or the *people seeing* the redness?"

"The people seeing the redness."

"You mean you don't like to expose yourself before them?"

Perhaps this is what he had wanted to do with mother.

"That's right, or embarrass my wife by exposing myself before, before— When I went to a wake last night, I think I was in eight rooms and I'd just keep going from one room to another. I mean I just don't want to sit down in one spot and get *talking* with some people for a length of time because I, well I mean—"

He sighed.

"Like I go out visiting I, before we'd go out to have coffee I'd go in the bathroom. I'd wash my face with cold water about eight times and cool off before I'd go out and have the coffee. I mean the whole *thing* is *ridiculous*. It's *stupid*, but it is happening and the way I look at it, I mean right now it's a physical reflex, a *conditioned reflex* and, uh, I can't see it."

He was a fine candidate for the Pavlovian tenets which simplify feelings tremendously. Ordinarily the therapist might have said,

"What can't you see?" or "What do you mean?" but first what did he feel was conditioned, and by what?

"What do you mean by a conditioned reflex?"

"Well, I mean, it's, it's, it conditions itself. It's happened so much now that it's got to a point where it's just a *permanent* thing. I mean I don't see how anything can be done about it. I mean, uh, like psychotherapy might help, but financially *I'm just keeping my head above the water.* I can't afford to go see a psychiatrist and pay the prices that I imagine most of you get. So I figure the next best thing is, I mean the reason, the main reason I wanted to see you was, I've heard, if there wasn't something I could take. Like I've been reading recently about five drugs that came out, chlorpromazine I think it is, some others, that have reduced worry and tension in people. I read about *some woman* who was *screaming* all night long because of what Mr. *Knock* was saying to her, an hallucination of hers. And she was given this chlorpromazine. She didn't scream any more at night. She could still hear him *saying* it but it wasn't *bothering* her. I mean it's supposed to reduce *worry* and *tension* in people."

Here he revealed an inadequacy in his work life which belongs in the sector of his relationships with men and in another interview. He expressed it like a bed wetter in terms of keeping his head above *water*. More primal-scene fantasy material appeared in disguise—a woman screaming being knocked while a baby urinated in excitement and fear.

"You mean about this worry of exhibiting yourself?"

"That's right. I mean, I, the way I feel now is this thing has gone on for so long that I keep, I'm in a state of nervous tension so much and for such a long period of time that sooner or later, as they say, something's got to give."

"You say when something's got to give, you mean you're afraid of what?"

"Well, that *physically* I'm going to explode. Something's going to happen."

This had meanings at every aggressive and sexual level. He feared exploding "prematurely" with an overlay of death and castration fantasies.

"That's what you meant by 'explode'? "

"Well, I guess so, probably, I don't know."

"Something will give and what?"

"Well I mean I'm going to have a *heart attack* or I'm going to have a breakdown, something."

Like the previous patient, he had easily displaced his fears about his phallus to another organ that throbbed and changed with excitement.

"A heart attack?"

"What I mean is, uh—"

"You've heard of such things?"

"Oh yes, my father died of a heart attack! When I got out of the service, before I met my wife."

"Your father had a heart attack? How did it happen?"

This was one of the temporal factors in his attack of flushing.

"Coronary thrombosis."

The therapist was aware that patients often hide their fantasies behind medical terms.

"What does that mean to you?"

"The heart gave out. I don't know. A clot of blood. I don't know much about it."

"A clot?"

"The way I, I, what I mean is the human body can only take so much and, uh, I mean you read, er, you, you read the paper about those who had emotional strains and so on and so forth. Well, I don't receive the ordinary amount of emotional strain. I'm under a continual emotional strain."

He meant that, like himself with his wife, father couldn't "make out."

"You mean living with the mother-in-law?"

"Living with this *condition.*"

"Oh!"

"I mean from the time I get up in the morning until I go to bed at night I'm always *conscious* of it. I'm *thinking* about it. It's a *strain.*"

His conscious thinking was a strain but warded off depressing material related to men and his job, and, at a deeper level, passive homosexual wishes. This sector was too dangerous; he was not ready for its development. This was an example of sex as a defense. He could blame sex, wife, mother, or mother-in-law for his depressing feelings of inadequacy and hurt to his pride in not making enough at work.

"So you've had all kinds of strain?"

"That's right."

"The mother-in-law, and the wife and not being able to make out with her for a year and a half, but now it's okay?"

"That's right."

"She likes *it* now?"

"Yes."

"Any time?"

He gave a slight laugh.

"Well, now that's a, she's, she's been having morning sickness. She's pregnant now. She don't tell me anything about it and I've been *hopped up* now for three weeks trying to make out and I can't make out, and I find out she hasn't been feeling too well."

"You mean she doesn't want to? She won't let you, or what?"

"She doesn't want to and there's morning sickness and spotting."

"I don't understand what morning sickness has to do with it."

"Well, she claims that it goes on throughout the day, *or something*. She's feeling *funny* off and on during the day."

"And you say spotting?"

"She, she's spotting, a few spots of blood from the, appeared on her undergarments here and there and she's afraid of a miscarriage from that."

Regardless of reality, this had to be treated as part of his sadomasochistic fantasies about intercourse.

"If you have intercourse?"

"She was, yes!"

"And so you haven't made out for three weeks?"

"That's right. I've been, as I say, I've been trying for three weeks now but I think I'm going to just give it up and call it quits until she finally decides that she's in the mood. No sense in *fighting* it, I guess."

"She's not in the mood?"

"Definitely not. Her grandmother *died* two days ago so that's that!"

This would be a non sequitur if it were not for the therapist's awareness of the patient's anxiety over his rage and fears of his bad wishes.

"So you've had all kinds of *tension*, your face *flushing* up, feeling you'll *explode*, that your *heart* is going to develop a *clot*, and that your mother-in-law will be with you forever, and that your wife is never going to let you make out."

"Uh, well I can say this thing, this thing here, er, I don't see how you can keep going along under a continual tension."

Now indirectly the therapist could attempt to tie up the various mother figures through a confrontation. In this manner, if it did not fit in, it could be ignored.

"Tell me, how did your father happen to get his heart attack? Was he, did he feel *tense* too? Was he under tension? Because you mentioned your trouble making out with the wife, and then you mentioned about father's trouble making out with mother?"

"Too proper!"

"She was like the wife in a way, eh? Not too interested?"

"Uh, no, I don't think so. I mean my wife is, when she's in the mood she's all right."

"You mean she's more that way than mother ever was?"

"Oh yes, very cooperative when she's in the mood."

He laughed. Laughter is a good way of mastering strong affect.

"How do you mean very cooperative? She likes *it*?"

"That's right."

"But not mother?"

The therapist was really doing double talk, i.e., at two levels.

"I don't, I could never visualize it."

"That's what I mean, so you feel mother was never cooperative?"

"That's right."

"So I wonder if you feel that had anything to do with father's tension."

"Gee, I don't know."

"Because you said that tension might cause the heart attack."

"Well I figure, I figure that you got to, something's got to happen. I mean you just can't go on—"

"What was making father tense?"

"Oh, I don't know. Uh, he was always, he *never had a good job.* He always had *just enough to get by on.*"

This was material for future sessions. He had identified with the negative features of both parents. This is common in hysterical and phobic states.

"What did he do?"

"Oh, he did anything at all, worked in a box factory, he soldered, and he had just enough to get by on. He used to get himself half stiff every Saturday or holiday. He drank quite a bit."

The therapist wondered if the patient did also.

"Was that because mother was that way? Or was mother that way because he drank, or what?"

"I don't know."

"No, but you have ideas. You don't know whether they are right or wrong, but you have some ideas."

A therapist uses this phrase continually to elicit fantasy material.

"I don't know, uh, I don't know why he drank like that, like he did. I mean he'd ruin holidays, Christmas and everything else like that."

"Since you've wondered about it, I mean, what are your ideas?"

"Well, my mother made a remark the time he died, something about him. All of a sudden she, in the midst of her sorrow she got mad at him for a minute or two and made some remark about how he used to spend his time up at this *friend of the family's* house with this woman."

"Friend of the family?"

"Yes, *relation*, an *in-law*, so to speak. How he'd spend time up there. He used to spend time up there."

"A relation?"

"That's right."

"You mean her sister?"

"No, I don't know who she was."

"Cousin or what?"

"Cousin, yes, probably is."

"Mother's cousin?"

"Mother's, my mother's cousin's wife."

"Mother's cousin's wife?"

"Her husband had taken off somewhere."

The therapist wondered if he had ideas about making out elsewhere or taking off and felt guilty and in danger of punishment by a heart attack.

"And left the wife?"

"And left the wife."

"And father—?"

He laughed slightly.

"Evidently had spent some time up there. She just blurted this out during the time while we were waiting for the undertaker to come. Something popped into her mind and I more or less figured that he might have been up there spending a little time."

"Because he couldn't make out back home?"

He laughed loudly.

"I don't know. I can't say."

"You mean now you know how he felt, eh?"

"That's right! Well, uh, something happened, er, as I say I always had the impression when I was going with my wife that she was *carrying the torch* for a guy. I knew it was a sailor and I knew he was from out of state, and from little things I picked up here and there, but I never asked her what the story was. Six months after we were married I went through her wallet and was looking at some pictures and she had a picture of a sailor. So I *blew my top* and she tore it up. So, about, off and on, the mother has mentioned the guy's name and two weeks before this Christmas she mentioned his name again. We were talking about the weather and she brought him up and all of a sudden it hit me and it started. It just rekindled all *the old suspicions and everything else* I had, and it started everything boiling up all over again and I got myself all *hopped up.*"

This referred to oedipal jealousy and mother carrying father's torch.

"You mean your suspicions that it was partly because she was thinking of him that you had so much trouble?"

"No, not that. No, the only thing that ever bothered me was that I didn't want to marry her unless she loved me *more than anybody else* she ever met."

This was a basic feeling of the oedipal child.

"Yes, that's what I mean."

"I had it figured out that she had loved this fellow more than she did me, uh, but for reasons of either religion or something else, she had ditched him or he had ditched her, but whatever it was she was *unhappy* about it. So it *bothered* me so much, I had thought about *it* so much that I decided to ask her twenty-two-year-old cousin who lives in the same house with us, with my wife since they were born."

His speech, like a dream, contained a mixture of present and past, reality and fantasy. The cousin was an alter ego of the wife and himself.

"A girl?"

"Yes. And she's a very fickle kid. She's had two hope chests, seven boy friends. She's really having a hell of a time for herself. But uh, I ask her and she gives me this big story. My wife went with him for two years, broke off just at the time she met me. Everybody in the house couldn't believe what had happened and, uh, all this and that. The guy wrote to my mother-in-law for *three* years after we were married and all this story, you know. So it had me all shaken up, so I went home and I asked my wife what the story was. It was foolish after *seven* years of marriage but I just was curious. So she made little of it, said she went with him for *five* months and that was it. My mother-in-law said the same story. She went with him for five months. She told me one night herself—"

"One says two years and the other says five months, eh?"

"Oh no, they both said, yes! So then I asked her other cousin and I made the mistake of telling her what my wife said so she immediately coincided with my wife. I should have asked her, 'What do you know?' and then compared with what I knew of it."

He appeared to be part a mildly paranoid "sissy" and part jealous boy.

"So you had your suspicions?"

"So I got that out of my mind now but *it* had me. So it was immediately after that, Christmas was two days later, and I tried to have relations with my wife, no dice. Finally one night we have them and I may have as well forgotten about it. She was completely *passive*. So since then nothing has happened. So I attribute it all, this lack of interest in relationships, to my bringing up this *other guy*, but then she tells me it was *morning sickness*."

To him it had become a mourning sickness: the girl for her sailor and he for the father at one level and the mother at another. The passivity was his problem also.

"You feel it was a different kind of sickness?"

"That's what I thought but I guess I'm wrong."

This was one of the meanings of "I don't know."

"So you have a lot of things to make you tense."

"I guess so."

"All kinds of things, eh?"

"That's right, but, uh, I, I mean, *I don't know*. I, I just feel as though I've reached the point where I've got to get *this thing*, got to get over this reddening of the face. I can't stand it another day. I feel that I have reached the saturation point more or less in the last couple of months and the result is that the whole thing has even got worse than it was. So, uh, I thought there must be something that I can do to slow myself down a little."

This showed very clearly the defensive function of the symptom. It had consolidated so many problems, past and present. It had permitted him to forget everything and to concentrate on his body image. He could keep away from conscious painful relationships with himself, his mother, father, wife, mother-in-law, boss and his premature ejaculations and poor earning ability. It was necessary to get him to rebel against the image of the mother and father he had developed over the years.

"Yes, because as you said, you were always the kind of fellow who avoided fights, never wanted to blow his top and get in a fight and do violent things."

"That's right."

"All your life, eh? Was mother against your fighting?"

"Not that I remember."

"Well how come then?"

"I guess, uh, gee, I don't know. I often think back in my childhood and try to figure out what went wrong somewhere along the line from *eight* years on. It's too much for me."

The question was why eight, but this was subordinated. Such numbers must be remembered for later use.

"She didn't care if you fought?"

"Well, I don't think she'd approve of it."

"What makes you think so?"

He laughed.

"It's just that I don't think she would. *I don't know.*"

There was a long pause. Then he inquired,

"Can you tell me why these things happen like this?"

"Which things do you mean? About your mother, about your mother-in-law, or your wife? Your father? Or what? You mean just the flushing?"

"The flushing, the blushing, the reddening of the face all the time. I, I don't know. I just can't figure out—"

"Did your father ever get flushed?"

"No, not that I know of."

"He just had a stroke, and that happened after he had been going with the girl?"

"That was a long, long time ago."

"That he went with the girl?"

"Yes."

"Did mother figure that he had been playing around with this girl?"

"I think so. Just from what she said that day, in a few minutes of, of despair or whatever you'd say it was."

"But you never played around?"

"Uh, once. Down in California on V-J night. That's about the only time in my life that I guess I sort of let loose to any extent."

This was just before he got out of the service and possibly around the time his symptom began.

"That was before you were married and your dad died?"

"Yes, before I was married."

"What happened?"

"Oh I got *picked up* by a sailor, it was later in the night, I had had a few drinks. Everybody was stiff, so *a sailor picked me up and he had a girl* with him and, uh, he sat beside her and *pushed me* over to *kiss her.* Then he *pushed me down* to *kiss her breasts,* you know, and he was really trying to get me going. Then he got me in the back seat with her and I had an *ejaculation* and that ended that. I got out of the car and went to camp, went to bed and that's about the closest I ever came to anything."

This proved what had been hinted at. He saw himself as a little girl (sissy) and recoiled in horror from the attending concept of castration. He tried to deny his awareness by emphasizing his phallus to the extent he had become one. The sailor used him as if he were his penis. From another point of view, there had been an attempt at a "homosexual" relationship through the girl as a connecting link. His ejaculation was based partly upon castration anxiety and feminine identification. Being feminine implied not only castration but having no control down below. The therapist had to be careful not to go too fast. His communications were like the dreams of the naïve, wonderfully informative, but much of the information was useless. Premature confrontation would produce a flight from painful insights in the form of more regressive and complicated defenses. The sailor with the girl was a father figure. He was underneath a *passive* person like his wife, with a defective penis.

"You had an ejaculation?"

"That's right, from just *touching* her."

"Touching her where?"

"On the *breast* and down, down below. I think I just about got there."

"With your hand?"

"Yes, I mean *even now* I don't, it doesn't take anything to make it happen! I mean I just come like that!"

He snapped his fingers.

"How do you mean?"

"I can have an ejaculation even before I have intercourse now, if I get *hopped up* enough."

The aggressive and sexual components were clear. Normally they act together in concert. Here in this neurotic, regressive, defused state they clashed and blocked their own full development and discharge.

"Before? And then you're all through?"

He laughed bitterly.

"Yes. I mean I really can't enjoy the *prelude* as much as I'd like to because I get too excited. So I have to *watch myself*."

The prelude to him was a guilt-laden, infantile type of sexual activity once watched by the mother. He was like the girl in Chapter I.

"How do you watch yourself?"

"Well, I've got to keep my wife from *touching* me or, or *rubbing* against me or anything, because it will happen."

"*She* would like to *touch* you and would like to *rub* against you?"

"That's right. I mean more than she does; she probably does it at the beginning and *the thing mounts up*. I've got to keep her at a distance more or less because if she gets near me then I'm just going to go like that."

He snapped his fingers again.

"And then I'm all done. And she's all worked up and then there's not much sense to it."

His ejaculatio praecox was tied up with mother's threats concerning touching and rubbing and exhibiting and looking (watching and being watched).

"It's always that way?"

"Yes, I can't, I just can't do it. I don't know what the hell you have to do to do it!"

"You mean you don't do it again?"

"Geez, I don't know how long it would take me to be able to do it again."

"What do you mean?"

"I have the desire probably but I don't. It just won't come up."

"It won't come up?"

"That's right. Maybe the next morning. Usually I'm all right, but it's no use."

"Well, you mean the next morning you try sometimes?"

"That's right. Well, I've tried it a couple of times and it happened again."

"How does the wife feel about that?"

"Well, she has an orgasm at the same time."

"She does?"

He laughed.

"I think I got her timed about the same as myself, although at times I've noticed that, you know, immediately following she's, *she's not satisfied* and *she'd like to do it again*, but I, uh, figure that I'm done. There's no sense to fooling around and wasting any time because it would probably take a couple of hours before I had another erection."

There was a long pause.

"You wouldn't have a match, would you, Doctor? Oh, thank you."

He puffed at a cigarette.

"Well, you would like some treatment but you say you have financial difficulties?"

"Well, I mean I just got my head above water."

"Why didn't you go to the doctor you went to before?"

"I would have to go in a V. A. Hospital and give up my job, Doctor. In fact, they couldn't figure out how this doctor ever had the right to see me. I make about forty-two hundred a year but with a wife and kids it's not easy."

"I think you would be better off if you went to a good clinic. Would that be okay?"

"Well, actually I can get some help from my mother and would prefer to see you for a while."

"Perhaps we will try it for a few weeks and see how things go."

"That would be fine."

"Then it was after your V-J day affair that this blushing began?"

"It wasn't too long after that, probably six months."

"Six months? And then you met your wife?"

"About, uh, after I started blushing, about a month."

"About a month?"

"A month or two."

"How did you happen to meet her?"

"At a dance."

He paused.

"I mean I never thought that she'd marry me. I couldn't figure out how any girl would marry a guy that had *something like that!*"

So far an inadequate, hateful penis had screened an inadequate-feeling, hated and hating boy in the past and the man in the present.

"What do you mean, the guy who blushed or who came off so quickly? Or who could just keep his head above water?"

"No, *blushed*. I suppose to this day I probably got to figure it out how she stood it this long, I mean, that bothers me, too. How she's been able to put up with *embarrassment* like this."

"What kind of work do you do?"

"I work for the bank as a collector."

"As a collector?"

"Overdue accounts."

Even his work appeared to have a symbolic value.

"As you said, you have been under many pressures. In the past you felt like an inadequate sissy who stupidly didn't know the facts of life, and now you still seem to feel the same way. Then you didn't dare stand up to mother and now it's your mother-in-law. Then you wondered if mother loved you, and now it's your wife. I think you can be helped to find out more about your inadequacy feelings. Perhaps it isn't as bad as you think."

"It would be wonderful. Do you think that will stop the *flushing*?"

"We'll look at it together. I'll see you some time next week."

"Thank you, Doctor. Good-bye."

This patient was seen twice a week intermittently for three years. There were many interruptions because of his type of employment and a strong reluctance to face his feelings of passivity and masculine inadequacy. These were so intense that he developed overwhelming depressed feelings frequently, and occasionally was openly paranoid, accusing his therapist of trying to make him feel he was a homosexual. Later there was much material concerning his passive relationship to his father and his "sissy" feelings and feminine fantasies as a child. This had been foreshadowed by his story about the "affair" with the sailor which was, of course, his own rather than his wife's. He finally left therapy, claiming that it interfered too much with his work. At that time his original symptom had receded into the background but occurred occasionally when he was under stress. On the positive side, he was able to control and express his sexual and aggressive needs to a much greater extent. This had led to an ability to obtain more satisfaction in his personal relationships.

If an interview is properly constructed, not only will the therapist become aware of the dynamic and genetic factors but the patient too will begin to sense them. He will fight off his awareness, however, as long as he is unable to modify his behavior or the circumstances leading to it. If a symptom becomes untenable owing to exposure of its meaning, a new symptom may be developed. Why does insight make a symptom untenable? In one sense, it makes the patient feel foolish and his pride cannot stand it. When our ego cannot integrate and control glaring discrepancies in perception and response, we feel humiliated, anxious, shamed, mortified and depressed. Indeed, the situation is so unendurable that we will go to any lengths to change it.

The concepts of goodness and worth-whileness are bound up with attainment and ego mastery. Control and orderliness are basic attainments that all mothers reward. The control of irrational behavior and thinking is inevitably connected with feelings of shame and guilt by a superego core of sphincter morality. Besides this, pleasure in the mastery of the basic drives is probably to a large degree inherent.

The interviews that follow the initial one are structured in essentially the same way. We gather insights about the presenting complaints and reveal their unconscious meaning in terms of their origin, uses, defenses against them and their derivatives. As the interviews progress, however, we make use of material from former sessions and connect separate complaints. Unification and integration of the material composing the patient's conscious awareness is our goal. Each interview is not only a session of therapy but also a piece of genetic and dynamic research. This is obvious.

One aspect of psychotherapy cannot be stressed too much. The therapist should rely on the material and the patient's own words and not make inferences that are too farfetched. He must also rely on the patient's readiness for insight. For example, let us consider the homosexual interests and anxieties of this man who let himself get picked up and handled in such a passive manner. To pick up this material would be destructive to the therapeutic process. It would be taking advantage of the patient's naïveté and show naïve expectations on the part of the therapist. The material that is timely is plainly suggested; i.e., the therapist should get the patient to ventilate his frustration and rage about his sexual and work performances until he realizes that his preoccupation with flushing is only a sign of a more meaningful preoccupation with his personal inadequacies. He must then arouse the patient's curiosity about how he got that way and hint that the patient's present gripes at himself may be based upon old, legitimate gripes at his parents' attitude towards him in the past. Another way of stating this is to say that defects in his past relations with his parents had led to defects in his present relations with himself and those around him. This was expressed in terms of a defect in his relation to his body image.

IV

FRUSTRATION AND MASTURBATORY FANTASIES

A Counterphobia Concerning Childbirth

The losses that lead to pathological mourning, neuroses, borderline states, etc., also lead to intense feelings of frustration which may in turn lead to angry protestations, fears of punishment and loss of control, guilt feelings and a withdrawal into fantasy. Libidinal interest detached from disappointing objects tends to return to the self and become attached to one's body and various aspects of the self-image. Withdrawal is usually accompanied by an effort to get the tender sensual attentions that are so frequently missing in the neurotic parent-child relationship by autoerotic stimulation of one kind or another. Denial of loss is reinforced and maintained by a concentration upon fantasy reinforced by passive physical sensations. We describe these fantasies as masturbatory because the denied affects are usually attached to the masturbatory act and often ascribed to it, especially the guilt and anxiety over loss of control. Often because of this, and parental prohibitions, the physical act is renounced or hidden by displacement and distortion, etc., as in the naval officer with the shaking hands. The all-important fantasy, however, is retained and often acted out. Acting out, however, seldom succeeds in completely warding off the painful affects associated with pathological mourning and, as a rule, anxiety is always just around the corner.

The problem of the origin and nature of anxiety is complex. Many abstruse theoretical and clinical papers have been written on this subject, but little has been added since Freud's original contributions. From the clinical point of view, anxiety may be quite overt and con

104

scious, or masked by a detached awareness of shaking hands, tension, pounding heart, shortness of breath, dry mouth, restlessness, etc. Whether overt or covert, anxiety in the interview situation is associated with libidinal frustration and acts as a warning of the fulfillment of some chronic, unpleasant fantasies connected with the loss of beloved objects of great importance, with depressive aftereffects. These objects may be things animate or inanimate, persons, parts of the body, abstractions, concepts of oneself or anything that stands for one or more of the many things that made up our precious infantile object world. All of these objects were the early successors to mother and connected with the primordial breast-mouth-ego relationship. Once, all our interest was focused upon the mother-self duality. As in all affairs of great intensity, there are inevitable disappointments, frustrations and renunciations which promote an increasing interest in and recognition of other objects, mainly the home and other members of the family unit. If our libidinal frustrations are not too intense and remain in phase with our maturational capabilities and opportunities, the ego's pleasure in mastery makes the growth process a pleasant and rewarding one. Small doses of anxiety in conjunction with minor losses can act as a developmental stimulus and later, by association, become a source of pleasure. It is only in large doses that these losses lead to pathological mourning, withdrawal and all kinds of neurotic symptoms. Accumulated instinctual tensions are handled in a manner characteristic of each individual and in a broader sense characteristic of each diagnostic group. When a large amount of denied or frustrated libido is attached to a series of fantasies and tension is released and expressed concomitantly by means of masturbatory activities, anxiety and depression are only postponed and temporarily prevented from becoming overt and overwhelming. Often the act of masturbation itself becomes a focal point or symptom of the withdrawal process. In the adult it is often associated with impotence, frigidity, and other experiences leading to narcissistic injury. In hysterical types who are so much governed by their immediate feelings, masturbatory fantasies are usually easily recognized as sexual and oedipal in nature. Jealous love, exclusive possessiveness, idealized homosexual or heterosexual longings, loneliness, inadequacy and guilt feelings, rivalry, incest, death, punishment, castration, the eternal triangle—these are familiar themes and they can exist as such or in an inverted form or as a reaction formation to the opposite. For example, the manifest interest of the boy or the girl can be placed on the parent of the same sex. At times love is expressed by hate, and the boy who cannot be the great lover becomes a great villain like Richard the Third. Reaction formations often occur in connection with anxiety states, and instead of phobic avoidance there may be a counterphobic type of involvement, where the originally dreaded feeling state and conditions under which it occurs are sought after. In such cases conquest of the fear will give rise to enormous, if temporary, relief, but usually anxiety will persist and accumulate continually. This leads to a constant renewal of the attempts to master it. Fantasies of renunciation of sexuality or aggression, reward, eternal life, unlimited potency, are common. A life devoted to the fulfillment or to the acting out of an intense and complex series of masturbatory oedipal fantasies can easily lead to frustration and reality problems that are difficult to solve. We will now listen to a patient who entered treatment because her fantasy life had eventually led to a traumatic abandonment by her husband. Disappointments in her relationship with her parents had led her to withdraw into a dream world which she called her Marjorie Morningstar fantasies. Her detachment had been shattered by the abandonment so that her feelings were now intense. This patient revealed a series of childhood deprivations, extremely intense oedipal longings for a baby and daddy of her own, and many masturbatory fantasies built around the themes of suffering, tension and turmoil. A childhood trauma of witnessing her mother have a miscarriage led to a mixed counterphobic and phobic defensive attitude toward her aggressive problems, sex and pregnancy. The oedipal theme will appear in a form different from that of the previous cases, and the reactions of this patient will be less in the form of symptoms and more in the form of characteristic behavioral patterns. This interview will illustrate, above all, that the analytically oriented psychiatrist must avoid the so-called reality aspects of a patient's problems. The majority of neurotic patients have functioning adult potentialities and capabilities. The relatively mature parts of their egos are insulted if they are treated like the helpless infants they so often feel they are. Usually they will solve their own problems when the unconscious determinants of their difficulties are comprehended. This patient, Mrs. Jones, was an attractive young woman with a childlike, innocent appearance. She was in her late thirties but looked much younger. She appeared bewildered, distraught and tense, and talked quickly and somewhat breathlessly.

"Well, I, uh, I just don't know how to start."

"Start wherever you wish."

"Well, I have three children and my husband, uh, well, we were married fifteen years."

She paused, apparently overwhelmed by the amount she had to tell. As usual, the time elements were given priority.

"Fifteen years?"

"Yes."

"How old are you now?"

"Thirty-eight."

"Thirty-eight. So that would be when you were twenty-three!"

"Yes, and four of these fifteen years he was living with another woman!"

She said this dramatically and waited for the effect. The interview had begun with a familiar theme, i.e., the oedipal triangle, which was reflected back by the therapist.

"Four of these fifteen years he was living with another woman?"

"And I didn't know about it."

"Which four?"

"The last four years."

"The last four?"

"And I didn't know about this!"

It appeared important for her to impress the therapist with her innocence of this.

"He was living with another woman?"

"Uh-huh."

"As man and wife?"

"As man and wife!"

It was impossible for this to happen without *some* clues being dropped. Why did she have to ignore them?

"And you didn't know?"

"I didn't know. This woman was a wife of a friend and customer of his. He was a salesman. I didn't know he was running around with the wife himself. Now, uh, he used to travel quite a bit and he used to call me and tell me I love you and miss you and this is the peak of my career and I hope that soon I can stop traveling, and so I had no knowledge until a friend of mine came in one day and told me of what was going on. So I called. He was in Florida at the time and I called Florida. I also checked his home office. *I just couldn't believe it.* And when they told me Mr. and Mrs. Jones were in Florida buying a home, I, uh, I mean, the floor might have gone down!"

"You mean you never suspected?"

"I never, oh I mean *I didn't look for it*. Now that I look back I can see a lot of things that add up."

When someone doesn't look at the obvious, it is usually for mixed reasons, such as a secret enjoyment, a fear of disturbing the status quo, a feeling of guilt, etc. These had to be made conscious and worked out.

"For instance?"

"Oh, for instance, when I was having the last baby who is four and a half."

"Four and a half? That would be six months before he started."

"Well, he started *before that*. I say approximately four years. I mean *I don't know exactly when it started*. He didn't want this last baby and he wanted a doctor to abort it! When he'd go away on trips and I'd call, I wouldn't call very often, but if his mother or father were ill they would ask me to get in touch with him. I'd call and they'd always say they never heard of such a person. He would tell me where he was staying. I'd call this place and they'd say they never heard of such a person, and when he came back I'd say, 'Fred, I tried to get in touch with you because your father was sick or your mother was sick, and they told me they never heard of you.' "

"This was—?"

"During this four-year period."

"Oh!"

"And he'd say, 'Well, I was registered under my firm's name. I wasn't under my own.' I mean I wouldn't suspect these things. These things could happen. There was a time when he said his car was stolen and he came home. You know, he came home in a taxi for about a three-week period. And I mean he told everyone in town the car was stolen. Later on I found out *she* was using the car while ordering a *foreign sports car* and having to wait for it to come through. I mean these things I found out later, not during the time."

Here was the first hint that the rival was to be envied for her possessions. It was important to keep a steady pressure on her to get into the past.

"But you say you suspected even before as you look back?"

"Well, no. As I look back, I *should have suspected*."

"Why?"

"Oh, because of these things that were happening, I mean that I know now that I should have added things up."

"You mean before this four-year period?"

"No, during this period."

"Oh, just during it?"

"No, I mean before this I was very happy *as far as I knew.*"

These qualified statements are often the best lead to the past or some valuable bit of information.

"What do you mean?"

"Well, I mean I thought I was happy. When I found this out and the thing came to a head—it is difficult to describe. He said he wanted to stay home and yet, uh, it is so hard to make a clear picture, there are so many little details that must be put into it."

She was confused by the complexity and extent of the roots of the problem in the infantile past.

"Say anything you wish."

"Uh, he wanted to stay home, uh, then he had a customer in Texas, he said, and was going to Texas and he was *giving her up* because he knew this was *no good.* This woman had been married *four* times before. She was a woman that when she saw a man she would start preening, you know, just for the man's sake, no matter what man it was. I found out and I said, 'Look, *you can run around with women but don't tie yourself up with one woman,* uh, you have children.' "

It was of interest that "four" recurred. Did she suffer a trauma at *four*? This may hint at it. Why would she not mind many women? *Four* could be taken up later.

"You didn't mind if he went around with many women?"

"Well, I did mind, I did mind, but I, there is no woman in the world who doesn't mind, but it is certainly worse for him to tie himself up with one woman completely because then he *loses all his ties with his children,* and the children, if you saw the children now and saw *their need for a father,* and every day, I don't have one day go by that *the little one,* who is *four* and a half and was almost *aborted,* keeps saying go *get me a daddy,* I want a daddy. Go get a *policeman* to get my daddy back. I mean you'd think the little one wouldn't mind as much as the others, whereas the others knew him more. Oh, the others do mind. The *little girl* keeps saying she feels completely *confused* now. She is, uh, the two older children are very very bright children. I don't know what their I.Q.'s are. They range somewhere in the 150s and they are very bright and *adult-thinking children,* adult and yet they are children. I mean mental capacities but *not grown up yet.* I wonder sometime if I am."

These children represented different facets or ego states of herself as a child, and her last statement confirmed this. It was a valuable piece of insight to be expanded and nailed down.

"What do you mean? Why do you ask yourself this?"

"Well, I don't know, I, uh, maybe uh, uh, this thing that happened, I went to a psychiatrist. Oh, well, there's something else that should have made me suspect. Two years ago, about two years ago, two or three years ago, I've forgotten the exact date. I went to a psychiatrist —well, my husband said he wasn't living with me the way he should."

"Three years ago?"

"Yes, and, uh, I didn't know why. I mean, we weren't living *as man and wife.*"

"By man and wife you mean you weren't having sexual relations. How come?"

"I didn't know! I couldn't understand!"

"You mean this was nothing of your doing?"

"No, no!"

"It was his doing?"

"He kept saying he was *too tired* all the time when he came home. He used to travel, be home very infrequently, come home maybe three days in two weeks, or something like that. And, I don't know, just was unhappy this way and so I said I didn't know what was wrong with our marriage, and he said it was my fault. He said I had a *mother attachment,* uh, and I didn't want to *leave my mother.* Well, I made a discovery on that too. Well, anyway, so I spoke to my *obstetrician.*"

This was an excellent opportunity to get into the past and not to be missed.

"What do you mean by mother attachment?"

"Well, the first child I had, uh, *died.* I had *toxemia* and it was full-time, full-term pregnancy. After that the doctors told me couldn't have any more children and I wasn't to have children but wanted them. I'm an *only child,* so *I wanted children more than anything in the world* and I just *wanted a family.*"

So many questions were contained in this speech. What in her fantasy killed the child? What is toxemia? Why couldn't she have more? Why was she an only child? What did she mean by a family? Did she want children more than a husband? The loneliness problem was the simplest.

"You mean you wanted lots of children because you had had no brothers and sisters?"

"That's right, because I had *no family at all.*"

By this she meant she had no father and mother either.

"No family at all?"

"Well, I mean, just an only child and that was all the family we had."

"How come?"

"Well my father when he was a child lived in Poland and it seems he went to the hospital when he was very little and when he came back his mother, and his brother and his grandmother, and his, I don't know who else was there, they were lying with their *heads severed from their bodies* and it was during an *uprising*, I don't know just what it was. He came back and *saw* that."

This could be regarded as a very sadistic fantasy about an overwhelming loss. All such fantasies are partly the property of the patient. How old was she when she beheaded them? How did *this* explain being an only child? Did this fantasy screen what happened to her potential siblings?

"Beheaded?"

"Beheaded, yes! Right in the house he saw them."

"How old was he?"

"He doesn't know exactly but he thinks between *six* and *eight*."

"Six and eight?"

"And then he went to live with his stepaunt. The uncle was his but the aunt was a stepaunt. She had some children."

"He was between six and eight and he came home and he found his mother—"

"His mother, his grandmother and his brother."

"And his grandmother and his brother?"

"Uh-huh, he had a younger brother."

"Where was father?"

"I don't know. He doesn't know if his father is alive, dead, or just what has happened to his father and, uh, *where was I*—well, anyway—"

"So he went to live with his aunt?"

"His stepaunt, and the stepaunt had children of her own and also children of his uncle. The children of the uncle were *mistreated*. There was one girl whom she was supposed to take care of and she was *dropped as a child*. The child *didn't walk* until she was *seven* years old and is today a *hunchback*, but when she dropped her she didn't seem to *care* that the child, you know, wouldn't walk when she was *three* or *four* or *five*, and the child today is deformed, I mean the girl, the uncle's daughter. I mean the children were very much *mistreated.* I've met them since, but of course they have gone off to different parts of the States, and my father used to go to work through the forests and he has on his legs, he has round circles. You can still see the impressions of eagles in them. He'd go through the forest and he claims they were dogs, he didn't know what they were. I suspect they were *wolves,* and they would *bite* a *hunk of flesh* out of him and he would put a silver coin in the wound and when the skin grew over it it would show an eagle."

Another sadistic fantasy series revolved about cruel losses. This could be echoed profitably and the oral-sadistic mood amplified.

"It must have been terrible having pieces bitten out of him."

"When he went to work, yes!"

"And getting pieces bitten out of him?"

"Not every day, it didn't happen, but there were *four* or *five* times. He went to work at a place where you buy food and when he would come home he used to give her his pay and she used to throw the *scraps* from the table to him."

Another sadistic fantasy had appeared. Her aggression was obvious.

"You mean on the floor?"

"Yes! And he remembers getting cholera. An epidemic was going on and, uh, she called in a neighbor, and the neighbor said he's going to *die* soon anyway so don't bother. So he crawled out and they had haystack there. He went to sleep in the haystack and he dreamt that his *mother* came to him and gave him *water* and took him on her shoulders for a walk in the fields and said, 'Now my son, you are better.' He woke up next morning feeling better and he went back to work and finally saved up money and he came here. He was about *sixteen* I think at the time and there was a special offer for *sixteen dollars* or something you could come to America in the hold with the *cattle,* and that's how he came here, and *that's why he had no family.*

Here was a non sequitur with certain kinds of possible meaning. The good and bad nourishing mother figures were sharply separated.

"I don't understand."

"He came here alone to this country."

"Oh, he had no family?"

"They were all gone!"

"I should think then that, just like you, he would have wanted family."

"He did! I mean, uh, he, or he wanted a, *I don't know.* Well, I'll tell you—*basically* he's a kind man but, uh, very *brusque.* He has no patience whatsoever. Uh, if things aren't just the way he wants them he talks *loud, curses* all the time, it doesn't mean anything, but it, but it is hard to live with."

This was the first "I don't know" signifying her ambivalence to father as well as mother.

"You mean hard for mother?"

"Oh, hard for my mother, very hard, and she too, in her way, I mean everyone has their *faults*, nobody is perfect. I'm not perfect, nor is she perfect, nor is he perfect, nor is anybody else in this world, but somehow or other I'm an *outsider*. I'm not an outsider but even I myself can see where things should have been *different* in the house."

All oedipal children feel like outsiders. Who was to blame?

"What do you mean?"

"Uh, she tries to be understanding. She's very, they are both very loyal but, uh, he likes people. She *lives with herself*. She is, I think she is *basically afraid*. She doesn't dress. She doesn't invite people over to the house. She doesn't go to the other people. She would like to. I know this, but she is *afraid* that she can't make it."

Here one could investigate her basic afraidness, but the business of no children was possibly more important.

"She didn't want any children either?"

"She wanted children. She was pregnant again. She was pregnant at other times but just didn't *carry through*. I mean she used to *work with him*. They had a *butcher* store and they used to *work together*, and in those days when I was young they used to work Saturdays, Sundays, nights, and they used to both *cut meat*, and you know sell poultry and things, and she got *pregnant* a couple of times but *lost the baby*, and they didn't have much money then. They were very poor."

Being around a butcher might encourage all sorts of sadomasochistic baby-making fantasies. Why did mother lose a baby?

"How many times was she pregnant?"

"I don't know. I just know, I know of one more time besides myself, I mean, but I was about *nine* at the time."

"You were nine?"

"Yes, and I had seen the baby that was miscarried."

"You must have seen a lot of terrible things for a child then, the animals being butchered and mother having miscarriages?"

This was a trial connection to reinforce the fantasy life.

"Well, he didn't butcher the animals. He was just a meat cutter. Of course he cut off the chickens' heads and *things like that*."

This was the second time this fantasy had appeared. The analyst would say that this not only was a reality statement but had hidden fantasy and screen values. It fitted in with her general sadomasochistic fantasies of father's role in making babies. A meat cutter was also a castrator. The concern about a fantasy phallus she felt she once possessed had been displaced to the head. Father's violence and temper led to her having fantasies of his having violent sexual relations with mother. These were distorted to fit her infantile conception of sexuality.

"The heads?"

"Well, yes, He used to take me out to the slaughter house. Of course, the first time I saw it I couldn't eat meat but you get used to those things. You know that they are for food. Those things don't disturb you after a while; but it was my *mother* he *cursed* all the time. He *yelled* and my mother would stay there and take it. There was *constant bickering*. There was never any peace. I just don't remember peace in the family but, uh, I got sidetracked there. I was talking about something else. Well, anyway, my children have that now; my mother, I tried to get away, oh, how I got onto that was, when I *lost the first child*, uh, the doctor told me I couldn't have any children and *I wanted children*. I didn't want to be alone. I wanted a family."

This was an important revelation. The emotional climate she grew up in was one of constant bickering. This had much more effect upon her than anything else, led to her susceptibility to being traumatized and shaped her fantasies into a sadomasochistic form. Loneliness led to the need for fantasy; bickering led to a certain type of fantasy.

"You were lonely as a little girl?"

"Yes, very lonely."

"Really?"

"Well, I was all alone. My mother and father worked and I used to stay up in the house all alone, and we used to live over the butcher store. I was ashamed to bring people there. It, it was never kept orderly, just once in a while during holidays and things like that people would come, and many times I would try to, you know, clean it up but whatever I did was not the way it should be done, and when I tried to cook or bake it was never the way it should be when I was small, and *whatever* I did *somebody else* always did *better* than I did."

This amplified her oedipal inadequacy feelings. It must have been easy to give up and turn to fantasy.

"You mean mother?"

"Mother and father both."

"They both did better?"

"I mean they did better or *other children* did better."

"Other children?"

"I mean there was always another girl friend of mine or somebody."

"You mean you always felt inadequate?"

"Well, I mean whatever I did it was not, it wasn't like the other child did, or wasn't like it should be done."

"Who said so?"

"Well, I remember in school we took up *cooking* in the sixth grade, or fifth grade, I've forgotten what grade, and I made some kind of bread pudding, and I did it according to the directions and I was so happy that I had made something for the folks. They were working in the store and I wanted, I had it ready for them. They came up. I guess I put it on a seat to cool or something. It was one of these fancy things where you put it in water or something. I mean it is supposed to blow up like an egg soufflé. Then when I gave it to my mother and father, my father said, 'Ugh, this is awful,' and my mother said, 'Why do you waste good stuff on this kind of stuff.' Well, I mean, gradually I stopped doing it. I didn't want to any longer. Now I got sidetracked there again."

Actually she was competing hopelessly with mother.

"But you said you had a problem about *mother!*"

"Oh, well, anyway, oh, when I was pregnant, when I lost the baby and then I wanted children, and so I went, I tried, I, we were, at the time we were married we went to Texas for a year. He was in the service. When we came back, it was during wartime and there were no houses. You just couldn't get an apartment in those days, so I moved in *with my mother*, which I shouldn't have done but I did, and that's the year, I mean I lost the baby that year."

"You felt you couldn't even do that right?"

"Well, the doctors had told me, uh, I had gone to some doctors in Texas and they told me I was built *too small* and that I couldn't have children. They didn't tell me anything about *toxemia*."

All little oedipal girls feel too small to have babies.

"Too small?"

"Yes, well that's what they told me down there, but I didn't believe anybody. It wasn't that at all. I just got *toxemia* and I don't know how I got toxemia, but I remember in my *mother's* house the furnace had smoked up and the walls were all *black* with soot, and here I was pregnant, and there was a little room off the kitchen that I wanted to have fixed up for the baby and nobody seemed to want to hire anybody to paint the walls or anything, so I remember I bought some paint and I painted the room so it would be ready and there was no child after all. But what am I crying about? I haven't done this for a long time!"

What was toxemia to her? Obviously it had something to do with mother's dirty house. She was crying because she saw herself as the neglected child her father used to be back in Poland. Neglected here also meant castrated—beheaded in her fantasies. At another level what she really mourned was her lack of a close relationship with a mother who cared.

"But this is what you say, you felt like sort of a little girl, an inadequate little girl, huh? As you said, doctors said you were too little and you felt too little too, or thought something was wrong with you?"

"Well, *something is always wrong with me.*"

"Really, what do you mean?"

"Well, then I did get pregnant finally. After I lost the baby, the doctors told me no children, that I mustn't have children, and I went to several. Finally, I got pregnant. I wanted a child so I went to another doctor. He was a big doctor and he said *you must abort* and he started telling me about adopted children."

"He said you must abort?"

"Yes!"

"Why?"

"Well, because of the case of *toxemia* and the history of toxemia, and I still had *high blood pressure* and my *kidney* was so *damaged.*"

"You mean by toxemia—what does that mean to you?"

"Well, all it meant to me was that I couldn't have children. I get high blood pressure when I get pregnant and I could lose the child or I could lose my life."

There was a deadly rivalrous relationship between mother and child. In another sense, her sadomasochistic fantasy life distorted all her relationships.

"You mean that the child might kill you?"

"Or the child wouldn't be born alive anyway."

"Born dead, huh?"

"Yes!"

"Mother or child, one or the other?"

"Yes, or both!"

"Or both?"

"Well, anyway, uh, I had tried to adopt a child. I went through the regular channels and nothing happened, so I was giving up on that and I wanted children; I wanted to try to have a child, so I went to several other doctors until I found a doctor who would let me and I did. Then I didn't want an only child because I know what I went through."

Doctors, marital partners, religions, etc., are all useful backgrounds as far as the neurosis is concerned.

"You mean as lonely as you were?"

"I didn't want an only child. She had to have brothers or sisters because I know what I went through without brothers or sisters."

"What do you mean? What did you go through?"

"Oh, the loneliness. You'd be up in the house all alone and there would be no one to talk to, or even when I was married, I mean, there's no family, like Thanksgivings and holidays, you like a family circle, or you—I thought I needed a family, that's all."

She felt something was missing that a family would provide. Why should she stay up in the house alone? What was in it for her? What sustained this type of behavior?

"What did you do while you were alone?"

"God! Make believe or write poetry. I used to try to clean the house but I used to give up because nothing was put where they wanted it put, when I was little that is. Oh, I used to go out. I used to look through the window and try to make friends. I had some friends but then they'd have to go off with their brothers or sisters and I'd be left alone again."

Tears rolled down her cheeks.

"I wonder what you thought about why mother didn't have children? What did you know about miscarriages and so forth? Why did you think that mother didn't have children?"

"Well, in the first place, having seen a miscarriage and knowing how ill she was, I knew that she tried and couldn't."

This must have been a traumatic nucleus for all kinds of anxiety-laden sexual and aggressive fantasies.

"You saw it?"

"Well, I saw the miscarriage."

"What did you see? You were nine, weren't you?"

"I was nine. I don't remember too well, only vaguely, but I remember the house was *cold*. We never had much *heat* in the house. We had a stove and that's it. And I remember she started *bleeding* all over the floor and then she got in bed and I called the doctor.

The doctor came and gave me this pan with sort of, it didn't look like a *baby* to me. I don't know. It couldn't have been more than the third or fourth month or fifth month because it was all, it looked like a *monstrosity* with veins and *stuff like that* and it was blue, and there was no skin formed on it yet or something. I don't remember too well."

"How did you feel?"

"Well, I was worried about my mother because the doctor told me how *sick* she was, and I just remember that the doctor said to me, 'Somebody will be her nurse.' Of course I'm afraid of *blood*! I can't stand the *sight of blood*! And he said to me, 'Somebody will be a nurse, you're very good,' because I was helping out with things that he needed. We couldn't afford a nurse in those days."

"But at nine you knew how babies were made, where they came from, you knew all that?"

"Yes."

"How come?"

"Oh well, I was always *curious* as a child and little girls in the school used to tell, and when I used to go to the store when my father had the butcher store, oh, *I didn't really know. I don't know if I really knew* because I remember one woman making fun of me and saying something that I thought was very *filthy* and I called it filthy at the time, *these things* you know that babies come out the same way as you move your *bowels*, you know."

"I didn't know" meant there had been confusion between the anus and the vagina which was maintained to ward off anxious and sado-masochistic castration fantasies.

"Like a bowel movement?"

"Yes, and oh, I thought she was a very filthy person to have said that, and uh, then of course little girls whispering and I always thought they came out of, uh, the *navel*, because I mean I remember once my mother went and took me to one of those turkish baths where all the women go naked and I remember they all looked wrinkled around the navel and I thought that's how babies must come out, but then *after I saw this* I knew that they don't come out through the navel."

When she could no longer believe in anal birth, she used the navel. The vagina must be denied as it implied the existence of castration. The sight had acted as a trauma, as she was not prepared to accept a feminine role at this age and stage in her development. It had the effect of augmenting her sadomasochism and fixating it. In another sense her infantile sexual, aggressive and narcissistic fantasies appeared externalized and actualized by the sight of the miscarriage, giving rise to fears that she was responsible and would be punished in a similar manner. She probably became phobic about sex and babies at this time and developed her counterphobic tendencies later.

"You saw her having the miscarriage?"

"Yes."

"From where?"

"Well, I mean I saw it come out from between her legs. But, well, anyway—"

She paused and appeared anxious.

"That was the first time you knew babies came out through there?"

"*I don't remember.* I really don't remember how, I mean I had the knowledge but not from my mother or father. They never told me, but the other girls would buy books to read and some mothers bought them a book on sex and your genital or something like that."

"The reason I asked was I was wondering how you felt after you saw all this?"

"*I don't know how I felt.*"

"About?"

"I felt *badly* but it didn't *repulse* me."

"I wondered if you felt that mother didn't have any children because—?"

"I thought she couldn't. I thought since she had this miscarriage, I knew she had tried so I thought she just couldn't. I really *never questioned it.*"

This was hardly likely since she was so curious.

"I wonder what your ideas were?"

"Well my ideas were that if circumstances were so that she could have, she would have, but circumstances were, she *worked in the store.* They couldn't actually *afford* another child."

"So you mean they didn't have them because they felt they couldn't afford any more?"

"*I don't know.* I mean she worked in the store. When she was pregnant even, she *denied she was pregnant* and tried to keep it a *secret* all the time. When some people would say to her, 'You are pregnant,' she'd say, 'No I'm not. I'm just getting *fat*, you know.' "

The neurotic guilt feelings and dissatisfaction of the child made her feel she too was an unwanted child who was the cause of bickering. As usual, "I don't know" meant "I don't know which of the many thoughts and fantasies I have is the correct one."

"You remember?"

"Yes."

"How old were you then?"

"Nine."

"Nine, this was around that time?"

"And I know she tried to keep it a secret."

"That was the only time she was pregnant?"

"*That I know of.* Anyways, well, so I didn't want to be an only child. I was a very unhappy, lonely child."

Left unsaid was "and it was *all my mother's fault.*" At the same time she felt it was all her fault.

"So *you* wanted another child after you had the little girl?"

"I wanted *as many as I could have.* If I could have had a dozen, I would have had them. I love children anyway, and anyway, so, at the time we couldn't get an apartment and I lived with my mother, and then when I got pregnant I held onto the child and had a little girl."

"You didn't have any toxemia?"

"Oh, yes, I did."

"With the little girl?"

"With all of them!"

"With all of them! How do you mean?"

Aside from the possible reality of the situation, it would be surprising if all of her sadomasochistic fantasies concerning pregnancy, miscarriage and childbirth did not result in a chronic anxiety, the manifestations of which could augment or be treated as a toxemia.

"Well, my blood pressure starts going up or something and they take me in. I never know when I'm going to be delivered because they *force* the labor. In fact the last one was taken out the end of the sixth month because he was due in March and he was taken out Christmas Eve. The doctor was going to be away Christmas Day and didn't want to trust himself not being around if anything happened, so they gave me Caesareans but they just *anesthetized the legs* because they said if they anesthetized further that it might *kill the child.* This way the child might have a chance, so it was a dreadful thing to go through! Talk about Hitler and torture! I don't think I could go through that again!"

Her sadomasochism had utilized the childbirth situation to the utmost.

"Talk about what?"

"About what Hitler did, the tortures, you know. I mean they just cut and the *things going in* and you can feel the *flesh being cut* and being *pulled* and you can *see it* because they put the bandage on, but you can see right under it, and it was *horrible!*"

"You had seen a lot of that?"

"No, all I saw was my mother."

"But I mean the slaughter house and all of that."

"Well, that, well I don't associate that with human beings. I mean that's different but a human being suffering. I couldn't stand, I can't stand to watch a person being given a *needle*. I mean it *scares* me. I look the other way. I mean I'd never be a nurse. I just couldn't be a nurse because *I feel it's me. Everything that happens to somebody else I feel it on myself practically!* I don't know if that's bad or good. In fact when I first got married I was scared of needles and when my doctor had to give me the Wasserman I ran around and he had to run after me for about *two hours!* I just wouldn't take a needle. And as a child in school, when they used to give the Schick tests, mother used to have to sign a note so that I wouldn't get the Schick test because I was afraid of the needle."

While she appeared to emphasize the sadomasochistic aspects of the hysterical character, she also illustrated the tendency of this type to identify too readily with anyone and anything that could be found useful to maintain these fantasies. The problem remained to determine what were the pleasurable aspects and guilt feelings that kept things going. It was noticeable how her sadomasochism was organized around the miscarriage in a way that made it resemble a primal coital scene.

"You must have suffered a lot?"

"Outside of that I was very normal. Nothing bothered me. I was never sick as a child except I had the flu, when the flu epidemics went around, but I was never sickly as a child. I remember I had a little girl friend who had scarlet fever and I slept with her and they wanted to give me a needle for that in those days and I wouldn't take it because I was afraid of needles and I never came down with it."

"How about your other babies? Did you have any trouble with the deliveries then?"

"Yes, with all of them."

"All?"

"Three I have."

"Painful?"

"Well, the first child the doctor didn't give anesthesia either and I could feel the head and I could remember waiting for the doctor to come and you could feel the head *banging* and all that, *terrible pain*, and you know they had to put *their hands in* to take the baby out. It was, I don't know, it was forceps eventually anyway. It was way up, and it had to be induced."

"So you really had a terrible time with all of your deliveries?"

"Yes! *Having children*, and they told me during pregnancy I had to stay in bed so that you couldn't use up energy. It seems something to do with *energy* and *toxemia*, I don't know what it is, but you had to stay in bed. And for that reason *I lived with my mother* during the pregnancies because *I was afraid* that if I moved away and I had to do anything I wouldn't be able to have children."

This "toxemia" led to her receiving much care from mother and lessened her separation anxiety. Now she revealed the phobic component of her neurosis. The inner fantasy was that they had to protect each other from their aggressive and evil thoughts. She was afraid to move from the dirty place that had made her lose her child!

"How did mother feel about this?"

"*I don't know. I know she wanted me to have babies* and I *know* she didn't try to *tie me down. I know, I know*, whenever I threatened to leave *or something*, she got all upset and *frustrated* and would say *I don't have anybody, I'm all alone*, and you're *the only one* I have and things like that!"

She needed continual proof that she was wanted and that her badness would not injure the baby (self) and/or mother. She also wanted to be mother's only one, but what had happened to the rest could happen to her. At one level it was mother who had gotten rid of them. At another level it was her bad wish to be the only child.

"Father is dead?"

"No, father is alive."

"Then what did she mean she had nobody?"

"Well, because my father is brusque and always yelling at her, and *they don't get along*, you know."

"So you were always close to another?"

"I was close actually."

"Really?"

"I don't feel myself being close. I like, I loved her, she's my mother."

"But she wanted you there?"

"She wanted me there and I am *very selfish* and I felt I would stay there just until I had my children."

"How long would you stay in bed?"

"Well, I wouldn't find out I was pregnant until about the third month usually and I would never, I never carried more than seven, so it was actually four months I stayed in bed. With the last one I was in the hospital four months."

"How come you never found out you were pregnant until the third month?"

"Oh, I'd find out but I'd just, uh, it didn't, I didn't worry about toxemia until the third month because toxemia doesn't set in until about the fifth, sixth or seventh month."

Probably this was the age in years when her fantasies set in.

"How did you feel about your sexual relations? You were in bed so much and he was away."

"I don't know. I mean, at first it was the way you'd expect it, I guess."

"What do you mean?"

"Well, I mean they were real pleasant but it was when we started to live with my folks that it became not quite so pleasant and not quite as frequent and gradually, but, of course, also I was pregnant. For five years, rather *within five years there were three pregnancies* of which most of the time I had to *stay in bed*."

"So you mean you never had relations very often?"

"I couldn't because of the pregnancies and also, well, *I don't know*."

"What do you mean? This is what your husband meant by a mother problem?"

"Yes, because he thought that I was *attached to her*. I don't know if he realized I wasn't. I mean I *love her*. In fact, if today I could see my way clear *I would go to her* even without my husband. He's now living in Florida *with the woman*. He's had a *baby* with *her*. Uh, when I found out it was too late. She was already pregnant. He said he wanted to stay home with his children, you know, but then he went off to Mexico, this was where *I got lost,* and then he went, I didn't know, he called up and said he was going to go to Texas for a while or Mexico for a while, to do some fishing, and he did, and from there he sent me gifts, a bag, and a skirt, shawl and everything. The next thing I know I get a Mexican divorce. The next thing I know he doesn't come back. He's living in Florida with this woman who, she took, and this was talked about openly in front of me, my husband and her ex-husband and I were there, she took from her ex-husband $150,000 he had saved! It was black market money but could not be shown. Then when they were having the divorce, her husband was a very wealthy man, she got from him $75,000 for the children plus $200 a week for life for her. She convinced her husband she might come back to him. Well, I mean, this was fast talking and her husband said, 'Well I'm going to give her everything. She's going to come back anyway, what difference does it make?' This I didn't know, finally when I did find out he was living as man and wife with her, I called up her ex-husband, who had remarried since, and the ex-husband said, 'My God, what are you bothering me about now.' He said, 'I've been sending her alimony for three years now since I started.' So that, oh yes, they have a home now in Florida. They have a swimming pool, I understand. It's quite a large estate in the nicest section of Florida they could go to. All the millionaires live there. He claims he's not working but he was making, when he was living up here, around $40,000 a year, $30,000 to $40,000 a year. Now he sends no money for the children. He claims he's not working and is living with her on this estate. She had this baby, oh I guess, five months after or six months after he went, you know, after the Mexican divorce decree. So, I don't know, I'm giving an *awful mixed-up picture.*"

Her ambivalence towards mother was apparent. Mixed with reality was the oedipal envy of the wonderful pleasures parents have in their baby-making sexual relationship, colored perhaps by an idealized infant-mother fantasy. Being cut off from her husband was the reality problem. Being cut off from mother was the neurotic problem to be solved by the therapist.

"This is a difficult predicament. So you came here because you feel mixed up?"

"Well I came here because I don't want the children *to grow up the way I did.*"

"What do you mean by that? What do you mean grow up the way you did?"

"Well, right now I feel *calm,* but generally in front of people *I look very calm* and I look as though nothing disturbs me."

"Surely, but it is really different?"

"It is actually *tenseness* and *turmoil!*"

"Tenseness and turmoil?"

"Just inside of me. I, I, I'm *like my father* in that I don't have patience but I try to keep it in."

"You mean this is an old story?"

"Yes, always tenseness and turmoil especially now!"

"What do you mean by always? How long have you been so tense? How long is always?"

"As far back as I can remember."

"How far back can you remember?"

"Well I can remember back to childhood, oh, I guess to seven years old."

"You can remember?"

"I can remember going to school. I can remember being ashamed to invite people to my home because my mother and father were not like other mothers and fathers. I tried to find one little thing about my family that I could show off about like other children could."

She had lost her heroic dreams of her parents too early. Another trauma!

"You mean they were not like other fathers and mothers because they fought so much?"

"Fought so much and weren't English-speaking people. I remember going to school and in the first grade the teacher wanted to keep me back because I couldn't speak English and, uh, finally the teacher called my mother up and told her that she would have to keep me back and my mother did finally get some book in the five-and-ten and I did get promoted because I did catch up finally."

"You learned with mother?"

"Well, she taught me of course. Today she says, you know I try to correct her and today she says 'Well I taught you English.' But I remember having to go to the bathroom. I raised my hand to tell the teacher in Polish that I had to go to the bathroom and the teacher wouldn't know what I was talking about, and *wetting myself* and being so ashamed because the teacher wouldn't understand me, and oh, I remember as a child I used to *wet my bed* and be so ashamed. My mother used to tell everybody. She used to go around telling people."

Girls also can be fixated at a phallic-urethral level where fantasies about exhibiting, shame, urinating, being cut, pierced, stabbed, etc., in both active and passive versions are of primary importance. Phallic masturbatory fantasies can be expected to play an important role in her life.

"She did! Up until when did you wet the bed?"

"Oh, I must have been about eight years old."

"Eight?"

"Eight or nine."

"Nine?"

She had problems controlling herself in many areas, especially her rage over her feelings of libidinal frustration. We could guess that her wetting referred to fantasies about her "inadequate" phallic genital and also fantasies about babies which she gave up temporarily after the "miscarriage." This made her repress her rage and increased her anxiety. The therapist had noted how she tended to spare her husband and father and show her anger at the "other woman" only halfheartedly.

"I don't remember. I know it was way past babyhood, and I used to, I used to, *I still do,* I used to *grind my teeth* in my sleep, and I would wake myself up hearing myself."

Grinding the teeth can be an aggressive symptom, like enuresis.

"Grind your teeth?"

"At night. Well, you know, I tried to, of course I grew up and I see people around here. You see what they should be, and so I tried to make changes in my life but, uh, finally after I did have the children, I had my house, this was two years ago too. I don't know why he built me a house when he had these plans, I guess, to go away. He built this house!"

"He said the reason he went away was because you had this attachment to your mother and were in bed so much?"

"He couldn't take it."

"You mean couldn't take what?"

"*I don't know what happened there.* I, I just *don't know.* I, I just, there's a lot more. I can't put my finger, I mean, I can, well it would take hours and hours and hours trying to figure things. Why I came here, well I started telling you about the psychiatrist and about not sleeping together, well we were going to this psychiatrist, oh, yes, so I called my doctor who delivered the last baby, and asked him for the name of a psychiatrist. I told him my husband thought I needed one."

"He thought you needed one because—?"

"Because of the mother attachment."

"Because of the mother attachment!"

"And he didn't want to sleep with me."

"Why?"

"I don't know. He said that I had a mother attachment."

"No, but what do you suspect?"

"Now, now I know he was living with this other woman and didn't want to use up his energies. I mean he wanted to show what a man he was."

"For her? You mean he enjoyed going to bed with her more?"

"Well, she, yes, well she *lied to me.* I don't know. I'm not a psychiatrist. I'm not a psychologist."

It was hard to tell which woman she was talking about, mother in the past or the woman in the present, or her husband. Hysterical women often treat their husbands as substitute mothers.

"No, but I wonder what you thought."

"I feel that she is a *nymphomaniac*! I mean, *we used to socialize together* and I remember sitting at the bar at the club, and I remember we'd just sit and talk, and the minute a man walked into the doorway she would go, there was a fireplace there, she'd go for the fireplace and start posing and do things, and she wore her hair long, and start doing things to her hair. And if the man walked out, she'd sit down again. I mean just as though nothing had happened."

This woman was a substitute for her devalued prostitute mother and also her own insatiability for making babies.

"By nymphomaniac, you mean she wanted intercourse and babies all the time?"

"I feel that. I mean she used to, uh, well she'd been married four or five times let's say."

"Never could be satisfied you mean, huh?"

"It seems that way."

"But you were different, you feel?"

"Well, *I don't know*. I mean I, well whatever craziness I have, and I am not crazy, I shouldn't say that, but whatever, *whatever I'm mixed up* it is not in that particular—"

"You mean sex didn't mean that much to you?"

"Oh, no, sex did mean something to me."

"What do you mean?"

"Oh, sex did, does, I mean I sure felt *the lack of it*. Otherwise I wouldn't have gone to a psychiatrist."

"Really? You felt the lack?"

The therapist could have asked her "What do you mean by sex?" but this would have been too direct and tactless. In reality she longed mainly for a mother-baby relationship. This type of relationship was a substitute for the dreaded sadomasochistically tinged concept of genital sexuality. It also defended her against a full participation in any love for her husband. In this sense she had anticipated abandonment and was prepared. This was part of the reason she did not show more overt rage. Of course there was also the element of guilt and "it is my just reward" for causing mother and father not to get along and the other babies to die. She concentrated on defeating her bad evil part represented by the toxemia.

"Well I mean, I, I used to ask him why we weren't sleeping together the way *we should*, and I was getting tense and emotionally upset. I just didn't want to do any work. I had *no desire for sex*, but I wanted *some love* and I wanted, I *thought I wanted* affection. *I didn't know what I wanted!*"

"What do you mean?"

"Well, I never had affection as a child. My folks are not demonstrative. They don't know how to say I love you. They don't know how to take you and give you a hug or a kiss. They don't know how to do it to each other, and they don't do it to me either. Maybe because my father never had love he doesn't know how to express it. Even to try to demonstrate it, I mean to take you and let you say I love you daddy, he shies away and says don't bother me. He gets brusque."

"So you mean you were always starved for this. This is what you mean by tenseness and turmoil, huh? That you always felt tense and full of longing for this kind of affection and felt hurt and angry because you were never getting enough of it?"

Her needs in these areas augmented the oedipal needs, rivalries and antagonisms.

"That's true."

"From?"

"Anywhere."

"From father, mother or husband?"

"That's right. Well, at first from my husband. I was always looking for it in my husband and soon I didn't have it in him either. Maybe that's *why I wanted children* because I felt children would give you affection."

This clearly showed how baby-mother love substituted for adult relations.

"Your husband never gave you enough affection?"

"Well, he did *in the beginning* and then it stopped, uh, and that's when I started to miss it."

"When did it stop?"

"Oh, it stopped, as I say, *right after the baby was born*."

The therapist wondered, was this herself and her parents?

"The first one?"

"No, the third one."

"The third one? You mean before that—."

"Before that it had gradually decreased but not stopped. I mean he traveled a lot. He wasn't home. When he was at home, he was affectionate. It was just after this last baby."

"You missed having relations with him?"

"I *guess* I did."

"What do you mean? You didn't know?"

"Well, I did. I mean I was very, I was satisfied if that is what you mean."

"No, but you sound like you were not sure."

"Well there were times, of course, when I didn't, but I mean we were brought up in a prudish manner so it was difficult to talk about these things."

"You can talk freely here."

"I know I can, It's just that, uh, well, uh, when he'd ask me, you know he was very thoughtful that way, I mean, in sexual life. He'd ask me if I were ready, you know, things like that. If I felt he was *overexerting* himself and felt that he himself couldn't and that he was trying just for my sake I would tell him I was ready when I wasn't."

The word "overexerting" suggested a fantasy of injury in coitus.

"You made believe?"

"Well, I wouldn't say made believe. I did it so that he wouldn't get *more exhausted himself.* I mean I didn't want to *hurt* him in any way."

Her sadomasochism naturally included all aspects of their relationship.

"Hurt him! I mean how would he be hurt? What do you mean by hurt him?"

"Well, he kept trying to hold off until I was ready."

"And so?"

"And I didn't know just how long a man could possibly hold off."

"That's what I mean. You thought he might be hurting himself?"

"By holding off. I mean not enjoying having intercourse if he held off too long, and not wanting him to lose the joy I would tell him that I was when I wasn't."

"You were more interested in him?"

"Oh yes, this was always so *in everything.* Even when I had the children. Another thing—."

She paused for a few minutes.

"It's not easy to talk!"

She suffered silently. This was the masochistic side of the picture. Everything would have been fine if the husband had played the allotted role.

"These things are very *painful?*"

"When I was having this last child, I will never forget. The other two children came into the house, the other two children would run up to him and say, 'I love you Daddy' and all that sort of thing, and I was thinking to myself I think he's going to love this child because he seemed to love children. But afterward this woman said that she, we socialized as I told you, she said I just had these children *because I wanted children* before *I was too old, not because I love my husband.* She said I had them because *I wanted them* and not *him.*"

This was a form of insight disguised by a projectionlike defense— "she thought it, not I."

"But I thought you said you wanted children so your children wouldn't be lonely."

"I wanted children for a happy marriage. I didn't want one child, and I wanted children for a happy marriage."

"So you mean you wanted the children for him?"

"No, I *wanted children,* I wanted, *maybe I was selfish* too, sure."

"What do you mean?"

"I wanted a family. I wanted a family *unit.* I wanted a family *group.*"

"You wanted something that would make up for the past that, you said, you didn't want to go through again in a way, not to be lonely, etc., is that what you mean?"

"Well, well what I wanted, and the way I felt at the time was, I wanted a family. I wanted a family unit. I wanted a mother and a father and children, and I wanted the children to have a *modern* mother and father."

"Not like you had?"

"Not like I had."

"That's what I mean. You wanted to make up for the past, huh?"

"I don't know if I wanted to make up for the past but maybe so. I wanted something different, something that I didn't have."

"That's what I mean."

"Well, anyway, I wanted these children for him I thought. I really was thinking that. And then of course afterwards he accused me of having children *just for myself* and of course that *hurt* because I didn't. At least *I didn't think I did. I might have, I don't know!*"

Now she was ripe for pinning down and further developments in the slow process of achieving conscious insight.

"What do you mean you might have?"

"Well I mean I might *talk about childhood* and all that but I *really never believed it,* and *still can't believe it* because now I look

at these children and actually pity them because they don't have what
I so much wanted them to have."

This referred to the husband. She must have turned to her
father and been disappointed there also.

"You mean they don't have *a daddy* to show them the tenderness
and the love and the kisses that you wanted from your daddy and
never got—is that what you mean?"

"I guess so. I mean *I didn't refer it to my father at all.*"

"But you said you never got these tender things from father, and
father didn't even give mother this?"

"That's right, but I didn't, well when I look at the children now,
this is the first association I have with myself and them and all. It's
just that I look at them now and *realize they want a father.*"

This was another area of growing insight into her own problems.
She actually had needed both mothering and fathering to resolve her
oedipal problems.

"So you look at them and you pity them because you feel they are
not getting actually what you never got. Your life was full of tension
and turmoil and feelings of frustration and not getting the kissing and
the petting and the handling and the tenderness that a child needs,
and so you didn't get this all the way along, and then you went to the
psychiatrist."

"Well, anyway I called my obstetrician and asked him for the name
of a psychiatrist so he said, 'You don't need a psychiatrist.' So I said,
'My husband feels I do.' He said, 'Well why don't you come and talk
to me. I say you don't need a psychiatrist.' So, well, I kept insisting.
I said, 'Please Doctor, for the happiness of the family. If my husband
feels I need a psychiatrist, then I want a psychiatrist, so please. I don't
know whom to go to, give me the name of a psychiatrist,' and so he did.
He gave me the name of a psychiatrist to whom I went, and my husband went also. He went to some other psychiatrist. My psychiatrist sent
him off to somebody else, and then I went to mine and on one visit
mine said to me, 'Did you ever consider divorce?' This was about my
fourth visit, and I said, 'A divorce?' I said, 'If I wanted a divorce I
wouldn't be going to a psychiatrist!' "

This also had to be treated as part of the fantasy structure.

"Why did he say that?"

"I didn't understand."

"No, of course. I mean what ideas do you have?"

"I was telling him about how my husband wasn't sleeping with me and seemed displeased with me for some reason. I didn't know why, and so I was going to see what in *my background* made me the kind of person that would be *unpleasant to a man.* I was going because *something must be wrong with me.* So if something is wrong with me, help me cure myself, help me to make myself the kind of person that a man does want."

There was a sarcastic note in this masochistic statement but she appeared unaware of it.

"You mean you felt that if anything was wrong it had to be wrong with you. Did you ever think it was wrong with him?"

"No, I felt it was wrong with me."

"That's what I mean. You mean you always felt like an inadequate little girl who couldn't cook and couldn't do anything."

"Oh, yes, always, of course, I *am inferior* in a lot of ways and I know this."

"How do you mean? In what ways are you inferior?"

She paused.

"Well, I'm not, *I hate housekeeping.* I do it but I'm not the best in the whole world."

It was probably certain aspects of femininity that she hated more than housekeeping but had to hide it from her conscious awareness. She had said she felt so inadequate in this area.

"How do you mean?"

"I hate housekeeping. I do it but I'm not the best in the whole world. I, I don't know, I just don't do it well."

"And you feel inferior?"

"Well, I'm going to school now. I took, well for instance even when I went to school I was a *lazy* kind of person, very lazy. I went to high school, took the college course in the first year, got on the honor roll but I had to work for it. I was too lazy to work for it so I took the commercial course and as a result I didn't have to do any work and got on the honor roll that way. Then when I had to go to college, I didn't have the credits for college. You needed certain credits to take the College Boards or something, well I couldn't because I didn't have the subjects you had to take College Boards on, so the principal of our school asked the Dean of the college to try me out for six months without the exams. Well, I went to college without doing any work in the past, so that *I am basically lacking.* Things used to come easy to me mentally but basically I am *lazy* mentally."

This was a disguised expression of her feelings of phallic inadequacy as well as of being an inadequate oedipal mother substitute. It also was part of a passive-aggressive and masochistic defense.

"Is this what you mean when you say you feel you are inferior?"

"Well the thing is, I took the courses in college, just the things I liked the best. I took sociology and psychology and philosophy and such things."

She had been in a flight away from her failures.

"You liked these better than housework?"

"I don't like anything *practical*, I guess. I like *theory*. I mean I can *talk* theory forever or philosophy."

A "talking cure" could run into difficulties with this woman.

"But housework?"

"I would do it if I had to. For instance, after I had the children and my husband was coming home, I did it with a *vengeance* and enjoyed it. My husband used to at one time come home for quite a while and I used to do it and enjoy it, enjoy setting the table, the *centerpiece* and all this sort of thing, you know. But then when he left I lost *the joy of it again*, and all for what? I don't know."

The vengeance was directed at mother and so was having babies. She even made mother care for her while she was doing it. The loss of her husband was a kind of castration betrayed by use of the word "joy."

"You mean this was the way you felt back when you were a child—what's the use?"

"That's true. When I was a child, of course, you know how you have a grand illusion about yourself. You hope you are a princess or something, you know."

Now she was bringing up elements of what is known as "the family romance" so common in all children. They make believe they are someone else. Then they can entertain certain forbidden fantasies more easily with less guilt and often with the aid of masturbation.

"Did you?"

"Oh, I used to read a lot of fairy tales and hoped some day someone would take me out of this shambles, and I don't know if you read *Marjorie Morningstar*. I guess every girl is a Marjorie Morningstar."

She laughed.

"I'm not even that because I'm not even a housewife."

Marjorie had loved the older man too.

"When you had these fantasies, did you ever have any sexual feelings?"

"Oh yes!"

"What do you mean?"

"I didn't touch myself but I would get all *tensed* up."

The word "tensed" gave away something, as she had said she had had this feeling all her life as part of her turmoil, which was a mixture of hatred and defiance, longing and love.

"How do you mean you got tensed up?"

"Oh, crossing my legs and I would do it hard."

"And squeezed?"

"That's it! Is that what masturbation is?"

"So that was with the fantasies?"

"I guess so, I don't remember."

"But you were always full of tension and turmoil!"

"But I didn't enjoy masturbating, no!"

"Why not?"

"I don't know. I just didn't enjoy it."

"So it would just be part of the fantasy?"

"No, it was not a fantasy, it was just I'd get so tight."

"To relieve the tension?"

"To relieve it, I guess, uh, it wasn't enjoyable."

"It wasn't part of the fantasy?"

"It had nothing to do with the fantasies, no. A fantasy is just wishful thinking."

"A good name for it, Marjorie Morningstar fantasies?"

"I guess so, I mean it was just, I mean fantasies were something separate. I mean I was just hoping to get out of the hovel."

She was too close to certain painful insights. It was best to go along with her.

"To get out of a mess and get someone who would give you these good things that mother and father never gave you."

"That's true. God, I'm *excited*! I never thought I'd get myself so *wrought up.*"

"But as you said you have always been more or less tense and wrought up."

"I didn't show it actually."

"Tell me, how do you relieve the tension now? Do you still—?"

"No."

"When did you stop?"

"To relieve the tension?"

"Yes, by crossing your legs and squeezing."

"Oh, I guess shortly after I was married. *I never was satisfied.* It wasn't pleasant at all."

Her marriage had been a form of acting out a masturbatory fantasy with many unreality elements out of the past running the show and constantly creating new problems.

"Not pleasant?"

"Not doing that, I mean, actually intercourse is pleasant but not this."

"But it relieved the tension?"

"It didn't relieve it, no. This was always during, when I, I don't know. It happened when I was the *loneliest,* when I felt the *sorriest,* I don't know, it never, *I didn't stop to think of why or when.*"

"What did you do afterwards when you were tense?"

"What I did then? Oh, I'll tell you what I did then. I smoked instead now."

"You smoked instead?"

"That's it. I mean if I could have smoked when I was a child I probably would have smoked instead of doing that, something to keep you busy. I don't know. You want to be busy and yet you have no desire to work. I can't describe it. If you want to do, if you want to accomplish, if you have a motive, like now I'm going to school. I went to school all summer."

All these activities prevented her from facing depressing thoughts but also prevented her from facing and mastering her problems.

"You mean by motive, what?"

"A reason for doing."

"You mean someone who cares or—?"

"Or something, somebody to do something for."

This type of longing characteristically develops during the oedipal period and was a good sign in her prognosis.

"Somebody to do things for?"

"Well, that's what I always wanted, somebody to do things for more than anything else in the world."

"You mean even when you were little?"

"Always."

"Whom did you want to do them for then?"

"Oh, I wanted somebody to do them for. I had nobody to do them for then. I mean I tried for the folks, you know."

"Mother and father weren't interested?"

"They weren't interested. They just didn't take it the way I would have liked to see them take it. I would have liked to see them happy but it just didn't work so I stopped. Oh, I don't know, things are coming out not exactly like I think them, maybe more true."

"What do you mean by that?"

"Well, I don't know. I never stopped to think about myself this way. I studied psychology so I could understand it in other people. When it comes to myself, I'm not that good. I guess I can't do it as well."

"It is very difficult. Maybe we will learn more about your Marjorie Morningstar fantasies and hopes. We then might understand more about this relationship with mother and father."

"Well."

"And the relationship with your husband? Have you given him up or do you hope he'll come back?"

"Well, I should give him up. I mean I know he's gone and it's over yet, and this is something I should see. It's the handwriting on the wall and I don't want to look at it. I mean I look the other way and I keep saying to the children, 'He'll come back,' but I think I do, *really believe it might happen.* I believe the children should have a father and I believe that the natural father is the most sympathetic and most understanding of them."

"But if the natural father isn't coming back?"

"Well, that's what *I can't face!*"

"You mean to get them another father? Why can't you?"

"Well, see with him for instance, I went with him for *ten years before we got married.*"

"Ten years?"

"We went together *as children.* We started going together when we were twelve years old. We knew each other as well as anybody can. In fact, *I used to want him to date other girls* once in a while, to date somebody else, so we would double date and I would say he was *my cousin,* and of course he would end up, you know, *coming back,* or something like that. He couldn't take it, he said."

The secret was now out in the open. Her husband was a father figure to a much greater extent than is usual. The word *cousin* showed the incestuous connection. At puberty, as is usual, the old oedipal conflicts came to the foreground with renewed intensity. She had never solved her oedipus complex. At puberty she needed to oscillate between girls and boys, homosexual and heterosexual love, until she could renounce her family as a sexual love object, and she could not.

"What do you mean?"

"Well, he used to have, oh, ever since I've known him he has always had *headaches*. Since he was twelve years old, and he's had headaches even before that. He always had headaches and always had colitis or, not colitis, loose bowels."

We now remember the beheaded woman and the anal birth theories. The husband was also like herself, partly a narcissistic object choice. She might have developed colitis or migraine.

"Loose bowels?"

"He would get cramps when anything upset him, and this has been so always. And I used to *worry* about that a great deal, but he'd go to doctors and they'd say there was nothing wrong. But the thing is we did go together for a long time and we got to know each other *like a brother and sister*."

She had made him an incestuous object to complete the family and become the boy she couldn't be. Every only child must be both a boy and girl to externalize their parents' conscious or unconscious fantasies.

"That's what I was going to say. He was like a cousin or a brother."

"He was like a brother in a lot of ways."

"You mean you don't think you will ever find someone to take his place?"

"Right now, no, I don't think so. I mean in the first place I'm not in condition. I'm not, I wouldn't *even want anybody* right now because I'd want to mentally adjust myself so that, I mean so I wouldn't be *mixed up*, I don't know."

Her sexual identifications were mixed up as a result of lack of oedipal renunciation.

"But this is what we are going to find out. I mean these are some of the problems that you have really never faced and settled in your own mind, huh?"

"I've never even thought about them!"

"Never even thought about them this way? All right, maybe this will help you to understand. I'll see you Wednesday."

"I wanted to ask, you see now I'm going to school, I go to college to get the credits for teaching, and I am interested in teaching. I am substituting now and going on as a permanent substitute in November. The teacher is *pregnant* and she is leaving and they are appointing me, so it is difficult, as I don't know if I am ready yet. I need this, I know, Doctor. At least I feel I need it badly."

Even this expressed her infantile inferiority feelings and fantasies about the anticipated future.

"Let's talk about it Wednesday."

The patient received treatment by a student therapist at a clinic She was seen on a twice-a-week basis and talked freely about her re sentments and feelings of deprivation, referring particularly to "tha other woman." Throughout her therapy, which lasted ten months, sh remained convinced that her husband would return. She called he rival's ex-husband repeatedly in an effort to obtain information abou his former wife until he became thoroughly incensed and refused t talk. Her treatment was complicated by the emergence of anxietie of an agoraphobic nature that complicated her educational training and by depressive episodes when she felt "He will never come back.' She broke off therapy when she took a position as a teacher in a cit some distance from the clinic. At this time she was socially withdrawr and moderately depressed but functioning well at home with he children and at work. Put another way, she had to express consciousl the depressive longings, hates and fears concerning her parents an self in the past that she had evaded by means of her masturbator fantasies and activities.

This interview was constructed so as to highlight this patient' sadomasochistic fantasies, ambivalence and oedipal strivings. Her fru trated infantile genital libido was the main source of her trouble an was manifested by her masturbatory practices and fantasies. This wa reinforced by a general passive masochistic component. She showe this by the way she managed to obtain an ambivalently regarde mother-daughter-baby relationship. Mother was necessary as a prc tecting and gratifying object but her "dirty place" led to the mi carriage. There appears to have been a phobic element connecte with sex and babies and a flight into a counterphobic type of actin out, leading to an insatiable desire for babies and mothering. Con tinually having babies allowed her to externalize in the present he past anxieties about intercourse, childbirth, miscarriage, beheading castration, oral-aggressive insatiable longings, etc. To a large exten intercourse was used for the same purpose. Fearing she had bee responsible for mother's miscarriage was synonymous with a fear tha she had injured mother's insides and her own had suffered a simila fate. The sense of incompleteness and loss thus had been referred t all areas of the relationship with the world. Everything points to he having a form of chronic anxiety hysteria. For example:

She appeared to be governed mainly by her feelings.

Her ego was always balancing between restricting herself and attacking her parental images, including her husband and his mistress.

Her tension and turmoil were a danger signal of psychic helplessness in the face of overwhelming stimulation, mainly by her sadomasochistic fantasies and interpretation of reality. The main traumatic situation that organized and shaped her fantasies appears to have been the miscarriage of mother's baby, but there must have been earlier traumas. In the therapy of this woman we would expect to find that the constant bickering of her parents had augmented the development of a whole series of sadomasochistic coitus fantasies concerning the parents, leading eventually perhaps to a sadomasochistically interpreted primal scene. We would expect every form of intinctual modification to be used to defend her against her anxieties concerning her sadomasochism.

Repression seems to have had a special affinity for her genital organization. She had a problem of frigidity which she tried to hide. To solve this it would be necessary to resolve her castration complex expressed as a feeling of being a defective person with anxieties about being inadequate, defective, cut and torn, etc., and to resolve her homosexual fixation on her mother. This was also directed toward the rival who had taken her husband. We can be sure that one of the reasons she was unable to realize for four years that her husband was with the other woman was her unconscious participation in the act. This she did not want to learn, as it fitted in well with her unconscious needs, both defensive and instinctual. In a sense she was re-enacting the oedipal situation with emphasis on the negative homosexual side of the oedipus complex as a defense against positive heterosexual elements.

Her counterphobic behavior has been mentioned. In other words, counticharge was directed mainly toward the external stimuli that aroused the inner excitation. Otherwise she would have avoided having babies. This was brought into focus by the traumatic miscarriage experience with mother.

She showed a typically hysterical tendency to idealize her parents which quickly gave way to hostility with ideas of loss, injury, depreciation, inferiority and humiliation.

Present events were elaborated and used as a defense against awareness of her chronic problems. The interview was so constructed, however, as to allow these to emerge.

An attitude of hostile dependence was present with both parents and husband but she was only dimly aware of the hostile elements.

The main difficulty in therapy with this patient would be the complication caused by her masochism and her sensitivity to libido changes. She could not give up her husband who was a "cousin" and a "brother"—the brother or masculine part of herself that she lost somewhere along the line. Her husband was both a mother and a father figure also. In any case, her sensitivity had been accentuated by the traumatic miscarriage experience and her accentuated fantasy life. Her frustration accentuated her tension and could lead to panic attacks and overt phobic states. In another sense it could be inferred that all her life she had maintained a hostile-dependent relationship with her parents by means of converting real grievances into guilt. This had helped to bind her excessive sadomasochism.

This woman could not afford psychoanalytic therapy, which is so much better equipped to handle the panic states, sticky transference, depression and secondary gains that would complicate her masochism. She warned us that she would love to discuss intellectual insights and theory. There would be a constant need to stress the importance to her of her feelings and to analyze the transference *indirectly* in a psychotherapy situation. How this is done will be discussed in more detail after we have discussed some of the differences between psychoanalysis and the so-called abbreviated psychotherapies in Chapter VII. Psychoanalysis is the ideal treatment for the hysterias. If it is not feasible, we must expect increased difficulties in handling the patient and a decrease in the expected goals and results; that is, there would be more symptom amelioration and less fundamental character modification. Without the latter, symptom changes tend to be transient and reminiscent of the old adage, easy come, easy go. It is also difficult to show the patient that *"passive"* masturbatory fantasies must be renounced in favor of *active* attempts to modify the reality of here and now.

V

DISPLACEMENT AND
SCREENING PROCESSES
A Job Phobia

In psychoanalysis, displacement refers to a shift in the energy of the forces behind mental phenomena, especially that connected with the sexual wishes. Thus, libidinal energy can be displaced to other types of impulses, such as aggression, or to objects that are associatively connected or simply convenient. A therapist or analyst detects displacement by looking for the *common pattern* in a series of communications. This chapter will deal mainly with the detection of displacement patterns and the problem of choice of substitute objects. Displacement is closely linked with problems in screen development, object perception and affect dilution as well as with the separation or isolation of affects from objects.

An object is always perceived in terms of the past and in relation to other objects. Perception is therefore associated with a comparison of things in the present outer reality world with complex ideas or concepts of things in the inner world of past memories and fantasies. Comparison in its more simple and primitive aspects appears to be equated with sameness and concrete objects in an ideational sense, and pleasure and displeasure in terms of affect. In its more evolved and complex aspects it is linked with such concepts as similarity, abstraction, and symbolization. The perception of similarity differs from that of sameness in that it departs from a relationship that is primitive, static, identical and simple, and becomes more evolved, dynamic and complexly patterned. This latter type of perception is accordingly less associated with the violent, all-or-none reaction typical of the

141

primary processes. Eventually a perceived object is related by the perceiving part of the ego to similar objects in all possible categories. These comparison processes are for the most part unconscious. The shift in emphasis from objects to patterns of relationships has had certain consequences for both the theory and practices of analysis. A brief clinical illustration will clarify certain characteristics of this attitude toward displacement which are of theoretical interest.

A twenty-three-year-old youth with a chronic behavior disorder was unable to work or attend school, as he was obsessed by anxiety concerning his body. The upper part, he said, was too weak and underdeveloped; the lower part was overdeveloped. Exercises for the weak upper part had not resolved this discrepancy. After describing his plight, he drifted to his service experiences. He was disgusted by the married officers whose (higher) ethical principles were so weak that they had failed to control their (low) animal desires and, when overseas, had affairs with foreign girls. This patient masturbated often and went with prostitutes without conscious guilt. He was shy in the presence of "nice" girls and had never had a "steady" girl friend. This did not worry him, as marriage and love were "dull traps." Shortly afterwards he volunteered that he collected pornographic literature. For amusement, he kept by his bedside a copy of *Forever Amber* next to *The Pilgrim Hymnal*. When this "discrepancy" was linked with the material in other categories, he appeared agitated, paced the floor and spoke about "farfetched" connections. Later, with much anxiety and depression, he recognized that there was a large discrepancy between his sexual behavior and accomplishments in school and his ideals. He feared he could never control or reconcile the needs of his "upper" and "lower" parts and that this would eventually lead to abandonment by his parents and "nice" people.

To say that this patient had displaced a conflict concerning his superego and his id onto his body would be only a partial truth. In a conflictual situation, all the various spheres of relationship of the ego at all levels become involved in the attempted resolution. The affect in such a situation is diluted and isolated from its original ideational components by being displaced to various spheres of relationship that change its significance and prevent its recognition by the conscious portion of the ego. In another sense, affect is displaced by being concentrated in one ideational sphere and thus withdrawn from other spheres. The ideational and affective residues remaining in various areas are then handled according to their intensity. Thus a sort of drainage occurs that allows a varying proportion of affect

ıd ideas in each sphere to be handled in what amounts to a totally
fferent manner.

Affect residues can be reacted to by reversal, phobic withdrawal or
ıunterphobic acting out. For example, in the preceding case, the
ıtient was very anxious about the condition of his body. He was
nical and indignant over the behavior of the officers and thought
.e contrast between the books attractive and very funny. He was
ıaware of any problem in the sphere of his superego until the
nilarities in all these spheres of relationship were repeatedly linked,
tegrated, and a pattern made conscious. The pattern here referred
a lack of balance and harmony and was closely related to the
mmon problem of ego control in the adolescent. He then reacted
ıth depression and began to produce material concerning various
ʾpression-laden discrepancies in the behavior and speech of his parts as well as himself, in the past as well as the present.

The screening of one area by another is a well-known clinical
ıenomenon. It is often expressed in terms of reaction formation or
ʾpposite" relationships. The patient who is continually preoccupied
th relationships to material objects or gadgets often will be found
be escaping from problems in his relationships to persons. Similar-
the introverted patient who dwells continually in an inner world
self-images and daydreams may be in flight from the outer world of
rsons, concrete things and reality events. Many times the opposite
the case, and the extroverted busybody, who is always concerned
out persons and events, is unable to examine himself and his fan-
ʾy life critically and in depth. A pattern of relationship is often dis-
rted by negation as well as reaction formation in the process of be-
ıning conscious. Words used to describe bodily difficulties often re-
ıl intense, hidden, emotional patterns connected with personal and
f-relationships. The patient who fears he has a "bad" heart is a
nmon example. The words are symbols of an affect pattern in one
ʾa which foreshadow what is also occurring unconsciously or about
occur consciously in another area of greater significance. In many
ʾes, a patient will complain only of difficulties in relationship to
ʾsons. These complaints will be repetitive, shallow in emotional
ıtent and stereotyped in form. Usually, it is necessary to wait until
ʾ patient refers to ideals, self-images or body images, and then ex-
ıd these relationships. In this way, affects attached to these areas
ı be mobilized and then transferred to personal relationships that
ı now become more meaningful. Relations with persons are pat-
ıed upon relationships between a person and his self-images and

also attitudes toward his body and substitute material objects. Thu
castration anxiety is one element in a pattern of loss that refers mai
ly to the body image and a level of development. It can be expresse
or aroused by losses in any area. It is never an unconnected entit
and simultaneously refers to the loss of vital persons or things an
concepts of the self. What is of chief importance is that the loss tha
becomes conscious almost always assumes a screening function for th
other areas and elements in the loss pattern. It is this process tha
allows affects to accumulate and summate and discharge graduall
and it insures a protracted working through of material in the ps
chotherapeutic situation. The importance of any of these consciou
patterns will vary from one situation and level of development to ai
other. None of the areas used can be relegated to a role that is
lesser or greater importance except in an isolated clinical, historic
and statistical sense. In terms of the therapy situation, by the tin
we have made a loss conscious in any one area it has already lo
much of its therapeutic importance and has begun to screen othe
losses in other areas. Any vital loss in one area or category will l
expressed consciously in terms of the one most suitable, according
the level of ego strength, psychosexual maturity, need for a scree
and the momentary availability of objects. The concept of depe
sonalization and estrangement can apply not only to the ego's rel
tion to the self but also to the body image. As an example, a ma
who is physically able to copulate may have no feeling in his genita
experiencing it as dead and apart from him. Such cases are not u
common in men whose chief problem was originally one of loss of
mother. A child may have a painful (bad) relation with her bladd
which represents a displacement of an image of herself as a bad litt
girl. Later there can be a displacement of her feelings onto bad adu
sex relationships. In any case, the conscious preoccupation acts as
screening type of defense associated with dissociation and isolatic
of affect from intellectual content.

Another well-known aspect of displacement and the reaction to tl
opposite relates to time. An escape from present problems can I
made by a flight into memories of the past; a chronic preoccupatic
with past terrors and losses can be temporarily relieved by conce
over persons or things in the present where tensions can be relieve
by acting out.

The integration, recognition and reconciliation processes by whi
the ego, through insight, orders and masters stimuli from the vario
areas to which it relates are mainly conscious. These processes are

complished by the referral of minor and major details of objects and patterns of relationship to holistic patterns of an inferential nature. These are idealized in both a good and bad sense. Such concepts are considered "reality" by the conscious or "I" portion of the ego, which plays the role of an observing audience. Another referential and ordering process by which the ego relates objects to reality is to a large degree accomplished by arranging stimuli in time. Both of these conscious approaches to reality are always only preliminary and relative in nature but tend to be taken as absolute and definitive expressions of the factual. Any new conscious or unconscious concept which threatens to destroy the security and complacency that is the result of previous integration processes meets with resistance until it too has become integrated and become part of the "real" world, that is, until it is patterned or coded in such a manner that it can become invested with affect displaced from a former pattern of relationship; i.e., a new concept must have a screening potential. This is simply another way of stating that we perceive what we are interested in and are interested only in what is useful for us.

In psychotherapy the working-through process requires an integration of related patterns of behavior in all the chief areas mentioned previously, mainly through a conscious recognition of their similarity. Working through is associated with a complex emotional state called conviction. The qualities of conviction and insight appear to be directly related to the number of spheres of relationship that have been integrated, as well as to feelings of trust and to the undoing of the displacement and concentration of affect in important areas which are ripe for discharge. Integration implies not only the recognition of pattern similarities but the necessity for reconciling various contradictory elements in the pattern and the antithetical areas. Some of these areas are part or qualitative aspects of the inner and outer worlds mentioned previously and include good and bad elements, part and whole relationships, the abstract and the concrete, the infantile and the adult, the nonverbal, prelogical and the verbal, logical thought processes, sexual and aggressive urges and even various levels of psychosexual development, such as oral, anal or phallic. Here, reconciliation implies the redistribution of affect in harmony with both the inner and outer reality that characterizes successful maturation.

A reaction to the opposite is frequently observed in many of these qualitative aspects. A patient is concerned with doing good deeds in the outer world in order to cover up bad, sexual or aggressive wishes in the inner world. Conversely, he acts "bad" to hide what he considers effeminate desires to be good and kind. Sexual responses are limited to organs or body parts in order to deny anxieties about a more general and mature emotional commitment. Interest in personal relations is used to cover gross sexual or aggressive interests; infantile patterns aid the evasion of adult responsibilities; magic thinking thwarts a depressive recognition of logical consequences; aggression is disguised by sexuality and vice versa; genital drives are expressed in terms of orality and vice versa. One of the most common examples which occurs in everyday life, as well as in dreams, is found in the displacement of large meaningful relationship patterns onto small and almost meaningless details. We are also well acquainted with the compulsive or schizoid type of patient who talks only on an abstract level and cannot be pinned down to concrete examples. Such antithetical relationships are part of a therapist's everyday experience.

Through conscious integration of the patterns in the various spheres of relationship of the ego, we strengthen it and make it capable of withstanding the vicissitudes of life to the limits of its constitutional endowments. In this sense, the term "weak ego" means one in which the various patterns in different spheres are poorly integrated or are dissociated. Such a weakness originates in connection with the accumulation and summation of narcissistic injuries and losses of essential persons and objects. It is related to the maintenance of and need for denial and the production of trauma screens. A *traumatic event* is often conveniently found and used as a screen to bolster up the processes of denial, isolation and dissociation. This means that when an event in the outside world occurs that is potentially harmful it may be perceived consciously as a tremendous threat because of the opportunity it offers for a displacement or transfer of inner tensions. This reaction is also the basis of the phobic state. The traumatic event and phobic reaction focus conscious thoughts on a threatened reality loss in the present instead of actual losses in the past. The former type of experience can be phobically avoided; the latter cannot be so easily evaded. Traumatic occurrences and phobic states often represent a flight into reality as well as an externalization of previously existing traumatic fantasies. Traumas are also related to counterphobic behavior and acting out. In each case, a sphere of relationship is created that permits displacement, isolation, denial and dissociation to work in an effective manner, at least temporarily. From the point of view of therapy, displacement must be undone and the various narcissistic injuries and losses worked through and faced realistically and consciously. A final settlement of past feelings of grief, hate and yearning must be made before reality and the present can be handled adequately. This can be done when the ego is strengthened by integration and the borrowed ego strength often induced by the transference.

Adult relationship patterns are modeled mainly upon the relationships formed with both primary objects such as parents and siblings and with various important things which later or simultaneously serve as substitutes for primary objects, such as transitional and fetishistic objects, pets and prized possessions of all sorts. The degree of affect invested in a relationship, whether pleasant or unpleasant, is of major importance in the determination of the shape, importance and survival of a pattern. A certain type of emotional climate or family attitude is also necessary for the continuation of any pattern. A pattern must also have a pragmatic and adaptive value or secondary gain in order to persist.

We are accustomed to think of character traits as being patterned or organized by traumatic events. A change in character may then occur in the direction of a phobic type of avoidance reaction or counterphobic mastery attempts. These are ways that character traits may be developed. In this sense, character traits can be looked upon as frozen remnants of traumas which are themselves a condensation of previous traumas, both large and small. Of course this is simply another way of stating that character traits and reality perception are based upon inevitable losses and frustrations and that traumatic events are an intermediate link in the chain. Losses and narcissistic injuries can be ultimately "traumatic" in effect but should be differentiated from the traumatic events and traumatic neuroses which occur in order to screen them. "Secondary" traumas that occur after the full development of the instincts should also be differentiated from those that occurred before this time. The latter are "primary" and diffusely organized traumas that occur in connection with major losses, fragmented egos and the narcissistic injuries attendant upon the defective relationship patterns established by the ego with primary objects. "Secondary" traumas are better organized and more dependent upon previous traumatic events. They refer to threatened rather than actual losses. The dividing line between the two types is obviously not a fixed one.

A twenty-two-year-old girl entered therapy because of difficulty in her relationship with her father. Ostensibly she hated him and had a close, affectionate relationship with her mother. In reality, she felt mother distrusted her and she distrusted herself and both her parents. Her character traits were largely influenced by her reaction to a traumatic event which occurred when she was seven. She and a schoolmate had visited a man who undressed them and induced them to perform various mutual oral licking perversions with him. They received candy for this and were allowed to look at his collection of pornographic pictures. This occurred repeatedly over a period of months. During these seductions, she was depersonalized. She remembered vividly being sent upstairs by him and told to undress and wait; she also remembered his alcoholic breath. After this man moved away, she had nocturnal anxiety attacks and traumatic nightmares in which she re-enacted the seduction. She became a model child until puberty, when the revived seduction scene became associated with a struggle around masturbation. This led to a flight into both homosexual and heterosexual acting out. Difficult emotional scenes with her parents persisted until she came into therapy. The complexity of the events leading up to the trauma and its effect in organizing her character would make a paper in itself; only certain points will be mentioned in order to demonstrate the displacement of relationship patterns.

Prior to the traumatic event, she had seduction fantasies combined with anxiety-laden dreams; all concerned herself and her father. These resembled the traumatic event and hid a series of defective and depressive relationships with her parents. Her relations with them were marred by their "progressive" attitude toward sex. As a little girl she had witnessed many provocative sexual scenes between the parents in which the father stormily accused the mother of being cold and unresponsive. The child felt that this accusation was just and applicable to her own relation with mother. Both parents were obsessional persons who were ambivalent toward each other and towards their little girl. The summation of a series of seemingly prosaic events was of primary importance in connection with the involvement in and the reaction to the traumatic event, and it was this material, as well as her character traits, that was organized by the traumatic event. Long talks substituted for affection as well as punishment in the household. Occasionally, however, the mother decided to beat her and went about it in a compulsive, as well as cold-blooded and methodical, manner, beginning by ordering her daughter to go upstairs, undress, lie on her bed and wait for a beating. The description of these events was strikingly similar to the seduction scene and they were also traumatic in effect. Beatings were followed by guilt, reconciliation and a feeling of closeness. The father occasionally drank too much wine and then played a game where he held the child tightly and tickled her by licking her ears and neck. In both cases, she often depersonalized. He brought home candy for her and owned many marriage and medical books with sexually arousing pictures which she often looked at and which appeared repeatedly in her masturbation fantasies. The analysis of the traumatic seduction revealed how well it had served as a screen by allowing inadequate, frustrating, anxiety- and depression-laden aggressive and sexual relationships to be transferred from her parents to an outside source. In this manner, a large number of major and minor psychic debts and separate events involving the skin and mouth, for instance, were screened and consolidated. In the present, she was involved in sadomasochistic, teasing relations with boys and girls. These involved biting and scratching. There were also episodes of compulsive stealing of candy that substituted for sexual acts and were accompanied by feelings of depersonalization. She could not touch her parents or kiss them. Her dreams and transference fantasies showed plainly her longing for oral and skin satisfactions that became increasingly apparent to her as time went on. A linking of the material led to preverbal affect memories expressed by sporadic episodes of deep depression and angry outbursts in the manner that is familiar in most analyses. She then recalled being "told" that as a baby she had had skin and feeding problems which had required constant attention. Such "secondary" memories are often of great importance as precursors for others which occur later in life when the affect is less isolated from the intellectual content. In this case her entire relationship to her father and mother was involved, as well as the traumatic event, and her memories were detailed in structure and experienced more intensely and in the first person. Thus, being "told" represented a form of depersonalization.

In the "neurotic" person, one organ or sphere of relationship tends to become overburdened by the necessity for discharging a large amount of painfully intense aggressive and sexual affects that do not properly belong to it and which it is often poorly equipped to handle. Reduction and discharge of tension in this case are ineffective. Frequently this difficulty is combined with a depletion of ego resources as energy is constantly being expended to maintain displacement coupled with dissociation and isolation of the various spheres of the ego relationship. Isolation can often be partly undone by a confrontation or interpretation that leads to a temporary undoing of a displacement and its associated emotional repression. Such a process must be repeated many times before any effective and persistent results in terms of ego integration and reduction of pathological mourning can be obtained.

The role of displacement in the therapeutic process will now be illustrated by the case of a rugged-looking young man with a work phobia. He appeared to be in his early thirties and was about six feet tall. He was markedly ill at ease and somewhat defiant and aggressive when the interview began.

"Could you tell me something about the problem that brought you here."

"Well actually I was sent by a neurologist at the———Clinic. I had been going there for treatment for a *low blood count* and *skin disease*, and I kept having these *dizzy spells* and finally they sent me to the neurologist and he recommended that I come here. He said I had some kind of a *fear complex*."

There were many words of interest. The last one had the most promise.

"A fear complex! What did he mean?"

"I don't really know."

"No, I know, but I mean what was your idea of this."

"Well, it was a complete *shock* to me because I didn't expect him to think I had anything wrong with me *mentally*."

He avoided discussing the *fear complex*.

"That's what it meant to you, huh?"

"Yes. Of course as soon as he said that and recommended that I come here, I was anxious to come and get it straightened out whatever it is because I've got a *wife* and *three children*. I don't want to have to give up *my job* or have *this problem* that I do have."

He showed indirectly that wife, children and job were related. Which area should be chosen for development? It was too early to decide. The therapist hesitated and had him repeat the sentence to see which area the patient would emphasize, as he would talk more readily about the easiest or most superficial problem.

"Pardon?"

"I don't want to have to change *jobs* and it looked as if I was going to have to change *jobs* the way I was going."

"Why?"

"Well, I kept feeling I was going to *faint, pass out*, and of course I thought it was because of the low blood count and the type of job I do, as before that I was fine."

"What do you mean by *job*?"

"Well, I deliver milk. I am a wholesale milk delivery man."

"You deliver milk?"

"Yes, to stores and restaurants, etc., and if I went into a store where there would be any great amount of *confusion* or I was rushed or trying to hurry or anything, I would start to feel dizzy and I'd have to sit down and take it easy for a while. I thought I was going to pass out."

"When there was *confusion?*"

The confusion was subjective—a projection of his inner feelings.

"Yes, it seems that when, you know, I was doing *big stuff* in a place where there were a *lot of people* around and so forth."

He would have liked to talk about bodily symptoms but words were picked leading to persons. *"Big stuff"* is interesting but *people* had better probabilities of development.

"People?"

"Yes."

Two key words were now combined.

"People would make you feel *confused, lots of people?"*

"Yes, it seems so now that I think of it, but then I didn't know what was doing it. I didn't have any ideas. I thought I had something wrong *organically.*"

The therapist was not lured away.

"In a *crowd?*"

"Yes, and it got so *to eat* in a restaurant or anything like that is almost impossible for me now."

This was another decoy of interest but not relevant now. One of the principal troubles of the beginner is that he is easily sidetracked by a patient.

"Because of the *crowd?*"

"The *crowd,* yes!"

"Lots of *people* around?"

"Yes, *that seems to be the trouble,* feeling they are *looking* at me. I was never bothered that way before."

"Before what?"

"Well, I've always worked on a *job* where I was amongst *people.* I've been on the same job for the last ten or eleven years, and I've never had any trouble that way."

"Up until when?"

"It seems about a year ago in January."

"Until a year ago from this January?"

"Yes."

"That would be January 1960."

"Yes, as near as I can remember back. Well, at that time I had a bad cold that developed into a chest infection and I was out of work a couple of weeks. From then on I felt *lousy* and I figured it was from that."

There was only one multidetermined word.

"How do you mean lousy?"

"Well, dizziness, feeling I was going to faint and so forth."

These words were still of secondary importance.

"That's when you began to notice *the crowds?*"

"Yes, but I still didn't associate it with anything mental. I don't know."

"And you say it made you feel *confused?*"

"Yes, you know, when I get real dizzy, I get so I can't *think very* good. Adding up a row of figures is difficult. I'm not as good as I used to be at them."

"You mean your ability to add figures was sort of interfered with by other thoughts that were on your mind?"

This was part confrontation and part interpretation. A similar maneuver was made in the first case, in Chapter I.

"Yes, it seems, yes, yes, now that I think about it."

"What do you mean? Do you remember back then?"

"Well I remember that I was sick for a couple of weeks. I was out of work for a couple of weeks. That was all."

"But you agreed you were thinking about other things, or you might have been at that time, or had begun to, or what?"

"No, I don't really know."

The resistance was obvious. The therapist expected it.

"Because you said you felt confused and you felt your mind was thinking of *something else?*"

This was the ultimate meaning of a *confusion.*

"Ever since then, I'd say, that I've been *confused* and I didn't realize it until this doctor told me to come in here. He said I had a *fear complex.* Now I've been trying to analyze it myself and think back and frankly I don't see why I should have any *problems.* I get along fine *at home.* I've got a *nice wife* and no *arguments* or *troubles* and I kind of hope this will be my first and last visit here."

This phobic situation interfered with his working. It was important to restore his work capacity. The wife appeared involved also, but this problem was a deep one and could be explored cautiously and by-passed for the present.

"I hope so, but we'll see."

"I really don't think there is anything wrong."

"At least you have a nice wife, no arguments and no troubles?"

"No. That's right!"

"You just live with your wife?"

"My wife and *three kids*."

"Three kids?"

"Yes."

"How old are they?"

"One is nine and a half, the other will be seven this week and the baby is six months."

"Boys or girls?"

"Two boys and the *little one* is a girl."

He had said his trouble began a year ago, when his wife was three months pregnant.

"Six months?"

"Yes."

He paused.

"Quite a crowd!"

This confrontation was a test.

"Yes, a nice family. *The little girl is just what we wanted.* We had the two boys and were looking forward to a girl."

"You wanted a girl?"

This was also a test and led to great resistance immediately.

"Yes, sir. What actually am I supposed to do now? I mean is this what I am supposed to be doing?"

"How do you mean?"

"Well I don't know. It looks like I'm carrying the bulk of the conversation here!"

He was irritated. He really wanted to be simply reassured that his "mentality" was fine. This would not last. If the therapist tried to be ingratiating or soothing, it would be fatal to the interview, as the patient would turn it into an argument and retreat to his physical complaints or answer questions perfunctorily.

"Certainly! You are the one who has the problem. We want to put our minds together to see if you can be helped because I don't know anything about you except what you tell me. You said, what did you call it, you said you had a *fear complex*."

It was necessary to be a strong father figure but also to change the subject from home to job.

"I told you what this neurologist told me *he* thought it was."

"Why do you think he thought you had a fear complex? What does that mean to you?"

"Well to me, I didn't really think he was going to tell me there was anything wrong with me, or I thought maybe it might be a *thyroid* disorder or something which was causing these dizzy spells and so forth."

This was purely his own thought and could lead to an interesting fantasy.

"Why thyroid? I mean do you know anyone who has had a similar disorder?"

"Yes, yes, I do know of a man who had a thyroid trouble and he seemed to have a lot of trouble, nearly fainting."

"Who was that?"

"Oh, a friend who came to the house *when I was a kid.*"

This was the first chance to get into the past and then to personalities.

"What do you mean? How old were you then?"

"Oh, *fifteen* or sixteen. I played with this fellow's son. We used to play ball together and so forth, and I remember one time his *father* had this thyroid trouble."

"His *father* had it?"

"Yes, and he had quite a time with it, and I thought possibly that might be what I had or something like that. I never expected him to tell me I had a *fear complex*. I don't really even know what this is."

He was not ready to remain in the past.

"But you just said, I mean in a sense you felt it had something to do with this fear of *crowds.*"

This would probably lead to the work area rather than the crowd at home.

"Well, it seems when I am bothered mostly I'm with a crowd or I'm very busy on the road in amongst a lot of people or delivering a large stock where there is a lot of *confusion* and now that I've started thinking about it, those are the times when I'm bothered."

"So then our problem is how come, because *what's a crowd?* You know they say two is company, three is a crowd, and there are *crowds* of four, five, six, all kinds of *crowds.* You said you never had any trouble with *crowds* until 1960."

"Well I'd say until a year or a year and a half ago, *something like that.* I think I've *always* been a little bit *uneasy* or not as *confident* as a lot of people are."

This was the opportunity the therapist had been waiting for. It was a *real* lead into the past and to the basic soil in which the symptom had sprouted.

"What do you mean? I mean how long ago?"

"Well, ever since I can remember, I guess."

"How far back is that?"

"Oh, I don't know exactly. I've always gotten along all right. I was in the Navy four years. There certainly were plenty of crowds there."

He was continually fighting to deny his underlying fears about himself.

"That's right."

"I never had any trouble in the Navy."

"But you said you were not always as what?"

This would *make* him repeat the key word.

"Not quite as *confident* as a lot of people."

"What do you mean by that? Could you give me an example?"

"Well I never seemed to have confidence when it came to *doing things.*"

"You mean even when you were a *little boy?* You say *always!*"

"Well, for a long time, yes."

"That's what I wondered. I mean how far back do you trace it as you think back?"

"All right. Well, well, ever since I, I suppose *since my mother and father were divorced.* I was about *thirteen* years old, I would say."

It was important to pin down the *time* first and not jump too quickly at such a gift.

"Around thirteen?"

"Yes."

"Before that you had lots of confidence?"

"I would say so, yes. I had *infantile paralysis* when I was *ten* or eleven. Up until that time, I can remember I always had all kinds of confidence."

This was even better. The divorce could wait. Of more interest were the years leading up to it.

"Up until ten?"

"Possibly that was when it started, I don't know."

"What happened?"

"Well, I had this infantile paralysis and I couldn't *talk* very well. I had it in my *throat.*"

"In your throat?"

"Yes, the bulbar type, and I used to have trouble *talking*. I used to talk through my *nose* and my *face* used to *twitch* and possibly that made me *self-conscious* at that time, I don't know."

"You remember?"

"I remember back then, yes, when I had the infantile paralysis."

"When you were *ten*, huh?"

"Yes."

"Then you were in about the third or fourth grade?"

This would pin down the time in more detail.

"Yes, I think it was the third."

His age could have been eight or nine.

"And you say you couldn't *talk*."

"Uh, well, no, I used to talk through my nose and it was hard to talk well."

"And your face would twitch?"

"Yes, I used to have a slight twitch in my face."

"Like what?"

"Well, my upper lip used to twitch and my nose at times."

"Can you show me how?"

This would help to reactivate old gestalts even better than words.

"Well, no, I don't think I could do it."

"Your nose would twitch?"

"Yes, my mouth used to also."

"How long did you have that?"

"Oh, I'd say off and on for close to a year."

"A year? That's a long time, for a ten-year-old especially!"

The therapist remembered that he was sensitive in crowds to people *looking* at him.

"Yes."

"And the other kids would *look at you* then?"

"I didn't have any *trouble*, no. I used to go to a one-room country school and there were never any kids making fun of anyone. It wasn't like in the big cities, and I can't remember anyone making fun of me outside of my *brother*."

First the details were important.

"You have a brother?"

"Two older brothers."

"Two older brothers! How much?"

"My oldest brother is forty-one. He is six or seven years older than

I am and the other brother is thirty-seven. He's a little over three years older than I am."

"You were the baby?"

"Yes."

"No one else?"

"No."

"And so you feel that you were a little less confident after that?"

"Yes, I think so, because I can remember when I was just a young kid in the first grade. I was always *big*, bigger than most kids."

"Pardon me, in what grade?"

"In the first."

"In the first grade? You were five or six?"

"Six, yes. I can remember I was bigger than most kids and could do things better, play ball better than most kids."

This was a pleasant memory serving to deny those about to emerge. The fact that he needed it was a signal to go easy.

"So you must have liked going to school?"

"Yes, I did, I liked going to school."

"Even from the first day?"

"Yes, I didn't have any trouble like most kids do."

"You were bigger and stronger?"

"Yes."

"Were your brothers big and strong?"

"They were both big, yes, but I'm the biggest one in the family now!"

"Now? Which one of them made fun of you?"

"The middle one."

"What's his name? What shall we call him?"

"Dick!"

"Dick? The oldest one was—?"

"Don."

"So there was Don and Dick and Dick made fun of you?"

"Yes. I guess that's typical."

"That's right, sure. He was still bigger than you then at ten."

"Yes."

"He would have been thirteen?"

"That's right."

"How did he *make fun of you?*"

"Well, he used to always pick on me constantly *even after* I had that paralysis."

"You mean even before?"

"Yes, I think even before but not as much as after I had been in the hospital that time. I came home, and he used to talk through his nose, mimicking the way I talked, and, you know, make fun of me that way."

"How did it affect you?"

"Well, I used to get all upset."

"There was not much you could do about it?"

"No, I couldn't. I tried a few times but never could beat him. I tried a lot after that but he could always *take me.*"

"He could always take you, huh? So you feel that might have had something to do with the loss of confidence around that time?"

"It could have, and I suppose my mother and father being divorced and me being the youngest one."

Now he wanted to shift the subject. The therapist could permit this and gain more information. A brother is a substitute for the oedipal father.

"What happened?"

"Uh, well they, uh, got so they couldn't get along. I don't know really why."

"You mean they got so over the years?"

"Yes."

He then told how his parents had argued and fought ever since he was a child, and how this upset him. After his polio, the family moved from Vermont back to Massachusetts, and father left when the patient was twelve. Originally they had lived in Massachusetts and had moved to Vermont when he was five. Father was manager for a milk company, the same one that employed him. Actually father was his "boss." Mother was a wonderful cook but not very neat or well dressed, and father went out a lot with other women. This was the cause of the fighting. When he heard them, he was very upset because he was very close to mother—her baby—but also father's favorite. Father "whacked mother around" occasionally. His older brother, Don, would stop him, as he was bigger and stronger, but unfortunately not always around. When he was twelve, father had thrown mother out of the house one night into the snow. He felt too impotent to help. He was really confused about whom to love and dreaded the day when the home would break up. The therapist encouraged him to talk about his oedipal feelings of impotence and inadequacy and confusion over his negative and positive oedipal components. After the separation and divorce, he and mother were alone in Massachusetts. His two older brothers had left home. He could hear mother crying at night, and he cried himself because he too missed his dad. This led to how good dad had been to him. He really lost his confidence in himself around that time. Both he and mother were depressed. She even became hypochondriacal, visited doctors a great deal, and had a couple of operations. This was worth investigating, and the interview continued in this direction until he was vaguely aware of his identification with mother, and how, of the three brothers, he was the underdog (the girl). As this part of the interview is important, we will begin with his mother's operations.

"What happened? What operations do you mean?"

"She had a gall bladder operation and a *goiter* operation."

"Goiter?"

"Yes."

"She had thyroid trouble?"

"Yes."

"How do you mean? What do you remember?"

This was part of the mother he had identified with.

"Nothing; not too much. She had a broken hand and had to have it in a cast. This all happened within that two or three years before she finally, I guess it was two or three years we were living in Massachusetts, and then she went to work."

"How did the goiter affect her? What kind of symptoms did she have?"

"*Nervousness.* She was very nervous."

"In what way, do you remember?"

"Gee, I don't. Well I remember her saying, this day I had been talking with her about this trouble I had been having and she mentioned that she had had that operation and before that she had been very nervous. I told her there was nothing like that with me because I had all kinds of tests, and there was nothing physically wrong with me."

"I see what you mean now. You were wondering when you had your dizzy spells and nervousness whether this was because you had a goiter too."

"Yes, I guess maybe."

"You remembered mother and you remembered that man who had it, the father of your friend?"

"That's right."

"Because that was around the same time, fourteen."

"Yes, I'd say so."

"And she was sick, depressed, crying, and you felt pretty bad too, so you feel then it goes right back there?"

"I would say so, yes. If that's the trouble?"

"I don't know. You say that as if there was an abrupt change which you felt."

"Yes, yes, I do."

"Why? What makes you think so as you look back?"

"Well, I was big, and strong, and I could play sports well. I got along in school well."

"You were bigger than the other boys?"

"As a rule, yes, kids my age."

"Yes, because you *are* a big guy. How tall are you?"

"Six, two and a half."

"Six, two and a half? How much do you weigh?"

"About two hundred and five or two hundred and ten."

"About two hundred and five or two hundred and ten. And I can see it's all muscle!"

This was just what he needed at this time.

"I grew awfully fast after I had that sickness when I was a kid."

"After ten you mean?"

"Yes. I began to stretch out then. I played baseball with the kids in Massachusetts and football and everything and I was good in all sports, but I didn't have the confidence to be very good in high school. That is, I went out for football and I made the first team my first year. Everything looked terrific for me. I was getting all kinds of praise from everyone. Then all of a sudden, boom, I just *quit* like that."

"When was this?"

"When I had gone into high school, I was fifteen years old."

"Around fifteen?"

"Yes, and *anytime it seemed I was doing good,* exceptionally good at anything and I *began to get any praise* at all, then all of a sudden I'd just *give it up.*"

"When you got praised?"

"Yes, and I couldn't understand it myself. I felt I guess that I was *hurting somebody* but actually you are only *hurting yourself.*"

The fatal identification with the passive suffering mother won out. He couldn't be a man like father.

"What do you mean hurting somebody?"

"Well, I don't really know. It always seemed funny to me that I was going along good in something but I would never finish it out, you know. I seemed to either *lose interest* or *get mad* or *quit*. I did fairly well in school up until I went into high school and then I just gave up in school, gave up on the football team."

"You mean by lacking confidence and giving up, you mean when people praised you you sort of didn't believe them?"

"Yes."

"You felt you couldn't live up to that kind of stuff?"

"That's right, exactly."

"You mean you didn't believe you were as big as you were?"

"That's right, yes. As big as I was, I always felt that I wasn't, that I was smaller. Well, I was always helping out the *underdog*, you know, *kids that other people made fun of*. I used to try to help them. I might have been better off if I hadn't been."

This was a disguised way of rescuing the mother. The kids were alter egos of himself identified with mother. The relation to the brother was obvious.

"If you what?"

"If I had made fun of kids and not been so sympathetic!"

"But, after all, you knew what it was to be made fun of."

"Yes."

"Was that the first time Dick made fun of you when you spoke with that nasal manner?"

Dick did to him what father did to mother.

"Yes, that's the only time."

"He never made fun of you before that?"

"Well, no."

"Bigger brothers can be pretty cruel to their kid brothers!"

"That's right, no more than, you know, any other brother."

"Did he really give you the works at times?"

"Uh, well, he used to make my life miserable, there's no two ways about it."

"In what way? What did he do?"

"Well, I can think of quite a few things. He'd always get me to do his dirty work. I remember one time on the farm Dick was building a camp, he and another fellow, so they got me to haul all the wood with the promise that they would give me a nickel. I hauled all the lumber for the place. Then afterwards they just laughed at me and sent me away. At times when they would be working in the fields why they would call, I remember one time particularly, they were spreading manure, this friend of his and himself, they called me over with the promises that they would give me something, and when I got over there I got a face full of cow shit! Things like that constantly, you know."

The analyst would call this a passive anal-sadistic fantasy.

"We could even say you had to take a lot of shit in a way from your brother."

"I certainly did, yes!"

"You must have been *furious!*"

"Yes."

He laughed.

"You were made to feel like the little *prat* boy?"

A prat boy is a slang term for a little page-boy sycophant who holds his behind out to a man for a pat or spank.

"That's right, that's about it."

"Because you wanted to play with them, I take it?"

"Yes."

"With your older brothers, and you tagged after them?"

"Well, not the oldest one, Don. He was so much older."

"That it didn't count. It was the one who was closest to you, huh?"

"Yes, that's right."

"But with Dick you always felt like the little inadequate kid, huh?"

"Yes."

"Who always got the shit end of the stick?"

This is a passive anal-sadistic mother-father coitus fantasy to enrage him and arouse his masculine protest.

"Right! Exactly!"

"Here you were getting big and now you are bigger than they are?"

"That's right."

"Now, how big are they?"

"They are both big fellows. My oldest brother is six foot and the other fellow is six foot one. My oldest brother weighs about one hundred eighty-five and the other fellow weighs about one hundred ninety-five."

"You know their weights and sizes so these things are important?"

"That's right, yes."

"Because now you are bigger but you don't feel it."

"That's right."

"You feel like the poor kid, and as you say you took care of the *underdogs*."

"That's right. Gee, I've got an *awful* feeling like I'm going to *cry,* you know."

"Those things hurt!"

"I mean now!"

"I know, just talking about it brings it back."

"I feel *terrible!*"

He fought hard to control himself.

"Don't be afraid. You know it won't hurt you. Kids can feel that way. I mean evidently from what you feel you have had a lot of this stuff stored up for a long time, huh?"

"Jesus!"

"What do you remember about it because I take it nothing happened after that, or did it?"

"No! I feel so *embarrassed!*"

"Oh, don't be embarrassed. A lot of very *strong* men cry at times."

"I never have since I was a kid."

"You've never cried since you were a kid?"

"No."

"How come?"

"I don't know."

"You mean you wanted to hold it in and never show it?"

"Yes."

He blew his nose vigorously.

"When you say kid, how old do you mean?"

"Well, since I was probably fourteen or fifteen."

"Fourteen or fifteen, up to then did you cry?"

"Yes."

"Often?"

"I think so."

"They made life pretty miserable for you, huh? Dick and his friends, huh?"

"Yes, yes!"

Now another key word could be used with telling effect.

"So you mean it sort of made you feel left out of the *crowd?*"

"Oh, yes!"

"And no matter how hard you tried and you worked hard in the Navy and since, but you were never quite sure of being accepted by *them*, huh?"

"That's right."

"As one of them?"

"You know, that's a fact!"

"I mean it shows how important it is that you haven't cried since you were fourteen."

"Jesus, I never thought I'd do that here! It's *embarrassing*!"

"Here you don't need to be that big."

"Well, it's a good thing, doctor, I'm alone with you here. I'd be ashamed worse if there were others around."

"It would be the same as a crowd then, huh?"

"It would be terrible!"

"So maybe these *crowds*, you know there are different kinds of *crowds*."

"That's right."

Now with the feeling state ripened and attached to the past, he could be faced with the present.

"Because you said your trouble was this feeling about being in crowds."

"Yes, yes, I seem to get *confused*."

"Tell me what did you do when you felt this way when you cried? Did you go off by yourself or did you go to mother?"

"Uh, no, mostly I went off by *myself*."

He was both mother and baby by now.

"Cried to yourself, huh?"

"Yes. Any time that I ever did it."

"You didn't want to show *them* how you were feeling, huh?"

"That's right."

He blew his nose again.

"You would feel too ashamed to have *them* looking at you, huh?"

"That's right, and to my knowledge that's the first time I've cried since, up to right now!"

"Yes, you were a proud kid!"

"I didn't want anyone to see me."

He probably meant particularly father.

"That's right, what you felt was a weakness?"

"That's right."

"Of course, I take it you've been fighting for a long time against feeling weak and little?"

"Ever since, yes."

"A long time."

"That's true."

"Because this, as you said, had something to do with the fact that you lost *confidence*, but it must have been coming on; I take it that Dick and the polio and then the divorce, all had a hand in making you feel more helpless."

"That's right, yes."

"So the problem is then how come that it started up again. Were you that way ever since? You said you weren't that way in the Navy."

"No, I didn't have any trouble in the Navy."

"You got along all right with the guys there?"

"Oh, yes, fine, never had a bit of trouble."

"But you said you began to lose your confidence then. When did it come back?"

"Well, when I was in the Navy now I got along fine like I told you. I got along with the *guys* all right, but when it came to advancing in rate I had all kinds of opportunities but I wouldn't do it."

"What do you mean? How come?"

"I just kept telling them I didn't want to be *rated*. I didn't want to have any *responsibilities*, but actually I really did want to, but I kept putting it off and not taking the examinations and not *getting ahead*."

This might be a clue to job difficulties. Success was too aggressive, and frightening. He would be taken by other Dicks, cry and be exposed.

"You mean?"

"I just had the thought if I did get the rate I wouldn't be able to handle it."

"Live up to it, huh?"

"So I went through the Navy without advancing my way up."

"You mean then you had some kind of image of yourself of getting rated and not being able to handle it right and they'd make fun of you and laugh at you?"

"Yes, that's what I was afraid of."

"They did that to you as a kid!"

"Not other kids, just my brother and his friends."

"Just your brother, you must have hated him?"

"Jesus, I guess I did in a sense, you know, and *in another sense I didn't.*"

The masochistic mother identification was again the fatal flaw preventing him from fighting back.

"I know what you mean. You mean—"

"This is awful hard, the son-of-a-bitch."

His eyes began to water again.

"No, it's not awful. This is part of the problem because you must have had the same problem in relation to dad too, because here he was doing the lousy tricks, throwing mother out in the snow, when you loved her so much, and here he was a nice guy to you at times too, huh?"

"Yes!"

"You were really confused."

"That's right."

"And here you were, part of you wanted to get ahead in the Navy and another part said no, I don't want to be *hurt*."

"That's right."

"So what happened when you got out of the Navy?"

"Well, I went back to high school for a while because I wanted to get a high school diploma."

"This was in Massachusetts?"

"Yes, so I went back to high school."

"When did you get out?"

"December of 1947. I went back to high school and got my diploma and then I went down to the University of Georgia for, well I stayed a half a year, and that's the only time I had trouble with *nerves*."

"What do you mean?"

"That I was aware of."

"Yes, what happened?"

"Well, I was going along pretty good. I went out for football and I was doing good. There were about three hundred guys out for football in a place like that, you know. Of course I hadn't played since I went into the Navy, but I was doing all right and I wanted to stay with it but the same thing happened. I didn't want to. The coach praised me a few times and I wanted to stay on and then—"

"You couldn't believe it?"

"Yes, so I quit, but I kept going to school and Jesus I began to have *pains* around *my heart*, you know. I thought I was having a *heart attack*. I couldn't sleep nights."

He had quit an activity symbolic of masculinity—the attack was of castration anxiety displaced from the phallus to the heart.

"Why did you think it was your *heart*? Did you know anyone who had any heart condition?"

"No, no, I just kept getting pains around there. I know I went to sick bay one night, stayed overnight, and they said it was neuritis, but anyhow I began to get real *depressed* and I finally went to see the Dean of Men and he advised me to take off and come back the following year."

The anxiety was a defense against and a warning of depression over a vital loss of a boy's ego ideal of manhood.

"By being depressed you mean you were confused and depressed over part of you which wanted to play football and be with the boys, and another part sort of just didn't feel he wanted to have that kind of competition?"

"That's right."

"I mean you still felt like that little kid again?"

"Yes, that's right, because I know even though I hadn't played ball outside of, you know, scrimmage in the Navy, I knew I was as good as any player on that team, and I was. If I had gone out and stayed out, I would have made the team. I don't know if it would be the *first team*, but I would have played in games I'm sure. The *coach* had noticed me even though it was a short period that I was out there and it is rare when he notices one of the scrubs because there are about three hundred guys trying out."

Two brothers had now become three hundred.

"That's right, they come from all over the country."

"And so I know that I would have made it, but yet, Jesus, when I was just beginning to get in shape and feel good I didn't go back. I took a day or two, I got *kicked* in the *mouth* so he came over and patted me on the shoulder while I was in the dressing room and he said, 'I want you to take a couple of days off.' "

This was where he got hit by the manure and was part of his talking equipment.

"In the mouth?"

"Yes, I got kicked in the mouth, right here."

"You had some trouble talking for a while?"

"Yes, for a day or so! It was kind of swollen and I had to have a couple of stitches. I was in the dressing room anyhow and the coach came over and said, 'Why don't you take a couple of days off and then you be sure and come back.' I remember I couldn't answer him because I couldn't talk too well."

"You were right back like the guy with polio again, huh?"

"That's right, so I took two days off and then didn't go back. I wish now I had."

"Then, when you had that polio, it was more than just a guy who couldn't talk in a sense with Dick doing all this mean stuff, imitating you, must have felt pretty *depressed*?"

"Yes."

"To be put in this kind of a spot?"

"That's right."

"Because you were really on a spot, huh?"

"That's right."

"You've never forgotten it, have you?"

"No, I guess not. In fact there are a lot of things concerning my brother Dick that are very vivid and they really should be forgotten because they are that minor, like the cow shit in the face, the time in the barn when he got mad and we were wrestling because I began to get the better of him and he picked up a pitchfork and jammed it at me. It stuck in the floor but it looked as though it stuck in me so *I rolled around it* and he got all upset and *started crying.*"

"Stuck in you, where?"

"Well, he took it and jammed it at me and I rolled over so *i looked* as if he *stabbed* me in my *stomach* and I remember that I got *great satisfaction* out of the fact that *he* was *crying* and *screaming* and pretty near hysterical because he thought he had *killed* me, you see. I mean things like that are so unimportant but somehow they have *always* been *vivid* in my mind."

His sadomasochistic fantasies were now out in the open.

"What does he do now?"

"He drives a trailer truck, still lives in Vermont. He has a farm where he raises cows and a few hogs and he is more or less a minor junk dealer. He buys and sells cars and things like that along with his regular job. He has two or three things he's always doing."

"Do you ever see him?"

"Yes, I see him about once a year."

"How do you get along with him?"

"Very good, very good."

"So you are in a tough spot, sort of, in a sense. I mean you haven't forgotten the past and yet to show any of it would make you feel real silly?"

This is what makes neurotic problems appear unreal and alien to the "I" part of the ego.

"That's right, yes it would."

"But now of course you have a different kind of trouble, in a sense. You are in the same spot, in a sense, *with father* because as we say you must have had the same kind of reaction to father—furious at him and angry at him for treating mother this way, and at the same time you loved him in a sense because he was your father and he was good to you."

"That's right."

"And I take it Dick wasn't bad to you all the time?"

"Oh no."

"Of course, sometimes he was good. At least he was kind enough t you occasionally so that you had hopes of being allowed to be part of the *crowd*?"

"That's right."

"He teased you, huh?"

"Yes."

"And this is what happened to father in a sense. It amounted to this much, didn't it. He made you feel he was a nice guy at times and then he quit and left?"

"Yes, that's right."

"When a boy needs a dad."

"That's right, exactly."

"Did you see him after that, after fifteen?"

"I didn't see him, I saw him just once or twice while I was growing up in Massachusetts. I went down to see him myself in Vermont one time and another time I went or rather I think he arranged to meet this friend of mine and myself, a kid I played with. He took us to Canobie Lake or some place. We spent the day with him, ate, etc. Then he brought us back. Outside of those two times I don't think I saw him at all until I went into the Navy. In fact I had been in the Navy a couple of years and hadn't seen him all that time, only twice."

He stopped talking and blew his nose.

"Then when I got out of the Navy I started going to see him quite often."

"This was after the University of Georgia?"

"Yes."

"After you left there and came back home, huh?"

"Yes, came back home and went to work. I was working on construction and I liked it."

"Whom were you living with then?"

"I was living with my mother."

"You were living with your mother and Dick was in Vermont?"

"He had never left Vermont."

"I see. And Don was—?"

"He was living in Boston."

"So there was just you and mother in Massachusetts, and where was your father?"

"Well, right after they were divorced, a year or so I would say, he had remarried and bought a house in Salem and he's been up there ever since."

"So you saw him then a few times?"

"Yes, yes, I used to see him. I used to go up there."

"How did you feel about that?"

"I didn't feel at ease with him at all. I still don't. I was working on construction and I liked it. It was not much of a job. There wasn't much chance for advancement or anything but I liked it and my oldest brother talked me into going to work for my father's firm."

"He knew father was there?"

"Yes. Both of my older brothers worked for this firm because of that reason. He talked me into it."

The ambivalence was very apparent.

"How come?"

"Well Don thought I had a chance to get ahead there. It was a good job, etc., and so I went to work for them. I couldn't get a job around here. My father at that time was district manager and he had control of the Brockton area, so I went to Springfield to work. I stayed there about a year and a half and got married there. Then I transferred to Brockton."

"This was back when you were twenty-two?"

"Let's see, yes, just about, so I moved up to Brockton and went to work. I wanted a transfer somewhere else but I couldn't so I got one to Brockton."

"How did you feel about working for father?"

"Well, everything was fine there when I wasn't working for him. Everything was fine up until, let's see, two or three years ago when he became my *immediate boss*."

"A couple of years ago, huh?"

"Yes."

"Back in 1959?"

"Yes, I think it was 1958 or 1959. See although he was over the branch where I worked he wasn't my immediate boss, but you know now that you've got a lot of this stuff out, the fact that I was working and my father a *big shot*, I wasn't accepted by the others, you know what I mean. I've always had the feeling that I had to do something extra or be an extra *nice guy* in order to get along with the guys."

The guys were the *crowd* at work. At home the crowd was the two boys and the little *girl* he was identified with. This is another reminder that in a group of children there is a "pecking order" as in fowls, and in the unconscious it is felt in terms of masculine and feminine attributes. Being a *nice* guy led inevitably to playing the baby brother role.

"You mean it brought back the old feeling you had when you were a kid, huh?"

"Yes, and I really don't think I should ever have gone to work for him."

"You mean the rest of them felt that you were sort of father's pet?"

"This guy's father is giving him everything, you know!"

"Because I take it that your brothers must have had some kind of envy of you in a way since you were mother's baby, you were her last-born, and your father liked you best too, in a way?"

"Yes!"

"So they must have really envied you and taken it out on you, huh?"

"Not the oldest one."

"Well, he was too old, as you say. He was big enough to forget it."

"That's right."

"But Dick was the one who was really envious, huh?"

"Oh Jesus!"

"He wouldn't even come down from Vermont?"

"No, no he didn't!"

"And this is the reason that Don said, go ahead, go with dad. I won't do it but you go ahead."

"Yes."

"Because he was the oldest boy. He was too much *in competition with him,* huh?"

"Yes."

"So you found yourself back with the boys and you felt the other guys looked on you again as sort of teacher's pet, a prat boy?"

"Yes, that's right, that's right!"

"That's the way you felt, you really don't know whether they did but it was the way you felt."

It was important to distinguish between *his* reality and that of the outside world represented by the therapist who will eventually be imitated (introjected) by him.

"That's right."

"You thought they were *looking* at you?"

"Yes."

"There was another crowd?"

"Of course there are always a few guys who regardless of what kind of a guy you are why they will hold it against you because your father is a big shot."

"So this puts you behind the same kind of eight ball you were behind as a kid, huh?"

"That's right, yes."

"Only you weren't quite aware of it then."

"Funny, I wasn't aware of it until now!"

Nothing could better illustrate the psychotherapeutic process, but it is wise to remember that the effect is transient and needs repetition.

"So you must have been thinking about those things without being too much aware of it."

"Without being conscious of it, yes. Of course right now the feeling I have is I better get the hell out of there and get another job."

"That's not easy."

"That's right, not after eleven years."

"Eleven years and you have a wife and three children. Good money."

"The money is good."

"So this thing was coming on then since father became your immediate boss?"

"I would say so, yes, without my knowing it. I thought when he came there, you see this is a lesser job than what he had because he's *near retirement* so they give a man a manager's job for the last year or two before he retires, so I figured it would be good working for my father, it would be all right."

"You mean you felt you might sort of get acquainted with him?"

"Get acquainted, yes, get to know him, you know."

"You had always sort of missed that?"

"Yes, and so he was only supposed to work until last June, at least he had mentioned that he was going to retire then, but hell he has held on ever since, you know."

"He was going to retire last June?"

"Yes, I think it was last June he was going to retire. As it has turned out, he is not going to retire until the end of this year. So *had he retired when he was going to, I think I would have been all right.*"

Retirement is a prelude to dying. His oedipal death wishes were part of his anxiety. He couldn't afford to lose father yet as he still felt too much like a little boy.

"Last June?"

"Yes."

"When did you find out he was going to retire in June?"

"I think he mentioned it to me. I'm not really clear but I think he mentioned that he might."

"Before?"

"Intended to retire in June."

"When did he mention it?"

"When he first came to work over there, when he first became my boss."

"In 1958?"

"Yes, I think he said then 'I expect to retire a year from this June,' something to that effect."

"That would be around June 1959?"

"June 1959, well I would say it was June 1960."

"That he said he would retire?"

"That he planned to retire."

"He told you a year before?"

"Yes."

"You said he told you a year before, so that would be around June 1959?"

"I'm not really sure of the dates."

"The reason I was wondering was I was wondering how it affected you?"

"Of course when he said he was going to retire, although *I wanted him to be there in a sense, I was glad he was going.*"

"That's what I mean. This is part of the *confusion*. As you said, you wanted to sort of get acquainted with the guy and you were fond of him in many ways and you wanted him to stick around in other words, and another part wished that he would get the hell out."

"Yes, that's right."

"Tell me, were you that way when they got the divorce? I mean did you feel originally now maybe mother would have some peace and then another part of you hoped he'd stay because you needed him. I mean I wonder if you were a little confused then?"

"I really *don't think,* uh, no, *I wasn't at all happy to see him go.*"

There are no negatives in the unconscious where the deep oedipal death wish is contrary to the more adolescent longing. The ambivalence was plain.

"Because when he was so mean to mother and threw her out in the now, I wonder if you hadn't wished sometimes that he would get the hell out?"

"No, I really didn't have that feeling, no, because when he did go never mentioned that he was gone or discussed it at all. I really wasn't happy that he was gone. I wish the hell he had been there."

"I was wondering at the beginning before you knew what effect it would have on mother?"

"No, I don't think I ever had that feeling."

"Whether you thought it would solve her problems?"

"No."

"I wonder because it is obvious that this is a bit of the confusion now. You have mixed feelings over his leaving, huh?"

"That's right."

"Did you get acquainted with him after he came down?"

"Yes, pretty well but—"

He paused.

"I know what you mean. It wasn't the same?"

"No, no, it isn't right now. You know when I was in the Navy I got two letters from him and they weren't *father and son* letters, just full of advice. And what the hell does a seventeen-year-old kid out fighting a war need advice for, you know what I mean. And I know my oldest brother was a prisoner of war for two and a half years, had made several missions and all, and he got a couple of letters from him while he was in prison camp and it was the same way. The letters were full of advice."

"No understanding, huh? All from the head and not from the heart?"

"That's right, that's right."

"That's not what you really needed?"

"That's right."

"So you mean the old yen to really get to know him and have a heart-to-heart talk together and all that never got satisfied?"

"No, no. It's the old *bull shit* every time—I this, and I that, you should do this, and I don't want to seem to be giving you advice but, uh, this is it and so forth."

"Was he still that way after he became your boss and you tried to get acquainted with him?"

"Yes."

"What was he advising you on then?"

"Well he is always shooting off about something, you know."

"You mean about getting ahead, what to do to get to be *district manager?*"

This might be part of the oedipal fantasy.

"Yes, yes, how he would manage this and that, like for instance if I am broke at times, as young people are sometimes you know, he can't understand why you should have any bills or anything like that. You're making $130 a week, etc.!"

"Treating you essentially like a kid?"

"Yes and 'When I was your age I was making $20 a week.' "

"So you were confused about a lot of things, about dad and mother and your brothers and yourself when you developed your fear of the crowds?"

"Come to think of it, it first began when I'd be with the fellows in the building where dad's office is and I'd wonder if they were talking about me."

"You didn't feel like one of them?"

"No. You wouldn't believe it but I felt like a little kid sucking round for favors."

"Well, this is all we have time for today. I'll call you as soon as possible and we'll get together on a regular schedule and see if we can find out more about your problems."

"Well, I hope so. The sooner the better. Jesus! I feel I've learned a lot already."

This interview illustrates very well how the unmastered remnants of the past can affect a patient in the present. There is much here that is characteristic of all cases. First, let us consider the origin of his anxiety attacks. In the first place, he was confused among the three crowds. There was the past family and the crowd of brothers, more specifically Dick and his friends; then there was the present crowd at home. The therapist kept away from this area but realized that one of the dates around which his trouble began marked a time when he first became definitely aware that his wife was pregnant (three months). The crowd he was immediately concerned with, however, was that of the other milkmen. They were obvious symbols of the brothers, especially Dick. It was in this area that the most intense effect appeared. Dick envied *him*. The milkmen thought, according to him, that he was the boss's pet. Around the time his trouble began, father was going to retire. He wanted to become a "big shot" like father but he never could accept being a big man. He wanted to give up his job. By the time the interview was ended, the patient had developed quite a bit of insight concerning his job phobia and his passive little-boy problems. Left unanswered was the problem at home. It is possible that passive homosexual libido was the main agent behind his symptom and that his fear of crying and being a sissy, as well as the yearning to be loved by dad and the "brothers," and his feminine masochistic mother identifications would have been the sector for development. However, there were some hints that his home life was not as rosy as he painted it. The father and mother aspects of his ego were suspect. Father cheated and mother was a simple housewife whose sole asset appears to have been her cooking. It would be important to know something about this patient's sex life *with his wife.* Did he want any more children? How did he handle the problem of contraception? How much anxiety did his baby girl and her relations with the two older boys and wife arouse in him?

In the therapy of this patient the principal task would probably consist of enlarging and repeating the material already furnished. Actually, a week following the interview the patient telephoned to relate he had no symptoms at all at work and saw no reason for continuing therapy. While part of this change was a flight into health to avoid further "embarrassment," such a result is perfectly laudable and desirable from the point of view of psychotherapy if not that of psychoanalysis.

In terms of pathological mourning, we could formulate his problem in terms of repressed yearnings for a lost father-son relationship repressed rage and yearning, rivalry and fear concerning a lost brother relationship. Repressed oedipal guilt elements were also obvious. In other words, the oedipus complex gave form to the pathological mourning. Fixation at a passive phallic level would ultimately lead to more symptomatic difficulties which could be treated only when he was ready for it.

VI

THE NATURE OF THE
SECTOR EXAMINED

A Food Phobia

A sector in psychotherapy usually refers to a single pattern of affects throughout a patient's life and his relationships with the various objects used to discharge these affects. In some cases a single affect such as fear, disgust, shame or guilt, will be central in the plot. For example, in this chapter a patient will center his difficulties around a fear of food at first. By the time the interview has ended, he will see his fear in a much broader sense. Often a sector develops around a relationship with, let us say, a series of mother, father or sibling figures and a number of affects are involved. The major affects that appear are anger, yearning, guilt and despair. From the discussion of pathological mourning, it will be apparent that such feelings will always be connected ultimately with the anticipation of loss or abandonment. Primarily this means the loss of an essential and ambivalently regarded person. As we have seen, displacement and regression complicate this simple picture considerably.

Through the proper selection of material by the interviewer, the pat story that the patient has evolved as a defense is broken up and increasingly fragmented until basic abstract feeling patterns can be recognized and then followed into the infantile past where they substituted for and were fused with primary object-related sensory perceptions. Repetitive abstract feeling patterns that are a part of the organism's response to the primary losses and traumas of infancy and childhood are in constant need of new objects upon which they can discharge themselves. The neurotic person tends to attach so-called

177

free-floating anxiety onto various objects with some degree of relish; i.e., anxiety and depression are diminished when we furnish strong feeling patterns with objects that can be mastered by action which leads to discharge of tension. These patterns may appear in the interview situation in the form of sensory sensations before they appear verbally, and the more so as the interviewed person drifts to lower and more infantile levels of expression.

In most neurotic persons, the various spheres of the ego's relationship are dissociated from each other, that is, there is no conscious recognition of their similarity. In this manner, strong affective charge attached to certain areas, such as the body or possessions, cannot be spread among and absorbed by many different spheres of activity of the ego as they are in more normal persons. For example, most of us are interested in and able to express ourselves in many ways relating to the uses of our body, objects and persons. The discharge of affect in the normal person is regulated so that intra-ego tension is kept at a relatively low level and the ego is free from the anxiety that appears as a response to the threat of being overwhelmed by intense masses of stimuli. It is assumed that this type of dissociative defense, that is separation of various spheres of activity, originates in the main as a response of the ego to deprivations and traumatic events. Following a trauma or loss a reorganization occurs in all spheres of interest and activity of the ego. The reorganization fits in with the previous one like a minor detail added to a Rorschach ink blot which alters the holistic organization to only a slight degree, according to its size, i.e., the intensity of the reaction to the loss or trauma. In this manner, the new event and the precipitate of past events reciprocally modify each other. What has happened in the past thus modifies what happens or is preceived in the present and is anticipated in the future. In another sense what happens in the present modifies our recollection of the past; what is anticipated in the future modifies our recollection of the past and our perception of the present.

When personal relationship difficulties are mentioned, it is implied that these are *not* of the ordinary kind, which do not lead to neurotic symptoms. They have come about as a manifestation or projection of an intrapsychic disharmony in the relationship of the "I" portion of the ego with various self-images. The only way to separate "ordinary" from neurotic personal difficulties is to note whether the emotion or the importance attached to the difficulty is disproportionate.

When a technique is obvious, a patient may tend to fall in line with it and isolate what he says during his session from his everyday life. More, we may believe an ingratiating patient has insight when he does not have it. A therapist may use a technique also to isolate himself from any and all emotional participation in the relationship or to disguise or hide from himself countertransference feelings toward the patient. This can only be done at the expense of certain over-all and vital insights and understanding, especially in relation to the timing of the confrontations. Actually, correct timing tends to be the last thing the beginner learns to do well.

Ordinarily the sector concerns itself with the presenting symptom. Frequently it is concerned principally with only one area of relationship, for example to other persons or to the self. However, in the initial interview it is often necessary to cover a wider range of areas which are concerned with the genesis and dynamics of a symptom. Later interviews can focus upon a single symptom or feeling of primary importance. This resembles the scientific procedure in the laboratory when a pathological slide is examined with a microscope. First it is examined under low power to a wide extent, and then a portion of it is examined in detail.

After the study of the first five interviews, it will be apparent that it is necessary for the therapist to listen to ordinary speech so that he can detect in it qualities that the psychoanalyst usually ascribes to dreams, fantasies and primary thought processes. Thus, in everyday speech we heard words and especially numbers that were multi-determined symbols, that is, we heard examples of symbolization and condensation. We also heard many examples of displacement and expression by the opposite; in addition, referents in time, causality, and location were lacking. Affirmation by negation, which of course is a way of expression by the opposite, was also heard. Loose connections between ideas and their charge of affects was another quality much in evidence. This manner of expression is also usually associated with the primary processes. Psychoanalysts are accustomed to the manifestation of these qualities in free association where they are more obvious than when they occur in the more ordinary verbal exchange of the psychotherapeutic interview.

We will now consider an interview in which these qualities of speech will be illustrated again in detail.

When this patient entered the office, the first impression he gave was one of angry confusion. He appeared to be a young man who was determined to tell everything but terribly embarrassed by his own need.

"How do you do. Come in and sit down."

The therapist indicated a chair and continued.

"Your doctor told me something about your case, but I'd like to have you tell me more and in your own words."

He was sturdy, broad-shouldered, and just above medium height. There was iron gray hair with the suggestion of a curl above a young boy's face, with alert and somewhat furtive dark brown eyes—the mélange somewhat Latin and attractive, which was disconcerting as the voice was unpleasant, querulous, and somewhat whiny.

"In regard to what?"

"How you happened to come to see me."

"Well, uh,"

There was a long pause and then he continued.

"If I can pinpoint the matter—I am *afraid*, I, uh, I have had *trouble* with *eating*."

"Afraid? Afraid to eat?"

"Afraid to eat."

"How come?"

"I don't know."

The therapist made the usual retort.

"You mean you don't know exactly but you have some kind of ideas."

"Well, I was afraid to eat."

An airplane passed overhead and drowned out the few words he was saying.

"I was afraid not to eat also, afraid of the aftereffects and—"

His voice died away.

The therapist continued to carry him along.

"You were *afraid* to eat because of the *aftereffects?*"

"Well, my food was coming up on me all the time."

He said this a little aggressively.

"That's what you mean by the *aftereffects?*"

He nodded.

"Yes. I'd have a hard time digesting my meal and that's not all of it. I was just afraid to eat. I was afraid to look at food. I was afraid to eat, period. I was afraid mostly of, well, after I did eat, the gastric effects of food."

He looked knowingly at the therapist. It seemed that he was reluctant to talk and felt trapped.

"Could you tell me something about what were the *gastric effects* of the *food* which made you afraid to eat?"

"Well, uh, if I had a friend out on Sunday, I was afraid I'd *burp*

Sometimes I couldn't burp. It used to stay there and, uh, I mean it's so hard to explain. Maybe it's, uh."

He looked helpless. The therapist encouraged him.

"You're doing fine."

He laughed in embarrassment.

"I'm trying to but I can't even pinpoint it. I mean, a lot of these things happen. Let me put it this way. The past two days were rough. I don't know why. Certain foods I'm afraid to eat like, uh, yesterday I had eggs for lunch. I usually have eggs, you know, just for breakfast, or maybe a couple of soft-boiled eggs for supper. But I had eggs in the afternoon instead of, uh, I know I didn't expect to get eggs. When I saw the eggs there, geez, I was happy that it was eggs rather than meat. Then afterwards I felt bad about it because I said, who am I kidding. I'm only kidding myself by not, you know, having different foods. I usually eat two or three meals a day, naturally, but the fact that I had eggs yesterday—"

There was a long pause.

"What do you mean by *kidding* yourself?"

"About this food business. I know that *meat* is important to eat, *fish* is important, *vegetables* are important foods, but the fear is still there."

"Fear of certain kinds of food, you mean? What kind?"

"*Meat!*"

He said this quickly.

"Meat?"

"Period! And I have a rough time with vegetables, unless they are *puréed,* or *something* not to worry about. But meat particularly. Uh, things like, uh, certain foods. I've been afraid to eat almost anything for quite a while."

He lowered his gaze and shifted about in his chair uneasily.

"How long is quite a while?"

The therapist wondered why he wanted what were essentially baby foods.

"For a period of almost two years."

"Two years? Since 1953?"

"Well, uh, it started around July the third, two years ago. Mind if I tell you the whole incident, would you like me to?"

He acted as if the therapist had been stopping him.

"Sure, go right ahead."

"Well, it started on Thursday night, as I recall."

"In 1953?"

This was two years ago. In his own words, he was really "pin-pointing" it but he would have been quick to deny this as he was probably confusing similar events or feelings that had occurred at different times.

"The exact year I don't remember."

"You mean it could be even more than two years?"

He shook his head.

"No, I don't think so. Approximately two years ago but, to my knowledge, the way I *feel*, it happened a couple of years ago and, uh, my wife, of course had, I want to verify this statement. *My wife* had been home with *the baby*. By the way, it wasn't a week, the baby had been home almost two months."

This was so confusing that the therapist tried to get him to repeat it. The first person who appeared, that is wife and baby, were probably at the root of the problem.

"Pardon me, I can't hear you."

He began again.

"We had a new baby in the house. It had been home about two months. Well, anyway, the incident was on a Thursday night. I had come home from work. I started *eating* and the *baby* started *crying*. So I got up quick and started rocking the baby. My wife was in bed. She was *sick*, a diabetic, and, uh, I had to baby-sit next door, the neighbor next door. July the fourth fell on a Saturday so I had to double up my route on the following day. I do recall I had a very severe case of *indigestion* that night. It lasted throughout the *night*."

The psychiatrist and the detective have much in common. They piece together evidence and have to read a great deal between the lines and pay attention to insignificant details. Neuroses, like crimes, usually bear a striking similarity to one another and, therefore, contain an element of predictability. The therapist realized, that the patient's symptoms and fears were a screen that hid a problem dealing with a baby and a sick mother. What did diabetes mean to him, and indigestion too? He was obviously uneasy.

"What do you mean by *indigestion*?"

"Well, the food was laying there and it was heavylike, it started running around in me. What did I do, eat too fast or what caused it, I don't know. To me I thought it was indigestion. Perhaps it could have been *something else*. I just don't know."

"What do you mean?"

He was treating the food somewhat oddly, as it couldn't be there and run around at the same time.

"Well, I do recall that I, that whole evening, and the whole night I was walking up and down and I couldn't sleep, and it was *murdering* me. I took Alka-Seltzer, Bromo-Seltzer. I couldn't relieve that feeling, that heavy, that terrible feeling I had inside of me, a *gastric feeling*. When I did burp, pieces of food would come up."

A new theme, "murder," had now appeared.

"You mean you had this while you were taking care of the baby?"

He nodded.

"Well, I had this when I was baby-sitting next door, as I recall. I went next door to baby-sit."

This was confusing.

"*Your* baby had just come home?"

"Oh, he'd been home for a few months."

"And your wife was in bed?"

"She's rather weak."

"*Weak?*"

"I had a rough time with her during the pregnancy."

He said this very slowly.

"I used to find her in *diabetic comas.*"

Now it began to get clearer. She was probably the murder victim.

"How did she get that way?"

He frowned.

"During that period of time, while she was pregnant, before this thing happened—my mind isn't clear. I'd like to get it as straight as I can."

His voice died away. His thoughts obviously made him uneasy.

"What do you mean?"

"Well, before the baby came I used to have, I found her *twice* in diabetic comas, unconscious. One time I found her on the floor in the afternoon when I came home. Actually I never used to come home from business during the day. I used to be out on the road you know, but I did come home this particular day. I don't know why or how."

He appeared puzzled.

"Out on the *road?*"

"Out on the road. When I'm on business I never come home for *lunch*. I used *to go out and eat*, you know, have a sandwich in restaurants, come home the regular time. This particular day I came home early and she was unconscious, in a diabetic coma on the floor."

He wiped his forehead.

"How did you know it was a *diabetic coma?*"

"Well!"

As he replied, his voice rose with excitement.

"I recognized it from *before*. I mean, she had another coma previous and, uh, it scared the daylights out of me. In fact, she was laying there on the floor, and if I hadn't come home—my oldest boy was just four at the time, he was *running around*, just a kid—and, it got to a point that I used to call her on the hour, every hour. I used to come *running home* at noontime!"

"After the second one or the first one?"

"The second one."

"Not after the first?"

There was much material to investigate in the meaning of comas and diabetes, but he had all kinds of diversions to offer.

"After the second one, after the second time I caught her in one, yes. And I used to be *afraid*. That's the way it turned out. I used to be afraid of the *kids choking on their food*. It started about that time."

Now "afraid" applied to wife and babies openly.

"You mean when your wife had her coma you were afraid the *kids* would choke?"

He didn't reply.

"Had you heard of such things?"

He nodded again slowly.

"I think it was—I'm trying to think if I can remember this distinctly when I was afraid—before she had the baby or after she had the baby. I mean this being afraid of the kids choking on food started. I had found her in *comas* because she was *pregnant* at the time."

"You mean the first *baby*?"

"My second one."

He made no offer to unravel the puzzle.

"If it was before she was pregnant the second time, it must be that it was the first baby who might choke on his food."

"I was afraid of both of them choking. It happened afterwards. I mean this choking effect happened after, you know, the baby was started."

"You had heard of such things?"

The therapist hoped to get a revealing fantasy to explore, but the patient was too upset to remember.

"Had I heard of, well, I'll tell you, the last time I was having a rough time *eating myself*, in fact I used to have *soups* all day long, soups and *baby foods*!"

He appeared to be confusing himself with both the mother and the babies.

"When was this?"

"That time."

"What do you mean by that time? You mean before she had the baby?"

"No, no, it happened after she had the baby. The fear of food happened after I had that indigestion that night."

"What do you mean by you'd have trouble where you had to have soups?"

"Well, when I came out of the hospital. That's a, well."

Here he appeared puzzled.

"That's a period I just can't pinpoint right now, exactly when I don't know."

Ther therapist ignored the slip. It was probably his wife who had been in the hospital but he was confused enough in his identifications.

"You mean that was before you had the *indigestion*?"

"No, it was after I had the indigestion that all that business started."

Here he appeared quite definite.

"After you had the *indigestion*, you had to have the soups. That was when you were afraid your boys might *choke*?"

"That's right. I was afraid to eat solid foods."

"You were afraid that they might choke?"

"Both of them."

He spoke emphatically. This meant all three of them—himself, child and wife. Both of the latter were obviously alter-ego figures.

"What made you think of that, of them choking? You had heard of such things? I mean, *children choking*?"

"Children" was picked as it might lead to the past.

"No, this thought just happened to come to my mind."

"That they might *choke*?"

"Especially if they were crying."

"Why crying?"

"If I see a child, if I see my boy with a mouthful of food, and crying, it scares the daylights out of me."

"Why?"

"Well, if he's been a *bad boy* and my wife tells him to be a good boy, not to make any *noise* at the table, or something like that, and if he starts being wise or fresh and then starts crying, then I get, Geez, I feel like—"

He gave a slight laugh.

"I'm ready to pop out the window. I get all excited. I get *nerved up*."

Unconsciously he was resurrecting a childhood image of himself and seeing it as his own child.

"You mean over someone *crying* with something in his *mouth?*"

"In his mouth, correct. Or if he gets something to eat and starts running around in the house, it scares the daylights out of me."

"Running around?"

"Well, the kid I mean, he wants to start playing with his toys or cars. It *scares* me, gets me *nervous*, especially while he's *eating*. I mean, of course he's *not supposed to be doing that anyway*."

He became excited.

"I mean, er, we, er, we don't stand for that. I don't get mad for the fact that he's running around the house. I get mad for the fact that there's a mouth full of food in this kid and it scares the day-lights out of me, or I'm afraid to let my youngster have *any small objects, aggie*s, or a *nail*. I'm always telling the older boy don't let him have anything like that. I'm always *hiding things like that!*"

Now he appeared to be developing a phobic history. Playing with things, symbolized by marbles and a nail, appeared coupled with dangerous oral wishes and showed the nature of the aroused infantile fears and longings.

"You mean he might put them in his *mouth?*"

"That's correct, Doctor. I'm afraid he might put them in his mouth."

"You've heard of such things?"

He shook his head and raised his hands helplessly.

"Uh, where these fears came from the good Lord knows; I don't. But they did come."

"You've heard of boys and children putting things in their mouths?"

"You bet I have."

"Where? What have you heard?"

"Well, I've heard of kids *choking* to *death* on certain things, nails, pins, *things like that*."

"And *die?*"

"That's right."

His voice sank to a whisper at the very thought.

"And die! That word there sort of made me shudder."

"What do you mean?"

He grimaced.

"And die. I mean you made it very emphatic. Die! If it happened to my kids! Who's going to take care of them and watch over them?"

Now the infantile plot apparently was enlarged to include the anxiety over a mother or a child dying. What might kill her in the mind of the child? The therapist tried to make his reply fit both the possible past and the present.

"So once you came home and found her in a *diabetic coma* and nobody watching over the children?"

He nodded assent.

"Right! Right! I was kind of scared and I was afraid for the boy and I was afraid for my wife. I was afraid that she might not come out of it."

"She might die too?"

"Right! I was afraid she might *die if I didn't come home*. Of course I was more afraid for *her* than I was for the little one."

This appeared to be an afterthought.

"What was a *diabetic coma* to you?"

"What is it, you mean?"

"Yes."

"Well, uh, I don't understand what it was, period! I happened to see it twice."

His emphasis belied the statement. Perhaps he didn't want to know.

"So you had some idea. You don't know whether it's correct medically or not, but I wonder what you thought a *diabetic coma* was?"

"Well, she wasn't drunk. She doesn't drink. I saw it happen just a few times before meals and she'd start acting like drunk and I didn't know what it was. I thought maybe she's having a slight reaction. But, uh, the first real serious reaction she had, a coma, happened during the *middle of the night*. I noticed that she wasn't *moving* and I don't know what happened, I just happened to wake up. It was about *four* o'clock in the morning."

In the clinical practice of psychoanalysis, there was a time in every patient's life when, as a small child, he awoke in the night and saw sights or heard sounds and fantasied sights that were horribly scary and that produced lasting impressions in his character, especially in relation to his sexual life. These events are called primal scenes. Such occurrences have a nightmarish quality and are usually repetitive. They are in a sense traumatic and act as focal points which screen a whole series of losses or injuries and organize reactive character traits. What now appeared to be coming up in his story had a reality value, but also could be treated as a fantasy which would give away other important things to come.

"When was this?"

"During the pregnancy of my second boy. And I playfully pushed her and I thought perhaps that, I tried to *arouse* her, you know how it is. A person usually moves in their sleep. You know, one way or the other. But I don't know how the hell I woke up but—"

He stopped and appeared perplexed. The therapist wondered how he had acted playfully. Was it in a sexual sense? This would result in much guilt later. The therapist also wondered if "her second pregnancy" applied to his mother as well as his wife, that is, in the distant past. Many children have nightmares when their position as mother's baby is challenged by their mother's pregnancy and the turning away from them that often accompanies such an event. These nightmares accompany a reactivation of the primal-scene memories or fantasies and tend to incorporate them into their structure.

"This was the first coma?"

"Yes, sir, The first coma and I snapped on the light and there she was with the eyes wide open. No comment!"

"What do you mean?"

"Scared to death."

He was sweating freely at the thought.

"I was scared to *DEATH*!" I was scared to death! Period! Geez, I called the doctor and asked him what to do and he said pour orange juice down her gullet. So I went out for a bag of oranges and that didn't seem to help, so I called the doctor back. Oh, I was scared, very scared!"

"You knew before she had something wrong?"

"I knew there was something wrong. To me she had a coma. She had a reaction, a diabetic coma!"

"You knew she already had diabetes?"

"She had it for *FOUR* years!"

"Four years? Since 1951?"

It was necessary to pin down dates to keep confusion at a minimum.

"She had it approximately, after my oldest boy was born, maybe almost two years after he was born."

"Two years after he was born?"

"In that vicinity."

"How did it happen?"

"How did diabetes happen?"

He shook his head and shrugged his shoulders.

"Of course, I don't expect you to, I mean what were all your ideas?"

"My ideas about it happening?"

There was a long pause.

"Well, I could say that I felt *guilty* about her being diabetic. Then again I could say I didn't."

The therapist wanted to know more about this guilt.

"That's what I mean, you don't know whether you are right or not but you felt guilty at the time anyway?"

"I don't recall."

This was resistance to be gradually undermined.

"But what do you mean? Then how could you say you felt guilty?"

"Well, I just made the statement now. I could say that."

He could not deny his own words as they were used too recently.

"What makes you say that?"

"Well, I'm the father of her child. I figure it came from damage to one of her organs."

"That's what I mean. You felt that something had happened to one of her *organs* when she had the *child*?"

"Causing diabetes, naturally."

"That's what I mean, this is what I want you to tell me about."

He answered quickly.

"That I felt guilty about it?"

"You thought that diabetes—?"

He started to get angry and interrupted.

"I want to get well and get the hell out of this mess. That's all that matters."

He appeared to feel trapped and it was necessary to be careful.

"All your answers are right. Just tell me what you thought. Did you think then that the pregnancy that she had, the first, had caused something to happen to one of her *organs*? Is that correct?"

"Uhhh, no! What had happened, I don't know why it happened. I didn't feel anything about it at all. I just, well I just didn't know why it happened and I was very, I had no idea why it happened!"

"How did you find it? How did it happen?"

"Found it? Well, she started losing weight and was becoming very irritable."

"She lost *weight*?"

"Lost weight, she used to eat quite a bit of food."

"She ate quite a lot of food?"

He lost his suspicious attitude and talked quickly.

"Yes, but she kept on losing weight and drinking a lot of water. I had a hint. I really, I detected it when she had trouble *urinating*. Her organs used to *burn* her tremendously. She told me that and I got scared. I didn't say anything to her about it, I wasn't sure, but, uh, her face became very drawn and thin and, uh, I became alarmed, naturally, and so did she. I sent her to a doctor and that same night when I came home from work she was crying. She told me she had an acute case of diabetes."

The injured organ was a sexual organ. Who was responsible? Behind the reality was a fantasy at a phallic urinary level, as was seen in previous cases.

"Then you think this might be due to some injury of the *organs* when she became pregnant?"

"Definitely."

"What do you mean?"

"Well, maybe the baby, being pregnant, might have moved one of her organs and caused the diabetes. But *I'm the one to blame!*"

This was the important element. Hidden behind this concern about his wife was his anxiety about injury to his own organs and guilt over certain wishes. In any case, where did he get this idea?

"You mean for making her pregnant?"

"Well, naturally, having children, certainly!"

"You'd heard of such things? That a woman is injured, one of her organs becomes injured when she has babies?"

He answered quickly.

"No."

"Then where did you get this idea? You say, naturally, certainly."

He pondered over this for a few moments.

"Well, I've heard of women having trouble having children, yes, after birth they've had trouble, yes."

"What kind of *trouble* do you mean?"

"Well, sometimes, well my *mother* had trouble. She had a serious operation. I imagine they can't explain it."

Naturally this would be connected with sadomasochistic birth fantasies that he couldn't explain to himself.

"After *birth* mother did?"

"No, within the past ten years: she had an operation. My mother's rather old but, uh, I think her stomach, some part of her fell down or something. I don't know what happened exactly."

"Her *stomach* fell down?"

"Her womb or some part of her body."

His statements made a kind of sense. A child doesn't know the difference between organs in the abdomen.

"One of her organs?"

"I'm not exactly familiar with medicine, doctor, so I can't explain."

This was a typical way of evading anxiety-laden fantasies: by pleading ignorance. Most likely it was more than ten years ago, so the all-important time intervals were taken up again.

"Ten years?"

"Well maybe longer. I mean that vicinity, within ten or fifteen years. Around ten years I think that operation was."

Here he appeared frankly puzzled.

"You mean around 1945? Around then?"

"I think it happened before I was in the service. I just don't remember. I'm not very sharp these days."

By "not very sharp" he meant confused by similarities.

"Due to having *babies?*"

"I don't know. That I don't know."

"But you said you'd heard of women who were *injured* after *babies.*"

"Well, yes, I've heard of women having trouble, I mean naturally, with children. I mean having trouble with their organs."

The process was tedious but he was slowly edging in the right direction.

"And you wondered then if it was due to mother having *babies* when her *stomach* or *womb* dropped down."

"Possibly. Well, those things don't happen to every woman. I mean some women are stronger than others. My wife is a very strong girl. Of course she, during pregnancy she had no trouble having the baby. Not in the least. Never had a sick day in her life. *I never had a sick day in my life.*"

His identification with his wife was again obvious.

"You mean you didn't know, or you wouldn't have had her have *babies,* or what?"

"If I had known what was to come, I certainly would not have had babies under any condition. Naturally! Definitely! Of course my kids are here, God bless them, thank God they are here. I wouldn't trade them for anything in the world, for all the tea in China I wouldn't trade them."

He was protesting too much.

"Even if your wife became well?"

He frowned.

"You and I are a little mixed up here."

The therapist became more explicit, as the patient's ambivalence in this area was an important focal point.

"You mean you wouldn't trade them for anything, but if it were to make it so your wife didn't have *diabetes*, you could have done without them. Is that what you mean?"

This posed a cruel dilemma.

"Not in the least!"

He snapped.

"I mean if I were to say to a guy, what would you rather have, your health or your money—health is more important. Whether you have money or you don't have money—"

"So do you mean the same with your wife? If she had her health, could you get along without the *children*?"

"No, I won't say that either. That's *your* way of putting it. You've really got me in a spot here. No, I think I'd rather have my kids, too."

He laughed and broke the tension.

"That's putting a guy in an awkward corner, isn't it?"

"That's what you're in, isn't it?"

"Yes, you're right. Yes, I guess maybe you're right. Uh, here on one hand I have a wife who has the diabetes and here on the other hand I want my kids."

Now the therapist could get to the point.

"But I understand that when she had her second baby she not only got *diabetes* but she got a *coma*, too?"

"I was afraid to have the second one! I was very much afraid to have the second baby. I didn't want, I didn't want to have the second baby."

This was probably only a partial truth, otherwise why should he identify so readily with the pregnant wife?

"*She* wanted it?"

"She wanted it badly and I kept on putting it off and she kept on insisting and the reason I was afraid of having the second baby is the fact that I was told that nothing would happen to her. I wasn't counting on reactions or stuff like that, I mean those things, I wasn't thinking about that. I was worried about how the baby would come out. I heard how the baby could come out deformed someway."

"Come out what?"

"Deformed. During birth."

"*Deformed?*"

"Deformed in one way or another."

"How do you mean?"

"Well, I mean, deformed. That's what I was told. I was told a baby could be born deformed."

"By *deformed* you mean?"

"Well, I don't know, a *leg* or *arm missing, or something*, I don't know."

From the point of view of the unconscious, the "something" was more important. He must mean he wanted a girl baby, which, in his mind, was associated with fears of castration through identification with the baby as well as with the mother.

"A leg or arm missing? Is that what you said, a leg or arm missing?"

"Well, not missing but—somebody told me how the baby could be born deformed in some means or manner. I don't know exactly."

"But what does *deformed* mean to you?"

"To me it means, uh, a paralyzed arm or a paralyzed leg. *Something like this.* God forbid—blind! *Something to that effect.* And I was kind of scared of having another baby."

He stopped and looked uncomfortable. As in the story of the blind Oedipus, the loss of eyes or eyesight is one of the most frequent ways that castration is represented in the neurotic fantasy life.

"A deformed baby, you mean?"

"You're right, a deformed baby. If I had any *conception* that she could *die* from being *pregnant*, I wouldn't have had the baby if she stood on her *head*. But I was told by her doctor that it was all right as long as she was careful, so I took a chance and we had a baby."

"And then she went into *coma*, and you were really scared—as you said, scared to *death*."

He agreed somberly.

"Those comas kind of scared me quite a bit, there's no question about it."

"You were scared then of her *dying* or the babies *dying*?"

"Well, uh, what I was afraid of was the fact that—she was unconscious and in a coma and there's *nobody there* to—after all, who's going to walk into the house? She was lying there from eleven o'clock in the morning, and I know with diabetes you just can't throw a bucket of water in a person's face to take them out of it. And I didn't know what length of time, what time it would be before a person could succumb in a coma. I don't believe I ever asked anyone about it, how long—or any doctor. Maybe I should have but I didn't."

"So you were *scared*?"

"But it scared me, yes, I was afraid of her dying, let's put it that way, if I *hadn't come home*."

This sounded as if he were going in circles again but it also was reminiscent of an agoraphobic type of separation anxiety with mother in the past. The therapist tried to get into the past but the attempt was premature.

"So mother had an operation on her womb ten or fifteen years ago because of her pregnancies?"

"Yes, but I'm not worried about that."

"But I was thinking, at least you had experience in the sense that you knew *pregnancy* could cause things to happen to *women*, huh?"

"No, except in her case of diabetes. While she was diabetic, I was afraid of her having a baby, afraid that something could happen to the baby. I wasn't afraid of her dying at all, no, not in the least, while pregnant."

"Who? Your wife or mother?"

"My wife. I was just afraid of the fact that I found her in comas. That's when I became afraid."

"I thought you were afraid for the *baby*."

"No!"

He started to fidget uneasily.

"The *deformed* baby?"

"That's one thing I was afraid of, and the fact that I found her unconscious also made me very afraid. If I didn't come home, what the outcome could have been, I don't know. I was scared stiff. That's why I used to call her every hour on the hour."

The therapist returned to the present to give him a rest and to look for a better opening.

"Well, then it was on this Thursday night you say you were taking care of the baby and your wife was feeling weak and in bed?"

"Yes. My older boy had to be put to bed. I had to go next door and babysit."

"How come?"

"How come what?"

"You had to go next door and baby-sit."

"Well, we used to take turns. We'd baby-sit for them; they used to baby-sit for us. But we did more baby-sitting for them than they used to do for us."

Obviously this could be connected in only one way.

"So your wife was in bed and you had to *leave* your kids and your wife and go and baby-sit?"

"Yes. I stopped that real quick, all that crap. It was a rough night!"

"What do you mean, *rough*?"

"It was a *rough* night, I remember. It was a *ROUGH* night! Very bad night. I had *indigestion*."

"So then, you mean by *indigestion* this feeling in your *stomach*, s that what you mean?"

"I don't know what you want to call it. I'd call it indigestion. All I <now it was *heavy*."

Here was a new word to explore.

"Heavy?"

"It wouldn't come up and it wouldn't go down and it was *murder*. Every once in a while a piece of food would come up on me. If I bent a certain way, I tried to get it to come up, it would, a small part of t might come up. It was a *nervous feeling*. *Terrible feeling*. The next lay I still had it. I had a *nauseous feeling* there. I went to see a doctor and he thought I had a *heart* condition and he sent me in the hospital."

More new words. When they are connected with the body image, they are especially important.

"When was this?"

"The very next day. The very next day. I was in the hospital for two weeks. Gave me X-rays. Nothing wrong. But that's when the of food, that's when the fear of food really started. That's when the vall started rolling down the hill."

"The fear of meat? Was it meat that you had been eating?"

"No, it wasn't meat."

"What had you been eating?"

"As I recall, I was eating sardines."

"Fish? How come meat?"

"I don't know. That's a good question, how come meat. I'm afraid, I'm *afraid of meat*. I see it, to me it's *bulk*. I'm afraid that I won't be able to digest it."

The sexual symbolism of a *piece of meat* was, of course, not obvious to him. How could it be made conspicuous? The reader may remember the meatman from *The Interpretation of Dreams* and from the previous case where the father was a butcher.

"Can't handle bulk?"

"Yes, I'm very much afraid of *bulk*."

"Bulk?"

"Bulk food."

"By bulk food you mean?"

He made a long pause and then continued.

"Steak! Meat! Meat, period!"

"A piece of meat?"

The sexual meaning might be more apparent when the words were used this way. He would understand unconsciously anyway.

"I'm afraid of the *meat,* yes!"

He became excited.

"I'm not much afraid of *hamburger.*"

"Hamburger isn't meat?"

"Hamburger, I have trouble with it, but I can digest it. I'm not much afraid of it. But I'm still afraid of meat! I don't know why the hell I'm afraid of meat."

He raised his voice.

"It happened yesterday. I got eggs and I wanted to throw the God damn things down and go down to a restaurant and get a piece of meat but I couldn't do it."

The therapist decided to return to the touchy question of the pregnancies, which were connected with guilty thoughts about a piece of hard meat.

"Your *wife* wanted the second baby?"

"*Desperately,* yes."

"Why desperate?"

"Well, she was *lonely,* she wanted another child."

"Does she feel two is enough?"

"Huh?"

"Does she feel two is enough now?"

"Does she feel two is enough? I don't give a good God damn what she feels! Does that answer the question?"

He laughed heartily at his own bravado.

"What do you mean?"

"I wouldn't have another kid if she stood on her *head!* Period!"

"How can you stop it?"

"Well, uh, in plain English, use rubbers or condoms or whatever you want to call them."

"But they can break!"

"I use *two* at one time!"

It was plain that having a baby or making babies was connected with sadomasochistic fantasies of deformity and death.

"Two?"

"Yes, I'm baboo!"

The therapist had not heard the word.

"What?"

He laughed.

"I use two at one time."

"What did you say, I'm what?"

"I'm baboo! I was only kidding."

"What do you mean by that?"

"Well, any fellow with nervous condition, they're all *baboo*. I mean they're all *bananas* or a *nut*! Well, it's a kidding expression. I haven't heard any, I haven't used any rubbers for quite a while, by the way."

Now this meant he had some insight concerning his anxieties over babies.

"You mean by using two rubbers you show you are nervous over getting her pregnant?"

"Oh no! Are you kidding? Yes!"

The ambivalence was obvious.

"I don't know, you'll have to tell me."

"Yes! I just told you, I use two and then sometimes during the, how do you say it, during the moment of pleasure, of *excretion*, uh, you know how sometimes I take it out just before—"

The word *excretion* was a slip showing an unconscious urinary fantasy. In psychotherapy such words are *not* taken up. This would not be done even in psychoanalysis until the patient had a great deal of understanding of his difficulties in the past. Beginners often make this mistake in an effort to impress the patient with their cleverness.

"You mean you put two rubbers on and then pull out?"

"Right!"

"Not very pleasant?"

He was on a spot between contradictory wishes.

"Not to me it isn't, anyway."

"What do you mean?"

"Well I don't get the full pleasure of the intercourse, naturally, by doing that. It's obvious, but, uh, I don't want any more children, Doc. I'm afraid to have any more children, scared to death!"

"So you go without the pleasure?"

"HELL NO! I DON'T GO WITHOUT!"

"But you don't feel safe with two rubbers."

"Sure! I like it as well as the next guy and, uh, we get along fine. Of course I could always use more."

"If you felt safe with two rubbers, why would you pull out? You mean there might still be a possibility?"

"Yes, I'm afraid that could be. I'm just afraid, period!"

This statement confirmed one of the meanings of a piece of meat but had to be expanded.

"To have intercourse with her, you mean?"

"HELL NO! Have intercourse with her? Are you kidding? No, I love it!"

He talked loudly as if trying to convince himself.

"You are sure?"

He turned a bright pink.

"So do you! We all do! That's bad if you don't like, uh, am I embarrassing you, Doc?"

This was an obvious signal for the therapist to slow down.

"You mean you're afraid to have intercourse with *her* but not of intercourse?"

"That's not real intercourse, naturally."

"That's what I mean."

"That's right. I'm afraid of knocking her up. Period!"

"That's what I mean."

"THAT'S IT! Sure!"

"Not very nice, huh? For a guy who likes it, like every man would?"

He appeared relieved and relaxed in his chair.

"Well, this is a world where you got to give and take and suffer. And then again, even if she wasn't pregnant, I mean even if she wasn't diabetic, all right, maybe *I'd have a third child.* But I don't think we'd want any more. I'd be very careful. I think I'd use more than two. Probably two, be careful. I don't want *all those kids parading around.*"

"What do you mean?"

The therapist was waiting for the moment when they could get into the past. In one sense, they were still just getting started, but at least they were getting away from *object* to *personal* relationships. Did his discontent lead him to cheat on his wife on the road?

"I don't want a houseful of kids, period. Of course you've got to give a little in this world and take a little, too, you know."

"So I mean sometimes then you must have felt that it would be nice if you could take a little yourself."

"Be wonderful."

"You've thought about that?"

"About what? If I didn't have to use any?"

"That's what you meant when you said wonderful, didn't you?"

"It doesn't give me convulsions. Not that I know of. I don't think about it at all, no."

His ability to repress his thoughts was being demonstrated remarkably well.

"Well, what would be wonderful? What were you just talking about? What would be wonderful?"

"Well, I mean to have an act of intercourse without using rubbers. It certainly would be wonderful."

"That's what you mean?"

"It would be wonderful to any man, wouldn't it? I think it would."

"You think of it sometimes?"

"Of, uh, what?"

"An act of intercourse without rubbers."

"Do I think of it? Not in the least."

The seesawing was too obvious for him to hide it from himself for long.

"You don't care?"

"Doesn't bother me, no! I'd love to have intercourse. Well, you know, when I'm in the mood for it. It doesn't bother me, no. As long as I get the sex act off my mind, well, if I enjoy it, I let it go at that. I still get the pleasure out of it. To my mind, I do, anyway. I mean I don't get as much pleasure as nature in the raw, that's obvious, but I get the, I get the full value from the act."

He paused and then said doubtfully—

"I think I do."

"You mean, you're not sure?"

"There's nothing like nature in the raw, that's obvious. I can remember when we had our children I enjoyed intercourse. I felt like one of the boys. Well, the wife's pregnant. Well, I can go for a free ride. Why not? Lots of fun. But, uh, maybe we can't take the consequences, you know. Especially now with her being diabetic, I'm kind of scared of having another child."

There was a long pause.

"That's the way I feel. Something wrong in that way or—?"

"Well, I wonder how she feels about it because she was the one who wanted the second."

"How does she feel about what?"

"Another child."

The therapist felt he could probably talk more easily about himself in the guise of his wife.

"I think she'd like to have another child."

"That's what I thought. She really would like more."

"I think she'd like a *little* girl. But I don't think she, uh, we talked about it but I don't think she'd, she would like it but not now. *She's afraid.* She's afraid *herself.*"

Now it was she. Of course, it was really he, as far as therapy was concerned. The next step was obvious.

"How about you, would you like a little girl?"

"Would I? Naturally. *I'd love it!* Sure!"

"Why?"

"I love kids."

"Since when?"

"Since when?"

He paused.

"What do you mean, since when?"

"I mean some people do, some people don't. Usually they have always wanted to have a big family."

"Well, I'd like to have a family of two or three. I think it's nice, yes. I got two. A little girl would be nice. I think three is a nice family."

The answer to why three must lie in the past.

"How many in your family?"

"Three boys."

With three boys there must have been a parental wish for a girl, and one of the boys must have felt more like a girl than the other two. This could be part of the patient's problem; i.e., he was afraid of his own feminine passive side, his little-*girl* longings for a baby. If he had a little girl, he would externalize and satisfy these longings.

"No girls?"

"No girls."

"Mother wanted a girl?"

"Mother had a girl!"

"What happened?"

"I think the girl died."

"When?"

What did he mean by he *thought* she died? Did she remain alive in him or his fantasies?

"Uh, I think the *first child* that she had was a girl."

"The first child she had?"

"Yes. Exactly when I don't know. It was, uh, I think it was, uh, *I was very young when it happened.* I don't know exactly."

"You were young? But I thought she was the first child?"

He hesitated.

"The baby was very young."

He was really confused in his identity with this girl.

"The baby was young? It came before you? It was the first child?"

"I've got to check up on that and find out. I'm not exactly sure."

"No, but you have ideas. You don't know whether you're right or not. What are your ideas?"

"About what?"

"About the little girl."

"About a little girl?"

"About *the* little girl."

"What little girl? My mother's little girl?"

Hysterical patients often behave in this uncomprehending manner. The confusion is based upon resistance concerning the little girl part of himself. So far four separate ego states were apparent, namely, the adult husband, the pregnant, injured, castrated mother, the little girl, and the crying boy who was injured by something he took in his mouth.

"That's right."

"It didn't even dawn on me. I've no idea at all. In any respect!"

"I mean did she die at birth?"

"I don't know. I'd have to ask."

"You mean mother never talked about it?"

"She never did. She really never did."

"It must have been a sore point with her, huh?"

Obviously this was the biggest island of resistance in the entire interview and the key to his problems.

"Maybe it was to her, yes. I wouldn't be surprised."

He said this slowly and cautiously.

"How did you know about it?"

"It got around somehow. I just happened to hear it. Where exactly, I don't remember. But I did hear it."

He paused suddenly, rubbed his forehead and appeared confused.

"What have I got a *headache* from? Geez, I'm all upset! I'm all nerved up! If it was ten minutes earlier, I'd think I was going to throw up. I don't know what it is! Geez, I guess I've had a *headache*, I don't know, since I've been here!"

Here was a conversion reaction. A headache represented his anger at being pushed in the directions which revealed his shame-laden secrets and his anxieties over his infantile, sexualized, passive feminine longings, his identifications with a little sister, his guilt over her death, his fears of his own death and his identification with an injured mother. Technically speaking, he had displaced a castration threat from his genital to his head. There was also a fantasy of getting rid of the dead little girl baby inside his stomach. This fantasy is connected with the anxiety over the pieces of meat being burped up and that of the little boy who runs around with dangerous things in his mouth. Like much technical knowledge, it could help to shape the therapist's responses but was not communicable to the patient this way or at this point. At the most it pointed out the right track.

"You have a headache now?"

"I don't know why. I mean I'm not, uh, *tensed* up, but I feel, uh, I don't feel relaxed like I should be. *What* am I *afraid* of? I've been feeling lousy. I had a rough ball game yesterday. I had the Yankees in mind. Do you like the World Series?"

This was an obvious escape which could be ignored. Now instead of being afraid of a piece of meat, he asked himself, "What am I afraid of?"

"So it just got around that this girl had been born and mother had a girl and she died?"

"I don't know where the information came from but I got it from somewhere in our family."

"That this girl had died?"

From the point of view of therapy, the death was a fantasy. Had he suspected that she died from swallowing things or that the bad mother had let her die or that she had choked? Had he wanted to bite her and devour her?

"You really have got me inquisitive. I'm going to find out about this. I don't know exactly what went on. I mean it dawned on me but I never wanted to probe into it."

"Why?"

"Well!"

He hesitated.

"I never probed my mother. In fact, I felt kind of self-conscious asking her a question like that."

He had felt too guilty about his probing fantasies obviously. Making babies is synonymous with intercourse and guilty, masturbatory, infantile, sexual fantasies and pursuits.

"About a baby?"

"About having a, you know, what happened. You know."

"What happened, you mean?"

"What happened to the little girl, what happened to the first child, you know. I didn't want to *bring it up in any way*."

Bringing it up referred to the stomach as well as to speech. There were other levels also to which it could refer, such as the phallus. He could have the fantasy that a part of himself had died, a defective part, and that he was unlike other men, but this material was not present clinically and therefore inadmissible at this point. When and if it did appear, it would be in conjunction with embarrassing, shameful erections, etc.

"Why not?"

"I didn't want to embarrass her or embarrass myself."

"Embarrass?"

"Yes."

"You mean talking about babies?"

"Well, with my mother, yes."

"Why to your mother?"

"My MOTHER?"

He was annoyed by the therapist's apparent stupidity.

"You mean you couldn't talk about such things to her? About babies?"

After a long pause he replied.

"Gee, I even got embarrassed when I told her my wife was pregnant, too."

"Really? When you told mother of such an ordinary event?"

"Yes."

"How come? You mean you never could talk to her about such things?"

"Never talked to her, period!"

"Really!"

The therapist acted as if it were incomprehensible.

"Really."

"Why?"

"That's a good question."

"What do you mean?"

"It's a good question. You know—"

Here he became very emphatic.

"It's a God damn good question. I couldn't talk to her in any respect!"

"What was wrong?"

"Old-fashioned."

He said this as if this explained it all.

"Old-fashioned, in what respect?"

"Well, I mean she was very stubborn. She had her mind set on everything she wanted, you know, her way, in any respect. Like the time I told her, well, I was *afraid to get married*. I was even *afraid to tell her* I was *engaged!*"

In all probability he felt that it was mother who wanted him to be a girl and that he should not have or use his penis or let it come up He felt he had to take the place of the girl baby his bad wishes had killed.

"And when your wife had a baby?"

"I was *afraid* to tell her she was *pregnant!*"

"Afraid of what?"

"AFRAID! AFRAID! AFRAID!"

He shouted, full of anger at his timidity. His symptoms defended him from the realization that he was basically a frightened, timid boy The acceptance of this was too severe a blow to his pride (a narcissistic mortification). The full realization of his over-all fearfulness was the first step in therapy.

"You mean that she wouldn't approve of these things?"

"Yes!"

"About your marrying and going with girls and using your penis?"

"No, no, no, she wasn't afraid of me going with girls but, uh, she didn't like my wife. I know that. She didn't like my wife."

This was another manifestation of his identification with mother Both were afraid. This was also another suggestion that he was hostile towards his wife, at least the mother side of him was. The first hint occurred when he talked of his panic over her "coma." From the point of view of his unconscious, he was responsible for her coma.

"How come?"

He didn't answer so the therapist repeated,

"You have some ideas?"

"I'm trying to, I'm trying to think of the idea why. Uh—"

There was a long pause.

"Well, let's put it this way. My mother's got a phobia that people don't like her. I know that if one of my brothers doesn't call her up twice a week she gets teed off. You know! That is if you don't pay *enough attention* she gets mad about it and she shows it. In other words, I imagine she expected the same type of consideration from her daughter-in-law that she does from her own children, which I try to tell her, remember she's not your child; she's my wife; about my brother's wife, it's the same way, you know? She also doesn't like my brother's wife."

Patients are always talking about themselves in the guise of others Here it is especially revealing. Obviously, this could mean his wife didn't pay enough attention to him and he was jealous of her, his children and his brother's wife. It was easier to let him bring out this material indirectly.

"She didn't want your brother to marry either?"

"No, she didn't like my brother's wife and, uh, she doesn't like my kid brother's wife either."

"Your two brothers?"

"Yes."

"She didn't want you boys to be married?"

The brothers also could be regarded as aspects of himself.

"Well the young one, he was not in a condition to marry, or he *shouldn't* have married. There's no question about that."

"What do you mean?"

"Well, *financially*. He wasn't working and had no job."

"Is that why mother didn't want you to marry, on account of finances?"

Instead of replying he turned his head and belched.

"Food is coming up."

"What do you mean?"

"I just happened to burp and it comes up kind of *sour*. It doesn't taste very good."

The therapist changed the subject to take off the pressure.

"So you weren't very close to mother?"

"Excuse me. What do you mean, close to her? I was very close to my mother."

Now he wanted to deny any and all hostility to any woman. He was a "sissy," a mother's boy.

"You said you couldn't talk to her."

"Oh yes, I couldn't talk to her about, uh, about how to *play ball*. I wanted to play ball in school. I wanted to play *minor-league ball*. I had a chance to go down there."

"You were very close to her but you couldn't talk to her about real boys' problems?"

"I was afraid to tell her I wanted to play ball instead of going to work. I didn't want to go to work. I was afraid to ask her, you know, about things like that. I know she would, you know, *beat me murderously*, if I mentioned anything like that. She'd get *excited* and yell about it and I'd let it go at that."

The symbolism of the bat and ball showed the problem he had with his wife. Marriage for him was all work and not enough play. The word *"murderously"* connected wife and mother and self.

"She used to yell and beat you?"

"Tremendously, yes."

"Really?"

"Yes, really. She had quite a temper really. Yes, a very bad temper."

"What did father do about that?"

"He was as mild as a baby! He did nothing!

"Mother wore the pants?"

"Two pair."

"Two pair?"

This was like two condoms!

"All the time. She was the boss. She was the boss like you're the boss. You know what that means?"

He gave a slight laugh.

"She was the boss. Oh yes. Sure was. She was the head man. Whatever she said went."

He saw the therapist as a strong father to whom he could express his anger at the mother. It was directed at the therapist too but could be deflected to the women easily.

"Is mother still alive?"

"Thank God, yes!"

The therapist suddenly remembered the time was nearly up and returned to the food problem.

"She was a good cook?"

"Excellent. The best." He paused and then said, "But I think my wife is a little better cook, really. Better than my mother. Of course, I recall I could always eat. And I always had a good appetite."

The therapist felt vaguely stymied. Time was running out. The problem of the little girl should have been pursued more intensely. It should be possible to get more knowledge in this area without making him too anxious.

There was a long silence.

"So mother had a girl who died; then she had three boys?"

"Uh, huh, that's right."

He appeared mildly suspicious.

"She never tried again for a girl?"

"I don't know. I DON'T know. That's a good question but can't answer it. I just don't know."

This subject obviously aroused him.

"Because I wondered about what were your ideas?"

"Really it didn't dawn on me."

"You mean you didn't care about having a sister?"

"No!"

He shook his head vigorously.

"Never even dawned on me. Sometimes I think—"

He waited a full minute and then continued.

"I used to care about her having another kid. I used to wonder about it."

"What do you mean?"

"It would be nice to have a girl in the family. Yes, sometimes I wish I had a sister. Something to mull over, you know. It's nice to have a female added to the family."

It was apparent that at one level the female would have been himself.

"Nice to have a female added?"

"A female in the family, somebody you could, you know, fight her battles for her and all that, you know, things like that. Gee, that question hasn't been asked me for a long time."

Who had originally asked him? Could it be that mother with her two pairs of pants had treated him like a little girl?

"You mean if you had a girl in the family you could have taken care of her, fought her battles and been tender with her?"

"That's right."

"Because you didn't have this relation with mother, I take it?"

"Well, my mother was, oh yes, my mother was very tender with us."

His eyes became slightly moist as the other side of mother appeared.

"She was?"

This was said as if it couldn't be believed.

"Yes, always was and still is. But I was just tremendously *afraid of her* and of *different things*, of *everything*. I was *afraid* to break *my glasses* and was *afraid* of being *late* for school, *afraid* of getting a *bad report card*, *afraid* of not *working*."

He was much attracted by the role of a girl yet it filled him with terror. Being *the* girl that mother wanted, and that in part he wanted, meant giving up his penis, being castrated. He had displaced his castration anxiety onto all these substitute activities. From another point of view, he could not accept being mother's little girl. That would be tantamount to accepting the role of a sissy (sister) and a mamma's boy. He secretly wanted a baby girl himself to mother tenderly. At another level, he wanted to be the oedipal boy who saved the poor dying castrated sister and injured mother but was in danger of castration himself by a primitive father. His early concept of father must have been entirely different. These various concepts are not at all contradictory in the unconscious. However, we have to follow the clinical material which will always indicate which of our theories is most important at the time. At present it would seem that at some vital stage he did not get enough tender mothering and later felt that he had to be a girl to get it. He also needed encouragement to defy mother. To do so he would have had to be backed by a strong father with whom he could have identified.

"You mean afraid of mother?"

"Afraid of *mother*, afraid of *everything*. If my *kid brother* broke his glasses, *I'd* get afraid."

This indicated the main problem area. The kid brother was a baby of whom he had been jealous. All babies are "girls" in the sense of passive-receptive things with an insatiable mouth-hole to be filled. The wish to be mother's baby was equated with being mother's girl that wanted to kill and castrate his brother, which is symbolized by "break his glasses." Originally his hatred and murderous wishes had been directed at this rival. The little girl fantasy was a secondary reaction. He envied the little-girl state of being the mother's baby he had been before his brother came along. This was the *real* little girl who had died. The bad mother was responsible, also the bad-boy part of himself. He was jealous of his own babies too and full of unconscious death wishes which "leaked" out in all directions.

"So now the only thing you're afraid of is—?"

"I'm *not afraid of anything*."

The hour was ending. Now it was time to confront him with the material that had been gathered and at a level that he could accept.

"Now you're not afraid of mother any longer, are you?"

"No, I'm old enough not to be afraid of mother."

"So the only thing you appear to be afraid of is a hard piece of meat, or of using your penis and making your wife pregnant, or of your wife or kids dying? Which are you afraid of the most?"

His face flushed.

"I'm not afraid of using my penis!"

"But you said you are scared to death of using it. That's why you put on two rubbers."

"Oh yes, yes, but I'm not afraid of using it. Don't get the wrong idea. I use it like a *baseball bat!*"

This revealed the sadistic fantasies he had in connection with intercourse and referred also to his minor- and major-league fantasies.

"You use it like a baseball bat! What do you mean?"

He squirmed as he talked.

"I'm just kidding. But I use it like any man does. I'm afraid of knocking her up, sure. I just don't want any more children, especially with her being diabetic. I'm *scared*!"

"You mean it might kill her?"

"No!"

His confusion was apparent.

"But then what are you afraid of?"

"I'm afraid of those reactions, those diabetic reactions."

"That's what you said. If you damage her organ and make her pregnant, she might get one and die."

He paused again, struggling with his thoughts.

"No."

"You don't think it would kill her?"

"No! No! I'm not afraid of that."

"You don't think she would die if she had another baby?"

"No, I'm not afraid of that, her dying, no. I'm afraid of the baby coming out deformed *again*."

Now what did he mean by *again*?

"You mean you'd like to have a girl baby but you're afraid it might be a deformed girl or the mother's organ would be damaged?"

Evidently his infantile theory was that one or the other was deformed (castrated). Making babies was a struggle over who kept the pants or penis.

"I'm afraid, yes."

'That's what you mean?"

"That's right. If she should become pregnant under the same circumstances, I believe I would call every hour on the hour to see how she was, no matter where I was."

He would have to reassure himself because of his hostility.

"But I thought you said you wanted a girl?"

"She really wanted a girl. I think I'd like a girl, too."

"So this is your dilemma, huh? You want a girl and she'd like a girl, but if you ever had a girl it would be deformed?"

"It doesn't scare me. I don't want to think about it. I don't want any more kids."

"What do you mean?"

"I don't want any more kids. I'll admit it. Let me put it this way. *What you don't have you don't miss*, is that correct?"

This was a cryptic statement referring to many things, such as a tender, loving relation with his parents and siblings, wife and children, a relation to men and women as a real man who had a big penis, big brain, earning capacity, etc. His present fantasies hid other depression-laden fantasies about his inadequacies.

"But you think about it now and then. You mean you don't miss it all the time."

"Don't miss what all the time?"

"What you're talking about!"

"Well, uh, well let's put it this way. Now that *my kids* are here, I'm thankful to God, but I'm *scared*."

"Scared of what?"

"Well, what might happen to, scared of it. Now that I understand what her reactions are I, uh, I still believe I'd be afraid if I saw in a coma."

"Afraid of her dying?"

"Well, that's what I'd really be afraid of, yes."

"So you're afraid of your wife dying and in a coma, and you're afraid of the kids going around with food in their throats, dying, choking?"

He sensed that the interview was ending and appeared both relieved and sorry.

"Well, I'll tell you. One thing has subsided tremendously. I'm not afraid of the kids choking on their food any more, except when they're crying, or if they are running around with food in their mouth. I I am distinctly afraid of letting my youngsters play with aggies, the baby, or any kind of hard object. *Scared*, really! *Afraid! Afraid! Always afraid!*"

"Are you afraid of everything?"

"I'm not afraid of food."

"Even a hard piece of meat?"

"Even a hard piece of candy. I tell my wife it's so long since I've had any hard candy."

After a long pause he added,

"I'm afraid of it."

"Of a hard piece of meat? Of intercourse? Of someone dying? What?"

"Of a hard piece of candy!"

"In more than one way. Perhaps we will find out why you are so afraid."

"You're right, doctor. Afraid! Afraid! Afraid! I have always been afraid."

"Well, this is all we have time for today. I'll see you Friday, same time?"

"Okay. I'll see you."

In this man whose wife had diabetes, the key words at first referred to food and eating. The associative material led from eating to intercourse and from a relationship with his body to one with his wife, and later one with his mother. (See the following illustration. Key words are italicized.)

afraid to eat .... afraid to have intercourse
afraid of aftereffects .... afraid of aftereffects of intercourse
food *coming up* .... sex and babies and penises coming up
pieces of *meat* .... sex and babies
meat important .... sex and babies important
afraid of food *lying there* .... wife lying there in coma
food *murdering* him .... wife being murdered by sex and babies—babies dying—mother beating him murderously
choking on food and .... balking on sex
baby foods .... girl babies
injured organs (stomach) .... injured womb-penis

The patient ended the interview feeling depressed and stating, "Afraid-afraid-afraid. I have *always* been afraid." Afterwards, eating lost some of its importance and his problems became broadened to include other spheres of his relationships. This highlights the often repeated statement that patients have to face and master their problems, which means feel worse, before they can arrive at better solutions and feel better.

From now on the therapeutic task would demand that we gradually make conscious his confusion and ambivalence in respect to persons, such as—

1. Mother, father and brother in the past, especially mother and the baby brother.

2. Wife and children in the present.

3. *Himself* in the past and present—feminine and masculine parts.

4. *His body*, especially his penis.

5. *Objects* such as food, aggies, nails, etc.

As his ambivalent patterns of relationship in all these areas were developed and integrated, there would be an increase in the ability of the ego to synthesize, reconcile and integrate various contradictory elements; i.e., his ego would become stronger. In some cases of phobia, it is necessary for the therapist to force the patient to face the phobic situation. In this case, the initial symptom was resolved and disappeared without such effort.

Knowledge of a case should extend to all aspects of the total field of relationships of a patient, especially when a case drags on. At these times, a review will often show that an important area relating to the internal or external worlds has not been brought up, although this is not always the case. Frequently the persistence of the patient's symptoms implies merely the need for more time for the process of integration or working through. In most forms of psychotherapy, especially with hospitalized patients, therapists are too dependent upon the statements of their patients, who are seldom able to judge their own capacity to endure anxiety. When insight concerning a pattern of behavior is present in most spheres and the patient is able to cope with his remaining symptoms, he should be prepared for discharge. The ideal of the beginner in therapy that, when skillfully treated, all patients will improve steadily from the beginning and be discharged freed from all their problems and singing a hymn of praise about their saviour, is infrequently realized. When it does occur, we should suspect we have been dealing in transference magic rather than science, and magic is usually very transient in its effects. A rather common occurance is for the patient to continue to complain about his symptoms only when he is questioned about their existence. In these cases, the patient is usually loath to face the problem for which the symptom was a substitute. In hospitalized patients, there is, in the majority of cases, a reluctance to leave the hospital as well as the doctor. In the patient with the food phobias, as his displacements were abolished he was faced with other anxieties relating to such problems as his abilities in his line of work and his difficulties in living up to his ego ideals. This took about four months. He was seen orginally as an inpatient in a hospital. When his anxieties broadened, he became moderately depressed but could be discharged to an outpatient clinic, where he was seen at weekly intervals for two years. At the time of his discharge his fears were quite endurable and concerned the normal uncertainties of life.

In this case, the pathological mourning concerned the father-son and mother-daughter relationship, both of which had become parts of his sadomasochistic masturbatory fantasies. In another sense his passive phallic fixation made active phallic behavior too anxiety laden to be endured and his tough talk only demonstrated an anxious flight from adult masculine behavior.

VII

DIFFERENCES AND SIMILARITIES BETWEEN PSYCHOTHERAPY AND PSYCHOANALYSIS

A Case of Hysteria with Depression

The segment of patients who cannot be treated by classical psychoanalysis is a large, if not the largest, segment of the population. The dynamic psychotherapies by which they can be and are being treated are evolving and still largely done on an ad hoc basis. In some comparisons that have been made between psychoanalysis and the dynamic psychotherapies, it has been said that dynamic psychotherapy offers "an approach as strong, or stronger than psychoanalysis" with "a greater range of applicability"—based upon "new knowledge of ego psychology." Obviously, this judgment must have been made from either case reports in the literature or a consideration of one's own technique in these fields, as nobody knows with the slightest degree of certainty what any individual analyst's technique is like, let alone the technique of various psychotherapies where everyone is a law unto himself. This is therefore a statement which can be neither proved nor disproved. Basically it represents a judgment about one's own methods. It has also been hinted that both the classical analysts and the dynamic psychotherapists accept the *essential principles* of psychoanalysis, i.e., the significance of the childhood history for personality development, the use of the concepts of transference and resistance, and the im-

This chapter contains excerpts from a paper entitled "A Comparison of Psychoanalysis with the Dynamic Psychotherapies," published in *The Journal of Nervous and Mental Disease*, 126:441-450, 1958, and reprinted with the kind permission of the editor

portance of the unconscious as an integral part of the human mind. Therefore, any difference between the two types of therapy is chiefly based on the interpretation of these principles and is only a problem in semantics. While this is certainly true, it must be realized that this still allows for an enormous amount of difference in the fields of analysis and psychotherapy. Many psychoanalysts hold that these "principles" are so broad that they are meanlingless and that there are indeed definitive and actual differences between the two. In their view, the two types of psychotherapy are at the opposite ends of a scale and qualitatively different from each other, with a central area of instances where modified psychoanalytic techniques and those of intensive, dynamic psychotherapy resemble each other. In examining candidates for the American Board of Psychiatry, I found a tendency to explain the difference in vague terms: i.e., in one, the patient is lying down and is seen four to five times a week, and in the other he sits up and is seen only once or twice a week. One doctor volunteered that psychoanalysts are usually concerned with the unconscious and psychotherapists with more "practical" aspects of the patient's difficulties! This is mentioned because it appears to be a widely held belief that, in any technique other than analysis, dealing with the unconscious is impractical. It is hoped that these recorded cases will illustrate the impracticality of *any* approach that *ignores* the unconscious.

Dynamic or insight psychotherapy is considered in the main to be a derivative of psychoanalysis and is practiced by both psychiatrists psychoanalysts with the use of various techniques adapted from psychoanalysis. The varieties of this popular type of therapy are legion in number and name. In all of these procedures an effort is made to elicit a free flow of verbal material which will give the therapist some holistic perspective and understanding of the origin, development and meaning of the symptoms and difficulties which beset the patient. An effort is made during this procedure to communicate a portion of the therapist's understanding to the patient. How and with what additions or deletions these two procedures are carried out is largely dependent upon certain theoretical schemata and premises concerning the nature of the various mental illnesses and the therapeutic, technical devices that are useful in treating them.

For purposes of comparison, psychoanalysis can be considered a method of therapy in which conditions are made favorable for the development of a state called a "transference neurosis," which focuses the present neurotic patterns of relationship on the person of the analyst. The present pattern is considered a regressive restoration of one from the infantile past. It is usually considered that the acute symptomatology has arisen because of some traumatic occurrence, insoluble problem or excruciating dilemma which has aroused to an unendurable pitch certain basic, anxiety-laden, sexual and aggressive fantasies stemming from the infantile past. For practical and clinical purposes, all neuroses, psychoses, etc., may be considered as chronic processes with acute exacerbations; i.e., the symptomatic illness is associated with basic, characteristic attitudes, problems, and attempts at their solution. In the transference neurosis, unconscious memories and relationships become conscious by means of a reliving of the past with understanding. An awareness of unconscious relationship patterns is induced mainly by a systematic interpretation of the resistances of the patient. Finally a resolution of both the transference neurosis and its infantile prototype occurs, accompanied by structural changes in the mental apparatus of the patient which make him capable of a better adaptation to himself and his environment. The development of the transference neurosis is made favorable by a number of technical maneuvers, all of which have the purpose of creating a kind of sensory deprivation which tends to encourage the fantasy creations of the patient. The constancy and continuity of the time of the interviews, the prone position with the analyst out of sight, the neutrality and passivity of the analyst and the observance of the fundamental rule of free association and intellectual honesty are some of the devices which lead to the intensification and development of the transient and initial transference reactions of the patient into a transference neurosis. Interpretation, after a period of preparation and in a transference setting, creates dynamic changes in the patient's mental apparatus and enables the patient's ego to perceive its emotional experiences and its impulses and their vicissitudes at the moment of arousal. The immediacy of these experiences engenders in the patient a conviction of the truth of the interpretations. This is aided by the analyst's cultivation of an artificial splitting of the ego into a critical, observing portion allied with the analyst and sharing somewhat his dispassion and neutrality, and an emotional, experiencing portion. The analytic process also permits a reintegration of the ego at levels other than the regressive one and promotes an enlarged concept of reality, as well as an increased ability to recall the past. Interpretation also aids the resolution of the transference, which is considered the ultimate resistance to change. The termination loss of the analyst also enhances the identification of the patient with elements of the analyst's neutral attitude to the patient's problems.

From this brief summary, it can be realized that the transference interpretation is the chief tool used in the psychoanalytic method of psychotherapy. It can also be realized that the interpreted material is, to a large extent, dependent not only on the nature of the patient's disorder and personality and the production of material by the patient, but also upon the personality and theoretical beliefs of the analyst, as these determine to a large extent what is heard. Therapeutic experience, which is of major importance, is shaped largely by theoretical convictions concerning what is significant in the material produced by the patient. Such convictions play a major role in the important period of preparation that determines whether an interpretation "takes" or is rejected, or is accepted simply as an intellectual curiosity. Thus, if one holds the traditional view that a neurosis is due to infantile losses, denial and repressions, and believes in the libido theory and an unconscious mental life, the main work of the therapeutic situation will consist of undoing resistances, making the unconscious conscious, undoing repressions and reviving the original infantile, sexualized conflict situations as a necessary preliminary to a better adjustment. If one attributes a neurosis simply to the development of anxiety-laden interpersonal relationships in childhood, then highly significant fantasy material in connection with infantile losses, sexuality and the patient's relationship to his own body or the bodies of others, in part or in toto, might well be neglected.

When a resident begins to do psychotherapy, he has little conviction about theory and little experience. Therefore, transference interpretation is difficult, unreliable and too full of guesswork. For this reason, sector therapy substitutes for this procedure one called confrontation. This uses the words and the material produced by the patient. It is realistic in the sense that it depends upon factual productions of the patient which cannot be denied. It is effective, reliable and easy for both doctor and patient inasmuch as the doctor can shift the burden of proof onto the patient who can deny a relationship only by giving more valuable information concerning his defenses.

Theoretically and actually, any or all of the elements referred to in the description of psychoanalysis can and do appear in the dynamic psychotherapies, especially when practiced by analysts. However, as a rule, in the dynamic psychotherapies there is little consistency in the approach and a great variability in both the techniques used and the goals desired. Psychoanalysts are trained in psychoanalytic institutes for three to five or more years in addition to their psychiatric training. There are few psychiatrists using dynamic psychotherapy who have received more than the basic three-year residency training in psychiatry. These are general differences.

There are more specific differences. An important one is that of the role of the therapist. In psychotherapy the therapist tends to be much less of a neutral figure than in psychoanalysis. Due in part to the vis-à-vis position and the infrequent number of sessions, and in part to the uncertainty of his role and technique, the dynamic therapist is inclined towards activity, i.e., teaching, setting an example, proving a point, establishing a friendly atmosphere or developing confidence. This diminishes the free-floating attention characteristic of the psychoanalyst and encourages a greater interest in the *manifest* content of the patient's speech rather than in the unconscious import of his words. This is even more pronounced in the case of the chronic, extensive note taker. There is also a tendency for the dynamic therapist, when facing the patient, to become a reality object in the eyes of the patient. This tends to complicate the development of the various transference states. Some analysts believe a transference neurosis seldom occurs or appears minimally in the majority of dynamic psychotherapies. This is highly debatable. Actually many patients who should be treated by analysis from a psychically economic point of view are treated in psychotherapy only because they cannot find or afford an analyst, and a transference neurosis of great intensity can develop in some patients on a two- or three-times-a-week basis. In sector psychotherapy, transference problems can cause considerable difficulty. There are times in any brand of psychotherapy when transference cannot be ignored and must be interpreted. In dynamic psychotherapies the therapist-patient relationship is frequently made obscure by many forms of activity of a highly complex significance, ranging from the offering of cigarettes to the exchange of gifts. Positive transference states are encouraged and maintained as useful adjuncts to the therapeutic process. Psychoanalysis considers such states as a resistance to be ultimately analyzed in order to encourage the patient's autonomy and free him from infantile dependency needs projected on his therapist. In psychotherapy these needs may remain hidden or not focus upon the therapist or become so violent or ambivalent that they will not respond to treatment. Analysis basically is dependent upon the existence of a well-operating and mainly intact ego. This often is not the case in psychotherapy. There is a general tendency in psychotherapy for symptoms to change, but to persist in a chronic form as the underlying infantile neurosis expressed in the transference states cannot be resolved. Psychoanalysis is the only form of therapy that consistently analyzes the transference in all of its aspects and attempts to resolve it, believing that its continued existence interferes with the final resolution of the infantile neurosis. This is not a slap at psychotherapy, because some infantile neuroses simply cannot be resolved by psychoanalysis or any other form of therapy based upon the present state of our knowledge. One of the earliest fallacies to be dropped by the beginner is that all cases can be cured by the right kind of therapy. This is often an overidealized form of psychoanalysis. This impossibility of cure should not deter us from attempting to do more with the tools at our disposal.

Another aspect of an increased attention to the reality problems engendered by the vis-à-vis position and the tendency toward active measures and manipulative techniques on the part of dynamic psychotherapists is the development of complications in the working through of important pathogenic material. Psychotherapy in general is sometimes described as a process whereby a complex series of projective and introjective relationships of an individual are gradually untangled. Stress upon reality elements of the type mentioned above and the use of manipulative techniques dim the perception of projective-introjective relationships considerably. This is especially the case with therapists of limited experience in the recognition of the great extent of every patient's projections. In fact, while experienced therapists and analysts can experiment with manipulative techniques, beginners should avoid them, as they can be too easily confused by the complexity of the situations that develop. The non-manipulative techniques must be learned first. They are easier and more rewarding in insight for both the patient and the therapist.

As a rule, the goal of dynamic psychotherapy is symptom removal or reduction in symptom intensity, and only secondarily character change. The lack of a clear-cut transference neurosis that can be used from the point of view of obtaining effective interpretative results, coupled with infrequent sessions and the stress on reality elements, reduces the chances of deep personality changes in most cases of psychotherapy. Whether this applies to those types of psychotherapy that are used by analysts or by well-trained or gifted persons who use extensively the techniques of psychoanalysis and see the patient over a long period of time is, of course, debatable. A great deal also depends upon what happens in the patient's reality world outside of therapy. New opportunities may appear, and slight changes in the patient may permit him to use them. This is particularly so in those fortunate cases that are enabled to find and accept a satisfactory love object. In these cases, the progress in therapy of any type can be exceedingly rapid. Usually in these cases the therapist is perfectly willing to take all the credit and minimize the element of plain luck.

The neutrality of the analytic technique is seldom practiced in dynamic psychotherapy. Therapists untrained in psychoanalysis and unanalyzed themselves tend to try to "convert" their patients. Frequently they get annoyed or uneasy when a patient is quite religious, socially snobbish or racially biased and waste much time poking into irrelevant areas and attempting deep character analysis when only simple symptom removal or change is indicated. The analyst reflects the patient's individuality and does not seek to remold him in accordance with his own ideals. The analyst avoids giving advice and instead attempts to arouse the patient's initiative. The inability to make use of his "personality" at times puts a limitation on the immediate effectiveness of the analyst's work. The analyst also does not attempt to act as teacher, model or ideal to his patients. Such behavior is more in the realm of dynamic psychotherapy as there are many types of cases that need and can profit from such pedagogic influences. Often psychotherapy of this type can be and is used as a preliminary for psychoanalysis.

Classical psychoanalytic technique is intended primarily for the treatment of certain types of cases. Owing to what has been called the "widening scope" of psychoanalysis, the classical psychoanalytic technique has been used with cases for which it was not originally intended, e.g., in some cases with severe regressive features or certain character types prone to develop such features. Such cases may call for the modification of the classical technique or fall within the realm of the dynamic psychotherapies. However, this is not a reason for modifying the classical technique in all cases or the theories upon which it is based.

Although interpretation is the basic tool of psychoanalysis, there are many patients suffering from grave ego weaknesses in which this tool must be supplemented by advice, command, prohibition, suggestion, etc. Such cases may or may not be treated by minor modifications of the classical technique. Eissler calls any modification of the basic tool of interpretation a parameter; i.e., a common parameter used by Freud with phobic patients was the advice or command that the patient, after a preparatory analysis, expose himself to the phobic situation. Eissler (1953) has laid down four rules for the use of a parameter which he feels allow for a scientific evaluation and exact description of any deviation from the basic psychoanalytic techniques. These are as follows:

1. A parameter must be introduced only when the original technique does not suffice and must never go beyond the unavoidable minimum.

2. It can be used only when it leads to self-elimination.

3. The final phase of treatment must proceed with no parameter.

4. The effect on the transference relationship must never be such that it cannot be abolished by interpretation.

Eissler feels that any parameter increases the possibility that the therapeutic process may be falsified inasmuch as it may offer the patient's ego the possibility of substituting transient obedience or adjusted behavior states for a structural change in the mental organization. The nonobservance of such rules allows the dynamic psychotherapist to enjoy many clinical successes that the analyst cannot obtain; i.e., the proper psychoanalytic technique works against much heavier resistances than the more versatile, catch-as-catch-can techniques of psychotherapy. Every introduction of a parameter increases the danger that a resistance has been only temporarily removed rather than analyzed. Eissler gives the impression of being theoretically vague and somewhat precious in this instance. Clinical success is important. This is what analysis and psychotherapy have been primarily devised for. Changes in mental organization are useless unless linked with clinical success provided these terms are understood correctly. The concept of clinical success is more complex than it appears at first glance, and will be discussed in chapter XI in some detail.

In the classical neuroses, i.e., of the hysterical, phobic or compulsive types, and with the classical analytic technique, a transference neurosis usually tends to develop spontaneously. In the psychoses and the narcissistic neuroses or so-called borderline conditions, transference reactions are unpredictable and a transference neurosis when it occurs is a tenuous, unstable thing which often must be aided, induced or produced by specific actions, gestures or words. It can easily be lost sight of, remain undetected, or fail to develop. The therapeutic situation must frequently be manipulated to preserve any positive transference state that occurs. The introduction of "parameters" is ordinarily more within the province of dynamic psychotherapy or the so-called modified psychoanalytic techniques which cannot be separated very well from the dynamic psychotherapies, simply because the few case reports where "parameters" were used have been inadequately described and evaluated. Anyone who has done much listening to the differences between the statements of therapists about their procedures and their recorded interviews will suspect that any therapist or analyst would have little difficulty finding "parameters" by the score in a recording of any of their own and their colleagues' sessions with patients. In the case of analysts, however, most of these would be inconsequential owing to training and experience.

The psychotherapist in many respects is in an advantageous position as compared to the analyst. His behavior can be readily modified to suit changing circumstances or behavior on the part of the patient. He can be active rather than neutral; he can limit his goals; he does not have to foster a regressive transference neurosis; he can be flexible in his techniques; and he can take on practically any type of case he wishes, and if transference complications do develop he can manipulate circumstances to suite any exigencies that arise. In the case of a "weak" or "fragmented" ego, he can act a role, provide support and manipulate the environment as much as is possible. Symptom amelioration, resolution of a crisis and assistance through troubled periods may be the only goal of the dynamic therapist, or his goal may be as ambitious as that of the psychoanalyst; i.e., he may seek to change or modify the patient's characteristic outlook upon life. There is nothing to prevent this. However, the nearer the goals approximate those of analysis, the more likely the therapist is to run into technical difficulties for the elimination of which the classical technique of psychoanalysis was devised. At such times the best knowledge, experience and inherent psychotherapeutic skill may be severely strained. It is obvious that in this area modifications of psychoanalysis may blend with psychotherapy. Undoubtedly advances in technical skills may come from the efforts of the dynamic psychotherapists in the realm of so-called deep psychotherapy, provided that a careful account is kept of the technique employed. No psychoanalyst will ever claim that the last word has been said about either theory or technique in a realm as vast as psychotherapy. The objection is to the substitution of the guess and pseudo-intuitive technical devices for tested standards of technique, and semantic quicksands for a precise and working technical vocabulary. The primary aim of much of the technique of psychoanalysis is to *prevent* complications from developing rather than to handle them afterwards.

It may be that as more psychiatrists are trained in the basic theoretical concepts and techniques of psychoanalysis, and as more research is done with various types of psychotherapy, new and more efficient methods will supplant the classical psychoanalytic technique, especially in the treatment of serious behavior problems and the psychoses. At this moment, however, nothing startling has occurred. The use of hypnosis, narcosis, tranquilizing and potentiating drugs, physical therapies and mechanical devices, such as the tape recorder, have added little to the effectiveness of individual psychotherapy, and even less to our knowledge of mental disease. Here I am not speaking of acute symptom modification, where many of the newer tranqulizing agents have proved effective, although even here the modification of symptoms may be more transient than the early reports and the advertisements of the various drug firms would lead us to believe. As dynamic theories postulate that the neurotic's and the psychotic's symptoms are the logical result of a pathological way of life, it will be of great interest to observe the complications of behavior that may arise and are inherent in the modification of symptoms by chemical means. This is especially so in connection with psychosomatic illness. In the case of the psychoses, the use of chemical agents has permitted therapy to take place on an outpatient basis. They have actually increased the use and value of psychotherapy rather than become a substitute for it.

It is obvious that the more the technique of psychotherapy approximates the ideals, if not the practice, of psychoanalysis, and the more the psychotherapist is well-grounded in the theories, techniques and types of experience of the psychoanalytic school, the more difficult it will be to distinguish the procedures and results. Eissler (1953) has formulated the belief of many psychoanalysts in his statement that "psychoanalytic scrutiny will disclose that the majority of cures by psychotherapy have been based on elaborate rationalizations which depend for their effectiveness on what is dynamically a repression of the basic conflict after some partial solutions of derivative conflicts have been attained and accepted as a compromise." In this sense psychotherapy has simply effected "a change in the content of the neurosis or a rechannelization of libidinal energy based on displacement, or has led to a new repression, or an exchange of illusions, the building up of magic beliefs or the development of an imitation of health." Of course such "cures" may be extremely worthwhile, lasting in effect and economically more feasible than results obtained in analysis. Whether or not an ego incapable of psychoanalytic modification is also incapable of any other kinds of change than those mentioned previously has not as yet been ascertained. The criticisms mentioned are applied mainly to the briefer and more superficial psychotherapies. In one sense they are a reaction to what Gill (1954) terms "the glib claims of those who measure the therapeutic results in terms of symptoms and (social) adjustment and overlook at what cost to and limitations of the ego." Obviously, again we have a problem in evaluation.

In skilled hands or with experienced and gifted therapists, many psychotherapeutic techniques carried on over extensive periods of time can achieve outstanding results; however, the theoretical explanation of such results can easily be defective due to bad reporting and unsolved or emotionally based attitudes and countertransference problems on the part of the therapist.

Bibring (1954) has approached the problem of the differentiation of the psychotherapies from the most practical point of view. He has distinguished five different groups of basic therapeutic techniques: (1) the suggestive; (2) the abreactive; (3) the manipulative; (4) the clarifying and (5) the interpretative. These are employed in various mixtures in all of the therapies. There are also five basic curative agents related to these techniques: (1) induced beliefs, impulses or actions, etc., brought about by suggestion; (2) relief from acute tension brought about by abreaction; (3) learning through experiences brought about by manipulation, and (4) and (5) insight brought about by clarification and interpretation respectively. He distinguishes four major types of activities in the psychotherapeutic process: (1) the production of material; (2) the use of the produced material (mainly by the therapist); (3) the assimilation by the patient of the results of this use; and (4) the process of reorientation and readjustment. The various curative agents can be used in a technical sense to promote the treatment process or to produce therapeutic changes, although as a rule the two procedures overlap; i.e., suggestions can be used to produce dream material or be used directly to remove a symptom. Clarification refers to preconscious material on the periphery of awareness, whereas interpretation refers exclusively to repressed or otherwise warded-off material. In general, and in analysis particularly, it represents a prolonged process preceded by a period of preparation, meeting unconscious resistance and followed by a period of working through. Interpretation differs dynamically from clarification and initiates a reorientation of the personality resulting in efficient solutions of the basic infantile, as well as derivative, conflicts. Although psychoanalysis makes use of all the above mentioned principles, insight through the transference interpretations is the main therapeutic tool. In the various dynamic psychotherapies, a change in the selection or combination of therapeutic principles implicitly goes along with a change of goals; i.e., clarification can be stressed and combined with manipulation as in Rogers' client-centered therapy or abreaction can be stressed as in various procedures employing hypnosis or intravenous barbiturates. As a second differentiating point, the various dynamic psychotherapies tend to modify one or more of the therapeutic processes and procedures of analysis in an effort to accelerate therapy. The *production* and the *use* of material by the therapist are the processes most easily modified, and the processes of *assimilation* and *readjustment* are the ones most difficult to change. It is of great interest that the activities which accelerate the production of material tend on the whold to interfere with the assimilation of it by the patient. In fact this is one of the difficulties that occurs in any attempt to abbreviate the psychoanalytic method of psychotherapy.

Bibring feels that in most current dynamic psychotherapies there is a shift from insight through interpretation to experiential manipulation and an attempt to alter the theory of the neurosis by reviving the original trauma theory of Freud and replacing the concept of repression by that of dissociation.

One can readily agree with the idea that a short psychotherapy based on psychoanalytic knowledge would be of great value. Alexander (1954) feels that an analyst should be able to establish a dynamic diagnosis which would enable him "to predict with a certain degree of probability what the patient's reaction to certain measures will be." Thus, "combinations of limited interpretations, provocation of certain types of transference, provision of well-chosen substitute outlets, alteration of the environment, suggestions or prohibitions of unconsciously tempting or reassuring situations or activities, the verbalizing of actual conflicts and advice about mental hygiene can very well be systematized." This appears easier on paper than in actual practice. Actually too few reports of cases of dynamic psychotherapy by analytically trained therapists are available, especially where the technique is clearly described and thus available for criticism and duplication. To my knowledge, the sector therapy of F. Deutsch is the only one of this type that is based on the theoretical postulates of classical psychoanalysis. In this case a therapeutic maneuver midway between clarification and interpretation has been described, called confrontation. An overconcern with results and the tendency to report only successfully treated cases in all forms of therapy often confuse the issues. The great majority of analysts agree that insights through interpretation is the main curative factor in psychoanalysis and the experiential manipulation in or outside the transference setting serves the secondary role of a "fixative" as in photography.

The most outstanding characteristic of the dynamic psychotherapies is not the lack of interpretation but the neglect of the period of preparation and the working-through process. In these preparatory phases leading to insight through interpretation, both clarification and confrontation may be used freely. In one sense, clarification and confrontation deal with partial relationships. Interpretation can be conceived as related to inductive reasoning. It supplies a missing factor which permits the comprehension of a relative totality of relationships. Although interpretation may be used in some of the dynamic psychotherapies, a lack of training, experience or a coherent theory creates a tendency to cut short this vital period of preparation. If and when this occurs, an interpretation may then be accepted on the basis of logic or suggestion and the positive transference, but such an acceptance tends to be an evanescent and superficial one.

A detailed analysis of the defenses and resistances involved in working through is seldom if ever accomplished in the dynamic psychotherapies and some types of psychotherapy called psychoanalysis. Depending upon the theoretical background of the therapist, certain spheres of relationship may be slighted or ignored, and these spheres may contain the key to the patient's deep feelings. Such evasions militate against what Alexander calls "total interpretations." All interpretations should include as many spheres of relationship as possible.

A question that is now frequently raised concerns the necessity of a regressive transference neurosis. The answer to this is dependent upon the goals and the type of case. Alexander asks whether or not transference is an attempt at belated mastery of an unsolved conflictual situation or a regressive evasion of a present-day reality situation, and then gives the correct answer, that both aspects are present in various combinations. He then asks how can one counteract the regressive evasion portion of the transference, and proposes certain manipulative techniques. To this the classical analyst might reply that unfortunately both aspects of the transference neurosis are inextricably conjoined and that the best weapon for solving such a problem is the transference interpretation preceded by the type of preparation and working through that have been mentioned. Actually, the appearance of the so-called regressive transference neurosis is only one indication of a general regressive tendency on the part of the patient in dealing with all spheres of his relationships. What has been covert is now in the open and available for inspection by both analyst and patient. The persistent regressive tendencies of all patients are present in psychotherapy as well as analysis but are more hidden, and part of the therapeutic task is uncovering them. Analysis here has the definite advantage of unmasking these regressive tendencies in a more convincing manner, chiefly through the medium of the transference.

To illustrate the difference between analysis and psychotherapy based upon psychoanalytic theory, we will listen to another initial interview which found a patient quite ready for a whole series of insights which helped her temporarily to reorient her life. Occasionally a patient comes into therapy who is ready for this kind of insight. It is not true that patients do not profit from experience. Life teaches us a great deal, but for some it is too little and too late to be useful. As in all healing arts, psychoanalysis and psychotherapy simply hasten and intensify tendencies in the direction of mental health which are too feeble or too overwhelmed to assert themselves. In sector psychotherapy, the technique remains the same. We go back into the past as soon as possible in order to understand the present. We look for broad patterns of behavior, link and integrate material, and, most important, we take advantage of our opportunities.

Carol Ann Pepper was unable to work, eat or sleep. She couldn't bear the sight of the office and the pity of her girl friends. She was a tall, well-proportioned blonde girl with her hair done up in a heavy braid and looped neatly over her head. She walked erect and firm-footed with an aggressive tilt to her chin, but there was a softness and fullness to her mouth and her gestures were quite feminine. Since her divorce, which was only a month behind her, she had been depressed and anxious and often found herself sobbing uncontrollably, which annoyed her, so that by the time she stopped she could hardly decide whether she was crying in anger over her behavior or from grief. Her doctor had first given her tranquilizers to help her work and Seconal to help her sleep, but her depression had only deepened until by the time he suggested a psychiatrist she was more than willing to comply. When she entered the psychiatrist's office, she was quite composed and without a trace of false modesty, guilt or shame. Taking the indicated chair, she glanced around and remarked:

"My, what a beautiful office."

The therapist smiled.

"Come right in. Sit down. Your doctor has told me a little bit about your problem but not too much."

She nodded quietly.

"All right, Doctor. Well, the reason I, well probably, I guess, maybe what brought this on was my leaving so spontaneously and then coming back yesterday. I just walked out, and I walked out on my doctor and I wouldn't blame him for wanting to crown me. It was just that up until yesterday I have never been able to face the fact that I really was getting a *divorce*. I just, I've been *fighting other persons, hating* them and everything else because I just couldn't believe it. I didn't, I don't know, everybody else was wrong but Dick."

She began to cry.

"I was wrong, everybody else was wrong but Dick and after all it was the first time. It was just like I got *cut*, you know, just baldly and bluntly but it was *cut*, you know."

A divorce represents the loss of a projection of part of oneself, an alter-ego figure. It is a *cut* at many levels. The analyst would be placed on guard for material concerning disguised castration fantasies with feelings of rage and hate ensuing.

The therapist looked sympathetic.

"Cut?"

"I married a man, a soldier, that I met in the service."

"When was this?"

"This was back in 1946, no!"

She paused uncertainly.

"My gracious, this is 1950, 1948."

"Two years ago?"

"It will be two years this June, that's right, and so, uh, we were separated immediately, uh, because he was so *young*."

"How old was he?"

This was a variation of "What do you mean?"

"He was twenty-four then, now he's twenty-six."

"And you?"

She paused before answering.

"I will be thirty-five in May."

"This coming May?"

"That's right."

The therapist gave no sign that he recognized the age discrepancy or considered it important. Her readiness to burst into tears was apparent. Her readiness to emote in one form or another very quickly and her deep involvement in a situational difficulty of a sexual nature warned the therapist to expect the type of difficulty associated with hysterical syndromes. Emotional commitments in the present prevent awareness of the role of the past and perspective in depth.

"And then you were thirty-three?"

"Then I was thirty-three, that's right."

"And he was twenty-four?"

"Yes, he was twenty-four."

The difference was treated as unimportant for the moment.

"So there was just eight years difference?"

"Yes, eight years difference."

"But you say you separated because he was too young?"

She looked pained at being reminded of the cut.

"Well, Dick had a very *abnormal* home life. His father and his mother were, his father had been in the Army and his mother had persuaded him to get out. He was very miserable. That's one reason, no matter what, I really admired Dick. I always will because I, I thought when I married him nobody would be able to be a better Army wife than another WAC."

Her eyes became moist.

"Than another WAC?"

"Than a WAC. I was a WAC in the service. I was an officer, a WAC, but Dick was a private, and their tour of duty is three years at an overseas base for one here, which is a very *abnormal* existence. I think that is probably why the Army has the highest divorce rate of any of the services and I think percentagewise of probably any group of people. I think I read something where servicemen, particularly Army, and salesmen are supposed to have the highest divorce rate. You know it is because of the extremely *abnormal* conditions under which family life is trying to operate."

The therapist was caught by surprise over the slip about "another WAC." He realized it immediately. The word "abnormal" would be best for exploration. It had been repeated three times. This type of emphasis on key words often gives away the nucleus of a complex.

"You said he had an *abnormal* background?"

"Well, his mother persuaded his father to get out of the Army. The man was very *unhappy* and never was able to find the kind of job that he really wanted, and he had loved the Army very much, and I don't think, I think subconsciously he never forgave her for that, you know, and I think that Dick was always *afraid*. I know we both were. He went into marriage *terrified* that he was going to end up like his father because his father lived a very *unhappy* life, took to drink. When he was in the service, he did, took money from the commissary, took supplies and was finally *kicked out* with a *bad conduct* discharge, and Dick was absolutely convinced that he would never ever, that that wasn't going to happen to him come hell or high water, you know. So he went into marriage, I think, subconsciously *terrified* of what a woman could, what he thought a woman could do to a man because he had seen it, and I went in for exactly the same reason."

It was clearly apparent that Dick was an alter ego, but it was important not to take any insight on her part for granted. All patients tend to stress their insights to their therapist and to themselves.

"How do you mean?"

"I was *terrified* of him because of what I had seen in my family of what a man could do to a woman because my father and mother have never slept together since I know."

Her voice became tremulous.

A therapist must listen to *words* as well as sentences. Oft-repeated and affect-laden words have a continuity and meaning beyond that concerning the object they are attached to. The italicized words tell a story about the *patient* as well as her husband and his parents. She must have been unhappy, terrified and afraid as a little girl about her parents' marriage and what they were doing to one another. All kinds of defenses were used to deny this, especially the sexual elements. The defense begins with a denial that they ever had relations!

There was nothing to do, as this non sequitur itself demanded an explanation without too much interference by the therapist.

"Really!"

"That's right."

She crossed her legs tightly and seemed reluctant to talk, so the therapist smiled and said,

"But they must have once."

"For Frannie and I, but I mean since I can remember. I never ever once in my life, when we first moved to California, when I was the age of five, so it must have been when I was around five or six, only once did I ever see my father and mother in bed together. You know, kids like to come in in the morning; just once, never since then have I ever."

Her voice became low.

"And I know, I mean I know they have never slept together. They are two of the most, I mean my father was very *strong*. I think probably he was born that way and bachelors run in the family. I mean we have two. There were two bachelor uncles who didn't marry until they were in their late fifties or sixties."

"Father was strong?"

"Father was, that's right. He could *do without*."

Hidden behind this innocent appearing statement were probably elements of a primal scene and evidence of a repression of all sexuality on her part. The therapist wondered whether to continue with this theme, and decided it would be premature. Here the problem was to delay and dilute her emotions rather than to intensify them.

"You didn't tell me, you have a sister?"

"Yes, I have a sister."

"Just the two of you?"

"That's right, just the two of us."

"And she's younger?"

"She's younger, that's right."

"How many years?"

"Two and a half, and my mother had her because she was bound and determined that I was not going to be an only child. She had been an only child, so that wasn't going to happen to me come hell or high water, and all of our lives she tried to make Frannie and I so *close*. Well, we just *never were*, that's all. The more she tried to push us together, why, well we are happier as sisters, probably as happy as we ever will be, get along, we do better if we are far apart."

This was an attempt to make believe mother had a baby just for her. There was too much envy. When two children of the same sex are in a family, one tends to be more masculine in relation to the other. This can be due to their parents or to their own wishes. The younger of two girls would find the feminine passive position easier to maintain. The therapist now felt she was possibly hinting about the "other WAC" and the "abnormal life," but this material was too loaded. He continued cautiously.

"Why didn't you get along together? What was wrong?"

"With Frannie and I? I don't know, just personalities or something, both of us."

"You never got along?"

"Well, I can't say we never got along. We just never had very much in common. We weren't close. I never *confided* in Frannie and she never confided in me. When we were kids, we *fought* and scrapped a great deal, but when we got older it was more of an acceptance of ach other, you know. There was *no real closeness.* There never has een amongst any of the members of my immediate family."

Her eyes filled with tears again.

"You weren't close to anyone?"

"No, no never. I've *cried* all my life. I've never been able to *confide* n anybody."

Her lips trembled. The doctor decided to shift to another area and et her emotions subside for a while.

"And your parents also? You said father and mother never slept ogether?"

"No."

"Why?"

"Because, uh, my mother was of a very affectionate nature and she vanted love and affection and intercourse, which is a symbol of love nd affection and, uh, my father—I think *intercourse* just absolutely urned his *stomach.* I really do."

She said this in a matter-of-fact manner with no reservations.

"What makes you think this?"

"Because of the, because of, for one thing, sex couldn't be mentioned n our family *at all, never, ever!* The only thing, well I found out he actual facts of life at *eighteen* and from a *smutty paper,* and it ust left me sick!"

She became indignant at the thought. There was a feminine side f her like mother and a masculine side like father. What had sickened he father part?

"What do you mean a smutty paper?"

"Oh, I mean, it was some kind of a, oh, I don't know, something on, can't even remember. All I can remember is the feeling I had after eading it."

This is one of the problems in hysteria. Only feelings are remem- ered, which constantly demand objects for their discharge.

"A newspaper, you mean?"

"Oh, no, no, no, it was, oh, a college something, it was a typewritten hing. I think it was supposed to be a joke or funny, or something, and had gone down to a girl's room to pick up some history notes, and he was out of the room and this was on her desk and I thought it as the notes and I picked it up and I started reading and I was so umbfounded I kept on, and I was just *nauseated!* I think that had n effect on me that took me months to get over."

"Nauseated" was a key to her identification with her father. It was empting to probe and find out what it was and if it was abnormal.

Nausea also suggested an oral sucking and licking fantasy but i
would be terribly premature and would probably be met by an "I for
get." The best line would be the time axis. So far the material coulc
be "tied up" only by the theory that she envied her baby sister'
position and oral satisfactions with mother, had hated her and turnec
to father and masculine goals and fantasies.

"You were eighteen and you had no knowledge?"

She nodded again emphatically.

"All my mother ever told me was don't sit on a *boy's lap* and neve
slide down the bannister, period! No reason why, I know nothing.
did just what she said and I never had any trouble with men at all i*
that way. I mean, I knew, if I ever did, I, boy! I just got *rid of him*
got *rid of them* some way or other. I mean I just didn't know and
just didn't much care, *I don't know*. I mean it never even really entere(
my head much, one way or the other. I can't explain it. I know whe*
I was a kid one of the first things I wanted to know was where a *co*
got its calf* and I wanted to get *The Book of Knowledge* so I coul(
find out, but the folks instead of, like it would seem to me the *norma*
thing to do was maybe use that as a slight opening wedge to futur*
knowledge or something. Why they just laughed and *cut it off* and
well as I said, gee I was the joke of the crowd when I was sixteen
The *remarks* would go around and it was just as though I didn*
know why or what they were even talking about!"

Mother had forbidden her to become conscious of a penis or t*
masturbate. She got rid of all phallic sexual thoughts. The curiosit
about the cow referred to her sister's birth.

"What remarks do you mean?"

"Well, I remember once this boy I was going with, the first boy
was ever really fond of, that was when I was sixteen, and there wa
a gang of us up on a front porch of a girl's house, you know, ther
were a whole gang of us and we were talking about love and every
thing and how to plan a house and all that, so little Carol pipes u*
with her great big loud voice for God and everybody to hear an*
said, 'Well, when I get married I'm going to have my own room a*
by myself, that's one of the joys of being married,' or something lik
that."

This was like her parents. She wanted to keep father and mothe
apart in one sense. There was an opportunity now for a superficia
comparison.

"You mean like mother?"

"That's right. Oh, I didn't know it then but that was my idea of the way it should be done."

"The way mother had it?"

"That's the way mother had it and daddy had it. Frannie and I had to *share a room* and I didn't think that was so much fun. She and I, I mean I always thought oh that would be wonderful to have your *own room*. Well, so everybody looked around at everybody else and I could see I had made a faux pas in some way but I didn't know why."

At another level (oedipal) she wanted a mother and later a father of her own. She was protesting her innocence too much. The doctor decided to test this thought.

"But you had already seen your parents in bed when you were five, you said."

"But that was just that one time, never since."

"But what did you feel then when you saw them?"

"I didn't even think."

"You didn't even think?"

"No, I didn't think about it one way or the other, no. I mean your folks can do no *wrong* when you are a child!"

It was hard to tell whether or not there was an element of sarcasm in this statement. Apparently it was not conscious. Wrong must refer to sex.

"You saw them having intercourse?"

"Oh, no! Oh, heavens never! I can't even imagine such a thing! Children seeing their family? Well, I don't know, maybe—"

Her voice died away.

"You said you walked in on them?"

"Well, this was early in the morning when they were stretched out in bed with the covers over them, and that's all. You know just as if they had waked up out of a sleep or something."

"And you wondered then?"

"Never!"

She answered abruptly, paused and then continued.

"Nothing ever entered my head in that way at all to wonder or even think anything about it one way or the other until I, well, I guess perhaps when my sister got married. Then it started to percolate."

Theoretically she had begun with hate for her rival and probably shifted to the more masculine role, and then cared for her and felt hurt by her marrying. It was not only an insult to the feminine side of her ego but the loss of a sister. Perhaps it was this loss that set off the abnormal reaction.

"How old were you then?"

"Well, let's see. Frannie got married when she was twenty-five, so that would have made me about twenty-eight."

"But you had already learned about sex at eighteen?"

"Well, I had read that paper and everything, but as I say it only had some sort of a sickening effect on me."

"That was about intercourse?"

"Yes, but I mean, it just made me slightly ill."

"I don't understand, you mean the description of intercourse made you ill?"

"Yes, I *guess* that was what it was."

She frowned.

"Really!"

"Certainly it did at the time."

She paused.

"But I was only eighteen and I had never known anything about it before."

"Well, I wondered, why should it make you ill?"

"I don't know. It just did, probably my nature because I don't know, I *never* have cared for *dirty* stories. I just don't care for them"

"You mean even before then?"

"Even before then and since then. It's just my nature."

It would be better to know more about the past so the doctor tried to get her there.

"You mean before that you had heard?"

"No, no, I never had!"

"You had never?"

"No. If I had, I didn't know because I didn't know enough about it."

"So you feel if your parents had slept together and if they had let you be educated in *The Book of Knowledge*, it would have been better?"

She paused.

"Well, that I don't know."

"I wondered, because you said that they never did, you seem to feel that there was something wrong. As you say, you felt they were abnormal, just like Dick's family."

"Well, isn't it considered normal for people to sleep together?"

The doctor ignored this attempt to take away the initiative.

"You feel it would have been better if they had?"

"I think probably there would have been a warmer atmosphere in the house."

"And then you feel it would have been a better atmosphere?"

"In which to bring up children, yes."

All this was too general and needed emphasis on the specific.

"That would have helped, you feel, in *your problems?*"

"I think I would have been more *secure* or *something*, I mean, I think that, uh, why I just think maybe I would have, probably I think I would have had more *confidence* with *men* than I did have."

"You didn't have any?"

Her confidence had been undermined *first* by feelings of rejection as a baby by mother and *second* by rejection as a girl by the father. *Third*, her hate and rage had led to a whole series of sadomasochistic fantasies about relationships between the sexes which made her anxious.

"I had a sort of, uh, *artificial*, I guess you might say, *confidence.*"

"How do you mean?"

"Well, I mean, I did outside as far as being gay and charming and attractive and everything else, you know. The minute anybody got *seriously* interested in me I'd break if off some way, *subconsciously*. I would just erect a *barrier* like that. I'd make a wrong remark or something would happen, but invariably they would just drift away. I've always been like the belle of the ball or something like that, but for a guy to get *serious* then I would just sort of back away."

Her narcissism had been seriously wounded by her "rejection" by first mother and then father. A *serious* affair would have revived the old angry and depressed feeling gestalts and lead to forbidden awareness of sexual feelings too. She could not *trust* anyone or believe they could really care for *her.*

"So even at twenty-eight then, you say, when your sister got married, you gave it some serious thought—what do you mean by that?"

"Well, I certainly didn't dwell on it or anything, I mean, it just suddenly, Frannie and Tom went shopping for a double bed so I thought, well I guess that's the right thing to do. I didn't think much more about it one way or the other. It's never really been too much of a problem one way or the other."

"You mean with Dick?"

"No, it wasn't with Dick, no!"

"What do you mean?"

"Dick was a very wonderful man, very kind and very understanding. The most wonderful man I ever went out with in my life."

"You mean you didn't mind sleeping with him?"

"No, I didn't mind it. Do you mind if we didn't, I mean I would rather not, I, I you are getting a little *close to home* so soon."

She burst into tears. This had a double meaning which was unconscious to her.

"I don't understand. Could you explain?"

"It's very hard to put feelings into words, Doctor. This is very hard."

The therapist felt, however, that this material was easier on her than the abnormal material about the sister.

"But I don't understand. You separated because he was so young and you say you separated from him right away. How did it happen that you married such a young man?"

"Because I fell in love with him."

This young man was a masculine version of herself.

"You mean you fell in love with him before you erected these barriers. With Dick it was different?"

"Yes, because Dick kept coming back. He didn't go away. He scaled the barriers."

"And you felt that was because he had the same kind of a family or what?"

"He had grown up in an abnormal atmosphere. Yes, I think he was looking for love just as much as any normal human being."

"Well, of course, but you mean more than any normal—because you said he was different from the rest?"

"He was just a little bit more determined that I was the answer to his, that he wanted me for his wife more than the others were. The others weren't that determined."

"And you feel you had something in common because of the parental setup? You feel that his parents didn't sleep together either?"

"No, I don't know anything about that. That I really, I can truthfully say I don't know anything about it. I know they were *separated* because for a while he would be in the Army and then they'd *fight* and then they'd go *back together* and then they'd *fight* again, and so I can assume that it was an *abnormal* atmosphere in that they were *parting* and *separating*, and *parting* and *separating* so much."

To the therapist it was apparent that Dick was not only an alter-ego image but that the "parting and separating" pattern was most important. Was it a fear concerning her parents worked out on her sister Frannie and now upon Dick? He returned to her family. She had acted out her parting and separating tendency upon her marriage.

"Your parents didn't do that?"

"Never. There's never been a quarrel in our family, never. Our family operates strictly on good manners. Everybody is very polite and very gracious and very, well they just run on good manners and good breeding, period. And that is not love. It was not a *warlike* atmosphere, but all emotion was just put in and *bottled up* and kept there completely, no, never any display of affection and never any display of anger, no display of *any emotion* whatsoever."

This was really a chronic deprivation leading, in her, to an hysterical type of narcissistic withdrawal.

"In all the family?"

"In the whole family, that's right. Well, Frannie and I growing up, naturally, you're children and you haven't learned the self-control you know that is put on you by your upbringing and your parents and we were intelligently brought up."

"So you *fought* and *separated* and *came back* yourself, too?"

"Yes, that's right, to a certain degree."

"But now would you explain to me what happened. You got married you say almost two years ago?"

"That's right."

"And then you said he had to leave?"

"That's right."

"What happened?"

"He had to leave within fifteen days because that was all the leave he had."

"Well!"

"And so, he just, I mean you can't go against the Army's orders. He was stationed in Germany and this was what we both knew was going to be the pattern of Army life, and so naturally I mean I had to let him go, and he did. But it was the letter situation, I think, that got it started first because I was all alone and I wasn't leading a *normal* existence."

The fateful words, *normal* versus *abnormal*, again appeared.

"What do you mean by normal?"

"Well, all my friends were married and uh they didn't want, I mean most of my own friends were newly-weds. They certainly were going through their own problem of mutual adjustment. They didn't want a third party, you know; they had to keep remembering to invite me for supper or you know, they just weren't there, and the only friends I had were both older women."

"Both? What do you mean?"

"Two, well there are *two sisters*, uh, one in her early fifties and one in her late fifties. They were very fine women and they were just bricks to me. I probably would have landed here with you much sooner. Whether that's good or bad I don't know, but they were very fine, very *strong personalities*. They gave me a lot of good advice, but the thing was I, *it* was just *cut off* from a *normal* life. I mean I'd go to work and I'd come home, and it was the apartment and me and books or the radio you know, and so I would sit and write and I'd get very *depressed* at work because, well I'm not usually depressed. I love working with people better than anything else. I had a job. I was an executive assistant and I enjoyed it very much, but working with people, while I find I enjoy it very much, it also takes a lot out of me. I'm just tired, very tired at the end of the day, just as I think you men probably must be, having to talk and accommodate yourself to the different personalities, so when I went home though I *didn't have a wife* waiting there for me, or anybody else fixing the supper or making things comfortable for me. I had to do it all myself, you know."

The two sisters had appeared again. She was ripe for some confrontations.

"You had to be your own wife?"

"I had to be my own wife, that's right."

She laughed.

"And that is just an added drain on your physical and mental energies and everything, and so then I'd feel like I had to sit down and write Dick, you know, dutiful wife, and I got to keep going and writing Dick, so *my depression* crept into the letters, I couldn't keep it out, and he didn't write as often. He was very busy there and they had a lot of good entertainment and everything, and after all he, well, I shouldn't have expected him to sit around and worry about me. He never, *nobody ever worried about him in his life* so *he never worried about anybody else and it was just—*"

She sighed.

"Just one of those things. So the letters were what started it."

"What do you mean?"

"Well, I mean *depressing* letters I'd write and then I'd get *mad* at him and, well, I mean I just would blow up, just be as mean and nasty as a *snake.*"

With no man to project her phallic attributes upon, she became a phallic aggressive girl.

"For instance, how would you be mean and nasty like a snake?"

"Well, I'd, oh, gosh let me think, oh, it sure took me a long time to get over the *lieutenant colonel* thing, just ordering him to start getting an education and blah, blah, blah, blah, blah, blah, blah, just an order, not will you please or drop a suggestion or anything here and there; so naturally no man on God's green earth—"

The "lieutenant colonel thing" was a sort of illusory phallus that interfered with her playing the feminine ideal role with her other phallus substitute from which she felt cut off; i.e., Dick was not only the phallus but the little boy whose parents were mean and nasty.

"The lieutenant colonel thing?"

"I was a lieutenant colonel in the WAC's."

"He was a *private* and you were a *colonel?*"

"Right!"

"And so you ordered him to get an education?"

"Yes. You can't blame him for wanting to throw me out!"

"He wasn't educated much?"

"No, he didn't have *as much as I.*"

"You had?"

"Oh, I've got twelve semester hours on my *Master's.*"

"On your Master's? So you have a college degree and a Master's?"

"No, no, I've *only got half my Master's.*"

This was a wonderfully revealing statement. She was bisexual in another sense.

"Half your Master's?"

"Yes."

"And he?"

"Uh, hadn't finished high school."

"He hadn't finished high school?"

"No."

She paused.

"So you wanted him to get his education and catch up with you?"

"Because I think, I mean whether I'm right or whether I'm wrong, think that was one thing that was a contributing factor to my folks' unhappiness in marriage. It was the fact that my *mother* was a college graduate and my *father* was not. In fact he had just, well he had his high-school degree but he walked out before it was handed to him."

"He didn't finish high school either?"

"That's right! And my mother was a graduate in arts from Columbia and I think that subconsciously there was resentment becasue dad always used to keep throwing it up."

"What did he do, your father?"

"An engineer."

"He was an engineer?"

"Um. My father is a real great man. He's an excellent artist, and he's an excellent engineer but he just unfortunately never liked the human race and he just can't get along with people."

"Did mother try to educate him?"

"No, because that's the trouble you see, my father is subconsciously *afraid of women too!* He's *terrified of women!*"

"What do you mean too? *Dick* was *afraid* of *women?*"

The castrating figure behind all this was a woman—*mother!* She found herself acting like this to Dick.

"Dick was too because Dick had seen what a woman can do to a man. You see the same thing happened in my father's family."

She then described how selfish and cruel her father's mother had been. Her garden came first, her children second, and they were trained like dogs. Father was determined never to let mother dominate him, and so was Dick.

"Yes. They had an awful lot of money, my uncles, I mean my grandfather did at one time. He was a financier but he made a mistake. He also had a great deal of engineering ability and he invented important things that they have in subways, back then it was in trolley cars, and so forth, and he made a very bad error of trusting a friend without getting it patented, and he invested money in it, and all of a sudden they went from great wealth to practically nothing. Also close to the same time their family home was condemned by the city so that they could build a school. Well, my *grandmother* was a gardener. Her *garden* and her *plants came first* and *children came second* and, uh, she had always disciplined the children very well up until they were around twelve or thirteen. I mean they were made to mind, they were fed the right foods, and she stood on her ear to see that they were well-disciplined. Again it was like, all I can think of it was like *training a dog,* you know. You teach him to do this trick at this time, down Rover and that sort of thing. This is all hearsay from what I gathered over the years from my mother and father."

The grandmother represented the bad side of mother to the child. She paused and then continued.

"So, when the house was condemned and everything lost, she just became absolutely enraged. She was a person who could, granddad didn't want to fight that public domain bsusiness. My grandmother did. She persuaded him to fight it and he lost. Not only did he lose but he didn't get nearly as much as he would have, you know, if he had been willing to sell in the first place. Well, everything contributed, why they came out on the very short end of the horn compared to what they had had at one time, and my grandmother never let grandfather forget it for a minute for the rest of their lives; and I think my father just hated it, and he went into marriage absolutely and completely determined that *no woman* was going to *do that to him,* just as I think *Dick* went into ours the *same way.*"

As a child, she must have loved mother up to the birth of Frannie. Then everything changed. She needed to be a boy but found that she wasn't well-equipped to play the role of a little colonel.

"He hated what mother did to father?"

"Mm, I believe so."

"And so then you put the pressure on him to get an education. I don't understand. You knew all of this, why did you do this?"

"Well, I guess there were several forces fighting, now I can see but then I couldn't. If I had only had an older person in my life, I wanted my *father,* I just begged my father to help me out with this because I thought maybe he could because he had *always before* been able to help me out pretty well."

"Before?"

"Well, when I was at home, well like once when I wanted to go into *nursing* and he said *no,* and he said don't ever even think of going into nursing because you've got too much, well he said, a response of a sympathetic nature to ever be *any good* as a nurse. He said you'd start nursing some poor soul and you'd feel so pitifully sorry for them that you would just be drowning in tears and they would get sicker and sicker from all this pity, you know, that you were not fit for it."

This was the same as telling her she could never be a woman. He must have driven her in the direction of being the boy.

"He said you were too sensitive to ever be a nurse?"

"That's right, he said far too sensitive in nature to ever be a nurse, right, and I didn't have any strong calling for a profession or anything, not so that I would just grit my teeth and go. The only thing that I ever really wanted to do that I did *buck* him on was being a *school teacher.* That I wanted and that I majored in in college, and while they tried to set up some barriers to reason me out of it, they were completely unsuccessful."

This was a good sign except that the sex of a teacher is indeterminate.

"So father was a little bit upset, as you say, about Dick not having finished high school?"

"Yes, that's right."

"And about his being younger?"

"Well, I don't know, I think they were a little worried about that, yes. They really never discussed it with me. I tried to get them to when I was home while I was sort of trying to make up my mind whether I should or whether I shouldn't marry him, and I was talking to my mother in the kitchen. She had met Dick and she had liked him very much. She told me when I told her I was going out with him, she said, 'Well I can truthfully say he is one of the most attractive men I have ever met in my life. I don't blame you a bit.' But, when I was home that time she said, 'Carol, you should never marry any man unless he loves you more than anything else in the world, unless he loves you that much.' And I told her, 'Well mother the only man that has *ever loved me like that* has been Dick.' She didn't advise me, I mean instead of the way I would have if I were a mother—"

Here she began to sob violently. The therapist changed the subject from the nursing-mother-father relationship to Dick and added a doubtful note. The idealized lost object has to be degraded.

"He *seemed* to love you like that?"

"That's right, that's right."

"But then what happened? When you wrote him those letters telling him he had to get an education—?"

"All the time we were going together I was afraid it wasn't going to work because those things *were* bothering me, his lack of education and the fact that he was younger. All those things were bothering me terribly, and I kept telling him that I was afraid that it wasn't going to work, you know, but all the barriers that I kept throwing up and everything he just, it was just like a little bull dog *hanging on*. He just kept coming back and coming back and coming back and saying how much he loved me and everything. Well finally, because I did love him very much, in fact I felt that I loved him almost *too much to marry him*—"

She was obviously afraid of her sadistic magic powers.

"How do you mean that?"

"Oh, there are a lot of women like that, Doctor, yes, sir, they will love him, but I was afraid I would *ruin* him, that once we were married that, uh, because I was older and had all this education that I might, I don't know, I didn't know what the future held."

What she meant by ruin him was castrate him, ruin him as a man, break his manly pride. Mother had done this to her when she was a little girl.

"That you might what?"

"Well, I might be a *dominating* person toward him or something. I don't know, but it just seemed—"

Her voice died away. She felt overwhelmed by sadness and dread as her old sadomasochistic fantasies were revived.

"You have known such women, you said?"

"I have known women who have refused to marry a man because they said they loved him too much to marry him. I finally decided that was a pretty weak excuse."

"Loved them too much, you mean, to ruin them?"

"That's right, if you thought you were going to."

"And you thought you might ruin him by dominating him?"

"Yes. Finally, Doctor, the way I figured it out, I went home and I started thinking by myself, well I can't ruin him *unless he lets me*. He has made the decision that he loves me, and if I really love him I've got to love him enough to marry him and let us just find out for ourselves. The proof of the pudding is in the eating. That's all I could see to do."

This offered an excellent chance to show her that Dick needed her and she him in order to solve their mutual problems. *"Unless he lets me"* was a welcome show of readiness for insight.

"So what happened then? You wrote to him and told him to get an education?"

"Yes, the old lieutenant colonel business. It was a habit I guess. I had been in for two years. I was, my father had tried to bring me up to be a *man* and I tried to live up to it."

Now everything was out in the open. From the point of view of the therapy, this was *her* fantasy and her own wish.

"How do you mean?"

"Well, I don't know. Dad would sit and he'd talk about how wonderful, who was that character in the Army that finally became Secretary of the Army, anyway he threatened to shoot a doctor who was going to *chop off a leg*, and he was the only general in the United States Army who had *a game leg*. I mean dad used to hold up these tremendous ideals of great figures."

The angry, "castrated" feelings were obvious.

"Army heroes?"

"Yes, always Army heroes, that's right."

"Dad liked the Army?"

"Dad liked, in fact dad tried to get in the Army in the First World War. He wanted to be quartermaster and they didn't call him, and they didn't call him, and finally the Air Corps was formed and some of his buddies were going in, and they said why don't you see if you can't get in the Army Air Force, and he was always talking about all his exploits as a man in the service. Part of them, I don't know, as men get older, maybe some of it I'm sure now is colored by imagination, but he was always holding up this ideal and I, he was just my God. Dad and God were synonymous practically with me when I was young."

She had turned away from the disappointing mother and allowed her sister to be the girl.

"You were closer to him than to mother?"

"Right. I always have been, until the last, just the *last few years* when I began to be able to see him as a person and the influence he had on me."

This was another sign of being ripe for insight.

"How do you mean?"

She burst into tears.

"The ideals he held up were awfully high for a girl to try to, I mean men can be so much more objective about things. I mean I think that's why men like you, and I don't know what it is, but I can't do it. I just can't, I can't, I think I went so far and I think that's why I'm here now. I went into the Army and I tried so hard. I don't know. Some of the men must have really shook their heads sometimes because I was so—"

She sobbed uncontrollably.

"Because *you* wanted to be a man?"

"I just tried so hard to be a man, you know, and I just didn't succeed too well. I guess what I probably wound up being more than anything else was a *scolding mother*. It was the nearest to it that I could come."

"You tried to be a man?"

"That's right. And I kept throwing it in Dick's face this isn't like a man, that isn't like a man. The poor guy!"

She moaned in an agony of repentance.

"You told him he wasn't acting like a man?"

"Yes! Oh, how awful, how awful, how awful!"

She was reliving her own childhood agony.

"So what you mean then by man is this *image* that your father had created, huh?"

"The poor guy didn't have a chance! Poor Dick!"

"So what happened?"

"Well, he started, I don't know, he started asking for a divorce, and then I was frantic because I don't believe in divorce. I mean I do now, I can see where it probably, all in all, it *happens for the best*. What did you ask me?"

"So you got angry and hurt at being *left alone* and being *lonesome* and *depressed* and you got *irritable* and then you sort of—"

"Reverted to—"

"Reverted to the man role?"

She had duplicated what had happened as a child.

"Reverted to the pattern that had been, you know that I had been living for so long. I mean I think subconsciously I was trying to live up to my father's ideals of what an officer was, you know, an officer and all this Stonewall Jackson stuff and all these generals, and George Patton!"

She cried brokenheartedly, then suddenly asked clearly—

"And what man wants to be married to another man?"

Now was an opportunity, thought the therapist.

"Dick wanted to marry that kind, didn't he?"

"Yes, because he kept coming back all the time!"

"That's what I mean!"

"Evidently he grew past that or something, I don't know."

"You mean he changed?"

"I've signed divorce papers!"

Again she sobbed uncontrollably. The therapist shifted the subject.

"What happened? So you tried to be a man and an officer, that's what you mean by a lieutenant colonel?"

"Yes, that's right."

"You tried to tell him what to do?"

"That's right."

This was repeated in order to get to a point where there could be no retraction. The remainder was logical and inevitable.

"Like a man would a woman? So you mean you had been living two roles?"

"Yes."

"The man and the woman?"

"Yes, and I just want to drop the man's."

"You went to work as a man and then came back and had to be the wife and cook for the man when the man came home, and you got sick of it?"

"That's, well, he wasn't there!"

"That's what I mean, you got sick of playing both roles and you wanted him to come home and play the role of the man so you could be a woman again?"

"Yes, that's right, exactly! That's what I want more than anything in life, just to be able to play a woman's role in life because what's more normal for a woman."

The insight proceeded according to plan.

"Surely, you know, but you must feel that what was wrong was that when you played the role of a woman you wanted to be married to a man like the man that you wished to be and like father had idealized, hm?"

"Yes, I think so, that's right."

"Sort of a Stonewall Jackson?"

"Yes, and be together."

"And Dick was no Stonewall Jackson, I take it?"

"I think that Dick will be some day!"

"Really?"

"Yes, I think so."

"How come?"

"Because he's that kind of a guy."

"But I mean he's two kinds of a guy then because you said that—"

She interrupted.

"And I was two kinds of a girl."

The therapist continued.

"Because you see there was one kind of Dick who was sort of a little bit on the feminine side who needed a masculine woman, who came back again and again, and who wanted a lieutenant colonel, and then there was the Dick you say who was sort of a Stonewall Jackson."

"Well, we just proved I was two kinds of woman, so why couldn't he be two kinds of a man?"

"That's what I mean. Do you think he was?"

"Yes, I think he is to this day."

"You think—"

"I think together *Dick and I will ruin each other now*, but he's *never been loved in his life by anyone.* He now knows there is one person in this world who loves him more than anything else in the world. I loved him enough to marry him and I love him enough to divorce him. I couldn't see, I mean I don't even regret one minute of these past two years because they've been—"

Her voice died away and she began to sob again.

"But I thought you only had him for fifteen days?"

"I'm talking about being married for two years."

"But you only were with him for fifteen days?"

"No, for the honeymoon, yes. I mean altogether I think we've been together for approximately *three weeks.*"

"Three weeks?"

"And I *don't regret* one minute of it because if I had just, I mean, well the girls kept saying if you quit now, you know, and let him go why don't worry he'll be back, he'll be back, just don't worry, you know, but there wasn't anything to it. It was just kind of like a trick or something and I didn't want, I mean I thought well if I do that then he'll never know whether I love him or not."

"What do you mean a trick?"

"That, well, I mean if I could just cold-bloodedly quit, just say all right it's a divorce and maybe go on and get it or pretend or something, I don't know, then maybe he would come back, but it seemed to me that then *he would always doubt* whether I *really loved him* or not."

The little-boy part of her could never believe in mother and trust her. She felt ruined and castrated by her. She also doubted father's love for her as a girl.

"So you mean you got a divorce?"

"No, I couldn't, I couldn't get the divorce. I tried and I tried and I couldn't do it. Dick had to eventually. I couldn't. I went to a lawyer and I could hardly even talk to him, and I told Dick I just couldn't do it. That's why he had to get it because I can't."

This was a defense by reversal. The little boy had left mother!

"He got it?"

"That's right. The divorce came through the other day. I couldn't do it, but at least he knows I really love him and I always will and he knows that too."

Now was the time to reduce the reality Dick to size, or place matters in perspective.

"What makes you think he'll be a Stonewall Jackson? I mean after all you only knew him for three weeks?"

"Oh, I've known him longer than that. I've known him, I've only slept with him probably, I mean we've only lived under the same roof for three weeks but we've been under each other's influence for about five years."

It must have seemed to her that she had known him all her life. This was since the time her sister got married, but this was a loaded area and it might be better to shift back to the early emotional climate that determined her needs.

"So you feel that if you had lived with him you wouldn't have slept apart, like father and mother?"

"Oh, heavens never, never. No, I'm taking, I've learned a lesson from my parents, oh, never, no, after all. No, that isn't what I mean at all. I just meant that we had known each other, but most of our relationship has been strictly by letters."

"That's what I mean. You never had a chance to live with him like father and mother ought to have lived?"

"Yes."

"You weren't disgusted to sleep with him, like father and mother?"

"No, not one bit, not one bit, no! He's the only man I ever met in my life that *never made a play for me* or *never made a pass*."

Now why was this necessary? She was a normally attractive girl.

"He never did?"

"Never. I admire a, I think a man is more of a man for having that much self-control. I don't admire a man that makes a pass at me because to me it shows a lack of self-control on his part."

This referred to her own repression of sexuality.

"He had such good control?"

"Excellent. He certainly did."

"Even after you were married?"

"*Even after we were married* and one night when I was going to have to go to work the next day I was willing, he wouldn't. He just said, 'No, I know you've got to go to work,' and he was that kind of a man, and I admired him."

"What did he mean by that, you've got to go to work?"

"I had to go to the office the next day and I was tired and exhausted."

"From what?"

"From work that day. That's the reason I don't believe in working wives."

"You mean you were tired and exhausted after you got through working?"

"Exhausted, always, and that's when we'd get, I don't know we'd get into fusses, and I don't know, it was just an *abnormal* existence any way you looked at it."

Actually she was exhausted from the two sides of her fighting, from fighting her sadomasochism. Dick was not man enough for the feminine side of her, so she secretly hated him.

"You fought?"

"We just quarreled, no, we always, I mean any time he wanted to go to bed, I was more, well, I loved him. I mean I can't understand why *sex* is supposed to be so *sinful*. If you love somebody, you are just giving them what they need. Each is giving to the other what they need and what else is love but giving yourself to the other person."

He wasn't giving her what she needed and obviously couldn't play the role of the man who could truly make her into a real woman. He could only be a little boy with a mother and this was not enough.

"You were giving him what he needed?"

"True! Love and affection, that is only one expression of affection, isn't it?"

"Instead of being a man, you could act only like a mother?"

"A mother, yes!"

"Some kind of a mother. What was it, an irritable mother?"

"No, not irritable."

"What was it?"

"Well, a mother who wants a child to do such-and-such because it is good for him, you know. I don't know what you'd call that, but that's the description of it anyway, but that was the thing I enjoyed more than anything."

"A scolding mother, sort of?"

"I mean, well, look, if Johnny does something wrong, Johnny gets spanked, because she knows, I mean if your son starts, say, smashing furniture or anything, why you are going to spank him."

"Were you like that with the boys in the Army?"

"If they stepped out of line, I was. I think discipline is discipline anywhere. I certainly didn't spank very many but if they did anything wrong that was against their best interests and, first of all the best interests of the Army—"

"Were you like that when you had these fights with Dick when you came home exhausted?"

"Oh, no, not so much, I don't think"

"What do you mean?"

"Oh, I don't know, it would be like maybe a dish would drop or something and, uh, oh, I'd get a little nervous and maybe snap at him and then cry or something like that, I mean, you know that's the only thing I can think of."

She had been unhappy without realizing she needed a hard, spanking, strong man like father, but she had hated him for making her be the castrated boy. Yet she had loved and pitied him because he was a version of herself. She had been trapped and chronically discontented and always waiting for the breakup she had feared would happen to her parents.

"You were crying then with him?"

"Yes, some of the time. It was all, for one thing there was always this knowledge that this wasn't permanent, that we were only living for today and tomorrow he went back to the Army, which is an awful— I mean no idea of a permanent existence ever entered our heads. I think it was definitely a sort of feeling like you are living for today and not for tomorrow, something like that, which is, well, I don't know, the only existence I could think of that could even come close to it would be something like wartime, you know, where you have that constant feeling you're living for today for tomorrow we die type of thing, and it was always, whenever we were together, always with that deadline that we knew was coming, and we would just try to cram in as much love and everything as we could before that deadline hit and we were stuck with it again."

She broke into tears again. The love-death, loss and castration theme always interfering with her taking a normal role. The therapist now shifted the sector to the past and her parents to allow her breathing space. Weaving back and forth between the present and past is one way of integrating a patient's ego.

"Tell me, how come your parents never broke up?"

The stratagem worked. Her eyes dried quickly and she answered. "Pride!"

"Pride? But when you were a little girl did you ever hear them fight?"

"They have never fought in their lives I am sure! It was all kept inside!"

It was impossible to separate fact from her fantasies and fortunately unnecessary.

"Did you ever expect them to break up?"

"My sister and I did discuss it. We talked between ourselves, how we thought it would be a good idea if they did, when we were, oh, I guess she might have been around twenty-three and I twenty-five, I think it was while I was in the last year of my service and home on a vacation from the Army. We were too young to know, we didn't realize then that they were a *habit with each other. Either* would be *lost* without the *other* now, and they are just a *habit*. I can't imagine either one of them married to anybody else."

She was talking about her abnormal relation with her sister as well as her parents but this could not be taken up now. The therapist returned to the appropriate question.

"But now tell me one thing else. Why do you feel that he is going to be a Stonewall Jackson?"

"Why do I think Dick is? Now, I could be *very wrong* there, Doctor, and it is none of my business. That's his life to lead, and I kept telling him that. I said, 'Don't you ever make me responsible for your life because I won't be. You are your own master and you are to be so,' and, uh, because I think he's got the brains for it. I think that Dick is one of these multifaceted men who has difficulty in finding his place."

This was her own problem, multiple and poorly integrated identities.

"At the same time you feel he has another side too?"

"Certainly."

"You mean the side that needed the strong lieutenant colonel?"

"At the time, but he has outgrown that *I think*. Dick needed it because it was the way he was brought up."

"You mean he had that side then?"

"Yes."

"And that was a sort of weak side, you felt?"

"Not a weak side."

"What would you call it?"

"I don't *want* to call it a weak side."

"What kind of a side would you call it?"

"I would just call it a side."

"A dependent side, or what?"

"Maybe at the time but—"

"That's what I mean."

"Yes, but he's a man now."

"Surely, you mean he grew up?"

"With me, that's right."

"You mean he turned into a man and you became a woman?"

"That's right."

"Because you said that like you he had been a mixture of boy and a girl?"

She was unable to continue with this pressure of reality without attempting some solution.

"Yes, but the real thing is that *this little girl has grown up into a woman* because while I've been a big education to Dick, believe me he has been a big education to me!"

This was said with feeling. In a sense this was a crystallization of insight. Now was the time to take advantage of this mood, fix it, and intensify it.

"In what way?"

"Well, one thing I know that if I should ever marry again it will be a *man* who is interested in a home life and not some type of job where we are going to be separated for great lengths of time."

"That's what I mean. Because it seems to me that Dick sort of was almost like a version of yourself in a way, wasn't he?"

"That's right."

"He was a Stonewall Jackson. The only difference between the two of you is he was a real man in a physical sense."

"That's right."

"He had a penis!"

"Yes, that's right."

"So he could really play the role and grow into it. He had a chance in the Army. I mean he could make the grade with the fellows and he could become a man's man with the boys, but you never had a chance because no matter what you did, no matter how masculine you behaved or what a Stonewall Jackson you would be, you always ran into the biological difficulty that basically you were a woman."

"And the mental difficulty!"

"Of being a woman, right!

"Because mentally men and women are also different, very different."

"Although it took you a long time to realize that?"

"Yes, it has, and it has taken experience, believe me, and that's why I'm here, because any time a woman tries to be a man—"

She shrugged and spread her hands in mock helplessness.

"That's right, or any time a man has this weak feminine side and needs a woman who is a man, huh?"

Now more insight that she had denied previously could become conscious.

"But I *knew when I married Dick that he was this type.* I knew this was coming because—the only thing was I hoped it wouldn't."

Her eyes became full of tears once more.

"You knew that when he grew up—?"

"That he was so masculine that he was never going to be able to put up with this type of mothering thing. There are quite a few men who have been very happily married to older women, but I knew he wasn't going to be this type. But he thought it was at the time!"

The situation was the reversal of her little girl oedipal problems.

"So then Dick represents something that you needed for a time as he needed you for a time in order that you both could grow up."

"I think possibly. I was cold on my wedding day, the first day we had, Dick was the first man who ever kissed me on a first date, believe me, and I just looked at him and I said, 'Dick, I could just never bear to write you a *Dear John letter.*' It was just like, I don't know whether you psychiatrists believe in women's *intuition* or not. I do, and on my wedding day I was scared stiff."

She had had a premonition. It was like a déjá vu feeling. The past was repeating itself.

"Scared?"

"I was scared that we were going to get a divorce eventually."

She realized that to be a woman she had to give up her masculine attributes, penis, career—the little boy of the past.

"You were aware of all of this?"

"But not, I couldn't have talked about it or explained it then, Doctor, like I can now."

The goal of therapy had temporarily been reached.

"That's right. Well we have gotten to understand it a little better, I think, by talking it out."

"Yes, that's right, that's very true."

"So in other words when you mourn for Dick really in some ways too you are mourning for that lost little boy that you were with daddy in a way, hm?"

"Well, probably, it feels that way."

"It was a nice relationship while it lasted, wasn't it, but better if he had accepted you as a girl?"

"Yes, in a way it was. It would have been very nice to know somebody cared that much for me."

"That's right, you needed him because sister had mother."

"Yes, I did. I really did."

"I think so. I think you'll understand it and when you do, maybe, as you say, you can play the role of a woman who demands and wants a real man who wants to work and live at home with her."

"Right."

"I think so."

"Thank you very much, Doctor."

The key word that gave away the pattern in all spheres of her relationships was *abnormal*. In a family with two boys (or girls), one is usually more masculine than the other, more often than not the older one. This is often encouraged by the parents, especially those whose narcissistic needs to reduplicate themselves are greater than average. Neurotic parents also have a greater need for this type of reduplication in order to redress their own childhood grievances by proxy. In her case, her parents were "cold" and "distant," and the normal oedipal needs and relationships of the little girl who turns to daddy when mother has the new baby, or disappoints her in one way or another, were intensified. Her relationship with father was *abnormally* strong. It was *abnormal* in that she had to relate to him as a general or man with a game leg—really a castrated boy. She was rejected as a woman or nurse by him. Her parents related *abnormally* to each other in her eyes—no love—no intercourse—only a distant politeness devoid of feeling. They were separated *abnormally* by education and so were she and Dick.

Why was father terrified over what a woman does to a man? He was like Samson after Delilah had cut off his hair. He was a castrated general himself, as she was with half her Master's. She said early in the interview she had been cut off. She meant she had lost her Dick. Really she was afraid of her own castrating tendencies in the present toward Dick. Who did it to her in the past? The mother, most likely aided later by the father. She visualized herself once as a boy who had been ruined or castrated by her mother. There was another side, however, that wanted to be a nurse or mother, which father crushed. She had identified with both her parents, but it was a hostile, sadomasochistic, disgusting relationship she could not trust. Each ruined the other. She introjected this type of relationship from one she had with her sister in the infantile past as well as from her parents and then projected it onto Dick and herself. Earlier in her childhood she had withdrawn from her disappointing parents into a somewhat narcissistic solution of her problems. She became father and mother and a brother and sister herself. She was bisexual. However, the dissatisfactions inherent in her marriage with Dick reopened the old wounds—her marriage with herself became unsatisfactory. The rejection implicit in the divorce revived (1) the rejection by mother when her sister was born; (2) the castration by mother or the body-image representative of the loss of her baby-mother relationship; (3) the rejection of her feminine side by daddy; (4) the fantasied rejection by the crowd where she was a laughing stock because of her naïveté; (5) her rejection of herself as a feminine person like her sister. Her sister can be looked upon as an alter-ego figure representing her feminine side that longed for a close relationship in a double bed. Dick was another alter-ego figure representing her masculine side which was often manifest and never closely united with the feminine sister side.

All the future sessions would tend to revolve around essentially the same material, with additions, deletions and variations on the above themes. Her daily experiences would usually determine which theme would be brought up and her reaction to these experiences would be determined in large measure by her reactions in the past. Depressive lonely feelings would complicate the picture and the therapist would be seen in many roles, those of father and Dick being more prominent if he were seen as a man, and mother and sister if he were seen as a woman.

In psychotherapy such transference reactions are best handled by early recognition by the therapist and then bringing up indirect but similar relationsships in the past with the original cast; that is, the therapist would keep himself out of the situation as much as possible. In the case of psychotherapy, a vis-à-vis, sitting-up relationship encourages a reality relationship and lessens the likelihood of violent transference reactions developing. This would be disadvantageous in the case of a psychoanalytic patient who possesses a well-developed rational ego, as in this case the impact necessary to produce conviction would be lessened considerably. However, in psychotherapy we cannot count on the patient's possessing such a relatively healthy ego and are often more interested in the establishment of temporary control over impulse and feeling.

The activity of the therapist during this interview, while not remarkable, was far greater than is possible in an initial psychoanalytic session where time is more abundant and greater wariness more in order. The transference reaction of this patient was obvious. She saw the therapist as a father figure and it was unnecessary to mention it.

The mourning reaction, including the grief, anger and guilt, had been combined in a masturbatory fantasy, the main theme pertaining to a love affair with a Stonewall Jackson, the opposite of her parents. She had acted it out. As is usual in neurotic acting out, reality elements were ignored to such a degree that the marriage was doomed from the beginning. She intuitively realized this. In another sense, they had both acted out, but the relationships were out of phase with one another. When this occurred, hidden negative elements were aggravated and positive benefits were cancelled.

VIII

PSYCHONEUROSIS AND BISEXUALITY

A Case of Hysterical Bisexuality

In Chapter VII we saw how bisexual identifications played a large part in the origin and development of the problems of a young woman with hysterical character traits. Many young men have bisexual identifications that can lead to attacks of anxiety or various ego-alien defense measures against this anxiety when their urges conflict with their ideals. Many young men have a tendency to fear their homosexual aspects unduly. When their character organization is primarily of the phobic and hysterical type, they are often amenable to sector psychotherapy. Some obsessional characters who are facultative bisexuals and oscillate between male and female object choices during late adolescence and the early twenties are also readily helped.

The case to be presented is that of a young man of twenty with some mild phobic and obsessional symptoms connected with sporadic homosexual activities of the mutual masturbatory type. He could not afford psychotherapy and was sent to a clinic by his physician to whom he had frankly told his story. He was seen in consultation. It will be noted that for all purposes the "consultation" was the same as an initial therapeutic interview. It is better to have the basic problem clearly outlined in depth than collect masses of information, much of which is irrelevant, or at least uneconomic in terms of therapy. One of the reasons why short-term therapy takes so long is that the elicited verbal material is left disconnected. The therapeutic process begins only when chaotic feeling masses and their verbal representations become organized and integrated in time, depth and over-all patterns. The therapist is more interested in unconscious *relation-ships* becoming conscious than in the appearance of forgotten memo-ries. If such memories cannot be integrated into the structure of the interview as a whole, they serve little useful purpose. The *relation-ship* of the recalled memories to the present problems must be ac-tively made clear and demonstrated ad nauseum. When a patient remembers a long forgotten incident he usually feels, "Oh, I have always known this but I just haven't thought about it for a long time." It is the duty of the therapist to demonstrate or, still better, get the patient to demonstrate to himself, the meaning of such an incident. Such incidents must be developed and the verbal material expanded, as in the case of dreams and fantasies. When homosexual feelings come to the foreground in psychotherapy, we tend to treat such feelings as a childhood problem in obtaining narcissistic supplies from the parent of the same sex (see Chapters XIV and XV). We also treat the often severe problems in detachment and withdrawal as-sociated with pathological mourning. In overt homosexuals, the detach-ment and withdrawal are of a much greater magnitude than is found in cases of anxiety hysteria, the ambivalence is more intense and the ability to tolerate intimate personal relationships is much less. In anxiety hysteria, masturbatory sexual fantasies are a defense and often acted out. In some cases of homosexuality they are a way of life, a desper-ate last-ditch stand that frequently defends against psychotic episodes. These are usually a mixture of depressive, schizoid and paranoid elements. We have to specialize in one small area in order to pene-trate in depth and establish sufficient connections between the past and the present so that insight acquired during the session will stick. In this respect the therapeutic process is like a brand of glue—some result in insight that sticks tightly; some have no adhesive properties at all. Even in the first interview the therapist who tries to learn everything in all areas ends up with a mass of material that is only a representation of the patient's and his own confusion. A patient is usually allowed to proceed freely for the first part of the interview while the choice of an area or sector is being made. All patients take some time to communicate the essential and important feelings of that day. In the case of the present patient, the relationship between his "homosexuality" and a father "fixation" was developed. There were many other areas that could have been explored if time had permitted, but it was felt that at this moment other areas were of secondary importance. Let us listen to the interview.

"Good morning, Mr. Doyle. Sit right down, please. Would you tell me something about your problem?"

"Well, uh, a few weeks ago, about, oh, I'd say *Christmas time*, uh, I was confronted with this homosexual problem. I was, I'm an organist, part time and, uh, *this fellow*, he's in the choir, and he confronted me with this, this, *these acts*. I mean I had never even given thought to *anything like that* and so, naturally me being a little green to that, I didn't stop where I should have stopped and before he advanced. And so it got just so *confusing* I didn't know *which way I was going*. I became afraid to leave my room, so I decided to look for treatment, to see if I could get any aid. And that's why I came here. In fact now I am *afraid* to go near *the place* I work."

Right away the therapist was confronted with a wide choice of words to pick up when he dissolved this statement into its components. Ordinary "sensical" words are often of much less interest than those that are *nonsensical*. For example, *"Christmas time"* as a symbol relates essentially to an adored baby who gets gifts magically from an all-good father figure. It was now early in March and the patient had said, "a few weeks ago." Again, what is an *organist*? In the everyday world it is simply a variety of musician. Here it stands a good chance of being a person who enjoys mastering and playing with an organ of a particular kind. It is a straw pointing toward a phallic level of fixation. Such indicators may turn out to be relatively useless, but they should be *listened for, heard* and kept in mind for future use. Most of the words that are *heard* in this manner *cannot* be used at the time they are revealed. Many of them are better suited for the development of other areas. In this case either of two words could be taken, e.g., *"confused"* or *"these acts."* The first one was very good; however, *acts* dealt with the chief area of the *"homosexual problem."* Right away the goal had become that of the therapist giving the patient and himself a good understanding of what this meant in terms of the patient's life experiences.

"What *acts* do you mean?"

"Well, he, he was, well, first he suggested that, he used to ask me all kinds of questions about how many girls do you have, and all this, and how many relations, sexual relations, you've had and, uh, and then one night he decided to advance on me to, uh, to, you know, just play around my *private*, and you know, well I told him to get out, he's *crazy*, you know, and so naturally, *I don't know*, I didn't *repel*, or tell him *not to stop*. And then he just *went on*, and then I *forgot about that*. And then the *second* time, well, he used to come ooking for me after rehearsal. And so I used to begin to try to dodge im, to get out of his way and just, I, I wanted to stop it *at that point* efore it got *worse*. Now I can't go near the *church* and I don't like o leave home!"

The other man was a threatening aspect of himself that he could ot control. The slip about stopping had to be ignored. At this time : would produce only resistance and anger. He was apparently de-eloping phobic feelings about the church.

"What do you mean *worse?*"

"Well, I mean, it might develop into a million other things."

He appeared timid and uncertain.

"Like what? You can talk freely. I understand your feelings."

"Well, I mean I don't like to go out on the street, and then there's he *other acts* that they commit. I don't know."

"Well, have you got any ideas?"

"Well, I mean *masturbation,* that's what he was *primarily* interested n, but it just seemed wrong to me. I mean *abnormal,* and I didn't vant to be involved in it."

He had already been masturbated. The fears were possibly also bout more regressive areas.

"You wanted to stop before you went, you said, *further?* And did vhat other kind of acts?"

"Well, I mean, he wanted to act, you know, just as if you know, *iale* and *female,* I mean the way they what was the un..."

He began to stammer.

"I mean, the contact of the *two organs* together. That's what he vanted! But I didn't, you know, want to go that far."

"Contact the two organs?"

"Yes, his organ against mine."

"You mean touch his organ to your organ?"

"That's right."

He began to tap his foot nervously. What kind of contact did this onscious *manifest* sexual act represent in other areas now uncon-cious? On first thought an organ could represent many areas of the ody. The safest area for an initial interview was to consider the organ as a penis. He tapped his foot more nervously. The tapping vas a rhythmic act symbolizing the masturbatory process. Here it epresented a confirmation that regressive and mainly phallic mastur-atory fantasies were his problem at this time. In some silent or verbally evasive patients the tapping would give away the important eelings and fantasies, Mentioning or drawing attention to such actions must be used cautiously and sparingly or it will only produce a "So what?" type of response. It was of no practical use in this case like much of the verbal material.

"Why not?"

"Well, it just seemed *abnormal*."

"You were afraid of being abnormal?"

"Yes."

"That's what you thought he had in mind?"

"Oh, no, I mean, that was his *next move*. He would, actually I go angry with him and *left*. I mean, he, I have an automobile and I used to offer to ride him home, you know, home from rehearsals. That was during the Christmas preparation. And, uh, so, I mean, he just got, I *don't know*. I *don't know*, it's confusing to me, really!"

This meant he was both attracted and repelled. Making the meaning of each action clear in areas other than sexual would resolve his confusion and then he would *know* what to do.

"Confusing? How do you mean?"

"Well, it just seemed so *wrong*. It just didn't seem *right*. I mean I didn't *know what to do*. It's just that, uh, I mean, I didn't have the *will power* to say stop right here. I didn't have that, I just couldn't do it. And so, then it began to worry me. I mean, should I or shouldn't I? It was a *constant battle* always."

Will power is in part a function of conscious awareness and integration of the ego. We cannot fight an enemy in the dark. Recognition is necessary. The word itself signifies the above necessary conditions.

"Should you what? Let him?"

"Oh, *no*. I mean *masturbate*. Or even have *any contact* at all with me. I mean I couldn't *resist*. I mean if he ever got certain, uh, within a *certain range* of me, I mean if he just came and put his hand on me like that I got so I couldn't resist. And so I'd *stay home* and battle it out, or try to *dodge him* as much as possible. I got so I didn't dare to go out at all!"

"You mean couldn't resist what?"

"I mean he had this act of coming, I mean like you, when you're alone he'd make a *sly touch* or *advance* at me and he'd want to commit this act."

"You mean to masturbate?"

The meaning of masturbate was the important thing. Masturbation is a complex act often combining tension discharge with avoidance reactions. Many conflicts are displaced onto masturbatory fantasies and all areas of relationship are involved. For example, a patient can attempt to relieve tension arising in a nonphallic area by means of phallic masturbation, or ward off the impulse to play with his penis by playing with his belt.

"Yes, well I mean, *I don't know*. It's *confusing* to me. And I wanted to know, is there anything that you could possibly do to alleviate this, *this desire*."

"You mean the desire to have him masturbate you?"

"Well, yes. Well I mean, I mean, like he comes up to me and I want to have the *power to say 'No'* and get *on my way*, or *something like that*. I mean like any *normal* person would do."

"You mean a normal person would resist and wouldn't let him?"

Here the therapist could say "You mean by normal a grown-up man who knew what he wanted and didn't need another man to lean on?" But this would be unconvincing, disconnected and premature.

"Yes."

"Do you feel you're *not normal*?"

"Well to *that extent*, yes."

"Was this a new feeling?"

"Yes! I never even thought of anything like that before. I mean, this was different, that's all."

"Before that you felt everything was *normal*?"

The therapist stressed this because obviously it could not be true. "Never" usually means "hardly ever."

"I did. I mean I never, *not exactly*, thought of it."

"What do you mean?"

"Well, I mean, waste my time thinking of anything like that."

"And you were afraid that you might be *abnormal*?"

"I might get *worse!*"

"How do you mean *worse*?"

"I mean to go off into *other fields*."

"Could you give me some idea of what kind of fields that you were afraid you might go off into? Have you heard about such things?"

The second sentence was to make it easier for him to talk.

"I never heard."

"Well surely you must have, what were you afraid you might do?"

"Well I don't, I don't even know. I mean I just, I, I, I don't know, I was just afraid that I might, might just become a *disgrace*. I don't know, just a *disgrace*. I mean this might turn out to be *nothing*. I mean that's what I was afraid, I don't know what it could have turned out to be!"

"No, but you said *other fields*."

"Well, I mean there's, there's, there's *other things* that they do."

There was a long pause.

"I don't know!"

Often "I don't know" means "I don't want to know or think about it."

"Like what? What have you *heard*?"

"Oh, I, well, I've heard of, I don't know. Oh! There is one. Uh, oh well the other fellow puts it in the other fellow's mouth and *things like that*."

The "things like that" were more interesting. Fundamentally they were derivatives of a dependent, passive, infantile sucking relationship that conflicted with adult feelings of shame, control and independence.

"He sucks his penis, you mean?"

"Yes!"

"You were afraid that he might?"

"Oh, I didn't want to get involved in *nothing like that*."

"He might want to get you to do this?"

The question of active or passive roles was purposely left uncertain. Actually both sides are a part of him and both are important.

"No, I wasn't going to do, no, I just didn't want to get *involved* and have him do that to me either."

"This is what you were afraid of?"

"Well yes, that could lead into *something else*, I don't know. I didn't want that."

The therapist could say "What else?" but it was better to be indirect and give him some rest.

"But you were afraid that you couldn't *resist*? If it goes any *further*?"

"If it goes any *longer*, yes."

The use of a different word showed resistance to this pressure toward the instincts, so the superego was stressed.

"And then you thought you would be a *disgrace*?"

"Well I mean in my *work*, if anybody ever *found out* I was doing that, well, gee, *I don't know* what they'd say."

"Well, you must have been thinking about this quite a bit."

"You mean recently?"

"When did it happen?"

"Oh, well, it was around the first of December, I *think*."

"So about three months ago?"

"Yes, and when I thought of coming here I was really afraid, disturbed, but it seems to me since I confessed this thing to my doctor, I felt better. When he was outlining the history, I became a little embarrassed. It hadn't been bothering me too much during the week; as long as I keep busy, or have a lot to do, I'm all right, especially if I stay home. When I rest at night if I'm tired, it just seems to dwell on my mind."

"What do you mean?"

"I mean just the act of that, that whole thing, just some sort of sexual act just dwells on my mind. I mean when I'm tired, or when I'm *alone* or *unoccupied.*"

It was not the sexual act per se that was important, but what it signified. Dwelling on the *act* prevented recognition of ita *significance* in other areas of the patient's life.

"The act of masturbating?"

"Well not necessarily that, just, just to have the *sexual desire.*"

"To masturbate? Or have him masturbate you?"

"Well no, *I don't have him in mind.* I just have an *urge* to do *it.* I feel *tense,* and I have just an urge to *relieve my tension.* I mean it seems to me that's the only way to *relieve myself.* And I mean, it's not as bad, I don't have the desire to have nobody, no other man or nothing like that. It's just that this, this person has come and twisted, seemed to *twist me around* so, I mean it just seems abnormal to me and I just wanted to see if there was any help."

This highlighted the meaning of his fear of involvement with a man. What kind of involvement did he *not* want for which masturbation was a *substitute?* What kind of intense feeling? Often masturbation represents an abortive attempt at self-sufficiency. It is a narcissistic type of defense against unwanted dependent longings and object needs.

"*Twisted* you around what way?"

"I mean from the normal way I had been thinking. I have never given thought to that, of doing such a thing, such a thing as that before."

"Masturbating?"

"Oh no, not of that. I mean with somebody else! No not that, no."

"You mean you've masturbated before?"

"Oh yes!"

"But this was different?"

"Yes!"

"Different in what way?"

"Well with *somebody else*. I never did that with anybody else."

"You mean it was more pleasant with someone else?"

"No, I'm not saying that!"

"Well I don't understand you then, in what way did he *twist* you around?"

"Well, it was just *abnormal* for him to do that to me. I mean, *I had never been close to another male before.* I mean—"

Now was the chance to get into another area of his feelings either in time or person or both. Being *close* and being *touched* have tender, sentimental as well as physical meanings.

"NEVER?"

"Well not like *that*, no!"

"You'd never been *close* to any male?"

"Not to *touch* me like that except, no, there is one incident I forgot, I'm sorry. When I first started taking organ lessons."

He laughed.

"That's what the *teacher* did and I went and told my grandmother."

"When was that?"

"Oh, that was in 1953, *something like that.*"

"Five years ago?"

"Yes."

It was important to pin down these events in his time scale.

"How old are you now?"

"Twenty."

"Twenty. And then you were only fourteen or fifteen."

"Yes, but he didn't go any further because they fired him at the church."

"What do you mean, what did he do?"

"Well he, he used to tell me about, well he used to ask me my age and *everything, every year* he'd ask me my age and why I was taking music."

"Every year?"

"Yes."

"You started going to him when you were how old?"

"I started taking music about, uh, from him I started when I was about thirteen."

"Thirteen. So you were with him about two years?"

"Two years. Each year, every so often he'd ask me how old was I. So this particular time, it was a *Saturday*, it was after *choir* rehearsal and he was, I was *interested in the organ* so he used to give me lessons. So this evening he, uh, he said, 'Gee, I bet you have a *big one*,' and I said 'Why?' And so he was *playing, showing me,* and he let his hand slip down on my lap, and I didn't like that and *everything.* The pastor came in and he saw us sitting there and he took his hand off right away. So I went home and told my grandmother. And they knew of *other incidents* that involved this *organist,* so they got rid of him. So I never saw him again. But other than that I never had any other *close,* I mean relations like that. I was just wondering, uh, I'm not trying *to help you diagnose,* but I try to figure out ways to get out of this, *all kinds of ways* and I can't think of anything to relieve *this thought.* I mean the thought of that thing just lays in back of my mind. And, I was wondering is there such a thing as being born, and it just comes out, I mean something like an inherited *trait,* or *something like that.* Is that possible?"

He was like many psychiatrists. He wanted to place all the responsibility on heredity, in part to get away from his superego (the pastor). He was afraid of a defect (twist) in his masculinity. A twist would be in the direction of the passive, feminine, castrated female or baby. Passive baby traits are the antithesis of the usual concept of active phallic masculinity.

"You mean were you born that way?"

"Well, why did I yield? Would I give rise to something, yield to that? I mean all of a sudden? Was it just hidden in me?"

These were valid questions that had to be answered by the interviewer.

"You mean why did you let *this* fellow—?"

He interrupted in his eagerness to know and to avoid.

"Yes, yes!"

"Play with you when you didn't let the organ master do it?"

"Yes! Well I mean, *no!* I mean he probably would have. I mean, if the minister didn't come in. See he came in and saw, I don't know. Because I didn't know *anything* about *sex* then."

"So you mean you're wondering if it was something that you were born with?"

"Yes. I mean I don't know."

"Is this what you mean by some kind of a twist?"

"Yes. I mean, not knowing though."

"Just coming out?"

"These past three months or so."

"Just coming out now?

"Yes! I mean why did I yield to that just then, and why didn't I resist it like *probably* a normal person would do?"

"Well what do you think?"

"Well that's what I'm trying to figure out."

"Surely, let's figure it out together. What do you think. You said you couldn't resist."

"No, I couldn't, and I figured, I'd *shift* everything around and I can't come out with any remedy. If I could have cured myself, I wouldn't have come here!"

He wanted to be told, but he had to find out himself in order to accept it so it would stick. If the therapist tried, he could only talk in vague generalities and be asked repeatedly "What do *you* mean?"

"Of course! So you can't resist him?"

"No, I mean, I, that's probably why I stay home."

"Stay away from him?"

"Yes. I dodge him. I stay home. I don't want to be bothered."

"He plays the organ?"

"He's a *singer*."

"He's a *singer*? How old is he?"

"Twenty-three."

"An older man?"

"Yes. You'd never know! I never knew he was like that. I mean he has no *feminine* traits about him. I never even knew he was like that!"

"You mean people who do these things are feminine?"

"Well, I mean you expect things, you see these *sissy men* walking around and you expect things like that out of them."

"You've seen such men?"

"I've seen them walking around the streets."

"So you felt that anybody who did these things was a sissy, eh?"

"Well, yes, probably something wrong."

"So you mean you wonder if there's some kind of a *sissy twist* in you?"

This was premature, but when asked as a question it could easily be dropped.

"No, I never thought of that."

"It's just I wonder what you have been thinking?"

"It just seems *abnormal*. It never occurred to me whether it was *feminine*, no, I don't believe that. It just seems *against nature* to do something like that."

"Well what are your ideas? One of your ideas you said was that you wondered if there was something wrong right from the beginning."

"Yes. But I can't think of anything."

"And then the other idea that you had, you wondered if the man had anything to do with it who touched you when you were *fifteen*."

"No, I didn't wonder whether he had anything to do with it. I wondered was it there, I mean, would I have, *I don't know*."

"But you had been around men before and that never happened, huh?"

"Oh no. I never even thought of it."

"Never even thought of it?"

"Oh no, not that, no. Because I've had *girl friends* and, as a matter of fact, I just met one about a *few days*, well, about a *few weeks* ago, and I forgot about that guy until I went *home* and then the thought came back and reminded me, '*You did this; you did that!*' "

Now came the problem—was this a flight into heterosexuality, or was his difficulty in restraining the man part of a flight away from the girl? Both problems could exist side by side. He had said his problem began a couple of weeks ago! Mentioning home allowed vital information to be gathered that might explain why he told his *grandmother* about the man and not his mother.

"Home? What do you mean by home?"

"Well, where I stay."

"Where's that?"

"I live on Washington Avenue now. I was formerly boarding in Brookline but I live down there now."

"That's your home?"

"Yes. No, it's not, you mean my *birthplace*, or what?"

"Where you live?"

"Yes, that's where I live."

"You're not living at home?"

"No."

"Brookline was your home?"

"No, it was where I was boarding. I'm from Maine. I'm originally from Maine. I came down here to go to school."

"Your folks are in Maine?"

"Well, I have a *split-up family*. The people that raised me were my grandparents, but my mother, and my father was up there. My mother lives here. She's been remarried. She's here. And I was living with them and, uh, I mean due to *family problems*, uh, I mean my *stepfather*, we don't get along too well, so I started to room and board out."

A split family was part of the confusion about a split self. The therapist decided that as his trouble was primarily with a *man*, the mother sector would be mostly ignored. His past was then taken up in more detail.

He said that he was now living alone because he could not stand his stepfather. His father and mother had separated when he was a child of three or four. He had lived with mother and her parent until he was five or six, and then mother had left home to come here. Every summer he visited his father, who was a high-school teacher in Maine. Lately father had become interested in him and had offered him money for school, which he needed badly. He had angrily refused it. This led to childhood anger at father's indifference when he yearned for him. Grandfather was too old. He would see father driving a car around town. He had never forgotten or forgiven the desertion. Ostensibly he loved mother much more than father and had written once a week to her from ages five to twelve. He could never remember father living at home, but had a vivid memory of the first time he had seen him. He was around eight or nine. It was Christmas Eve or morning around four or five o'clock. Father arrived dressed in an imposing Army uniform loaded with presents. He had thought and dreamed about him off and on ever since. He was not sure, however, whether father came to see him or mother. This was part of his confusion. The father sector was so important in terms of loss and pathological mourning that he was kept in this area. Let us continue after the Christmas episode.

"You mean you saw him afterwards ever since that time?"

"I've seen him *riding in his car*, and he'd come by at *Christmas time* and leave some *money*."

"It must have been quite a surprise for you."

He saw him just enough to fantasy about him and long for him continually.

"Oh well, I always used to say, 'There's my father,' and point him out."

"He was a nice looking man? I mean you were proud of him?"

"Oh yes. He was a *teacher* and a lot of the other kids, their fathers weren't teachers."

"That's right. He was an educated man. He'd gone to *college?*"

He really had three fathers—the grandfather, the idealized good teacher-father, and the idealized bad, snob, mean father. He also must have had the usual fantasies; e.g., he left me because *I* was bad or *he* was bad, or *mother* (women) was at fault. The main fantasy would be dictated by confluent circumstances.

"Yes."

"What happened? Why didn't he take you?"

"Well he married again. Oh he's married *two times* since then."

"He was married then when he came to see you?"

"No, he wasn't. I don't think he was. *I don't know. I don't know.* I haven't figured it out. But he has had two wives since then."

"He's had two wives since then?"

"Yes."

The problem was whether he, in his fantasy, was one of these wives in the sense of being a sissy, a sister, or father's little girl.

"You've been to visit him?"

"Every time I go to Maine I visit him and he takes me around. He's very nice."

"He's good to you?"

"Yes."

"He has other children?"

"Uh-huh."

"How many other children?"

He sighed deeply.

"He's got about six, I guess. Three by the first wife, I mean after, the one *that I know of*, and then he has a set of twins and another one."

There was a strong possibility he had identified himself with these children at various times, both sexes. What did he mean by "the one I know of?"

"Boys or girls?"

"*I don't know.* I think, *I don't know.* Oh yes, those, the *last* three are three boys. The first three *I don't know what they are* because they live in another part of the city now, and I just really met his last wife, I mean his past family."

His statement mirrored his sexual confusion in the past.

"But you were sort of angry at him in a way because you longed for him and wanted him around like the other boys and he never—?"

"Paid any attention, no!"

"Really didn't, huh? Why?"

"I never had the *nerve* to ask him why yet, but I probably will."

The obvious question was, "What were you afraid to find out?"

"Well, what ideas have you had? I mean you thought about it, I can see."

"What ideas did *he* have?"

"What ideas did *you* have why he didn't?"

He sighed again.

"*I don't know.* I just, *I don't know.* He seemed sort of *fickle minded* to me, the way he does things. One minute he's like this, the next minute he's changed his mind. I don't know why."

Now the therapist had to test the limits actively. "Fickle" was an odd word in this situation.

"But I was wondering if you felt there was something wrong with you?"

"Wrong with me?"

"Yes."

"Well, no, I didn't think so."

"No? But I mean, *then.* Of course, you know better. I wondered if you thought that he might think that there was some kind of twist, or something wrong with you."

"No, I didn't."

"Then?"

"No, I didn't think there was anything wrong with me."

"Because at least we know of one thing that was different *then.* You were different from the other boys."

"Yes."

"I wondered if you ever—"

"Well, no, I never even considered that."

This area of the *twist* was too difficult at present.

"So you mean you've had no man to guide you, sort of?"

"Well *yes. No.* I mean I had to learn things on my own, like, you know, the way you throw a ball, the way you do other things, nobody to wrestle with when I go home or *things like that.* I never had that. Practically everything that I learned was, I put more effort into learning things from my *grandmother.* I mean, everything I'd go to her, I'd take things straight to her. I mean I didn't have any confidence at all in my grandfather either."

He meant that as a boy he felt rejected by both father and himself. He projected these feelings onto grandfather too.

"Why?"

"Well, he seemed so far away from me. It was just that way. He seemed to be a *cold* person too."

"You wanted to take things to him?"

"Well I would have liked to, yes. Hell, a lot of things I would like to go to him about, but I'd look at him and I'd say, 'No, I'll go to her,' and he would get angry when I would go to her and tell her things."

"He got angry?"

"I mean, yes!"

"He wanted you to go to him?"

"Yes. Well, everything I asked her, when I wanted to take music lessons, she made the last decision. I told her first. I didn't say anything to him. He'd say, oh, you don't need to take that. He didn't want me to take them."

"You were interested in music even then?"

"Yes. Well, I *always* wanted to play the *organ*, always did."

"How long ago? Even when you were a little boy?"

"Ever since I can remember. I always did."

"How far back can you remember?"

"I mean, going to church. I guess I was about school age, about *five*, about four or five. That's indefinite, I don't know."

This was when his mother left. He solved the loss partly by withdrawing, and developing a narcissistic type of independence as a deense. In doing this he identified with the mother in part and loved his "organ" or phallus as he wanted her to love him; then, feeling it to be inadequate, he identified himself at this phallic level with the man with the big organ and learned to master it from him as soon as possible (at thirteen). The teacher-organist took on the attributes of the idealized father-teacher. Another way of saying this is that the "organ" took the place of mother. In playing it, he mastered his helpless feelings and became like father with mother in a happy togetherness. When he was "seduced" at fifteen, he suffered a minor trauma which had been revived by the present affair.

"Yes, but what do you remember?"

"I just remember that I always wanted to do that, play the organ."

"At four or five, when you went to church?"

"Oh yes."

"With whom did you go to church at four or five?"

"Well the family, we'd go together."

"You mean mother and you?"

"No, not my mother, my grandmother and grandfather."

"Your grandmother and your grandfather and you? Then mother hadn't moved, had she?"

"Well I guess she had. I don't ever remember going to church with her, no."

"And even then you liked the organ? You wanted to play with it then?"

"Yes."

"You can remember?"

"I can. I always did love music, especially the organ, I love it."
He made a long pause.

"See I mean, this conversation helps me. Now if I could stay in this *state of mind*, I would never be bothered."

"What do you mean?"

"I mean *talking* to *somebody*, but I know I can't talk with someone always, I mean if I could just stay in that *mental state*. Even when I go home, or even when I'm alone I'd be all right."

"What mental state do you mean?"

"I mean just *talking* with you. I mean my mind is *occupied* on *something else*. But it's just those times when I go home."

"But do you mean it's only when you think of this fellow playing with your organ?"

"No! It's not the idea now of *thinking*. It's the idea of just wanting to get *rid* of this *tension* and that *always* comes, *sometimes* comes into my mind and sometimes it doesn't. Sometimes I just want to *get rid of it*, the *tension*."

"What do you mean by *tension*?"

"Well, you just feel *depressed*, that's all."

The tension represented a longing to possess a lost object. He had defended himself from depression over the loss of mother by turning to the organ. This was probably a development of an earlier inadequate relationship with the mother which had been handled by phallic masturbatory activity; i.e., good feelings warded off depressing thoughts and feelings. Turning to the organ meant identification with an organist who was a teacher and a version of the idealized father. Thus, the homosexual fantasies became a refuge against depressing heterosexual losses and disappointments in connection with the mother.

"Depressed?"

"Well that's the way I feel, and I get a feeling about every, it seems to follow a cycle, *once a week* or *something like that*. It's not always, no."

"Once a week?"

"Yes, I'd say about that."

"What days does it come?"

"Oh, about *Thursdays*."

"Around Thursdays?"

"Yes."

"You begin to get depressed?"

"Well it seems that way."

He paused.

"And sometimes I get these *terrific headaches* every night, *the day before that.* I just get *headaches.* I have some medicine the doctor gave me for *headaches.*"

This was a conversion symptom connected with what? A conversion headache is usually thought of as a somatic equivalent of depression or an anxiety state and a warning of danger of losing control of one's head. This could refer to many things. For example, this patient will describe two types of headaches which might refer to two different object losses, e.g., mother and father. The analyst would also say that he had displaced phallic libido onto his head as an "organ" as well as the church organ, and the headaches were equivalents of loss and castration anxiety. Another way of seeing this problem would be in terms of anxiety leading to tension and rigidity, fatigue and pain, which were focused upon in order to avoid painful thoughts of loss leading to hate and rage and/or depression.

"*Headaches?*"

"*Yes.*"

"When did you get the headaches?"

"Oh, well, these, these, they started about this year, about *four weeks* ago or *something like that.*"

"Something like that" might easily refer to the fact that he had said he met a girl a few weeks ago. This was when he said his trouble first began.

"Four weeks ago?"

"I mean these constant aches, they really ached. I never really had any headaches but they really ached."

"You never had any headaches before?"

"Well, not headaches like *these.* These were just, the headaches before, *they* would go away, but these were really aches."

"What headaches do you mean? You had some before?"

"Well, yes, headaches before, something that aspirin would easily take away, but then aspirins wouldn't do any good. So he gave me some other pills."

"So for the past four weeks you've had these headaches?"

"Yes. They hurt very much."

"*Headaches? Depression?*"

"Well usually the depression, well yes, that would, I would just be all *nervous* and a *nervous wreck* at that time. Sometimes I'd worry."

"Worry over the *tension?*"

"Well I don't think it's due solely to the *tension* but I think that's involved. It comes on too, at times. And I think the *only way to escape* this *feeling* is to *commit that act* or *something*, the *masturbation act*, or go out looking."

The reference to looking was missed. It probably referred to looking for the man. If this had been developed, it would have led nicely to how his masturbation got rid of his tension concerning his passive longings for the man and his anxiety over playing a sissy feminine mother role.

"You mean you masturbate to get rid of it?"

"Yes, or sometimes I'd have a nocturnal emission."

"Does it get rid of it when you masturbate?"

"Well, I have that sense of *gratification*."

"I mean does that get rid of the *depression* and the *headache*?"

"Yes. Well I might be fooling myself, but it does."

"It takes the *depression* and the *headache* away?"

"Well the *headache*, no. It doesn't take the *headache*, no."

"The depression?"

"Yes. I feel more *relaxed* and—"

"And the *tension* goes away?"

"Sure."

"But the *headache* stays?"

"Yes, that's what I said. It goes away after I take these pills, eventually."

"Where is the headache?"

"It's right along here. I'd say just about my *eyes*. I wear glasses too, but I don't think that's from not wearing glasses now."

This was connected with *using* and *protecting* his eyes. He was bringing in all kinds of organs onto which phallic libido and castration anxiety had been displaced.

"What do you mean?"

"I mean I take them off and I wear them."

"You don't think the headaches are from glasses?"

"I think it's just a *nervous condition*, I mean just a slight nervous condition, because I'm very *nervous* and I *worry* about, uh, *just common things*."

"Like what?"

"Oh, I've an *automobile* to pay for yet."

"Have you?"

"A bill to pay, or just, just, just worry about *things*. I mean I just constantly think about them, and which I shouldn't worry about."

He was constantly fearing some loss concerning objects that were a substitute for the old objects whose loss depressed him.

"You feel that you are a *nervous* person?"

"Yes, I do."

"How long have you been so nervous?"

"Oh dear. Well, I became really nervous, I mean outwardly since about 1956."

"Fifty-six?"

"Yes."

"Two years ago. When you were eighteen?"

"Yes."

"How do you mean?"

"Well I mean even like rehearsals I'd get really steaming *angry* and I'd *yell*, and I really didn't mean it. And I'd really start *fussing* about nothing. I'd just get steamed up quickly but not now as much because I noticed there was no reason for that. I'd just tell myself that there's no reason for that and I'd sort of try to stop it, but before that I was really, to my idea, I was terrible."

His rage was originally at his parents. Being angry and *yelling* would lead in the direction of creating *loud noises*. This would involve a voice organ. Did he yell and rage when his mother left? He could have been asked this question now.

"But tell me, you said you were interested in playing the organ when you were four or five?"

"Yes."

"You wanted to then?"

"Yes, I did."

"What did your grandfather think about it?"

"Oh well, they just, I mean, they didn't, he didn't. I don't know what he thought about it then. I mean I didn't even ask about it. I didn't inquire can I take lessons because, I mean, they knew I was too young, but when I became of age they began to investigate and that's when he outwardly said that I shouldn't take it."

"He said you shouldn't?"

"Oh yes, he didn't want me to take."

"Grandfather didn't want you to play the organ?"

"No."

"Why not?"

"Well I don't know. I guess he figured that a *young boy* shouldn't be *in the house practicing* and *things like that*. He didn't want me to take it."

This referred to the feminine passive components of organ playing
and was part of the confusion and the many "I don't know's." In
playing the organ he could actively control his longings to yell and
make angry noises. He could be the big man with the mighty organ,
admired by mother. He could be the mother who played with his
instead of father's organ. He could also be the boy who learned from
a father how to use the organ. Father was a big man with three wives.
These feelings were derivatives of or had their origin in infantile
masturbatory fantasies. The seductions at fifteen and at Christmas
time threatened to undo the sublimations. These were not well established, and if they broke down, all the infantile anxieties and de-
pressions threatened to recur. Before any boy can be *truly* independent, he must play a passive role toward his father and get know-
how from him. This passive attitude was a threat to his narcissistic
pseudo independence, which was in part and among other things a
reaction formation to his passive longings.

"How about your father?"

"Oh, I don't think he knew anything about it."

"You never ever told him?"

"Well, now he does. Then he didn't know that I wanted to, I
don't think he did."

"But you saw him every now and then."

"Yes, but I never told him."

"Never mentioned?"

"He'd always ask me how I got along in *school*, or something like
that. That's all."

"So you never could *confide* about the organ?"

"No."

"Only to your grandmother. You told her about the organ."

"Yes, I did."

"She didn't mind?"

"No, she thought it was a wonderful idea. In fact, she paid for
everything and, uh, she bought me a *saxophone* when I was in the
high-school band, and she was just very interested in me in taking
music."

"What about mother?"

"Well, I don't know what part she was playing. But she was right
she knew that I was interested, but I don't know what kind of support we got from her. Of course I wasn't writing her any business
letters or anything like that."

"You couldn't confide in father or grandfather?"

"No, neither one."

"Stepfather?"

"Oh no, not him."

"But didn't you have any boy friends?"

"Yes, but I never did, well, we'd talk over things, but gee, I mean just *some things*."

"No real closeness?"

"Well, we had, we were buddy-buddy."

"Who?"

"Kids at school, and then the kids in the neighborhood."

"But not like a father?"

"Oh no. *Some things* you just wouldn't say. I'm just saying that *some things* you wouldn't say, you wouldn't go up to your friends and tell them."

"What things do you mean?"

"That's what I said, just *some things* you wouldn't say."

"Like what?"

"Well, I couldn't think of anything. I just feel that way, that some things I wouldn't tell."

He won't tell about his anxieties about his organ and his intimate little-girl feelings and longings to sit on his knee. The resistance to talking about these fantasies was by-passed by the resident, who could have been more persistent in this area.

"So you mean there are lots of things that you felt that father could have helped you in?"

"Yes."

"And you were never able to get close?"

"No."

"Then this fellow has been sort of closer to you than any other man?"

"Yes."

"The first man you ever were really close to, huh?"

"To that extent, yes."

"And now it's hard to get him out of your mind."

"Yes."

He made a long pause, while this thought was mulled over, and then continued.

"So what do they do in cases like this? I mean is there any help?"

"What do you mean by help? I don't exactly know what you have in mind. You mean to forget him, or what?"

"Yes. I don't know what to use. I don't know what you do."

"No, of course, you don't, but I just wonder what your ideas are. What is it that you want help for, to forget him, or what?"

"It seems like I've been in an *abnormal* state since then. I mean it looks like *I don't think the way I thought before.*"

"That's what I want to know more about. In what way do you think differently?"

"Well, you just become *conscious* of *things* you never—"

His voice died away.

"That is just what I mean. Conscious of what things?"

"Oh, things that, I don't know!"

The organ had been an escape, like many other things, from his longing for an intimate physical relation with father, which had been partly denied rather than adequately mastered. The denial elements of the relationship had now been aroused.

"You mean of a sort of longing?"

"Well, yes. I'll tell you, there's *something* within me that doesn't want, *that doesn't want to do this,* and there's *something that does.*"

"That's what I mean. And how about the part that wants to do it?"

"It sometimes seems greater than the part that doesn't want to."

"And you mean you have this kind of longing and wish that he was close to you and would touch you again?"

"Yes! Yes! But then that repulsive part comes up, too."

"And says no, I don't want anything to do with it?"

"That's right. Sometimes that's greater than the other."

"Surely. Did you touch him?"

"No, not, well, the second time, well, no, I didn't do what he did to me, though. What I mean, well, he was just like he was sitting down and he's there and I'm here and so, I was just sitting *on his* his knee more or less, and, uh, *he seemed to like that.*"

He was acting the role of the little boy with his dad and liked it.

"So you mean he played with your penis until you had an ejaculation?"

"Yes."

"And you just put your hand on his knee?"

"No, well I mean, just sitting there, usually when you say touch, I mean, I didn't want you to get the idea that I was just sitting there with my hands folded or anything like that!"

"No? I was wondering, were you playing with his penis?"

"No, I wasn't."

"What were you doing?"

"Well I was just sitting there. I don't know what reactions I had but—"

"I don't know, but I wonder what you were doing with your hands."

"Oh no, I was just sitting there. I don't know what I was doing with my hands. I mean, I wasn't thinking about my hands."

"What were you thinking about?"

"Well I was just, you understand, there was the feeling, but, uh, I wasn't positive what my hands were doing."

"But you said, the reason I ask you this is because you said this was a different feeling than when you were just masturbating yourself."

"Well, it actually was."

"You mean by different feelings that you felt close to this man?"

"Yes."

"Sort of intimate?"

"Yes."

"And you mean this was what you were thinking about, that really the only difference was—"

He interrupted and finished the thought for the therapist.

"Yes, closeness! That's all."

"Because after all if you only wanted someone to play with your penis you could do that yourself."

"That's right. That's exactly right!"

"But there was something else, which was this sort of closeness to an older fellow."

"Yes. Oh, but I don't confide in him in any way though."

"You don't?"

"No, no, I don't."

"Why not?"

"Well, I just don't. In fact with very few people I do, very few."

"How come?"

"Oh, decisions I make myself. I'm so used to doing that that I just make them myself. I figure I can reason things out."

He really meant that he was afraid of and starved for close contacts. The loss of a parent will often initiate a withdrawal from close relationships with people. This may appear as a pseudo independence and self-reliance. It is a lead from weakness and fear of being hurt rather than one from strength. Often such persons stress sexual masturbatory relationships in order to escape from tender feelings which would resurrect past depressive feelings that once overwhelmed them and were repressed only after a severe struggle. In this case the pubertal seduction exploited his hidden longings for a close contact with both parents. It also allowed him to focus on a man and penile masturbatory feelings to ward off dreaded sentimental dependent cravings that were rooted in his loss of the *mother*.

"This is what you mean, that once you longed for a father and wished you had someone you could confide in, you wished you had a father like the other boys, and then later when he wanted to help you, you said 'I don't want it. I had to go for so long that now I'm going to be independent.' "

"Yes."

"So this is what you mean that you don't confide in people. You're independent, eh?"

"Well yes, to a certain extent. I mean that, things like, well, you take, well, 'Father, what should I do in this case?' or should I do this or that. I mean rather than confide I just make decisions myself."

"You had to be your own father?"

"Yes."

"But you mean that it wasn't enough and there is a part of you that sort of longs to have some sort of a close relationship to a man?"

"Yes. To him."

"To whom? To that other?"

"Oh, no, now, I thought you were speaking of now. I mean to this other fellow, this other individual."

"You mean it used to be in the past to father, and now it's to this guy."

"No, well not, I mean to be close to someone. I mean before this time it was just for, uh, *consolation*. I mean for just *advising* me what to do. I mean it wasn't any, uh, I didn't desire any relation like now, to another individual."

"Now all you think about is how wonderful it felt to be close to him sexually?"

"Yes, and after the act, oh, I'd feel terrible. I mean I'd be ready to *hit him*, just get him out of my sight."

"*Angry* at him?"

"Yes."

"Why?"

"I don't know, just the *idea of him*. I don't know. I do get *angry*, and I try to *rush him off* and get him out of *my sight*, and usually after the act it worries me all night. I say, 'Why did I do it?' "

Everything was reversed. He actively rushed the man off instead of the man leaving him. He wanted to *see* father then, and now it was the opposite. Before, it was "Why did he do it?" He must have masturbated to forget. Playing the organ was a substitute. The seduction crippled this defense and prevented it from being really sublimated or desexualized.

"Would you stay up all night?"

"Well, not all night. Maybe I'd get up and turn the *radio* on, or I'd *read,* and I'd get back. And I might go down and *practice the organ.* There's a *little organ* in the house, studio, and I teach there on Saturdays. And, I'd go down and practice and I'd come back, and I still can't go to sleep without *thinking about this,* just the act of doing this. I don't, when I think about it after the *act,* I don't think about I wanted to do it. It's just the idea that I'm sorry that I did it. That's all I can think of."

"By the *act* you mean of being *close* to him and sitting on his knee like a little boy."

"Yes!"

"And feeling his hand on you?"

"Yes!"

"Then you say on Thursdays you get depressed."

"Well, I'd say about Thursday, yes. That's usually when my week slows up."

"When you're not busy?"

"Not busy, yes. See on weekends I'd be very much occupied."

"Busy playing?"

"No, you see I always play at church parties, just on weekends".'

"You mean on weekends you are busy with the church organ?"

"Yes I am."

"Then it's in the middle of the week, on Thursdays?"

"Yes, when I don't have anything to do."

"Then you play with the *other organ?*"

"No, I don't. No, I dodge him."

Both the longing and the rage and rejection were intense.

"But you said—"

"Oh myself, oh myself, yes."

"And you become nervous and tense, and you get these headaches?"

"Yes, I do."

"So then you play with it yourself."

"Yes!"

He laughed heartily.

"Well, when do you see him?"

"I don't. I don't. I haven't for, oh, well, I saw him once after that, I mean we met up."

"When was this?"

"Oh I'd say about January."

"About two months?"

"Yes."

"That's six weeks ago, and you've been having your headaches since then?"

"Yes, I don't, I figure they were from too much work or too much worrying, but I didn't say they were directly from that."

"No, I don't know either, but you've been having the headaches since then?"

The headaches were an expression of his tension and anxiety over his passive-dependent longings to be babied and his rage at himself and this man who evoked the old needs, frustrations and rages. His dependence was a blow to his adult pride.

"Yes."

"And worrying?"

"Yes."

"About?"

"Bills."

"And also you said whether or not you had a twist?"

"Yes."

"You mean you still kind of miss him?"

"No, I mean—"

"Part of you?"

"Well, it's just when this desire comes, *I don't know*."

"Well, that's what I mean. There's a part of you that sort of misses him?"

"Oh, yes, the feel of *it*, yes, the *idea*."

"That's what I mean, the feeling of being close."

"Yes."

"And it's this *feeling* that you're really concerned with?"

"Yes."

"Not the masturbating, because as you said you could do that yourself."

"Well, that's all part of it, I mean."

"That's what I mean, it's the feeling of closeness associated with it too."

"Yes."

"But you were furious with him and yourself because as you said you've always been an independent guy."

"I've always kept a lot to myself."

"What do you mean?"

"Oh, these things that I want to do. If I ever became interested in, like the organ, I'd sit down and figure out things, how is this, and how is that, and I'd really come out, my answers were always right. I mean I wouldn't go and *inquire*. I'd always figure it out myself."

"How the organ worked?"

"Well, not how the organ worked. I mean just like timing in a certain song."

"How to play it?"

"Right. I mean other individuals would go get the records and copy rhythm off the records and things like that. I'd just sit down myself and figure it out, as to the reason why and how."

"So you were so proud of yourself in a sense, huh? At least you could do these things by yourself."

"Oh yes, I am."

He laughed again.

"Sure. Why not?"

"Believe it or not, I am."

"Surely."

"But I don't know whether I should be or not, but I am. I just feel like that within myself."

"So I take it that's one of the reasons why you were worried about becoming attached to this fellow like a little child."

"Yes, it seemed to lower my *morale* by doing something like that."

"You didn't feel so independent?"

"No, I didn't. That's it. That's right. I didn't. Not that I'm trying to live independent in every way, but *I don't want to depend on something like that.* And I couldn't find anybody else to go to discuss this thing with. I mean I'd feel funny talking to the minister."

"Surely."

"He might not want me around any more, if I—"

"And you couldn't talk to mother?"

"Oh no. I wouldn't dare tell her. I'd be embarrassed telling her that."

"That's what I mean, or go to grandmother?"

"Oh no!"

"You wanted to talk to a man?"

"Well, I mean someone that I knew, that I thought that was sure to have some remedy."

"You mean a remedy for this part of you that—"

He interrupted and laughed again.

"Uh, yes! I don't know."

"That sort of feels lonely and wants to feel close to a man?"

"Yes."

"Because you said, I think, that you, as a child, used to feel lonely and wished that you had a daddy like the other boys."

"Yes."

"Did you get depressed then in those days?"

"Well at certain times, yes, when they had some special gathering at night for just a father and son."

"*Father*-and-*son night?*"

"Yes, but I didn't want to take my grandfather because he looked too old to me. He wasn't really old, he was only about forty-eight or so."

"He wasn't like the other boys' fathers?"

"No, he wasn't like them. I didn't want to take him."

"So you'd feel different?"

"I know I did."

"You really felt abnormal?"

"That's right. That's right."

"So you didn't go?"

"Well, I'd go but I'd feel bad."

"By yourself?"

"No, I'd tell him. I'd have to tell my grandfather because I'd get a whipping if I didn't tell him."

"So you felt bad both ways?"

"Oh yes, I felt, all during reading hour, whatever it might be. Like at football games, he never used to take me to those or anything. The only times I'd go, I mean I'd play when I was at school, I'd participate in that sport, but my father would never come and when there was a big football game every year, he'd never take me. Or anything like that, so—"

"You must have missed him a great deal."

"Oh yes, I thought of a lot of places I could have used him."

"That's what I mean, you thought about him a lot?"

"Yes. Well I guess so."

"So then in a way it's almost as if there's a part of you that keeps thinking all the time about a father and longs to be close, and to have this man do this to you. It is like a sort of little boy part that feels lonely."

"Yes, well it's, yes—"

"But this is a different kind of relationship."

"Yes, but it is the closeness I guess I miss."

"That's what I mean, because as you said the distinguishing feature was this *closeness* that you never had."

"That's right. I would say so."

"So it's as if this part of you still needs it, eh?"

"It needs the closeness? You mean there's something missing?"

"Still something missing."

"Oh yes, I mean, sometimes I feel very *lonesome*, not necessarily for *him*, but just *lonesome*, period. I just need, you know, somebody close, that you can talk to, you know. The majority of my time is spent telling *somebody else* what to do or something of that sort."

"Only now you're sort of angry at father?"

"Well, I don't want to be *bothered*. I mean it doesn't matter if I see him."

Consciously he did not want the old wounds to be reopened, but also he wanted to go back and complete the past.

"It's too late?"

"Yes, it's too late."

"Too late? But part of you evidently doesn't think so?"

"Huh?"

"Part of you doesn't think so?"

"Well, I don't, that part doesn't want him, but it's just the intimacy."

"That's what I mean, you're repulsed by that part now."

"Yes."

"You don't want to be a little boy?"

"No."

"Sucking around a man?"

"No! No!"

"Because you thought that this might lead to even worse?"

"Yes."

"And by worse you mean abnormal sucking?"

"I mean I'm that way. When something new confronts me, I go and try to find out everything I can about this thing, so that's what I did. I read a book that outlined what it does, you know."

"What book?"

"Oh, one of Freud's books."

"You read one of Freud's books?"

"Yes."

He laughed.

"What book was that?"

"I don't know, something on psychoanalysis or something, I don't know. I don't remember."

"And what did the book say?"

"Well, it just said that some people do those different things, you know, and I didn't want to be involved in anything like that."

"That they touched their organs together?"

"Yes. that's what he said."

"And you meant by touching the organs, you mean—"

"Well, I mean just like *a man* and *a woman* would do, you know. I mean get on top of you, you know."

"On top of you. You mean he'd get on top of you?"

"No, no! I mean that's what I didn't want to happen!"

"I know that. I mean that's what it meant to you. He'd get on top of you and do it to you?"

"No! Well it didn't happen to me that way because it would be *the other way around!*"

"Which way would it have to be?"

"Oh, if it was, *I would have to be on top.*"

He laughed at the idea and at this aspect of the dependence-independence theme.

"You'd have to be on top, eh?"

"This is, uh, no, I don't want anything to do with that, it's too *confusing!*"

"That's the part that confuses you. You mean who does what to whom and which part of you wants what?"

"Yes."

"And you don't like to think about that?"

"No, I don't like to think about any of that."

"But, as you said, when you get home and you start to have those thoughts, you can't stop thinking."

"Yes, well that's just the, not the, I don't have to do the *act.* I just have the thought. I want just the feelings of being close you know."

"And you can't get it out of your mind?"

"No, I can't. I've tried every gimmick, but I can't."

The obsessional thinking was a way of keeping busy. By thinking of the sexual act he didn't want, he could keep the more painful yearning feelings and thoughts at a distance.

"What have you tried?"

"Well I mean, I just try to stop thinking. I just try to keep as busy as I can."

"Try to keep busy?"

"Well, then, yes. I mean that's usually during this depressed cycle. Yes, but I mean Monday nights and all that I'm never bothered. I just go straight to bed. I'm so tired I just flop on the bed."

"And on Thursdays you can't sleep and you keep thinking about—?"

"Well, this, now sometimes, it's very peculiar, sometimes, some weeks I might just, like when I'm busy I don't even think about it, but when I'm not busy, it comes on, just about Thursday or Wednesday. And if it does come into my mind on the weekend, I just drop it easily. I always have something to do to replace that thought."

"What do you have in mind?"

"Well, I met a very nice young lady about two weeks ago and, uh, and see this happened between the time that I had this fight with my old girl. I didn't have a girl friend when this happened. I had just quit her."

"You had just quit your girl friend when this happened?"

"Yes. Well not exactly just quit but, uh, we had broken up for about, uh, I had been away for about four weeks."

"Steady girl?"

"Yes, we had gone together for two years. It started when I was in high school."

"Did you ever feel close with her?"

"Yes, occasionally, but she wasn't much for sex."

"She wasn't what?"

"She wasn't too much for it. She was scared of the risk, you know."

"Did you have any trouble in your sexual relations with her?"

"No."

"And with this girl that you're going with now?"

"Oh no, she, we haven't gotten around to that."

He laughed.

"Haven't gotten around to that yet, eh?"

"No."

"So what you would like then is to find out what confuses you, what it is that you want?"

"I want YOU to see if you could, uh, just help me get rid of this, this *other person* that keeps telling me, yes, *to do this thing.*"

"You mean that side of you that longs for a man."

"Yes. It might seem farfetched to you, but I do."

"A man, you mean?"

"Yes."

"For a *father?*"

"Well, no, it's just this *act,* no, no, no, not the longing for a man, I mean for a father, but it's this act I don't want to have anything to do with, this sexual act. Now that's the part I don't want."

At times it was more galling for him to admit he had a little boy's longing for his *father* than to admit he wanted a sexual relationship. He wanted to feel like a big independent man. He was a teacher himself. This contrasted heavily with his little-boy yearnings when he sat on the man's knee. He used masturbatory sex as a screen to cover up his tender longings, but was willing to say he wanted closeness and not sex as long as it was *not* attached to father.

"You mean *that kind* of a longing?"

The therapist was purposefully vague.

"Yes, I want to get rid of that. I mean the other, I don't, I mean I figure you can discriminate the two. I mean the *longing for a father* and the *longing for that act,* but if you could get rid of the whole, just the act, I mean I'd probably be all right."

"Well, I think you can be helped. I will find someone for you if you would like."

"Yes, I certainly would. I don't want to go near that church and often I don't feel like going out at all."

"I will get in touch with you as soon as possible."

"All right. Thank you, doctor."

The central problem of any neurosis in the male can usually be reduced to his inability to accept his passive feminine wishes in respect to other males. This is from the point of view of the distribution of libido. The patient in this interview was filled with and repulsed by tender longings for a close contact with an older man, a father figure. He sat upon his seducer's knee and passively allowed his genital to be handled. He said he did not want this, but later admitted he longed for the sexual part of the act even though he could masturbate himself better from the gross point of view of technique. He wanted the intense, condensed feeling of intimacy that the act represented in order to make up for past deprivations. The "act" he talked about allowed him to concentrate on the sexual or sensual aspects and deny the more painful aspects of the relation, that is, the tender passive infantile yearnings that are epitomized by the act of sitting on the man's knee. Later he could admit his longings for a tender relationship but with little intensity of feeling. It was obvious that this type of feeling was a tremendous threat to his feelings of independence and masculine pride. More will be said about the physical basis of these feelings later. From the point of view of the ego, we could say that from this interview we could deduce the following construction of his development. He lost his mother around four or five. Around this time he turned to the church *organ*. The psychoanalyst would feel that most likely this memory was a screen, valid as a memory but a cover-up for an unhappy period when he turned away from mother towards men and his male organ. Around this time he had probably started to become "independent" more than his age warranted and began to fantasy about his father with longings that reached a high point around eight or nine when father visited him. Afterwards he felt deserted and disappointed again; he turned more and more to his "organ" and became more withdrawn. This "independence" was more of a pseudo independence or narcissistic withdrawal and a lead from weakness rather than strength. In one sense this meant his "organ" became his love object. He was ripe for seduction by a man at puberty, because at this age his oedipal conflicts were reactivated and intensified by genital and biological developments. He had lost mother and "discovered" the "organ" at four or five, if not earlier. At puberty he would have been an easy target for a male organ teacher. This man would be an obvious father substitute, a teacher like father, interested in music unlike the grandfather, and an "organ" player like himself. In other words, this man was a narcissistic object choice. It was likely that this experience was traumatic and that he dwelt upon it in fantasy as it was useful in the sense that an interest in his organ, father and men allowed him a greater measure of independence from a need for mother and women. He said that he had known a girl for two years and had changed, had become angry, yelling and fussy. Perhaps this indicated that he was "thawing out" and giving up his phallic independence, and that his childhood unexpressed anger was coming to the surface. He connected the recent seduction in time at

least with the fact that he had left his girl "three or four weeks ago."
He had also left his present seducer. These two acts also appeared
temporally connected with the development of a conversion symptom, headaches, and obsessional thinking. To understand this we
have to think of the terrible blow to his self-esteem he had suffered
from being abandoned. The painful thoughts were, "Why did they
do this? Did they consider me worthless? Am I twisted, defective, abnormal?" These thoughts must have been present continually. He
defended himself from them by saying that at least this girl and that
man are interested in me. The presence of the father in his home
town allowed him to soft-pedal the issue of his abandonment by
mother. The first sexual seduction allowed him to concentrate on the
"organ" instead of the person. The issue of the girls protected him
from the men and vice versa. Finally, he was the one who left them—
the master of his fate and not passively overwhelmed. He now had a
new girl. In essence he appeared to be running back and forth between men and women at one level, between male and female roles
at another level, and between "organs" and persons at still another.
In this interview an attempt was made to give him some insight into
the fact that what he called his homosexual problem was in reality a
failure to complete his psychological growth and old unmastered
tasks, a failure to accept and adequately control childhood injuries,
loves and hates. He had attempted to solve these problems by denial
and the development of a reactive type of independence.

Later interviews brought out some further historical material that
was of great interest but did not basically alter the conclusion that
his defective relationship with his father was the main sector to expand in any attempt at psychotherapy.

His phobic feelings had begun around the time mother left. He
had developed a school phobia which had persisted off and on for
three years. Thus the ages of five or six and eight or nine again
showed their importance. Prior to eight or nine he had also been
extremly phobic concerning thunder and loud noises. This was of
great interest in respect to his interest in the organ. It turned out
that ever since his initial seduction at fourteen or fifteen he had had
homosexual fantasies which had become obsessive in the past two
years, or ever since he had left his mother and had known his girl
friend. He claimed later that he had gone with his girl and had intercourse in order to get these fantasies out of his mind. The fantasies
were mainly those of being passively masturbated by a man who

loved him. The girl he had gone with annoyed him because she was "gossipy" and didn't care for science, music and serious subjects. Later this turned out to be a good description of his mother. He had left Maine right after his initial seduction and had lived with his mother and stepfather. He mentioned that around the time his father had visited him (at eight or nine) his mother had also paid a visit. He mentioned bitterly that she came to see her mother more than him. She was not at all interested in the organ, unlike his grandmother, and not at all overjoyed to have him around after puberty, as she had three children by her new husband and was financially strapped most of the time. He had arrived at her home with high expectations and was extremely upset by the difference in the real and the fantasy mother. This drove him further toward the homosexual role.

In the fourth session a new and important fact came to light. The age of eight to nine was important for another reason. A girl cousin, who was a year younger, came to live with his grandparents. For a long while he was jealous of this girl, then finally they became fond of each other and played duets together on recorders. He hinted that there had been some form of sexual activity which helped his grandmother to decide that when he turned twelve the time was ripe for him to live with his mother. One of the reasons he found mother disappointing was that she acted and looked so young he thought of her like a girl friend and found himself constantly thinking about and intensely aware of her intimacies with his stepfather. This led to a furious feeling of jealousy and hate of the stepfather. For this reason he had moved out two years ago. There had also been a half-sister in his mother's home who was around five years younger and he hinted that he had felt very close to her.

At the end of a four-month period, when he had been seen approximately thirty times, he was acutely aware of how he ran from women to men and his organ. He had no particular anxiety about home or church or homosexuality, and was able to accept a "loan" from his father of $100 a month. He complained bitterly, however, about his general feelings of depression and moodiness. He would burst into tears and feel furiously angry over what he called corny movies and television programs which always seemed to concern lonely, abandoned people, especially children. At this time he was transferred to a college mental-hygiene department and was seen on a weekly basis. Before his transfer he was prepared by weaving material concerning his attitude about therapy into his fears and fantasies concerning abandonment.

In summary, we can see that his therapy was primarily concerned with the analysis of phobic symptoms and narcissistic character traits that interfered with his psychosexual growth. Therapy was not concerned with his morals or his choice of a career, although these are always influenced. As is so often the case with phobics, his "independence" was too much a reaction to a passive phallic fixation.

IX

THERAPY TECHNIQUE AND THE PERSONALITY OF THE THERAPIST

Case of Hysteria with Conversion

A good knowledge of formal psychiatry, including history taking, administrative duties and a recognition of the overt neurotic and psychotic syndromes, may make a beginner feel less anxious with patients and able to assume more easily the *role* of a therapist. Unfortunately, these qualities are of no more help in enabling him to undertake this role than is a knowledge of neurology, medicine, psychology or sociology. Theoretically, an important factor in determining the ability to learn and use the "analytic" type of psychotherapy appears related to the ability of the therapist to imitate the patient in the following way. Ideally the patient is induced to split his personality into an adult, rational, observing and controlling portion and a feeling, remembering, infantile part. It is necessary for the therapist to do the same thing but somewhat differently. Ideally he must possess an over-all emotionally stable and psychosexually mature personality that can permit a controlled regression of a portion of itself in the therapy situation. This allows the therapist to participate in the patient's thoughts and feelings to the extent that he comprehends with conviction the rationale and the connections of the patient's manifest difficulties with their unconscious origins. This also enables him to cultivate a sense of awareness for what is relevant and important in the welter of material presented by the patient. He can then literally hear better. There is a wide range of ability among beginning therapists in spotting important key words and phrases and relevant material and in relating details to large patterns of behavior. Paradoxically this can be done only by paying attention to minor details, by always suspecting manifest historical material and the obvious, and by always considering the possibility of defense by reaction formation. The majority of those whose personalities are mature enough to finish medical school or its equivalent can learn to be effective therapists with many types of patients. Those to whom this ability comes naturally can always improve their skill.

There is a good deal of nonsense, believed mainly by lay people, to the effect that psychiatrists are or should be persons of superior intellect, personality integration, maturity and breadth of outlook, etc. While it would be nice if this were so, actually psychiatrists in general have shown little difference from other groups of technical specialists. They tend to be no wiser or make better judgments outside of their field than do surgeons, etc. The rate of neurosis and psychosis in this group is probably little different from that of other groups and may conceivably be worse. This may not reflect too severely upon their ability as technicians. A lame man can become an excellent orthopedic surgeon.

Many if not all people, who for the most part are mature in their appearance, thinking and behavior, have periods of transient regressive thinking and acting with varying degrees of control over it. Even Freud was not immune to this. The ability to permit a portion of one's ego to regress in a psychotherapeutic relationship, however, implies on the part of the therapist the necessity of leading from strength rather than weakness. This implies having a reasonably well-integrated personality and being free from glaring emotional blind spots and complexes. Although this is always a relative matter, few residents are so loaded down with emotional problems that they are unable to be fairly objective and controlled in their dealings with the majority of their patients. Freedom from the thought-constricting effects of anxiety, on the part of the therapist, is important for a number of reasons. The majority of those who wish to take up psychotherapy as their specialty do so in response to deep-seated personality needs. This applies, of course, to the choice of any career. In psychiatry these needs are usually similar to those that send patients into therapy. Just as patients fall into diagnostic groups with various problems based upon different character traits, so do psychiatrists. Like patients, therapists can be divided roughly into hyperemotional, feeling persons and those whose intellectual processes are dominant and isolated from their emotional convictions. One is all heart and no head and the other is the opposite. There is also a third type whose tendency is to derive much satisfaction from a sense of power in manipulating patients. They have an exaggerated need for admiration and clinically successful results. Each type has its own set of problems.

In medical circles, the hyperrational and unemotional type is relatively more common. His main weapon in dealing with his own and his patient's problems is his ability to intellectualize, rationalize, verbalize and organize his thoughts neatly. He makes an excellent impression upon his colleagues or supervisors, especially when they are of the same type. He is usually able to present cases with apparently good understanding. Unfortunately, whether resident or supervisor, this type is often so far off in his timing and choice of the material that he discusses with his patient that the insight he imparts causes little conviction and cases drag on interminably. One of the first things the beginner learns is the futility of intellectual insight without conviction. There are few therapists of the intellectual type who do not try this kind of "cure." Another tendency of this group is to interpret too frequently and too deeply. When more experienced, they develop a reaction formation to this tendency, play too passive a role, and do not dare to interpret deeply. It is too illogical.

The most common tendency in all groups, and the third one in particular, is to confront the patient with the therapist's understanding. This is often evidence of a kind of anxiety found in persons whose age or lengthy past experience in psychiatry as measured in time forces them to demand better than average results from themselves. In many cases this is manifested by authoritative interpretations and a pinning down of patients with keen if futile logic. Hostile responses of the patient can then be regarded as a triumph in exposing hostile transference states. Another characteristic of all beginning therapists is their tendency to exaggerate the importance of details without regard to their over-all importance.

At the opposite pole from the intellectual type are the hyperemotional therapists who are keenly alert to all the nuances of their patients' feelings and the over-all situation, but deficient in organizing the material so that it can be understood in terms of recurrent patterns of behavior and needs. This makes it difficult to help patients who need some organization of chaotic masses of feeling material in order to control and moderate their anxieties. A certain subspecies of this type of therapist is not happy unless down on their knees wrestling with the unconscious for the salvation of the patient's ego. They gravitate towards encouraging intense abreactive episodes and become impatient when such events do not cure their patients. They are annoyed when their patients relapse or do not dredge up any particular traumatic events and memories. Amytal interviews, hypnosis and related procedures are quickly adopted by this type and just as quickly dropped. Ill-founded enthusiasm or pessimism concerning the prognosis in such cases is common.

The three types mentioned are similar to the hysterical, obsessional and narcissistic types of characters. Undoubtedly there are many other types of therapists, such as depressive, paranoid and schizoid, whose behavior and mode of thinking resemble those of patients. We could also classify therapists as predominantly motherly, fatherly or brotherly. The first type tends to be overpermissive, warmly involved, sympathetic and understanding. The accent is on intimacy, giving and free expression of feelings, especially aggression. The fatherly type is more constrained. There is a greater emphasis on reality problems, control of impulse, postponement of pleasure and use of aggression. Fatherly therapists are usually more tolerant of sexual impulses and less tolerant of aggression. The big brother or sister type is common among psychiatric residents. It is often expressed by the formula, "I know because I have had similar experiences and feelings." All of these types have their own kinds of advantages and problems. All patients have intimacy problems due to distrust and an overt or covert withdrawal from realistic personal relationships. Many cannot tolerate mothering, or react to it with regressive behavior. Fatherly therapists frequently have difficulties with obsessional patients and problems in masked aggression. The admission by the therapist of problems similar to his patient's is almost always a mistake and may evoke only contempt and increased distrust. Other classifications of therapists can be made but this would be belaboring the point, which is that until psychotherapeutic procedures can be fully described, examined and evaluated, subjective impressions based upon personality characteristics of the therapist will always cloud the issue of who is doing what to whom.

There are two types of behavior that are incompatible with success in any type of analytically based psychotherapy, i.e., that due to acting out and that due to an isolation of the therapy from real life. These can be done by therapists as well as patients and are best dealt with by good supervision or self-analysis.

When a therapist listens to a taped interview of himself treating a patient, especially after a week or two, he will often be amazed to hear how irrational or anxiety-motivated or inconsistent many of his responses appear. This will be especially apparent if a supervisor is present, as he will identify with him and be more critical. The simpler process of listening to himself is an exceptionally valuable one if analysis and supervision are not available. There are some difficulties inherent in this method. Recordings may be collected like sheaves of notes and never used. This may be owing to compulsive tendencies or narcissism on the part of the therapist who is unconsciously bent upon saving everything that has the connotation of being a valuable part of himself. Many therapists find it difficult to listen to themselves critically enough to make this procedure worth while, and are either carried away with admiration of their efforts or feel that nothing is any good. In any case, the only penalty is wasted time. The question that should always be uppermost is, of course, "Why did I say that and what did I mean?" This will never be a popular process, as it takes two to three hours to review a fifty-minute interview.

It is difficult to recognize acting out on the part of the therapist, since rationalizations are plentiful. There are also many subtle ways of showing aggression or being seductive which are almost impossible to detail but may show up in a handshake and above all in the handling of time and money. Few of these do much harm, but they can cause annoying complications. A therapist can also isolate an interview just as much as a patient, mainly through an inability to be friendly and at ease.

Many beginners find their narcissism wounded by playing second fiddle to persons important in the patient's past. They overestimate the therapeutic importance of their unique presence and see transference everywhere and as a natural reaction to themselves. However, the most common error is that of allowing the patient to manipulate the transference states by playing upon the therapist's prejudices, which most patients quickly ascertain. In terms of personality type, no therapist has an overwhelming advantage over any of the other types, although it is easy to postulate ideal combinations of intellectual organizing ability, as in the compulsive, feeling for what is appropriate, as in the libidinal type, and ability for cool detachment, as in the narcissistic type. Most therapists feel they possess the ideal combination of these three qualities. Medical technicians who do much work on blood-cell counts have their tendency to err on the plus or minus side evaluated in terms of a correcting coefficient. The only way we can approach this is in terms of a therapist's personality is through analysis of character traits. As psychotherapeutic techniques become more effective, it may be that long-term psychoanalytic procedures will become more a part of research and medical training for therapists than for psychotherapeutic purposes.

Let us listen to a patient who attempted to take the control of an interview away from a resident who was an experienced therapist but was momentarily disconcerted by the frankness of the sexual material.

This clinic patient was an attractive and somewhat hard-looking married woman in her early thirties with a bored, cynical expression in her gray eyes. She had dark brown hair with a touch of blonde put in and was carefully made up. She appeared moderately ill at ease, blinked her eyes occasionally and passed her left hand nervously across her hair above an ear. The therapist waved her into a chair by his desk. He was a young man of pleasant appearance and in his late twenties.

"Could you tell me how it happened you came here."

She licked her lips nervously.

"Well, I don't know. I had *pains*. Let's see, about two years ago in March my doctor thought I had a *fallopian pregnancy*. Then my *nerves* gave way and I had that awful attack of *pains* and came to the hospital. You know I get this horrible *twitch* in my eye lately."

The therapist hesitated for a moment over the aside remark and then decided to use the obvious key words.

"Your *nerves* gave way and you had an attack of *pain?*"

"Yes, *pain*. They suggested to me I had a *fallopian pregnancy*."

"What do you mean?"

"I was four months late in menstruating. My husband was also a patient in the hospital at that time. We had hospital insurance. I had just had the kids' tonsils out."

The therapist decided the information about her family took priority.

"You have kids?"

By now the young therapist appeared to be no threat to the patient. She had recovered her composure and her voice had become calmer and more relaxed. The therapist sensed the change.

"Yes. I was still covered by the insurance over at the hospital and I figured I'd go there. I didn't know it was my *nerves*. I thought, gee, maybe I am *pregnant* because I hadn't menstruated in four months. So I went over there and they told me, they examined me and they said my uterus was *normal* and would I please bring a sample of urine. I guess they do a rabbit test or pregnancy test or something and, so, I went over there and I didn't put my name on the bottle. I saw the girl sweep all the bottles up in her arms like that, you know, and I didn't think anything about it. Well, somewhere along the line my urine got mixed up with some pregnant woman's because when I went over two days later for a report on it they said to me, 'Congratulations, you're pregnant.' So I said to the doctor, 'What do you mean, congratulations; you told me if I was pregnant I would have a *fallopian* pregnancy.' By that I mean a pregnancy of the *tubes* and the way I understand it the baby forms in the tube and then when it gets so far along in a pregnancy if you don't have the tube removed, you know the operation, then the baby growing makes the tube split open and *peritonitis* sets in, you go into a *shock* and you can *die*."

"Peritonitis sets in?"

The therapist realized that she would make frequent attempts to clothe her fantasies in medical terminology.

"Yes."

"How? How do you mean, peritonitis?"

"*Poison.*"

She said this in a matter-of-fact manner.

"Poison?"

"Yes."

"If you—?"

"If you don't have, if you have a fallopian pregnancy and the tube ruptures, you go into a shock, peritonitis sets in and you can die!"

"How do you mean *poison?*"

"*Poison, peritonitis,* you know, something like *gangrene* I think."

"But how does that come from the tube splitting open?"

"Well, all that, the baby and everything is in there and it splits the tube. I don't know. I don't like to talk about *those things!*"

Now the mood induced by the repetition of key words brought other fantasies to mind.

"What do you mean?"

"Like the *brain wave,* what did they give me a brain wave for? The first time they gave it to me was because I *cracked* my head. The second time they just gave it to me. What I can't understand is I've got a *sore* spot right there."

She put her finger on her head.

"Why doesn't that show up in a brain wave? There must be *something* there."

She felt threatened by her feelings of defectiveness and badness in some area.

"What do you mean?"

"I think that *sore spot* is what causes all these *spots* in front of my eyes."

"What do you mean by sore spot?"

"Right there. There is a sore spot right there and if you press it I get this sharp pain in my head. I have these spots right now. I've got them all the time."

Now the therapist began to realize that there was probably a different sore spot in her life, possibly in her relationship with herself or others, and that this was displaced onto her body.

"Really!"

"Yes, I've got them, I can point them out to you, all the time."

"You've had them all the time?"

"Yes, I've had it for, oh, I don't know how long."

"How long do you mean?"

"I can't think how long I've had them. I've had them for an awful long time."

"Really! How far back?"

"I had them when I applied for a veteran's pension two years ago. I had them before that. Gee, I've had them for an awful long time."

"Can you remember back to when it was you had them?"

"Well, all I know is I got them all the time."

"Really!"

"Yes, I can see them on the wall. I can see them right out there. I can touch them."

"Touch them?"

"I can point them out, the spots."

"The spots and the pain?"

Here she became confused, as these two words were too distantly related to her.

"What pain?"

"You were talking about the pain you had too."

"Oh, in the head?"

He realized he had been in error.

"Hm. Yes."

"Oh, that's if I touch *this spot* on my head, not *those spots* that are floating around out there. You don't think I'm crazy, do you?"

"What do you mean?"

"Well I mean now do I sound a little bit nuts?"

"How do you mean nuts?"

"I don't know. Ordinarily I don't have an *inferiority complex* and yet when I sit here with you I do."

Now there was a chance to find a more important sore spot in her life.

"Inferiority complex?"

"Yes! I feel *foolish* when I am talking to you."

"In what way do you feel foolish?"

"I don't know, real *childish*. Am I a *hypochondriac*?"

"What do you mean by a hypochondriac?"

"Now look! A hypochondriac to the ordinary person means you *imagine pain*. I actually *have* the pain! And I've got to figure all these *problems* out myself. If that's the way, I'll be here for years you know trying to figure out what makes me tick. I know I get very *nervous* and when I get *nervous* I get this *pain* here."

The therapist wondered if he should return to the inferiority complex, but was unsure.

"Really? When you get *nervous*?"

"Yes. When I was working at a hospital, I said to a girl one day, 'Oh, I'm getting *nervous*,' and she said, 'How do you know?' I said, 'I've got that *pain* again.' I don't know what it is right there."

She pointed to her abdomen.

"When you get nervous?"

"It must be because I went to a doctor once and I had the pain all the time. Every time he pressed it, I got the pain."

She showed him where on her abdomen.

"But, of course, he felt a little bit lower."

She smiled coyly and then said seriously,

"But you know if I just touch my stomach it is so sore. They will check me again to be positive I'm not pregnant?"

The therapist felt intrigued by the other doctor's behavior.

"What do you mean you got pain every time he touched you?"

"It hurts there."

She pointed to the region of her navel.

"Every time he touched you? "

"Yes. But I mean it hurt me all the time. I'd get attacks of it."

"Attacks?"

"Yes, sharp pain right there."

He ignored her invitation to feel it himself.

"You get attacks of pain? You've had attacks of pain for quite a while?"

"Oh, two years I've had them."

"Really? Since then?"

"I went to work in a candy factory two years ago, let's see, a year ago, or something. I worked there four months. I had the spots all the time I was working in the candy factory. I could hardly see the candy for the spots. Then when I got sick the day after Thanksgiving a year ago I was working in the candy factory, and I went to work, and ooh, I got such a sharp pain and it was, oh I felt like I was so weak. That's when I came over here and I had a 19,000 white count and was hospitalized on the medical ward. I laid in there a week. They sent for my X rays. The X rays had been taken in the last five-month period previous to that, like from August on, and they told me I was a hypochondriac."

"Where was the pain?"

"That spot right there."

She pointed towards her abdomen again on the left side.

"Oh, it is so sore to touch it."

"What is that spot, where is it?"

She was all wide-eyed innocence.

"I don't know! What is it anyways?"

"Where do you locate it?"

"Right there."

She indicated the same spot again and looked annoyed.

"What do you mean?"

"*Kidney!*"

"Well, you must have thought about it a lot."

"Well, I'll tell you. When they gave me the gall bladder X-ray, I thought it was my *gall bladder*. I worried over that. When they gave me the stomach ulcer X-ray, I thought it was that and worried over that. They gave me kidney X-rays and I worried over that. This all stretched over a period of time. You know they had to arrange appointments. Then they gave me the *barium enema* X-rays. I nearly died on that thing! I told you on the kidney X-ray my *eyes* swelled shut."

She put her hand to her forehead.

"Oh, my *head* is splitting. Can't you order aspirin or something for my headache?"

"Well, as you were saying, you thought then it was this or that, but you must still wonder about it."

"Now I think I have *cancer*."

"What do you mean?"

"I think I have cancer."

"You think you have cancer?"

"I think I've got it. I've got too many pains not to have it."

"But I mean particularly this pain, is that what you are thinking of?"

"Yes, I think *whatever* is there has *spread* all through me now causing all my *pains*."

Something bad, malignant, harmful and devouring festered within her. She spoke correctly, but because of displacement onto her body the source could not be discovered.

"What do you mean by cancer? What are you thinking of when you wonder about that?"

"I don't know, I always have that thought."

"How do you mean, that thought?"

"That's why I came here. I didn't come here by force. I was told to come here to help myself. They cut me open in April with acute *appendicitis*. They said I'm *all right inside*. Then the pains still continued. Then I thought I had *adhesions* but they said it is too early to have adhesions."

"What did they mean by all right inside?"

"They said they didn't find anything *wrong*. All my organs were *good*."

"Nothing wrong *inside*?"

"Um, just acute appendicitis."

"You must have wondered about what might have been wrong inside."

She began to wonder if the doctor was confused or teasing her, then said sarcastically,

"When?"

"When you said they cut you open?"

"For appendix?"

"Yes."

"They did an exploratory operation. They said they did an exploratory because when I came in here to have my appendix out I was three weeks late menstruating then!"

"Oh?"

"And they explored me to see if I had anything wrong with me, *some kind* of a *female disease* or something."

"You must have had some thoughts about that."

"Oh, I figured they might find a *cyst*. I've heard people talk about cysts on their *ovaries* and things like that."

"On their ovaries?"

The therapist could have said, "What did that mean to you?" The result would have been the same.

"Yes, I've heard people say they've had them."

"And this caused the pain?"

"Well, all I knew then was I had the pain in my side. When I came in here then, they took my appendix out."

"For a pain in your side?"

"Well, this will *kill* you, you know when I—"

She clapped her hands to her forehead.

"Oh, I'm dizzy. You know I came up here in November. They told me I was a hypochondriac. They told me to go to a psychiatrist. I went there. I was working in the candy factory over three months and I was covered by insurance so the psychiatrist and a medical doctor signed the insurance papers. I collected the insurance for twelve weeks, and each time they made out the new form they put down *Anxiety Hysteria Complex*."

The therapist wondered how much her insurance entered into the picture and slipped off the track, losing the thread for a minute.

"You were covered by insurance?"

"Sick insurance."

"Well, what sort of insurance was it?"

"Oh, I don't know, some kind of factory insurance or something."

"For what possibility?"

This was a correct way of returning to her fantasies, although the therapist was not aware of it.

Again she became sarcastic and condescending.

"I couldn't work, you see. Okay? So I went to the doctor, I don't know, for four or five months and I got awful *nervous!* I got these awful *headaches* and I've got a headache talking to you!"

Suddenly the therapist realized he had gotten off the track and that the insurance could wait.

"You had these awful *headaches?*"

"Yes. Gee, I wish you could give me something for the *spots*."

"How do you mean *awful* headaches?"

"I've got one right now. I get *lightheaded!*"

There was a long pause.

"What happened?"

She continued.

"So, anyway, after I stopped going to the psychiatrist I stayed home for a couple of months and I was a nervous wreck, every one of my nerves."

"For example?"

"What? Oh, everything! I had pains in my head and I couldn't sit still. I was drinking coffee. I couldn't sleep nights and I still can't. I slept two hours last night."

The therapist ignored her attempt to drag in this symptom.

"You were a nervous wreck?"

"Yes, I'm a nervous wreck everywhere! So anyways I went over and got a job at a hospital. I was working there three weeks and I got the bellyache, a pain, you know, in my stomach."

She continued before the therapist could ask her to enlarge upon this statement. He smiled, trying to show that he was aware of how heavyhanded he seemed.

"Where was that? Show me."

"What? Right here! Oh, that spot, every time I touch that. You know for years that's been hurting me and they haven't done anything for it."

"For years?"

"Yes!"

"Ever since when?"

"For a long time I've noticed that. When I touch right there, I get nauseated."

"And this was since when?"

"What? I don't know, I don't know how long."

"You have some ideas?"

Now the therapist's persistent refusal to get involved began to pay off.

"Well, I had pains and aches—*it all started in the service* when that psychiatrist used to make me go on *sick call* when I wouldn't *menstruate.*"

"How do you mean it started?"

"He used to make me feel like a *nut.*"

"What do you mean?"

"He used to make me feel like a nut sending me on sick call."

"When you didn't menstruate?"

"It was something new to me! They said it was my physical reaction to *adjusting* myself to *military life.* Of course, we had a pretty *rough* military life, you know. I'm *not knocking* the service. If I had it to do over, I'd do it. I *loved every minute* of it. Gee, I was happy when I was in uniform."

It sounded more as if she were ambivalent.

"You remember?"

"What?"

"You remember?"

"Oh, yes, oh how I remember! My psychiatrist brought that all out. He said that, uh, I was happy when I was in uniform because I'm a *tomboy* and that's why I liked to wear the uniform."

This was a wonderful lead. Patients remember what has *meaning* for *them*.

"What did he mean *tomboy*?"

"I don't know."

"Were you a tomboy?"

"Yes, when I was a kid, I had a *tool chest* instead of a *doll*."

She was then really interested more in the phallus tool than the baby. What was the reason for this tomboyishness?

"Really?"

"I had a *bicycle* instead of a *doll carriage*."

"You remember that time?"

"I've heard the family say."

"What did they say?"

"They said that I was a tomboy."

"Who do you mean by family?"

"My mother, father."

"Your mother and father?"

"Yes, I remember—"

"They were the only ones?"

"Yes, well we're not, we don't bother with the relatives."

This sounded suspicious. There were important relatives!

"You were the only child?"

"No, I have a *sister*."

She had to deny her sister until a direct question was asked. This hinted at the origin of the cancer within, i.e., devouring hate and jealousy.

"Really? She's younger?"

"Yes, she's younger."

She seemed loath to talk. This was the original sore spot.

"How much younger?"

"What? Uh? Two years."

She paused in a reluctant manner.

"What were you going to say?"

"Uh, she's more the *female* type."

"In what way?"

"She's a *lady*!"

"What do you mean a lady?"

"Well, she is. She is *frilly* or *something*, I don't know. She dresses beautifully. She is very beautiful. She went to buy a coat in a store and they offered her a job as a model. Now don't go telling me I'm building up all kinds of *resentments* because my sister is pretty or something! But we are not close."

"What do you mean no resentments? You're not close?"

"No, no, I just call her up on the telephone. Guess she got kind of *worried* when she found out I was coming in here though."

"What do you mean no resentments?"

"I never had too much to do with her."

"You remember?"

"Well, I mean, what I'm saying. Oh, when I was in the Army and I got a telegram saying her *baby* was born, I went out and got *drunk* to celebrate."

"When? Her first baby?"

"First baby! And then I wired her $10 to buy some flowers or a new hat or something. I don't know. When I went home on leave, I brought home gifts. I felt like the big shot. I was in *uniform* in the Army. Yes, that's a *good feeling*, you know."

She now had an illusory phallus to make up for sister's baby and beauty. Now the therapist understood the baby problem in more detail. She could still her envy of sister as long as she could play the man, but she really wanted to be the frilly girl who was mama's baby.

"How do you mean?"

"I don't know. I was just proud I was in the uniform. They used to write me letters, send me packages and all that."

"But you say that—"

She interrupted.

"Oh, let's get back to my bellyache!"

This was an obvious example of how her physical pains were a displacement from other pains relating to persons.

"You say that your sister was pretty?"

"Well, she is, beautiful!"

"You thought so even when you were a kid?"

"Yes, but she never could *ice skate* or *ride* a bicycle or *anything like that*."

Her envy was almost overwhelming.

"Really?"

"No!"

"How much younger was she, by the way?"

"I *don't know*. I think she's two years younger than me, I *don't know*. I *never inquired*! Isn't that funny! She's thirty or thirty-one, I honestly don't know how old my sister is! She looks so much younger than me sometimes I guess, I don't know."

"In what way?"

"She's got a nice build. She's tall."

Here she slumped down in her chair as if she were depressed.

The therapist felt she needed support, and encouraged her to talk about her skill.

"She never could ice skate?"

"No, couldn't even roller-skate."

"Whereas you could easily?"

This was the best kind of ego support at this time.

She laughed and continued.

"Yes, she used to go out on dates with boys and they used to have to give me nickels to get rid of me."

"How do you mean?"

"Yes, he's my brother-in-law now, he's very good looking. He's the Gary Cooper type, a wonderful fellow. He's the type you go in his house and he makes you feel right at home, you know, one of those types, and uh, he, uh, they kid me about it. When I was a kid, I *didn't feel wanted*. I was a tease."

Obviously she felt unwanted as a girl by her parents and forced into the boy's role.

"You didn't feel wanted then?"

"Well, sure I, no it wasn't that, it was the idea I was an awful tease. I'd sit on the doorstep or in the parlor with them or something."

"You remember?"

"Yes, I remember that. They used to pay me to get rid of me."

"Because you were an awful tease?"

"I'd sit there if they were spooning, you know like if he was courting her."

"You did?"

"And, uh, I don't know, different things like that, but uh if *she died tomorrow* I'd cry, I'd *feel bad* but I'm not that close to her. She made a *crack* when I got a pension. Her husband is not a disabled veteran. We own our own home and we've got a car and they live in a project."

Again the therapist wondered where to go. The material about the husband was of great interest. Did she feel like a disabled veteran, neither fish nor fowl, girl nor boy? But the reaction was also one based on her inferiority complex concerning her sister. Perhaps her attitude to husbands, brothers-in-law and father could wait.

"She made a crack?"

"Yes, I can't, it was just uh, she found out I was, I told her I was going to a psychiatrist and she said, 'Oh, you're a nervous wreck,' something like that. I don't know, it didn't strike me right. It sort of built up like uh, like a *funny feeling* in me."

This "crack" was symbolic of her inferiority feelings. She feared she was physically and mentally abnormal and unlovable. "Funny" was a way of denying hatred.

"What do you mean, a *funny* feeling in you?"

"Well, I'm a very *funny* person. I don't kiss my mother and father and I never kissed my sister."

It was obvious that the relations with all were inadequate and hateful.

"Even when you were a kid you didn't kiss your mother and father?"

"Oh, I guess I might have when I was a kid. I don't know but I don't now. I can't relax around anybody, can't relax with my husband; I can't relax with my kids!"

"Really? How come?"

"Yes, I can't relax with *you!*"

The therapist ignored the personal touch.

"At home you can't relax with your husband and kids?"

"Nobody, no. People come to visit or something and I wish the heck that they would get up and go. Like last night I tried to sit down and watch television and I couldn't."

"You can't relax?"

"No, not even with my own kids. If the kid comes around and wants to kiss me, I push him away!"

"Who do you mean?"

"My daughter is like that. She always wants to kiss me. I say all right, kiss me and go to bed, get out of here."

"Your daughter? How old is she?"

"She'll be seven in May. She's beautiful."

It was probable that she was envious of her daughter also. Her hatred was like a cancer devouring all her relationships.

"Really! She's beautiful?"

"I'll show you a picture of her the next time I have my wallet with me. She looks just like the angel on a Christmas tree."

"How do you mean?"

"She's got long gold curls, natural curls."

"But you say you push her away?"

"Yes, I don't know what it is! I get embarrassed!"

Once she must have wanted to be her parents' little angel and be kissed, and then she felt rejected and became a tease.

"What do you mean, get embarrassed?"

"The only time I kiss my husband is when I want to tease him."

"How do you mean?"

"I'll say, 'Give me a lover's kiss,' something like that."

"When you want to tease him?"

"Yes, when he's reading the sports section in the paper, I go over and say, 'Give me a lover's kiss,' or something like that."

She was probably frigid sexually, i.e., at the level of the body image —like her pains.

"Does this apply too when you have relations?"

"Well, you know something, this is, this is, ooh, I got a pain."

She clutched her left side and grimaced.

"Really! Where?"

"A *pain* in my *side*."

"Yes?"

"When my husband. Oh, that *eye*! If it doesn't stop twitching! When my husband was courting me, I had butterflies in my *stomach*. Maybe it was *hot pants*, I don't know. I'm very blunt. Are you married?"

She looked searchingly at the therapist, as if he were a little boy, until he became embarrassed.

"Yes."

"Oh, that's good because if you weren't married I think it would be kind of a shame the things I come out with! See, when I went in the service, I got away from home. I didn't have anybody watching over me and to keep up with the crowd I drank a lot and I did a lot of *foolish things*."

The therapist realized that she was the one who felt little and ashamed, and recovered his poise.

"How do you mean foolish things?"

"I guess I *fooled around* a little bit."

"Fooled around?"

"Oh, when I'd get drunk."

"How do you mean?"

"I guess I had sexual *intercourse*. I can't remember anything specific. Oh, yes I do. I remember once, when I first got to the Army Hospital and this, he was a good-looking guy, I didn't know any of the fellows, you know, so this guy had a car and he asked me to go out with him. When I think about it afterwards, what a dope I was. He all but forced me to have intercourse with him. He didn't even use a prophylactic. He pulled out and caught it in his handkerchief. Well, I got so nervous over that!"

The therapist wondered if she meant pregnancy.

"What do you mean?"

"I, I, I was, they had been drilling into us venereal *disease!* Venereal disease! You know how they do in the service, so I got to thinking and I guess you know. I went on *sick call* the next morning for them to take a smear because I had this white discharge, leucorrhea or something, and so what did this guy go and do? He got a discharge and he went up for a smear and he made some kind of crack to me!"

Another crack, the therapist felt, about her guilt over her badness and worthlessness.

"Crack?"

"Yes, he tried to say he got the discharge from me and I didn't have venereal disease!"

"Well, what did he mean when he said he got the discharge from you?"

"See, in the service, they show us all these pictures about venereal disease and when I got the discharge, well I had it off and on you know, so this guy said something about *he* got a discharge and kept on looking at me funny you know, well I went on sick call to make sure I didn't have something!"

"Didn't have *something*?"

"Yes, venereal disease or *something*."

The disease was a sort of cancerous dead-child part of her.

"Well, you must have wondered about what it was though, since you didn't know."

"Well, I saw pictures of it in the Army. They showed us a movie of it, what it does to you."

"What sort of thing does it do to you?"

"It *cripples* you, *blinds* you, it *burns* when you urinate and you get *sores* all over you!"

It does to her what she wanted to do to others as a bad child. She offered the therapist the choice of many physical areas. He finally decided the eyes would be of most interest and represent the others.

"How do you mean it blinds you?"

"They showed us pictures of, uh, I guess it was syphilis that people get crippled and blind if they *touch themselves* and then they *touch* their *eyes*."

To this aggressive, masculine girl, this touching business was obviously important in a masturbatory sense.

"Well, you must have wondered what it meant?"

"Well, I was afraid the guy might have been out *horsing around* with *somebody* else and might have given it to me. I went on sick call anyway and when the smear came back it was negative."

"What did touching themselves and touching their eyes mean to you?"

"I was a medic. I had to learn this."

"So you must have thought about it."

"You know I never knew about venereal disease until I went in the service."

She laughed.

"I never knew there was such a thing!"

"You must have wondered a lot about what sort of things—?"

"Well, in the service, we were taught to put the rubber gloves on when they were sterile, not to *contaminate* a *sterile area* and all this. See all these things now, just talking to you now, now I'm beginning to, all this Army training it all reverts back to different things that associate themselves with me now."

She was still occupied with touching herself but it was in a different sense, i.e., touching a sore spot. It could be past or present and concern many areas beside the genital.

"Touching yourself was a problem?"

"Yes, like that now that I think about it, touching yourself if you have syphilis and putting it on your *eyes* or something like that."

"As you say, it *blinds* you?"

"Yes, syphilitic sores get in your eyes and it blinds you."

She had mentioned a number of sore spots before, involving abdomen and head.

"And sores?"

"The discharge from somebody with syphilis or gonorrhea or something, there's another one, I never could think what the other one was, chancres?"

"What are those?"

"Those are sores they said."

"Well, what sort of sores?"

"They showed pictures of the men's penis and the women's wombs with these big runny sores on them!"

"Sores! Where? Head? Stomach?"

She squirmed uneasily.

"I just told you, on the men's penis and the women's womb from sexual intercourse."

"On the woman's womb?"

"Around the *mouth* of it, the *lips*, you know the outside, like *leprosy*!"

This was indirectly connected with the sore heart and not being kissed.

"Like leprosy?"

"Sure. I don't know. All I know is they showed us pictures of them in service."

"You must have wondered about it?"

"I don't know but I wasn't taking any chances on getting it."

"Sure, but you must have had a lot of thoughts about these things because you remember it so vividly."

"Yes, but you know I haven't thought about that in a long long time. You just brought that back to my mind."

This was the function of a therapist.

"But you thought about it then?"

"Yes, but anyway I went on sick call and I didn't have it so I never spoke to that guy any more!"

The therapist decided to return to the newer version of her hypochondriacal complaints.

"Tell me, how would it cripple you?"

"Well, it's *poison* that gets in your bones."

"Poison?"

"Hey, look now, we've been on this poison business twice, haven't we, what with fallopian tubes?"

This was a form of insight that she recognized but was unsure how to use.

"Really!"

"Yes!"

"How do you mean?"

"Look, look at this, look what I get when I get nervous! I break out in that horrible sweat."

"When you get nervous?"

"Yes. Ooh, those spots are driving me nuts! They, it bothers me more sitting in here in this room with you, seeing those spots."

Why with me, the therapist thought. He wondered if he should ask more about her present troubles, but decided to continue with her Army life in order to lessen the pressure.

"But you were told it did a number of things, like you said it cripples you, and I wonder what you meant?"

"Something like arthritis, I guess. I don't know."

"In what way?"

"It cripples you. You can't walk. It gets in your bones."

"You say it gets in your bones! How do you mean?"

"I don't know. Hey, before I forget, talking about bones, you've got to get me X-rayed for that hip."

"The hip?"

"Yes, I haven't had it X-rayed in over a year now so—"

"What do you mean hip?"

"I've got a density in my left hip."

"A density?"

"Yes, and I know what a density is! I looked it up. It's an accumulation of calcium and it's in the bone marrow. I've got one on that left hip and I haven't had it X-rayed in over a year. I was supposed to come back periodically and I haven't felt like going back. I've got all these pains and everything and all they tell me is that I'm a hypochondriac and I don't want them to keep on telling me that."

"What did this *density* in your left hip mean to you?"

"It didn't bother me. It's funny. It doesn't bother me."

"In what way doesn't it bother you?"

"I don't want it to bother me so it's not bothering me. I just know there's a *density* there and when the doctor gave me the paper to go down or something I saw it. It said *osteomyelitis*."

"Osteomyelitis?"

"That's a disease of the bone."

"What do you mean?"

"I don't know. I think they have to *cut your leg off*. That's why if I had a pain there I would never tell you."

The therapist realized that her fears of losing an important part of her body were the core of her neurosis. The pains were thus a warning signal of this possibility. Had she as a child felt she had been a boy who lost his penis because of touching?

"Having to cut your leg off? A disease such that you have to cut your leg off! What do you mean?"

"You are getting awfully excited when I say these things."

He hesitated, embarrassed at first by the truth of the statement. Then he realized this was also a projection of her own excitement.

"Excited, in what way?"

"You're going so fast! Anyway it's nearly dinner time."

It was obvious that she was ready to conclude the interview right now and felt pushed.

"Well, we were just talking of what you were thinking about, the osteomyelitis."

"Oh, I like you. I'm not *getting mad* at you!"

The therapist ignored her anger, but decided to veer away from the lost leg.

"Oh, I see. Anyway they told you all these things about V.D., that it cripples you and blinds you?"

"That's all I know, that's all I know what they told us in the service."

"You said you saw pictures?"

"They showed us all kinds of pictures. They showed us everything."

"Really?"

"Yes, you know I was the best map reader in my company!"

She wanted to change the subject, but this was also a sign of the importance of this area so intimately bound up with her castration fears.

"What did they show you?"

"Didn't you ever see the pictures?"

"Maybe you could tell me about them."

"Uh, they showed how, uh, what did they show anyway? Oh, they showed the pictures of the syphilitic sores and with gonorrhea you get a discharge, and it showed pictures of the women's wombs and the men's penises with sores all over them. Then they showed us these people hobbling along crippled and blind."

"People hobbling along crippled and blind! What do you mean?"

"From getting syphilis and not seeing about it."

"From getting syphilis and not seeing about it?"

"You know, letting it, it gets a hold of their body."

"Well, how would it get hold of their body?"

"I think it made mental patients too out of them."

"In what way?"

"Affect their mind? I guess it must spread through the blood, yes, it must because when you take a Wassermann you can tell."

"Well, how would it affect their minds?"

"I don't know and I don't care to know and I don't even think about it!"

"But you must have wondered about it at that time?"

"I don't care because I didn't have it. I just forgot about it. You were the one who got me on the subject!"

She was angry and excited.

"Well, anyway you were telling me about the fact that you remembered it so vividly and you remembered that sometimes you thought that it made mental patients out of them and affected their minds."

"Because they showed us movies."

"Really! Were you scared?"

She relaxed in response to his empathy.

"All I know is we all sat there and were red in the face."

She laughed.

"Our ears were burning and everything! Nobody looked at anybody else when they came out."

"What do you mean?"

"We didn't joke about it. It wasn't anything to joke about when you saw those realistic pictures."

"I should think so!"

She nodded emphatically.

"Yes!"

"What do you mean it was nothing to joke about?"

"It's nothing to joke about if in a moment of passion or hot pants or *something* you get exposed to it!"

"In a moment of passion?"

"Oh, passion, love-making or whatever you call it. *Playing house!*"

Playing house must mean playing father and mother making babies. At the same time a moment of passion could refer to hate and the wish to kill or hurt.

"How do you mean playing house?"

"When I say playing house, I mean sexual intercourse."

"In a moment of passion or love-making?"

"Well, yes, the only time I ever did that in the service was when I was drunk. The *liquor* brought it *on in me!*"

She could only feel passion when her superego guilt was numbed.

"And it embarrassed you?"

"Yes! Any time I ever did it I never saw the guy any more! I couldn't *face him*. I was terribly embarrassed."

"You couldn't face him?"

"Of course all the other guys I ever went with like that they used prophylactics."

"And you felt embarrassed?"

"Sure, the guy would think you're an *old bag*."

An old bag is a reversal of an orally insatiable baby envious of her sister. More feminine means basically someone more desirable in the mother-baby sense.

"How do you mean?"

"Well, he'd figure if you do it once with him you do it all the time."

"What do you mean an old bag?"

"A *whore!* Someone they say is an *easy piece*, or however they say it. Anyways, I was always careful. I didn't want to get pregnant and get caught because I didn't want to *disgrace the uniform*."

By having (being) a bad baby! Now it appeared that getting pregnant would do two things: (1) It would give away her longing for a baby and to be a baby, which was connected with her yearning for a man as mother and sister had; (2) It would mean the end of the uniform, which stood for the illusory phallus or the phallic active identity she assumed as a defense against her infantile passive feminine wishes and fears. It too would shame her to expose her penisless state.

"It would be a disgrace for you to get pregnant?"

"Yes! Gee, you know, some *odd* things happened to me in service." She laughed.

"How do you mean *odd?*"

"One time there I went on a pass. I got arrested."

"Arrested?"

"I got arrested."

"Really! You remember it?"

She laughed.

"I remember it as clear as day. I got drunk, and these two civilian fellows—I went to the hotel in town by myself. I went to the bellcap and asked the bellcap—you know it almost seems when I'm going to talk about myself *it's like I am just telling a story*. It's, it's really a scream when you get to think about it, you have to *laugh* about it! And the bellcap said they didn't have any rooms, so he says wait around maybe there'll be a cancellation. With that, these two fellows, one was a soldier and one was a civilian—the civilian fellow he was handsome! Oh, he should have been in the movies! He was really cute! So they were staying at the hotel. So they said to the bellcap—I was a good-looking girl then!"

She had nicely demonstrated the mechanism of depersonalization. By seeing herself as someone else in a story, it didn't matter. It also demonstrated reversal, i.e., from sadness and guilt to humor and enjoyment, from embarrassed shame to exhibitionistic pleasure. Finally, it demonstrated a facet of the infantile withdrawal process.

"What do you mean?"

"I was good-looking."

"You mean you're not good-looking now?"

"No, I'm a mess now, and uh—"

She paused.

In the service with her uniform, she was a phallus girl. She felt whole and desirable. Obviously she didn't now in her married state, with a disabled veteran and in comparison with her sister and her sister's good-looking husband. She was full of the old hate and envy.

"Oh, I just feel like a mess."

"In what way?"

"I got spots in front of my eyes and I got a headache."

"That makes you a mess?"

"Yes."

For a minute or two she was overwhelmed by her sorrows. The therapist decided that she was bound to return to the "humorous" story to escape this depressing material.

"The headaches and the spots in front of your eyes make you a mess?"

"Yes! These pains, everybody looks at me like I'm crazy because I've got pains. Well, anyways, let me tell you the story. Uh, anyway, the fellows came over and said would the WAC like to come up to their room, they were having a party. So we went up to the room. They were the nicest fellows you'd ever want to meet, no kidding! No monkey business!"

"What do you mean?"

"No, no fooling around."

She paused.

"They never came near you?"

"No. It was all on the up-and up! They didn't try to have intercourse or anything. They were just having a good time. I was one of their *buddies* like that, you know!"

She was accepted as a male in a sense.

"A real buddy?"

"I mean it is *so hard to believe* actually under the circumstances. That's what made it so *funny.*"

She laughed loud and long. To the therapist the denial of the painful, defective, little-girl state was clear, but to her for a moment the wish had again triumphed over reality and the underlying shame, guilt and dread were robbed of their terrors.

"Funny, in what way?"

"Well, this will *kill you.* Somebody poked me to *wake me up.*"

"Yes?"

"The MPs were standing there! The lieutenant of the MPs and two big MPs and they said, 'Okay, corporal, get out of the bed and put your clothes on,' so I looked, you know. I hadn't done anything wrong, so they took me away!"

"And you'd just been buddies?"

"Buddies with the fellows! And they had said next day we'd get up early, I had the pass you know, and we'd have breakfast and it was all going to be very sophisticated, you know. They were going to take me out to breakfast, get a car and take me around the city, and the red-headed, it was a red-headed soldier, I don't remember, but I know he wasn't good-looking. The other fellow I don't know what he was to be perfectly truthful, and they were going to take me around to the fellow's house, you know. Oh, I was just like a *long lost sheep* they had picked up."

In being accepted as a buddy, she had a loving parent (phallus) restored to her.

"How do you mean a long lost sheep?"

"They were just friendly with me, you know. Well I'm a character anyway, I'm full of *laughs*, cracking *jokes* and that, you know."

Her method of denial of her lost, depressive, hungry, guilt feelings.

"But by long lost sheep you mean?"

"Yes, so anyway—"

All this was a little too much for the resident's moralistic self.

"Really, a *black* sheep?"

She took his judgment easily and without anger as this area was relatively uncharged at the moment. This premature type of response is *not* productive of any change and usually is injurious to the therapy situation.

"No, *you put that word in my mouth. I didn't say that!* So anyways they turned around and the MPs made me go and get my clothes on.

They marched us out of the hotel and they put us in the MP car and the lieutenant gave me a cigarette and, of course, by that time I had sobered right up. I wasn't really drunk, I don't think. I was just tired. So, uh, anyways they turned around and took us out to camp outside the city and they put me in jail in a WAC detachment. They put me in a room with bars. The civilian guy, the cops took him to jail and they took the soldier to the MP station. They took me to the WAC station. They had WAC military police. I never knew they had them! They put me in a room with bars and they let me wear my uniform. I could see through the door and there's these WACs going through my overnight bag. They took my wallet and were counting my money, and they were looking at the balance in my checking account and everything, and I happened to be going with a boy whose picture was in the wallet. He was in the Marines. Then they called out to me and asked me whose picture was in the wallet. They were just nosy."

"How do you mean?"

"Well, they said, 'Who's this?' I said, 'My boy friend.' They said, 'What would your boy friend think if he knew you got picked up in a room with two fellows?' I said, 'I wasn't doing anything *wrong*!' So they said, 'All right, go to sleep.' Well I sat there. They let me have my cigarettes and I just sat there."

The therapist seized on this.

"They thought you did something *wrong*?"

"Yes, they were nosy, looking at all my belongings. So anyway, they turned around and the next morning they came in. It was pretty late then anyway. Maybe it was 9:00 or 10:00 in the morning. I had seen dawn come up. I had seen all the fellows marching by, so anyway they took me to the mess hall and gave me some breakfast. By that time I was a nervous wreck! All I can do is drink coffee! They got me in a WAC car. They took me down town. They left me sitting in the WAC car and who did I see but the civilian guy. The cops brought him in!"

The therapist by this time had realized he had made a mistake. It was necessary for her to realize she felt guilty and why, but in her own way and time.

"The guy who was very cute like a Hollywood guy?"

"Yes, and they brought in the red-headed soldier too and I think the red-headed soldier came over to me and he told me they had done some kind of a test on him to see if he had sexual intercourse and, uh,

I guess they did the same thing to the civilian guy. The hotel had thrown him out of his room."

"What sort of a test?"

This was an error, a side issue. She relished this story because, although she appeared guilty, she was *really innocent*. The therapist should have said as much, and added that she must have felt different at other times when she did things.

"I don't know. I don't know anything about it."

"You must have thought about what sort of test they did."

"No, I didn't care because I *didn't have anything to do with them.* So the red-headed guy came over and told me, he said, 'Gee, we're awfully sorry what happened.' He says, 'This civilian kid has had so many parties in his room that they have been waiting to throw him out and that's the excuse they used, finding a military woman in the hotel.' So then, uh, so the WAC MPs came back to the car. They let the red-headed guy come over to the window to talk to me, you know, and they went in and filed charges against me—picked up in a hotel room with two men. They didn't do any tests on me, or anything!"

Her pretense of being a buddy could not be maintained.

"Really?"

"Nothing at all!"

"What do you mean?"

"They took my word for it. I guess they tested the guys and found out there was nothing wrong with them!"

"Well, what sort of tests?"

"Examine their penis or something, take their blood pressure or something, I don't know! All I know is they didn't do anything on me. They took me back to the WAC detachment."

"You wondered what they were going to do to you?"

"By that time I was *numb*! I was so *embarrassed*. So they took me back."

"What did you think they were going to do to you?"

"Court-martial me! By that time I was scared stiff, so anyway they took me back."

"You were scared stiff?"

"I was scared stiff what the commanding officer was going to say."

At one fantasy level she was scared to be caught "playing house" for fear mother would cut off her "uniform."

"The commanding officer?"

"Sure, the WAC commanding officer!"

"Oh, the WAC commanding officer?"

"They took me back to her, they marched me in, they reported that I was under arrest and left me in her hands and I had to go up and I had to salute and say 'Corporal Kelly reporting.'"

"You were scared stiff of that?"

"Sure! I was embarrassed!"

"You were embarrassed?"

"That I got caught like that and I hadn't done anything wrong! So anyways I checked in with her and she says, 'At ease, corporal, and tell me what happened.' It was the lieutenant. The C. O. wasn't there, it was the lieutenant in charge. She was a good scout. She says, 'What happened?' I told her how the porter, I figured he had called the MPs you know and that; so she says to me, 'Well,' she says, 'you've got your choice between company punishment and a hearing before the Board.' I says, 'Give me the company punishment,' so I had to police the area for a week."

"Company punishment?"

"Police the area, go around picking up the cigarette butts!"

"You had a choice?"

"I think it was that I would have to go before the Board for court-martial or something. They would break me, they'd make me a private! I'd be embarrassed. I'd be *ashamed* of myself! Boy, I never did that again!"

"You said you were scared stiff?"

"Sure I was. Wouldn't you?"

By now she was in a good humor. The escape in the past augured well for the present. The veiled disapproval of the therapist did not annoy her, as she felt older and wiser.

"In what way?"

"If you were caught in a room with two women."

She laughed.

"Wouldn't you be scared stiff? Oh, you probably wouldn't! You'd probably enjoy yourself."

The therapist mastered a mild anxiety and tried to continue.

"Caught in a room?"

"If you were caught in a room with two women, and they took you, how would you feel? You won't answer me, I know that!"

The therapist felt vaguely trapped by her.

"I didn't hear what you said."

"I said if you had been caught in a room with two women and they had arrested you and you weren't married to either of the two women, what would you do?"

The therapist found himself unable to think momentarily.

"Oh, I see."

"What would you have done?"

She laughed triumphantly.

"Well!"

The therapist forgot his technique.

"I don't know!"

"You could dream, I suppose."

She said this sarcastically.

The therapist caught himself and recovered his position.

"You felt scared stiff?"

"Scared stiff! I was embarrassed! I was ashamed! I was ashamed because I had on a WAC military uniform. Now can I go to lunch?"

The therapist decided he had to continue until he was more in command.

"I wonder what you mean when you say scared."

"Scared! Sick! Sick! And I never told the other girls what happened. I just said I got reprimanded and I was on company punishment."

"In what way were you scared sick?"

"*Sick, nervous, upset* and *everything!*"

The therapist might have returned her to the present now by saying "This is how you feel now. I wonder why? Are you embarrassed over anything you have done lately?"

"You remember?"

"Oh, yes! When I get nervous and upset, I get this horrible *nauseating* feeling."

"You do?"

"Yes, and with all the talking about it, I bet I won't be able to eat!"

"You get a horrible, nauseating feeling?"

"A *sick feeling* inside of me. All I know is I don't feel *good.* I don't feel *good* now when I talk about it."

The therapist realized she meant this literally. Her bodily feelings represented a threat from her superego.

"In other words, when you feel scared stiff, you feel horribly sick and nervous and you are afraid others will think you are not *good?*"

"I don't know. It's a sick feeling. It's a horrible sick feeling."

Now the therapist felt on the right track.

"You mean when you feel you are not *good* it is as if you were *sick* in one way or another?"

"Maybe I've got stomach *ulcers*. I must have stomach ulcers, getting that awful feeling in my stomach."

This was like her saying, "Let's get back to my bellyache." Now the therapist felt in command and able to end the interview.

"*Awful feeling? Not feeling good?* We'll talk about it again."

The therapist stood up as a sign that the visit was over. She arose, frowned and said,

"Well, now I have a *headache*. Do you think I'm a hypochondriac?"

He smiled reassuringly.

"Perhaps we'll find out together why you don't *feel good*."

She nodded slightly and shrugged doubtfully.

"I hope so. Good-by. See you tomorrow."

"Good-by."

One mistake this therapist made was obvious. He ended the interview knowing too little about the patient's past, especially in relation to her parents, and the present in terms of her personal relationships, especially with her husband. She displaced her painful, frustrated and guilty feelings in respect to her self and persons onto her body. If we knew something about her relation to her husband and parents, our understanding of the painful relationship with her body would be more complete. What was driving her to the psychiatrist now? Actually, it was difficult to keep this patient away from her physical symptoms and the doctor handled the interview quite well. She would like to have been a Christmas angel like her daughter but felt bad, frustrated and lonely. She was neither a buddy nor a beautiful girl in her own opinion. A shell of hardness covered a soft-hearted center full of ungratified longings. Knowledge of the problem outlined the steps the therapist had to take in her therapy.

It would be necessary, as tactfully as possible, to lead her away from her bodily complaints and pains to the important areas concerning her self-regard and her relations with persons. This would entail, especially, knowing more about how and why she compared herself so unfavorably with her sister. What were her infantile relations with mother that made her feel her femininity was so much less than sister's? What role did father play in reinforcing the earliest defective body and self-image feelings she had in her relation with mother? She must have hated not only her beautiful rival and herself but also her parents. What successes she had with her parents as a tomboy was also an important point. What everyday special events in her relationship with her daughter and husband brought back those poignant, anxiety and depression laden memories of past conflicts? She was probably, very early in life, before her sister's birth, a Christmas-tree angel herself who fell from grace after her sister arrived. It is probable that shortly after the birth she began to become fixated at a phallic tomboy level. The use she made of her body and of sexy teasing would be labeled as narcissistic and hysterical, and most of her bodily symptoms could be called conversions. From the point of view of therapy technique, however, diagnoses are unimportant. She could not help being influenced by a therapist's benevolent attitude which would help in mitigating the severity of her self-criticisms in connection with the past. All her life she had been rebuffing people who offered her tenderness and yet longing for it. She was an excellent example of the old adage concerning neurotic patients that tells us they run away from the very things they want the most. When she could accept tenderness, she probably would not need the hypochondriacal defenses (once handled by sexual acting out) that served as a poor substitute for affection, and the relationship inside her family circle would then suffice. This would not happen overnight no matter how well insight was imparted, but once she had been made to face and understand what her real problems were she would never have the same conviction about her bodily symptoms that she had at present. Psychotherapists disagree about how long it is necessary to work on the defenses of this type of patient. As far as this patient is concerned, knowledge of her relationship with her husband was not adequate to ascertain how much he, as a disabled veteran, reinforced her neurotic patterns and what the secondary gains were. Often such factors are decisive. We can only make these factors conscious and then let the patient fashion her own destiny. The therapist made one bad mistake when he called her a *black sheep*, and she reprimanded him in a manner he deserved. This might get him in trouble later, when her guilt feelings become more conscious, but in any case correct technical procedure could handle any problems that would arise. There are no analysts or therapists who do not make many mistakes of a similar nature in their daily practice. With experience, however, errors of commission will be less than those of omission, which are usually more numerous and due mainly to fatigue. The repetitiveness of case material, however, guarantees unlimited opportunities to redress this type of error.

The wartime sexual behavior of this patient was a kind of acting-out of a phallic masturbatory fantasy loaded with longing, defiance, guilt and anxiety. The tomboy, phallus-girl, castration aspects were obvious. The most accessible area to work in involved the envy and rivalry with the beautiful sister. She was already conscious of it but needed to work it out in great detail and with feeling. Girls want to have a phallus or become boys for complex reasons. There was a lost, Christmas-angel, tender mother-child relationship, a yearning for a phallic masculine independence, a me-and-my-buddy (phallus) relationship, a defiance, an escape from competition with the sister and mother, and often there is a push by one or both of the parents in this direction. Making this material conscious would be a vital part of undoing the pathological mourning and loss reaction.

X

SOME CHARACTERISTICS OF THE HYSTERICAL PERSONALITY

A Case of Anxiety Hysteria

The case recording in this chapter will illustrate many of the characteristics associated with the classical concept of the hysterical personality. No patient of this type can be treated for long without showing anxiety attacks, conversions, phobic states and tendencies to become overconcerned or even traumatized by everyday events. They go from one crisis to another like Eliza, pursued by bloodhounds, crossing the river by jumping from one treacherous cake of ice to another. This usually permits only superficial concern with the past. It often means that more than average difficulty will be experienced in getting the patient to return to and develop memories of the past. The superficial nature of the emotionality, the histrionic attitudes, the transient and easily-made identifications, the lability of feelings and shallow concerns are all evidence of a frantic flight into the present to avoid remembering the past.

Most cases of hysteria show two points of fixation, a fundamental but hidden one at an oral level, and a more obvious one at a passive phallic level. The oral aspects of hysteria and other related problems will be considered in some detail in the last chapter. The case in this chapter will illustrate the phallic oedipal elements nicely. Theoretically we would expect *personal relationships* to be concerned with morbid jealousies, death wishes, rivalrous hatreds, passionate yearnings and chronic fearsome expectations of being rejected, cut off and abandoned. In connection with *inanimate objects,* we might expect the concern with sex, castration and the phallus to affect re-

327

lationships to the "things of life" in an obvious manner from the point of view of symbolism. When we turn to the *body image,* we can expect a sadomasochistic sexualization of all the component organs, orifices and projections. The themes of guilt, punishment, renunciation, confession and ultimate forgiveness and acceptance are always present. The ultimate goal seems to be a unification of an all-good mother, father and child into a perpetually contented unity or trinity that will nullify all previously existing losses and injustices.

The patient was a moderately attractive young housewife. She was a little on the plump side and had a plain-Jane appearance because she used no rouge and little lipstick. Her hair was curled neatly, however, into a mass of ringlets, which was a little at variance with her plainness. She could not wait until she sat down and began talking the minute she entered the office.

"May I say something that happened last night that might give you a good idea of the way I feel. Before I start from the beginning, some girl friends and I had a little get-together last night, and one of the girls—I mentioned that I had mononucleosis and one of the girls said, 'Oh, that's the kissing disease,' she says. 'You know where that comes from, mostly the college kids when they go away on weekend parties,' and I started to blush. I have no *guilty conscience,* I haven't been kissing anybody that I shouldn't have been kissing, but that is just how stupidly *self-conscious* I am! She must have noticed it because she said, 'Of course it doesn't have to come from that,' and I said, 'Well how come *children* have it,' and she said, 'Well of course it doesn't have to come from that.' I don't know whether she noticed I was *embarrassed* or whether I just felt that way. That is the way I feel *at home.* Now with those girls it doesn't bother me."

The therapist felt it was too early to take up her guilty conscience and chose a safer word.

"You mean *self-conscious?*"

"Yes."

"What do you mean by *self-conscious at home?*"

"Now, if someone had said that in front of my husband and I had blushed, then afterwards I would be thinking now Jim is going to think that I have a *guilty conscience,* that I had been kissing somebody, that I had caught the mononucleosis from kissing, and I haven't got a *guilty conscience* because I haven't, I haven't the faintest idea where I got it from, but that is how stupid I am."

The therapist decided to mention her conscience obliquely.

"This is the kind of thing that you would think about?"

"Yes, yes."

"That he might be thinking that you—"

"That he might, yes, that someone close to me, my husband, other people it doesn't bother me, I don't care what they think and yes, I would be thinking and I would dwell on it."

"Is that who Jim is, your husband?"

"Jim is my husband. And I would dwell on it and it would build up in my mind until I couldn't *eat* because I get the most self-conscious when I'm eating, and the last few days I wasn't able to *eat at home.*"

A guilt-laden problem of some kind was being displaced onto eating and made it necessary for her to watch herself. The therapist knew that in hysteria a genital sexual problem was easily displaced in this manner.

"You get *self-conscious* when you are *eating?*"

"When I'm eating."

"How do you mean?"

"I just do. When I sit down at the table to *eat,* I think that somebody might *say something* that will *embarrass me.* I act as though I have a *guilty conscience* about everything and I haven't."

"A guilty conscience about what?"

"Nothing in particular."

This answer was to be expected.

"I mean what do you think?"

"Now, well, it might have been connected with this deal about Jim's brother."

"What happened?"

"I had the feeling that I needed someone who was interested in more things than my husband. I have always been interested in everything and Jim has no interests. He is a very quiet person with simple tastes and he is not interested in *things,* and we visited his brother and his wife all the time."

"When was this?"

"Well, we've been married ten years and it started—I met my husband in service by the way. I was up at camp and he was my boss. He was the chief storekeeper and I was a storekeeper, first class."

"You were in the—?"

"I was in the WAVES, yes."

"When was that?"

"Let's see, I went in in 1943 and I got out in February 1946. I believe it was about June 1944."

"So about 1944 you met him?"

"Yes, and we were married in June of 1946."

"Tell me, how old were you then?"

"Twenty-three, almost twenty-four. I was born in 1923 and my birthday is in August. I was almost twenty-four when we were married, and I guess I was pretty *immature*. He is eleven years older than I am by the way."

"That was ten years ago?"

"Yes. I'm thirty-three now."

"And he's eleven years older?"

"Yes."

"That makes him about forty-four."

"That's right."

"And you were pretty immature?"

"Yes, well he got out of the service three months before I did and I would come home once a month during those three months and we would visit. We would go down to his brother's house and spend the weekend. He didn't have any friends and he was very close to his brother. He and his brother never spoke until his brother got married. They lived in the same room and never spoke, but all of a sudden they got very close after his brother's marriage, which was a long time before we ever met, but anyway they got very close and that was the the only friend he had. And we used to spend all our time there."

"And you were very *immature* at that time?"

"Yes."

"What did you mean by that? What do you mean by immature?"

"By, by thinking of *other men*, by thinking I hadn't *found what I wanted* in *my husband* in spite of being in love with him. I always have been! I've never been out of love with him, but by thinking that I—"

She paused in her protestations. The therapist decided to reinforce her guilty mood.

"You were thinking of other men then even though you were married to your husband?"

"Yes!"

"This is what you meant by immature?"

"Yes!"

"What were you thinking about other men?"

"Thinking that, that his *brother* was more *interesting*."

"Interesting?"

"Yes. I was looking for *excitement*. All of his friends are older. His brother is two years *older* than he is. I guess I shouldn't have married someone so much *older* than myself. I wasn't ready for it."

The question was what kind of excitement was missing in her marriage, and how her marriage did not fulfill her fantasies.

"You weren't ready for marriage?"

"I guess not. I guess I wasn't."

"Is that the way you felt?"

"No, I didn't at the time."

"But this is the way you feel now?"

"Yes."

"Looking back?"

"Yes, that's right."

"But what sort of excitement?"

"Oh, I wanted to go *bowling*, I wanted to go *dancing*, I wanted to do *anything*, but all we did was sit and talk and I used to be so *bored silly*. He wouldn't take me, he wasn't interested in bowling. He can't dance, he hasn't any rhythm, and I was just so full of life. I've calmed down a lot now. I'm thirty-three and I've accepted things more, but I *resented* it very much."

"You resented the fact that he wouldn't show you a good time?"

"Yes. Then I got thinking, oh, his brother would perhaps say something humorous which Jim seldom does, and I just got all *confused*."

"You were confused?"

"Yes."

"About what?"

"Well, we were both in love but Jim thought that we shouldn't marry and *I was the one who talked him into it*, that it would be a wise thing to do."

This was a giveaway of her ambivalence toward the marriage right from the beginning. Hysterics are frequently women who fall in love with a strong, aggressive, older man who is too much a representative of the oedipal father. In a sense they feel threatened by the violence of their emotions and by their own sadomasochistic conception of sex and love. They run away and marry on the rebound. Usually they pick a passive, quiet man whom they regard as no threat and who is seen unconsciously as a motherly figure. Through their nagging, they reduce him to a state where their emotional and sexual relationships are chronically impoverished. They then complain to their psychiatrist and accuse the husband of being the cause of all their troubles. The therapist wondered if this was her problem. Then there was the question, was she really using her husband as an alter-ego figure representing her own hated passivity?

"He felt that you shouldn't marry?"

"*He* thought that he wasn't *good enough* for me. He used to cry. He would go up to the Chief's Club and sit and we would have a few beers and a hamburger, and on the way across the field he'd be taking me back to my barracks and he would cry and say that he wasn't good enough for me. *He* was the one who felt *insecure* then, and I don't know which of us was the most *immature* to tell you the truth. I felt very *grown up* at the time, but as we get older we find out that we are not so grown up. It takes a long time to grow up, but at that time I didn't feel immature. I thought I was the *wiser* of the two of us, and he would say he wasn't good enough, and I knew that he wanted to marry me. Whether it was my intuition or what, I knew he was in love with me but I was the one who had to talk him into it."

"You had to talk him into marrying you?"

"Yes. I mean I certainly wouldn't have if I didn't feel he was in love with me. I don't mean that, but I just felt that he needed the push. He just didn't have the *self-confidence*, and I felt he *needed a push*. Maybe I'm wrong, but I know he is deeply in love with me as I am with him now that it has grown over the years."

The ambivalence was now more sharply focused. Why did she pick such a passive person? Was it in order to deny these qualities in herself in terms of the part that had not grown up?

"You felt he wouldn't have asked you to marry him if you hadn't—?"

"Yes, yes and I felt that *time was flying* and *he* was well on his way to being a *confirmed bachelor*, and that if I didn't be the *aggressor*, which is very foreign to my nature, I'm not *aggressive* at all."

The therapist knew this could hardly be the case. The hysteric is aggressive and the qualities of the both aggressiveness and passivity are pronounced, even though antithetical.

"You are not aggressive?"

"I am not aggressive at all, no. That is the only instance in my whole life I know that I have been aggressive, and I *resented* it that I *had* to be, but I felt that it was necessary."

This is a way of stating the problem that she picked a passive man and then aggressively resented his passivity for the duration of the marriage.

"To do what?"

"To be aggressive and talk him into the fact that it would be wise for us to be married."

"Because you wanted to marry him?"

"Yes, yes, and I felt that he wanted to marry me but he kept saying that he wasn't *good enough* for me and I knew that he was."

"What did he mean by not good enough?"

"Oh, he was down in Panama and he used to go around with *trampy* girls and *things like that*, and it *bothered* him. He told me all about those things."

The question now arose, did she fly into marriage for fear of her own "trampy" impulses going out of control? "Things like that" referred to prostitution fantasies which are common enough in hysteria, with slave-girl, hypersexual, sadomasochistic feeling tones. It was these fantasies and longings that were part of her missing excitement.

"What bothered him?"

"Oh, I suppose he felt that since he had been with girls like that that he wasn't good enough for me or something."

"He felt *guilty* about that?"

"I think so, that's *my feeling*. He never came right out and said that, but that's my feeling, and then about six years ago he took me to, he went to a course, he's in the industrial real-estate business. They sent him to New York for a week for a course and so forth, and I went with him for a few days. He went ahead and I went later, and I was the only wife along and one evening he and the fellows who were in the course, we all sat around this hotel room laughing and having a nice time, and as I say Jim being a quiet kind and I felt as though I needed something else, there was this fellow there, one of the fellows there who was real jolly and he had the funniest jokes, suitable for a woman hearing them, and I thought gee whiz I wish Jim were like that, and that was all there was to it, but once in a while after that—I never saw him or heard of him again—once in a while I would think when I was real bored, gee whiz I wish Jim were more like Dick is."

"Who is Dick?"

Dick was a man who had been working with her husband for six months. She thought of him continually as more "jolly" and attractive than her husband, especially when she was *bored*, which was often. She then wept as she went on to tell how she would blush when her husband mentioned Dick's name. She would think she was *ruining her marriage* or *something* was *lacking* in her. Somehow this made her *stop eating*. The eating material was obviously a non sequitur, representing a displacement of sexual interest from genitality to orality. Giving up eating was an atonement for "trampy" masturbatory fantasies. After a few remarks on her fears that she and her husband were incompatible, she complained of being *stuck at home* with her two little girls, aged nine and six. She blamed all these thoughts on her "mononucleosis" which had begun six months ago. This was around the time she met Dick. She had gone to a doctor for a growth in her throat and felt herself going to pieces over "the anxiety of wondering." The interview continued as follows.

"Wondering what?"

"Whether I had *cancer* of the throat or not."

To the therapist, cancer, tuberculosis, ulcer, etc., are bad attributes growing and devouring and threatening the ego ideal with various losses.

"What happened?"

"So I waited two weeks. I got this *fungus* in my throat. I went back to him to ask him about the fungus and he gave me a prescription for some little pills which turned out not to touch the fungus. At any rate, I reminded him that he was going to take the test for mononucleosis and I know he was just humoring me. I don't believe from his attitude that he really thought I had it, but he humored me and took the test. That was on a Friday and the next Wednesday he called me and told me that I did have it. But that very morning on this Wednesday I went to pieces before I knew I had the mononucleosis. It wasn't that, I wasn't frightened of that, but when he called me in the evening about quarter of six I was so *relieved* to hear I had something physically wrong with me and that I wasn't going crazy, because that morning I was vacuuming—"

She paused, lost in thought.

"You thought you were going crazy?"

"Well, I thought I, well a *nervous breakdown* at any rate."

"What made you think that?"

"I was vacuuming and the idea came into my head that I *would be responsible* if my *sister-in-law* died. About two months ago she had, went to the hospital. She was *bleeding*, had been bleeding for a month, went to the hospital, and on Monday they operated and found a very *active fibrous tumor*."

"When was this?"

"They found a very active fibrous tumor in my sister-in-law."

"When was this?"

"About two months ago."

"About two months ago?"

"Yes."

"You said about six months ago, or about then, was when you went
o pieces."

"No, six months no. Six months ago was when I first started the
ore throat. About six weeks ago I went to pieces."

"About six weeks ago?"

"About six weeks ago, yes. But before that, before I was feeling
erribly panicky, I was going along all right. I was calm and perfectly
ormal. My sister-in-law had this operation and on Monday they oper-
ted and found a very active fibrous tumor and I called her husband
o find out how she was, and he told me they were sending a specimen
o the lab and they wouldn't know until Wednesday whether she need-
d another operation or not, and she did. She had another operation
n Thursday."

"Fibrous tumor?"

"Yes."

"What kind?"

"I don't know. That's all I know."

"Where was it?"

"Down in her, I don't know, in her uterus somewhere."

"In her uterus?"

"I don't know, I don't know where it was."

"What made you think it was her uterus?"

"She had a complete *hysterectomy* on Thursday and the doctor
old her husband that it was not *cancerous,* and I sent her flowers
nd I felt sorry for her. I told her I went to church and prayed for
er and *I didn't have any,* any *guilty feelings* and all of a sudden
his Wednesday morning—"

Now it was obvious she did have these feelings. There are no neg-
tives in the unconscious.

"You didn't have any guilty feelings?"

"No."

"What do you mean?"

"Well, I'm trying to explain, this Wednesday morning the day that
found out I had the mononucleosis, but before I did find out, the
hought came into my head from out of the blue. *I hadn't been morbid.*
hadn't been *thinking about it.* The thought came into my head
hat if she *died,* that if she had *cancer* and that if she died, I would
o *out of my mind.* I felt as though I was responsible because all those

many years ago when I had been thinking about her husband, I wondered in my mind if I ever had wished that either she or Jim were *out of the way.*"

This was a real, up-to-date version of the old oedipal theme.

"So that what?"

"So that I would, so that Harry and I could get married or *something*. I don't know whether I, I honestly don't remember if I ever thought that or whether I was daydreaming all those many years ago. I haven't had those thoughts in a long time."

Dick and Harry were both representatives of the aggressive, "jolly" man she wanted.

"But you wondered what it would be like to be married to Harry?"

"Yes, yes, yes I did."

"And so you wondered—?"

"So I wondered—this time six weeks ago the thought came into my head, did I ever have any thoughts of their not being here, or their being out of the way, and I thought if anything happened to Betty I would go crazy wondering if I ever had terrible thoughts, and I told my doctor that, I told Jim, I told my minister, I told my mother. I just felt as though I had to tell everybody to clear my conscience. My minister was no help!"

This was a nice example of obsessional thinking, common in anxiety hysteria. She had to confess to everyone, as this guilt-laden wish was only a derivative of deeper longings out of the past.

"You told everybody?"

"The people I mentioned. I told my *mother*. That was the morning I got panicky."

It might be possible now to get into the past and back to an earlier triangle situation.

"Your mother?"

"Yes."

"Was she with you?"

"Yes, she's got the children. She brought me here yesterday morning. At first when I got that terrible panicky thought I couldn't get it out of my head. It came out of the blue and it stayed there, and I called the minister and asked him if he would please come over right away. I was terribly upset and I told him my thoughts. He had no words of consolation! He was speechless! He's a young minister and I guess he just didn't know what to say to me. I guess he hasn't lived long enough to be wise and comfort people. He had no words of comfort. I'm an Episcopalian. I asked him if he would please read from the prayer book with me. I even had to suggest it. He didn't even suggest it. He took me, he said, 'I'll come back at 1:30 and pick you up and take you to a doctor who helped me!' He had had trouble being nervous before sermons. His *throat* would kind of *close up* on him and this doctor had helped him with some *white powder* so he thought maybe he might help me, so I went to his doctor and I told him."

Any person with throat symptoms is close enough to her to be considered worth investigating. The minister was another despised passive man, but also an alter-ego figure.

"His throat would close up on him when he became nervous?"

"Yes, and so he just from the lack of a better idea wondered if this doctor might help me also. He is a homeopathic doctor, whatever that is."

"And you said also about six months ago this person, Dick, was transferred into town here?"

"Yes."

"And you had sort of admired him that one night?"

"That's right."

"And you blushed about that too?"

"Yes."

"As soon as you heard his name?"

"Yes."

"Because he was the type of person you felt you would like to spend some time with?"

"That's right."

"So the problem seems to be related to your feelings about being with other men?"

"Yes."

"And possibly what it would be like to be married to somebody other than your husband?"

"Yes, but I feel guilty about it."

She broke out crying.

"I shouldn't because I know I've never had any *horrible* thoughts but then when I was sick the thought got into my head and I just felt so guilty. I felt like I was the worst person in the world."

"What do you mean by horrible thoughts that you haven't had?"

"That I might have wondered at one time, what I might have wished that, that I didn't have now, that if Harry didn't have Betty, which is a terrible thing. I tried and tried and tried to think and remember back and think whether I actually thought that at the time or whether I am just building it all up in my imagination."

"So you couldn't decide whether or not you had actually wished them out of the way?"

"Whether I had actually wished, yes. My general practitioner that I've been going to, I finally went and told him this. He said, 'Gert, even if you wished that they both went up in an airplane and were killed,' he said, 'you've been forgiven for it long ago.' I said, 'Well I know I never wished anything that horrible!' He was more comfort to me than my minister because my minister didn't have one word of comfort to say to me, and I believe the doctor when he said that. He said, 'You've been forgiven for that years ago!' "

The tendency to magic thinking was characteristic, as in all neuroses.

"And your feeling was that your wishes, if you ever had them, might make it come true?"

"Yes, well I thought it might!"

"And your wishes might be responsible?"

"Yes, exactly. It just made me feel so awful. I'm not a mean person and I don't think I ever thought that but being sick and being *weak* I couldn't get the idea out of my head."

Now weak had a double meaning; it could refer to things moral as well as physical.

"What do you mean being weak?"

"From my mononucleosis. It has weakened me terribly."

"How do you mean?"

She quickly switched the subject to her husband. She had been confessing her fears to her husband, who had panicky attacks now and then himself. She felt *responsible* for them. He must feel bad over her *"easing her conscience on him."* It turned out that he just felt *"powerless and frustrated on the job"* and was cured by reassurances from his boss. This led to how he was often away from home. They had lived for five years with his mother—a *"cold woman"* who said nasty little *"cutting"* things. She described herself as different, i.e., *warm* and *close* to people.

Now the therapist could have developed the theme of the cold, cutting, nasty mother, which was repeated twice. This was the logical thing. She was also quick to deny the possibility that *she* might be *cold* too, whatever cold meant to her. Then there was the problem of "cutting things." What was cut by these things? The therapist chose to approach the cold problem from the point of view of the patient's image of herself. He continued as follows.

"You like to be close to people?"

"Yes."

"How do you mean?"

"I like people to like me. It's a natural emotion, I guess, but maybe I am more outgoing than other people. I would be very unhappy if I thought that people didn't like me and most people do like me. I go more than halfway when I meet people."

This behavior was probably a reaction formation.

"You have always been very outgoing?"

"*Yes*, oh *no*, no, I've had to *force* myself. When I was small, I was very *shy!*"

Now was an excellent time to get into the past and hear about the original cold mother and passive father (like her husband).

"You were shy when you were small?"

"Very, yes, and I still am basically but I try not to be."

"What do you mean by when you were small? How old?"

"As long as I can remember."

"Even when you were a little girl?"

"Yes, yes, I've always been extremely *shy* and I've had an *inferiority complex*. I remember when I was in the first or second grade feeling inferior to other little girls in the class because we lived in a three-family house and I lived in Worcester and my folks worked in mills."

"Both your mother and father?"

"Well, my mother worked later. During the depression, my mother went to work for a while because my dad was very *infantile* and insisted on going into business for himself repeatedly, and he would put them in debt and then my mother had to go to work and get them out of debt. My father repaired radios on the side and nothing would do but that he start up a business and go whole hog, rented a great big office in Worcester and had my grandmother come in, installed at a typewriter, and he didn't know anything and he never will know any more about business than the man in the moon. And, of course, it was a complete failure."

"You feel that, sort of looking back, he was kind of immature too?"

"Oh, yes, and he still is."

"He is alive now?"

"Yes."

"How old is he?"

"He's about fifty-eight."

"How old is your mother?"

"She's the same age. My poor mother, what she's gone through trying to—every *two years* in my whole life *we moved.* I never went to the same school more than *two* years! I was constantly having to make new friends."

The basic confidence in her environment had been undermined by some event now represented by moving.

"By we you mean your parents and yourself?"

"Yes, and my brother. I have one brother."

"Oh!"

"It was a family of four."

"Is he an older or a younger brother?"

"*Two* years younger."

This was the original move. She had been cut off from her passive baby relationship with the mother. She longed to be actively handled —to make up for her loss.

"He's two years younger?"

"Yes."

"So you're the older?"

"Yes."

"You always moved?"

"We moved every two years."

"Why was that?"

"Because my dad was *never satisfied* with his job, pressure, pressure, pressure, he'd say, I can't stand it! Or greener pastures on the other side of the street—and we moved. We moved here and there in Worcester."

Now this could refer to herself and her interest in other men.

"He always felt the grass was greener elsewhere?"

"Yes, and he still does at his age. He is working at Newport as a machinist."

"This is sort of like your problem in a sense?"

"Yes, yes."

"That the grass might be greener?"

"Yes."

"With somebody else?"

She interrupted.

"That's right! That's right! In spite of the fact that I'm very much in love with my husband! Pardon?"

She took a cigarette from the pack on the therapist's desk.

"And you felt you were kind of immature when you were married? This seemed to be a problem, and you characterized Jim as a very immature guy?"

"Yes, and he still is. I hope and pray to God that I *grow up before he does.*"

The passive-father and baby-brother hatred had poisoned her relations with her husband. Here the therapist decided that the relation to the cold mother might be more rewarding.

"What was mother like when you were young?"

"My mother?"

"Yes."

"My mother—?"

"You said she had to go to work when he—"

"I have never been *close* to my mother."

"What do you mean close?"

"I never felt close to her as other mothers and daughters feel close to each other. I have never been able to confide in her."

"Why was that?"

"Because she is not an outgoing person."

"She is not outgoing? How do you mean?"

"She is not outgoing. She would never come over close to me when I was young or since and put her arms around me or anything like that, never. *She* was *shy* and I know she would have liked to but *something held her back.*"

She was describing herself as well as mother.

"You mean she didn't show affection?"

"That's right, that's right. But she always did everything for me."

"How do you mean?"

"I had, they were poor, but I had better clothes than any of my friends. I was given everything. I never had to—I didn't know *the depression* was on. Other people knew the depression was on and I should have but no matter what I asked for I was given. My brother wasn't given as much as I was, and then I was called *selfish.*"

She was denying her own economic depression. When a patient makes this type of statement, it usually means the opposite, especially when a girl says she received "things" and her brother never did. This, of course, was an oblique reference to penis envy.

"Why was that, that your brother was not given things?"

"I don't know why. And another thing—"

She talked fast and excitedly, then stopped suddenly.

"Of course you don't know why but you must have had some ideas about why they would give things to you."

"And another thing, once when I was very tiny, maybe four or five,

heard my mother tell a friend that she *loved my brother* more
she loved me, and that bothered me."

his was what she felt in any case. From another point of view, this
is one thing brother had that she did not have more of!

"How do you mean?"

"Wouldn't it bother you if you heard your mother say that she
loved one of her other children more than she loved you?"

"What did you feel?"

"I don't know what I felt. I naturally was *crushed*. Anybody would
be to hear that, and when I was in my teens I told her about it. I kept
it in all that time!"

This must have been a chronic fantasy and a source of anger, depression and envy.

"You mean as you said before you should have known the *depression*
was on and yet you didn't?"

"That's right because they gave me everything I wanted and then
they never taught me to give, in other words. I received all the time
and they never taught me how to give, and because they didn't teach
me how to give to people I was called *selfish*, and I don't think it
was my fault. They didn't teach me how to give. And I don't think
I deserve the label of being *selfish*, and so ever since I have been trying to *compensate*. I've been *giving* and *giving* for ten years, and the very
day I got sick I was going to start—my town has an adult education
program in the public school and I was going to start an oil painting
class, and that very day I got sick, and that just tore me to pieces. I
said to the minister I've been *giving* and *giving* and *giving* for ten
years and now I finally had the chance to do something I wanted to
do, and I *got sick* on the *very day* I was going to start it."

This was an admission of an obvious side of her that was poorly controlled. Oil paintings are a sublimated form of smearing. If she were
in analysis, we could think in terms of toilet-training problems around
the time brother came along.

"And you said as a child you were always taking?"

"Yes, so I tried, and when I knew that, when I realized that, I tried
to compensate when I grew up to know better, I tried to go the other
way."

"You mean you tried to make up for all that taking by giving?"

"That's right."

"It sounds as if you felt a little bit *guilty* about having *taken so
much* and that your brother *didn't get as much* as you did?"

She was really guilty about her jealousy and death wishes which later intensified her oedipal longings and inadequacy feelings.

"Yes, and because at the time I didn't know I was getting, it was normal to me. I didn't know that I was getting more than my share at the time. It was only later that I realized."

"But you said that there was a sense in which you weren't getting as much as your brother. You overheard your mother say—"

"Yes! I was getting the material things and he was getting the *love*."

"And the material things didn't really count?"

"That's right."

"The things that really counted he was getting and you weren't getting at all?"

"Yes, because material things don't mean that much to me. I would rather have other things."

This was probably another denial to be investigated later. Often one of the important factors in the hysterical woman's symptoms stems not from her love life but from her competitive and exhibitionistic relationships with other women which are thwarted by her husband's inadequate salary. She can then displace her own inadequacy feelings in respect to women onto her husband in respect to other men. Basically her husband is seen as an inferior phallic object that cannot be developed or made big. So she is correct when she says she'd rather have other things.

"Why was it that she preferred your younger brother?"

"Because there is a reason, there is a very good reason, because of her mother-in-law, my father's mother. She lived with us until I was fifteen years old, and she is a son-of-a-gun. She has been wonderful to me but I had very mixed feelings about my grandmother. She is still alive but *very sick*. I believe she is seventy-nine."

"She is sick?"

"She is sick now, yes."

"What is she sick with?"

"*Swelling* of the *legs*, she has a very *weak heart*."

These words also refer to fantasies, but only a small percentage of cue words can be developed meaningfully in any *one* interview.

"You said you had mixed feelings for her?"

"I had mixed feelings for my grandmother because my mother had told me how horrible she made her life. She lived with us until I was fifteen years old and then she *married my mother's brother!* My mother told me recently that they were carrying on together! And that's another thing I thought, suppose I'm like my grandmother underneath!"

The quality of incest was now of primary importance.

"How do you mean?"

"That I had *bad instincts*! I was a virgin when we were married and I thought to myself suppose I'm having these thoughts because basically I'm like my grandmother and my mother told me my grandmother was kind of *trampy*."

Now she had brought up a familiar word.

"Trampy?"

"She went around with men, and when her first husband was alive he did too. My mother says she doesn't know who started it—whether he went with other women because Gram went with other men or which way. Of course Gram blames him."

"Yes, but the important thing is that you seem to feel that you might be like her somehow, that you might be sort of *trampy* as you said. But you mentioned the word *bad instincts,* what did you mean by that?"

"Well, isn't that bad instincts?"

"Well, in what way did you mean it?"

"Couldn't you inherit something like that?"

"Apparently you felt you might!"

This was the correct way to respond.

"Lately, since I've been so upset I thought my goodness, I have never gotten over her influence!"

"That actually you might have bad instincts?"

"Yes!"

"You mean having *sexual affairs*?"

"Yes, and I don't want to!"

"Is that what you have been thinking?"

"Yes, and I don't want to. I'm very satisfied with my *relations* with my husband."

Relations was a multidetermined word.

"How do you mean?"

"We have a, our sexual intercourse is very satisfactory in every way. He gives me all the love and affection that anybody could want. But my mother told me that, and I told Jim, I said, 'Suppose I got it in my blood from my grandmother.' I know it is irrational. I know I haven't. I have always had enough character to know how to handle myself."

This denied the other "weak" side displaced to her body.

"Of course you know rationally, as you said, but *one part of you* is very rational and seems to understand these things, and says why of course these things aren't inherited. Of course I'm in control of my feelings and I don't want to have affairs, but there seems to be *this other part* that you are concerned about."

"And the only time it comes out is when I get physically run down, that's right!"

"That this part may be weak when you get physically run down and you might be like your grandmother?"

The therapist had begun to split her ego. Usually this can be and should be done in the first interview.

"I don't think, I don't dwell on that too much actually."

"But I mean these are the things that you have put together?"

"Yes, it came into my mind once and then I let it go. I mean that hasn't been bothering me terribly because I know better. I know I've got more character than my grandmother has. That hasn't really, really that's not basically, that hasn't bothered me terribly because I know better, and I know that I'm not like that because I know that during my growing up, if I was like that I certainly had *plenty of opportunities.*"

"How do you mean?"

"Well, anybody when they are dating, could be bad if they wanted to and I never even had the *desire!*"

This was an interesting confession of the presence of repressive forces.

"How do you mean bad desires?"

"Oh, well having sexual intercourse before you're married. I never had the desire to. In fact, I didn't even *understand anything* about sex. I had, I had, they say that *some* girls have a *terrific sexual urge!* When I went out with boys, they used to tell me how *cold* I was. I never had *any sexual urge* at all. I have now. I'm not abnormal in that way. It was just *late* in *developing.*"

Her *terrifying* sexual urge was strongly repressed.

"You never knew anything about sex?"

"I didn't know, well, I wouldn't say *nothing*, but my mother never told me anything."

"She never told you anything?"

"No."

"How did you find out?"

"From other girls that were all wised up, but it still didn't *interest* me. I still never *thought* about it. I had very *healthy interests.*"

The question was, was this also a reaction formation to an earlier period?

"Healthy?"

"I mean normal interests of any sort, well, I don't know, is sexual interest healthy too? I didn't think it was."

"Well, I wonder, because you see the words you used—sexual interest are *bad instincts,* that they are *abnormal,* that they *aren't healthy,* and the implication—"

"Yes, but I have gotten over that now. I haven't brought that into my marriage."

"Was that how you felt before marriage?"

"I suppose. I didn't have any *horrible* feelings about it, no. I didn't have any feelings that it was, I just felt that it was just—"

She was unable to find the right word.

"Why should you have had *horrible feelings*? You said you didn't know anything about it?"

"That's right."

"And you had no experience?"

"No, no. I didn't have any horrible feelings about it. I thought it was just something that was morally wrong. I had always gone to church and *everything* and I knew that it was something that was morally wrong and so I just didn't do it. So it didn't occupy any large area of my mind ever."

The later moral teachings made a convenient screen.

"You were never tempted?"

"No, I was *never tempted in the slightest.* I was never tempted in the slightest."

"Because as you said you had plenty of opportunities that you could have taken advantage of?"

"That's right. In fact, to show you how little I know about anything, when Jim would bring me back across the field at night from the Chief's Club and he would kiss me, and now I know what he was doing—I don't know what the term is—he would start jiggling against me and he came off in his underwear. I didn't know what was going on! I didn't know that that was what was happening. Then he'd say 'I'm sorry,' and I'd say 'What are you sorry for?' I hadn't the faintest idea of what was going on. I don't know whether that's important or not, but it shows I had no knowledge!"

"Of course, as you say you had no knowledge and no feeling?"

"I had no feeling!"

"Is that so?"

"Yes."

"When he was jiggling up against you?"

"Yes. I had not, no, I didn't! I didn't! It might seem strange and I was twenty-two at the time and I had no sensation whatsoever."

This was true hysterical frigidity or anesthesia.

"How do you account for that?"

"I don't know, just late developing sexually, I suppose. Well, other girls, I'm sure, had developed to the point where they would respond at twenty-two as far as I know, but I didn't, but I responded *when we were married.*"

"All at once?"

"Yes."

"You responded when you were married?"

"Yes."

"How did you develop so fast?"

"Oh, well, about, oh, about a month or several months before we used to go parking after we were engaged and we didn't have any intercourse but I'd guess you'd call it petting, and that was when I learned what it was all about, but I had no *guilty feelings* about that because I feel that's not morally wrong."

"Why should you—? By petting, you mean just touching?"

"I was still a virgin when we were married and I thought *that* was the important thing. I had to find out about life sometime. Petting is not morally *wrong* and I never did it with anyone else. I only did it after we became engaged, so I had no *guilty feelings* about that."

"It is almost as if you have to reassure yourself of that?"

"Yes, I guess so."

"Why?"

"I don't know, I just feel as though I want to be frank and tell you—"

"That you had *no guilty feelings?*"

"No, I'm not trying to reassure myself, I don't believe. I'm just trying to be frank with you and discuss my life with you."

It would be premature to continue along this line.

"But you said your mother never told you these things?"

"No, she didn't."

"I presume this was because, as you said before, you were never very close to her?"

"That's right. She was shy. Once she gave me a book on menstruating, maybe I was about eleven or twelve, and that's the only thing and she couldn't even discuss it with me. She was so embarrassed. She gave me the book and said, 'Here, read this.' And that's the only thing that ever happened. And naturally since she was embarrassed, I was. So I read the book very shyly and probably with many blushes, I don't remember."

"You even blushed then?"

"Yes. Oh I *have always blushed* very easily."

"Have you?"

"Yes, yes. I don't know whether that is something physical, whether your *blood* is close to the *surface* or whether it is strictly emotional or what, but I've always blushed very easily."

"You were embarrassed when she gave you the book on menstruation? What did you think?"

"I don't remember thinking anything. I knew about it. The girls had told me about that, older girls that were already menstruating. They told me about it, yes. I didn't know the reason for menstruation."

"So actually the girls had done what mother was supposed to do?"

"Yes, that's right. I think that happens in a lot of cases. I think nowadays it doesn't happen so often. I'm certainly going to try not to be like that with my girl."

"You feel that a mother should—?"

"Of course, that's where it should come from."

The normal line of development from here would be "If my mother had told me things. I would have known better and have married a more exciting man," but this would come much later.

"How did you feel then not knowing as much as the rest of the girls, the girls talking about these mysteries?"

"I have always felt very naïve compared to other girls."

This feeling is derived from the oedipus complex—"too little and too late."

"Have you?"

"Yes, yes, and as I started to say, when I was young, then I felt inferior to these other girls. They lived in *single-family houses* and we lived in tenements and *multiple-family houses,* and that made me feel inferior, so you can see how sensitive I am. It wouldn't bother a lot of other people, I realize that. I just was *born sensitive.*"

Single and multiple family probably referred to the grandmother living with them. She had multiple mothers.

"To where your family lived?"

"Yes!"

"And the fact that you knew less than the other girls about sexual matters and you weren't close to your mother so she could share these things with you?"

"Yes, I don't remember that that ever bothered me terribly though."

"But, sure, the fact that she wasn't giving you the things that a girl, you felt, should have gotten from mother which apparently your kid brother was getting."

"Oh, yes, as I started to say, because of my grandmother, when I was born my grandmother *took me over* and she wouldn't let my mother change a diaper for me. *I was her baby,* so that my mother, because she was *namby-pamby* and wouldn't stick up to my grandmother, let her take over and I became Gram's baby. To this day she says, 'Oh, you're my baby.' When my brother was born two years later, my mother had gotten up a little gumption and he was her baby, so it is not my mother's fault except for the fact that it was her *weakness* that she couldn't stand up to my grandmother. *I don't blame my mother terribly.* My mother was just too weak to stand up to my grandmother. My grandmother was a very domineering woman and still is."

Now it was plain that her husband represented the passive weak mother, and the material suggested this even more because the question arose. Did she really miss mother before brother? Was this the meaning of the multiple-family house that made her feel inferior? Was she gram's baby because they were two of a kind?" She obviously did blame the mother terribly!

"So you were the baby of your grandmother and your brother belonged to your mother?"

"Yes, yes, my mother has told me that since. That was the way it was. When I finally confessed to my mother that I had overheard this conversation of my mother loving my brother more than me, when I finally confessed to her many years later when I was in my teens probably, she said, 'Oh, I don't remember saying that.' Well, maybe she doesn't. Maybe it meant nothing to her at the time but naturally it stuck in my mind because it *cut me!*"

The *loss* of the mother was the personal representative of *castration* feelings in connection with her body image. From her self-image point of view, she called it an *inferiority complex.*

"But you said your grandmother was somewhat of a problem in running around and this type of behavior."

"Yes, but I didn't know it."

"You didn't know it?"

"No, I never dreamed it, no, they certainly kept it a close secret from my brother and me. I never dreamed it."

She appeared to have worked her precursory oedipal relations out between a grandma and a mother. Everything must have come to a head after brother's birth. Grandmother was a representative of the primitive father.

"You never saw her?"

"No, no, but recently my mother told me that they had a talk with my mother's brother. It hurts my mother and it hurts my father too. My father's mother, whom I have been talking about, married my mother's brother who is about *fifteen* years, or something like that, younger than my grandmother, and my mother and father have never gotten over it, but they practically forced them to get married because *they were carrying on together.*"

"When was this?"

"I was *fifteen.*"

At this time, the old oedipal jealousies were revived by pubertal changes. She was like the child who had discovered his mother was having a sexual relation with father and felt left out, inferior and full of rage. Pubertal conflicts are usually a reliving of old oedipal problems. More questions were in the therapist's mind. Had she seen and heard things previous to this age which were a giveaway concerning Gram's affairs? Was this even a pubertal trauma? Did it organize her character and make it necessary for her to repress everything sexual? Did she feel to blame?

"When they were married?"

"Yes. That was when they left our house and started housekeeping for themselves."

"What did you think?"

"I didn't, I was embarrassed because I knew something was wrong with a grandmother marrying—there were a lot of jokes about it. I'm my own grandmaw and grandma married, oh he was our uncle and then he became our stepgrandfather, and I supposed it *embarrassed me.*"

"Incest?"

"Well, is it? They weren't in the same family. They were from two different families."

"No, but I mean as far as you were concerned, it was all one family?"

"I suppose, I don't remember."

"Of course, they aren't related by blood actually, but as far as you were concerned they were two people in the same family?"

"Yes!"

"Sexual—?"

"No, I didn't know it then!"

"Of course not, but as you look back on it?"

"It was all very innocent to me. The only thing that embarrassed me was because I knew my folks were embarrassed because of the relationship, and that was the only way it affected me, but I knew my mother was so glad to have my grandmother out of the house, that that was my main feeling—one of relief. If mother is glad, I'm glad. You know, it she's so glad to have grandmother from under her feet, then I'm glad. And that was the only way it affected me at the time. I had no terrible feelings about it. It was quite, I was quite casual about it, good-by and have fun, you know. So I don't remember feeling anything terrible about that."

The essence of the oedipal situation is the triangle. The matter of displacements and substitutes frequently complicates things. Grandmother was now old and dying and adding to her problem of guilt, remorse and apprehension over her future.

"So the problem at the moment is that there seems to be a conflict that you are going through between, let us say, two parts of you—"

"That's right."

"One part looks at the other and feels that it is not fully in control of this other part, which seems to be looking elsewhere—the grass is greener elsewhere—it is concerned about sexual matters with other people, and this is the part which you told me possibly is like that of your grandmother."

"Uh-huh."

"That she was carrying, that she married a man in a trampy manner and that you yourself may be turning into a trampy person."

"That! No, I don't believe I have felt that strongly about it. I feel more in control of myself than that."

"But the point is that this is why you have to be in control because you are afraid this is the type of thing that might take place."

The therapist wondered if he were not making it too strong.

"I'm not sure how strongly I feel about that. I really don't think that that is the basic thing. I really don't because I feel as though I am morally strong enough not to be like that. I truly don't think that."

"What do you mean?"

"I truly don't think I'm afraid of going wrong, no, I don't believe I am."

"But that is what you told me."

"I told you that that thought came into my head."

"That's what I mean."

"After my mother told me what my grandmother was like, I thought about it for a few days and then I said to Jim, 'Suppose I got bad blood in me,' but it wasn't bothering me terribly, I don't believe. I don't think it's something deep inside of me that I'm terribly afraid of it, no."

She seemed to be protesting more than necessary.

"But the point is that it has occurred to you."

"Yes."

"It has concerned you—that this is the part that may have the bad blood from your grandmother, that may have the bad instincts, that may think, if not act, trampy."

"It's the thought, yes! I know very well, I'm not afraid of acting like that."

"Because of the other part?"

"Yes."

"The other part that looks at yourself and says, now look this is silly. I know that I didn't inherit that blood. I know I'm not responsible for my sister-in-law getting cancer. I know I'm not responsible for Jim's brooding about such and such, but there still is this conflict between these two parts?"

"Yes, and when I'm well, I don't consciously think about that, but it must be way back there somewhere so that when I get sick as my doctor said—"

This was such a convenient sickness. The therapist decided to confront her with it.

"When you get weak?"

"As my doctor said, he said, 'You're trying to blame this on mononucleosis.' He said, 'Everyone who gets mononucleosis doesn't get like this,' and I said, 'No, I know that.' I'm not trying to blame it on the mononucleosis. I'm just trying to say that I truly don't have these thoughts at other times. I have a healthy mind at other times."

"That's what you tell yourself?"

"That's what, that's, I honestly believe it! I'm not just telling myself that. I honestly don't have such thoughts!"

"But as you said, you must have them somewhere?"

"In my subconscious, or whatever, yes, that's right."

"Of course."

"But I don't consciously."

"Because the mononucleosis doesn't suddenly produce these thoughts?"

"No, I know that."

"The thoughts must be there somewhere?"

"Yes."

"And come out—"

"Two years ago I had the *flu* and I was more or less like that then, but I got over it quicker because the flu got over quicker. They gave me Aureomycin and I got over it quicker."

The time was finished so the therapist stood up.

"Well, these are things we will have to talk about."

"All right. Good-by."

"Good-by."

The central theme of this interview was a guilty conscience. The interview also showed very well how all the so-called reality material that is dredged up by a patient can be examined to our advantage for its fantasy content and hidden meaning. In this sense, the reality material can be considered as manifest material with hidden symbolic and associative values subject to the same laws as dream material, i.e., condensation, distortion, displacement, reversal to opposite, etc. For instance, she talked about how inferior she felt because she lived in a three-family house. We could not understand this feeling in terms of her infantile past without realizing that she grew up in a multiple-family situation in reality. Father was a passive man who was dominated by his mother, who became his secretary and took over his child. She must have loved Gram at one time and identified with her in part. She must have missed her real mother, however, who worked, which means essentially "left her." She felt mother was cold and rejecting like her mother-in-law. Everyone knows how in-laws in general and mothers-in-law in particular are targets for the projection of married persons' hostile feelings about their bad parental images on their own bad and unwanted traits. Often the opposite is true, and many persons marry in order to obtain a mother (in-law) or the kind of family they wish they had had in the past. The patient was full of jealousy and resentment toward her brother. She told us how selfish, aggressive and withdrawn she used to be as a child and how she suppressed and repressed this part of herself. In the present this part had returned and would have liked to get rid of her husband and sister-in-law. Whom did she want to get rid of in the past? At one level it was probably her brother. Later it was probably mother or grandmother or both. Her father was a man with big ideas and at one time must have seemed to be a real charmer to the little girl. We might speculate that material things did not make up for the absent mother and that early in her life she turned to father and became his baby. The relation with the grandmother, who was father's mother, was in this sense a precursor of her relation to her father, but the shadow of her basic mistrust in and dislike for her mother fell on her relation with her father and grandmother, and with her husband she felt again the old loneliness, dislike and guilt.

Now let us look at the material in another way. There was an "immature" part of her that embarrassed her, a part that wanted "excitement," that was "bored silly" and felt frustrated, "resentful" and "aggressive." What kind of "excitement" did a child want? It could have been something simple like playing ride-a-cock-horse on father's foot, but these innocent games as well as many others are connected together by feelings and fantasies which can be called masturbatory, as the sensations that occur during these games are of a sexual or sensual nature and readily associated with the masturbatory act itself, which is especially common as an antidote for loneliness and boredom in children. In another sense there was a "terrific sex urge" which she had to deny. This was associated with "trampy" prostitution fantasies representing insatiable longings for sensual feelings in the genital area which took the place of longings for tender intimacies of a more poignant and yearning nature and closely connected with depressive empty feelings. By dwelling on the relation of the ego to the body image, she could avoid or minimize the affect associated with other more painful areas.

She stated that she had no guilty feelings until her marriage. This meant the time when she could no longer ignore her genital and the "terrific sex urges" she "never had." Why did she have to remain so sexually "ignorant"? Later sessions revealed an interesting incident she had failed to mention. At the time she met her husband, she had been going with an officer for whom she had developed a passionate longing. The strength of her feelings for this "gay, talkative and charming fellow" panicked her and made her feel like a stupid and unattractive little girl. She was sure that when he found her out she would be deserted, so she deserted him first and made her new male friend, Jim, marry her. Here the situation was reversed and *he* did not feel good enough for *her*. Actually, she had gone with him at first to throw her girl friends off the scent of her affair with the officer, as he was a much older man who told her he was about to divorce his wife. She did not trust him but was fascinated by him. This kind of story is not uncommon in hysteria, where the triangle type of relationship is always in the offing.

In psychotherapy we would be faced with making the past conscious and demonstrating how it influenced her thinking, feelings and behavior in the day-to-day present. We would have to show her how the spoiled, selfish, materialistic, envious child was still very much in evidence in her and isolate it so that it could be freely criticized and controlled. We would have to discover what kind of masturbatory fantasies or substitute actions kept alive the longing for the special kinds of guilt-laden feelings of excitement she needed in order not to feel "bored silly."

Actually, the majority of hysterical women have a defective relationship with other women because of their envious and competitive mother-daughter fantasies and unresolved "homosexual" type of tender longings. No man can fill the bill in this respect. Her relation with her two little girls would have to be critically examined also, as she would tend to duplicate with them the cold mother-daughter relationship that followed the "sexy" Gram's baby-relationship, and she would feel guilty and anxious and depressed over this.

Ultimately we might have to uncover the incestuous fantasies of the Gram's baby-relationship. This could have many meanings, as "Gram" was her father's secretary. Is she daddy's and Gram's baby or Gram's and mother's brother's baby? Then her father would no longer be her real father and she could have a nonincestuous love for him. The fantasy of being the child of other parents than one's own has been mentioned (the family romance). It allows the child to degrade the parents and at the same time become more tolerant of his own forbidden aggressive and sexual longings. In this sense Gram and mother's brother could be considered her own devalued mother and father.

Of course there are many questions unanswered in this interview. What were her relations with her brother like? In the interview, Dick, the exciting, gay, lively one, was a brother figure. In her therapy it turned out that she had given up her jealousy of her brother at an early age and turned all her rage onto her mother and grandmother. Early in her life she had become fascinated by her brother's ability to urinate differently and they had played exciting, exhibitionistic games together. Around nine or ten she had made many attempts to seduce him away from mother and they had become close confidants, this relationship lasting until she went into the service.

Although many facets of her oedipal problems and relationships were not explored, developed, or worked through, this patient learned a great deal about herself, integrated much of her past with her present, and established a more realistic relationship with her husband and with various female acquaintances. During her therapy she became quite depressed. Such a feeling often accompanies the acquisition of painful insights and is often a prelude to certain necessary renunciations of infantile attitudes. It is not always necessary to treat a patient deeply, investigate every facet of his life or continue therapy over the years. Once the therapeutic process begins it often continues unaided, like any other healing process. In this case the therapy lasted fourteen months. At the end of this time the patient was given a six-months vacation. A follow-up showed her to be symptom free and therefore therapy was not resumed.

XI

THE EVALUATION OF
RESULTS IN PSYCHOTHERAPY
A Case of Anxiety Hysteria with Depression

The importance of the evaluation of results in psychotherapy and the incompleteness of our present studies in this field are at present of much concern to psychoanalysts and psychiatrists. An enormous amount of time, money and energy is being channeled into efforts to relieve the emotionally distraught and mentally disabled, yet there has been little effort to evaluate scientifically the results of the therapies that are the keystone of all these efforts. This is not due to laxity but to the difficulties inherent in the evaluation. The figures that are usually given in this field are dubious, especially when we deal with the neuroses, because terms and criteria can at present be only poorly or inadequately defined. This is due to the great number of variables present, as well as to problems of a philosophical and semantic nature. These difficulties are not so apparent when we deal with grossly psychotic persons treated with a drug or easily defined physical therapy, in whom results are measured in terms of great changes, such as need for custodial care, etc. With the psychoneuroses and character disorders without grossly observable behavioral difficulties, a demonstration of the results of therapy is more difficult. The subtlety of the symptoms as well as the results in many cases make disagreements

This chapter contains excerpts from a paper entitled "Evaluation of Psychotherapy with Modified Rorschach Techniques," published in *The American Journal of Psychotherapy*, 6:471-483, 1952, and reprinted with the kind permission of the editor.

inevitable; i.e., the less severe the psychiatric illness, the more difficult it is to effect changes and evaluate results. Theoretically the most difficult of all cases is that of the nearly "normal" person. The experience of training analysts is in agreement with this statement.

To evaluate results properly, we have to be able to define first what we are treating, second the method of treatment, and *then* the effects of the treatment. In the present state of psychiatry, agreements in all three of these categories are not easily arrived at. The system of nomenclature is highly unsatisfactory. In psychoanalysis, where cases are studied the most intensively and extensively, diagnosis tends to become vague or considerably broadened by the time the analysis is in full swing. Getting to know the patient makes it harder to pigeonhole him and the classical categories appear more and more procrustean and inadequate. When it comes to describing technique, it is difficult to get even the classical analysts to agree upon the importance of its various aspects. In the case of the other schools of psychoanalysis and the many types of psychotherapy, each person is a law unto himself. The word psychotherapy has been stretched to mean practically *any* contact with a patient. Simple counseling, advice, reassurance, passive listening, narcosis, hypnosis with or without suggestion, wild, incomplete or abbreviated or modified psychoanalysis, persuasion, exhortation, retraining, role replacement and re-experiencing singly or in groups—all these are considered valid forms of psychotherapy and all are equally obscure descriptively and practiced according to the unique ideas of each practitioner. This means that with the exception of psychoanalysis none of these methods is "well standardized." Techniques even amongst the most orthodox of psychoanalysts varies from analyst to analyst, and not in any inconsiderable sense either. These are honest differences but they should not be minimized. For example, let us consider the basic tool of psychoanalysis, i.e., free association. One analyst may consider it unlikely that any patient can free associate well until he is in the closing months of his analysis. Another may feel from the beginning that what is going on is not analysis because of the inability of a patient to free associate with ease. There are almost no points of technique on which there are not violent disagreements among reputable analysts. The differences in the field of other therapies appear to be even greater.

The experience, character structure, maturity and objectivity of a therapist by necessity play an important role in the evaluating of a therapy, which means essentially that at times it will be difficult to differentiate between the evaluation of a technique and the evaluation of the therapist. The type of case chosen is of considerable importance. This has been mentioned in comparing the results obtained with psychotics and neurotics. Under this typological heading we must include not only the diagnosis but such factors as ego potentiality based upon past accomplishments and also secondary gains. A therapy that yields excellent "results" in the case of university students may be almost useless in the treatment of pensioned veterans, etc. The setting in which a psychotherapy takes place is also important. A hospital milieu may be so conducive to the development of passivity and dependency that any attempts at therapy may be nullified. The time factor itself is also of considerable importance, as the longer the duration of the therapy, the better the chance there is for outside factors to influence and confuse the results.

The problem of a control series is something that everyone thinks about from time to time. The feasibility of controls will differ according to the type of therapy. With the longer types of psychotherapy, such as psychoanalysis, it appears at present to be impossible. However, with short-term therapies, say for example those under six months in a hospital setting, it could possibly be combined with research in the field of group therapy.

All in all, the value of an evaluation of a psychotherapy will vary directly in proportion to the elimination of imponderables. Figures concerning such an indefinite thing as the results of psychotherapy in the neuroses are of little or no value, whereas figures on the results of treatment of, let us say, one hundred cases of migraine headache with sector psychotherapy as used by third-year psychiatric residents in comparison with one hundred cases treated over a similar period of time with Ergotamine would be meaningful and of pragmatic value.

There is, further, the problem of who and what determines the "results" and what the word "results" means. Reduced to its simplest terms, a patient comes to a psychiatrist for a better solution to a problem or for a dilemma concerning his relationship with other persons, and with himself, objects or his body. If overt symptoms are prominent, they are usually looked upon as partial if unsatisfactory attempts on the part of the patient to solve his problems; and the psychiatrist must ascertain their meaning, communicate this with conviction to the patient and then help the patient decide what can be done in a realistic way that will alter either the problems or his reaction to them. It is difficult to separate an evaluation of the results obtained from the goal that is consciously and unconsciously set by both the patient and the therapist. In the beginning this goal is often obscure. It may have to be changed during the course of therapy or as knowledge of the case increases. It may vary from an attempt to alter the basic character structure of the patient with long-term analysis to simple change or modification of a disabling symptom through the simplest of supportive measures. Obviously therapies with such dissimilar goals cannot be evaluated together.

Should the therapist, the patient, or both together decide when a goal has been reached? Some have felt that the therapist who sets the goal rather than the patient should decide whether or not it has been reached. There are reasons for this statement. The opinions of the patient during therapy are unreliable, as the development of insight necessarily involves the production of much anxiety and depression in spite of efforts to control its dosage. Transference relationships with the physician may promote a transient and deceptive disappearance of symptoms. There may also be the so-called flight into health to avoid anxiety or depression in guilt-producing situations. At the conclusion of therapy, the patient's estimation of the results may be confused with difficulties in handling situational problems which cannot be altered. The opinions of the patient's friends and relatives are often only of value when they are considered as a group and unreliable if taken individually. The wife of a Demerol addict whose husband was "cured" of his addiction and able to resume his previous occupation stated that her husband was "much worse" because he expressed a great deal of aggression against her and would not tolerate her attempts to remould him into the image of her father. The opinions of doctors without psychiatric training or doctors who have not known the patient over a long period of time are worth little in spite of their scientific background, although the impressions of the family physician may be an extremely reliable guide as to a correct evaluation of certain sociological aspects of the results of the patient's treatment. Although the impressions of the therapist may be distorted by wish fulfillment, they are on the whole more accurate than those of the patient and his friends and family, as his knowledge of the patient is more intimate, as a rule, than that of the patient's family or any of his associates.

The flaws in the above line of reasoning, however, are obvious. An impression or opinion of a therapist, or a patient, or his friends is hardly an objective evaluation and is always open to criticism. Ideally, we might submit data furnished by the patient, the therapist and, let us say, a social worker who is acquainted with the social milieu of the patient, to a committee of psychiatrists. Here again we would have

to accept the impressions or opinions of a number of people or com-
mittees and, even though it is a step in the right direction, it is somewhat cumbersome; i.e., verbal, descriptive opinions are difficult to handle
statistically, and statistical evaluation is a practical necessity if we are
to take advantage of its ability to cancel out and eliminate many
variables.

To illustrate some of the problems encountered when we try to
estimate results verbally, let us consider the following case: A female
patient, age thirty-two, entered the hospital because her eyes felt heavy,
dull and painful, lacked luster and moved too slowly. She had an
enormous fear that her eyes would never be the way they used to be,
i.e., lively and sparkling. She was seen for sixteen weekly interviews,
using the sector psychotherapy of F. Deutsch. The associative material
revealed that her symptoms began around the time of her thirtieth
birthday when she was pregnant with an unwanted child and had
developed some ankle edema. She admired and valued her legs more
than is usual in women. She had a great deal of hostility toward her
husband, who was partially deaf and refused to buy or drive a car.
She felt tricked into marriage, and a feeling of inadequacy about being
the youngest of three sisters was increased by the fact that her sisters'
husbands were financially better off and drove cars. She had never
been in love and apparently could love only an idealized image of
herself in her youth, when she had been extremely fond of dancing
and showing off her legs. She was in part consciously aware of her
enmity towards her husband, and stated frankly that were it not for
her religion, social disapproval and the children she would divorce
him and return to live with an over protective mother. Her concern
with her eyes appeared to be connected with forbidden exhibitionistic
tendencies and anxiety over the injury to her narcissism incurred by
the swelling of her legs during pregnancy and the birth of a girl child.
It also warded off depressive feelings about her inability to be a young,
teen-aged girl with a chance to marry a more romantic and wealthier
husband or have a succession of charming and attentive lovers. "My
eyes will never be the same" meant "I will never be young and gay
again." At a deeper level, her anxiety about her eyes represented
her anxiety about feeling that she had an inadequate husband and
an inadequate girl child to display and was herself an inadequate
being without a phallus like that possessed by a younger brother. She
felt she had been rejected by mother on this account and was extremely
suspicious about mother's reactive overconcern for her in childhood.
She also felt she had been pushed into marriage by mother and had

again received an inadequate phallus or man who was unable to supply her with phallus substitutes (cars, etc). The goal that was set in psychotherapy was that of strengthening the ego by making consciou and abreacting the affect-laden material connected with her eyes Following psychotherapy, the patient no longer had trouble with he eyes but became exceedingly aggressive toward mother and husband with a tendency to be moderately depressed. She became increasingl hostile and left at the end of sixteen weeks, refusing any furthe therapy and feeling disappointed with the results. Her husband, whil grateful that she no longer ran up large medical bills, felt that thi "result" was little better than the disease.

It will be readily apparent that there are many things to be cor sidered in evaluating the "results" obtained with this patient, eve though the goal had been reached. At the onset of the treatment, i was felt that the patient was extremely narcissistic and not very ir telligent and that there was a definite danger of precipitating a sever psychotic depression. During the early interviews, however, it becam apparent that her husband was not only identified with her inadequat phallus but also with rejecting parental figures, an aggressive, ove protective mother and a weak father. The emergence of aggression manifestations of withdrawal and depression could thus hardly b avoided. From the point of view of symptom disappearance, she wa able to leave her mother's home, take care of her child and resum living with her husband. From her own point of view, she had obtaine little relief. She finally partially solved her voyeuristic and exhib tionistic needs, anxieties and guilt feelings by becoming overconcerne about her baby daughter, who, she felt, resembled herself as a chil and devoted much time to exhibiting the child to her friends an family. From her husband's and mother's point of view, she wa sullen, still depressed and disagreeably aggressive.

The above case is described to show that in spite of the philosophica problems and subjective uncertainties mentioned at the beginning this chapter, it is possible to delineate certain spheres in a patient life where there are disturbances and in which there are chang which can be evaluated. The dynamically oriented therapist usual considers the following factors, needless to say from a relative poi of view.

1. The disappearance or lessening of symptoms. This is not si nificant unless the symptoms have been present for a long time ar do not recur. The difficulty here is that frequently symptoms reappe in a different form or are covered up by problems in acting out

withdrawal from society. A twenty-one-year-old boy complained of phantom-limb symptoms and continuous and excruciating pain in the stump of his amputated arm, unrelieved by local injections of Novocain. He was spared a neurosurgical operation and this symptom was completely alleviated following some insight into the significance of an approaching marriage and the relationship of his symptom to the loss of his mother when he was a child. However, he returned a few months after his discharge complaining of depression, acid stomach and epigastric pains relieved only by constant eating. From the point of view of the neurosurgeon, his treatment had been successful. From the psychiatric point of view, this was not so. Following more treatment he lost all of his complaints, gained weight and was happy and well-adjusted for a two-year period on the outside, living by himself and associating mainly with fellow amputees. Although he had given up attempts to marry and showed signs of a narcissistic regression, it was quite evident from a follow-up interview that from the point of view of the patient and his friends, as well as his immediate family, his treatment was considered by many doctors to be strikingly successful. The problem remains, however, how can this success or change be measured?

2.   An absence of further need for therapy. The ideal treatment envisages a maturity manifested by a freedom from a parasitic attachment to a physician, spouse or parent, but this also is difficult to measure or judge and is seldom obtained in psychotherapy owing to the absence of a working through of these attachments.

3.   The development of insight. This refers to the intellectual understanding of the relationship of the patient's symptoms to repetitive conflicts in the past as well as in the present, plus an emotional conviction of the reality of these relationships. It also implies a recognition of the necessity for the abandonment of infantile beliefs and modes of adjustment. This means insight with conviction.

4.   The ability to use acquired insight and act more objectively and in accordance with reality and with greater freedom of choice. One might also include an increase in the capacity for dealing more adequately with and sublimating or channeling into constructive fields aggressive and sexual instincts with an increased satisfaction and success in relationships with other people, less ambivalence in interpersonal relationships and love life, the capacity for contributing more to the happiness of others and an increased ability to find satisfaction in work and recreational activities. This highlights the fact that from a performance point of view a therapy can be evaluated properly only

after a period of time, and illustrates the complexity of the material involved in making a decision about "results." It also illustrates that we are concerned with measuring the amount of reversal in a regressive process in terms of an approach to a theoretical maturity.

In the case described previously, the patient ceased talking about her eyes and, when asked about them, stated, "They are not my real problem, so what's the use of talking about them?" It was evident that she had developed conscious knowledge of the meaning of her symptoms but was still reluctant to accept the fact that her wishes were unattainable. She had become able to displace some of her libido from herself and her eyes to her child. She "submitted" herself to her husband but remained anesthetic sexually. From an over-all point of view, she behaved more like a mature adult. Here again, although one might claim that therapy was moderately successful and that the patient's condition had improved, this is still only a subjective opinion, and we are still begging the question of measuring the reversal in regression quantitatively as well as qualitatively.

Many psychotherapists, in an endeavor to assess the multiple functions and potentialities of the effective ego and regressive changes, have turned to the psychologist and test batteries, which theoretically are able not only to evaluate ego functioning but to give one an idea of the types of ego defense mechanisms used, the amount of anxiety and guilt feelings present, and the rigidity, flexibility and potentiality of the personality as a whole. Actually, little has been accomplished in using these tests before and after therapy to measure changes in the depth of regression. Such tests have tended to be cumbersome and certainly not divorced from subjectivism. In many cases, there has been merely a change from psychiatric to psychological terminology. With some of these tests, such as the Rorschach, evaluation following insight therapy has been difficult due to the increased introspection and preoccupation with old, infantile material which produces a pattern difficult to evaluate. In spite of this, test batteries remain to date the most successful attempt in the field of psychology and psychiatry to place on paper, in an objective and abbreviated form, a series of formulae which demonstrate to a remarkable degree the multiple aspects and potentialities of the personality. However, even a series of formulae is cumbersome, and what is needed is a simple, practical, well-defined method of evaluating personality functioning in terms of maturity and regressive elements, one that can be evaluated quantitatively and can be used in the many clinics and hospitals now established all over the country. There is a great need for more refined successors of these tests. Variations in "normal" people over a period of time might be determined, following which it would be possible to measure a therapy and contrast it with other therapies. Such a measurement would not be concerned with the therapy as a tool of investigation, of course, but simply with its efficacy in stopping or reversing regressive tendencies in personality and, when results were pooled, some of the variables which, as has been pointed out, make a therapy so difficult to evaluate would be eliminated.

It is apparent that much more work must be done at basic descriptive levels before evaluation procedures can be made useful. The problems of nomenclature and diagnostic categorization are exceedingly complex and will not be discussed here in any detail. This is a fundamental area for research. As far as psychotherapeutic techniques are concerned, we shall never get anywhere until therapists are willing to permit an analysis of samples of their own techniques. This is another fundamental area for research loaded with disguised, displaced, conscious and unconscious anxieties on the part of the psychiatric and psychoanalytic profession. Even after the doubts and fears concerning such studies and evaluation procedures have been resolved and reliable reports have been made by competent people, it will be a long time before this data can be made useful. The main usefulness of such reports will be in the area of aiding teaching procedures and cultivating a generation of better therapists. There is an old dictum that where many remedies exist for the treatment of a disease it is usually because few of them are very effective. The truths of the psychoanalytic theory of the neuroses are so self-evident that a rational and effective method of treatment based upon them, such as sector psychotherapy, can readily be demonstrated and perhaps later evaluated with accuracy. At present, those who make use of it will soon observe its superiority over the more vaguely outlined methods of treatment.

Let us now consider a case that will highlight some of the difficulties of evaluating results.

The patient was a moderately attractive, plainly-dressed woman in her middle thirties who had telephoned for an appointment. Nothing was known about her difficulties. The interview began as follows.

"Could you tell me a little bit about your problem?"

"Yes, well, it's kind of difficult to get started. First of all, the chief problem right now seems to be that I can't seem to stay in *my own home*. I get up in the morning and after an hour or so I'll have to *leave*."

Already there was a problem, namely, why she had to leave and where she wanted to go. In this sense the sector was already defined.

"Who is in your own home?"

"Well, my son and myself. Of course there is my husband also."

The husband appeared to be an afterthought.

"You have a little boy?"

"I have a little boy three and a half and there's my husband and myself."

"Just the three of you?"

"That's right. And of course my husband goes to work every morning and as soon as *he leaves* I become very tense because I have been struggling terribly ever since we bought this house."

"How do you mean?"

"Well, we bought it two years ago and after we moved in I felt I couldn't be there *alone*. I wasn't feeling well then. I was seeing Dr. X at the time. I've always been, since my *breakdown*, I've always been afraid to be *alone*. I become very *confused*. At times I've been *afraid* to *look* in the mirror, *afraid* of *myself* and *what was going on inside me*."

"What do you mean?"

"I would just be in a *panic*, perspiring, and very *frightened* and *wanting someone to be with me* until the *worst* was over, and this had been going on for a while. So when I bought my home, I still had these feelings."

Her reaction was like that of a claustrophobic person threatened by an internal danger which was projected onto the house when her protector left her. In such cases, the protector is usually regarded very ambivalently. The word *alone* appeared to be a key to her problem in the past revolving around a loss.

"This has been going on for how long?"

"Since *my son* was *born*. Shall I start at the beginning? I suppose I should."

"If you please."

"Well, in 1955 I had a child, in May 1955, and just before he came I was *crying* a good deal. I had become *depressed* and I called my doctor, and I began to see him. And after the baby came, for a few months I was able to go on, for about four months. *My mother* was with me. She stayed with me because, well she's *quite alone herself* and *she should be with me* and I could use the extra help anyway."

"She is *alone*?"

"She is *alone*. She is a widow. She makes her home *alone*. And she

was with me during the time, for four months. I broke down completely. One day I just went to pieces and this has been going on
since 1955 in different stages. I have been feeling *ill*, very *tired*, and
can't *cope* with *it* any more."

The most important theme was concerned with the loss of a close
baby-mother relationship and at a time when the child's ego was in
symbiosis with that of the mother.

"Since the baby?"

"That's right. Since my son was born in 1955. Well, after I broke
down in the fall of 1955 I began to see Dr. X *again* but we weren't
getting anywhere and I think he thought I should try to *go on myself*,
well, just go on seeing if I could handle it."

"Pardon me! You saw him before the baby?"

"Yes, I did. I was seeing him actually off and on, I had been seeing
him."

"Well, then you mean it really began before?"

"Well, in those days I don't think I was really ill. I was feeling a
lot of *tensions*. I was *insecure* with my husband and that's how I
started to see Dr. X. I think that's all in the past, Doctor."

This type of statement merely underlines the connection of the
material.

"Surely, but I would like to hear about it from you, you know."

"Well, I get confused trying to remember everything."

"There is so much to think of?"

"There is quite a bit."

It was apparent that she had a problem with a mother and her
husband. Freud has remarked that many women spend their married
lives battling out with their husbands their past problems with their
mothers.

"You were *insecure* with your husband?"

"Well, yes. Early in our marriage he had gone to a *party*. It was an
office party."

"When was this?"

"It was in 1952, I believe."

"Nineteen-fifty-two, six and a half years ago?"

"Yes, that's right, and I used to *cry* a great deal about that because
I felt my husband was at this party and drank a little too much and I
thought he might have met *some other women*. I felt *insecure inside*.
I found this out later, I mean why I felt insecure."

"What do you mean?"

"Well then, it goes back to my childhood."

"Well, you can go back there if you want."

When a patient has been in therapy, the therapist takes advantage of it and gets his fantasies about what was learned and how he reacted. The therapist can be forewarned of what is to come and build upon the former insights.

"This is coming out all in pieces, just the way I didn't want it to come out. Well, when I saw Dr. X we worked together and found out a great deal about my childhood that more or less brought up *this other thing*. I guess I was *unhappy* as a child. I didn't know this until now, until recently, but I guess I wasn't too happy."

"How do you mean?"

"Well, I lived between *two homes*. I used to sleep at an aunt's home. I lived part time between my aunt's house and my mother's home."

"An aunt?"

"An aunt."

"Mother's sister or father's sister?"

"Mother's sister, and she was extremely close to her and our homes were close together."

She had already used the word *confused*. This probably meant between two mothers and two homes—which one to hate and which to love. Her childhood situation was a perfect setup for intensifying the usual infantile tendency to split the world into all good or all bad.

"She was a married aunt?"

"Yes, she had a daughter of her own and a husband and a nephew living with her too, and I used to sleep over every night with my cousin and I would spend part of the day with them and part of the day in my own home. I was shifted between *two families*."

"How come?"

"Well, it started this way. My mother had five children and I was the fourth and when the fifth came along they were *crowded* in the apartment. My aunt was making her home with my mother at the time, so when I came along they thought it was too crowded and my aunt rented an apartment of her own. Their daughter was about three years older and they thought that I should keep her company more or less. They were crowded in my home so why not let Jean sleep over there. That was my cousin's feeling and that's the way it started. It's just one of those things that happened gradually."

She must have hated the new baby that displaced her.

"How old were you when it began?"

"Maybe five."

"Five?"

"Four or five."

"Four or five? You mean then you were home up until four or five?"

"Yes, I was at home up until then. I remember being in the house until my younger sister was born."

"You remember these things?"

At this time her oedipal longings for exclusive possession must have been intense.

"Well, I've been saying them so often, I have them pretty well set in my mind. I have a very good memory and I'm sorry I have because I remember a *lot of pain* I have felt and I would like *to forget.*"

"What do you mean, for instance?"

"Well, the *horror* and *panic* I have felt. Well, in the past few months, I can just look back on certain things when *my baby* first was born and I can remember how terrible I felt."

"When your sister was born?"

"Yes, I know about that because I know what year she was born. I was three and a half when my youngest sister was born."

She was at home with her sister at least a year before going to her aunt's. Every detail in the past was important in determining her reactions to her own baby and husband.

"But you don't remember?"

She remembered the day her sister was born. Mother had the baby at home. She knew "something big" was happening and was anxious. She clung to her fourteen-year-old sister's skirt. She also knew a new baby had come. This memory screened a lot of anxious, jealous, resentful and depressing material revolving around a loss of her baby position. From then on she felt like a has-been. Shortly afterwards her aunt moved out and a year or so later, when she was around five, she began sleeping at night at her aunt's home. She shared her cousin Mary's bed. She "shuttled" between two homes. Now it seemed like an "impossible" situation. She would never let this happen to *her* child. When she was with Dr. X, she had found out that it had *"really affected"* her life. She went on to explain.

"In what way? Well, I never became *really close* to my mother because of that. I never *really* got to *know her,* and *even my father* for that matter. At age fourteen I wanted to come home myself and I came home and said, 'Mom, I'd like to stay here at night. I want to sleep here!' And I did, but when I turned fifteen, I *lost my father.* He passed away. So it wasn't the same, but that's another thing."

The new loss made it impossible for her to work out her oedipal problem during puberty and revived the old hurt.

"So you mean there always was a feeling then that you had never completely belonged to either family?"

"I found out later on. At the time I didn't realize it. I thought I belonged quite a bit. My people were very affectionate and very closely knit, and I thought I was all right until everything *blew up in my face* after I was *married* and *problems* started to come up."

This meant after she had to leave home. Why did she leave? She must have been ambivalent about both homes and mothers and everyone around.

"What do you mean, what problems?"

"Well, I started to argue with my husband because of that party. Now I don't think I should have minded his going to that party and drinking and wishing the women Merry Christmas and kissing them, which is quite the thing to do these days. It seems to be the normal thing, but in those days I couldn't take it."

"You mean you were jealous?"

"Extremely, extremely, I was *miserable*."

Her jealousy was based on the old mother-baby relationship and therefore irrationally violent.

"You couldn't forget it or forgive him?"

"No, I was miserable. I felt he *didn't love me any more* and, of course, I found out later working with Dr. X that it stems from the fact that I never got any love from *my father* and I more or less expected my husband to give me the love my father should have given me. Of course, this didn't happen overnight. This insight didn't happen overnight. This happened gradually. But after a while things more or less settled down and I felt well enough and I had a child. I wanted a baby. My son came along and after my *son* came along I went to *pieces*, really went to pieces. It was a complete *breakdown* as far as I could see from what I was feeling, and of course *when I broke down I remembered* the things I had learned from Dr. X and I began to resent my mother a great deal."

Actually the reverse happened. The birth gestalt revived the old jealous and depressive memories. She really meant her mother but the pattern, of course, radiated to the father and she could feel "Mother let me go so I missed getting love from my father." At a body-image level she was accusing mother of castrating her.

"For letting you go?"

"Yes. In fits of anger I told her right to her face that she had been unfair to me. Of course my mother was very hurt. She didn't have any education. She was born in the old country and had no formal education or learning, and this was very strange and new to her. What harm was there in leaving her girl with an aunt, a loving aunt, and she cried and was sincere with me. She said she never realized what it could do to me. After this suffering I had been through and this pain, I knew that, I believed my mother."

"Surely."

"I know my father and mother didn't do it because of lack of love. They loved me all the while but they were, I believe, caught up in bringing up their family. There wasn't much money during the *depression* and *having more than one child to love*."

"It's hard to forgive them?"

"Well, *I think* I have. I love my mother a great deal now and three years ago I couldn't. I was very hostile towards her, but she has stood by me. My mother is a wonderful person. I've found that out now. She has stood by me and has taken all my *assaults* and when I say assaults I mean the lashings that I have given her and my father too. I mean I *lashed out* at her husband and my father, and she has taken it and has repeatedly told me that it wasn't from lack of love. And I have come to accept that."

This was impossible or she would be symptom free. The conflict must have been displaced or shifted to other areas.

"But now something else—?"

"Well, now it seems to be *the house*. I have a *fixation* or an *obsession* about the house I'm living in. I feel that I *can't live there* and I don't want to *give it up* and sell it and I'm *caught*. I'm all caught up on what I should do."

The displacement was from persons to things. The house was a symbol for the mother, but there were two of them. She was unable to renounce the longing to be mother's only baby, and she couldn't give up the aunt either.

"I don't understand, what do you mean you can't give it up?"

"Well, I bought my home, as I say, and I found it very difficult to be there and momma came again and stayed with me. She had been living alone. No one needs her *at home* and she felt 'My daughter needs me' and she stayed with me for a while, and after a while I couldn't *stand her* because it just pointed out to me that I was *ill* and I wanted so much to be *independent* and *on my own* because I *never needed anyone* up to the time I broke down. I was *ex-*

tremely independent and I never needed any other member of my family. Of course, I was *never close* to any of them really."

This was a wonderful description of the past. She had felt rejected when mother sent her to the aunt and had developed a pseudo independence. She had become her own mother and had taken herself as a love object. To do so her libido was withdrawn from those around her. She could only care for herself and that wasn't enough. She was lonely and depressed but these feelings were denied. Her therapy with Dr. X was successful inasmuch as this defense was broken through and the old loneliness, panic and feelings of depression and abandonment returned. This illustrates the old lesson that patients often must get worse before they get better. With a person of this type, intimacy, dependency are loved and craved but feared because of the resurrection of the old gestalts that were connected with the abandonment by the originally loved person or persons.

"Like mother and father?"

"Well, like my other sisters. I have three other sisters. There was just one I was close to."

"Which one was that?"

"My youngest sister, Florence."

"The youngest?"

"The youngest. I became very close to her after I was married. I somehow became close."

This was a reaction formation to her original hate. She solved the loss of mother by becoming mother. Florence was then *her* baby. We might even suspect she wanted a girl instead of a boy baby to work out her problems.

"But you were close to Mary?"

"Yes, but not in the same way. I can't explain it but it wasn't the same type of closeness. But actually *when I broke down it seemed I became closer to everyone* in my family. My brother and sisters proved very understanding. They seemed to understand me and I just naturally drew close to them and they drew close to me and *I began to love them* a great deal and *because I was changing* I found them different too."

She paused.

"Well, I think I'll go back to the house again. My mother was with me and I couldn't stand her because I felt this proved to me that I wasn't well and I wanted so much to be well again and not leaning on momma, and I sent her home."

Her longing for mother and ambivalence over her "rejection" intensified her oedipal rivalry with her and feelings of shame.

"You mean by sick then as against well, that you didn't want to be—?"

"Alone."

"And also a little baby, momma's girl?"

"Yes."

"You wanted to be a grown up, independent woman?"

The adult part of her felt mortified also. Of course, this sensitivity was interwoven with the oedipal inadequacy feelings.

"That's right. A constant panic and *confusion*, a great deal of *confusion* that sometimes I couldn't cope with. I would just break down and I would pick up the telephone and I would talk to someone. I used to call my *aunt* up a great deal. I used to gain a lot of confidence from her."

This was the hub of her confusion. Her infantile goals were incompatible with her adult ones, and her wishes in connection with the aunt incompatible with those in connection with mother. If this is true, the difference must be clearly revealed in order to effect a reconciliation.

"So you mean momma lived with you and you called up aunt?"

"I used to call up auntie a great deal."

"So you were still sort of between both of them?"

"Yes, until the past six months. I have been describing the relationships right, I think, because I have begun to accept the fact that my aunt is my aunt and momma is my momma."

"You mean you hadn't before?"

"No, I was *mixed up* until now. I think I have been all along."

"You mean that's the basic *confusion*?"

"Yes, a definite *confusion* and if I needed help I expected my aunt to come running to me."

"As if she were your real mother?"

"Well, yes."

"Is that what you mean?"

"Yes, probably. You see I grew up with my aunt and I *could talk to her* and she gave me a great deal of *understanding*. As a matter of fact, when I was growing up, I would go to my aunt and talk to her and she would give me understanding."

She felt safe in not having all her eggs in one basket. She didn't have to commit herself fully with either one and didn't trust either one completely.

"She was different from mother?"

"Well, yes, they are not of the same temperament, not really, but my aunt is a very *sensitive* woman an *understanding, quiet* sort of person, very *controlled,* and I could talk to her."

"Mother wasn't that way?"

"No, my mother was very *warm* and *spontaneous.* The other one was more controlled. It's hard to explain."

There must be two similar parts of herself.

"Mother wasn't controlled?"

"No, she was just the opposite of my aunt."

"In what way?"

"Well, my aunt was very *reserved* and *calculated.* Everything she does she thinks about it and deliberates on it and she, my aunt, can read and my mother can't and somehow it seemed like being with her just drew me to her and it was easy to talk to her, but in these past few months when I've been in need, when I would need someone, well my aunt just wasn't there. She had *her own problems* at home and she wouldn't respond the way I expected her to. That was very hard, that was very hard for me to take, but I finally accepted the fact that she was my aunt and I had no right to demand things. She was just a good aunt. She loved me a great deal but I wasn't her daughter. She had one of her own. But I've been through *hell* in order to *change* these *feelings* I grew up with, and it has gone the other way. I'm giving everything to my own mother. I love her a great deal and I understand her a great deal and she stands by me, as I say. She is always there when I need her. She's a very unselfish person. She will baby-sit for me at any time."

"But you still feel confused?"

"I'm confused? No, I'm not confused about *that* any more."

"About the house, I mean?"

"Well, I'm confused about *myself* and the *house.* That's why I'm here. I think I've resolved the past. A lot of that has come out and I more or less have *settled* it but the present, today, that's why I'm desperate. That's why I've come for help."

What she meant was that her insight needed more working through, accompanied by reconciliation and acceptance of discrepancies in her attitudes toward the new areas on which she had displaced old problems. It was impossible to solve her problems in terms of the mother loss, penis loss or any other separate loss. All of these areas had become bound up and united by the fact that her infantile ambivalent affects had been and could be shifted readily from one area to another. This displacement allowed her to postpone, evade and dilute the process of working through. To paraphrase Freud (1937), once the building is on fire it is necessary to do more than remove the overturned lamp that started the conflagration.

"What do you mean confused about the house?"

"Well, first of all I'm confused about *myself*. I've *changed so much* these past three years, not *basically* but *emotionally*. I'm *not the same person* at all, and I don't even *know myself* at times. I don't know what I'm going to do next and what I'm going to want next. I have changed a great deal."

This was really a fine tribute to her previous doctor, but this change had penalties attached which made further therapy necessary.

"What do you mean?"

"Just everything, just about everything."

"That's a lot!"

"And that is a lot. I've been through hell in three years."

"Could you give me an example of how you have changed?"

"Yes, as an example, I grew up in a tenement and I always wanted to escape and run away. As a girl, I dreamed that one day I would live in the country—I love grass and *growing things*, trees and flowers —that I would have a home of my own."

She wanted a baby of her own so she could realize her longing for a baby-mother relationship, a just-us-two relationship. This part of her resented her siblings. Tenement means a crowd. But another part felt lonely.

"In the suburbs?"

"In the suburbs, that's right, and it happened that when I married I was fortunate enough to marry a man who wanted what I wanted. We both wanted the same things, and we were able to have this home, and now that I am in it I am not happy. I'm not happy and when I'm down in the city I look at these empty flats, cold-water flats, and I picture myself living in them and wonder if I would be happy there because I wouldn't be so *alone* and *isolated* and I could *walk out* any time I wanted and be in the city or go to church if I wanted to go to church, or *visit* a *friend*. You see I feel *I'm cut off* where I am. I ought to tell you that my house is in the suburbs but I have to walk about three blocks to the bus. I *haven't got a car* at my disposal. My *husband needs the car* for business and *I'm not close to anyone* in the neighborhood so I feel very much *alone* there, very much, very very much, and sometimes this feeling of isolation gets so great I feel I can't stand it. I want to run away. And that's what I have been doing since September. No, not really, since I bought the house, I don't think I have stayed in a whole day. I always manage to leave part of the day. I find it *intolerable* to be in all day there anyway."

This showed the relationship between the feelings of abandonment which related to persons and castration anxiety which referred to the body image. The feeling of defect was displaced everywhere.

"So you mean this is the confusion between the childhood parts of you, one that longs for your own house in the suburbs and the part that longs for the tenement and the closeness of these two families with all these mothers and sisters?"

"Well, I have changed so much. I wanted just the opposite when I grew up and now that I have it I don't know myself."

"You don't know which one you want now?"

"That's right and this *endless indecision* is just *driving me, driving me*. I go through these *terrible moods, depression, crying, fear, panic*. It's *hitting* all over since my son was born. Well, I should tell you I managed to stay home by myself in my own home for about a year. I managed, and I struggled a great deal to do it but I managed to be in, to run my household, take care of my son, wash, cook. I more or less formed a *pattern* for living, but as I said I always had to leave the house for *part of the day*. Then last September I broke down one day. I told my husband I just couldn't live there any more. We had to leave, we had to sell and I had to get out. When this happened, I couldn't sleep at night. I thought this is it, I just can't cope with myself. I would go for periods of not knowing myself. I'd look in the mirror. This has been the thing that has brought forth my illness, the mirror. When I'd look at myself, I'd be confused. It started that way. When my son was born, I'd go to wash and comb my hair and I'd be all mixed up and I'd think, who am I? I talked to Dr. X about this. Now I don't say that any more after three years. It is just that I am mixed up."

She was literally a split personality between past and present, child and adult, two homes, two mothers. Such a split can occur in a single home between good and bad images. Simplifying this relationship and making it conscious would ease her anxiety to a degree.

"So do you mean 'Who am I' in the sense 'Am I auntie's child' or 'Am I momma's child,' or what?"

"No, no, that's not it."

"Who am I, in what way?"

"I changed a great deal."

"Physically?"

"No, *emotionally*; feelings; what I wanted as a wife, what I expected as a wife; what I demanded of myself. I was a perfectionist in everything."

"Perfectionist?"

"Yes, oh I demanded that from myself. I just had to be perfect. My home had to be perfect. John had to be perfect. This party that he went to, that wasn't right for us, you see. I've always wanted to be perfect, and that's how I changed. I'm not that way any more. I don't expect to be and I don't want to be and I don't demand it or ask it of anyone any more, and most of all myself. So I've changed in that respect, and also in the way I want to live. I wanted that home in the suburbs and now that I have it I don't want it. I'm miserable. I'm going crazy. This is the thing, when I'm there alone, I start to imagine. I feel a lot of pressure. It starts to build and when it starts to build I get mixed up and confused, and when that happens I feel I'm losing my mind, that it's just a matter of time and I won't know where I am or who I am or what I'm doing any more."

There was a regressive return of all the old feelings of love and hate which now appeared in an alien and distorted form.

"Then what will happen? What do you fantasy will happen when you lose your mind?"

"I'm very much afraid of mental hospitals and I'll tell you why. My *oldest sister* had a *breakdown* after *she* married and I was exposed to it. I was exposed to her crying."

This trauma shaped her childhood feelings and fantasies into a different form. The older sister could be used as an alter-ego image also.

Her sister's marriage was not happy from the start. When the patient was twelve, this sister had a baby and became very depressed. She thought sister was suffering and insane, and was terrified that this would happen to her. She connected it with having a baby. Since twelve, she had feared marriage, babies and breakdowns. She had a friend who feared going blind. They would compare blindness and insanity and fear growing up. Actually her sister's depression had lasted only a month. She was aked why she felt her sister had suffered so much and continued as follows.

"Well, I could see the general *feeling* and maybe because *I was so unhappy myself*, I just—"

She meant she projected her own ideas and feelings onto her sister.

"You mean at twelve you were *unhappy* too?"

"Well, so I found out with Dr. X, I must have been."

This was a form of persistent denial. Intellectual recognition is not enough. Emotional conviction was lacking. Further insights and working through were necessary. Patients do not believe through suggestions and will not accept suggestions unless they ring true or serve as useful screens or escapes.

"How do you know? What did you find out about your unhappy past?"

"Well, even then I wasn't close to anyone. I didn't feel loved by my father and I wasn't close to my own mother. I was *close* to one *sister* growing up. She more or less acted more the mother than my mother did. I have an *older sister*."

"Who is that?"

"My sister Sally. She was very good to the younger ones. She would comb my hair and sew dresses for me and curl my hair, and she was the *little mother* in my life at home."

She was also a model and object for identification. This made her "breakdown" traumatic and very threatening for her.

"But not like a real mother?"

"No, but away from home it was *my aunt*, you see."

"Yes, so you had *all kinds of mothers?*"

The therapist should have pointed out how *confused* she was at this time.

"I guess I did. I guess I did, unfortunately."

"And then you were sad, you found out."

"Well, I found out I couldn't have been very happy not to break down like that."

"You mean with all of these mothers none could compare with what you really wanted from your real mother?"

"No, no one can take the place of a *real mother*."

By this she really meant an idealized mother. Having so many mothers allowed her to displace bad and good qualities freely and postponed the necessity for reconciliation.

"How do you mean that?"

"Well you know that, Doctor, don't you?"

"But *my* knowledge doesn't do *you* any good. It is what *you* felt."

"Yes, well, I don't know, I probably, well, yes, now that I look back, now that I think of it, I think as a child you have to have someone you are close to."

She longed for complete possession of the mother. She had an unsolved and primarily negative oedipus complex. The oedipus complex actually oscillates between both parents. It is a push-pull sort of thing.

The boy or girl cannot possess the parent of the opposite sex without getting the know-how or the "tools" to do so from the parent of the same sex. Morever, the child still needs to be "babied" by the parent. The physiological mysteries concerning sex and babies are too frightening. *Both* parents are necessary for their proper solution through introjection, identification and role learning.

"In other words, you always felt that something was missing, huh?"

"You mean while I was growing up? I didn't feel it, no. I grew up completely unaware of it."

"But I thought you just said you were so miserable yourself that you could understand—?"

"No, I *found out* I was *miserable later* when I had *therapy* with Dr. X. I learned these things from *insight*. I didn't know that I didn't feel loved. I found out later."

"How do you feel now about it? What do you believe now?"

"I believe now that I was loved."

"But do you also believe that you were miserable?"

"Yes, I *think* I was miserable. I don't think I would have broken down the way I did—"

"You mean you just think it sounds logical?"

"Think, yes."

"But you don't remember feeling miserable?"

"Yes, I remember feeling miserable."

"What do you remember?"

"I remember on my sixteenth birthday crying and crying."

"What were you crying about?"

"I *don't know*. My *father* had been *dead* about a year and in those days families believed in mourning even for the younger girls and my family gave me a black corduroy jumper and, well, I was crying. *I don't know what I was crying about* but I cried that day. That's what I remember, that black jumper they gave me and also I was made to wear *mourning* clothes in high school among all the other students and I was the *only* girl in class in black and if that wouldn't give anyone a *complex* I don't know what will. I felt *different* from my *high school chums*. I was draped in black. I remember one of my teachers called me up to her desk one day and she said, 'How's your mother?' She probably figured why does she insist on this, I don't know. I told her she was well but was *grieving* over my *father*."

This paragraph shows how much work remains to be done. She avoided grief for father by resurrecting her old feelings of *being dif-*

ferent from her sisters and brothers (classmates). She could also do the opposite when and if it were necessary during therapy. The social situation was used as a screen. The analyst might also say that an external narcissistic mortification in the present screened an internal narcissistic mortification from the past.

"So you mean from the word 'go' then you always felt *different?* You were the only one of your sisters—"

She finished the statement.

"That was sent away!"

The therapist continued.

"That was sent away and you were the only one who had two mothers. You were different to start, huh?"

"Well!"

She sighed.

"Well, I suppose now as I look back it seems that way but while I was growing up I was unaware of what was going on inside of me. I found out later, I found these things out later when we started to probe and dig in, Dr. X and myself, why I was unhappy, why I cried and *I expected so much from my husband*, why I was insecure, that's the main thing that came out, my whole childhood came out."

It was clear that she expected her husband to make up for both mother and father.

"I don't understand. You say you understand these things. You mean they sound reasonable to you but you don't really remember how bad you felt?"

"No, *not really.* I remember certain feelings and certain memories in my mind that I was unhappy about."

Intellectual pseudo acceptance is often used as a defense, like the child who shuts out unpleasant truths by yelling, "I know! I know! I know!" This is why it is necessary to test a patient's insight ad nauseum.

"Like what?"

"Well, I'll have to, do you want me to think back?"

"Surely, if you wish."

"Well I was miserable, I was miserable in high school."

This was after twelve. Before this time, she remembered nothing other than nice things. On Sundays her aunt's and her mother's families would all be together. She was at her aunt's home until fourteen, and then she decided to come home and be with her mother. She put it this way.

"Well, I must have felt *when I got older* I don't *belong* here. I told my mother, 'I want to sleep at home now. I want to be here!' My mother didn't object. It just became very natural for me."

Now was the time to interweave or integrate the *past* and *present* feelings and events. This is an essential part of all interviewing.

"You mean so this is the same old problem now. You don't know where you belong, whether in the tenements in the city or out in the suburbs?"

"Well, that's *one way of putting it*. I'm very *confused* and I'm afraid of insanity and mental hospitals."

"By insanity you mean you are afraid of losing something and becoming *depressed*?"

"I'm, well, yes."

"And *crying*?"

"I label what I *feel* is *insanity* even though I've been told by more than one doctor that it isn't insanity. I'm just afraid of the *word*."

This illustrates nicely how futile it is to treat patients with semantics.

"Well, that's what I mean. I'm trying to get *your ideas* of what insanity means. Insanity means to you, I take it, crying and being depressed like your sister?"

"Yes, Doctor, because I think when I saw my sister acting that way when I was a little girl, I labeled it in my own mind as being insanity, and when it happened to me I thought this must be it, this is insanity."

The therapist did not allow himself to be contented with this rational but superficial agreement.

"What did you see?"

"Crying, oh a great deal of *crying* and *anguish*, a great deal of anguish. She wasn't able to go to work. My mother had to *take care of her baby*. She was with us a great deal. She cried all the time, and that's what I've been constantly doing, and I just labeled it insanity."

Mother had to take care of *her* baby as well as her sister's to satisfy her own need for babying and make restitution for the old losses. At the same time insanity means castration in a different sense—a mother loses her baby. This is another expression of incompatible drives, like longing for independence and mothering at the same time.

"What was her baby, a boy or a girl?"

"A little girl."

"A girl?"

"Yes, and she's married and has a child of her own now. A lot of water has passed over the dam since that time. My *sister* will be a *grandmother* in two months. Isn't that *wonderful*? Well, anyway, it hardly seems possible, and *I* will be a *great-aunt*. Well, I was twelve when she was born and she married at twenty, and now she's going to be a mother. Well, anyway I labeled myself insane. The anguish seems to be so deeply buried in me."

The anguish she mentioned meant that at twelve she had experienced a return of the repressed. This was the anguish experienced at five when she lost mother and her baby position. Her guilt and ambivalence toward mother and the new baby led to an intensified need for a baby by daddy and to increased castration anxiety and need for massive denial and reaction formation. For a time she became narcissistically withdrawn and self-sufficient. All of this was woven into her oedipal family romance. When it returned at twelve, the unconscious alien quality and anxiety over a loss of control and a massive eruption of id material made her feel insane. There is also a hint that being a great-aunt is not as wonderful as she claims. Lost youth is one of the commonest screens for other losses.

"You mean you are afraid of being anguished?"

"Of feeling this way, of *not being able to stay home*. I was very *efficient* and *highly organized*. I didn't need anybody and I'm just the opposite now. I don't know myself this way, so consequently I'm always confused. I am, I'm terribly *confused*. Sometimes I feel as if I'm, I am beginning to see myself as I really am, as I am, I mean with these moods and feeling happy and crying. Somehow the *feeling* is that as I get *older* I have to *face myself as I am, not as I was* but as *I am today* and I hope this feeling will take hold and keep growing because I think that *is how I can get well*."

Her kind mother and husband and her therapy had invalidated her old compulsive and narcissistic self-sufficiency type of defenses. Her readiness for insight appeared quite good.

"How does your husband feel about all this?"

"He's been wonderful, very patient and understanding with me. He is very good to me. I have been very fortunate. I don't know where I'd be if he hadn't been this good to me for hours when I felt tense and he told me over and over again that it would be all right. He has been wonderful to me and that's why I have a great deal of, *not guilt* but I'm very anxious over it. I want to give him a good life and also my boy. He's three and a half now and he can understand and see *what's going on* and that has me *worried*. That really does."

This was fortunate for the husband, although the therapist would have to watch out for secondary gains in her illness.

"But you said you felt totally different about *everything*. Do you feel different about *him?*"

"About him, I grew up in regards to my husband!"

"How do you mean?"

"Well, he's a pretty wonderful person."

"You mean before that you didn't think so?"

Before her therapy, she had fought continually with her husband. She was extremely jealous and ready to feel deserted at any time. Her relationship with her father was also described as deficient.

"I was always shy in the presence of my *father*. He was, well, in his generation they didn't *fondle* children too much. I don't ever remember being held by him but my *mother tells me I was* when I was an infant."

This was material for another interview but could also be examined briefly. The therapist used the least anxiety-provoking statement to echo back.

"You never got much fondling?"

"Sitting on his lap, not too much, nothing like that. I remember as a little kid I would kiss him goodnight. When I was in my own home, I couldn't approach my father. I was almost *awe-struck* by him. He was a big man. I never felt close to him."

She would tend to long for awesome men, as the loss of her father prevented her from reducing him to a normal size during latency. A kind husband might not be enough.

"And mother never *fondled* you either?"

"Oh, yes, when I would, oh yes, once in a while. She loved me more than my father did, but my father never laid a hand on us to *punish* us. He would just have to look at us and we knew we would have to be good. He *never struck us* or *hit us*. He had a loud voice and when he'd get angry he would yell. I was *afraid* of that *loud voice*."

"And you wish you had been *closer?*"

"Oh, I certainly do."

"Why, what do you mean?"

"Well, because I have found out that, well if what I have discovered is true and if I had a better childhood—"

"You mean with father?"

"With father and mother, and shown a little bit more love."

"By showing love you mean physical affection?"

"No, no, there are ways of showing love besides physical affection. You don't have to be kissing a child every minute."

"Surely."

"Give the child *understanding, time* and by *talking* to them."

"So you mean you didn't get these things? Or was it only from aunty?"

"I stuttered in my childhood a great deal and I found it very hard to recite in class. When I went to high school, it became very hard for me because I was growing up and becoming aware of boys and I wanted to be *pretty*, and it was very hard for me to get up and *recite* in front of the classroom. It was *torture*. I remember in one class in particular you had to get up in the front of the class and recite and it was very hard for me to do that. And I was dressed *in black* at the time so you can *see*."

Voice problems often screen feelings of genital inadequacy. Here her speech gave away her ambivalence, guilt and feelings of defectiveness. Her stuttering probably began at three when the baby arrived. Her guilt over the death of her father was augmented by his being another rival for mother. This was suggested by the association between stuttering and being dressed in *black*. High-school problems may intensify but do not *cause* neurosis. They simply screen the unconscious infantile problems.

"It must have been very difficult?"

"It was."

"Did you spend much time by yourself?"

"No, I had friends. I belonged to a gang, a *group of girls*, but I felt I was *different* because I *stuttered* and they didn't. I was self-conscious. They were spontaneous and I was reserved. I was *always the reserved one* in the *crowd*, and I was very self-conscious of my speech, extremely so. It wasn't until after I got through *business school* that I seemed to gain *confidence* and boys began to find me *attractive* and I was *dating* and I became *confident* and *didn't stutter*. As a matter of fact, I didn't stutter any more. I went out into the business world and got a *good job*. My first job was in a small office. I was the *only girl* there. I had a whole office to myself! I was a *secretary* and *bookkeeper* and I had confidence then."

She was *the* one and only. She was also self-sufficient narcissistically. She had her career which made up for her old losses, especially mother and father.

"You were happy?"

"Well, yes. I think that was *the happiest time of my life* between eighteen and after I was married."

"You mean from eighteen up *until* you were married?"

"I was happy after I was married *until I started to see Dr. X.*"
Now she wanted to blame Dr. X. If she was so happy, why had
she gone to him?

"As happy as you were from eighteen up until your marriage?"

"Well, up to the time that I saw Dr. X. I was very happy after I was
married up to the time I saw Dr. X. Then it started to reverse."

"You mean?"

"I mean, well, uh, I began to feel confident and sure of myself
about eighteen when I graduated from business school."

"From eighteen up until you got married, you were doing fine?"

"Well, yes."

"You were the only girl in the office and everything was fine?"

"Well, that wasn't the only job I had. I had *other jobs* where I
worked in an office with a large group."

There were other mothers too, even in this situation.

"But you felt independent?"

"Well, I was independent, yes. I stopped stuttering and I felt sure
of myself and I was found *attractive* by *fellows* I was dating and my
mother was very proud of me. She had a *bookkeeper* in the family and
she was, she was extremely proud of me. I didn't go to college. It
was *business* school. I went for about eleven months. I was certified.
My mother was proud of me then."

This undid her castration state. Her mind was now invested with
phallic libido as in the case of obsessive compulsives.

"You were certified?"

"No, well, just a minute and I'll explain that. I was certified for
the speed I had in shorthand. I'm not a certified accountant. I don't
mean to give you that impression."

This meant that she had not become quite self-sufficient like a
real boy. She gave the impression that this was a lack in her. The
therapist reassured her.

"But you had accomplished a great deal?"

"Yes, I was happy then."

"And then you got married?"

"And then I got married and I was still happy then *up until the
time I began to feel insecure* with my *husband.*"

At this time she evidently felt as complete, mature, independent
and secure as she ever had been but, like her speech, her position
was shaky and insecure. The feminine role and motherhood also meant
giving up her career, which symbolized her phallic and narcissistic
defenses.

"And then you had the child?"

"No, I should tell you my son came *five years later.*"

"*Five years later?*"

"I didn't have a child *right away.* I didn't have my son right away."

"How come?"

"Well, about a year and a half after I got married this *party incident* came up and I saw Dr. X and I kept *seeing him off and on.* As I look back now, I really didn't need a doctor then. I think I would have worked out of it. I really think I would have. It's *now* that I am really struggling. In those days, *no one knew.* Then I used to *argue* with my husband and I would be *resentful* and I would keep bringing up the incident of the party to him and I would try to make *him* feel *guilty,* and that was the predominating thing that led me to a doctor."

"So you mean *really* you had *trouble then before?*"

"Well, if you call that trouble. In those days I was not *confused.* I was not *confused* and I was not *panicky* and I *didn't need anybody.* I didn't have a telephone and I didn't care to have one. I didn't see *my mother* for, well I would see her once a week. I never went to my mother's home. I didn't need any of *my sisters* and I didn't need *my aunt* either. I never call on *anybody.* I was *independent,* even *while I was seeing Dr. X.* If I had a problem then, believe me it was a very *slight one.*"

This was self-deception. Her problem then was her narcissism. As a defense, this had certain advantages but it also carried certain penalties. She could not love and trust anyone. She had made her husband take over all these roles and had become too dependent upon him. Having Dr. X allowed her to distribute her dependency needs, but she lost her ability to deny the past and had to face the repressed old painful affects and find a different solution in the present.

"You mean the problem you went to him for?"

"Yes, the problem I went to him for."

"It was a very slight one?"

"It was."

"That you were hyperjealous, critical?"

"*Insecure,* I was so *insecure.* I thought he didn't love me any more."

"You mean before the party everything was fine?"

"*Oh, I don't know.*"

"But you said that was the happiest time of your life!"

"Well, that was because I was really confident then and sure of myself. That was one time in my life I felt *independent* and sure of myself."

"And this began to change when you got married?"

"Well, it changed after the party incident, that's when it *really* changed and I saw Dr. X off and on for a while and after I tapered off seeing him, and the doctor would tell me all along to have a baby. He felt it would be good for me to start a family."

Now things were clearer. The baby not only revived the old gestalts but the loss of it acted like a castration. She was no longer a little boy-girl who could work at a career and be married to a mother plus aunt plus sister, but a little girl with a defect, i.e., no penis, baby, etc. She could now blame Dr. X for this instead of her husband.

"He did?"

"Oh, definitely. He thought having a child would be very good for me and he told me *not to wait.*"

"Didn't you want one? You waited, so I take it you had some other reason in mind."

"I, we didn't want, I didn't, there was *something in me.*"

"Something in you didn't?"

"Myself, *I didn't want it.*"

"You didn't want it?"

"That's right."

"Why didn't you want it?"

"I *don't know.* I just, I *don't know.* I think I felt I would have one *eventually.* I knew that. I would want the child eventually but I thought we will wait. We had the excuse that our *apartment was small* and we wanted *the money* and our *own home,* one reason or another."

She had to deny her incestuous wish for daddy's baby, and at the same time she didn't want another baby around. Here again her feelings were ambivalent. There was always a loss whichever way she went. This is the key to obsessional indecision.

"Were there other reasons why you didn't want a child?"

"Other reasons? Well, that's what the doctor used to tell me, that's not the real reason. He used to tell me there's *something more* and I don't know, I couldn't tell him. Maybe because I myself, as we found out later, *I had never matured emotionally* and maybe I myself *wasn't ready*, that *that instinct* never was *strong* in me because we found out when I completely broke down; after my baby was born I went to Dr. X and I talked several times and he said, 'You *never grew up emotionally.* It is *too intricate* and *too deep* to explain but you didn't have a chance to mature.' Maybe that's why. I don't know, I *never wanted one*. You know I never was introspective until I started with Dr. X. I never asked why I didn't want a baby. I just didn't want one. I just went along with myself. I never asked why I *don't want one* or brood over it. I didn't want to have one. It wasn't until after I had therapy that I became very introspective and now I might ask don't I want to do this, why don't I want to do that, but I didn't then. I was a lot better off too. I wasn't so aware of myself."

The therapist noted the massive nature of her denials and respected them, but some of her defenses could be tested.

"You mean if you had it to do over again you would have done things differently?"

"You mean not go to Dr. X? I *don't know.*"

"Not get married?"

"No, I *would have married.*"

"Have a baby?"

"No, my son is *worth every bit of it,* but I think if I had known I would have a breakdown I wouldn't have had the courage because I have been through hell, believe me, because I don't think any human being can tell another what he feels, but *I felt a great deal.* I've had a lot of *confusion* and *panic* and that's the way I can explain to you but that's not describing what is going on inside of me, but I think if I had known I would have a breakdown I wouldn't have had the courage to have a baby. But I didn't know and *I wanted my baby* and I went ahead and had him, but after I had him, oh four or five months later, I broke down completely, I went to pieces, and it's been this way ever since. Now it's the house I'm living in. I'm not happy there."

"But you can get rid of it?"

"Well, that's it. I'm in between. I don't know what I want. It seems like I am *two people.* Part of me wants to be at home in *my own* nice, neat little bungalow, and part of me wants to be in a tenement. Now this has been going on since September very very strong."

This was an excellent piece of insight but it had to be greatly expanded.

"Which tenement? You mean like where you lived when you were a child?"

"Any city tenement."

"That's what I mean, like where you used to live?"

"That's right."

"So you mean part of you is where you are now in your bungalow and another part of you is sort of back in the past where you used to be in the tenement?"

"That's right. And when I'm at my mother's home, *my mother* is still living in *the tenement where I was born.*"

The material then led to her being torn between her mother and husband and baby. She would like to have her mother live with her but it was unfair "*to cut her off from her own home.*" and she resented her being with them. She resented the baby allegiance which insulted her adult pride. She felt she had gotten over her deep resentment of her mother when she was with Dr. X, but it still hurt. She felt chronically cheated but couldn't say anything about it to her mother.

"See, she doesn't know that and I could never begin to explain because I don't think she'd *understand.* She could just turn to me and say, 'Look, I loved you and I still love you,' and she has proven that."

One of the main problems was that the real mother *felt* and the aunt mother *understood.* There was a similar split in her ego.

"But it is almost as if you say yes, I know that now but part of me when I was little—"

"I told her, I said, 'Mom, I know that now, I know you didn't do it to hurt me, but it did hurt me.' "

"And you still feel it?"

"Well, I feel it because I am still struggling. If I could begin to live again—"

"You mean that little girl part that was hurt so deeply?"

"Well, yes, but I'm still struggling because I'm not able to run my life, to live the way I want to live."

"But as you said yourself you know these things and yet you don't really remember feeling that way. It is as if you *understand* a lot intellectually."

"That's right, that's right."

"*That* you learned with Dr. X."

"Yes."

"He told you and you said that makes common sense and it sounded good but you really don't feel it and you don't remember it."

"I don't remember before twelve."

"That's what I mean."

"It's after twelve."

"You mean all of this real stuff that happened which was so important before twelve you only know it intellectually?"

"That's right, that's exactly right. It's true!"

"But it is a problem, isn't it, and you still have these feelings and all this intellectual knowledge doesn't help with those feelings?"

"Sometimes I wish I had never been enlightened. I have had feelings of just wishing I had never known anything and had just gone along."

"Where ignorance is bliss, it is folly to be wise, huh?"

"That's right. As a matter of fact, Dr. X and I discovered that what we would deduct together I would brood on and it would stay in my mind. I am sorry for that. That is why I wished I didn't know these things. In fact, I have said it to myself over and over that I wished I didn't know because *what you don't know can't hurt you.* I think that old saying is true. Of course, on the other hand, *maybe I have to know these things in order to grow up.*"

The therapist could not have stated it any better. The *activity* of the therapist should not interfere with the patient's autonomy if this is at all possible.

"To change and grow up?"

"That's right."

"So you mean there is a part of you that really feels happy in the bungalow and with your husband who is a fine man, and you have a fine baby, so that this part of you hopes it can master the little-girl part that longs for the tenement and her mother and hasn't solved these problems of the past?"

"It seems I'm just split in two right now. I mean that. Part of me a little girl wanting to live where I used to live and part of me wants to be very much in my own home. You know I used to dream of gardening and having a home and my own flowers and I can have that now but I can't enjoy it."

"Perhaps there was another part of you that dreamed of being alone with mother, being her only baby?"

"I don't know."

Now she had demonstrated her insight in this area and it was possible to move on in other directions and test the limits. Her attitude toward her aunt had also been insufficiently developed.

"But now there is no one at home except mother, you would be her only baby."

"Oh, when I'm there, *I hate being there.* You see I'm quite mixed up. I mean it. I'm there and at times I will just torture myself—I don't belong here; I should be home; what am I doing here?"

"In other words, what you mean is when you are with mother you still act as if you were back in the past?"

"I don't know. I don't remember."

"But you said, when you were home it was almost as if you said, ah, what am I doing here, I don't belong here, I belong with my nice kind *aunt*; and when you were with your *aunt*, you said what am I doing here, I belong with my real mother."

This was the core of her ambivalence—the root of her ego split.

"Now this is something I am hearing for the first time. I have never heard it put this way before."

This meant that the reaction to the aunt was of great importance and had been inadequately worked out. The therapist deliberately delayed exploring this area to prevent her intellectualizing and isolating it.

"Well, what do you think? How do you feel?"

"I'm just mixed up, doctor. That's what I'm here for."

"You mean everywhere you are, this is the basic feeling—what am I doing here, I don't belong here?"

"Well, when I'm, I don't go *any other place* besides my mother's home. At one time I didn't even want to go there."

Actually, she spent her time traveling back and forth between her mother's tenement and her country house, almost a daily trip. She was sick of it and wanted independence. She said this angrily. The conversation then returned to father, and she was asked about her uncle, the other father. She was "pathetically afraid of him." He was so stern. She was now just getting to know her brother, who is two years older than she. She related casually that this brother lived near mother and had lunch with her every day. She hinted that she was jealous of him. In any case, there were so many members of both families that she was just beginning to know. Her older nephew was like her brother. She could now look directly at him and talk with him. She could not before her treatment with Dr. X. She felt cheated out of all these relationships. So much of her energy was now devoted to undoing and repeating her past. This could only be done to a limited degree and involved guilty incestuous yearnings, anger at her own emerging dependency needs, and anxieties over controlling a host of sadomasochistic fantasies which, for the most part, were unconscious. Let us listen to the end of the interview.

"So you mean you are making up for all those things you said you missed in your childhood?"

"And it is too bad because my husband is paying the price and my son is too and I just came along with it and I wonder how I got it. I'm trying to fill in a *lot of gaps but it isn't there*."

This symbolized her feelings of castration and loss quite nicely.

"But you haven't filled them all in yet?"

"I don't know. *I've changed so much.* I went to visit my brother yesterday. They were having something done in their kitchen. They were altering the home and he asked me to go over and see it. When we walked in, they had company there and I find that *I am more spontaneous* than I used to be. I wasn't spontaneous before."

This also must have been the result of her therapy.

"What does he do?"

"He works for my uncle in the food and produce business."

"So you are more spontaneous?"

"Well, yes. Oh, I've made changes for the *better.*"

"Oh! How do you mean?"

"I mean I know that. I know *I've grown up a great deal. I've be come more spontaneous, I'm not afraid of people. I'll speak my mind.*"

"So you are even confused there about if you had to do it over again whether or not you would go to the doctor?"

"Oh, I suppose I would have gone. I *think I would have gone.*"

"You mean when you feel bad, this is part of the confusion?"

"Yes, I say I wish I didn't know these things because I remember every detail that *I don't want to remember.*"

"Like what?"

"Well, if I'm reading a book I can remember a sentence and what part of the page it is on, and I can remember having a good time well when I was courting with my husband I can remember the details of dates, where we went, what I wore, how he acted and how I felt. I remember thing very *vividly.* I wish that too was different because I remember the pains as well as the pleasant, good times in my life, so that is why, I mean, whatever I have found out about myself has stayed with me all the time and I *brood* over it and I can feel very sorry for *himself,* and when I do that I become very *angry and resentful.* I haven't had a chance and if I had a different life i would be different for me and this sort of thing. But right now, doctor it's the *house.* I've come for help."

The word slip *"himself"* had to be ignored at this time. Vivid memories in the *recent* past have a screening function for the in fantile past.

"And yourself?"

"And myself, the *house and myself.* I'm *very confused about mysel* and I think primarily it's because I've changed a great deal."

The new change in the direction of mature femininity was im

peded by her anxiety over her fantasy change or castration in the past.

"Not about the baby?"

"No I'm not *confused* about my *little boy*. I feel very upset over the fact that he's been *exposed* to this. I'm very much *aware* of this."

"Not about your husband?"

"No, I really mean that, no!"

"So you mean yourself and—?"

"The house."

"The house and your mother?"

"Well, maybe my mother. My mother must be part of this, yes, but it is really the *house and me*."

Very often when a woman with a castration complex is able to accept her female status she dreams she has discovered a new charming little room in her house. She has discovered her vagina and that she is completely in her own right. The house is thus a frequent symbol of not only the mother and the mother's body but one's own body— especially for a woman. By now the time was up and the relationship with the aunt would be a sector interview by itself.

"But you said you had those feelings about mother when you were there and when you weren't there?"

"Well, once when I told Dr. X I don't know who I am because I would get feelings about being *confused*."

The confusion applied to all areas, but had to be simplified to go along with the main point of the interview—the relation to the mother.

"By that you mean whether you are the grown-up woman in the bungalow or the little girl in the tenement, huh?"

"Well, he told me this about my home when I was living in an apartment and he told me when people change a great deal it happens to them, so I felt it must be that I have changed. I'm a *different person*, really I am."

"You told me that you felt it was very painful?"

"Yes, you see, first of all I'm *always confused*. I go around being *confused*. I live in a *constant confusion*. Then there are times when I don't know *who I am*. I am just very blank and *numb*. I want to lie down and just be *quiet* and there are times when I feel I can't cope with this and *I despair*. I go through horrible feelings of despair where I just want to *die*."

This statement was the inversion of her desire to kill her rivals. There was also a question of how guilty she felt about death wishes toward her brother.

"And you never felt those things before twelve?"

"No, oh, I never thought of this up to when I saw Dr. X."

"How do you know? You don't remember anything before twelve?"

"I'm sorry. I'm referring to what I'm *feeling* now."

"Well, I'm referring to when you said you don't remember anything before twelve?"

"No, I don't, no!"

"That's what I mean. So you really don't know whether you felt this way or not when you were shuttling back and forth between auntie and momma?"

"I wouldn't remember if I felt them; I didn't know it!"

"That's what I mean."

"I don't remember. What I found out about the period between four and twelve was through the insight I gained with the doctor."

"Purely intellectual?"

"That's right, purely intellectual."

"Maybe we will help you to remember these things and it will really come back—how you felt then—and maybe we'll find out that you also felt that way even way back then, and a lot of these feelings that you have now are *your way of remembering things* because as you said your memory is awfully good."

"It is good."

"And yet before twelve it is not so good, huh?"

"Well, I remember a lot of things but I don't remember feeling bad."

"You can't remember much about your feelings?"

"No, not too much. The problem now is the house and I came for *advice*."

Advice was an intellectual trap. She would blame the new therapist then, and transfer to him the old anger and resentment she had at mother, aunt, Doctor X, etc. Actually, no matter what the therapist did we could expect this type of complaint, i.e., *confusion*.

"Well, we'll see. I think we can help you a great deal. Part of you wants advice but part of you wants to be independent and make her own judgments."

"You're all done, doctor?"

"We're all done for today. I'll see you Friday at 3:00 p.m. if that is convenient for you."

"All right, doctor."

When we listened to this woman's story, we got the impression that the birth of her sister, along with her being sent to her aunt's, signified to her a traumatic rejection by her mother. Her feelings were hurt so much that she became mistrustful of everyone and everything. She had tended to withdraw and deny her anxiety, depression, rage, hate and need for a loving close attachment to mother. Worse, a unitary concept of herself had been injured. A symbiotic relationship with her mother had been broken abruptly. The sudden loss of what amounted to part of herself had left her confused about whom to trust and love as well as hate and blame for this loss. This confusion had irradiated to all areas of her relationships with her body, self, things and persons. It had intensified her normal oedipal and castration feelings and fantasies to such a degree that they could not be mastered.

We see that there was a whole series of losses which had led to an anxiety, indecision and confusion about where to turn, as all her selections contained the threat of some kind of loss and a revival of all the old hurts. Her anxiety acted as a signal warning her of some impending loss. Unfortunately, this threatened whichever way she turned. Basically this loss was that of the mother. It was felt as the loss of a piece of her own ego and at a body-image level it signified a castration or loss of the most intense *feeling part*. Boys were then seen as having a kind of independence she longed for as a shield against being so vulnerable to losses. The interest attached to the phallus was later partially invested in the mind and a career and still later invested in the new baby-mother relationship. A chronic inability to feel close to anyone, masquerading as independence, led to a constant longing to restore the old child-mother unity that pregnancy had taken care of to a great extent. In her childhood, she had been dissatisfied with the aunt, as she was not her true child and had had a rival constantly around to remind her of this. The aunt seems to have given her values in the form of understanding and verbal communication but without satisfying her emotional needs to be mother's one and only. An interesting parallel could be drawn between the aunt and Dr. X, the psychotherapist. This would have to be worked out later in the therapy as an old transference problem. She also had an obsessional interest in talking and ruminating and a tendency to shift back and forth between obsessive-compulsive thinking and hysterical feeling mechanisms to defend herself against losses. Her ambivalence and indecisiveness had been expressed during her childhood by her stuttering.

When she turned to her mother, she had been overwhelmed by

feelings and at a loss about how to express them without reviving overwhelming anxieties about a loss of control. By this time, her mother was also a devalued (castrated) person when compared to the aunt, who had a "mind." She apparently achieved a shaky phallicized independence when she was a career girl. Marriage itself, by emphasizing her feminine passive-dependent needs, had acted as a partial castration but there was the compensation of the unitary husband-wife relationship. The delicacy of the balance had obviously been a large cause of her pathological jealousy. The ambivalently regarded pregnancy upset things to the extent that the birth signified a baby-mother separation and the old fatal division of interests. The baby's being a boy may have revived and emphasized her confusion about her infantile wishes concerning her sex to quite a degree.

Her ambivalence connected with knowing about her past was interesting in connection with the evaluation of results. She had enjoyed the new-found ability to express herself and be spontaneous, but the return of the denied and repressed painful thoughts had not been welcome. However, one without the other was impossible. She was an excellent illustration of how most patients have to feel worse for a while in order ultimately to feel better. Knowledge and ignorance each have their special gains and types of pain, just as do love and loneliness.

The therapy of this patient would revolve around the establishment of a trustworthy relationship with a therapist who would make every effort to aid her in establishing a fusion or integration of knowledge, memory and feelings. It would be necessary to integrate all the known losses as well as others that remained to be discovered. When she discussed things, such as homes, the therapist would integrate this with people and her changing concept of herself as well as them. Her changing concept of her body would also frequently enter the picture. Finally she could say about any and all of these areas, "Now I know and feel that this is truly so." The danger would be in permitting her to establish an aunt type of relationship with the therapist where feelings of sibling jealousy would lead to intellectualized discussions. This, from what we have heard, was the tendency with her previous therapist. Another danger might occur if she became so full of feeling that she was unable to talk. There was a strong possibility that she would alternate between hysterical and compulsive defense mechanisms as well as between the two mothers of her childhood.

Ultimately we would arrive at the level where the loss of the father would be a chief concern rather than the loss of the phallus or the mother. This was expressed somewhat mildly in this interview, and the accent would probably fall more heavily on this area later on. She also mentioned the brother, who, like herself, was going to see mother. We would undoubtedly find rivalrous feelings here, with the possibility of sexual overtones when and if she strove to deny her hate; that is, she might cover up aggression with sexual material and vice versa. Separation from the therapist would have to be a prolonged process, handled with delicacy and tact, as she would have the same insecure feelings with her therapist as she did with her husband and perhaps be ready to leave the present therapist frequently and return to the previous one. Also, we cannot take her word for certain that she loved her husband, let alone her mother. There was a possibility that, like her sister's, her marriage was unhappy. Some of the material suggested that her husband was too much like mother or father and not enough like an aunt. In any case, she needed all three to complete her psychosexual growth. As long as she could not feel like a mature woman, she would always secretly wish she had been a "certified accountant."

Above all, this interview shows how easy it is for a patient to blame a therapist for the growing pains that are part of the treatment. Much nonsense has been written on this subject and believed by critics of insight therapy and often, unfortunately, by therapists themselves. It must be realized that few patients are harmed and many are helped even by beginners. The worst possibility is lack of any result and the waste of time and money. Many patients are never seen until a downhill course is inevitable, yet only experience and a trial of therapy can determine this, and no one can be sure.

XII

THE ROLE OF THE BODY
IMAGE IN PSYCHOTHERAPY

A Case of Peptic Ulcer

A manifest conscious complaint about a defect in object relationships in one area always hides or screens defects in other areas. When the affected sphere is consciously that of the body image, the patient's major difficulties lie either in his personal relationships or in various images of himself. Such is the case with patients who have psychosomatic illnesses.

The various relationship spheres of the ego with the outer reality world of the present and the inner world of the past and the expected future can be considered as the psychotherapeutic field (see Table 1). The body image we are conscious of is usually much younger than in reality (usually ten to fifteen years), and is often distorted. At times both the body image and the self-image are chronically and obviously at variance with reality.

Psychosomatic patients usually begin an interview with a description of their bodily defects and miseries. The words used to describe their bodily difficulties also apply to their more important personal or self-relationships.

The repetitive nature of the person's patterns of relationship with other persons is well known and more or less easily demonstrated clinically. However, the extent and importance of the person's repeti-

---

This chapter contains excerpts from a paper entitled "Some Clinical Aspects of the Body Ego," published in *The Psychoanalytic Review*, 44:462-477, 1957, and reprinted with the kind permission of the editor.

tive relationships with his body image have only lately come under intensive scrutiny. Bodily sensations are used by the ego in both expressive (instinctual) and defensive (ego) aspects. Postural, kinesthetic, auditory, visual, skin and visceral sensations can be looked upon as, among other things, preverbal accompaniments of preconscious and unconscious thought processes. These may or may not be expressed verbally at a later date. The perception of these sensations is modified by the ego to maintain its stability. In this sense, the ego is self-regulating.

For example, a patient became preoccupied with the visual image of a shadow on the wall, which he traced in detail, and then with the noise of a clock ticking. These sensory preoccupations were substitutes in the present for the recollection of a past trauma concerning the loss of a parent. They aided him in the postponement of its remembrance, and in a gradual approach to the material. Noises and sights in the present defended him from noises and sights in the past. Sight may also defend against sound. Another patient became preoccupied with the painful effect of light, and resorted to dark glasses after hearing his parents discuss a portion of his infantile past of which he was very much ashamed. This discussion concerned his anxiety over *noises* in the night and particularly his mother's asthmatic attacks which he had even then associated with *visual* fantasies of sexual attacks upon her by father. Then as now, preoccupation with sight defended against hearing. Kinesthetic sensations associated with muscular activity are frequently used as a defense against awareness of unpleasant affects. Such defenses are especially prominent in the histories of athletic, hyperactive and acting-out personalities.

These concepts have practical importance and clinical applicability in psychotherapy. The body ego from the point of view of its development and use is the gateway to the all-important affects in the therapy session. This can be illustrated by the case of a married woman of twenty-eight who began therapy complaining that she had become seclusive and unhappy and could not get along with people because of her low I.Q. Actually she was of college background and her tested I.Q. was in the superior range. Her father was a scholar; her stepmother, a school teacher, had entered the household when the patient was seven. For many hours this patient gave a dry, intellectual and discursive account of her personal difficulties with little affect until the problem of her "small I.Q." led to her inability to absorb knowledge (words) through her eyes. This led to defective eyesight and sensations in her eyes. She had received glasses at three because of an internal strabismus which was operated upon at seven. It had then become an external strabismus, and for many years her schoolmates "pitied" her. The area of eyesight led to dry eyes at her mother's funeral and to her choking up. Her trouble in the present had, in large part, been due to her having married at twenty-four when she felt "too old to wait any longer." She had "accidentally" acquired a kind and understanding husband and had two very fine children. She felt she did not deserve them. Whenever she thought of them, she felt a rush of tearful emotion, and in the past year had developed a chronic blinking of the eyelids and a mild blepharitis. Shortly after her marriage she was able to dispense with her glasses frequently except during periods of fatigue. Now she wore none. During the initial phase of her treatment she blinked her eyes frequently and showed some redness but no evidence of strabismus. The eye sensations, sparked by the words "burning," "redness," "strain," "watering," led not only to her mother's death but to her inability to compete as a boy or a girl with a learned (phallic) stepmother for father's love, and anxiety over competitiveness in general related to her "bad" behavior as a tomboy and to the "good" mother's dying. All this was a prelude to her fears that her bad behavior, defective eyes, or low I.Q. must eventually lead to the loss of her maternal husband. It appeared that she viewed a happy marriage as a fulfillment of a guilt-laden, oedipal wishes in both positive and negative aspects, her husband being in the main a motherly figure, yet also a good father. Her cup had run over. Wishing to appear more beautiful in his eyes, she stopped wearing her glasses and after a short while found to her amazement that she could dispense with them. The eye symptoms became minimal. This relative "disappearance" of her eye trouble invalidated an area she had used defensively in the present to avoid conscious thoughts about a defective, ambivalent relationship with both her mother and father in the past, and to deny grief over their loss. Another way of looking at the same problem is that her marriage acted like a successful transference type of therapy and induced her to give up a narcissistic, body-ego defense, oriented around the eyes. But it led to the emergence of castration anxiety and depressive and guilt-laden material associated with her parents, especially the mother, which clouded her relationship with her motherly husband in the present. In the main, the material revolved about masturbatory fantasies, her defective genital, and voyeuristic activities (seeing "bad" things). The patient's dispensing with glasses following her marriage is reminiscent of cases described by Bettelheim and

Sylvester (1949), who stress the magical and protective function of glasses.

In 1928, while lecturing on psychoanalytic techniques, Glover (1955) discussed how difficult it was to deal with cases of character disorders who complained only of personal difficulties. He noted that when complaints of bodily sensory symptoms appeared, it was a good sign. These symptoms or feelings could be nurtured and expanded as a key to the pertinent affect-laden relationships. This rule still holds good and is now understandable in terms of what has been formulated about the body ego. In psychosomatic cases, body-image material should be used to develop personal or self-relationships which are momentarily important from an economic point of view. Here the word "economic" refers to what is ripe for use in therapy. For instance, a patient at one time may complain of heart symptoms which are associatively and economically related to father figures, and at another time of stomach symptoms related to mother figures. The problems of a psychosomatic patient complaining of low back pains may concern fears of and a desire for a passive, anal relation with the father. Later the same patient may suffer from peptic ulcer symptoms with problems economically related to a passive, oral relationship with the mother. This is of importance in relation to the frequently misunderstood problem of syndrome specificity. A choice of symptom or organ is made according to the defensive needs of the ego at that moment. A patient stopped having epileptic seizures and was able to fight off or "control" them only to develop migraine headaches which were so severe that she "surrendered" to the aura, and the epileptic attacks reappeared. She claimed these attacks were more endurable. It could be demonstrated that although the basic problems in this patient's life remained the same, the migraine headaches were, from an economic point of view, related to overwhelmingly painful, anal and oral, sadistic material concerning the mother, and the epileptic attacks were related to less painful, phallic, sadistic material concerning, in the main, the father. One would expect to find material economically aligned with the mother when cavities and growths are involved, and to the father when extremities and projections are of primary concern. However, such generalizations are clinically of little value to a therapist and none at all to a patient in the interview situation.

The therapist has the task of integrating all spheres of action and relationship throughout a patient's lifetime. The over-all importance of the sphere of personal relationships is well known and has been made the center of some schools of psychotherapy. Some of them attempt to deny the importance of infantile sexuality, the libido theory, the body ego and the biological foundations of psychoanalysis and psychotherapy. This is not rational. Castration anxiety and penis envy are ubiquitous phenomena in clinical material because they are bodily representatives or symbols of a personal loss, i.e., a reaction to the loss of the primal mother or her substitutes. They are primitive, affect-laden, narcissistic, body-ego manifestations of such a loss, and therapy without their conscious recognition and integration as part of an over-all loss is like a plant without roots. An analytic patient of Dr. Ernst Kris (1955), who desired a circumcision while in analysis, asked his doctor whether it was true that some rabbis bit off the foreskin. Dr. Kris interpreted that at one time the patient had wanted to bite off his father's penis. The patient thereupon felt he had always known this and developed the somatic sensation of a cap (foreskin—rabbi's cap) over his head; i.e., his body image of himself at one level was that of a phallus. The rabbi, of course, was himself and also Dr. Kris. In an active sense, the patient feared that Dr. Kris would do to him what he himself wanted to do to the doctor in the present and father in the past. Thus, ideational, mnemonic and sensory material could be brought together so that past and present personal relationships, intraego relationships and body-ego relationships could eventually be integrated in the genetic as well as the dynamic sense. This type of interpretation can seldom be used outside of psychoanalysis.

The concept that the body is the earliest object of the developing ego has many implications in psychotherapy. The initial patterns of relationship of the primordial ego are those with bodily organs, parts and systems, including that group of organs called the brain. Patterns of relationship that occur between bodily organs precede the mouth-breast-hand relationship and will ultimately be projected into and reciprocally modified by the outer world. These organ sensory patterns exist in phylogenetically, ontogenetically and hierarchically ordered structures. The body ego in the case of the patient of Dr. Kris was perceived at the time predominantly as a penis. At other times in the analysis it could have been perceived in terms of feces, breast nipple, mouth, etc., depending upon the momentary needs of the ego. The earliest patterns of relationship, for example, might be those between the limbs and the hollow viscera, as such patterns appear throughout life in connection with the solution of problems concerning masculinity and femininity, activity and passivity. In any case primitive sensory patterns can be regressively, reactivated during epi sodes of stresss or when loss of a body part leads to an alteration in the economy of the body ego. From a structural, economic and dynamic point of view, such reactivated sensory patterns may be similar to each other in different cases, but each will possess unique properties. Phantom-limb pains are an excellent example of this. As F. Deutsch (1954) and others have implied, sensory impressions are never perceived in isolation but always in groups according to the level of psychosexual development and associated with various objects and organs, and antagonistically and synergistically balanced, as in purposive, muscular behavior. In the course of ego development, awareness of the body image has become so much a part of object relationships that various abstract, sensory perceptions, such as a certain type of pain, may represent the entire past history of a specific object relationship in capsule form. Thus the meaning of painful sensations in phantom-limb cases differs from case to case from time to time. Words used to describe such pain, i.e., crushing, burning, annoying, twisting, grinding, tearing, drawing, etc., are always significantly overdetermined. Despite the possibility of "organic" elements, such descriptive words can readily be used in the interview to develop associative material concerning these past object relationships. The following case will illustrate this.

Phantomlike phenomena may appear in situations where no physical amputation has occurred but where the function of a part has been impaired or completely lost. A thirty-one-year-old female with a partial deformity of the left leg since an attack of polio at the age of three perceived her leg as painfully twisted and cramped. Two years after the occurrence of her polio her mother had become psychotic and had been committed to a state hospital where she remained until the present. The patient remembered with great longing her mother's rubbing her body and especially the affected leg, but completely denied love for her in the past and spoke continually of her resentment of her mother's prudishness and general coldness when she had come home on periodic visits.

In a dream, she twisted the left arm of a girl friend who reminded her of her mother, and in another dream a male friend and phallic alter-ego figure had his left leg placed in an iron boot and twisted by Communists. Like many who have been thrust prematurely into self-sufficiency, she placed a very high value on an active, masculinized, independent role in life, and had an exaggerated fear of passivity as well as a great capacity to deny or minimize the reality-object world.

During the dissolution of her pain sensory-pattern complex, it could be demonstrated that the loss of the mother had been equated with a loss of bodily function, i.e., the cramped leg. In this case the pain was an abstract precursor of material dealing with an ambivalent relationship with the mother. This patient warded off depressive feelings of passively longing for the mother's attention by a great increase of activity and use of the defective leg. This led to feelings of fatigue and stiffness in the leg which were preceived as a tremendous threat, forcing her into a dreaded and guilt-laden passivity. The pain was associated with an "overuse" of the defective limb, which, like the activity of the patient in general, served to deny castration anxiety and passive longings that were finally perceived consciously as an oral, homosexual threat; i.e., the pain represented a protective mechanism against anxiety basically connected with oral, devouring wishes. The stimulus that determined the appearance of the painful phantom was the tentative decision of the patient to leave the part of the country where her sisters lived and her mother was confined. Secondary material revolved about the loss of two older girl friends or motherly sister-substitutes. The pain, of course, prevented her from leaving. Thus, in this patient's childhood, the affect associated with the loss of the mother was denied by displacement to a loss of bodily function. In the present, the pain and loss of function were reactivated and served as both a warning signal and an aid in the denial of the new and the old repressed grief concerning her losses. A cramped leg had become the equivalent of a cramped life. Cathexis that was once invested in an object on the outside had become phallic, narcissistic cathexis of the body image which had been increased by the loss of the mother substitutes. The somatic sensation of pain appeared as a substitute affect, mainly for grief, but also for love, hate and anxiety. The denial of a loss, regressively reactivated by stiuational problems and losses, was handled through the ego's use of various sensory feelings connected with the leg. Other clinical material strikingly demonstrated that the left leg represented her defective genital and was actually an "illusory phallus." In this case, immediately after the mother's loss she "discovered" masturbation. She had become envious of her brother's penis, and turned from feminine activities with dolls to tomboyish activities in which her defective leg was perceived as a painful handicap. The material suggested that the investment of this bodily part with phallic narcissistic cathexis occurred secondarily to the genitalization of the libido and the awareness of the possibility of castration, and that the loss of her mother had the effect of crystallizing or intensifying this investment as a needed narcissistic defensive measure on the part of her ego; i.e., the child needed a penis in one sense to caress as she would have liked the mother to caress her, and in a related sense to furnish her with good sensations to neutralize bad ones and fill a gap in her needs.

The case material is similar to that in cases of phantom-limb phenomena where amputation has occurred. As a rule, in such cases the lost part has served to represent both a lost child and a lost parent figure, and both the part and the representative figures have been ambivalently regarded. Szasz (1954) had remarked that the "natural" and almost universal phantomization of a lost body part is like normal mourning, and phantom pain is more like melancholia. In these cases also the shadow of the "annoying" lost object or part has fallen upon the ego. The mechanism of projection also, he points out, makes the analogy to paranoia a striking one, the patient being persecuted by the annoying limb. If anything, these analogies show the artificial nature of the separation of the body ego from the ego proper.

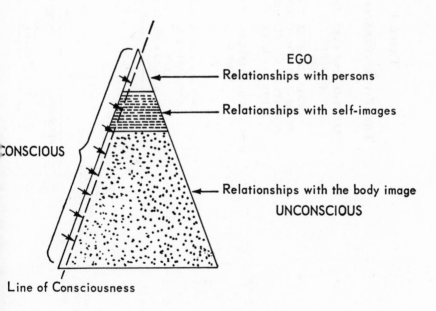

FIGURE 2. IMPORTANCE OF THE BODY IMAGE

Relationships to the right of the line of consciousness apply to the unconscious portion of the apperceptive ego.

Table 1

The Psychotherapeutic Field

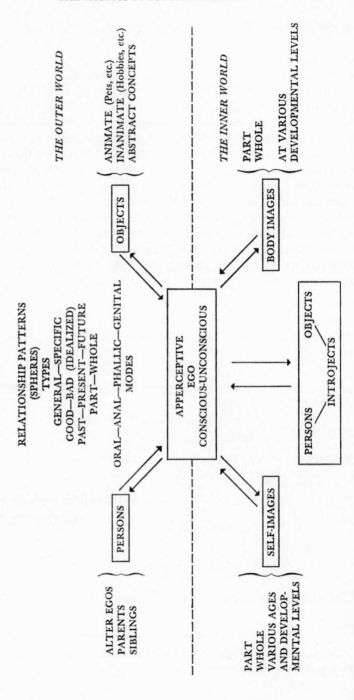

The psychosomatic type of case is so common and so important that it will be discussed in more detail in the next chapter. An example will now be given which concerns a man with ulcer. This case will illustrate how to thread one's way through a maze of material and how the affect expressed by a painful relation to an organ serves as a screen for a series of painful and defective, past and present relationships with persons and with the self in terms of losses and frustrated ambitions.

The patient was a man in his early forties who had a bleeding ulcer and was threatened by an operation which to him meant that his stomach would be cut out. The X-rays had shown a large, partially healed duodenal ulcer. He talked rapidly and appeared to be in a hurry. The therapist began the interview.

"Suppose you tell me your story and we'll see if we can't put our heads together and help you, because I take it you want to be helped?"

"I certainly do. Well, uh, where do you want me to start? Right from the beginning of this trouble? Well, of course, I was *poisoned* overseas."

The key word was obvious.

"Poisoned?"

"Poisoned, yes, sir."

"When was this?"

The important dates and ages had to be pinned down, as they usually play a crucial part in making confrontations.

"Nineteen-forty-four."

"Nineteen-forty-four?"

"*October*, I believe, *around* that time."

"How old were you then?" How old are you now?"

"Forty-two."

"Forty-two? So that was eleven years ago?"

"Yes, sir."

"When you were thirty-one?"

This was said partly to impress these facts on the therapist's own memory and partly to get the patient back into the past.

"Yes sir. And since then a, during that period of the poisoning, of course, uh, I got terribly *upset* there, the ordeal that I went through. It was sort of an *odd* thing, I was *paralyzed*. As I sat there waiting to be taken into the operating room, wherever they were taking us, I felt myself paralyzed up as far as the *eyes*."

"Paralyzed up to your eyes?"

"Oh, right up to here."

He demonstrated with his hand just above his eyebrows.

"The last thing I'm saying to myself is no, not up, way up."

Obviously this meant death.

"Up to your eyes?"

"Precisely, yes, sir. I was saying to myself, well I know the other guys that I knew—there were *two dead ones* in the ambulance with me—I said, well I guess I'm next!"

The therapist returned to the two most highly charged words.

"They were *dying* from *poisoning* too?"

"Yes, sir."

"How did it happen?"

This was really a variation of "What do you mean?"

"Well, there seemed to be an epidemic in that section of London. There was *food* that it seemed a lot of us might have bought it in that neighborhood or in the service club there, and, uh, it definitely wasn't from *drink* because I hadn't that much left of a fifth in the room that I was in and the F.B.I. and C.I.D. and all that was brought in and they analyzed it and it wasn't, it certainly wasn't from *drinking poison*."

He appeared to feel that drink was good and food was bad.

"Poisoned food?"

"I, uh, that's what I guess at that time they diagnosed it as, or possibly I had a few drinks at the bar that might have been included in that. I never saw the medical report, you would understand that. Well, as I say, three days later I came to and with these hoses up my nose and pumps and all these Scotland Yard guys and everybody around, C.I.D., and everybody wanted to question me on what happened."

"What's C.I.D.?"

This was a simple point of information. There appeared to be a mild paranoid element present.

"That's, uh, pertaining to some form of secret police, I guess. That's what they call it. I don't know just what it was but I think that's what they call them anyway."

"They were interested in this?"

"Oh, yes, sir, definitely. They thought that, uh, well they didn't, I don't know what they thought to tell you the truth, but they were all around me."

He appeared to be unsure.

"No, but I mean you might have some ideas."

"Well, where I got it? They asked me where I got the booze."

"They thought someone was trying to poison you with booze?"

"Yes, all of us, in that particular neighborhood, that was in that neighborhood, because they seemed to be picking them up. They picked up one fellow out of an alley, you see I was in a room with this *queen* and I sent her out to get military police or someone who could get me to the hospital."

This was a symbol of the mother. This was probably the right track, as mother and feeding would most likely be connected with any stomach problem.

"You were in a room with a *queen?*"

"Yes, so, as I say, at that time I had the weakness. I don't know what it was and I couldn't hold anything on my *stomach* until they brought me to the hospital. Well, then they questioned me and I told them I remembered there was some drink left so they analyzed that, which showed them nothing."

Poison, drink and mother suggest a paranoid orientation so far.

"You mean figuring that the queen may have done something?"

"No, no, no. Definitely it wasn't her because they really went over her good. I went with her all the time I was there practically. You know, all I was able to, shacked up."

He was definitely not ripe for this kind of material, yet it was important to get into this area of his relations with persons.

"With this girl?"

The therapist now said "girl" instead of "queen" to take off the pressure.

"Yes, yes. So they took her over the coals."

"You were shacked up with her?"

"Yes, she's the only one I had while I was there. So that wasn't it and the booze was okay. Well, they discharged me from the hospital and *since then* I've become inclined to be *nervous*. Now, at that time, I was a duty sergeant. I had charge of a whole group of men in the officers' B.O.Q., and all that. I didn't have to work hard. It was just my job to see that things were okay, but I used to go out *even with men*. I used to say to myself, 'Take it easy,' but I had the tendency *to worry*. I thought maybe going out would help me to *sleep*. From then on I started missing a little *sleep* and I find I'm being a little bit *nervous*."

"By *nervous* you mean *couldn't sleep?*"

This was a feedback of two of the most likely words. The therapist could also have referred to *worry* and asked, "What were you worrying about?"

"Couldn't sleep, uh, after I got out of the hospital. I was *nerved up,* that was all, from that time on. Well, then I noticed I couldn't go out and do things I used to do. For instance, I couldn't go out and have a few *bottles* and be *safe,* and, uh, everything started to go *wrong.* Well, then about that time the war was practically over and I said well I'm coming home. Hell, I can throw this whole thing over."

It was no longer safe to drink from the bottle. What did he want to throw over—the queen? Were his feelings about her "unsafe"?

"That was back in '45?"

"The year of '45, July I think I came home."

"When you were thirty-two?"

"Thirty-two, in the States. Well, uh, I had *trouble sleeping,* but I didn't say too much. I kept saying to myself, oh, hell, I only got another two months to *sweat it out* and I'm getting out. So, I did get out and I went right to work. I went back to the company I had been working for almost *twenty years.*"

"Doing what?"

"A milkman."

This offered a wonderful field to expand in connection with drinking and mother. It was a symbol as well as a reality.

"You were a milkman?"

"Milkman. So I went back to work and uh, I couldn't sleep. I had trouble sleeping, but fortunately one of my brothers, he got home from the service. I had him for a helper."

"You have brothers?"

Now was the time to learn the family constellation.

"Oh yes, I have several."

"Several—how many?"

There were three sisters and four living brothers. One brother was dead; all were about two years apart in age. He was the oldest child. The dead brother was the seventh child. He died from pneumonia when the patient was eighteen or nineteen. After learning about his sibling relationships, the therapist returned to the time when he was at home unable to sleep and very nervous. A doctor on the milk route gave him phenobarbital pills which did not help. Nervous meant irritable. Finally he had to resign from his job. He hated to do so, as he was making $130 a week. He thought he would "step out for a year and get acclimated to civilian life." This betrayed the fact that he could not, and that he had changed. He also talked in terms of waiting for himself to "cool off," which suggested anger. Around this time his stomach really "acted up." It had been bothering him right

along to a lesser degree. He was asked what he meant and the interview continued as follows.

"Since I, well right *from the time I was in the hospital* that time."

"From the time you were *poisoned*?"

"Yes, but I never paid any attention."

"How does it *act up*?"

"Well, uh, it didn't in this respect. I wouldn't call it acting up, it,
uh, things that I used to be able to do, *eat* for instance, and *drink*
and *stuff*, I just couldn't do it like I could previous to that time."

What was stuff? The therapist could not find out now. In later
sessions it turned out to mean partial impotence and withdrawal of
interest in women. Later we will see that it meant to have the relationship he had with mother when he was her baby and sole concern.

"You were always a good eater before?"

"Oh, you bet your life. I drank plenty of *milk*. I drank in the
summertime three or four quarts of milk a day. You know in the hot
weather when I'd be peddling it, I'd put plenty of that away."

"You lived at home with mother?"

This was the obvious substitute for milk and said in order to get to
personal relationships.

"I lived at home with her up until the time I was twenty-five or
twenty-six, I guess."

"Then what happened?"

"Well, uh, my father was getting, you know, kind of old so they
moved nearer his job and I roomed with some friends. And the
family went out there with him, but I still gave my mother five or
ten, you know, every week. I still helped them but I wasn't living at
home."

"Anyway you could drink three or four quarts of milk a day then?"

By then, milk substituted along with drinking for a boy's lost relationship with his mother.

"Oh, gee! With no trouble at all."

"But then after you got poisoned—?"

Poisoning was an event with a special meaning for him. It ushered
in the stomach trouble and nervousness and symbolized the loss of the
oedipal mother-relationship fantasy expressed at a regressive oral
level. After being poisoned, it was no longer safe to live and drink
with the queen.

"Well, I could still drink the milk. I *always* drank the *milk* even
when I went back, you know, on the milk team, I used to drink a pint

of light cream at home almost every morning. If I felt tough, well it put a *lining* in my stomach. That was my theory, and then I can *eat* and I'll feel better. So I used to drink that pint of light cream, break it against the end of the platform, see, and say, 'Cracked bottle,' and they'd give you a fresh one and it wouldn't cost anything. That's a little trick of the milk business. So, uh, as I say, when I thought, well a few years or so ago, I'll step out for a few months or a year, and I'll go back but, as I say, between the stomach working on the nerves and vice versa I'm gradually *going down*. I mean to say I'm not getting any better and I'm *slipping* a little bit. In other words things that, uh, were easy for me would gradually become a little more difficult to do."

He talked as if he had been steadily regressing to a more and more infantile helpless position.

"What did you do when you left the *milk* business?"

"Well, I uh, I did at that time odd jobs. There was plenty of work around. I would take, when I'd, you know, feel good, and I was able to sometimes get two or three nights good sleep or something like that, I'd go out and I'd always find a job. I mean to say odd jobs."

"You didn't go home? With mother, father?"

"No, I didn't go home. Oh, wait a minute, after the war, yes, I'm talking now about after the war. Yes, I went right home with my folks then."

This area of uncertainty pointed to the existence of a complex.

"Oh, I see. What do you mean?"

"I was home with them because my *father died when I was overseas*."

"He did?"

This was the key to an understanding of the onset of his difficulties. In his unconscious, father's death must be connected with the poisoning. Events related in time tend to appear related casually in the unconscious. This could be tested.

"Yes."

"Before you were *poisoned*?"

"Uh, right afterwards. Afterwards, I believe. No, before, before! Wait a minute, now, let me think. I don't know the exact months. I, uh, it was in the fall and my father had died just, I think *just previous* to that, in the month of October, something like that."

He now confirmed the above supposition. This might not be true in reality, but reality has little influence upon the existence of a neurosis.

"Just before you got poisoned your father died?"

"I believe, uh, well, I'm not sure on the dates but I can tell you it's—"

"Around the same time?"

This was like saying that they were connected.

"Yes, around the same time."

"What did he die from?"

"Cerebral hemorrhage. He was hit by an automobile. He died of a cerebral hemorrhage, that's all I know because I wasn't able to get home. That's what they told me. I was living at home then with my mother because my mother was a widow and after all, some of the family were married and only two or three at home. I had a young sister who was only a young girl then. This is ten years ago. She wasn't married. She was still in high school."

This implied that he didn't know the cause of father's death until he came home. The therapist was more interested in his fantasies before he knew this. Why did *he* have to be the one who took care of mother and, therefore, could not marry? Here a mistake was made. The therapist should have found out what he meant by cerebral hemorrhage and also what he thought might have killed him, but he wished to develop the relationship with the mother and not be sidetracked.

"So there was only you and mother and sister?"

"And one *brother*."

"One brother?"

"At home."

"A younger brother?"

"*The fellow next to me.*"

"Next to you?"

"Next to me, uh, at home. Well, he didn't make much money because he broke his hip when he was a young fellow. *We* were coasting down a hill and *we* ran into a tree and *he broke his hip* and his *leg* is a little bit *shorter* so he's *handicapped.* So he didn't command a big salary so I was *needed* at home to, you know, to help swing the weight. Well, I suppose—"

His guilt over the brother was one factor that kept him home.

"It was just you and the brother then. The other brothers were married?"

"They were all married then. We were getting by. I mean I was able to go out and work, but as I say, things were becoming more difficult. But I wouldn't give in, figuring that is, *never knowing what it's like to taste defeat in regards to anything I wanted to do, I was always able to do it."*

This was a wonderful chance to get into the past, which was missed by the therapist. The patient fantasied himself omnipotent, perhaps in order to deny an infantile defeat that was too traumatic to accept and resolve.

"By becoming more difficult, you mean difficulty *sleeping*, or with your *stomach?*"

"Uh, I'd say my *nerves in general* were becoming more and more upset."

"You weren't able to eat well?"

"Uh, I wasn't able to eat like I used to but I would say the weight I dropped in a period of a few years in there, about ten pounds, fifteen pounds, I guess. And, uh, I was getting more jumpy all the time because I'm thinking, well, I can't go back to the job and everybody, friends I would meet would ask, 'When are you going back?' and I know with all my heart and soul I was unable to go back to hold that job because I can't sleep and after all, *if I can't sleep, I can't work.* I mean it just requires a lot of bookkeeping and figures and you've got to have your mind wide awake. I just couldn't go back, so as I say, I fooled around and did about everything a man could do in regards to making an honest dollar. I wasn't paid well but I was always able to command a good day's pay and I mean I did. I mean I really didn't have any financial worries, but, uh, the *prestige of losing a job*, after all, and years, you know, on one job, that *upset* me a little bit. Well, uh, in the meantime the *stomach really* started to get *bad* and I went to the doctor a few times, told him about it. Well, several doctors I went to they'd say, I knew them all and they'd say, 'We can't tell you anything, you'll have to have X-rays. You're a veteran,' this is the part I want to impress on you. They'd say, 'You're a veteran, why don't you go to the V.A. and they can take X-rays?' Well, that I tried a few times. Over at the Soldiers' Home one day, and in the meantime at nights I'd be doubled up like this with the *pain*."

Of course the therapist did not know of his impotence at this time. Accordingly he remained with the stomach symptoms and the problem of how they were connected with a reaction to father's death.

"You had pain?"

"Awful, boy! Not too bad then but there were nights, some would be a little more than other nights. This is my procedure. I'd sit on the edge of the bed and hold my stomach."

He was like a mother with a sick child. An active, adult, sexual role was denied to him or forbidden, so he had regressed to an infantile role acted out on his body.

"Where was the pain?"

"Right in here, sir. So, I'd, uh, go over there, they'd strip me down and in the meantime the pain would probably disappear. It happened several times. I'd be sitting down waiting to be called and the pain would go away. They'd say, 'There's nothing wrong with you. You needn't bother to remain.' That's all. Well, I'd use up the prescription or something and maybe I would feel a little bit better. But in the meantime I started to lose some more sleep. I was down to about *four hours* a day sleep, *about four hours at one time.* I could almost tell the time by when I'd wake up. And, uh, I'd get irritable and everything and go back again and the same procedure. So I finally went into Court Street. A doctor in there knew me and he said 'You're a very nervous man. Why don't you take a little change in the scenery?' This was now drawing towards '49, I believe it was '49. I told my family the doctor said maybe that would help, so I went to Florida. While there, I don't know whether the *chlorine* in the water or anything, but I got so I hardly wanted to eat at all and I had a job with a friend of mine."

He had now regressed to a baby's four-hour feeding schedule. The chlorine appeared to be connected with a revived fear of poisoning and was a mild paranoid defense against a depression manifested by anorexia and insomnia. Some feeling of loss was in the background and had to be explored cautiously.

"Chlorine?"

"Chlorine. The water down there's supposed to be full of it, chlorine, oh you know what it is. I mean my question is the stuff they purify the water with. Isn't that what you call it, chlorine?"

"And that made you—?"

"Well I had an idea that that might have helped."

"You mean it made the water *taste* bad?"

This was probably the way he knew something was in the water.

"It tasted terrible. Your mouth would be awful *dry*, you know, in the morning. Oh, terrible, terrible dry. Well, I went on—this friend was a friend of mine so I worked part time for him. I never held a steady *route* because I couldn't."

From a reality point of view, the dryness might have been due to anxiety, or possibly his medication contained belladonna, but from the point of view of therapy and fantasy it was a recrudescence of the same trouble he had overseas, i.e., poisoning, depression and anxiety. Why? Did he blame himself for his father's death? Did he long for his mother or her substitute, the queen?

"*Route?* You were working a route?"

Was this a substitute for the milk route?

"He had, this friend of mine had four *ice routes*, a fellow I was in the service with, see. So I would run a few days on one, sometimes I'd force myself and he'd say, 'Well stay on this one for a couple of weeks, will you.' Well, I'd try and if I picked up a helper or something I would make it. But I'm really starting to go down in the hundred and sixties. Middle one-sixties from an average one-hundred eighty-five to one hundred-ninety pound man all my life. Well, in the summers I did a little painting. I still wanted to hold my pride. *I wanted to come back with a few dollars* and I was bucking it down there. It got so that friends were saying, 'Gee, what's the matter with you, you look terrible. Why don't you loaf?' So I go over there and the same procedure. I guess you know my medical record."

"You mean pains in your stomach, couldn't eat, couldn't sleep?"

"Couldn't eat, couldn't sleep. I go to the V.A., nothing wrong! Same routine. More Amphogel or Gelusil or something."

"What did mother think about this?"

This was important. He wanted to look big in mother's eyes.

"Well, I didn't let her know. That is the three years I was down there I said nothing. I didn't let my family know at all that I'm suffering."

"They never know?"

"No, they never knew. Part of the time I lived in a hotel and towards the end when I started to get bad I made plans to move in with a private family."

"You never would let them know you had this? Why not?"

He has already indicated his answer.

"Because I was trying to battle it out myself, you understand. I was just trying to be *independent*."

This gave the therapist a chance to make a generalization that would lead to the past.

"You're that type of guy who has always been independent?"

"That's right."

"Who didn't want to go to mother with anything?"

"Oh, no, no. I *never* went to her."

Now the therapist could try again to go into the past.

"You mean even when you were a kid?"

"I never went to her, I never went to her. *She always* used to confide in *me* because I was the oldest. If something went wrong, I was like the *second father* of the tribe."

The oedipal problem was out in the open.

"You took father's place, sort of, when father wasn't there?"

"Yes, when he wasn't there, yes."

"She confided in you?"

"She confided in me, yes."

"About?"

"Well, uh, somebody would get out of line or at that time *money* wasn't too *big*. I guess around the early '20s and those days I used to go out and even as a youngster gather wood and worked hard all my life."

Big money stood for the bigness in all aspects, especially phallic, that he needed to impress mother and self.

"Really?"

"Yes."

"You worked when you were a little fellow?"

"When I was a little fellow."

"What do you mean?"

"Well, for instance, you heard me say twenty years on the milk team. I started in there, I guess, when I was a little boy, eleven or twelve years old. Got up about two o'clock in the morning and go to work on that until I became sixteen years old."

"Didn't your brothers, didn't they help?"

"Well, they were too young."

"Two years younger?"

"Well the one two years younger was lame."

"He was lame. And the one four years younger?"

"Was a sister, then there came another brother."

"Six years younger?"

"That's right, six years younger. But by that time they were little boys, five years old, and I was eleven or twelve."

"But father you mean didn't make enough money. You had to—?"

While he wanted to work for mother he also may have resented being forced to because of father's inadequacy.

"Well, we were middle-class, let's put it that way. We were a big family. He worked for the railway. They were, he was probably making $35 to $40 a week in those days. I don't know, I'm saying approximately, but I know when I was around nineteen or twenty I was making *as much as he was* and that was in the early '30s. But I *always* did help, you know, around the house."

"So you really were sort of a second father?"

"*Yes! I never knew what it was to enjoy a child life! I worked all my life! I mean to say always, every Saturday and Sunday!*"

This proved the therapist's suspicion that the patient's attitude toward his independence was decidedly ambivalent. There are all kinds of losses to be mourned.

"You missed it?"

"What do you mean? When I got out of it this time?"

This was a loaded question. What did *he* mean?

"I mean the first break you ever got was when you went in the service."

"From hard work, yes!"

"That's what I mean. When you were in the service, you had it easy and this nice queen."

"Well, no, no."

He laughed nervously.

"She was no *pal*. *She* was a companion, you know what I mean."

The prostitute mother was really not enough. He also needed a father who was a pal. Instead of identifying with the father, he was a rival, but he felt like a little boy who could never become a real man. After father's death it was highly probable that he had not gone through the complex process of mourning and solving the loss by identification. Instead, father had become a persecutory introject in his stomach. In another sense his retaliatory anxieties made him feel attacked by the greedy longings of his childhood. Hidden in the background was a melancholia, an agitated depression compounded of guilt and greed, loss and longing, anxiety and desires to atone. The infantile narcissistic basis of this will be discussed following its demonstration in the interview.

"Was she the first girl?"

"Well, uh, uh, over there, yes, sir."

"Well, because I mean you were such a hard worker here you really didn't have time."

"I know I never did. For a man my age, if I told you *I never went with a girl in my life*, you wouldn't believe it."

This meant he never gave up and resolved his need for his mother and his infantile fantasies, but the question "why" still remained. It was also another loss.

"Really?"

"That's right."

"You never went with a girl in your life, you mean except the queen?"

"Well, uh, I didn't *go* with her. She was *just a bed companion* over there, there was *no love.* It was just she treated me all right and I treated her—it was *tit for tat.*"

The relationship with mother was a monetary one.

"You mean a bed companion, you mean for intercourse?"

"Yes, that's right."

"But it was nice, she was a good companion?"

"Yes, a good companion. There was no love. She didn't mean anything to me."

"You mean you never fell in love?"

"Oh, no, no, no, never, and in my younger days I never had any occasion."

"So, you mean in your younger days you had to work too hard?"

"I did, yes."

"And turn your money over—"

"I didn't turn it all over. I always had a dollar in my pocket."

"How come you didn't have any love affairs, I mean what happened?"

"Well, for instance, in my teen years, when everybody would be *sleeping,* I'd be *working.* When they were *playing,* I was *sleeping,* so I never did have the time."

This was a variation on the oedipal theme of being left out, and also a measure of his somewhat narcissistic withdrawal.

"You mean because of this, uh, being a milkman you lived sort of an odd life in a sense that you were—?"

"Well, no, I wouldn't say that. I got it clean when I wanted. I knew where to go and take one out."

The word "odd" was too much like "queer," with connotations pointing toward an involvement with men, so he had to deny it.

"But it was odd in the sense that—"

"That I never had a girl friend? Yes."

"That's right. You could have had a queen. You mean you could go to a prostitute?"

"Yes, that's all. Frankly speaking *that is what I did most of the time.*"

"That's right. That's all you *could* do."

This meant it was all right and should not be a cause for guilt.

Going only to a prostitute signified his withdrawal, his narcissism and fear of emotional involvement.

"That's all because I never had time for girls, although I have met and had women customers say to me 'Gee, a nice looking fellow like you,' which I was, we'll say fair looking in those days, uh, *they couldn't get over it.*"

He had not been able to get over the loss of his narcissistic ideal self. He had become a second father to himself with all of the old yearnings and inadequacy feelings, as he compared himself with the infantile superman father he later triumphed over.

"So when you came home you were too nervous?"

"I uh, yes."

"I mean when you quit the milk route?"

"I uh, yes."

"You didn't have a girl friend then?"

"No, none."

"Too sick?"

"No, I was pressing all the time to hold the job. I didn't want to give the job up!"

"The job?"

"My milk job. I didn't want to give it up after all those years. I was only working *four hours* a day and making that kind of money. I mean, my God, five days a week, you couldn't beat that!"

"I mean after you gave the milk job up."

His underlying passivity and conniving were apparent. The job was taking care of mother. He had had a privileged niche in connection with mother but the magic feeling had worn thin since father's death. Possibly living with the "queen" had upset the balance and he was denying longings for a more adult type of relationship with a woman other than his mother and occasional prostitutes. But why was it necessary to deny this?

"Well, I still, uh, *women didn't mean anything to me!* I'd go down to the club or something where all my friends were. I'd go down and play cards, go down and have a couple of balls with the guys or *something like that,* go bowling or stuff like that. I mean I had my activity when I felt like it but most of the time I was getting this *tired feeling.* But I wouldn't give in to it as I said before. I never knew what it was to be sick. But now when I went down to Florida I went down to a hundred and fifty-seven pounds."

The statement about women was obviously ambivalent. Tired means a hidden depression. About what? What was missing? Probably when he said he had no real childhood, he meant no close relation with a dad and with other boys. Everything so far pointed this way. His rivalrous relationship with father and the brothers had interfered with his mastery of the homosexual side of his personality.

"In Florida?"

"Miami Beach. Right down near the dog track. I didn't bet them but that's where I was living, *down with the poor people.* I wasn't *up near the rich folks.* But, as I say, I thought I could come home. I was a *little coward* and had a *little pride.* When I had to give up the ice route, he gave me another route that he wanted me to run. I couldn't do it for him. I was *deathly sick.* I got so that if I did get a little sleep, Doctor, when I'd be leaving the ice plant and go on the route there'd be a series of lights coming over to the beach from Miami proper, and for no good reason at all, and when those traffic lights went against me, jeez, when I'd get over to the beach, boy, I was sick. Man, just the *aggravation,* I know it sounds foolish but things like that, that's the things that bother me."

The underprivileged little-boy part of him was talking now, the little boy who had done such big things. Now he saw he had paid a terrible price and was full of rage, death wishes, guilt and inadequacy feelings of the oedipal child. In another sense, an old narcissistic wound had been reopened.

"You found yourself blowing up, you mean?"

"Blowing up, for no good reason at all. The least little thing, a light would hold me up or I couldn't get *by a woman driver,* oh, foolish things, but I know in my heart and soul that there was something wrong."

Being held up by a woman had to be treated as a fantasy. Was it mother, her loss and his longing to appear big in her eyes that were responsible for his pains and losses?

"A woman?"

"Yes, you know how they are. They *hog the road,* you *can't get by them* and maybe you're trying to make a little time or something— *little foolish things* like that would upset me. Yet I had *no control* over them. I just couldn't help myself. I certainly would have tried if I could have because what I suffered in *pain* and everything else, get *all worked* up and *aggravated for* nothing! Now, as I say, I have come home."

This expressed well the ambivalent nature of the oedipal attachment to mother and his inability to resolve it.

"So your other brothers were really much more fortunate, huh? They were able to marry?"

"They're all married and have families."

"Except your brother next to you?"

"He's home."

"He didn't marry?"

"No, he's home. He's not able to work now, since the war. He hasn't had anything steady. But *he and I* now, of course my mother now is quite an old lady, we are the only means of support. He is doing nothing. She's been getting welfare, but now that my mother's an old lady it doesn't help much. With my brother's welfare from outside, we're getting by. I mean he and my mother are taking care of me. I've made about $300 in all this year. I'm ashamed to admit it."

A confrontation that was obvious could be made. It would have little effect now, but could be useful later.

"So you mean you used to take care of them and now they have to take care of you?"

"Absolutely! They *are*, well, they're helping me."

"Tell me, did you ever miss having good times like the other kids were able to have?"

"No, because I enjoyed the milk business. My heart and soul were in it. Today if I could go back, I'd be okay."

The milk business had been his magic route to becoming the rich, self-sufficient person. He gave the impression that he had been disappointed by mother and had withdrawn from relations with her and with persons in general or dealing with milk and money as narcissistic and fetishistic substitutes.

"How did you happen to get in the milk business?"

"Well, uh, I was just *overanxious to make a dollar* and a guy who was on a route took me on."

Now it was possible to explore the past more fully.

"Even then?"

"Even then. I was *always an eager beaver because my mother couldn't give it to me, anything like some of the neighbors' kids had it,* so I was always anxious to *make it all* myself."

The deprivation and source of the ambivalence were clear now. It sounded in one sense as if he were talking about milk as well as money and love, but obviously his narcissistic needs were involved.

"How do you mean always? As a little boy, you mean?"

"A little boy, even *younger* than that I used to go and set up pins at the bowling alleys, two cents a string, something like that. Any-

thing so I'd have a little money and *bring some home to my mother.*
That was just enough, *I've been that way all my life.*"

"So you mean you wanted to make money for mother?"

This was to clarify the picture. It was as if he had attempted to
reverse the roles and become the giver as a normal prelude to becoming the second father. The inevitable disappointments in any
child's relationship with his mother lead to some withdrawal and a
longing to be the giver of all good things himself. This drives him
toward the father who can supply the secret he needs to become big
and powerful, as in "The Sorcerer's Apprentice."

"No, not necessarily, for *myself* too."

"For you?"

"I mean I was willing to share it fifty-fifty, let's put it that way.
Plus the fact that *I didn't have as much* as the *other guys* I wanted
to work, which I did. I'd always get up and run errands, anything I
could do as a child, so that's how I got started in the milk business."

"You mean mother taught you to be like a father?"

"Yes, well my mother always gave me little chores around the
house, bring up the coal and the wood and stuff like that. I always
had little things to do but I was *ambitious. That wasn't enough. I
wanted to drive ahead.* That's why I can say at twenty-one years old I
was *foreman* for the milk company. I was only twenty-one years old.
That was right in the dark days of the depression and there were
college men and everything else there, and I was boss at only twenty-
one years old. I always had that go-go-go in me."

The basic oral insatiability showed clearly. It was as though he had
escaped from some injury to his infantile narcissism by a premature
flight into phallic competitive activity, which led him to become the
second father.

"And at nineteen you were making as much as father?"

"Oh, yes, at eighteen."

"At eighteen?"

"I made as much as him."

"But you missed a lot too because, as you say, a lot of the boys
played together and could go out with girls."

He had skipped too many stages that were a vital part of psychosexual maturation and also necessary for the mastery of basic anxieties
and needs in relation to men, especially brothers and father. His premature heterosexuality in the form of a second fatherhood had kept
him from an early normal type of homosexual problem solution.
Now he had to remain drinking with the boys. The anxieties connect-

ed with the tenderness and intimacies of love and personal relationships were never mastered.

"But I never missed it. *Something I never had I never missed.* I
wouldn't say I missed anything."

This could be tested safely, although it was connected with the
underlying depression.

"You didn't want to marry, have a home and kids?"

"Well, I never thought of that. *It's only in recent years since I've
become sick that I realize I've probably gone beyond the stage. I do
now these nights that I'm unable to sleep.*"

He stopped and looked puzzled. This material evoked anxiety and
depression and had to be handled carefully.

"You say since you've been sick you realize. When is this that you
began to realize?"

"Well, probably in the last seven or eight years."

"Seven or eight years, you mean eight years would be 1946."

"Approximately 1946 or 1947, around there."

"*When you came back home,* you mean, from the service."

"Yes."

One inference was that his guilt over father had ruined his relation with the queen, and life with the queen had ruined the milk
route.

"Then you began to wonder?"

"I began to wonder, huh. Well, now I'm getting up in the years.
Everybody else has gone but I'll have to stick with ma a few years, I
put it this way. Well, the others are gone. Well, I'll have to stick
with her until she's old enough to get her old-age pension. You know
what I mean, at least do that for her. Then when she started to receive it, here I am sick. And I'm helpless now. I can neither help
myself or help her."

He had regressed to the role of an orally insatiable, anxious, depressed and angry baby.

"You mean now when the time comes that you could go out and
get married, it is too late?"

"Yes, sir, it's *too late,* doctor. I feel as though I'm a sick man and
uh—"

He paused and looked anxious and uncertain.

"They've got to take care of you?"

"Well, they are. My brother has been very good to me, but still it
isn't enough in this respect. I always had my own money. I always had
a roll in my pocket. I had a car, traded it in every year. I took fairly

good care of myself, always had everything I wanted, and now I've just been getting by, doctor, if you understand what I mean. I have a couple of dollars in my pocket that my brothers gave me when I went home last week. They gave me $5, two of my brothers. You know, the twins, some spending money, something like that, but I've *lost that independent feeling* I had, you understand? Being this way and as time goes on I'm getting worse until this. I have known I was a sick man but I couldn't convince the doctors, so I got so that I've been sweating it out at home. I have seen a *black stool* several times in the last five years, as much as that. But I say to myself what's the use of going over there?"

He had a chronic feeling that he was going to be refused. Black stool meant black "pinpoints" in a normal stool. He also complained of chronic guilty feelings which had begun overseas when he was poisoned. At this time he felt the commanding officer was *"sore"* at him and thought he had done *"something terrible."* Now he was tired all the time and could only sleep four hours at a time. Everything hit him in the stomach. A new symptom, headaches, had also appeared. This dated from the time his mother had had a "slight stroke." It was obvious that he had felt frustrated and hostile to both parents, especially now the mother. It appeared that he blamed her for a missing relation with his father; i.e., he felt seduced into a premature, inadequate manhood. Let us return to the part of the interview where he described *what happened after* father's stroke.

"Yes, then he acted up. He only lived a day or something, a day or two, that's all it was. Then he died. While he was in there, I guess he was a pretty *violent man*, a *sick man*. It all happened within a period of three days. My father was never sick a day in his life."

A violent man and a sick man were equated. Then came a denial.

"Tell me, what do you think now that you look back? What do you think did all of this?"

The therapist was now taking advantage of the fact that there is always a time in any interview when a patient is willing to admit that he has all kinds of ideas, most of which are valuable leads. This type of question should not be asked prematurely, which means usually early in the interview before the patient's affects and memories are fully aroused.

"Myself personally? Well all I can attribute it to, never knowing what it was to be *sick* or anything, is that *poisoning*. Definitely my stomach was *never the same* afterwards. I've been *sensitive* and the fact that maybe *I should have been able to get*, which I didn't, medical treatment some years back, didn't help me any. It leaves me in the present state today. I mean that's all I can say. *I may not be honest with you.* I don't know anything else to say. I'm not afraid to have you ask questions because I'm making no stories up. Ask me anything you want to ask me and I'll answer to the best of my ability."

Following the war and living with the queen and father's death, things were never the same. He began to feel cheated out of something and full of resentment. He also doubted his honesty. This was a species of insight, but not very useful now. It also referred indirectly to the past losses which had "hit him in the stomach" and had been responsible for his narcissism and withdrawal.

"If you get better, what are you going to do?"

"I'm going to try and go *back on the milk route.* I don't know. It's going to be kind of hard now *at my age* to go back and *climb stairs.*"

He was only forty-three. The therapist knew nothing of his impotence. Climbing stairs is a common symbol of sexual intercourse in dreams.

"Would you get married?"

"No, I don't think so."

"Too late?"

"Too late, I figure. I missed the boat. That's what I say to myself anyway. I *missed the boat.*"

This little piece of insight could be expanded.

"When did you miss it?"

"Well, uh, about seven or eight years ago. Well more or less, let's say since my mother was half self-supporting. The little bit of money she gets from the old-age definitely doesn't support her."

"You mean seven or eight years ago, *right after coming back?*"

"Yes, when I found myself with the *burdens of running the whole show,* let's put it that way, and I wasn't physically able to. Believe me, it really upset me when I had to give the job up. They kept saying to me, 'We'll give you *something* else, give you the wholesale route.' I said well I'm perfectly well *satisfied.* What the hell's the difference whether I go on the wholesale route or retail route or what it is. I was only working *four hours a day.*"

He lived as a big phallic man through his identification with father. When father died, his identity began to diffuse and he regressed to an oral baby level, sleepy and hungry at four-hour intervals. He was poisoned by the father introject; i.e., he feared father's fate would overtake him. His experiences living intimately and sexually with the queen had made him more aware of his adult and genital sexual needs and feelings of love and hate. These feelings were attached to his family primarily and had to be repressed. This effort led to increased tension and exhaustion, but it was still unclear why his stomach had become the locus of his dissatisfactions. He was like the man who had sold his soul to the devil. He got his wish but it carried a punishment with it.

"You were supporting the *whole show at home?*"

"Well, then, yes. The other children were contributing a few dollars, but I was more or less running the show then."

"Did you get *fed up?*"

"No, I was content then."

He evaded the question by talking about the past.

"You didn't mind then, but now?"

"I've *always* had the disposition of just an *easygoing slob* as far as that goes."

"You mean it was easy for them to—"

He was stressing his lack of aggression. He had also used "always," so the past could be brought up again.

"Yes, everything was easy for me all my life. Money came, work was always easy, nothing was difficult until this time since I started to get sick."

Now he was denying all the deprivation and inadequacy feelings he had in the past. He meant that around the time of the poisoning and his relation with the queen he had developed some insight into what he had missed and into the fact that he had been led to substitute money for love in his relation to mother, and that his bigness was a sham. He then had to deny the insight. Patients often have to get worse in order to get better, because loss, depression and reality awareness go hand in hand.

"You never felt that you were too easy?"

"No, sometimes I figure I have been, with people I didn't know too well, a little bit overgenerous."

This is a quality associated with oral types.

"And with your family?"

"No, I never felt I was. I figured anything I gave my family went to a good cause, that's all. Never had any feelings that way."

"With others?"

"Yes, I'm always known as a *soft touch*. I always had money, made good money, I was always known as a *soft touch* no matter what route I ever drove or where I was. It didn't take long for the boys to know that I'm a *soft touch.* I don't know what else I can say to you."

He had played the big shot, the bountiful mother and wealthy father, to assuage his feelings of deprivations. This was part of his narcissistic self-sufficiency and withdrawal. Now the therapist had to wind up the interview.

"So you have no regrets?"

"Well, the only regrets I have are I'm not well. I can't get up and work."

The therapist could play a truth-and-consequences game with him as a way of confronting him with himself.

"You mean if you could get back on the *milk route* you'd be perfectly okay?"

"Providing I had *my health,* yes. I'm content, yes, I like the work."

Health equalled not *sick,* which equalled being a satisfied man who was not resentful. It also meant being like his brothers and not a little boy.

"You could make a good salary and go back with the boys."

"Well, not necessarily the *boys,* I'm *older* now. If I went back now I'd go down and join the Elks. I'm a pretty good bowler. I could bowl on the team, as a matter of fact, and I could bowl on the team this year. I don't want to be sick but what's the use of kidding myself. All I can say is I'm going down real fast because I've been noticing this hemorrhaging more than any others. I didn't know at the time—"

He meant, "If I could do it over again, I'd have played with the boys and related to my father." The balls and pins in bowling symbolize the relation with men, both sexual and aggressive, controlled and safe. Any marriage would be premature for him until he worked through his homosexual loves and hates, needs and attachments to men (fathers). The hemorrhaging to him was a warning that he was giving up hopes of adult heterosexuality. It was a reminder of the imminence of castration (operation).

"What do you think will be the end result?"

"Well, I'm hoping, uh, to come in here, that's why I took the choice to come upstairs here to see if I can *save myself an operation.*"

"How do you mean?"

"Well, uh, downstairs the surgeon came up and talked to me. I don't know whether they intended surgery or not. They're not doing surgery on me but I told them I'm terribly *nervous* if they did intend to. I didn't feel as though I wanted it because I'll only develop *an-*

other ulcer from carrying these nerves. So I said I'll try the nerve plan and see a psychiatrist."

This type of superficial insight is common in patients and not very useful.

"You mean the *nerves make the ulcer?*"

"Well, it seems to me *one fights the other.* I attribute one to the other. It's a battle back and forth. *I'm feeling halfway calm, the stomach will act upon me and I get nervous and vice versa,* that's all, just one battling the other."

He had projected onto his body the struggle between his tense, restless, phallic, masculine part and his oral, baby, passive, stomach part. At another level, it was his father and mother, so the therapist could try for information in this area.

"How did father and mother get along?"

"They had their *little spats,* I suppose, now and then."

"They did. In what way?"

"Yes, *money* sometimes, the problems of a big family."

"Mother was complaining?"

"Well, if my mother bought something and father didn't like it, oh, boy! *My father was great on eats,* he really was genuine on the eats."

This was a good opportunity to explore the relation of food to father. It was also a surprise, as feeding as usually related to a mother.

"Well, he insisted, like I was the oldest, *he made me set an example* for the rest. Like *turnips,* I never liked them as a real youngster, and he'd say, *"You eat it,* if it's good enough for me, you eat it." And if I didn't, I'd get *a little tap on the behind,* see, to set an example for the rest."

The question now was, is this memory a screen for his getting the original poison? How did he react to "turnips?" Was a "tap" like a "stroke?"

"So you had to eat it whether you liked it or not?"

"I ate everything. *I learned to like everything.* There isn't any vegetable I didn't have to eat!"

"You learned to like it. You mean you didn't at first?"

"I didn't at first but I learned."

"Do you remember?"

"Oh, I, uh, I wouldn't say *I hated it,* but if I had a choice of potato or something I would take it rather than turnip. I remember turnip was one thing I didn't care too much for, or carrots. I didn't care too much for them but when they were put at me I ate them the same as the rest. My father was always great for the table. That was one thing we always were brought up that way. The table was *essential* in our house. We didn't have *fancy things* like some of the neighbors had maybe, but we always had *plenty to eat.*"

If the interview had not been ending, the therapist could have explored the things he didn't get.

"And you had to eat it? Is this what you mean?"

"Had to eat it! Yes!"

"He made you all eat?"

"He made us all eat. He enjoyed, I would say, more or less good health himself and he wanted his family that way. He was great on the eats. We used to get at that time, I think, six quarts of milk a day. That was the daily delivery off the milkman then."

"He made you drink milk?"

"Oh, a glass or *two glasses* almost at every meal."

"You didn't mind drinking milk?"

"Oh, no, no. I was always a great milk drinker."

"*Always a great milk drinker?*"

"Ever since I can remember I was *crazy for milk.*"

"How long can you remember?"

"I think back when I was four or five years old."

"You remember then even?"

"I always liked milk."

"You were also a great eater then?"

He ate, competing with father, but he was ambivalent about eating and later even about drinking.

"Oh, yes."

"Like father?"

"*Always a great eater.* Of course, I was the oldest and my mother had a couple of sisters that never got married, and they used to take me around, you know, to grandmother's to eat, and they always told me *I ought to eat chicken* and everything. Little pieces of steak they used to broil them like in the old country. You know how they used to do it."

"They gave you sort of the *special food,* you were the oldest."

"Yes, I was the *pride and joy* at that particular time, you know. *Of course, as we got older everybody was treated equal.* There was no, *never any* favorites."

When all the rest came along, he was no longer mama's pride and joy. He had to share food and drink (milk). His inflated narcissism was wounded and he must have withdrawn. He continually tried to do it all by himself and, aided by the environment, thrust himself prematurely into an adult role. He had constantly to deny the painful realization that he was no longer mama's favorite.

"And when you worked on the milk route you could drink all the milk you wanted?"

"Oh, yes."

"You had five or six quarts yourself?"

"Well, there were times, there were lots of days, no fooling, when I drank four quarts of milk."

"You were getting more milk than the others were?"

"Yes, I was drinking it while I was working."

"Well, there were many good reasons why your heart and soul were in the milk business—big money, lots of milk, easy life—but you really missed a lot too, didn't you? You have had more than one kind of pain, haven't you?"

"That could be, but I always figured what I never knew never hurt me."

"Maybe, as you said, you missed a lot of things. Perhaps we can find out more about them."

"I hope so, Doc. I'll do anything to feel better."

Let us see what lessons we can draw from this case and how we could proceed with a plan of therapy. We have to realize that each case is unique, and tailor our therapy to fit the clinical facts and not vice versa. This will prevent us from thinking and working with the patient at a level that has no meaning to him. For instance, if we are overconcerned with the relation of ulcer pain to a "biting, internalized mother," or a sadomasochistic birth fantasy, or even castration anxiety, we will be like the patient to the extent that we will "miss the boat." Thus, the material as far as the present interview was concerned might have led us to the following observations:

Before age two, our patient received special food and was mother's pride and joy.

After the others came along, times were hard. He felt deprived and guilty about his death wishes and jealousies.

He then not only became an eager beaver, second father to the others, but an overgenerous mother to himself. He found a narcissistic solution to his needs. This was accompanied by a withdrawal of interest in persons.

His pride in his independence and competitive bigness and unlimited milk supplies compensated for missing things until he went overseas.

His first real girl, the queen, gave him something different from prostitutes. Actually, she was the widow of a flier killed in the Battle of Britain and a "nice" girl. She made a home for him. After her, he felt lonely and discontented and began to realize something was wrong and missing in his life. This was painful or anxiety-provoking enough for him to deny and displace the associated affects.

The death of his father brought to the fore oedipal guilt feelings and longings for a missing boyhood relation with a father whom he needed in order to grow up. In psychoanalytic terminology, he felt persecuted by the lost object which had now become a persecutory introject.

The poisoned food syndrome was a reactivated gestalt connected with eating, drinking, ambition, passivity, dependence, aggression and orality in general.

Another, and supplementary, way we might look at this patient is in regard to his denial of his later deprivations by means of a regression to a pretwo-year-old, oral level and an almost fetishistic preoccupation with milk and being a milkman. His libido was obviously anchored here. This was his love life. Depending upon the material he furnished us with from session to session, our first task would be to stimulate and draw out his awareness of the many things he had felt deprived of or missed in the past. We have to undo his denial thoroughly. This means not only the recall of memories but the return of old depressive and anxious empty feelings, longings and the realization of wasted years. Good therapy demands the suffering imposed by reality awareness. While we endeavor to limit the dosage to an endurable amount, we must expect such reactions in our patients and help our patients to expect them and to become desensitized to them. Depression is not only a reaction to loss but a deflection of aggression onto oneself. We could help the patient with his internalized aggression by deflecting his rage and deprivation feeling in the present and against doctors in the past and old images of his mother, father and siblings. By leading him to the queen, we could also lead him to a realization of what he had missed in regard to marriage, love, children and a home where he could be truly independent and a real first father, i.e., to things in the present.

Sooner or later the problem of his impotence would appear and we would have to get him to see it as part and parcel of a general impotence in his relation to persons, women especially, and feeling in general. His feelings of being deprived would also involve homosexual persecutory or paranoialike defenses against depressive feelings. These would be connected with doctors, father, the brothers and persons who took advantage of his "overgenerosity," and ultimately with the bad, depriving mother who succeeded the one who gave him special food. Actually, her place, in one sense, was taken by the father who gave him turnips and forced him to eat. It is obvious that all this would take many interviews, during which we would come upon many new symptoms and problems. For instance, headaches might appear as well as material in connection with fears of strokes and hemorrhages and paralysis. Long before we reach the "last" session, we will have recognized that our main task consists of integrating the material in terms of an awareness of large over-all patterns of relationship that permit the development of a tolerant perspective of and detachment from the immediate problems without feelings of abandonment, isolation, loneliness and estrangement. The fundamental problem in any case is that we are dealing with a narcissistic solution to problems involving a loss. Pathological narcissism always involves withdrawal from involvement with persons and compensatory involvements in other areas. It also involves frustration. The withdrawal leads to further losses, just as loans at a usurious rate of interest lead to increasing debt.

XIII

PSYCHOTHERAPY OF
PSYCHOSOMATIC CONDITIONS

Case of Ulcerative Colitis

In Chapter XII we listened to a man with a peptic ulcer. We saw, in a fairly convincing manner, that his symptoms at first appeared associated with a great deal of conscious and unconscious emotional and ideational material connected with food, drinking and eating, and the stomach. Later in the interview it was clearly demonstrated that the manifest problems in this area screened hidden problems in such areas as his genital sexual life and a partial withdrawal from relationships with persons in general. How does emotional and ideational material come to be associated with the production of an ulcer? The available evidence is clear in some respects. We know conscious and unconscious emotional disturbances produce changes in the vascularity, friability and secretory properties of the mucous membranes of various areas in many persons and that there are no ideational complexes that are not associated with emotional components and physiological changes. The physical areas affected most intensely are unique to each individual. These ideational, emotional and physiological fusions are of long duration whether they are associated with one set of organs or another. They have been present to a greater or lesser degree since childhood; i.e., the "target organ" has been involved from earliest childhood days. Some initial interviews illustrate this in a striking manner. In this chapter, the case of a man with one of these fusions involving the lower gastrointestinal tract will be presented and compared with the case of the man with the peptic ulcer.

434

The development of our knowledge concerning stress, exhaustion and alarm reactions and their relationship to the pituitary-adrenal complex has greatly increased our knowledge of how certain psychosomatic syndromes occur, but, as an etiological agent, hormonal substances are only one link in a long chain. There is no general agreement about what is a psychosomatic disease. Some believe that all of medicine is psychosomatic, while others reserve the term "psychosomatic disease" for an obvious functional disturbance of an organ due to its inappropriate use for the solution of emotional difficulties. The patient's use of his skin in certain cases of excoriative neurodermatitis would be an example of an illness on a semivoluntary basis, and the use of the stomach to express intensified passive oral needs to the point where a chronic gastritis is produced would be an example of an involuntary process. Perhaps a better example of the latter would be certain cases of blepharitis that are connected with the denial of grief and which can be temporarily relieved by episodes of weeping. Such an approach, however, is somewhat atomistic and emphasizes the split in the concepts of psyche and soma. Still others prefer to use the term "somatization reaction," which can apply either to organs of motility or to internal organs. One of the better definitions is that given by F. Deutsch (1939b) who stated that "psychosomatic medicine is the systematized knowledge of how to study bodily processes which have become fused and amalgamated with emotional disturbances in the past and in the present." This should be explained, because its simplicity is deceiving.

Our understanding of psychosomatic disease rests essentially on our understanding of why some persons tend to become organically ill in response to overwhelming stress, whereas others tend to develop a neurosis or a psychosis or suffer a pathological character change which is mainly a disorganization of certain highly developed and habitual inhibitions. Although this question cannot be definitely answered, theoretical speculations might be summarized as follows: patterns of adjustment to stress are laid down in the early formative years of life and crystallize in certain character patterns or habitual reactions which are never purely psychic but are interwoven with somatic manifestations; i.e., mental attitudes and reactions are interwoven with complex vascular, endocrine and chemical reactions which are in part specific for the organism and in part a result of experience. F. Deutsch (1939b) has labeled this process "conditional dispositional fusion." This fusion involves the entire person, but may manifest itself chiefly in one organ or organ system. It involves more than the concept of the Pavlovian conditioned reflex and is nearer to the gestalt concept. Furthermore, like the gestalt concept, it is an entity in itself and can be reactivated either from the organic or the psychic side. Accordingly, all organic changes in the body, including illnesses, tend to activate certain psychic constellations involving thought, behavior and emotion.

Likewise, events arousing emotional attitudes previously associated with an "organic" illness will tend to activate certain symptoms and physiological changes associated with organ syndromes. This gives the phrase "character patterns" a much wider meaning in terms of habitual reactions on the part of both the body and the mind. Such patterns can roughly be classified from a developmental point of view as infantile, adolescent or adult. New patterns are constantly being superimposed in a facilitating or an inhibiting and controlling way over the old. In each case, they are an exquisitely balanced combination of action, structure, thought and feeling. These patterns can also be classified as abnormal or normal according to their appropriateness for the age of the person, the situation and the mixture of impulsive emotional elements with logically verbalized elements. The control of the rate of discharge and proportion of the emotional elements and their physiological repercussions are the crux of the psychosomatic illness. Throughout life, the emotions can be tamed and harnessed or denied and repressed. They cannot be kept from occurring, and are always associated with bodily changes. When they rage out of conscious control, they often lead to and appear as a psychosomatic disease. A psychosomatic illness in this sense means the revival of a distorted infantile character pattern of control of or defenses against repressed emotions linked with certain past unbearable situational difficulties, the organic physiological part being manifest and serving as a disguise or a cover for certain emotional and ideational elements which remain hidden. The term "adult" implies behavior in keeping with common and socially accepted standards. These standards, from the point of view of psychoanalysis, refer to such characteristics as genital maturity, resolution of the oedipus complex and maturational changes in keeping with one's age, such as outlined by Erikson (1959).

Every person is a kaleidoscopic mixture of adult, adolescent and infantile character patterns, all interlocked and mutually interdependent on one another for the maintenance of a unique personality. Adult character patterns are the first line of defense against anxieties, depressing losses and the vicissitudes of life in general, and they work hand in glove with hidden but persistent remnants of our infantile narcissism and comforting, if somewhat megalomanic, magical and irrational feelings such as "harm cannot occur to me as long as I live a certain way," etc. Emotional and physical traumas and losses of all kinds continually occur. Such traumas can accumulate and eventually may lead to a traumatic experience characterized by a disintegration of the adult character patterns and a revival of infantile anxieties, often with physical concomitants when one organ system bears an excessive load. One of the most convincing proofs of this is the shift in the balance of character patterns or the personality changes that occur as complications and aftereffects of the medical treatment of psychosomatic illness. Also, psychosomatic illness often follows losses, a severe injury, a narrowly escaped accident or even a temporary organic illness, as any of these experiences can be traumatic in effect.

Is there a type of person especially susceptible to a psychosomatic illness? Although any type can be affected, the compulsive and narcissistic person who appears overly self-sufficient and is unable to relate well with others or come to terms with his basic emotional needs is chiefly affected. There are many such persons who deny their emotions a satisfactory measure of expression and who tend throughout the years to have defective personal relationships and to accumulate anxieties and delayed emotional responses that press for discharge. This is particularly true when an expression of strong emotion is called for on occasions such as death, marriage, divorce, birth, love and experiences which throw the normal social order into a ferment. These persons place a great load on their stress-adapter mechanisms, and preserving mental and physical homeostasis becomes increasingly difficult for them as they age and face the inevitable frustrations of life. They tend through denial to accumulate minor losses, frustrations and traumas which only need an excuse to coalesce into a major traumatic event. A blow to the head, a physical illness or an emotional upset, according to their past conditioning, can act as the last straw to the overworked stress-adapter mechanisms, both psychic and organic, and precipitate a traumatic type of reaction of great severity. This reaction appears manifestly and ostensibly in only an "organic" form. When it does, it means that the "organic" illness is being used by the patient to deny certain emotional problems, derive gratifications and discharge other repressed and suppressed feelings. Many of the gratifications are defensive; i.e., the illness acts as a conversion process and prevents painful emotional material and memories from coming to consciousness. The affected organ, whether it is the head in patients with chronic, posttraumatic headache, or the lungs and chest in patients with asthma, becomes the central point of the patient's life, and feelings which belong to the past and the present are related to this organ. The illness itself becomes a part solution to the patient's past and present difficulties and a defense against the painful necessity of facing real or fantasied physical, social and personal inadequacies.

The relationship of physiological homeostasis to its psychic counterpart can be demonstrated in a different way. The homeostatic balance of hundreds of persons under intense emotional strain becomes so precarious that they show signs and symptoms of many incipient psychosomatic diseases. Such symptoms as musical rales, joint pains of a transient nature, injected sclera, headache, blepharitis, extrasystoles, diarrhea, back pain and phosphaturia are legion and few people in the course of a lifetime fail to develop one or more of them every now and then. According to past conditioning and its usefulness in solving past problems, any one of these transient physical states can be the early stage of a severe psychosomatic disease. One syndrome frequently observed by the author during the last world war among exhausted personnel from Guadalcanal consisted of the following stages: (1) an increased contrast in red and white mottling of the palmar areas, leading to (2) formation of pinpoint blebs in the white areas accompanied by itching, and (3) secondary excoriation and infection. With rest and local measures, most such patients recovered before stage three was reached. Many never reached even the second stage.

Prevention of chronicity is of primary importance in the treatment of psychosomatic disease. We should remove a patient from the stressful environment if at all possible and try to re-establish and reinforce the adult defensive character patterns as quickly as possible. Fortunately, this tends to occur by itself. Mild disorders, which comprise most cases of psychosomatic illness, need little or no treatment other than that given to the neuroses. The more severe disorders may need the cooperation of an internist or good general practitioner who will take charge of the physical treatment. Many can be treated only in a hospital. The patient's difficulties with his personal and self-relationships both in the present and past must be brought to his consciousness as a continuum. He must be encouraged to develop a more realistic solution to these personal problems. In this manner, the affected organ system can be relieved of its psychic entanglements so that its physiological responses will not be impaired or overburdened. Sometimes it is difficult to distinguish the mild from the more severe disorders because the apparent strength of the personality of those prone to develop psychosomatic disorders makes an evaluation difficult for many physicians.

What confuses the issue is that in our civilization we tend to overestimate the stability of narcissistically oriented persons, who are often compulsive in their habits, self-reliant and able calmly to intellectualize their way through life. This type appears to be especially susceptible to many psychosomatic disorders. A major therapeutic difficulty in dealing with these patients is their proneness to intellectualize and avoid emotional commitments. An even greater difficulty is the defensive reactions and the anxiety produced in them by any attempt to get them to discuss their personal problems with anything but superficial understanding. This is partly due to the great defensive use they make of the intellectual processes, the integrity of which is associated with deep-rooted anxieties and emotions concerning the integrity of their bodies. Insight therapy is technically difficult and time consuming. Transference reactions are difficult to detect. In one sense, the psychosomatic disease is the patient's last stand. The therapy situation itself not only threatens to deprive him of this defense but adds insult to his narcissism as well. The development of insight in the patient is accompanied by the discharge of an enormous amount of aggression, which may pose a difficult technical problem, or there may be a complete surrender and the patient rapidly regresses to passive, dependent, infantile character patterns which mean a greater technical problem for the therapist.

These patients will reveal a great deal of information that is psychologically relevant to their psychosomatic illnesses only if they are unaware that the therapist is interested in this material and especially if they are allowed to speak in an offhand manner. Sector psychotherapy is particularly adapted for obtaining this type of information.

Following a working through of the material, the patient must be encouraged to find new solutions to old problems. This aspect of psychotherapy is as a rule played down on the theory that once the patient has become aware of all the various facets of his problems he will act in accordance with his knowledge. This is more often than not a futile hope. The patient remains stymied and uses the therapeutic situation as the major part of a neurotic compromise. Advice, suggestion and command that a choice be made are often of no avail until a reasonable limit to the therapy is set. For safety's sake, this can often be introduced as a six-month vacation. In some cases a slow weaning process works better, i.e., visits at monthly intervals, etc. All psychosomatic cases must be played by ear concerning the recurrence of somatic symptomatology. As long as this is in abeyance, the verbal complaints of the patient who is ready for discharge can be treated lightly.

The history of a typical case of psychosomatic disease can be divided into the following stages:

1. The developmental stage—this occurs before the sixth year. The principal psychic problem is a qualitative or quantitative defect (loss) in the relationship between the pregenital child and the mother, characterized by pathological mourning and a partial abandonment of object relationships with a compensating increase in narcissistic relationships. This coincides with an organic affliction and a denial of grief, rage and guilt. F. Deutsch calls this a conditional dispositional psychosomatic fusion. Coupled with this there is usually a secondary gain which partially compensates for the defective (lost) mother-child relationship. This may or may not mean that the mother's care of the sick child takes the place of love. The child may and can act out the mother-child relationship on its own body or with other children.

2. A period of fixation then ensues between age five and puberty. During this stage, more conflicts and losses are drawn into the relationship with the afflicted organ, which in one guise or another substitutes for the mother. In some cases the father may substitute for the phallic mother, or the relation may shift back and forth between the two.

3. There is usually a period in the teens and twenties characterized by fleeting and often stormy attempts at intense object restitutions. These tend to be unsatisfactory in one way or another, and become progressively poorer after the first signs of difficulty appear.

4. A precipitating trauma then occurs which signifies the loss or abandonment of object relations, regression and the development of a severe narcissistic neurosis manifested by a painful relationship with some organ system that serves as a somatic screen. This bolsters up a denial of underlying and usually unconscious painful relationships with persons and the self. The failure to realize idealized versions of the self are of special importance.

5. Secondary complications may occur in an afflicted organ owing to accompanying vascular, hormonal, infectious and toxic changes. As often as not, the patient does not go to the doctor until these com-

plications are obvious. Often the secondary complications may be mistaken for the primary disease.

In the case of the peptic ulcer, the patient talked of an ideal feeding relationship with his mother and aunts, who were fantasy or alterego mothers. This was interrupted by the birth of many siblings. He described this in terms of various deprivations. Early in life he began to abandon a personal love relationship with mother for a monetary ambition-ridden one. The longing for an oral feeding relationship was hidden. He longed for sweet milk and got bitter turnips from father. Finally he solved his problem by a narcissistic self-sufficiency. With four quarts of milk a day and a pint of cream, he could keep his hungry stomach mollified. The oedipal overtones were obvious. He lived dangerously, with occasional illicit sexual relationships which he later conceded were mainly with dissatisfied married women customers. The poisoning acted as a warning about his powers for evil. The longing for a loving relationship with father as well as mother had never been fulfilled and his happy experience with the "queen" only resurrected all the old gestalts laden with depression, anxiety, uncertainty and inferiority feelings. After the "poisoning" trauma, he abandoned personal relationships along with the "queen." This was symbolized by his impotence, which expressed and augmented his problems but did not *cause* them.

From here on he regressed to a severe narcissistic neurosis. In the treatment of this case, transference reactions appeared in a fleeting and unsustained form and no transference neurosis occurred. With such patients the main job is one of undoing displacements, introjections, and being aware of their often disguised hypersensitivity to the smallest environmental events in connection with primary figures and their usually obvious substitutes. All of this can be more easily illustrated than described, so in this chapter we shall contrast the peptic ulcer case with one of a young man in his early thirties who came to therapy for a similar reason. He had mild to moderate attacks of ulcerative colitis and had been warned that eventually an organ might be cut off. He looked much younger than his chronological age and appeared calm. He had a faint and somewhat cynical smile. He sat down and waited for the doctor to begin. He had telephoned for an appointment six weeks before and appeared wary about accepting an earlier time. He began by talking about his *colitis* in terms of *runs, cramps* and *pain*. This led to how his hands were *shaking* and he was afraid of accidentally touching the electric wires of the appliances he worked on. He had had the runs for eleven years, which was the time he had left home to go in the Army. At first he thought it was due to something he ate or drank. Before this he had been *normal*. This meant going once every two to five days. The nervousness and shaking had begun only two years ago. He was *jumpy* on the job, *disgusted* and *angry*. Since he had telephoned, he had noticed that when he was *angry* he had the runs; yet this was not always true. At various times he had blamed different foods or drinking and he had quit liquor and various foods to no avail. The only things he knew that always bothered him were corn and cucumbers. At times, he volunteered, he could go up to sixteen days without a movement. He was then steered toward the past and asked how his mother reacted to his constipation. He immediately became very wary and noncommittal and declared he "couldn't remember." He was never close to her. This led to the fact that he was the oldest of eleven siblings. He recited their names with fondness and ease. Mother was a good cook but her food was too plain. Now he liked spicy food. He acquired a taste for it in the service. He was then asked where he ate now. The interview went on as follows:

"In a restaurant and at my mother's."
"At your mother's and in a restaurant?"
"That's right, more so in a restaurant."
"You're not married?"
"No, I'm separated."
"Separated?"
"Yes, sir."
"When did you get married?"
"Nineteen-fifty-three."
"Nineteen-fifty-three? Five years ago?"
"That's right."
It was better to approach the mother gradually through the wife relationship.
"Was she a good cook?"
"Yes, I'd say so."
"What nationality was she?"
"Italian. Do you mind if I smoke?"
"Not at all. Italian? You're separated?"
"Yes, sir."
"What happened?"
"Well, I blamed a lot on myself."

"How do you mean?"

"Well, drinking, for one!"

After a long pause he continued.

"Well, there's a lot of feelings to this."

He appeared wary and angry.

"Angry feelings, you mean?"

"Yes, angry."

"You mean you're angry at her?"

"Yes."

"What for?"

"Well!"

He sighed.

"That's another thing."

"What do you mean?"

"Well, I'm waking up to a lot of things that I never thought of before. I never dreamt that it could be right. I mean I always had some other excuse."

"What do you mean, for instance?"

"Well, a lot of *feelings* I had for my *wife*. I wonder if it wasn't actually my *mother* and I took them out on her."

"Could you give me an example? You mean *angry feelings?*"

"Yes!"

The therapist repeated the key words, allowing time for the mobilization of feelings.

"You mean you were angry at your wife but it was really your mother you were angry at?"

"That's right!"

"What were you angry at mother for?"

He paused for two whole minutes and indicated plainly that he didn't want to talk.

"Oh, for many things."

"You can tell me. I know this is painful material because I can tell from the way you are looking at me. This has a lot of feeling in it but I'd like to hear it."

"Well, I'm here to be helped, so—"

He paused again, still struggling with himself.

"That's right."

After another long pause he smiled apologetically and continued.

"Well, my mother *ran around* for a long time."

"Ran around?"

"Yes."

"With?"

"Other men."

Other men could mean him as well as father. Superficially this was beginning to sound like an oedipal jealousy problem. The question also arose, was running around connected with the *runs*?

"Other men?"

"Yes."

"How do you know?"

"Well I happened to walk in one place."

"Walk in on her?"

"That's right."

"How old were you?"

He sighed deeply.

"Say eleven or twelve years old."

"You mean you're not sure?"

"Well I'm not sure if it was when I was eleven years old or twelve years, but I know it was around that time."

When a patient makes this type of a statement, it usually means that other things happened around the same time that confused the issue, or that the event acted as a traumatic scene which attached to it other and similar traumas and important memories. This confused him. In some aspects it resembled a combination of a primal scene and a prepuberty trauma of the kind that could have marked effects on the structure and organization of his personality.

"And you caught her doing what?"

"Well, anyway I used to take it out on my wife."

"What did you catch her doing? You mean she was having intercourse?"

"All right, yes."

He seemed eager to drop the subject.

"Was she doing anything else?"

"No, it was intercourse."

It was necessary to get a clear understanding of an event of this importance.

"In bed?"

"No, it wasn't on the bed. It was, it was in the church. That's where it happened."

"In the church?"

"Yes."

"How come?"

"Well, see my mother's cousin worked there and we used to call him Uncle Jim. I used to bring his lunch over, and a lot of times I'd be hanging around my father's store and then take his lunch over."

Here he linked Uncle Jim with his father. This would be a point in favor of his using this incident as a screen for an earlier occurrence when he saw mother and father, which may have in time been linked to primal scene events, dreams and fantasies. But there was another point here. *He* took the lunch over and found the faithless uncle as well as the mother with someone else.

"Which uncle was this, your father's brother?"

"Well actually he's not my uncle. It was my mother's cousin by marriage."

"Mother's cousin by marriage?"

"Yes."

"And you called him Uncle Jim?"

"Well yes, we did. He was more of a, I don't know, but that's the way my mother thought about it, as a courtesy more so, and, uh, I just happened to walk in that night."

"Into the church?"

"Yes. You see he was the janitor there."

"And he was making love to her?"

"He was having sexual intercourse!"

He paused and then continued.

"When you say love, I mean to me it could be many ways."

"You mean it wasn't love as far as you were concerned?"

"I mean I'm saying it could be love sexually, oh, there's many ways."

"That's right, you mean what?"

"To me it wasn't love."

"It was just plain ordinary—?"

"I mean something was wrong! I don't know what but I knew something was wrong."

This something was the incestuous element as well as the blow to his narcissism, i.e., that *his* mother did such things by design. In a patient with colitis, sex probably had strong anal overtones.

"But as far as you were concerned you felt it was a *dirty* thing?"

"That's right."

"And you were *disgusted?*"

"That's right. I was hurt more than anything else."

The therapist decided to test the limits of his memory in this area.

"You never suspected before?"

"No."

"Yet I don't understand. She had eleven children by your father."

This had another meaning besides the obvious one which said, where did she find the time for affairs, because he must have known where and how the babies came. Here the question arose, did his colitis in some manner support a denial of his infantile fantasies concerning the sexual life of his mother?

"That's right. I don't understand it either."

"They were all by father?"

"I guess so."

"I wonder how you felt?"

"Well I always loved her."

"Up until then?"

"I still do."

"Really?"

"Really."

"Since you were eleven, you've done a lot of thinking about this?"

"Well, I mean I have many ideas."

"That's what I mean. What are some of these ideas? You don't know whether they are true or not, of course."

"Well I don't know. You can't say, in a way, I don't know, I guess I blame my father in a way because he never made, the money he made he usually drank, or he didn't work. I mean, uh, I mean the way things are today I'd say that that was one cause."

Father never produced much *money* for mother, so she had to turn to Uncle Jim like a faithless prostitute. The unconscious relationship of money and feces was also in the background.

"He didn't make enough?"

"Well you can say he didn't make enough, and in another way he did make it but he didn't do anything with it."

"That's what I mean. With eleven kids to support and a wife, he drank it?"

"That's right but, uh, I mean she still played around after he did make money and he quit drinking."

He paused and then added,

"So I mean I can't blame him there."

"By the time he quit you mean it was too late?"

"It could be so, I don't know."

"I don't know either, but it's easier to start things like that than to stop them."

"Yes, if you start that way you still run into problems because I don't know if I'm right or wrong."

"What do you mean?"

"Well, I mean I don't know why she did it. All I know is she did do it and I can't get rid of *that feeling* towards her."

"You mean things were never the same afterwards, huh?"

"Well, I guess the real thing that hurt me most of all was the *beating* she gave me."

"When you walked in?"

"No, it wasn't long after that. I don't know, either I *wanted something* or was just *mad*."

"What did they do when you walked in?"

"Oh, you know, they broke it up. I walked out. I didn't stay there. In fact I *ran out*. I just *ran out*."

"Ran out?"

This running out on mother had marked a turning point in his life. His life had become organized around his efforts to deny his dependence upon her. He called his trouble the "runs" for more than one reason.

"That's right."

"And you did what?"

"I went back to my father's store."

"You didn't tell him?"

"No, I didn't tell him."

"But you say later, what happened? You wanted something?"

"I don't know, truthfully I don't remember it. I know I either asked for something or I did something and she said 'No' and slapped me. And I said, 'I'm going to tell dad about it,' you know how a kid is!"

"You threatened her?"

He laughed.

"I don't know whether it was blackmail or not. I know I got the worst beating of my life. In fact, no one will ever give me half the beating that she did."

"How do you mean?"

"I'd never let them."

"How did she beat you?"

"I just remember that beating. Don't ask me how."

"But I mean what do you remember?"

"I mean with everything, a broom, anything she could get her hands on, and her nails."

"Nails?"

"Well, you know, her fingernails."

"Oh! She really went at you?"

"Yes. I'm *burning inside* every time I think of it."

"You were furious you mean, huh?"

"That's right."

"Angry!"

"Real angry because I didn't think I deserved that beating."

Now a linkage of two themes was made. It was to be expected that he would reject it, but it would have unconscious repercussions.

"Did you have the runs then?"

"No."

"You were just angry, huh? Burning?"

"That's right."

"It sounds to me as if that burn has been going on for a long time."

"That's right."

"You never forgot it?"

"No, but I mean, uh, I know."

He sighed.

"I know someone else that had to leave, you know, the same thing happened to him."

"What do you mean?"

"Well, uh, when I was in Korea, in fact we were getting ready to come home, this kid and I were talking and I asked him if he was going home and he said 'No,' and I asked him why and he told me why. You know, because of his mother, as he put it, shacking up with another guy and he caught them, see, and he was living with his father and his family is busted up. And, uh, I mean he has a hatred for her and he won't go near her, but, uh, I don't know, I can't do that."

"You didn't *run away*?"

"No."

"After she beat you, you stayed around?"

"Well, I *ran out* of the house."

"But you came back?"

"I didn't come back until about eleven o'clock that night. I just didn't want to go back."

"Why?"

"I don't know. I just didn't want to go into the house."

"How was she the next day? How were things from then on?"

"Well, it was awful quiet. I never stayed in the house much after that."

"You avoided her?"

"I'd get up and go down to the bakery like I usually did. I'd get the bread and the rolls and I'd get ready for school and I wouldn't come back until I came back with my father. I wouldn't come home from school."

"You stayed out of her way?"

"Yes."

"You ran away in a different sense, but you couldn't stay away?"

"No, I mean because she's my mother."

"You still care?"

"Well, that's it, I mean, uh—"

He choked up with feeling.

"You were the oldest boy?"

"Yes."

"Had you been her favorite before?"

"Well, I don't know, that's one thing I can't say about my parents. They never favored one more than the other."

This may have meant that the parents were equally indifferent to all.

"But you said she was a woman with so much temper. She was able to beat you like that."

"And there were times when she wasn't that way. I never saw her that way before."

He then painted an idyllic picture of life with mother before the beating. Babies were coming along all the time. He was the oldest and the natural helper. At this point in the interview, his wariness became more open. As the oldest boy, he would go to the store in the morning for milk and rolls and get breakfast. The therapist was leading once more to the golden period before he ran out on mother.

"So there were no more?"

"That's right."

"And you were, in a sense, the grown-up boy, huh?"

"If you're leading to something, I don't know what it is. I've been trying to figure it out."

What was it he felt guilty and suspicious about? It would appear that it was mainly his trying to be the second father, as in the patient with the peptic ulcer, and that his oedipal guilt was showing, but there were many other factors at work. The way he stayed with his father and the way he wouldn't allow his sisters to get the food were signs of negative oedipal facets to his personality. It might have been that his attachment to mother was in large part a symbiotic identification with her. With all these children, she may have been out of his life so much that he was hypersensitized to losses. This could also have led to a reaction characterized by partial withdrawal from object relationships, increased narcissistic preoccupation with himself and his body, partial identification with the lost object and somatic accompaniments. If this were so, it could be demonstrated.

"Really? Not at all! I just want to know. You were the oldest boy and there was quite an age difference between you and the next boy, wasn't there?"

"Yes, that's true."

"That's what I mean. Mother must have relied on you to be her man when father was away."

"Oh, my father relied on me too! I mean I actually stayed with him more than I ever did at home."

"Stayed with him more than you did at home?"

"Sure."

This was an ambiguous statement, as the time factors were unknown. When he ran out on mother, he had an infantile precedent. He must have turned to father as a child, probably many times and in a specific manner with specific somatic complaints.

"What do you mean, didn't he stay at home?"

He sighed.

"Well, you see after all this happened, you know, my father did make money. He was the head bookie in the city, and I'd come right from school and I'd stay with him until ten or eleven o'clock until he went home."

"You mean when he went home to mother?"

"I went home with him. What I'm getting at is I never played around the house or anything like that. I always went right down to the store."

Why did he have to tell this to the therapist? "Never" means never any more after a period when he always did.

"But I'm talking about before."

"Before?"

"Before eleven."

"Oh, I guess I stayed around the house."

"And helped your mother, didn't you?"

"Yes."

"That's what I was trying to get at. You were the oldest boy and naturally she must have depended upon you. You were a little closer to her than the other fellows, the other children."

"Yes, you can say that. That's true."

"So it was sort of a double shock in the sense that you had no idea what she was doing down at the church?"

"She had sexual intercourse!"

He said this bitterly.

"Yes, I know, but how did she happen to go down there? To meet him or was she working there?"

"No, my mother never worked."

"She just went down to meet him there?"

"I guess so, I don't know."

"She had known him? Had he been around the house?"

"I only saw him once in my house."

"The reason I ask you this I wonder what you thought. How did this happen? You said you had some ideas which were that father, for a while, didn't make much money or drank what he did make."

"Well, you see, now my thinking is different. You know as you're growing older you think differently, more so here with you than I ever did before."

"What do you mean?"

"Really I thought about things from time to time but never as much as I am doing here."

"It's too painful to think of things like that, wouldn't you say?"

The core of all traumatic experiences is the oedipal situation. This means that oedipal longings, jealousies and inadequacy feelings have organized and have superseded all early traumas. This is as true in psychosomatic and psychotic cases as in cases of neurosis. However, in the former, the oedipal elements are more affected and screened by preoedipal elements.

"That's right."

"Sure. What did you think from time to time as you tried to explain to yourself?"

"Well, I just never could explain it to myself."

"That's what I mean. You had all these different ideas and they didn't seem to explain it completely."

"No, none of them."

"What ideas did you have? You said one was because father drank the money up."

"Aw, she just had to go out and, uh, I mean—"

He stopped as if he just could not say it.

"You mean she was that kind of a woman?"

"Yes!"

"She had to go out and have more than one man?"

This was probably *his* trouble based upon chronic mistrust, hyper-sensitivity and vulnerability.

"That's right."

"And you said that you connect this with part of your problem when you got married?"

"Yes, I mean now that I see it more clearly."

"How did you connect that up? I don't get that."

"Well, uh, I mean now I can see where I wouldn't trust my wife because I always had that fear like if she went out with a bunch of girls, or if she went out with her sister, or regardless of where she went, even if she went alone, that's when I'd start thinking about my mother."

"You figured that if she'd cheat, anybody would cheat, huh?"

"That's just about it."

"You mean you don't trust any woman?"

"I guess I don't."

"Still don't?"

"I have to say that. Not that I have to, I mean I say that because really and truly I'm not sure if I do trust a woman or I don't."

"You didn't trust your wife?"

"I think I did and yet I don't."

"But what happened that made you separate?"

"I mean all these things used to build up in me and then I had a habit where, uh, I think it's because of that, I'm not sure, where *I wouldn't stay in the house.* You know what I mean. If I had to go home for supper, I'd want to get right out and, I don't know, just take a walk or something, *just keep going.*"

This was a dramatic admission with hidden meanings that described his bowel behavior as much as personal actions. Running out, keeping going, building up were all parts of the defense against loss and separation and the anxiety building up over the years. He must have been ripe for a prepuberty trauma. In psychoanalytic termi-nology, he had introjected the bad faithless mother and fecalized her and tried to rid himself of her, but the process had failed. As in the story of "The Sorcerer's Apprentice," the aroused demons could not be controlled. In this case the aroused, regressive, infantile gestalts had made him feel more helpless, dependent and mistrustful than ever. Another aspect would deal with the murderous rage which made him want to beat mother the way she beat him and possibly send her away or kill her.

"Just like you did back home with mother?"

"That's right."

"You wanted to keep away from the house?"

"That's right."

"Didn't you want to look at her and see her and be around her?"

"Well no, it wasn't that. It was, I know I tried to figure this one out but, uh, I don't know why but, uh, I could be lying in bed and we could be talking and start to go to sleep and then after a while I'd just get *an urge to get up and get out.* And if an argument would start, I'd just have to get out of the house."

"Did these thoughts interfere with your relations with her?"

"Well sometimes I'd have sexual intercourse and I wouldn't even think of it."

"Wouldn't even think of it, in what way?"

"I mean if I was having sexual intercourse with my wife, sometimes I'd think of an *old girl friend.* I mean that happened, I don't know, a couple of times."

"How come? I mean weren't you particularly interested in her?"

"Well, I don't know whether it was because I was mad at her or what. I don't know. I tried to find a reason for that, too."

It appeared that he couldn't allow himself to become closely involved. The old girl friend must have been a mother figure.

"An old girl friend?"

"Yes, like there was one girl in particular."

"Who was that?"

"Well, that's a girl I went with in Korea, *a nurse.*"

"What will we call her? I mean, just her first name."

"Betty."

"You were in love with her?"

"Yes, we wanted to get married."

"And you mean intercourse with her was better than with your wife or different?"

"Uh, no, I mean, uh, I thought my wife was better than anyone I've ever had."

"Better than Betty?"

"Oh yes."

"And yet you thought about Betty?"

"Yes."

"And you felt that was because you were feeling mad?"

"I don't know. I mean that bothered me. Why would I do that?"

"You mean in spite of the fact that she was good to you and very good in intercourse, you still thought of Betty or some other woman?"

"Well wait a minute. I mean, uh, when I say good I say I thought she was good sexually, but my wife *never wanted it.*"

This meant never wanted *him.* The pregenital anal elements were a disguise. The main fixation was at a phallic oedipal level.

"She never wanted it?"

"No, my wife never cared for it."

"And yet she was good?"

"Well, I mean when I did have it, I don't know. I was *crazy in love* with her and, uh, I don't know. I just don't go to bed with any girl. I mean I'm funny, I really have to like them. I mean some guys can go out and grab anything on the corner or in a bar but, oh, no, I have to know them. I have to like them!"

This would be fine except for the probability that this was a pseudoadult reaction and not a lead from strength. It was more the behavior of the anxious, mistrustful child. He had already admitted that his wife and his mother were confused in his mind. His concept of intercourse had unresolved infantile elements in it.

"When did you first have intercourse?"

"When I was thirteen years old."

"At thirteen? You started so young?"

"I guess so."

"And you were in love then?"

"No, I wouldn't say I was in love. I didn't know what love was."

That was quite true. He was on the run from a mother-child relationship and probably more deeply repressed passive feelings in regard to men (uncles and fathers).

"You mean you—?"

"The girl knew more than I did and I happened to be in the right spot, now that I think of it."

The discovery of mother's affair was a seduction and a prepubertal trauma. He must have run into a precocious affair as an escape—a displacement of sexual interest. Such precocious heterosexual activity usually occurs in conjunction with an avoidance of normal homosexually oriented relationships and their resolution. This can lead to an intensification of unconscious passive-feminine fantasies and the defenses against them, including paranoid feelings.

"So you didn't trust any of them?"

"No."

"Betty, too?"

"Well, no, I can't say I trusted her."

"You thought that—?"

"Oh, I thought everything."

"What do you mean?"

"I just, I don't know, geez I've been trying to figure this out for a long time."

"Yes, I know. I wondered if you thought because she didn't care for intercourse that—"

"Well, uh, if I wanted to go to bed and she didn't want to, and I mean it happened, say, five times that week, and if I wanted to go to bed five times and she said no, well automatically I thought *there was another guy*. I just figured something was wrong. It bothered the hell out of me. And she didn't want kids."

Who was the other guy? An uncle-father figure was in the recent background. At an earlier level, it was another child. More and more it was clear what he was doing when he ate corn and cucumbers (penises) and had many stools (babies). He was acting out a primal-scene relationship fantasy. Being the mother defended him from ever losing her. He might easily have become a homosexual or a paranoid character.

"She didn't want kids?"

"No, and I did. I wanted *a big family*."

Now the therapist could explore his maternal identifications.

"Did you have any?"

"I have two, a boy and a girl."

"You wanted a big family?"

"That's right. I like children."

"You grew up with a lot."

"That's right."

"Did you like to take care of them?"

"I *always did*."

"What do you mean?"

"Well, I used to *change the diapers, washing, wash* the kids and hold them. It never *bothered* me."

Now "the stool was out of the diaper" and the situation was ripe for some tactical work which would prepare the ground for future confrontations.

"To change messy diapers?"

"Yes, well I mean I'd do anything, wash them, anything. It never bothered me. *I liked it!*"

"Did mother let you?"

"Oh sure! In fact my mother would be *in the hospital*. My father would never do it so I used to do it."

Clearly he had played mother in a certain role. This must be slowed down to be fully developed. There was also the repetitive loss problem.

"You mean when mother had her babies?"

"Yes."

"In the hospital, that's what you mean. Was she sick?"

"You see four or five times after my mother had the babies she had to go back to the hospital."

"What for?"

"I don't know."

"What were your ideas?"

"She was just sick, that's all."

"Sick, in what way?"

"Because of the babies."

"Because of the babies?"

This was obviously himself, a sick person because of the stools.

"Yes."

He paused.

"Don't ask me, Doctor, because I don't know."

"But what were your ideas?"

"That's all I know. She was sick. I could say she had a hemorrhage because I know today they could have a hemorrhage or *anything like that*. I mean I *can't* say that because that isn't what I thought."

There are no negatives in the unconscious. Anything like that is a "mess," a "feces hemorrhage." What is the physical mechanism in such a case? We can assume reasonably that what he called "building up" was associated with localized capillary engorgement, increased mucus membrane friability, punctate bleeding and secretory activity. All of this was gradual and at first easily reversed. Then it became "habitual" or "learned" and somewhat autonomous. Secondary complications (ulcers) arose, healed and rose again. We could use a different analogy and speak in terms of a positive feedback. For instance, the bleeding itself could be associated with more anxiety, rage, distrust, etc., and beneath it all an ever-deepening defusion of his libidinal and destructive instincts.

"But you've heard of things now, hemorrhages, bleeding?"

"Yes."

"You knew how babies were born then? You knew about those things?"

"Well, yes, I mean I learned, you know."

It would have been interesting at this point to find out how he learned, but the therapist wanted to return to the fecal babies and time was running out.

"So you being the oldest one, you stayed home and took care of the babies while she was in the hospital?"

"Yes, that's right."

"It never bothered you?"

"No. If I went to your home and you had a baby there, and you were busy and your wife said, 'Would you help me,' I'd change the baby. It doesn't bother me where with other people I know it does."

"What do you mean?"

"I know a lot of people that just can't change a diaper. A lot of guys get married, they have four or five children and yet they never change a diaper. To me that's wrong because *it all goes with the baby. Maybe I'm wrong.*"

This was an admission of a dawning awareness that he had usurped the role of the mother and something was wrong with his masculinity. It was also a realization of a distorted birth theory.

"It goes with the baby?"

"Well, sure, I mean I can't see if you can pick a baby up and love it why can't you just pick it up and help clean it."

"Of all the crap?"

"Of anything."

"What do you mean anything?"

"Well, I mean the eyes, ears, nose, anything."

"Messes?"

"That's right, dirt!"

"I take it you didn't mind cleaning up."

"No, I've always done the dishes. I still do when I go into anyone's home."

"You had a lot to do when you were a kid then, I should think."

"Oh yes."

"Mother was away a lot, huh?"

"Yes, I'd say so, yes, or she couldn't do anything."

"What do you mean?"

"Well, I mean a lot of times she'd be sick."

"Sick in what way?"

"Well after the baby she always seemed to be sick, I don't know what way."

This all fitted in with the role he was playing, the sick mother with the stool babies.

"In what way did she complain, tired, weak?"

"Yes, tired, couldn't get up."

"She'd stay in bed?"

"Yes."

"And then you'd have to take care of things."

"Well, I didn't have to."

"No, but I mean you felt you wanted to?"

"That's right."

"You liked to?"

"That's right."

"You'd cook and do the dishes and clean the messes?"

This was a mistake. He was not interested in this side of a mother.

"Oh, I never cooked."

"You didn't cook? Who did the cooking?"

"The woman next door and my aunt, or someone my father would have come in."

"You cleaned up?"

"That's right."

"The house?"

"That's right."

"A lot of work?"

"I don't think so."

Now it was possible to test the limits, especially his need for masculine identification.

"You didn't mind?"

"No, I told you I didn't mind it."

"I was wondering. I mean wouldn't you rather have been outdoors with the boys?"

"Well, I guess every boy would. I mean if you knew they were playing ball you'd like to go out and play."

"That's right."

"I mean probably sometimes I did mind, but I mean I don't think it really bothered me as much as it would someone else. And I say I don't think, I don't know for sure because I don't know how anyone else would think about it."

He sounded troubled and uncertain.

"You got used to it?"

"Yes, that's true."

"I take it you started very early, when you were a little fellow, to do this. Do you remember? How far back do you remember?"

"Well, say eight or nine years old."

"Then at eight you remember cleaning things?"

"Yes."

"Washing the dishes and taking care of babies at eight?"

"Well, no, helping."

"You were helping mother then?"

"That's right."

"You were interested?"

"Well, I mean I'd watch *the baby*."

"That's what I mean, you were interested in doing things, in helping."

"Yes, that's right."

"Even then?"

"That's right, but I did do the dishes at eight. I don't know how good it was, but I did."

"You didn't change diapers?"

"No, not at eight, or at nine, I can't say that, but around ten or eleven years old, I'd say so, yes. Actually I wasn't around all the time up to ten."

"What do you mean?"

He sighed.

"Well, it started when I was born. I only weighed a pound. I was a seven-or eight-months baby. My mother fell over a chair. So, anyway, she sent me to my grandmother's until I was three. Then I came home. Then, of course, Eva was there. I can remember watching her being taken care of. So you see I was always interested in kids and caring for them."

This material hid a lot of feeling. At the tender age of three, he was in no position to stand by idly and watch a little girl get the mothering he must have longed for. He must have withdrawn, partially at least, and identified with mother as a lost object and the little girl as an envied object.

"And so you came home and found a girl in your place?"

"I wouldn't say in my place. I liked babies. She was having them all the time. I didn't mind. Actually I went back to live with my grandmother right after the hurricane for a year. It was around seven to eight, I think. Anyway by nine or ten I was home and helping with the diapers and keeping things clean."

At this time he was acting like an older daughter rather than a son. This period of his life had to be developed cautiously, as he was suspicious.

"How about when you were with your children, did you take care of them too?"

"That's right."

"She didn't mind?"

"Who, my wife? No, she'd either do it or I would. Like say, for instance, now, uh, I came home from work and she'd have the supper ready and she'd want to go in town. Well, I'd take care of the baby. I'd get it undressed for bed."

"But then you'd wonder?"

"No, not all the time."

"No, but sometimes you wondered what she was doing, huh?"

Here the therapist was trying to get at a memory of the faithless mother by arousing the appropriate emotion.

"That's right and I found I'd wonder more if I drank."

"Tell me, did you ever wonder about mother before this time that you caught her?"

"No!"

"What was wrong with her, what she was doing?"

"No."

"Away in the hospital?"

"No, I knew she was going to have a baby. I mean my father would say 'Your mother's having a baby.' "

Having a baby and making a baby to the child must have had all kinds of deep emotional significance for him, but he would have to deny these feelings at this stage.

"You knew how babies were made then?"

"No, not then, no."

"I wondered what you thought. What did you think? Kids have odd ideas. What did you think?"

"I know I never asked my father."

"Why?"

"I don't know. I just never did. I'd ask the kids on the corner, you know. I remember every baby she had we'd stand outside the window and try to see. Then I'd go up to the hospital. My father would always sneak me in to see the baby."

This fascination with the babies was probably part of the attempt to master the trauma occasioned by his insecurity at three, when he left one mother and home and went to a new one where he had to share the new mother with a baby girl. In all probability the losses of this period, and anxieties as well, were displaced onto his genital. This led to comparison with the "castrated" little sister. His envy of her and wish to be a little girl would be equivalent to a longing to give up his genital as well as his active three-year-old status. The unanswered question was, did he regress temporarily during this period as far as his bowel activity was concerned?

"When is the first time you went?"

"Oh, I think it was my sister Lorna."

"How much younger is Lorna?"

"It was Marlene, Lorna or Marlene."

"How much younger are they?"

"Lorna is three years younger than I am, three, no four!"

"So when you were three and four years old you were already getting introduced to the babies, huh?"

He had left out Eva, so it was possibly even earlier.

"Yes."

"Who took care of you when mother was away?"

"My aunt did. It was my mother's aunt but we always called her our aunt. She was a terrific person."

"She was?"

"That's right, the best in my life."

He had had three mothers. The aunt was for him the all-good, nonsexual mother. Now the interview was drawing to a close and there was more to be learned about the present time.

"So you wanted a large family? You liked babies and you wanted to have more than two?"

"That's right. First of all I couldn't see having a kid, having a baby three or four years apart like she wanted it, and I couldn't see it."

"How close did you want them?"

"I, I figure two years is perfect. I figured you could give it all the love and care and by the time another came up my wife would be rested and everything would be all right."

"How come you separated? What happened?"

"Well, uh, I started working two or three jobs. I just used to stay out of the house. I realize that now."

"Just like at home?"

"That's right."

"Why were you staying out then?"

He described how his wife grew lonely and they would fight, holler and argue like father and mother. They were always fighting about money, food, and kids. He and his wife had separated thirteen or fourteen months ago. He had been going with a nurse for the past three months and felt that he trusted her more than any woman he had ever known. He understood *her*. Since he had met her, he had stopped seeing his mother but still thought of her. Whenever he had visited her, he would sit down, get *restless* and have to get up and leave.

He was repeating again the traumas of the past. The first two times he had been sent away. The third time he had run out himself.

"Restless?"

"That's right."

"Is that what you mean by this nervous feeling?"

"And I'm not way up here in my head as much as in my stomach. I feel shaky in my stomach. Then I get cramps. Sometimes they are so bad I have to lie down and draw up my legs. Then again I get up and walk around."

"So then in a way your runs began the first time when you went in the service, when you left home? It was your first time away from home?"

"Yes, that's right, it was the first time."

"Did you miss her when you were in the service?"

"I missed my family when I first went in but after that, no, I really liked the service. In fact, to this day I'm sorry I ever got out because I did like the Army."

"In spite of the runs?"

"That's right."

Only a part of his ego was involved. His symptoms had spared him depression and separation anxiety.

"They didn't bother you too much?"

"Oh, I had them. It got so that I had them so often I just took it as it came."

"Did you write, when you were in the service, to home?"

"Oh, I did at first and then, uh, I quit writing."

"To whom?"

"My mother, my sisters."

"Not to father?"

"I wrote to my father and he was never good at writing."

"He never answered?"

"Only once and that was for money and I sent him the money, but I never wrote him a letter."

In one sense, he was producing for father like a mother, but the problem had to be approached lightly.

"Were you as close to him as you were to mother?"

"I think I was pretty close to my father."

"You were?"

"Yes, because I used to work with him before I went into the service."

"Doing what?"

"Well, he had the bookie joint and I had a fruit and vegetable stand of my own in the front of the variety store, and I did pretty well with it."

"He did the booking and you handled the store?"

"I handled the store."

"You handled the front and he handled the rear?"

"That's right."

"And you did well with that?"

"Yes, I did very well. I liked it very much. I bought my own fruit and vegetables, my own car."

"How old were you when you started working on the fruit and vegetables?"

"I think I was sixteen."

"Sixteen?"

"Yes, say fifteen and a half or sixteen when I started my own fruit and vegetable stand."

"So it was after you left home because, as you said, it was at eleven that you found mother and you said after that you started staying away from home. Then later, because she beat you up, you really started staying away from home, and it was then that you ran out and stayed with your father."

"That's right."

"Then you worked the store?"

"That's right."

"But you were always thinking about home and the babies, I take it?"

"Uh, yes, I mean, oh, it was a tough thing wanting to go home and yet you didn't."

"You wanted to go home and see the babies, help to take care of them and do the stuff that you were interested in?"

"Well they used to come down to the fruit stand and I'd see them and take them downtown."

"But it wasn't the same?"

"No."

"Mother had to clean the house, take care of the babies herself from then on, eh?"

"That's right."

"Did she ever miss you?"

"I don't know. I never asked her."

"You never could talk to her after that, huh?"

"No, my father couldn't either."

"There was sort of a wall between you?"

"That's right. My father's dead now."

"When did he die?"

"Two years ago last July."

"And mother, how is she now?"

"She's all right. I never see her. I mean if she ever wants anything I always make sure she gets it."

"How does she let you know?"

"Oh, somebody will call me or she will."

"She does call you?"

"Well this is the first time that she's actually called and the only reason why she called, it was very short, was that this very good friend of mine died and she said that I should make the wake."

"There is still that barrier between you, huh?"

"That's right."

"You've never forgiven her for her affair with the uncle and she's never forgiven you for threatening to blackmail her?"

"I don't know about that."

"What do you mean?"

"I mean I don't know if that's so or not."

"You don't know, but what do you think?"

"I don't know. I know she, uh, was always constantly asking my wife why I never went over to the house."

"She had forgotten?"

"I guess so."

"But not you?"

"But I, never! I don't forget easy."

"Do you think you'll ever forgive her?"

"I tried but I can't."

"Why?"

"I don't know."

"You don't know?"

"I mean I understand people do it—"

"What ideas do you have?"

"Ideas? I don't have any of those. I keep asking myself, why do you constantly think about it? And I do!"

"All the time?"

This was the key to everything. The preoccupation with the mother

of therapy in connection with various aspects of the positive side of his oedipal relationships with the mother. The really troublesome problems, however, were the negative oedipal wishes or those concerned with father and the men.

"Just go and drink with her?"

"Yes."

"And you never go to bed with her?"

"No. I went once."

"You went once?"

"That's right. I just don't care to."

"You mean you just don't care for her?"

"Not that way, no, but she is good company otherwise."

"How do you mean?"

"Well, she really is a nice person to talk to or go out with, and I guess I was fascinated when I first went up there. She was a call girl but I never dreamed she was one."

"Why? What do you mean?"

"I just never figured her for one. As a matter of fact, I didn't believe it until I saw her with a guy and she told me."

This theme could have been developed as it was obviously a repeat of the incident with mother, but it was time to end the interview.

"But she likes you?"

"Yes, she does."

"And you go and visit her?"

"Once in a while."

"And drink with her?"

"That's right."

"But no sex?"

"No. I did once, that's all. I mean she can't understand why but she never asks. I mean you know that she can't figure it out. She'd make a comment every once in a while. 'You're very unusual. Any guy I ever went with had to get a little bit off me, but you don't. You don't give a God damn.' And I told her, 'Oh, well, that's just the way I am.' I'd just drop it like that. In fact I know an awful lot through her, you know, because other call girls come up to the apartment. I could go out with these girls. I get along pretty good with them."

"Why do you think they are call girls?"

"Well, I know the guys that hang around and live with them."

Now he was ripe for the type of juxtaposition of material that is called a confrontation.

"The reason I ask you this is because you say the money trouble that father had led to it all, and I wondered if you thought mother was going with uncle to get money."

"I don't know. I can't say that."

"But you thought that?"

"I did think of that, yes!"

"That's what I mean, that she wasn't getting enough at home, and I don't mean sex. I mean money, because you knew that she was having so many children that she certainly was getting all the sex at home."

His physical symptoms were probably multidetermined and a defense against feelings of inadequacy concerning his earning capacity as a man. In another sense his many stools could be looked upon as his being more productive than father.

"Well, that's why I blame him for that."

"You saw in a way, or you must have thought that if he had made enough money and had given it to her, then maybe she wouldn't have had to go out, huh?"

"That's right."

"And this is why you worked so hard. You worked three jobs, you said."

"That's right."

"Well, suppose we see each other the same time on Friday."

"That's all right by me. Thanks a lot, doctor."

There are many ways in which we could compare this patient with the one with the peptic ulcer. Both were the first born of a large family. Both of them had mother problems. They had "lost" a favored relationship with her which was vitally connected with their infantile narcissistic needs, feelings of ego integrity and physical intactness. They had attempted to regain these vital needs in part by becoming independent, in part by turning toward the father and in part by deep unconscious identifications with the mother, manifested chiefly by alterations in the body image. This had repercussions in the area of physiological responses. Why did one patient choose the upper part of the gastrointestinal tract and the other the lower portion? One became a milkman and a kind of phallic mother who fed himself with unlimited supplies of milk and cream and made lots of

in age, attitude and outlook. The peptic ulcer sufferer was an older man whose personal relationships were minimal. He appeared to have given up. The prognosis was dubious and the most that could be hoped for his future was a stabilization at a nonovert homosexual relationship with the boys, in which he could bowl and drink. The man with the colitis was much younger and better able to relate to persons. In this sense he was more trusting of his ability to love and be loved. More outlets for his instinctual needs could then become available. He also appeared to have acquired insights by means of a type of introspection that was mostly lacking in the other case. The main area where information was lacking was in respect to men. He talked of shaking while working and the danger of touching. This area might have led to his relationships with men and his concept of himself as a man. His attachments to and preoccupations with women and mother were in a large part a defensive retreat from longings for a relationship with men which, because of their infantile narcissistic nature, were highly sexualized. He needed to complete his development in an area that had been largely by-passed. In the therapy situation we would have to expand the area in which he talked about his longings to go out and play with the boys, and interpret in a tactful manner, and in terms of the past, his anxiety-laden needs for male friends. This would probably be disguised, hidden and displaced to other areas. In connection with this we could develop the theme of his disappointment in his father and his two-timing uncle. Whenever the subject of his relationships with men became too hot to handle, we could let him talk about his relationships with mother and the good aunt or his wife and the nurses. This type of situation would be revealed by a growing negativism, disinclination to talk, manifest hostility and persecutory fantasies. We should expect him to be depressed and not be in a hurry to relieve his depression. These are necessary concomitants of the working through of insight. If they become extreme, antidepressant medication may be necessary. This often requires a great deal of experimentation. In cases where the somatic symptoms become potentially dangerous, we should refer the patient to an internist. While this will give rise to a certain class of problems, they will be of less serious magnitude than when the therapist acts the role of the internist himself. Problems cannot be avoided in any type of psychotherapy, and are especially complex in cases of psychosomatic illness. We must, above all, be careful not to be overoptimistic about the immediate effects of our therapeutic endeavors upon the persistence of chronic physical symptoms. In an ordinary uncomplicated case, when we develop the personal and self-relations, those with the body subside into the background and may not even be mentioned for long periods. In terms of the interview situation, the words used to describe the physical state have to be treated as having double meanings. In this case the words "runs" and "pains" stood out. In running out he was identifying not only with the bad mother who ran around, but also with the bad father who ran out on mother and on him. As in so many cases, the emotional climate of this household, where there was "always fighting," was the main problem inasmuch as it furnished a soil that nourished his pathological identifications and neurotic solutions to his problem.

maintain denial. Because of the denial, the original grief, angry yearning and guilt affects cannot be worked through. This does not allow the patient to become completely reconciled to his loss, rid himself of the old object and turn to a new love interest. It does not permit a healthy return to reality, a lessening of withdrawal and acting out, and a reversal of the dissociative process.

Actual loss of the mother or father should not be considered the only cause of pathological mourning, although it often initiates it. The loss of infantile feelings of love, omnipotence and trust in the environment can occur gradually because of sickness, accidents and chronic neglect. Turning away from persons to the self and the body is characteristic of the withdrawal and detachment reaction; i.e., pathological mourning leads to the consideration of pathological narcissism.

A basic problem of all patients, which is of special importance and severity in borderlines, is that of narcissistic sensitivity and vulnerability. This refers mainly to the area of self-regard or the superego's attitude towards the self-image. Of major importance is the discrepancy between the existent self-images and the ego ideals or idealized images of the self. When the analyst talks about pathological narcissism, he is not talking merely about self-love or self-regard; these qualities are an important and an essential part of everyone's personality. In order to understand the structure of pathological narcissism, we will consider a simplified hypothetical case showing the relationship of pathological narcissism to loss, its denial, pathological mourning and ego dissociation.

A child during the period from approximately six months to six years loses his mother in one way or another for a period of weeks or months. At this time of life he is especially vulnerable and reacts at first with grief, fright, and "angry yearning," and finally with withdrawal and fantasy formation. A pathological mourning characterized by a denial of the loss and a splitting or dissociation of the ego may occur. In this case, he apparently recovers and appears changed by the time the mother returns. The following symptoms may then indicate that a personality change has occurred, i.e., that he has withdrawn and has already begun to act out:

1. He may act more self-sufficient but may occasionally appear withdrawn. He isolates himself from other children or behaves in an antisocial manner. The mother may be ignored. There may be an indifference to affectionate gestures from the mother. At times such gestures may be accepted mechanically or with sugary affectation.

2. He may be neither trusting nor trustworthy in behavior, and steal, lie, run away, etc., depending on his age or the type of acting out.

3. He turns his main interest from his mother to himself and things, including toys and parts of his body, especially his genital.

4. Although he apparently neither wishes nor gives affection, he is hypersensitive to slights in this area.

5. He is able to and does deny large segments of reality, especially in the area of other persons' feelings and behavior, in the service of preserving certain omnipotent feelings, wishes and expectations.

All of these reactions and qualities are relative and gradual in development. They are related to the withdrawal process and need some explanation and expansion of details. The self-sufficiency is in many ways a pseudo self-sufficiency because the child has turned away from people to himself. In some distorted manner, he has identified with and taken over the function of the faithless mother or lost object himself. In the case of the mother, the most common way this is done is for the child prematurely to invest his genital with great interest and sensation and give it the sensual attention he once longed for from mother; i.e., he masturbates. Other areas or parts of the body, a doll, toy, or an associated act such as being tied up or beaten, another child, or an associated subject such as music may be substituted in part or in toto in this masturbatory relation to the penis. The basic lack of trust in the mother easily leads to a lack of trust in himself, as the ego of the child and his mother at this stage of growth are symbiotically related. He may neither expect nor give any quarter in this area of trust and honesty, and develop a pragmatic ethical system usually based upon animal cunning plus a shrewd ability to size up a situation and its possibilities. His lack of belief in himself and lack of any well-organized system of values leads to exaggerated longings as well as to basic suspicions and cynical feelings concerning his fate or luck. Because of a faulty and arrested development of the superego and reality testing, he is a prey to primitive wishes, hopes, fears and fancies. The adult superego is a comfort and refuge in times of trouble as well as a restraining influence. The lack of its development or its deformation, therefore, creates many possible serious states of danger, especially in the field of social situations and judgments. The hypersensitivity of the narcissistic character is of tremendous importance. It is tied up with shameful anticipatory and exhibitionistic anxieties over being unable to control himself and the world around him, as well as with the above-mentioned superego deformation. Control and regulation are important functions

narcissism leads to a faulty development of the ego ideal and the entire relationship of the ego to the superego. Reality awareness and the ego ideal originate from the earliest and deepest frustrations of the child's needs. The hope and expectation or despair of attaining the ego ideal is of enormous importance in the pathology of the borderline case. Just as the superego threatens with a stick, the ego ideal entices with a carrot. To a degree the superego represents the punishing and usually fatherly portion of the introjected parents, and the ego ideal the rewarding and usually motherly portion. When the ego "dwells apart" from its ideal, or the incorporated ideal is primitive and unrealistic, anxiety usually develops along with regressive efforts to evade it. Premature *ego* development is apparently associated with the obsessive character, and it may be that premature *superego* and *ego ideal* development is associated with the development of hysterical and narcissistic characters. Such characters require a thorough analysis of their narcissistic as well as their libidinal needs, inhibitions and defenses in order to help resolve their symptoms and problems. The main effect of a premature development of the superego and ego ideal is found in the harshness of the former and the seductiveness of the latter. Indeed, pathological narcissism in a child is frequently associated with such contrasting qualities in the parents. It is also associated with a weak tie to the male parent which ultimately leads to a weak tie with reality. Thus, in a reality sense, the superego can be portrayed by the father and the ego ideal by the mother. The ego ideal develops from the original narcissism and megalomania which allowed the child to feel self-sufficient. This narcissism is founded on an early and uninterrupted symbiotic relationship with the mother, and it is the interruption in this early relationship that produces withdrawal and pathological narcissism. Part of the pathology can be described as a failure of development of introspective and empathetic abilities to the extent that the ego, superego and ego ideal work in harmony and in tune with realistic perspectives. In this sense there may be either an abandonment of introspection and a turning to the external world and acting out of conflicts, or a withdrawal to an inner world of unchecked fantasy. Usually the two processes alternate or occur mixed together. The ability to relinquish characteristic attitudes associated with infantile feelings of omnipotence is only accomplished with much practice and always with great reluctance. In therapy or analysis the abandonment of withdrawal is associated with the revival of infantile gestalts laden with rage, depression and apathy. This may lead to failure and withdrawal of interest in therapy, or to a stalemate or an extremely long working-through process.

The pathology of narcissism, empathy and the relationship of the ego to the superego and ego ideal are intimately linked with the handling of homosexual libidinal components of the personality. The ego ideal is an aspect of the self image; therefore, the guilt and dissatisfaction which arise from the nonfulfillment of the ego ideal lead to ungratified homosexual longings, frustration and rage which are then transformed into an increased sense of guilt. This often manifests itself as social anxiety. Borderline personalities usually are unable to achieve a satisfactory expression of love and sexual impulses owing to the persistence of primitive attitudes and anxieties concerning intimacy. Attempts at intimacy are associated with a rekindling of the old conflicts that first of all led to the original loss and withdrawal. Often there are lifelong ineffectual and narcissistically injurious efforts to re-enact the original struggle in hopes of a better solution.

The role of the phallus, real or imaginary, as the substitute for the lost mother cannot be stressed too much. Narcissism is above all *phallic* in character. In some cases regression and displacement can easily distort and disguise this situation. In large measure the narcissistic character has become the mother, and the phallus the child. The early mother-child relationship can easily be reconstructed in terms of the sexual problems that are always present. As might be expected, castration anxiety is more intense than in the case of the neuroses where narcissism and withdrawal play a lesser and more ego-alien role. The social sensitivity of the narcissistic character is to a large extent based on *exhibiting* his defective genital or its substitute by displacement. He is easily hurt by comparisons with others. The voice, the head, the intellect, any part of the body may substitute for the phallus. In psychosomatic disease, an entire organ system is often involved. Such cases are primarily narcissistic in pathology. Because of the importance of the inadequate phallus, one can always find a secret defect, physical or mental, etc. The unmastered loss of the mother is the usual unresolved narcissistic injury. Eventually it leads to a compensating ego inflation, heightened aggressiveness and revenge fantasies. Omnipotent feelings based on illusory identification with a primitive mother image are no substitute for the feelings of self-sufficiency that, in the normal person, reveal an ego united with the ego ideal and supported by the superego.

In all neurotic and borderline cases it is characteristic for the patient

me back. I told her I wouldn't see the woman any more or anything else."

To the therapist it was obvious that he had a mother problem. This was probably why he was so intent on protecting the children from leaving the mother.

"To protect the children?"

"To protect the woman's children."

"That's what I mean."

"So she could keep them, yes."

"You wanted to protect them?"

"That's right."

"How's that?"

"Well, I mean, when I met her I didn't tell her I was married or anything else. I mean she found out I was married later."

He laughed mockingly as if disgusted with himself.

"She found out I was married later and I felt guilty. I mean, I don't know, I, she never asked me but if she had asked me I probably would have told her I was married. I lived *like a single man. I went out* any time I felt like it. There was no way she could tell I was married. And then when she found out I was married, uh, well *she's still in love with me* even now. She calls me up every once in a while. I mean I, she says she's in love with me or *maybe she just wants a man.*"

He had wanted to protect the children from losing their mother. He was protected from losses by acting "single." This meant not attached to anyone. In reality he was a mother's boy who was unable to trust her or any woman. He denied this by reversing the thought to "*she's still in love with me.*" It was he who just wanted a "mother."

"You say you lived like a single man?"

"I did. I don't now."

"But I don't understand, so you lived like a single man. Your marriage started to break up right after you married her. You started drifting apart, you said. How come?"

"Well, the first year of our marriage was good. We were both in the service together and, uh, she was a WAVE and I was a sailor *nine months.* And then she was discharged ahead of me, about two weeks ahead of me and, uh, I started looking for company then. mean right after I was married. And I didn't make out with one but I tried. I mean, you know, I actually tried."

"Right after you were married?"

"About *nine months* after."

The therapist noted all the references to nine. They emphasized the baby-mother problem. All such numbers have both an approximate numerical value and a symbolic value. Often they refer to significant ages.

"You mean when she—"

"When she came up here to be discharged. I was *left* in New London for a week or two, or something, I forget. But I was *left so many days* after she was discharged and I went around, and I wanted company and I went out and I met this girl."

Being abandoned, lonely and depressed was the problem.

"Were you lonely?"

"Well I don't, I guess I was *lonely*; I don't like to be *left alone.*"

It was important to pick up this admission.

"Really?"

"At times I do."

"How do you mean?"

"I mean when it's raining I like to walk around in the rain. I enjoy having the rain come down on me, I mean, and sometimes I'd want to get off by myself. I wouldn't want anybody around me!"

First he had to show that he was really independent.

"Were you always that way?"

"Yes, when I was a kid I used to bum on the road. I used to bum and I used to, just to get away from home. *I came from a big family.*"

There are different ways of losing a mother. Having her monopolized by siblings is one of them.

"How do you mean? How big?"

"Ten."

"Ten?"

"Six girls, no six boys and four girls."

Why the confusion in sexes? It would be useless to pick up this minor slip now.

"How many?"

"Six boys and four girls."

"Which one were you?"

"I was the fourth from the oldest; two girls and a brother are older."

"Two girls and then a brother? Then you?"

"Then me."

"Then six more?"

"Yes. And I get fouled up. I don't know too much about my family. It's an awful thing to say but I, I, I can't quite remember

"No, I don't remember. I mean I *might have been*, but I remember my father before I went in the hospital he told me to be a good boy, and I remember that I used to dream. I was up on a high, I don't know what it was, but it was like a *chimney* and it was bricks. I was walking around and I could hear *drums* on either side of me. And, uh, I heard my grandmother calling me. And they said I was ready to die. They gave me everything when I came out of ether. That was the time they didn't give you milk and ice cream and all that stuff. They *gave me anything I asked for* because they figured it was, I was going to die and for *five days* I just lay like I was dead, didn't care about anything. I was throwing up and then I got worse and they cut me open again and then I almost died again when they cut me open the second time. Well, when they took me to the hospital, they didn't even wash me. They rushed me right into the operating room. They might have, after they put me under, washed me."

This had all the qualities of a traumatic experience. He had been passively overwhelmed. The dream referred to a phallic symbol. The hospital experience probably consolidated the withdrawal and active, phallic, narcissistic fixation as a defense against passivity and castration fears.

"You can remember?"

"I can remember them taking me from the ambulance right on in. My father was running around beside it saying, 'Be a good boy, be a good boy; don't cry.' I *didn't want to go* to the hospital."

This had been one time he had not wanted to leave.

"You didn't?"

"Oh, I *cried.*"

"Really!"

"Oh, I didn't want to go."

"You didn't want to leave home?"

"That's for sure. That time I didn't *now that I think of it* because I was in great *pain*, I mean I couldn't *eat*, I couldn't *laugh*. I knew I was sick and the *doctor* came one day and I told him, 'I'm all right, I'm all right,' so he said 'Well, if you feel better in the morning, you'll be all right.' And he came the next morning and he looked at me and he said, 'This *man*, this boy has to be rushed to the hospital' and he called an ambulance. I guess I was just about gone then, I don't know. And my sisters cried."

He had showed his character then—full of denial and reaction formation. The slip about the man showed how much the present was mixed with the past.

"You cried?"

"No, I wouldn't cry. I swear. At that age I used to swear *every time I got a pain.* I'd start cussing. I'd bite my lip. In fact my lips were painful."

"You mean you had had *pains* before?"

"No, at that time I mean. Oh, I had the pains—"

"You say you used to cuss when you had *pains.* What do you mean?"

"All the time I was, for two weeks I had had *pains.* A *kid had jumped on my stomach.* That's how it happened, I think. I mean I don't know but two weeks before I was *fighting* with a guy and he jumped on my stomach, you know, cowboys and Indians, and I wouldn't tell my mother because I wasn't supposed *to fight.*"

He laughed amusedly. This was an important screen memory, probably connected with infantile homosexual, sadomasochistic theories about babies and intercourse. He also gave away the mother's boy sissy part of himself that he was also running away from.

"You weren't supposed to fight?"

"No. She didn't like me fighting, roughnecking."

"She was afraid you would be a roughneck?"

"Probably, I don't know, But I mean, as I say, after I came out I was always rough and tough. I traveled with this *guy.* I mean I, I was basically no good. That's basically what I think was wrong with my wife and me. I mean deep down inside I feel my wife is *too good for me.* I really do. Although she comes from the same type of family as I do, she's different. She reads and I don't know. I, in fact I thanked her for being my wife at times. I mean I, I, I *feel guilty.* I think she could have got so much better. That's exactly the way I feel inside."

This too was a reaction formation that allowed him to preserve his infantile megalomania and claims to special privileges. His real guilt concerned his past and his mother love and hate, not to mention his passive homosexual tendencies and failure to live up to his ideal of becoming a doctor. It was this ideal that was too good for him!

"Why? I don't understand. What do you mean?"

"What am I? I'm nothing. I mean I'm a first-class gunner's mate in the Navy. Is that anything? I mean that's the way I feel. I'm, she probably could have got somebody with an education."

"You mean a *doctor?*"

At fourteen, as a pubertal boy, he was panicked by his own ideas of what a man had to do sexually and competitively, and perhaps toyed with the idea of how nice it would be to be a girl.

"Even when you were fourteen?"

"Even when I was fourteen."

"You were afraid of being a sissy?"

"When I was sixteen, I remember we used to fix these lights in the theatre, and you know how high theatres are. I was assistant manager, and all the other guys were afraid. I was scared too, and I went up on a straight *ladder* and they held it at the bottom, about *five guys* held it at the bottom. I went up it but I was scared. But I wouldn't show them I was afraid, fix the lights, you know, when they'd burn out. I told them, 'Ah, you sissies,' but deep down inside I was just as afraid as they were."

Here it was necessary to ask, "Why *five* guys?" They probably symbolized the five fingers of his hand. Now we can remember the dream of the chimney. Most likely he had chronic masturbatory fantasies about being a daredevil hero. In the service, masturbation is often referred to as an affair with the Widow Thumb and her four daughters.

"You were afraid that you were a sissy then?"

"I was afraid that they would think that I was afraid, and I wanted to be thought brave."

"But that's what I mean. You called them sissies but you knew you were afraid, so you must have thought you, too, were a sissy, underneath!"

"That's right. I told them, 'Ah, nothing to it,' see?"

"That's what I mean, but you really were afraid you were a sissy?"

"I was afraid that they would think that I was the same as them, see, and I didn't want them to think that I was the same as them."

"Did you think you were a sissy?"

"Not when I conquered it, not when I went up. I mean I had to prove to myself, you know. Did I do it?"

"That you weren't a sissy?"

"That's right, because I was scared."

Now it was possible to return to the mother-child relationship for more information and testing.

"What do you mean by a sissy? Do you mean a mama's boy?"

"Not a sissy, uh, *afraid of something*. I mean, I can't explain it. I, uh, I just don't like to be *afraid of anything*. When I get *mad*, I *cry* and I don't know what I'm doing. I really don't. I go out of my head.

I mean that's the only time I'm not *normal*, when I really get *mad*. I say things. I've hit prople when I didn't even know that I hit them. Never in my life did I ever hit *her*. I almost did once and I hit the table instead because I realized what I was doing. And, uh, I just lose my head. And once aboard ship a colored fellow called me some names. Oh, normally it wouldn't bother me, but I was tired and everything else, and I told him, 'Smile when you say that,' and he said, 'I say it twice,' and it took about two guys to pull me off of him. I was going to kill him. Then he told me he'd get me when we went ashore and I knew *if I waited*, and *I thought about it, I'd be afraid*. So I says, 'Come on, we'll go right now.' He said, 'You don't have any liberty,' and I said, 'I'll make it,' and I just walked off the ship. And he says, 'Let's you and I be friends.' And we were friends from then on. He told me he'd get me with a knife."

He laughed and continued.

"And right now when I'm mad I want to take care of things myself. I'll take care of myself, you know."

He laughed again. The meaning of the impulsive behavior was apparent. Accordingly he might be afraid of sex and women because of sadomasochistic fantasies.

"What do you mean?"

"Well, I figured that if I was mad enough I wouldn't care if he came at me with a knife."

There was a chance that this experience had awakened old anxieties.

"You had already had a knife stuck in you twice."

"Well, that was a doctor. I mean they knew what they were doing."

He laughed uneasily.

"You didn't mind the doctor sticking the knife into you?"

"Oh, I don't mind a doctor at all. In fact I had myself recut open in the Navy too. They said I had an inguinal hernia, and they recut the scar. It doesn't bother me. Hospitals don't bother me!"

"How did you find out you had the hernia? What did it mean to you?"

"Well, my, my side *bothered* me and I used to get a *bulge* and, in one spot."

"Your side bulged? How?"

Operations and illnesses are convenient fantasy hideouts.

He said that when he got tired his right side would hang lower than his left, which sounded as if he were talking about his testicles. They operated on him for his pains—a hernia, they said. This was at

"Used to? When was that? You mean before you married?"

"That was before I had this Betty and it was, all our married life it was just me being satisfied. *She wasn't being satisfied.* Why she stuck with me, I don't know. I really don't know, except that I *worked hard* and I *gave her everything.* I mean I did, I, when I got out of the service, I was working fourteen or fifteen hours a day, so that she could have things. We lived with her mother and, uh, I used to leave at six o'clock in the morning and I wouldn't get home until twelve o'clock at night sometimes, and I mean it was a tough grind on me for a year. Then they, I heard they were taking station keepers at Edgerly and I got that. It was a little less money and I was, I was pretty tired. I mean I was pretty well worked out. I'm just *a little fellow.* I'm not a big guy, and I get tired easy, so I went there."

He must have been extremely competitive, and continually comparing himself with his siblings as well as identifying with an inadequate father. This could be made partly conscious.

"How tall are you?"

"Five eleven, when I stand up. When I slouch, I'm about five nine or nine and a half. But actually being measured for height I'm five eleven. I'm thin. I weigh, now I weigh one hundred forty-five but up until three years ago, I know three years ago I weighed one hundred twenty-eight pounds."

"Three years ago?"

"Because I boxed at a smoker at the station and that's what I weighed, one hundred twenty-eight pounds! No! I weighed one hundred twenty-six and they said I weighed one hundred twenty-eight one day because a guy was one hundred thirty-six that I was fighting. That's right! One hundred twenty-six!"

"You were always a little fellow?"

"I was always thin, wiry, strong. I was always strong!"

"Were you bigger than your brothers?"

"Bigger! I had a brother that was about five foot nine but I guess he weighs a hundred eighty-five or a hundred ninety, my older brother, and I've got another brother, Al, and he weighs about one hundred sixty. He's about my height. And another brother, Fred, he's about five foot nine or ten and he weighs about a hundred sixty-five. I mean they're pretty big."

"You were the littlest?"

"Thinnest! I'm tall but thinnest, more or less."

"That's what you mean by big and little?"

"Yes. I mean frail, you know? Everybody thinks I'm frail until they tangle with me. Dynamite comes in small packages!"

He laughed.

"Did your brothers tangle with you?"

"Well, only once did I ever really fight with my brother, my brother Dick, my older brother, and I was just a kid. He was picking on me."

"How do you mean? How old as a kid?"

"I don't even remember. I think I was about *nine*. I don't even remember really, and I was in a candy store and he was picking on me, and I hauled off and I only hit him once but his nose started bleeding."

He laughed and continued.

"And I didn't stop running for *nine* or ten blocks."

He laughed uproariously.

"I took off. He went after me for a while but I didn't stop running until ten blocks and he never caught me."

The therapist continued to test his and his brothers' relationship to the mother. He ate as much as his brothers but used up the food in nervous energy. By nervous, he meant his hands shook. Mother was a poor cook. His wife was much better. She was also good in bed. It was all his fault but he just knew she wasn't satisfied. He suspected she "wanted it all the time." He would test her. It was obvious that he was projecting his own insatiability onto his wife. He was chronically starved for the sexual contacts and sensuous masturbatory feelings that took the place of tender, intimate, personal relationships which he could not endure. These might make him cry and rage, feel guilty, or be depressed. With the barroom women, like Martha, he felt safe and very sexy in an unanxious manner. He was also more potent and suffered less from ejaculatio praecox with these women. He always felt challenged by these women, and at times wondered about the other men in their lives. This was an important area for another interview. The interview continued as follows. He had just remarked that his mother had continually called him a "leech." This described his oral insatiability well and also showed that his relationship to mother wasn't as simple as he described it.

"She did?"

"I can get anything out of anybody. I get on them and they can be mad at me at first but in time they have to like me."

This exemplified his feelings of omnipotence and infantile magic.

"A leech?"

North Carolina and travel with a carnival. She didn't like it but she didn't dare tell me not to because she knew I'd run away."

"You'd run away before?"

"Well, when I was sixteen, I quit school and I just took off."

"The first time you ran away?"

"Well, I'd go away for a few days. I'd go over to Beach City and stay there."

"You mean before you left school?"

"When I was sixteen. When I quit school."

"I mean when you used to go away to Beach City?"

"I was in high school. On weekends I used to go over to Beach City, and I used to belong to the *Drum* and *Bugle* Corps and I could stay at this guy's house. I could stay there."

This tied up with the dream of the chimney and referred to his phallic displacements and attempts to master his castration anxieties and anticipated losses.

"And mamma was worried? Because you were puny?"

"I don't know whether she was worried because I was puny but she always babied me. I can't explain it."

"She always babied you how?"

"Well, anything I said was all right because she was afraid that I would, you know, go off or do something."

He acted out not only to master anxieties but also for the secondary gains and perquisites.

"Run away?"

"Yes. I'd tell her, 'I'll see you. I'll see you in a week or so.' "

"Had you run away before?"

"To Beach City."

"When was that? The first time you ran away?"

"Ohhh, fourteen, fifteen, fourteen, I don't know. I don't even remember when I did it. I remember I used to go on weekends. I used to stay at this other fellow's house. He was an *only child*."

This was what he wanted to be so badly.

"You mean she thought you were puny and babied you, but at the same time she got mad at you and thought you were a leech, and accused you of taking money?"

"No. She never accused me of taking money or anything. Oh, well, borrowing."

"That's what I mean."

"But, when I was young, I never did. It was just when I went in the service that I started wanting money. *I never had enough!*"

Money was an obvious substitute for the other things he never got enough of from mother.

"But you said she began to baby you right after the operation."

"Yes. But I don't mean in the money matters."

"How did she baby you then?"

"Well, she'd give me, probably *extra food*. When the other kids wanted chow, she'd say fix your own. If I came in, she'd fix it for me."

"Special foods?"

"Well not special."

"Special care?"

"Special care. She always did and *I came to expect it*."

"Did you eat it?"

"*Half* the time, yes, *half* the time, no."

This showed his ambivalence over being mother's baby or like the brothers.

"Really?"

"That's right. If I didn't feel like eating, it's the same way now, if I don't feel like eating, I don't feel like eating. If there's something I don't like, I'd rather go hungry than eat it. If they had oleo, I always had oleo at home. We came from a big family and naturally, I won't eat oleo. I used to go without bread or anything, when I got mad I went without bread. Now I won't have anything but butter on my bread. My wife cooks with oleo, fries and things like that but on my bread I have to have butter. Same way with stewed chicken, I won't eat stewed chicken. I got *fed up* with it. Lobster! I'll eat lobster any time she'll give it to me because I enjoy it."

"Fed up? How do you mean?"

"My mother! Well at the time, as I said, I never thought of it. Now when I look back, no, she wasn't really a good cook. I mean in comparison with my wife, but at that time that was probably why I liked to go to other people's houses and eat there, because it was more attractive. To us it was put out there and that was it, you know, eat it!"

"So mother took care of you and gave you special attention but you still, in spite of it, were always lonely, you said. You went out and walked in the rain."

"Yes. I remember once I was going to Beach City. It was cold. It was actually hailing, and the rain was actually cutting into my face and I could feel it, and I actually enjoyed it, believe it or not. It was actually hurting me. It was stinging me, yet while I was walking I was thinking, this is fun. I was dressed for it."

In this situation he could safely feel like an inadequate boy.

"Were you cold?"

"No, I was dressed for it. I didn't like being stung. I mean I was covered up like this."

He put his arms over his head.

"But it was fun. I mean I was doing something. I was braving something."

"Not being a sissy, or puny, or weak?"

"I guess that's it. Basically I don't want to be weak."

"Were you always afraid of being mamma's boy?"

"That's it. Basically that's probably it."

"Not a man, like your big brothers who were so heavy?"

"Well, I was as good as any of them. I can take them on or anything, I mean if they want to fight or something. Like my brother Bob. Supposedly he had a heart condition. He wasn't, he couldn't go in the service or something, heart murmur or something, and he came up, he was a big guy, and he probably could hurt me, I mean even though he's younger than me. I mean you have to face facts. So he started messing around and I told him, 'Don't mess around.' He kept messing around until he got on my nerves."

"What do you mean, messing around?"

"Oh, he kept pumping me, 'Come on, let's wrestle,' you know, and all that stuff. and I said, 'Don't get on my nerves, keep away, don't bother me.' "

"He was a younger brother?"

"He was feeling his Cheerioats, you know."

"How much younger than you?"

"Oh, he was about twenty-one, I guess. No, twenty-two. He's about six years younger than me. This was three years ago, four years ago. It was before he went in the Marines."

"He was the child that came after you?"

"No, Jim after me."

"Jim came after you?"

"Jim is like me. He's small, not really small, but he's thinner than the rest."

"How old is Jim?"

"Three years younger than me, two or three. I don't even know. See, I don't know too much about my family. That's an awful thing to say."

"You were only two or three years old when they were born, eh?"

"Mmm. Well, we were a big crowd, I mean the whole family. Well she's still got young ones at home! No, I guess the youngest is, say, twelve, I don't know. I really don't."

"She had lots of babies?"

"Yes."

"How many children have you got?"

"Three, two boys and a girl. A boy, and then we had a girl, and then after I had that affair with Betty we had a boy."

"Betty? I thought her name was Martha?"

"Well, that was the first one, that one in the bar I told you I went out with, this one at the bar. I went on a party after I got the money from home."

"Oh, yes, the $50."

"Oh, I spent more than $50. I think I borrowed some at the bar."

"That was Betty?"

"Yes, that was Betty. When I came back to my wife, she said she'd take me back. We had always planned our family up until then, you know, and I told her I didn't like her using the diaphragm, so she became pregnant again."

"You wanted a lot of children?"

"No, I didn't want a lot. I definitely don't want a lot of children. I want to be able to *support* my children."

"Not like your father?"

"That's it, that's it basically right there. I can remember when I had nothing for Christmas and all the other kids had stuff. Not in my family."

"When was this?"

"Ohhh, fourth grade, or something."

"When you were nine years old?"

"About that, and, uh, all the other kids had stuff and, uh, I don't know. We had to write a story, a composition."

"A story?"

"A theme. That's it. On what we received for Christmas, what we liked best. Well, I had received one little book, you know, with stories in it, and I wrote a story on that, and they thought it was so wonderful that I thought it was the best gift that I had received. They didn't know it was the only one, and I wouldn't tell them. I wouldn't tell them, but it was the only thing that I could write about because it was the only thing I had received. And I swore, my kids will never *go without*. I mean I'd rather go without myself than let my kids go without. When I separated from my wife, *I'd send them money*. I mean she got the allotment check and I was sending her $40 a month, not a month, payday, $80 a month besides the check. She was getting $176 and the check."

This could be tied up with other areas.

"So you mean mother wanted you to be a doctor and make more money than father?"

"Yes, she basically did. I mean she wanted me to be a professional man."

"So you wouldn't be a weak man like father, who didn't make much money?"

This was said to test his fantasy about the father-mother relationship.

"I think basically, yes, I think so. I don't know."

"But, as you said, mother never thought too much of father?"

"Well, I don't know. They had *ten kids*. She must have thought something of him!"

In his unconscious, father was a terrific baby-maker, a big sexy man he could never equal. He too wanted lots of babies to beat him, but this conflicted with his wish to have a child who would get what he couldn't have, really an only child.

"What do you mean?"

"I mean, uh, I don't know. But yet she was always yelling at him. Once I saw her pick up a knife and throw it at him. Not at him, she threw it across the room. I don't know whether it was meant to hit him or not, because she, she gets very *nervous*, you know, *emotional*. My mother is like that."

This was the other side of himself, the sissy side.

"Like you?"

"I guess. I don't very often though. I don't let myself. I mean I walk out before I get mad. Now I reason things out."

"So you're afraid of being like father, being weak and not making much money, and taking care of your kids, and you're afraid of being nervous and emotional like mother?"

"Yes."

"You don't want to be like either of them?"

"That's right. I want to be average. I don't want to be above anybody. I want to be average."

"It's not easy."

"I know it."

"Of course, you've been saying right along, 'I'm just like my father was, look at me, I'm nothing,' and you're saying too, 'I'm like my mother, I'm nervous.' "

502 THE TACTICS OF PSYCHOTHERAPY

"But I'm not as nervous as I used to be. I mean, I, I don't know, you know."

He laughed.

"I am nervous with you but as a rule I counteract the nervousness. I talk to myself and, and, I stop myself from being nervous."

"How do you mean?"

"I guess I'm living in a dream world, if you want to put it that way, but I don't think so. I, I just, if, if, if I get scared about something, I reason, and I say, what are you afraid of?"

"That's what I mean. You make believe you are not afraid."

"That's it, I guess. I guess I do."

"You climb ladders, you do all these things, and make believe you don't mind."

"Uh-huh, and I laugh when I really feel like crying. I do, I mean, when I feel bad, I won't let people see I feel bad. I'm *hurt* easy. People say things to me that can *hurt* me. I just laugh about it. I don't let them know it."

"It's not easy? Were you hurt when you were little? Did you cry?"

"No, I don't remember before I had my appendix out. I forget."

"But now you can go out and drink and forget things?"

"I never drank to forget."

"What did you drink for?"

"Why did I drink? I think the reason I drank was because I can feel better than people."

"That's what I mean. You can forget that you feel so bad?"

"There are so many people worse off than me in a barroom that I can feel above them."

"You can forget yourself?"

"I can buy them a drink."

"That's what I mean, you can forget all about you and think of them."

"If anybody came up to me and said, 'Hey, buy me a drink,' I'd buy them a drink. They didn't even have to ask me."

"Just like you had a lot of money?"

"And if I didn't have the money, I wouldn't go in a barroom, if I couldn't buy somebody a drink."

"Another make-believe?"

"Yes. I knew at times I couldn't afford it, so I got loaded. When I got feeling good, I didn't care. I'd buy the whole barroom if I had the money."

"You made believe you had the money?"

"That's it. I always figured there's more where this came from."

"From mother?"

"No, not now. I work for it. I mean I even got spare-time jobs when I wanted money. I can always earn money. I've been very lucky that way. If I really want to earn a dollar, I can earn a dollar. I had my roof fixed. I knew nothing about roofing and I went up and helped the roofers and saved this money."

This was a side to be encouraged, a positive identification.

"But, as you said, father was a man who more or less always worked but didn't make much money. Anyway he worked hard, eh? He was a good man?"

"Yes, I think basically he was a good man but, as I say, I don't know. I can remember once something I heard about how he used to gamble. Well, I gamble a lot. I'd like to gamble but I don't now."

"Father used to gamble?"

"I love to gamble. Oh, I do! But I wouldn't lose. I'd enjoy myself."

"What do you mean, you heard father gambled?"

"Well, I can faintly remember something about a poolroom, and my mother told him to keep out of it, and I know in the back room they gambled."

"How old were you?"

"Just a kid. I don't know. I was really young. I was in Beach City."

"You mean before you had your appendix out?"

"That I don't know. I don't know whether it was before or after. I don't. I can remember the pool hall on the avenue, but whether it was before or after I don't know."

He laughed.

"Well, I think you can be helped. If you like, I will make an appointment at the clinic for you."

"Thank you. I would like that. I guess I really need some help."

"Okay. I'll get in touch with them and they will write to you."

"Thank you, Doctor."

We discussed in Chapter IV the case of a woman who, as a little girl, had witnessed her mother having a miscarriage. This had been a traumatic event in her life and a focal point and screen for a large number of sadomasochistic fantasies, as well as chronic feelings of tension and turmoil. The tension was relieved by a kind of masturbatory activity and by counterphobic attempts to undo the past by means of having many babies. She had attempted to create what she called a family unit, but somehow everything went awry because of her "mother problem." The present chapter acquainted us with a young man who also had a mother problem and a traumatic event in his life to which he had also reacted in a counterphobic manner. From the interview, we could tentatively reconstruct some of his past and see how it influenced the present. In the case of the woman, the miscarriage trauma screened sadomasochistic fantasies growing out of her parents' bickering scenes from the butcher shop and the lonely, angry feelings which she developed from being relatively neglected by her parents because they were always working. Her loneliness, anger, longing and depression had led to a partial narcissistic withdrawal. She acted out her problem in her marriage. The trauma in the case of the young man was the appendectomy, when he was so frightened, lonely and hurt, and also kept away from home and mother for such a long time. What did this trauma screen? We can suspect that previously he had been a mother's boy who couldn't fight, whose "stomach" was jumped on, one who felt deprived of his mother by a succession of babies. He felt he had never gotten enough for Christmas. This was symbolic of his attitude toward the mother-child relationship. He felt he had suffered and had been deprived and, therefore, had a right to run out to other women, a right to spend the household money on drinking and a right to take love or money from all women, and especially mother. We note that he used mother's money to drink and get a "woman" who would give him the sexualized, drinking, close relationship he couldn't get from mother or wife. Why couldn't he respond to his wife? We could deduce from his own words that he felt too much guilt and that his ambivalent feelings for his mother had been transferred to his wife. In this setting they appeared unreasonable and confusing to the rational part of his ego. He was so preoccupied with being left by the mother or wife that in his own words he had to "act quickly or be afraid." He really felt sexually inadequate and like a little oedipal boy. He feared his wife might leave him. His preoccupation with sex and his penis was foreshadowed by his phallic dream in the hospital, which was a denial of the castration anxieties aroused by the operative procedures. In another sense, his illness consolidated a fixation at a phallic oedipal level. This is tantamount to stating that the original mother-child dependency relationship pattern had been partially displaced to a narcissistic penis-self relationship. The two or more girls he went out with were interchangeable. They were pickups at a bar and in this sense more like himself; i.e., they were narcissistic love objects. He could relate to them with little anxiety. They were bad like himself. His wife was *too* good. We can recognize here a variation on the old theme of the whore-mother versus the madonna-mother that is so common in adolescents and that we saw in the case of the shaking naval officer. The bar girls were simply partners in the acting out of masturbation fantasies which reassured him that he was self-sufficient and it wouldn't matter if he were abandoned.

His aggressive and competitive nature was revealed by this knowledge of the sizes and weights of his brothers. He knew them the way an adolescent baseball fan knows batting averages. At the same time, he tried to forget their names and made a thinly disguised suggestion that his mother was always pregnant and still raising babies. His competitiveness was exemplified again when he called himself an "also-ran" and described how he used the barroom to play the role of a big spender. His aggressiveness and feelings of inferiority prevented him from having a close relationship with other men. This was in mind when he said he "always missed something" and "always wanted to be one of the crowd." We can surmise that unconsciously he meant the crowd of brothers. These feelings were displaced to the men in the bars. Like the bar girls, they were interchangeable. His narcissistic hypervaluation of his penis and his unrealistic idealization of masculine qualities in general could not fail to augment his need for admiration from and acceptance by men. This problem was to a great extent based on an inadequate father-son relationship. The father had been so devalued by the mother that the boy's identifications with him were composed mainly of negative qualities. This had led to a need to incorporate good and strong masculine qualities in order to grow up and made him vulnerable to longings for the attention of men. Unfortunately, this longing was passive, the way a little boy would feel it. This would be a blow to the more adult portion of his personality. He attempted to obtain love and esteem through drinking with the men. His fears of being a "sissy" in the eyes of these men was thus an expression of homosexual needs and anxieties. His ejaculatio praecox with his wife increased his sissy fears and showed that his reaction to her was like that of a little bed-wetting boy. This led to a frantic need to prove his potency. All this material was behind his running out and leaving his past and present homes.

In the psychotherapy of this type of case, the analysis of the patient's narcissistic needs, mistrust and withdrawal would take precedence over the analysis of libidinal and superego material. We would patiently have to go over his "sissy" fears and longings again and again and without undue haste. Patients of this kind are exceedingly vulnerable to depression and running out of therapy. They often exaggerate their misdeeds and damn or denigrate themselves in order to prevent the therapist from doing it. The attitude of the therapist in any case must be one that says, "I doubt that you are such a bad person, and there must be a reason why you behave like this. Perhaps when we find it, you won't have to dislike yourself and behave so unreasonably to yourself." This must be done convincingly, as such patients are extremely suspicious. They cannot be fooled by sham sympathy and detest false approval. The only thing they need from us is understanding of their needs for satisfaction and punishment. The greatest danger to therapy comes from their transference reactions and their extreme ambivalence. From the point of view of the patient, the depression that comes with insight constitutes the worst hazard. During these periods the chosen sector should relate to areas of the patient's life where he has been happy and successful. This is usually possible. There is no difficulty in obtaining material in the treatment of borderline patients. The real problem lies in their hypersensitivity to change and losses in any area, the inflexibility and stickiness of their attachments, and the necessity for prolonged periods of monotonous working through of conflicts. Confrontations must be made *sparingly* most of the time. Some patients of this type will react adversely to many sessions with a therapist, as they fear close relations of any type. Others need to be seen daily. Their endurance of intimacy depends upon their reaction to their oral insatiability and fears of swallowing and being swallowed up by the therapist. Knowledge of this characteristic is of little help to the patient unless he sees it in his own terms. A blanket rule for *any* type of patient is especially important with this particular type; i.e., "Don't *push* the patient in order to get results." We would eventually have to convince this patient that his wife was human and with her share of faults as well as virtues, and conversely that his father and mother were not as bad as he thought. He would have to find this out himself. Therapy in such a case is timeless, as in the case of any chronic illness, and can be most easily accomplished in many cases by means of divided doses. In some cases, treatment will have to be continued with another therapist owing to intense feelings of rejection. Such a change may be valuable in that similar experiences with other therapists may strengthen insightful convictions. However, when any patient changes therapists, regardless of the reasons, the first therapist tends to become a target for the patient's dislikes. Along with all professional people, beginners in psychiatry tend to believe the stories patients often relate concerning the stupidity or chicanery of their previous therapists. Even if they are true, they have to be treated as part of the patient's fantasies. Narcissistic patients with maldevelopments of their superegos tend to provoke strong countertransference reactions of either a positive or negative type. This often constitutes the chief problem in handling them. For obvious reasons, they are especially refractory to the pastoral type of psychotherapy and the therapist who does not thoroughly understand his own superego problems.

Borderline patients tend to make transient identifications readily, and have a whole series of pseudo selves or phony roles that the therapist must become aware of and eventually integrate by making conscious to the patient the contradictory nature of his thinking and behavior. This can be done very effectively by means of confrontations, but must be done gently.

XV

NARCISSISM AND OBJECT CHOICE

A Case of Pedophilia

The treatment of the borderline states includes the various sexual perversions. It is complicated by the need to understand the pathology of narcissism and the need to sense and analyze our countertransference reactions. Many therapists react to such patients with anxiety, envy, guilt and hostility. A narcissistic type of choice of love object is always present. The first task of the therapist is to reveal this to the patient with detached empathy. The love object in such a case is always a version of himself as he is now, once was, or hopes to become. It may be a part of himself, usually his penis in the case of a male and an illusory penis in the case of a female. It must be remembered that patients with narcissistic neuroses have very confused sexual identifications. This is so especially in their childhood. When we meet a male patient, for example, who is sexually seductive with a young girl, our first task is to reveal to him that the young girl is, in some way, a version of himself. This may take some time, as the relationship may be quite complex. A patient of this type is usually pressured by a relative or the court into coming into therapy. He will relate a pat story full of breast-beating clichés and phony guilt feelings. These must be tactfully exposed, ignored and circumvented. This can be done most easily by playing the role of the devil's advocate in some cases, and in all cases by supporting the patient's weak, reasonable ego. The following case will illustrate how this is done.

The patient was a man in his early thirties who had been sent

508

into treatment by his wife who had threatened to divorce him. Therapy is useless in such cases until the patient's curiosity and need for understanding is fully harnessed and exploited. He will then want treatment himself. This is another way of saying that the first thing we attempt to do in any type of therapy is help a patient save face. All patients suffer from an internal narcissistic mortification attendant upon the realization that they are not "normal" and cannot control their behavior. In the case of this patient, the mortification was also external. He felt helplessly *forced* to come by his wife's threats. The problem of face-saving must be handled with the greatest skill, as most patients are extremely adroit at sensing false reassurances. Frank and total acceptance of the patient is necessary. This can only be done if the therapist is fully aware of and in control of his own problems in the area involved in the patient's problems.

This patient had telephoned before coming and had tried to discuss his case over the telephone. He appeared sullen and at times angry during the early part of the interview, but by the time the interview was over he was eager to return. No false promises should be made concerning cure or help with any patient. Sometimes these are implicit. In many cases if not most, the patient expects all kinds of magic and it takes considerable time to make him aware of how unrealistic his goals are.

"How do you do. Won't you sit down. Could you tell me something more about your problem. You told me a little bit over the telephone."

"Well, mostly it has been the *nervousness* around the house, *fighting* with the *wife* and, uh, I'm just feeling plain nervous, that's all, and plus what I told you on the phone about the nine-year-old girl, Joanne, that I had *shown myself* to."

The symptomatic problem as well as the aggressive and libidinal elements contained in it were all present in this statement. The libidinal elements were of primary importance to the patient.

"Shown yourself to, how do you mean?"

"I exposed my privates to her."

"How did it happen?"

"Well, she was in the house and I had been drinking, so I guess I felt *sexually aroused*."

This covers a broad field. If the therapist asked, "What do you mean by sex?" the patient's narcissism would be injured and his anger aroused. The therapist instead appeared mildly puzzled.

"By a nine-year-old?"

"Well, that's what it seems like."

"You mean she looked more than nine?"

"Mm. Well, no, I guess she didn't. I don't know how to explain it except I did it, and that was it!"

"Sure, but I wonder what your ideas were. You've done a lot of thinking about it, haven't you?"

"Yes, I have."

"That's what I thought. Tell me what your ideas were."

"Well my ideas were—"

He paused, and frowned before continuing.

"It hasn't been too good of an idea with me since it happened, I'll tell you that much."

"How do you mean?"

"Well, I haven't felt very, very *good* as a human being since it has happened."

He was now beginning his pat account of his sin and guilt—his own *mea culpa*.

"Of course! I realize that you have been very ashamed, but nevertheless there must be a reason for these things. Let's not try to judge the act one way or the other until we understand it. We are both curious to find out how it happened and why it happened. When we know, perhaps you will be able to help yourself in case something similar comes up again because it probably took you by surprise. Do you remember?"

"I never thought I'd ever do anything like that, I'll tell you that much. It's just that the girl seemed *wiser* than ordinary."

"That's what I wondered. Had she been in the house before? What shall we call her?"

"Joanne. We were friends with her parents. We live just across the street from one another."

"Who is we?"

"My wife and I."

"You and your wife? Any children?"

"Three. I only had one then, a boy."

"A boy? How old was he?"

"He was about a year and a half old or two years old."

"And the little girl was nine?"

"Yes."

"How long ago was this?"

"About five years ago."

"About five years? How old are you now?"

"Thirty years old."

Now some of the all-important dates, times and persons were known
and the interview could continue.

"Thirty. That was when you were twenty-five. She was nine and
she seemed *wiser* in years, you said."

"Well, I don't know. It's, she seemed to be *interested in all the boys*
and *everything like that*."

He had probably projected his own interests onto this girl as well
as sensed her interest.

"How did you know?"

"She was sitting in the window and hollering to them all, in the
hallways all the time with them, and so on like that."

"Hollering what?"

" 'Hi, there,' and 'Hello, there.' "

He paused.

"I just don't know how to explain it."

"No, you don't know if you are right or not but you have ideas,
and you can say anything here."

"The only thing that I can say is I just, I did the act without, what
do they call it, premeditation? That was how it happened."

This was part of the pat story.

"How it happened?"

"Well, I just hugged her and I guess I got *aroused* by *hugging* her."

It would be nice to know what he meant by hugging but too tactless to inquire, "From in front or behind?" etc. The same went for
"aroused."

"She came in?"

"It was in my house. She came in and was running around. I was
wallpapering at the time."

"Your wife was out?"

"Yes. She came in, yes. Well, we always went back and forth to one
another's house."

"Some little nine-year-olds can be very wise sometimes. Was she
that way?"

"No, I don't think so. It was me more than her."

"I don't understand. What made you want to hug her?"

"I don't know what made me want to hug her."

"No, but again you must have been thinking about this and you
have ideas."

"Well, the only idea I can get out of it is I must have a *degenerate*
mind."

"How do you mean by degenerate?"

"Well, a person who would do a thing like that must have a *dirty* mind, that's all."

"Do you think you have a dirty mind? What do you mean by that?"

"Well, the ordinary thinking person I should think would be able to cope with it and hold himself back"

This meant that he assumed ordinary people had similar wishes.

"I don't understand. You hugged her and you got aroused. Do you mean you got an erection?"

"Yes."

"And so you took it out to show it to her?"

"Yes."

"What for?"

"I thought she wanted to see it, that's all. *She gave me that impression.*"

This was another projection. He wanted to see it himself or reassure himself that he had a penis that was admirable.

"How did she give you that impression? I mean in what way? How did she act when you hugged her?"

"She didn't avoid it or anything."

"You mean she acted as if she liked it?"

"She seemed to."

"Your just hugging her, not touching her?"

"Well, she didn't run away on me."

"You mean she didn't try to get away?"

"No."

"She just sort of, you mean, stayed there and took it, or what?"

The patient looked uncomfortable and confused. The doctor continued after a pause.

"I know this isn't easy to talk about."

"Well, I thought eventually I could bury it but I guess I never can."

"Bury it how?"

"Bury the thought of doing it."

What kind of a thought did he want to bury? The manifest thought was probably a screen for another.

"What makes you feel it is so—I think you have wondered and I wonder too why such a small girl. I mean you and I would understand it more in an older girl, huh?"

"Yes, sir!"

"What did she do when you took it out?"

"She just looked and I rubbed it against her and then she ran out."

"Rubbed it against her, where?"

It was extremely important that this act be broken down into its components and analyzed as if it were a fantasy.

"Her thigh."

"Her thigh! You didn't try to have intercourse?"

"No, she had a bathing suit on."

"She wouldn't take if off?"

"I didn't ask her to."

"Why not? Isn't that what you wanted to do, or what did you want to do? I don't understand."

The therapist was playing dumb to make him give the details.

"Well, I didn't, evidently I didn't intend to have intercourse I guess, I don't know."

"You mean you didn't know what you wanted to do? Did you want to have intercourse with her?"

"I don't know, to be truthful with you."

He probably didn't know and was afraid to know the truth.

"And you feel you must be *degenerate?*"

"Well, there certainly must be *something wrong some place.*"

"Well, that's just what I mean. Now you have been thinking it all over. How do you think it happened?"

"Because I was *oversexed,* I guess."

It was more face-saving for him to believe this rather than the truth—that he had failed to grow up.

"Are you? Do you think you are oversexed?"

"I don't know."

"What do you mean? I mean these are words that mean something different to everybody. I wonder what you think. What is oversexed? Does your wife think you are oversexed?"

"Well, after that I guess she had quite a few opinions of me."

"She said so?"

"Well, she brought it up quite a number of times."

"What do you mean? What has she said?"

"Well, about Joanne and so on. Every time we had an argument she'd tell me what a degenerate I was for doing it and so I had to live with it."

"But did she mind having intercourse with you?"

"She does. I think she endures it more than anything. I don't think she does it willingly. I think she does it as an act of marriage more than anything else."

"Ever since, you mean?"

"Yes."

"Before that?"

"Before that we had *natural* relations, yes."

This was an odd word to use. There must have been some defect in his adult sexual relationships.

"What do you mean natural?"

"Well, we got along good and so on, like that."

"Sexually?"

"Yes."

"How often?"

"Probably once a week."

"Once a week! You thought that was oversexed?"

"Well, I didn't think it was oversexed. I would have wanted it more but she wouldn't. She just wasn't in the mood or something and we just didn't have it more often."

"You mean she never cared for it particularly?"

"I guess not, no. Just when she felt like it, I guess."

This was part of the pat story. He would like to blame the wife. The therapist went along with him to make him feel more at ease.

"When she felt like it? And you never forced the issue?"

"No, I never."

"Why not?"

"I figured they had their rights as well as I did."

"Were you kind of shy in those days or what?"

"No, I just waited until I figured she was in the mood and then I'd *play a game* for her."

"You what?"

"Well, I played a romance game, they call it."

"What do you mean by that?"

This was part of his adult play acting. To him it was a necessary game.

"Well, get them in the mood, make love to them first, I guess."

"You mean it was playing a game though? You mean you didn't really feel like doing it?"

"Well, yes, I felt like it when I did it, *naturally*, but it seemed that I had to put more time into getting her aroused and getting ready for it than it took me to complete the intercourse act!"

Now it was plain that he had ejaculatio praecox, which was a chronic narcissistic wound in addition to its other meanings.

"You mean by the time you had her aroused you were through?"

"I was gone, yes."

"You were gone! So you mean you were unable to do it *naturally*?"

"It seemed that way, yes."

"And you were through too soon?"

"Yes."

"And she didn't like that?"

"Well, she never said anything. She'd just get up and go in and clean up and that was it."

"Did she show that she didn't care for it?"

"Yes."

"And ever since then she doesn't even want to do it once a week, huh?"

"Well, we've sometimes gone a month or a month and a half."

"What do you do?"

"Masturbate!"

He said this defiantly. Here again it was best not to ask "What do you mean?" but it was highly probable that his fantasies would be related to his perversion.

"Tell me, what do you think about when you masturbate—your wife, or some other girl, or who?"

Mentioning the wife and girl made it easy for him to talk *naturally*.

"I'd think of something I probably had intercourse with before or *something like that*."

He said "something" instead of "someone." This was a form of slip that was best not to take up—a reaction to a part object.

"Before you married?"

"Yes."

"Who? What will we call her?"

"It doesn't matter. Half of them I *never knew their names* anyway."

"What do you mean you never knew their names?"

"Like the Japanese, I never knew their names."

"Oh, there were Japanese girls?"

"Some of them were, yes."

"You mean prostitutes?"

"Yes."

"Or pickups?"

"Yes."

"They were the only kind of girls you knew?"

"Well, my first wife was an ordinary girl."

"This one is not your first wife?"

"No, this is my second wife."

"When were you married the first time?"

"When I was seventeen, in 1949."

"How did you get along with her?"

"Well, we didn't get along too well at all. In fact we only stayed together about seven months."

"Why? Did you have the same trouble with her?"

"No, I don't even recall our sexual relations."

"Don't even recall them?"

"Well, I, vaguely, but I don't remember them the way I would the ones today. I don't recall even what it was like."

"She was cold too?"

"No, I don't think so. I think she was normal."

"What do you mean by normal?"

"Well, she satisfied me, I guess, and so on like that."

"How long did you last with her?"

This was purposefully made ambiguous.

"Six months."

"And when you had intercourse?"

"Oh! I don't remember, to be truthful. I never seemed to bother around with them much as long as I was satisfied."

"You were always quick?"

"Yes."

"You never bothered around? How did you feel about this, coming off so quick?"

"Well, I was young and didn't know anything about it so I didn't think much of it."

"Did you last longer when you were with the prostitutes?"

"It didn't seem so."

"Just like with both your wives? Were you disappointed?"

"It was always the same, yes."

"When you masturbate, what do you usually think about?"

There was a long pause.

"Various ones, I guess."

"Like who?"

"I can't think of anyone in particular that I, well sometimes even my wife."

"You think about her?"

"Sometimes, yes."

This was extremely interesting. If he desired little girls, why didn't they enter into his fantasy life?

"Never Joanne?"

"No, I never thought of her and that's what makes me do a lot of thinking now. If I thought of it then, why wouldn't I think of it later on?"

"Well, how come you were caught?"

"I wasn't caught."

"You rubbed against her thigh?"

"I didn't have any sperm or anything come out."

"By thigh you mean?"

"Her behind."

"What happened?"

"She just went out. Her mother called her I think and she went next door."

"She didn't mind your rubbing?"

"No, she didn't."

"And her mother called her and she went next door?"

"Yes."

"But how come it was found out?"

"I guess she was talking to her mother one night about six months later and her mother called my wife and they got together and the girl told the story."

"And you admitted it?"

"Yes, sir."

"Why?"

"Because I was *guilty* of it. I don't think I could have looked anybody in the face then and said 'No.' "

"You'd been thinking about it?"

"Yes."

"And you thought you were degenerate?"

"Well, I thought a normal everyday person doesn't do things like that."

"Well, what do you think, now that you look back?"

"I think it is just as rotten now as it was then."

It was necessary to test the meaning of this type of guilt.

"What is so rotten about it? After all, she was fooling around too. I see this makes you feel very strongly. Here you are about to cry. Your eyes are getting red, but what is so rotten about it? Why should you feel so rotten, huh?"

He blew his nose vigorously before replying.

"Because it is wrong, isn't it?"

"What is so terribly rotten about it? It is somewhat odd for a grown man but—"

He interrupted.

"It's rotten to go off the—"

He choked up with emotion.

"After all, you know lots of little girls of nine fool around. You know that, don't you?"

"No I don't."

"You never thought little girls fooled around?"

"No I didn't."

"Or little boys?"

"I didn't know that, no."

"You never heard of such things?"

This was hardly likely. He must have heard of such things, if not participated in them.

"No, I didn't. I heard of boys when I was in the *orphans'* home playing with one another and so on like that, but I didn't think girls did."

This was the all-important clue to his past and to his infantile sexuality.

"You heard of boys playing with one another?"

"Yes."

"When you were in the orphans' home, what do you mean? I don't know much about you."

"Well, what they call having relations with one another or trying to when they are young kids, two boys, one trying to get into the other one's *behind*, and so on like that."

This was a giveaway. The girl screened a regressive longing for an anal, homosexual, narcissistic relationship with a boy such as he used to be—an acted out masturbatory fantasy.

"Get into their behinds?"

"Yes."

"Oh, is that what you were trying to do with Joanne?"

"No I wasn't."

It was possible that he was just being literal. The fantasy must have been there.

"Is that what you were thinking of doing, I mean?"

"Well, evidently I must have had *something* in my mind at the time!"

"So that is what you mean by degenerate?"

"Yes."

"That's what you thought about?"

"That's what we kids did then."

"Did anyone do it to you?"

"No."

"Did you do it to any of the others?"

"Yes."

"When you were nine?"

"Younger even."

"Younger? How young is young?"

"Seven or eight."

"Seven and eight?"

"Yes."

"Who were you doing it to?"

"I don't remember their names."

This sounded exactly like the relations with the prostitutes.

"How come you were such a sexy little fellow then?"

"Well, everybody else in the place was doing it!"

Why should he have been so active when he was so little? Was he denying his passivity?

"How come they didn't do it to you?"

"Well, I always had a, I don't know, the ones that I went with evidently were the weaker ones or something and it always seemed that I was the one who was on the top."

"You were the one who did it to them? But didn't you get curious? Didn't you want to try?"

"Try what?"

"To see what it was like yourself?"

"No, it didn't interest me."

"You were always interested in doing it to them?"

"Yes."

"So when was the last time you did it to anyone?"

"Oh, that must have been when I was in the orphanage, twenty or twenty-one years ago."

"When you were?"

"Eight or *nine* years old."

This was the age of the little girl.

"Eight or *nine*?"

"Yes."

"And you stopped when you were *nine*?"

"Yes."

"What for?"

"I was transferred to other places and so on like that."

"Couldn't find anyone after that?"

"My mind wasn't on it after that. It just seemed that there was a spot where they were doing it and in fact my mind probably cleaned up a little bit in the years afterwards and it was an offense."

"I mean what were you doing it for, just for excitement, or what?"

"Well, I guess it was a sensation or something at the end of it."

"You had a sensation?"

"Yes, a feeling at the end of it."

"At the end of it?"

"Yes."

"So you mean you came off without any sperm, huh?"

"That's probably what it is, yes."

"Do you remember, was it like that with Joanne?"

"Well, that's what it seemed like, yes."

"Seemed like? You couldn't remember?"

"I can recall."

"Getting a sensation at the end of it?"

"Yes."

"Just like as if you were coming off?"

"Yes."

"What did you do after nine?"

"Do you mean after that?"

"After nine?"

"I suppose I jerked off."

"Do you remember?"

"Well, I haven't talked to a man yet who hasn't."

"Well, of course."

"So I suppose I did, yes."

"Up until you met your first girl?"

"Yes."

"When was that?"

"When I was about fourteen, I guess."

This was too early, and probably a precocious flight into heterosexuality to screen his narcissistic homosexual fantasies.

"Fourteen!"

"Yes."

"Who did you get then?"

"Oh, she was a girl just my same age."

"Fourteen?"

"Yes, fourteen or fifteen, I forget exactly."

"How did you happen to get her?"

"We were baby-sitting for a couple."

"Both of you?"

"Yes. We were boy friend and girl friend and I started petting with her and the both of us were aroused and I took her in the bathroom but I couldn't seem to do anything with her. She was crying and I couldn't break the hymen partition or anything so I just let it go, so it wasn't actually intercourse."

"Couldn't do it?"

"That's right, yes."

"You didn't want to treat her like the boys?"

"No, I didn't want to do that."

"Why not?"

"I didn't even think of it where she was crying about it and so on, I, it just, well I guess I just wasn't aroused any more."

"So when was the next time? When was the first time you ever had real intercourse?"

"I guess I was about sixteen."

"The reason I ask these questions is I mean there were lots of boys with you in the service?"

"Yes."

"But you never cared about that from then on?"

"No, I had, we had the girls in Korea. We had intercourse with the Korean girls."

"Have you ever thought about those days in the orphanage?"

"Yes, I recall them."

"When you were doing it to the kids, you mean?"

"Oh, once in a while I think back on it but I just put it off as I wasn't the only one who had done it."

He recalled them with conscious guilt over his homosexuality. This screened many intense angry, yearning, guilty and depressing feelings —an acting-out defense.

"So that's what I mean. That's why I wondered why you felt so degenerate."

"Well, I'm sure there are a lot of people who did go through life without doing it. It must give them a better feeling when they are looking back than I have."

"So you mean you feel there is sort of a streak in you because you said she had a bathing suit on and you weren't thinking particularly of intercourse, or did you? I thought you said that."

"No, I think I was more afraid than anything else after I had started."

"Afraid of what?"

"I don't know, of being caught and so on."

"Being caught?"

"Or being afraid something would happen, or what, a wife and a child, and so on, like that, what would people think."

His superego development was incomplete and dominated by his narcissistic needs. It could be tested.

"You mean what they would do to you?"

"No, not so much what they would do, but I would hurt the girl and hurt my wife and my relatives and everything else, by the action, and up to that point in life I didn't think I had done anything that was out of the ordinary in that sense."

This sounded good, but was probably part of the pat story and invested with little conviction. The past had to be explored more fully.

"How come you went in the orphans' home?"

"My mother died when I was six and a half or seven."

"How come?"

"Childbirth."

"Childbirth?"

"Yes."

"Do you have any brothers or sisters?"

"Yes, four brothers and three sisters, one brother dead and two sisters dead."

"They are all older?"

"No, I'm the third oldest."

"How come you went to an orphanage? I don't get it."

"Well, we had a family auction when my mother died and one brother went here and another went there."

He said this with obvious bitterness. The therapist could sense that this episode probably began the period of narcissistic withdrawal.

"A family auction?"

"Well, they came from everywhere and one took this one and one took that one."

"Relatives?"

"Relatives and friends."

"And not you?"

"No, I went to the orphan home."

"They didn't want you?"

"No, me and my brother Charley, we both, he went to Worcester and I went to this one over here."

"How come?"

"I don't know how come."

"No, but I wonder what your ideas were."

"Nobody wanted me, I guess, that's all, or there was nobody there.

Mrs. Smith wanted the baby, Tommy, because he was so beautiful, so she took him, and my aunt had my brother Fred, so she took him."

"Why did she take him?"

"Well, he had been with her most of the time anyway. He stayed down there on the weekends and so on, so he was like her son. My grandmother took my brother."

"Why?"

"Well, he was born in her house and so on like that, and I was the one *they always said just couldn't get along.*"

The withdrawal process may have begun before his mother died— possibly when a sibling was born.

"You couldn't get along? How come?"

"I don't know. I had ideas of my own, I guess, even at that age."

The therapist laughed to lessen the tension.

"What do you mean?"

"Well, if they'd send me to the store I'd be *mad* and I wouldn't go or I'd *run away* and I wouldn't come back overnight, and so on like that."

"Mad? What do you mean?"

"Mad at my mother for sending me to the store or mad at, *just mad,* I guess, angry."

"At mother?"

"At everybody who tried to make me do anything."

"But you must have had a reason. What was the trouble?"

"I don't know."

"No, but what do you think now? Do you remember?"

"Well, I figured I was the one who always had to go to the store, it seemed, so I just felt as though let the others go for a while."

"They picked on you, how come?"

"I wouldn't say picked on me."

"No, but I mean—"

He interrupted.

"I was just the handiest one around, that's all, but it just seemed that way."

It was probably that he was a mother's boy who felt abandoned.

"How come you were the handiest one around?"

"I don't know, probably just circumstances that *I was there all the time.*"

"You were hanging around mother?"

"No, no, I was, I would be out playing and so on like that but whenever she'd holler she'd holler John."

This was a more face-saving version of the story.

"You were her favorite?"

"No, I don't even remember her actually."

"Don't remember her?"

"No."

At that age he must have wanted to turn to his father.

"And your father didn't want to keep the family together?"

"No."

"Why?"

"He wasn't capable of it."

"Why? What was the matter with him?"

"Oh, he died at forty-seven and he was twenty-one at forty-seven let's put it that way."

"He was what?"

"He had no sense of responsibility for anything else in life at all He just shunned anything that meant anything to him."

This was what he had actually been doing himself—and hating hi mother, father and himself for doing it. Something was behind hi ejaculatio praecox. His fixation was at a phallic urethral level lik the man with the erythrophobia, but the tendency toward narcissisti regression and acting out was much more intense.

"When was this?"

"Ever since my mother died."

The therapist returned him to the father sector.

"And he died at forty-seven?"

"In 1954."

"Five years ago? When you were twenty-five?"

"Yes."

"All that time he never cared, huh?"

"No. Whether he cared or not, he certainly never showed it."

This could be used to induce a therapeutic ego split.

"That's what I mean. It is not easy for you to think about, is it Because I take it that you didn't want to be the same kind of father huh, who would not care about what he did?"

"Well, he certainly didn't."

"You wouldn't want to be a father like he was?"

"He certainly didn't put any effort into giving anything to anybody.

"Into teaching?"

"That's right."

"You, you mean?"

"That's right."

"How is it that you came here *now*, because this is an old problem?"

"Well, it has been going on for five years. My wife originally agreed to stay with me on the condition that I seek help but I never did. Last year I went to a doctor but he just said I should have *outpatient* treatment, so I forgot all about it and I let it go. Then every time it seemed I could get the chance to come in, it was either money or something. I couldn't leave my job because we didn't have enough funds in the house or something like that, so my wife and I have broken up about twenty times."

Outpatient treatment was too much like the orphans' home. He needed a father.

"You broke up about twenty times?"

"In the last seven or eight years, yes."

"About what?"

"Well, mostly about this Joanne incident and my drinking along with it."

"You were drinking?"

"Yes."

"Since then?"

"Yes."

"What do you mean?"

"I don't know whether it was trying to forget or build myself up."

"Build yourself up, how do you mean?"

"I try to tell myself that somebody else might have done it too."

"How do you mean?"

"I don't think I know anybody who has done it."

"You never heard of it, huh?"

"I've heard of it in the papers and things like that."

"That's what I mean. What have you heard?"

"Well, every now and then a family man with three children has something to do with little girls, four or five or six years old, and then I hear on the radio, there was an announcement on the radio one day that said all these sex fiends should be caught and put away for life and so on like that."

In his fantasy he must have longed for his father when mother died, i.e., to be hugged and petted at one level and to take mother's place at another level, and at this age it would be an anal physical aspect of a negative oedipal longing, a relationship like those at the orphanage.

"You mean that's you. Is that what you thought?"

"Well, it certainly puts me in the category with them."

"But you never wanted to harm her?"

"No, I didn't want to harm her."

"That's what I wondered. I wondered what you wanted her to do because you said you didn't want to have intercourse with her. You see this is kind of a mystery, isn't it?"

"It is, yes!"

"Because if a man wants intercourse, I mean you know where to go."

"I'd go to Scollay Square."

"Of course, and you could get tattoed at the same time."

They both laughed heartily and the therapist continued.

"So there must be something in this besides intercourse that you really don't know about?"

"That's what stymies me!"

"That, of course, is what we are going to try to find out. I wondered if you had any ideas because here you've been a good husband, a good father. It seems to me that you have had two problems. One is that you never had very adequate sexual relations with anyone. The other relates more to your feeling that life has given you a lousy deal as far as your parents were concerned."

"Yes, sir. You said it!"

"That's one problem, and then there is this other problem of a sort of fatal fascination for a nine-year-old girl. Joanne might have been a bit of a tease. I'm not judging her because I don't know her, but we do know this, that we have a mystery here as to what you wanted from her and why you wanted it from a nine-year-old. You see you don't know this yourself yet! We will have to try to find out, huh? Perhaps we'll also help you to find out why your sexual relations with both your wives have been so unsatisfactory. Maybe things will become clearer."

"I'll try to make everything as clear as possible. I just can't figure it out by myself."

"We'll have to do this gradually. There are many things that a person doesn't know about himself. You have always been afraid. One of your big problems is that you have always felt that you were either a little degenerate or queer, or a little odd somewhere, huh? You've been so afraid of this that maybe you haven't even wanted to look. Maybe we will find out that you aren't as bad as you think, if you work at it."

"I certainly hope not."

"You can only do your best."

"Thank you. I'll try hard."

"Good! I'll see you next week at the same time."

This interview clearly demonstrated that the genesis and dynamics of this borderline patient were no more difficult to ascertain than those of the neuroses. What is difficult is the problem of undoing the narcissistic withdrawal, which includes the chronic mistrust of everyone and himself, the hypersensitivity to petty remarks and incidents, the chronic inability to satisfy his emotional needs for love and attention, and the chronic hate resulting from his daily frustrations. When the narcissistic withdrawal is analyzed, the old depression-laden gestalts of the past that led to the withdrawal are revived. Patients have to face months and years of extreme anxiety and, above all, a depression, which in many cases makes them want to withdraw from treatment. This may be done in anger, the therapist being seen as a frustrating or castrating parent in spite of transference interpretation. Such patients frequently do much better with a second or third therapist. The same applied to their married life. The improvement in relationship is usually due as much to their new insights concerning their own unrealistic wishes, sensitivities and guilts as to the personality of the new therapist, husband or wife. The therapist who embarks on the treatment of borderline and psychotic patients should make it clear to both the patient and himself that the therapeutic procedure is a limitless one and not set his goals too high. When acting-out problems are reduced or abolished, the patient is usually left with a chronic intractable residue of anxiety and depression which is quite endurable. Efforts to reduce it to the vanishing point are not warranted. In the usual case, improvement will be slow and steady with occasional long plateaus where progress appears to have stopped. These are usually only a sign that a long period of working through of insight is needed. If the ability to work and relate to other people is reasonably satisfactory, the patient should be discharged. Like patients, therapists frequently expect too much from themselves. Psychoanalytic psychotherapy does not have to apologize to anyone for its results. It can still claim to be able to accomplish more in a shorter time than any other brand of therapy when over-all results in terms of long range personality change, integration and maturation are used as a yardstick.

The patient in this chapter, like the one in Chapter XIV, felt full of chronic guilt. To understand why he, an "adult" man reacted "sexually" to a nine-year-old, we have to realize how unmanly, inadequate and frustrated he felt before he met the young girl. He was semi-

impotent, fighting with a dissatisfied wife, full of self-hate and ap
parently not doing well in or being satisfied by his working life
His unhappiness in the present had led to regressive ambivalen
longings for the more infantile masturbatory fantasies and practice
that had diverted and sustained him when he had been so cruell
auctioned off. That past was always with him, even to the exten
that he felt he was a degenerate who should be locked up in anothe
kind of orphans' home. He was expressing in harsh, adult terms th
feelings he had as a child when all the siblings came along an
when his mother died. These were condensed into a longing fo
sensual comforts and reassurances that he was not a helpless, castrated
sissy, mother's boy. He hated himself, to be sure, but he was also ful
of sullen defiance and feelings that he had a right to do anything t
make up for the past. He related to part objects in one sense, lik
the hero of Henry Miller's *Tropic of Cancer*, to whom all women wer
only genitals in which to lose himself from the cruel, uncaring worl
     Making conscious the origin and uses of this man's perversio
might not be difficult. It might be only an isolated incident tha
would not occur again. The semi-impotence would be a more difficul
problem in this case, and the superficial relationships might never b
modified to any large extent in any short-term therapy of a few year
duration.
     The relation of the Joanne incident to the death of the father wa
probably of primary importance, but there was not enough materi
to reveal its meaning. One could speculate that father's death revive
the depression he felt at the time of his mother's death. Actuall
it turned out that his father had died a month before the Joann
incident. Like many other cases of this nature, this patient was force
by economic pressures to leave therapy and work in another are
where insight therapy was unavailable. He was seen only eight time
and, while his relationship with his wife was eased and the groundwor
for future therapy was laid, there was no change in his psychologic
status other than a conviction that his problem was of long duratio
and related to his chronic feelings of depression and inadequacy as
man. His passive phallic fixation was complicated by passive analit
and an anxious guilty reaction to his yearnings. The narcissistic el
ments however were of primary importance.

XVI

GOALS AND THE
LENGTH OF TREATMENT

Four Interviews from a Case of
Anxiety Hysteria

The length of any therapeutic treatment is naturally tied up with the goals set by the therapist. Removal of symptoms is usually accomplished with ease and often in the space of relatively few interviews, provided they have had an acute onset, a relatively short existence, let us say three to six months, and when the precipitating factors have been mainly environmental and are fairly obvious. This chapter will be illustrated by four interviews from such a case. Chronic neurotic symptoms and difficulties are the end result of fundamental and interlocking pathological character traits or habitual methods of action and thought which are less difficult to detect than to change. Other pathological character traits ward off anxiety and depression. Many of them are associated with withdrawal and pathological mourning. They are often associated with secret overt masturbatory practices and fantasies. They may have developed as a substitute for these fantasies and practices or as a reaction to them, and remain isolated from the main stream of the patient's life and conscious thought. The relationship of certain character traits to masturbatory conflicts is often shown by patients who, when they attempt to renounce these traits, resume masturbating or obvious substitutes for it. Loss of any type of sexual pleasure arouses castration anxiety, rage, defiance and the depression associated with all kinds of old infantile losses. Another way of stating the problem is that pathological

529

character traits are usually tied up with residual infantile sexual longings which have become especially intense and masked by symptoms. We call such a state regressive, implying that some event or combination of events in the environment had blocked the patient's more mature hopes, wishes and responses. For example, consider the case of the lieutenant colonel in the WACs who had lost her Dick. She had developed aggressive, masculine character traits and fantasies. These were once concerned with getting her father's love but now tended to lead inevitably to a loss in the present that would set off repercussions in connection with past losses. After awareness has been focused on a character trait, the patient and the therapist have to explore together the origins and uses of it. This is usually done in a piecemeal fashion while working against all varieties of resistance, most of which come from the patient. A good example of this type of relationship was seen in the case of the milkman whose characteristic attitude toward his brothers and father in the past had led to anxiety attacks in connection with his fellow milkmen. In psychotherapy the modification of character traits is usually carried only to the point necessary to minimize symptoms. This implies that a great deal of working through of newly acquired insights must be left up to time and the patient. The fact that this is possible is not always recognized by therapists. The effects of well-conducted therapy extend outside the therapist's office and continue to operate long after therapy has come to an end. In some respects, it is more difficult for a patient to isolate vis-à-vis psychotherapy procedures from his everyday life than in psychoanalysis, because these procedures have more resemblance to everyday life experiences. Psychoanalysts are well trained to recognize this type of isolation and do not hesitate to use the vis-à-vis technique when they feel it is necessary.

The criteria for terminating psychotherapy differ from those of psychoanalysis. As a rule, psychotherapy deals with more difficult types of case material. It is less thorough and idealistic in its expectations, and potentially less effective. Psychotherapy is often used for borderline cases with severe problems concerning their narcissistic needs. They may remain distant in their relationship with the therapist and uninvolved emotionally in their own problems. Insight in any dosage may involve unbearable or traumatic quantities of tender or hurt feelings from which they run. Acting-out problems may strain the patience and technique of the therapist unendurably. There is a need for a prolonged period of working through of insight, and weaning is also a lengthy process. Such cases can drag on in a seemingly endless fashion. Long-term treatments can easily be confused with stalemate. The latter condition is characterized by lack of progress, continuous open or hidden negative transference states, and the patient's *adapting* himself to the treatment situation instead of responding to it. This means that the therapy situation may be used by the patient as part of his defense *against* change in a vital area by turning the treatment into a sexualized, enjoyable procedure, an act of atonement, a compulsion or a ritual. A patient may encourage the therapist to accept high fees or seduce the therapist into accepting dramatic or interesting but safe material that only obscures the sources of his anxiety and depression, or he may make minor changes in unimportant areas to distract his therapist. However, in any case, the main symptom complex will remain unaltered. The usual way a stalemate manifests itself is that the patient comes regularly and produces the same material repetitively like a cracked phonograph record without any particular change in any of his everyday relationship patterns. One solution to this problem is a long vacation. Some therapists and patients are temperamentally unsuited. Everyone knows this, but it is seldom admitted by a therapist once therapy begins, either because of pride or lack of recognition. During a separation, a patient often realizes the extent of his dependency needs and wishes concerning the therapist. Patients who have denied having any feelings at all about the therapist or having insights concerning their problems may develop enough perspective to return to therapy and work hard at it. This "fractionated" type of psychotherapy can be successfully used in cases of chronic and severely ill borderline patients who need long periods of working through of any insights that are acquired. Any discharge in psychotherapy should be treated more as an "au revoir" than a good-by. This assists the patient to tolerate the "loss" of a key figure in his life until he has found someone to take his place. The idea of a patient discharged from psychotherapy free of all symptoms, independent and fully mature is an idealized concept of patients and perfectionistic therapists. Symptoms as a rule tend to persist, drained of their affects, and can always recur providing the circumstances are right. They always increase in intensity whenever the relationship of the therapist and the patient is negative and when separation or termination is threatened. This should not deter the therapist from giving patients a trial period of being on their own. The weaning process is particularly lengthy in the case of borderline patients, as termination of therapy is regarded as an abandonment and can easily precipitate a temporary regressive withdrawal from personal contacts.

A change of therapists is a risky procedure. Strong negative feelings usually appear. Many mildly paranoid and chronically disappointed patients tend to react negatively to their first therapist in the same way that many hysterical women react negatively to the first man who deflorates or "castrates" or makes them a woman. The narcissistic and megalomanic defenses adopted by such patients are a last-ditch stand against overwhelming feelings of guilt, depression and inadequacy. The removal of such defenses should never be undertaken lightly or without expectation of a violent reaction. Many therapists, as well as patients, fail to credit their colleagues for having performed the initial excavations for the foundations of a new personality. The case in Chapter XI showed how effective therapy can evoke hostility. Many mildly psychotic or severely neurotic patients are chronic cases who must be carried along almost indefinitely in order to make a reasonably good social adjustment. A standard rule in psychotherapy is that the greater the preponderance of narcissistic defenses and withdrawal tendencies, the longer the treatment. There are some exceptions to this rule. There is a narcissistic component to all the neuroses. Many mild problems concerning withdrawal or the development of "genuine" or "meaningful" relationships must be left up to time, the patient and the vicissitudes of life. Occasionally perfectionistic therapists allow patients to cling to them in the hope that all their problems will be settled by a type of symbiotic relationship. While usually no great harm is done, such an arrangement is no better than an artificial neurosis and destructive to the extent that it encourages a regressive dependency. It prevents the patient from developing mature responses and the therapist from facing and mastering his own anxieties and narcissistic needs.

Most patients should not be carried along for years when there is an absence of any observable change in their condition. If this is done the procedure can become a very destructive one for both patient and therapist. The former becomes chronically negativistic, pessimistic and depressed, or regressively and aggressively dependent. The latter becomes cynical and technically sloppy.

There are certain warnings applicable to every diagnostic category in respect to length of therapy.

1. The psychotherapy of psychotic and borderline patients, when the outcome is favorable, usually leaves them with neurotic residues which should be left alone. There may be compulsions, mild conversions or anxiety, etc. Perfectionistic therapists may feel, "Now we have reduced the psychosis to a neurosis, and will reduce the neurosis

to normality." This can seldom if ever be done. Attempts in this direction usually lead either to stalemate or to a lighting up of the psychotic process once more.

2. There is a certain basic level of anxiety proneness in every individual which cannot be altered. When cases of anxiety neurosis are treated, they should be discharged when the anxiety no longer seriously interferes with their social conduct, work performance and love life. This also applies to mild residuals in psychosomatic, compulsive and phobic patients and is especially the case with middle-aged or elderly patients. Organic involutional processes frequently lead to an outbreak of regressive symptoms, acting-out problems, psychosomatic diseases, etc. A gradual organic deterioration may nullify or defeat therapeutic efforts. However, when the past performance of such individuals has been good, we can often expect a good clinical prognosis.

In severely disturbed cases we should not hesitate to use sedatives, tranquilizers and antidepressant medication as adjuncts to the therapeutic process. This is quite contrary to the usual practice of psychoanalysis. It is quite unnecessary and even dangerous to let patients who are seen infrequently suffer from intense anxiety and depression. In the psychotherapy of certain hysterical and compulsive patients, drugs would complicate the problem of symptom and transference analysis, but in the treatment of severe borderline states we can use them to great advantage. Residents in the process of learning the techniques of psychotherapy should use drugs of any kind sparingly if at all. In a hospital setting it is better to have a separate physician take care of the problem of drug administration and physical examination. In cases where this plan is not feasible, the resident must remember to isolate his medical duties and thinking from the therapeutic interview. Thus, a cold on the ward may be associated with problems dealing with viruses, aspirin, Kleenex and nasal decongestants, but to a therapist and in the psychotherapeutic interview it is associated with and its symptoms are a manifestation of depressive feelings of loss and inadequacy. This attitude applies to any and all illnesses. When drugs are not used sparingly, they can mask symptoms and encourage regressive dependency states that are associated with new and complicated symptoms. Thus, when anxiety is abolished, depression may appear. When depression goes, hypomania and acting out may occur. The pain of psychosomatic disease is often replaced by severe depressive states and episodes of unrealistic thought or behavior. Psychosomatic diseases are often associated with paranoid ideas and feelings. Many drugs have side effects that complicate or mask a situation still further. As a result, the original difficulty and symptoms associated with it may become completely obscured.

Symptoms persist long after their usefulness has ended. The patient's symptoms may be present minimally but are not mentioned unless inquired about, and the persons and events connected with the symptoms are eventually discussed dispassionately with perhaps mild depressive overtones. When this occurs repeatedly, we can test the reactions of the patient by cutting down his time. This will produce a flood of new complaints or a revival of all the old ones. Such a procedure is always on a trial basis.

An enduring change in the nature of the symptoms is another sign that weaning the patient can be considered. Common changes, for example, are those seen in depressed patients who may develop compulsive routines, compulsive patients who develop mild anxiety, phobias or conversions; hysterical or hypersexual patients who become inhibited in their psychosexual interests; or the acting-out type of psychopaths who develop anxiety and depression or compulsive behavior. When changes in routine are made in the weaning of borderline patients, they should be mild and discussed well in advance. In some cases we will find that the neurotic symptoms cover a latent psychotic withdrawal and isolation which has been developing for many years, usually following the loss of a key figure in the patient's life upon whom he has been utterly dependent, with or without conscious recognition of the fact. Such patients may react intensely to any loss of time or even a change in their routine, and in all cases such reactions should be expected. In some cases, when the time is reduced, the patient may cease to progress any further or put on a false front of independence and ask for a quick termination. This may call for a frank admission of having made a premature judgment.

In the cases of anxious or phobic patients, absence of symptoms should lead to encouragement by the therapist for them to face the anxiety-producing situation. This must be insisted upon repeatedly. At times we can assist patients by allowing them to use a tranquilizer and later wean them from it. Usually the mere presence of the pills in the patient's pocket will suffice as a substitute for the reassuring presence of the therapist.

Many patients attempt to preserve contact with their therapists following termination of their treatment. This is especially true of borderline or psychotic patients. Such patients will preserve some kind of contact either by mail, telephone or occasional visits. The latter are preferable and should be permitted freely. Many cases of psychotherapy are terminated because of impatience, boredom or overoptimism on the part of either the patient or the therapist. Such cases will naturally return frequently and should be freely permitted to do so.

The last few interviews should be treated exactly like the early ones. For that matter, each interview should be conducted as if it were the initial and final one. Leaving the therapist, for example, is linked with previous losses and changes in relationships. These should be discussed in detail. There is one small exception. If an opportunity occurs, a review and summary of the important material related to the chief difficulty of the patient can be attempted. Termination can be treated as only a long vacation. Transference reactions are usually unanalyzed in psychotherapy. Patients may be discharged who are more or less deeply and ambivalently attached to the therapist. This can only be revealed to them and resolved by them gradually. Long vacations frequently have the salutory effect of revealing to both the therapist and patient the extent or absence of transference manifestations.

When a strong transference neurosis develops, the therapist will find himself engaged willy-nilly in the practice of psychoanalysis. In such cases, it is difficult to avoid the stagnation and acting out that ensue when a fully developed transference neurosis is not interpreted correctly. Interpretation of the transference can usually be accomplished best at the end of a session, after feelings concerning figures in the past have been well developed, clarified and understood. It can often be demonstrated that these feelings and attitudes exist during the interviews and how they complicate the treatment process. This type of finale for an interview gives the patient time to think things over between visits and helps to prevent an automatic acceptance or rejection, often associated with some patients in psychotherapy. Too few interviews, as is often the case in psychotherapy, encourage an isolation of the therapy material from the patient's everyday life. When vacations and thorough reviews of case material, etc., do not help, either a change in therapists, help from a more experienced colleague, or an admission of failure is in order. The first is usually easier on both persons concerned, although the therapist should be frank about the difficulties to be faced and not imply that if the patient can only find the *right* person he can be "cured," as this is not likely. Many patients can be helped very little by psychotherapy of any kind.

In summary, in sector psychotherapy the accent is on ego integration and conscious control. It is assumed that pathological symptoms and character traits exist in all types of cases in varying proportions. These symptoms and traits are mainly based on or are reactions to infantile traumatic losses and pathological mourning states. The pathology involves dissociation, withdrawal from meaningful relations with others, and a denial of old griefs, hates, yearnings and guilts. Unconscious feelings and thoughts associated with these pathological states must be made conscious in terms of their development, meaning and use in everyday life. This insight must be associated with conviction and be useful as well as used by the patient. To achieve integration the therapist and the patient must understand the relationship of (1) the past to the present and anticipated future; (2) the self to others; (3) the part to the whole, the specific to the general. The therapist actively manipulates the structures of the interview to accomplish the integration process.

Anxiety hysteria has usually been considered the original neurosis of childhood. It is the fountainhead of all the later, more sophisticated and systematized adult neuroses. Mild anxiety states are present chronically with occasional acute and intense manifestations. Phobic states and hypochondriacal fears may alternate or occur in conjunction with mild conversions or obsessional preoccupations. This type of neurosis is more prevalent than any other psychiatric condition and may persist in its original form up to and during the adult years, but emphasis on one or another aspect is often foreshadowed in the preschool years. This emphasis often develops into a specialization in certain persons. An accentuation of one or more types of symptoms is developed by habitual repetition, by identification with various members of the family, who may have similar symptoms, by development in a certain emotional climate or by exposure to other environmental opportunities. Most of the cases that have been presented have been in this diagnostic category. Let us now consider four interviews from a case of anxiety hysteria treated in forty-two interviews over a period of one and a half years. The patient was a middle-aged man. He was suffering from a mixed neurosis in which obsessive-compulsive and intellectualizing elements acted as a façade for the phobic and hysterical aspects of his personality. There was also an accentuated narcissistic vulnerability and withdrawal from personal relationships and feelings in general. He was seen once a week, as this was all the time he could take off from a responsible job that involved much traveling around the country. At the time he came for treatment he was in his late forties and moderately successful in the business world, but handicapped financially by his refusal to take well-paid, responsible administrative posts, due, he felt, to a great interest in research. Superficially he appeared calm and pleasant, with a somewhat ingratiating smile. He betrayed his tension by chain smoking and a mild tremor of his hands. He had been referred by a doctor who was treating his wife. She had made suicidal gestures and, shortly after her treatment began, insisted that *he* see a psychiatrist for *his* problems, which she claimed were responsible for hers. When he called for an appointment, he claimed that his principal difficulty was migraine headaches. He had suffered from them since childhood and no treatment had been of much help. For quite a while he made no mention at all of headaches, but went directly to his relationship to persons, as shortly before his visit his wife had made an attempt at suicide.

First let us consider the initial interview. The patient began on his own initiative.

"Well, I suppose you would like to know why I asked for the appointment. I'm with a pharmaceutical firm. By training, I'm a chemist. There is no *crisis* in my own problems. My problems are *old* and well ingrained."

He laughed briefly and continued.

"And, uh, in a way, they have been usually livable with as lots of them are. I don't know if Dr. Smith talked with you or not."

"He told me that you wanted help with an *old* problem."

"So this is all the background you have? Well, my wife has been seeing Dr. Smith off and on for several years now, and well I think as usual the recognition has been awfully slow that *her problems are my problems*, and while mine are not expressed in *breakdowns* or *crises* nevertheless they are *mutual* ones."

This was apparently a piece of insight to begin with, but it had to be expanded and developed to mean anything.

"In what way?"

"Well, I mean they increase mine at a rapid rate. The very fact that I got accustomed to live with my problems has had a very bad influence on her problems, since they are a little more on the surface. So after long deliberation and several *shocks* I decided what I obviously knew anyway, that the best thing is not to think about it but to do something about it and try to resolve the mutual problems by looking a little more into mine. Just the very fact that I have not gone through any personal *crises*, nervous breakdowns or anything like that makes it a little harder to describe what I consider my problem. Maybe the easiest way to start is to perhaps quote a little bit from the few conversations I had with Dr. Smith when I consulted with him about my wife and my relationship to her. In the last meeting we had, after a rather severe *crisis* my wife had, he made a few statements."

He paused for a moment.

"A severe crisis?"

"I should say that having talked with my wife a lot there's a great deal of insight into my problems too, but at least one of the outward phenomena was that I'm, as you may have noticed by now, very difficult to start to talk, I am not very *forceful* and actually *avoid* problems by being *nice* to everybody and what not. Just to mention one rather superficial characteristic, I think this is one of the things that has created one of the greatest strains on my relationship with my wife in that I really do not *give* by actually not *demanding*. In other words, the relationship from the beginning of the marriage, which is approximately over nine years old, has actually *deteriorated* in *mental intimacy*, as well as *physical*, by the way, without any outward aggression on my part. I am always compromising and giving in, but actually not giving anything at all."

His circumlocutory speech was more concealing than revealing. He was beginning to talk of complex personal relationships. Why did he have to appear so nonaggressive? Possibly he could be led into important *physical* and specific areas where this type of defense would not work. The defense was also one of talking in generalities.

"How do you mean *physical?*"

He ignored the question and continued.

"There was another crisis and indeed a very bad one when my wife made a so-called *suicidal attempt*. It was a *typical* thing after an argument. After my leaving the room, she grabbed a few pills. She is a trained nurse. She obviously had no forethought about it. It was an emotional breakdown. There weren't even enough *sleeping pills* around to do anything, but it wasn't the question whether it was a *suicide* or not. It brought to my mind that, well, let me backtrack a little bit. After a particularly nice evening together with friends with very good relations between us and what not, I went into the usual intellectual tour de force, thinking this was a good time since the relationship was good to bring up a few points, you know, and I had to *rub it in* and *balance things up*. Of course, as the conversation went on, it *deteriorated* and the *fright* I had, as I analyze it back now and try to think over the whole rather *distressing* night there, is that during that whole time I was actually less concerned with the fact of the *suicide* attempt even when I called the doctor—I was practically sure in my mind that there was no *danger* to life and what not—but it became clearer to me than at any time before that this kind of interaction showed we were *terribly far apart*. Mary, that's my wife's name, has a natural tendency to be *withdrawn* as far as the inner emotional life is concerned, not socially but, as far as her real inner life is concerned, we had come to the point of *terrible isolation*, a terrible *loneliness*, and moved far away from being reached by each other, and this attempt to use this outwardly better relationship to really talk about our deeper problems showed me that our relationship had *deteriorated* very badly. My reaction was a very *rationalizing* and *intellectual* one. She is an *intuitive*, nonintellectual type. Our relationship had just deteriorated to the extreme. So then I decided since obviously she was going to see Dr. Smith, which she did—she had seen him once prior to this just a week ago—I felt that this was a *now-or-never situation*. We would start at the same time and at least remove the *unavoidable strains*, I mean the avoidable strains."

He laughed and continued.

"Because there are always some unavoidable ones I am sure."

The slip was ignored, as his wordiness showed much anxiety. He was already in a crisis; i.e., his compulsive rationalizing and intellectualizing defenses were not working well. His own *depression, isolation, withdrawal* and *loneliness* were apparent as well as his *rage* and *anxiety*. The therapist encouraged his talking indirectly about his problems. As in the previous case, his wife represented his emotional, intuitive part. He externalized it or projected it upon her person.

"She is just beginning to see Dr. Smith?"

"Again! I think this is her third start with him. She has been seeing him on and off in *crises*. It was therapy."

"Therapy for the *crises?*"

"Yes. Well, the first time she saw him she had a rather extended course of therapy."

This hinted at the depth and extent of his problem as well as hers. It might be easier for him to talk about his wife and give us some indirect information about himself until he becomes less anxious, and it was necessary to know some details.

"How old is your wife?"

"My wife is, uh, I'll have to figure that out. I'm *forty-seven* so she is *thirty-four.* I felt therapy would give us the best chance, and actually when you asked me what is the immediate need other than the fact that when anybody can afford to benefit by a therapeutic situation from what I know about it—, I lost my thought now. Well, that, yes, what the immediate need is, uh, the immediate need is that I *definitely need help* in finding an immediate adjustment other than a completely rational one in order to resolve the various problems with my wife."

The therapist noted that he made no mention of his "migraine" attacks. Some other problem was in the foreground.

"Are there just the two of you?"

"Yes. We have *no children,* and *this is of course one of the problems.* She at least says she wants children and I at least say I don't."

This represented a division in his own personality in regard to the emotional, depressed, withdrawn part of himself who wanted a baby-mother relationship.

"*She* wants them?"

"Oh, yes, she just generally would like to talk me into having children and I just generally *refuse* to. This is a rather vicious circle."

"She feels you don't want children?"

"Yes, we have never made any attempt to have them."

"And you don't want children?"

"No. It is one of my *long-standing* opinions."

This was the first chance to go into the past and at the same time take some of the pressure off the present.

"What do you mean by long-standing?"

"Well, I was almost *always* convinced I didn't want children."

"How long is always?"

"Well, I don't know!"

"You mean even when you were little?"

"Well, I think as long as I have ever had thoughts about marriage as a potential."

"When was that?"

"I would say late teens to early twenties."

"Back in your late teens? You remember back there?"

"A lot of little things, you know, remembering many instances, and this is something obviously for reasons which go way back. It's a topic I've always talked about."

"Since your teens, you have not wanted children?"

"I was vociferous about it. I always talked about it."

"What do you mean?"

"Let's say in normal social intercourse at a party."

An attempt was made now to find out something about his past.

"When you were in your teens? Where were you?"

"Let's say, well, with friends, sitting around with friends."

This was defensively vague.

"Where was this?"

"Oh, I was at that time, uh, I was born and brought up in Alabama."

"In Alabama?"

"Montgomery."

"Montgomery? You were in Montgomery then, in your teens with your friends vociferously engaged in arguments to prove that children were not wanted?"

"I was a little more philosophical than that."

He laughed.

"But anyway, what were your opinions then?"

"In those days I think they were based on the fact that the instinct for procreation and of reproducing oneself is actually an atavistic instinct just carried over from the *uncontrolled* mating instinct of the animal, and that type of explanation. Therefore, to the intelligent human being the fact that there is such an instinct has no intellectual validity. That's point one."

The anxiety was mainly about controlling his needs and longings.

"You mean you felt that an intelligent human being ought to be able to control his instincts?"

"Yes. In other words, he has a decision to have children or not to have children, not just because there is an instinct to have children."

"He should control his instincts?"

Restating the problem continually in these terms would make it easier later on when his difficulties with his instincts were clearer.

"Yes! So then the second point is why do I decide one way or the other, and there is a rationale that has been with me for a long time. It is actually only in the last few years that I personally don't think this rationale is really so damn clever after all. The rationale was always the one that I didn't like *responsibilities*. However, whenever I had one, I'd take it very *serious*. So in the situation of children I'm in a *quandary*. On the one hand I don't like the responsibility; on the other hand, in my personality make-up as I have observed it, once I have had one I am a *slave* to it. This is why I *shirked marriage for such a very long time*. I was thirty-eight when I finally married."

He was afraid of obsessional involvement and slavery or some fantasy of dependency and being hurt.

"How come?"

"I just evaded it very carefully."

"But what for? As you look back now? You must have done a lot of thinking about it."

"Because I said to myself I don't like the *responsibility*! I can have a lot of fun without being married, but if I were married then I could not evade it and I would be tied down by the *responsibility*."

"You mean you were afraid to become a slave to marriage or to children?"

"Yes, one or the other, yes, on a very similar basis."

"A love slave?"

"Or a responsibility slave. It's like for a long time I didn't like to have the same *job*. I actually still don't either."

People who have such fears have had a particularly difficult time with their first important relationships and have a chronic mistrust of everyone and everything, including themselves. The therapist continued into his past.

"What made you think you would be such a terribly responsible person who would become a slave? Had you done this before?"

"Uh, in a way, uh, of course you can only take my judgment for it."

He appeared unwilling to go on.

"You said you had this feeling already in your teens."

"Well, I had always lived up to responsibility once I had it."

"And at the same time you also had this fear of getting into a situation which would trap you and which you didn't have control of?"

"Right!"

"You felt you should have control over the instincts but didn't want to get into any situation where you might lose control and become a slave?"

"Yes, no. Of late this rationale doesn't impress me any more as being so damn clever."

His ambivalence was clearly in the open.

"Because you know more now?"

"But of course about having children unfortunately I have now a specific rationalization."

He laughed.

"How do you mean?"

"The trouble is that the difficulty with having an opinion on a slightly intellectual or rationalizing basis is that from having been *rather small* and being the *youngest* of *three brothers*—the others being four and six years older—as far as I can remember, actually thinking about impressions, I was *always* well trained in being a *great rationalizer*."

The factual elements demanded priority.

"Two older brothers? You were the baby?"

"Yes."

"No sisters?"

"No sisters, no. So I always, on the surface, could philosophize myself out of any difficulty. On the other hand I was always, this is one of the things I briefly discussed with Dr. Smith, I always and still am again outwardly controlled but inwardly have very strong irrational fears. I have a terrific *fear of thunderstorms*. I also *fear flying*. I do fly and I do go out in a thunderstorm but both of them frighten me irrationally."

The anxious phobic elements were now beginning to come out. His position in his family constellation was conducive to his becoming the little sister. Intellectual compensation for his "smallness" was probable.

"How do you mean?"

"Of late the emotional strains are greater or my resistance to them is less, whichever the case may be. I master them actually now as a grownup less well than I did when I was young, and this was another sure sign, in addition to the marriage problem, that I am *playing with fire*, because I have just seen too many people *snap* who were under very perfect control before."

He was beginning to sound even more like an anxious, phobic, hysterical person. He still made no mention of his headaches. This was obviously a mixed neurosis with a preponderance of compulsive intellectualizing defenses against anxiety and depression.

"Who do you have in mind?"

"I have seen so many people snap."

"Really?"

"Yes, and nowadays you see lots of people with nervous breakdowns."

"Who do you have in mind that you knew?"

"Oh, in fact there were *two guys* in our own firm. One is permanently gone."

It will be remembered that he had two brothers.

"What do you mean?"

"One of our former vice-presidents snapped completely. Others have had slight nervous breakdowns. Well, in business life, you see it left and right. I've seen my oldest brother. He had a slight nervous breakdown."

The brother was a part of his self-concept and had to be treated as an alter-ego figure.

"He did? When was that?"

"Yes, he was *always* nuts anyway in the normal sense of the word."

He laughed. Laughing can be a sign of anxiety and the necessity to minimize the meaning of a certain aspect of reality. The therapist permitted this by smiling and in this sense participating. The word "always" might lead to more past material.

"What do you mean?"

"Well, he was always what you kind of, what is colloquially called nuts, you know."

"Yes, but how? Different people show it in different ways. There are all varieties of nuts. Which variety was he?"

"Well he was the variety which not in a medical but in a colloquial sense you might almost call schizophrenic. He is either here or he is not. In one moment he might participate in a conversation with the greatest of *friendliness* and then be *completely opposite*. He usually has a very nice personality and doesn't bother anybody. His relationship to his children is the same. He loves them to death or he doesn't seem to know that he has any. He has had an awful lot of *psychosomatic diseases* from his teen-age on and stuff like that until he finally had a nervous breakdown. He did not go into therapy because he had as many people do, not a real prejudice, but pretended he thought it doesn't do any good. It's a nice interesting occupation for some doctors but it really doesn't mean a hell of a lot. Nevertheless when his son, who is a really *severely disturbed* child, who is now about twenty-one, got into real trouble, then for his son he suggested *he* go to a psychiatrist. So, I mean it is very easy to see just a lot of illogicality. Well, *my own wife* had two real breakdowns, to get back to me again."

His ambivalence toward psychiatry was now revealed clearly and also one reason why he feared having children.

"What kind of breakdowns?"

"Well, where she did completely *irrational acts* for very brief spells."

"What did she do?"

"Well, one time she just *threw herself out of the car* when I wasn't driving at any speed, and this *other suicide attempt* I mentioned, and, uh, when we have any of these arguments she becomes very *emotional*, becoming nearly *uncontrollable*, and our *physical relationships* have suffered."

This was probably an important area, as it was only mentioned indirectly. In all probability, his wife externalized his own worst fears.

"Your physical relations?"

"Yes, there is very little physical relationship."

"How much is very little?"

"Oh, maybe once every half year, as bad as that! There I personally got into a psychological trap."

"How do you mean?"

"Because I started to get the feeling that our relationship had *deteriorated* and, and uh, I always had the feeling that to start relationships I would have to pretend first something that doesn't exist."

"You mean that you loved her?"

"Yes, and then it started to get into a vicious circle."

"You don't love her?"

"Uh, this is one of those very difficult words."

His ambivalence and withdrawal tendencies and fears made it impossible for him to commit himself. He used the word *deteriorate* so much that it was possible that he feared he was deteriorating or aging and was hiding it by generalizations and sexualization of his problems.

"That's right."

"Well, I would say from the start of this marriage I never defined my relationship to her as, well let's say on an emotional level, as *some other love experiences* of mine have been."

"Could you amplify that?"

"Well I would, especially at the time I married her, I would not have defined my emotional feelings towards her as love."

"What do you mean?"

"I had loved more before."

"How do you mean that?"

"And yet hadn't married."

"Your late thirties? That was when you were married?"

"Yes. I'm forty-seven now. I was thirty-eight then."

"You were thirty-eight then and she was twenty-four?"

"Yes, thirty-four uh, twenty-four I guess."

The therapist ignored the slip, which suggested he was concerned over the disparity in their ages.

"What happened?"

"Well, when I was thirty-eight, I discovered as many people do, I think, that just horsing around starts to get rather boring. In other words, the thrill of an affair here or an affair there started to diminish quite a bit. Secondly, I had at that time gone, dated Mary for, let's see, I got out of the Army in 1947, shortly after Hiroshima, about that time. Since I was thirty-six at that time, I got discharged in the first batch, and I met her almost immediately after that and we dated almost continuously during that time. Neither of us dated *exclusively* with each other but mostly with each other, and, uh, I made a very *severe misjudgment* of the case. She was actually, when I met her, *on the rebound* from a very *unsatisfying love affair* with a *much older cousin* of hers who was of my age group, give a year or two, and something which doesn't lead to anything and what not. So *we* dated on the *rebound*."

"On the *rebound*?"

"I was on the *rebound* from the Army. While I didn't fight in the Army, I spent five days a week in uniform in a laboratory working from eight o'clock in the morning until one o'clock at night and sometimes through the night, didn't have any fun and nothing, and here I was back in a civilian suit. I was in circulation again. I had nothing to do."

"How do you mean?"

"Feeling a little lost! I was two years in the Army. I didn't know many people. I met her on a blind date and on a dare, both of us knowing it was a dare, and we had great fun fooling the other people who brought us together, so we continued dating. So the whole thing started as a big joke on both of our parts."

"A big joke?"

"You said it, and she still met this other guy, this cousin of hers, for quite a while. We laughed about that. Then she gave that up."

"So she was going with a cousin and going with you at the same time?"

This was important, as it probably foreshadowed some material concerning a triangular oedipal relationship that was still unsolved. The joking was a denial mechanism.

"Yes, as I called it in those days, the dessert, I was the dessert. This in my fancy-free situation at that time was just the right thing, so I thought."

"That was as far as you wanted to be involved?"

"Yes, sir!"

"Did you know the cousin?"

"I met him afterwards. I've seen him several times since. He isn't in this area now. He's an Army doctor and therefore is almost any place, or the Air Force I guess it is. So then after about a half a year I was intelligent enough to notice this thing on her part was getting more serious, and I met her family and was invited for Thanksgiving, etc., etc. I felt a *noose* around my neck and I did what I've done."

"A noose?"

"Yes, so I did what I had done *many times before*. One jolly afternoon I just said, 'Well, I'm afraid that this is getting you too much involved and me too much involved. We better break up.' "

"You had done this before?"

"Yes."

He laughed.

"So we officially broke up."

"When you got too close?"

"Yes. In my other experiences, when it was girls who were older than I, that was very easy. There was never that danger."

"You picked older ones?"

"Those were the times when I let myself go emotionally because there was a road-block anyway."

"You were quite safe?"

"Just as safe as hell! It was safe, but it wasn't emotionally safe at all."

"So there was a similarity of relationships. You didn't want to become *involved* or let things get out of *control*, either with *love*, or about *children*, or *intercourse*?"

"Or even having her fall in love with me! I thought at this time it hadn't gone that far."

"You hoped you could control it?"

"Yes, as a matter of fact now it comes back to me, I had a good rationalization for that too, as I always have for anything. I am a *professional rationalizer*, that's why I am reasonably successful in my business."

"How? What was your rationalization?"

"The rationale was that, uh, there is no moral reason not to have affairs but just to have affairs for sexual satisfaction isn't enough reason. If you have an affair with a woman, you should like her. This was a very simple rationale."

548   THE TACTICS OF PSYCHOTHERAPY

"You should like her?"

"Yes! But of course there are other reasons than that. Actually in my teens with the awakening of the sexual instinct, I didn't have much *access to girls.*"

"How come?"

"Well, my father was an industrialist of the old school in many respects. He had his factory in the suburbs where he bought a very nice house with gardens within walking distance of the factory, so that there were very *little social contacts.*"

He was suggesting that he had social anxieties in addition to his other anxieties. This hinted at a chronic withdrawal reaction of some kind.

"So you and your brothers remained isolated in a sense, huh?"

"Yes."

"With mother?"

"I was, well, *mother died* when I was *ten years* old."

"Mother died when you were ten?"

"She was severely sick for the last *three years* of her life."

"Since you were seven?"

"Yes."

"What was she sick with?"

"Cancer."

What did this mean to a child of seven to ten? He probably felt that she was sick over him. This type of feeling could also be related to his anxieties about his wife. The start of pathological mourning and withdrawal was probable.

"Cancer? For three years?"

"Yes, it was one of these, well, I don't know."

"Cancer of what?"

"It started with cancer of the breast and then metastases all over and it was a very slow *deterioration* process."

He had used this word before in connection with his relationship with his wife. It was probably synonymous with chronic loss and hurt.

"And before seven she was well?"

"Reasonably. She was a very high-strung woman."

"High-strung?"

"Yes."

"You mean?"

"*Nervous.*"

"Nervous? How do you mean?"

"Yes, but I think there was a deep love between her and my father, a very good relationship, although he was around ten years older."

This was a meaningful non sequitur showing that he had some doubts. Apparently "nervous" had a hateful significance. Then there was the present age disparity.

"Can you remember that far back?"

"Yes, I do because in the years of mother's severe disease I was *an awful lot with both of them.* Father preferably took me whenever mother was hospitalized, he took me along usually, and I saw them interact in this severe situation when mother wasn't well. I could very plainly see father's emotional reactions."

This was probably a screen memory for a very traumatic period, but it was too soon to get much out of it except the realization that he must have become sensitized to problems of closeness and loss and had probably become somewhat anxious and chronically, if partially, withdrawn around this period. This could be tested.

"Wasn't that quite moving?"

"It was."

"It was difficult to bear, wasn't it?"

"Well, no, since I always used to be a *snotty* little boy, rather *snobbish* and cocky, probably because I was *isolated.* I was an *empire unto myself,* but my interpretation of being *isolated* was being a *Little Lord Fauntleroy* and all the people who lived around kind of the *slaves.*"

He had spoken of being isolated before in connection with his wife, so this was the right track. It sounded as if he had withdrawn and there was a problem concerning his narcissistic needs. Lord Fauntleroy was an effeminate mother's boy with manifest ideas of grandeur, who really felt inadequate compared with the other boys (brothers).

"But you were mother's baby."

"No, there was very *little relationship* between my mother and myself."

This was probably denial by reversal to the opposite. It also described the loss.

"How come?"

"Because, well, in those days we always had cooks, governesses and what not."

"You mean you went to them?"

"We all had good relations but *didn't see our mother very much,* and of course in most of my memory mother started to spend an increasing amount of time being sick."

His memories of a close relationship with mother were associated only with sick, painful incidents. The loss at first was chronic and cumulative.

"So you didn't see mother much except when she got sick?"

"Yes. actually *I saw more of her then.*"

"After she got sick?"

"More of her then than I did before!"

Most children take the credit or *blame* for whatever occurs in their egocentric world.

"What did you think was the matter, because you didn't know anything about cancer and metastases?"

"Well, I only know that she was very badly sick. That was about all I know."

"Do you remember what you thought was causing her to be sick?"

"No, coming from—my father was a chemist. One of my uncles was a physiologist. There was a rather scientific family there. Even my brothers who were older were philosophically and technically inclined, so at a very early age I learned the lingo."

"You learned the lingo? You mean you could have said cancer and metastases? What did that mean to you?"

"There was enough lingo around so that I didn't build up any particular fantasies about it."

This was only a type of denial.

"Or at least if you built up a fantasy, you are not aware of it?"

"Yes, yes, I was educated enough to know there are diseases and doctors to take care of them and there are operations, there is this and that, and actually in this surrounding I was rather *prematurely* educated. I read Shakespeare when I was ten."

"So you mean you always had rationalizations to fall back on?"

"Yes, and in addition to that, I felt I knew it all."

"Because this is what you said you always did?"

"Yes, I believed that I knew the facts."

"That kind of comforted you a little?"

"Yes. I think I did know more than the ordinary child of seven to ten."

All of these statements betrayed his flight from anxiety-laden fantasies about the unknown terrors that made mother ill. A precocious ego development was suggested.

"Let's say then from seven to ten you had all kinds of rationalizations and could control your emotions even then, huh?"

"There was, as a matter of fact, a kind of pride when I went to the hospital."

"In controlling yourself?"

"Yes."

"How did you react to her death? Did you control yourself there too?"

"By and large. The, the, this I do remember rather vividly, while I don't remember all the other things which fall together in one big picture, but the day of her death—she died at home, not in the hospital—I do remember that."

The therapist now tried to awaken some feeling.

"They sent her *home to die?*"

"Probably, that was probably what was done. Nothing could be done operatively any more, and an uncle of mine, an uncle spoke to us children. Father was with mother when she died. My immediate reaction was one of terrific *hate* against the uncle."

The uncle was a bad-father figure. He was probably illustrating ambivalent feelings of long duration. His anger was due to mother deserting him. It would be surprising if he did not also blame his father and himself. The death guilt was in all probability sexualized.

"Why?"

"I don't know why, I just remember."

"You mean your rationalizations failed you?"

"Failed, and I went to the upstairs john and cried."

He paused, lost in thought.

"You remember?"

"Yes, and I was called down and, uh, then I was called down and I saw my father. My father cried, and that made me somewhat uncomfortable, but again it gave me a little bit of superior feeling of being the well-controlled boy."

He was already advanced along the road where his anxieties and feelings in general were controlled by isolation and other compulsive characteristics.

"You went to the toilet to cry?"

"Yes. That was the one place I could lock myself up. It's the only privacy a little boy has, the only one."

He laughed at the idea.

"That's the place for privacy?"

"Yes, to get rid of a lot of things."

"To get rid of a lot of things? What do you mean?"

"Well, of course, then it was our custom to lock the toilet. It has also a very strong symbolic meaning of privacy in addition to the strictly toilet fantasies. It is really the one place where no one can disturb you."

"What do you mean?"

"Many people don't. In many houses, if the bathroom door is closed, it is occupied. If it is opened, it is not occupied, but there is a real, very noticeable *bar* or is it a *latch*?"

"Latch or bar whatever you want to call it."

"As a matter of fact, in our upstairs john, I remember there was even an "occupied" or "unoccupied" sign like in a public toilet to make it even more symbolic."

This all fitted in with his compulsive character traits but could not be used now. He was treating the toilet as a place he could go and have "dirty," secret fantasies which he would only gradually reveal. The therapist had to be interested more in his *feelings* than his rationalizations.

"And you remember crying?"

"Then during the night, mother died during the night, well I'm sure being only ten years old I did sleep most of the time, then waking up in the morning I had the fantasy that it isn't true, perhaps it isn't true, even though I knew damn well it was. I didn't have to ask anybody. I just kind of thought by waking up the whole thing could be undone. Then the next day father asked me if I wanted to see mother and I did not, and I was just led into the room then and she was all covered up with flowers and ferns. That was about all I remember of that. But my relationship was always, before and after, well after of course but even before, was always a father-son relationship. I was *father's baby* from way back and remained so to his death."

This was hardly likely, but the material was worth exploring. Little Lord Fauntleroy was a mother's boy, a sissy. He probably meant he turned to father.

"When was that?"

"He died—of course, this enters *into the marriage picture too.* This is one of the things that *frightens* me. I analyze too easy. There must be something wrong. I get these things out awfully fast."

This was more correct than he believed. The affect was displaced. He laughed.

"But he died, uh, when he was seventy-six. I didn't show much concern. I believe. *I am very facile hiding my feelings even when I have them.*"

"As you said, you have controlled them ever since you were seven years old or before. So there was a good reason for it. Maybe this is what you had to do."

"I think so. So anyway he died."

"When he was seventy-six?"

"That was just at the time when I had broken up with Mary, during our going-together stage."

"What year was that?"

"That was around '47."

"Around '47! About the time you had come out of service, you had met her and then you went with her for how long?"

"We were going together around three-quarters of a year, let's say, something like that."

"So if you got out after Hiroshima, that would be '46, I think."

"That's right."

"So, around '47 father died?"

"He had been living in New York. I lived here. And during his last disease—I never really broke with Mary but then we just met a few times for lunch."

"You were on the rebound from father and she was on the rebound from a cousin?"

"Sure, and then father got his final terminal disease."

"What was that?"

"Heart."

"Heart?"

"It was, of course, during the severe nurse shortage and my father lived with my middle brother and his wife in New York. They couldn't find anybody. Oh, Mary was a graduate nurse, and I met her through her best friend, another nurse who at that time was in some other place but was available for a week anyway or five days, so we arranged for this other girl to come and take care of father, and then Mary got three days free from the hospital and came up with me to New York too to take care of father. My father, however, more or less refused to be nursed by Mary. He had met her before with me. He liked her very much, and that I am sure had quite a bit to do with our getting married."

"That he liked her?"

"Yes. He kind of indicated I should."

"What do you mean?"

"Well he rather strongly indicated that he would like us to get married. As a matter of fact, we never told him that we had broken up at any time. He sensed it a little bit, and I am sure that had an awful lot to do with that."

"So you married her right after he died?"

"Not too long after that. We made the, or rather as Mary likes to quote me anyway, I made the decision to get married rather than we."

"You made the decision?"

"Just quick one evening, uh, when we spent an evening together. She just had applied for a job in Detroit, which she only told me about later. So she canceled her job in Detroit after I indicated the idea that we should get married. We got married within a week after that. Unfortunately, it was actually from the time of getting married that our relationship *deteriorated*, at least it had an awful lot of ups and greater downs, and then a few ups and greater downs again."

"You mean right from the beginning?"

"Right from the beginning, yes!"

"You didn't get along so well?"

"Yes! Well, of course, obviously my particular personality make-up isn't the easiest to get along with and she had a lot of burdens to bear. She feels she could have gotten along with any *man*."

This must have stung him. It had the value of a self-accusation.

"With any *man*?"

"Yes. She now tells me that she was, of course, terribly upset by my very rational attitude after we got married. I kind of made it clear that I was going to be a good husband, and so forth and so on, but nothing about love and *that sort of thing*."

"She didn't know how afraid you were of that sort of thing?"

"Yes. That's right. But as people do, she also forgets that if such a game can work at all, two must play it and she also made me believe that this was a game she was trying to play anyhow. So we kind of muddled along most of the time and the only trouble was both of us were not getting younger, and well with gay parties and what not in the first years we could always overcome it by just ignoring it."

"And now you want to see if you can't salvage something out of this relationship?"

"Yes, definitely!"

"Because although you have been in control of your feelings for a long time, you are now wondering if you might have a breakdown?"

"Yes, but even here I don't feel strongly about it."

"You mean by breakdown that all this will come to a head?"

"Yes. That's true."

"And you won't have control over things."

"The breakdown may not be that I literally snap. I still may be going to work."

"How do you mean?"

"I'd lose all enjoyment of myself."

"You mean become depressed?"

"Yes, I mean I would just live on as a *lump*, as it were, with no enjoyment of life and no relationships. Many people do it, but this is certainly not something to look forward to."

"You mean without love or sex or feelings for life? As if dead?"

"Yes. This is something I have started to notice increasingly. Also I'm just repressing everything in myself. I *was never excessively aggressive sexually*. It didn't *bother me* in my bachelor years. I didn't have hundreds of affairs and what not, but I enjoyed the ones I had."

What he meant was that his aggressive sexualized fantasies about mother's death inhibited him. In another sense, *his* aggression had been the cause of mother's death. He did not trust any woman. This will be discussed in detail later.

"You could take it or leave it?"

"Right! But as luck had it, always when it started to get uncomfortably long and with no love interest around, something new would occur."

"Something would come along in the nick of time?"

"Yes. Something would develop more or less, but now it is at the point where I just have a desperate feeling, and *I'm not the type where my work is full compensation for me*, so that I just can see that if I don't salvage something from the relationship, well, of course, in a situation like that you do consider *divorce* at times. I hope you can do something for me."

Here he was hinting that his work relations (with men) were unsatisfactory too! In a sense, it was as if when he could not run away from a relationship it deteriorated into a condition that had once been traumatic for him, according to the law of repetition compulsion. There was a return of the repressed.

"Well, we'll see what can be done. Is five o'clock a convenient hour?"

"Yes. Unfortunately I can't see you more than once a week."

"Why is that?"

"It is very difficult for me even once a week as I am all over the country by plane. This is one reason I have come, my fear of planes, you know."

"Well, let's try it on a once-a-week basis and see what we can do. We'll determine where we'll go from there after we know more about your problems."

"Actually after this last *shock*, funny as it may be, I felt much better about it."

"What do you mean?"

"The shock resolved a few things which I think are less well rationalized."

"What shock do you mean?"

"The shock of seeing Mary do that."

"The shock of her making this suicidal attempt?"

"Yes. At least I think I understand her a little better and am a little more sympathetic."

"All right. Is Friday convenient for you?"

"That will be perfectly all right. First I must make it clear that I may have to go on business trips continually and what not. They usually do not come at the last minute and I usually have some influence on it. Fridays are fine. Well, I'm glad Dr. Smith sent me to see you."

"Thank you. Then I'll see you Friday. Good-by."

"Good-by."

This man revealed to us from what he said about himself and his wife that he was a lonely, isolated person on the verge of a depression of a type associated with fairly adequate defenses. He was predominantly an anxious, obsessional and phobic person who avoided highly-charged emotional situations of a sexual and aggressive nature. Intellectualization and isolation defenses were used freely by him. At the end of the interview, he let us know that he was afraid of becoming depressed and losing all his abilities to relate to others—a kind of dying. He also talked about his brother, whom he called a "schizophrenic" with psychosomatic problems. Of course, we do not know what his idea of a schizophrenic was, and the therapist should have asked him. In later interviews he developed the theme that he had a psychosomatic problem himself in the form of migraine headaches. His fears were primarily those of depression, loss and emotional involvement. He was terrified of becoming attached to someone and helplessly dependent upon them, and then losing them. He tried to avoid a loss of one kind and found himself involved in other kinds of losses. The attempted suicide of his wife obviously had aroused fantasies he had about his mother. He also hinted that he had physical problems concerning sexual intimacy as well as personal communication difficulties. Pathological mourning was suggested.

In the second interview he was wary, and tried at first to get the therapist to discuss psychological matters. He could only talk about his wife, how she needed guidance and relief from responsibility because she was so depressed. He said he had seen many of his friends' marriages break up and didn't want this to happen to his. He felt he was more like a father to a daughter than a husband or a lover. Neither he nor his wife was satisfied in one sense. For him it had been a marriage of convenience. He then said he had never been very passionate and was now more or less *impotent*. His wife had had two affairs. One was with a *"boy"* who told him he loved his wife. He told the poor boy he would have to "work it out." The other affair was with a "man," but she just "toyed" with him. Both affairs were hopeless, as she wasn't really interested. He too had had a few casual affairs. This led to how ever since his mother died he had been detached in his emotions. His wife was pictured as a naïve daddy's girl type who desperately wanted a child but was not capable of taking care of one and would only collapse under the effort and be even more depressed. All of these figures were part images of himself, as the material will illustrate.

The second interview, from the point of view of affect, revolved around his sexual impotence. He mentioned it quite casually at first and it was treated by the therapist as part of a general reaction tied up with his withdrawal from love and people in general. Later it was hinted that his casual attitude toward his impotence, extramarital affairs and his wife was a matter of protective coloration. He agreed with this and accepted it intellectually.

The third interview began with a discussion of a group-therapy project at his place of business. The group had discussed creativity. This concerned his profession at first and then drifted towards children and back to his profession. His father was tremendously creative, with over two hundred patents in his field. He and his brothers had only a few patents in their fields and he felt *his* creativity was frustrated. This led to children again and his wife's longing for a child. He then revealed that although he could not communicate with his wife he once could with an older female *cousin*. The therapist remembered that his wife had married on the rebound from a love affair with a cousin, so kept him in this area and the interview proceeded as follows.

"Actually that was quite a bit my pattern before I was married, to latch on, not to flippant persons, but to persons who in some way were not really available."

"How do you mean?"

"Well, they were safe. They didn't always turn out safe! I always thought, however, that if I ever really loved it would be a *terrific* thing and I was pretty damn sure it wasn't going to happen."

"Terrific in what sense?"

"Sexually, intellectually and what not. For many years I built this image around the girl I had my first affair with who was *eight* or *ten* years older than me, and when I was *very young*. I could build it around her very easily because she had an *outward attitude* which made any continuing tie impossible because of the age difference."

"How old were you?"

"I was, well actually I fell in love with her before a time when I had a good rationalizing vocabulary. I actually fell in love with her when I was ten."

This was around the time his mother died. He was on the rebound!

"And she was how old?"

"At that time she must have been at least eighteen."

"That's a big difference to a ten-year-old."

She was like an adult. It was probable that she had become a mother substitute. This permitted him to deny and evade the loss of mother.

"Yes."

"What do you mean by an affair?"

"Well, in a way she reciprocated. Of course this is the story of my life and maybe there are a lot of clues in it. She was my *cousin* and, to make life more complex, at a much later date I found out she was *desperately in love* with *my father*, who was a widower. And then eventually she married him, much later."

The situation was made to order for the preservation and intensification of oedipal problems, and had probably acted as a prepuberty trauma. He appeared to have some intellectual insight regarding this, but it was defensive; i.e., "I understand, so we can let the matter rest."

"She married him? Let's see, when you were ten, how old was father?"

"Oh, there was a terrific age difference of some thirty years."

"So she was eighteen and father was already forty-eight?"

"Yes, approximately. He married her when she was about twenty-eight."

"So he was fifty-eight and she was twenty-eight, and you were twenty?"

"Yes."

"And were you still in love with her during these ten years?"

"I think I was very much genuinely and extremely fond of her as *long as she was alive.*"

"When did she *die?*"

"She committed *suicide.*"

"How old were you then?"

"At that time I was, uh, about *twenty-eight.*"

"Twenty-eight? So she was only thirty-six?"

This meant that his mother died when she was around thirty-eight as she was ten years younger than father. These ages were inexact and overdetermined, and probably meant that the cousin was equated with the mother. This love affair fixated him at an oedipal level and affected his remembrance of the past as well as his future expectations. The suicide intensified a withdrawal reaction that had probably begun very early in life.

"Why did she suicide?"

"I wasn't there. I was up north when it happened, but I understand she took *sleeping pills* and *jumped out of the window,* both! She was Polish. I'm half Polish. My father was Polish and my mother was old southern stock, so-called, and being also Polish my cousin couldn't take certain social snubs. My father on the other hand was a very forceful and fearless man. He got along with everyone. After this, however, he got out of the state. He gave up everything, of course, and came to New York, but he got out in a very orderly manner. As a matter of fact, the people who bought his property personally regretted his leaving and paid him very well for the property, and the entire town turned out to say good-by when he left."

As he related this, he appeared very tense. The therapist, therefore, decided not to remind him of the similarity of his cousin's suicide and the attempts of the wife, and let him rest for a minute before continuing. The wife took sleeping pills and jumped out of a car!

"Pretty hard to compete with a fellow like that?"

"Yes, well this is of course terrific, one of the school-book problems, and in addition I was always very attached to him emotionally. I was his *favorite son* but although I was emotionally very much attached to him I fought him almost like *mad*, even on the verbal level. We would discuss things quite violently."

He had said that this was the story of his life. His cousin's marriage must have made him horribly hurt and jealous. The oedipal constellation could be linked up indirectly.

"By the way, how much younger is Mary?"

"Mary is, of course, thirteen years younger than I, I suppose I'm repeating a pattern in that."

This type of insight is excellent but transient unless it is pinned down and underlined.

"You mean that this young woman who suicides, or makes a suicidal attempt with pills and jumping is an old story?"

"But this seems to be more than coincidental because, of course, I am not my father. I have not got *his strength.*"

He felt like a little oedipal boy.

"You said he had two hundred patents and you only had a couple."

"Yes, and as an example of his relations with his wife, this girl, as long as she was alive, was just completely *devoted to* and *dominated* by my father."

"So he was able to play the role of the *man* in spite of being quite a bit older?"

"Oh, yes, I'm sure of that!"

"How do you know?"

"She was before that, well, she always played a game, entertaining, going to parties as any young girl would do, and after she married she led my father's life which was a, not very much of a social life and all that."

"She was willing to give it up?"

"Yes, and apparently very happily. She was not a well-adjusted person to start with, as one can see from the real suicide and breakdown under this social-pressure situation."

"How do you mean?"

"Of course the breakdown was under conditions which, although now it comes back to me! She did make one suicide attempt before!"

This was even more similar to the behavior of his wife.

"When was that?"

"When my father first refused to marry her, but that was just an attempt."

"How do you mean?"

"I think she was putting up a fight. I think the reasons why my father did not want to marry her was because of his old-fashionedness and feelings of his responsibility to his children, and all that."

"You must have been terribly hurt if you loved her ten years. Was that before father knew her?"

"No."

"She was around the house?"

"She was his niece. He knew her since she was born."

"So you were in love with her and she was in love with him?"

"Yes, but at that time he really didn't know it."

"How did she feel about you?"

"She always liked me very much."

"As a boy?"

"Yes."

"How do you mean?"

"There was a little more than just friendship, I think. I was there at the time when she thought she came out to be with my father. I was kind of a *substitute when he wasn't interested.*"

This had depressing oedipal overtones.

"So you mean she would come in and be consoled by you?"

"It was a very clear relationship in this respect. I was *ten* or eleven when I first knew her, because she lived in a different city. I really only met her for the first time when she was there for the summer, or something like that. I was *ten* or eleven, something like that. Ah, the relationship *deteriorated* after a very short affair of only one week."

"What do you mean?"

"Yes! A sexual affair."

"You had intercourse with her?"

"Yes!"

"How old were you then?"

"I was just eighteen."

"So she was twenty-six and it was just before she married father?"

"It was two years before, but my mathematics are not quite right. It was about two years before she married father."

"So you had an affair with her for one week, and what happened?"

"Well, that was quite understandable. I wasn't *stupid enough to think that she was in love with me.* It was under very *queer* circumstances, anyway."

This was probably a denial of the truth. There are no negatives in the unconscious. He felt stupid (narcissistically mortified) later.

"What do you mean?"

"Her father had just died a short time ago, and her mother kind of collapsed under that. I had just graduated from high school. My oldest brother and I went to visit them. It was kind of my graduation present. My oldest brother took me along or went with me for a weekend, and, uh, they invited me to stay there for a week. My brother had to go back to the university. I stayed the week. It was one of these very unreal situations which lead into things like that. Everything was in favor of it. Her mother was in a rather depressed state. She was more or less available for lunch and dinner in a superficial social way, but she wouldn't go to a theatre or anything because the family was still in mourning. Once I went to the theatre alone so I really wouldn't have to participate in that. There was very little going on while I was there. The whole family retired early in the evening; normally her sister and brother and I were put up in some kind of a sitting room which was next to her bedroom."

With the death of father, the daughter was on the rebound. She represented an oedipal object for him in a double sense. She was like a motherly sister and she also was an alter-ego image of himself; i.e., he too was in love with a dead parent and on the rebound.

"She already knew you cared for her?"

"Yes."

"Ever since you were ten?"

"There was no doubt in my mind that she obviously liked me genuinely and deeply. She was always very fond of me, and she talked intimately with me, even when I was twelve or thirteen years old, and this is a thing of course which at that age aroused my love terrifically. The very fact that she talked with me as an adult and with absolutely no chitchat about school books and what not. We talked about philosophy, the theatre, people, love, sex, what have you."

"You could really *communicate* like an adult with her?"

This was a way of linking the present situation with the past.

"It was a terrific experience!"

"To *communicate* this verbal type of love?"

"Yes. And of course on the other hand ever since I was *a little boy* she would put me on her lap once in a while, or kiss me goodnight and what not, and my mother had just died when I was ten."

Now he was ready for a simple confrontation. The implications would arise later.

"So really she took mother's place."

"Yes, and in a little while she showed me how to manicure my hands, etc."

"So you turned right from mother to her, and she became a better mother."

"Sure, in many respects."

"So you had a happy relationship with her that few boys are able to have?"

"Yes, a very useful way of learning about life."

This was a vague statement. The therapist could innocently test it.

"How did it happen? You were next to her room and she came to you?"

"How do you mean? The sexual relation? Well, this was of course accidental."

"Do you mean because her father died and she was quite distraught?"

This was a denigration of their relationship and had to be denied by him.

"She was actually not quite distraught. I think her relationship with her father was a fond, but not a very deep one. Her father was very typically, even though I didn't know him well, a rather dashing businessman. He treated his daughter always like a lady, that was his relationship, but it was not deep."

This probably referred more to his wishes and a denial of his fears. At another level he was talking about the little-girl side of himself in relation to his own father. At another level, it referred to the mother.

"But she married a man who was so much older, as if she needed a father to make up for what she didn't get from father."

This was a trial balloon. Actually it referred to him.

"Yes! Because her father was really almost like a caricature of a society journalist, dapper."

"You said that you, too, were sort of not close to mother?"

"No, not very close but it was a very good relationship. There was no *antagonism*."

Now things could be superficially clarified.

"So you sort of repeated in a sense what she did. You went for the older girl to make up for what you didn't get from mother, and she went from a father who didn't give her much to the older man to make up for what she didn't get."

"That is right. I *feel it is right*."

"And in the process your paths crossed?"

"Yes, quite obviously."

"For a week?"

"For a week."

"How did it seem to you?"

"Oh, wonderful!"

He laughed.

"How do you mean?"

"It was a terrific experience. I was cocky as hell after it."

"How do you mean?"

"Everything after that *was an anticlimax.*"

"She went to father afterwards."

"Yes, about two years after."

"You had her for just a week?"

"Oh, when we met afterwards, which happened several times, on neutral grounds as it were, she didn't refuse to be intimate with me but she avoided the opportunity. It was not even obvious that she did, but I think she very carefully did it."

"How do you know?"

"Well, I think she had the feeling there was no percentage in it for her."

"What do you mean?"

"I was too young and I think also there was a little bit of kindness towards me for worshiping her."

"So, it was a nice relationship in which you gave her comfort and she accepted it from you in this time of stress?"

"Yes, she helped me in the same manner as she did before in showing me how to wash my hands and keep my nails clean."

"She was like an older sister or a mother?"

"And she helped me to become an adult."

"An older sister and a mother substitute and yet on a much more intimate basis?"

"Yes. Somehow due to the *cousin relationship* we could go one step further."

"From then on, any relationship with a woman was an anticlimax?"

"In a manner of speaking, yes!"

"You've never again had it so good?"

"Yes, that's true."

"It affected your heart as well as your head?"

"I was never as elated!"

"And you've never been able to communicate with a woman like you could communicate with her in all spheres?"

"No. As a matter of fact, of course it went that way."

"You must have thought of her a lot."

"I built her up over the years."

"Ordinarily a boy who has had such a wonderful experience with someone and who was so close to a woman and who was able to have such communication, verbally, sexually, spiritually and emotionally, he would frequently daydream about her."

"Kind of, yes, I think I did."

"He might even have her as a continual daydream."

"I probably did, of course. Actually the fact is it was around the time when a boy thinks he will be *king of the world* anyway and hasn't had any *bad disillusionments* yet. The very fact that she then married my father was a *dreadful shock* and I conveniently forgot all about it."

His work relationship with men was involved as well as his love life.

"Do you remember?"

"What? When I was told? Yes! And I conveniently forgot in a relatively short two years, or whatever it was."

"Where were you when you heard?"

"That she actually told me that she loved my father?"

"Where were you when you heard about it?"

"I had just come back from a trip to Florida and stopped to see friends somewhere in the country and I got a wire from my father."

"You say it was a dreadful shock? In what way?"

"Well, it was one of the few times I just cried outright and what not. But when I got over it, when I collected myself, it was five minutes or so actually, after a short time I built up an image. I made even more of *a hero* out of myself. Here I was, a young boy, you know, in a very complex, romantic situation, an interlacing thing. It took me out of the ordinary and helped me to overcome the shock. Anyway I got over it."

He meant he retreated into narcissistic grandiose fantasies.

"But nothing ever touched you like that afterwards?"

"No, it's true."

"As you said, you more or less skipped around from one to the other?"

"Yes."

"So you really were *on the rebound?*"

"Yes, it was a very long bounce, and the funny thing here is that, and I think also very unfortunately, while in a flirtatious mood before I was married, I told this to Mary at one time. There was still, even as old as I was then, there was still a mixture of a very *warm remem-*

brance on the one hand, and also a little bit of the boy left who was very proud of the *unusual circumstances*. And the funny thing is then very shortly afterwards my feelings changed and my memory now in relation to this cousin is much more on a *story basis*. Up to that time, it felt like a *real* thing to me and then very shortly afterwards it just seemed *different*, and is now something I bring up in a therapy situation, but it doesn't mean much to me any more."

Going with Mary permitted this. Unconsciously he must have displaced the affect belonging to the past onto the situation with Mary, but by then he was exceedingly ambivalent. It would be necessary to reveal to him both the love and hate and connection with the past.

"You mean as if it had happened to somebody else?"

"Yes, it's not on my mind much if any now. Mary is my only problem."

"And yet it was such a shock to you that you really have never been able to feel like that again. I mean have such a depth of feeling."

"Yes, I did get upset."

"You must have been terribly hurt?"

"Yes, that's right."

"And you've wanted to communicate the same way with Mary, verbally and physically, and yet something has always held you back, and this is also obviously what Mary wanted from you, but you just couldn't trust her or any woman, in a sense."

"And of course she is very observant about things which matter. This story is very representative of the block in me, and she is very resentful of it."

"Of course. In other words, there's always that ghost of what was her name, what was your cousin's name?"

"Eve."

"Eve?"

He laughed.

"The original sin in other words."

"The primordial woman, the real mother of us all, she has always stepped in between you and Mary?"

"I was *always keenly aware of the symbolism*. The name itself had a ring for me and all that."

This pointed up the inadequacy of intellectual knowledge.

"Quite a formidable person for Mary to compete with?"

"Yes, you said it."

"I mean there was no competition. How could any ordinary flesh-and-blood-woman compete with a ghost like that?"

He nodded.

"Dead people are always hard to compete with."

"Right! Because usually you haven't lived with them long enough to devaluate them."

"And of course the, the queer thing is, both from a story value and I think somewhere the story value has a lot to do with it, that when Mary met my father, my father for one reason or another didn't like any of my former girl friends, but he *really went for her!*"

"So Mary in some ways then took on the role of Eve?"

"Probably. But of course I never did, or now don't admit it, and if I don't admit it, I mean I don't admit it!"

"No, we don't really know, but you must have been *dreadfully hurt.*"

"Well, I must have, of course."

Obviously he wasn't ready to face his aggressiveness toward all these frustrating women.

"This is the big problem. What happened? Your attitude must have changed. What you remember are only these nice things. There were two Eves, the one you loved and the one who left you and used you."

"Of course I went through the usual face-saving procedures and when I came back to Montgomery and first saw my father, well, I started to play a very romantic role, and I insisted I must talk to Eve once alone. That's the only time before and after I did that. Having reviewed in my mind probably all the classic literature on how you behave like a gentleman, I had but one talk and I don't know really what I wanted to talk about. It was a face-saving procedure. I thought to myself, I can face it! You know talking about all this has given me quite a headache."

He smiled wryly and felt the left side of his head gingerly. The connection of headaches with the mother-Eve-Mary constellation was obvious. The therapist decided to ignore the somatic symptom temporarily, as the personal relationships were more important.

"What did you talk about?"

He frowned and nodded.

"It's very, very hard to say and for that matter to even remember."

"You must have some ideas."

"Well, I don't know. We've gone over the story very quickly. As I said, I haven't thought about it since I met Mary."

"Mary attempted suicide the same way as Eve, and aroused a great deal of anxiety in you. It must have had some repercussions somewhere along the line in your fantasies of why Eve suicided. And *you* said you had a longing to communicate with Mary in the same way that you once communicated with Eve. This is only the beginning. As *you* hinted, we've only skimmed the surface."

"It all seems very romantic now. Actually, what surprises me is how well I've gotten over it."

"It seems like the same old plot with a new leading lady."

"Yes, but there are lots of differences too. By the way, this headache is killing me. I suppose it's psychosomatic, but it certainly doesn't help to know it."

He meant the same thing concerning this attempt to draw comparisons. Simply talking about Eve aroused anxiety which was felt as pain. His headache was a warning in connection with the revival of his old yearnings and frustrations.

"How long have you been having them?"

"Oh, they're an old problem. My mother had them worse than I do."

"Then you probably know how to handle them. Okay. I'll see you next week at the same time, if that's convenient?"

"I'm not so sure I do. I'll be very pleased if I get rid of them as a bonus in my treatment. Okay. I'll see you then. Good-by, Doctor."

Intellectualization, rationalization, communication, using the head were threatened by a massive eruption of evaded affects connected with the denial of painful losses. Through use of his "head" defenses, he kept his grief, rage, guilt, yearning, distrust, etc., in check or in control. The headache warned that this control was slipping. As it was the end of the interview, it was not necessary to do anything. Otherwise, the therapist would ease up and induce him to talk about other things where his control was adequate or excellent. Headaches in this sense can be considered a conversion symptom representing the defense against affects, as well as a symbolic expression of the affects themselves. In another sense, the headache symbolized the failure of a phallic narcissistic defense. The pain itself was probably mediated in terms of muscular tension and fatigue and associated vascular changes. The secondary physical effects of his chain smoking are ignored here, although they too are involved in the psychic elements attached to his oedipus complex.

Now, all the main details were out in the open. There were three important levels of relationship so far. These concerned mother, Eve and Mary. He must have had a bad relationship with his mother from the earliest days. Why had he taken over her headaches? Headaches are often tied up with repressed attacks of rage associated with passive longings for a baby-mother relationship, either directly or by proxy. In this case, he had identified with this aspect of the lost object. He was frightened by his wife's demands for a baby. The problem revolved around a gradual revelation of how his infantile narcissism had been injured and then integrating this knowledge in all areas of his life, past and present. He was able to talk very glibly about his past, as almost all his affect was tied up in his relationship with Mary and in the present. He was far more dependent upon her and angered by her than he realized and full of anxiety about the possibility of their relationship being ended. From the point of view of his body image, he was preoccupied with loss and castration anxiety, which appeared symptomatically as impotence and headache.

The next interview began with the patient's describing how confused he had become over a *double* situation that was occurring, meaning his *feelings* in therapy and in a form of group therapy that was all the rage in his industry at that time. At times he felt elated and on the verge of understanding something, and at times hopeless and depressed. The *double situation* where Eve and Mary were *confused* was then introduced by the therapist as his real problem. He then talked about a *double* switch he had made after Eve's marriage to his father. He changed his field of work and left home for New York City. There he was depressed. Whenever he smoked, he became dizzy. He felt queer, nervous and tense, thought he had ulcers, and was very restless. He had a short love affair with a sympathetic older girl but when he tried to have intercourse he was impotent and developed a severe nosebleed and *headache*. His nervousness led back to his childhood when he was three years old. He was always sickly and had been terribly overprotected by his mother. She too was nervous and excitable and fainted very easily. The first time he remembered her fainting he was very frightened. He had run away to tease her and had hidden in some bushes. He saw her faint and thought he had killed her. She fainted whenever father was late from work and often wore a black scarf. It developed that because of *mother's* anxieties and a school phobia on his part he had remained home with private tutors while his two brothers went to public school. At this time, he had severe nosebleeds, headaches and frequent colds. As his mother began to sicken from a slowly developing breast cancer, he withdrew from her and developed a whole series of compensatory masturbatory fantasies. In them he was better than his brothers, very independent and always had to be different. He had developed what he called a *double* approach to life. On the surface he was coldly rational, detached and amused and cynical in appearance. Underneath he felt hurt, depressed, sick, aging, fed up, angry and *uncreative.*

As this patient became aware of his passive feminine "creative" longings for a child and his sadomasochistic fears for his wife, based upon his experiences with Eve and his mother, he talked at first about how *his wife* wanted to leave *her* therapy, then how he wanted to "cut it off" himself. He grew more and more depressed as he realized his hidden hatred of women in general and Eve and Mary in particular. He remained away from his hour on occasion and felt more and more angry at his wife for giving him an ultimatum; i.e., "either we try for a child or get a divorce." He did not trust her to be a mother and feared she would suicide if he divorced her. This material was repeated in session after session.

The seventeenth interview began with a discussion of how he and his wife had sent his wife's sick and senile father to the hospital. He felt guilty of "selling him down the river." He then drifted to the matter of how shocking the *deterioration* of age was and how old he felt. He was convinced that *passive* people *deteriorated* faster than others. This was a body-image representative of his *deteriorated* relations with Mary. Finally he decided he would be *active* and dare to have a child. He became anxious to know if he could. He and his wife went to New York City and tried. He found himself potent, and both enjoyed each other's company as well as their physical relationship. In subsequent sessions he brought out his tremendous fears of aging and dying and unfulfillment—which meant no close family ties. He had always felt lonely and had never related well to either father or mother. The oldest brother had been a father substitute. He discussed his brother's families in detail, each of them having difficulties which he had anticipated would occur in any marriage he had. He declared bitterly that all he had dared to have was a pseudo marriage that was really only a legalized affair. At this time his anxiety and depression were very intense. He continued in this condition until around the twenty-eighth interview when Mary became pregnant and he became so panicky that he was put on small doses of meprobamate. He felt sure Mary would collapse if she had a child and that she would be a real suicide or really go insane. He readily saw that the same fears applied to himself. Around this time some important new historical material appeared. Let us listen to the thirtieth interview. At this time he was considerably less depressed and anxious.

He began the interview by talking about the death of his father-in-law. He had been comforting Mary. Neither of them could sleep. He joked with her over *her* attachment to daddy. The therapist used this material to go over his father's death in more detail than previously and how the death of father had allowed him to marry Mary. Her warmth and the way she got along with father aroused pleasant *warm* feelings in him. Father repeatedly hinted that he wanted him to marry Mary and treated Mary as if she were a member of the family. He would actually refuse to have any nursing help from her, although he did not mind getting help from his other nurse. The interview continued as follows:

"Yes, the other girl who was also a friend of the family actually and was very nice, he was just full of praise for the other girl."

"But it wasn't the same?"

"Yes, he had no objections at all to her very personal services."

"So you mean if he had been younger and not sick he might have married her himself?"

"This is Mary's theory!"

He laughed heartily.

"Really!"

"Yes."

"She thought that too, huh?"

"She always kidded about that. Well as a matter of fact, a joking situation like that has a lot more truth in it than is intended. She carried on an awful lot of chitchat with him about how they should pick out the wedding dress, and how they should get married and how much fun it would be for her to be my mother-in-law, my stepmother, really."

"Your stepmother?"

"Yes, this was an easy conversation topic."

"Or your mother-in-law?"

"No, my stepmother."

"Because if she were to be your mother-in-law?"

"Well the relationship is so *confusing* that I got confused."

"What do you mean by *confusing*?"

"I see what you mean, yes, it is a repetitive pattern."

"You get a girl, fall in love with her, have an affair with her and your father marries her?"

"Yes, yes."

"Then she becomes not your mother-in-law but your stepmother?"

"Yes, this was funny because it was carried out to a much greater degree because of an age barrier because a silly and established pattern is very—"

He paused and appeared confused.

"So you mean that in a sense she was married to father and had been like your wife and at the same time was your stepmother. If Mary were married to father and then you married her, she would be your wife and also your mother-in-law in the sense that she was like a daughter of Eve!"

"Yes, that's right."

He laughed heartily and then continued seriously.

"So it is almost as if in a sense she *was* a repetition of Eve."

By marrying Mary, he could deny the loss of Eve and mother.

"So you went from mother to Eve and from Eve to Mary?"

"Yes."

"Father was the common tie?"

"Yes. The funny thing is this pattern goes even further. I mentioned the other day my oldest brother with whom I used to have a very close relationship. He knew practically all the girl friends I had between my cousin and getting married, all the various and sundry friends and lesser entanglements, and he disapproved of all of them. He didn't like any of my girl friends at all. The first one he approved of was Mary, so this was a double approval."

"So there was a double approval between father and the oldest brother? You say you used to have a close relationship with him?"

The role of the brother as a father figure was worth exploring.

"Well, I think I mentioned the last time, as we grow older brothers don't communicate any more."

"That's right. How old were you when you were close to him?"

"Oh, it actually was, well it is still a close one only we don't take advantage of it."

"Was he like father?"

"No, not at all. None of us were. The middle one had the ambitions but not the stature. I think one never can inherit a strong personality because even if they had it, it would be *suppressed*."

"How do you mean?"

"It just can't come out. It just can't flourish."

"Because?"

"Under a very strong person."

"You mean father was like a tree. All the ones who grew under him were stunted?"

"Kind of stunted, yes."

"He was so strong?"

"Kind of. My oldest brother and I just escaped the competition because we just literally ran away. By choice we didn't enter our father's firm. The middle one did take the challenge and stayed with my father's firm, and he's the one who still runs it, and of course he was the one who was held down most. At least my oldest brother and I had our own professional activities and what not, but the middle brother professionally was always under him until he died."

"The middle brother now has the business?"

"Yes, the oldest one has the children. There is one in college and there are two little ones. As a matter of fact, the oldest brother without having been entangled was *very fond of my stepmother too.*"

"He was? How do you mean?"

"He just liked her very much."

"But he didn't have an affair with her?"

"Nothing was ever perpetrated, no."

"How do you know?"

"I think."

"That's what I wonder."

"I think up to the age of thirty as a minimum I know everything my oldest brother had ever done on any level."

"But after that?"

"Well, he stopped, I didn't see him quite so often and he didn't write diaries any more. If somebody keeps very complete diaries, it is very easy to be informed. At first, of course, I sneaked them out of his room, and then when my brother found out that I read them he would put signs in where it was interesting to read, so I didn't have to waste so much time."

"That was very nice of him."

He laughed.

"But I am reasonably sure or I have no reason to believe there is anything I do not know."

"Before thirty?"

"Yes."

"But after thirty?"

"I don't think much happened. I just didn't follow the detail any more."

"And your middle brother, was he interested in Eve?"

"No, no, she disliked him, or she took the same attitude as my older brother and I take. He is a nice brother who has his faults but we get along when we see each other and we get along fine when we don't see each other."

"He was somewhat a copy of your father?"

"Yes, but I think he was only a copy but not an image."

"And she didn't go for copies?"

"Yes! While my oldest brother and I are not a copy, actually the similarities are greater in fact, or interests and what not, but we weren't copies. The middle one tried to, just as one simply puts it, get into the footsteps of his father, so outwardly he could be the successful scientist, businessman, and all that on all the superficial levels, but my father really never had much communication with that brother. I was rather different from my father but in a very close relationship. We talked about everything and anything."

"About Eve?"

"Well, actually considering the times and his upbringing he faced that very well too. We had one or two talks about it."

"He knew you had had an affair with her?"

"Oh yes, yes!"

"You told him?"

"No, I think she did."

"She told him?"

"I never, this is one thing I never probed. Everything would be in guarded statements more or less. It wasn't in full detail."

"So why did you feel she told him?"

"Oh, because my father and I had a talk."

"When was this?"

"After he got married."

"Oh, I see, she told him after she decided to marry him?"

"Yes, because there was an obvious element of danger in it for her that I would get so angry I would start to tell stories or what not."

"So you mean she spiked your guns by telling him before?"

"Yes."

"If anyone was to tell, she wanted to be the one?"

"Yes. Nevertheless, I don't think everything was covered in Victorian language, as it were."

"What did he say?"

"This I don't quite remember, but I think, of course, he just intimated that he knew about my interest in her, as it were, and this shouldn't stand between us, that he understood it, and without saying it in any crude manner. I am translating that now because I only have a memory of it and not a recollection of the language, intimating that this was a very understandable and a very delightful *puppy love* on my part."

"How did you feel about that?"

"Of course I didn't accept it."

"You were very disturbed then?"

"Yet on the other hand I had always fixed my attitude that it was now my gentleman's duty to stand aside."

"That's easy to say intellectually, but you felt differently?"

"Yes, but of course in fact—"

He paused, lost in thought.

"You had to run away?"

"In effect I did."

"You did it and yet it cost you?"

"Yes."

"Because you were heartbroken?"

"Yes, and of course my father agreed very readily to my, uh, my going."

"Running away?"

"My stopping studying and going to New York for a year, but then I came back after a year."

"You had recovered?"

"And I had recovered."

"You had recovered to some extent but it still hurt?"

"Yes, but the outward adjustment was actually extremely well because I visited once or twice a week in my father's home, well at least once or twice for lunch."

"And you saw Eve?"

"Oh yes."

"How did you feel?"

"It worked out quite well because for one thing I think young boys are in many respects, uh, uh, are superficial as it were. For one thing, she did get older from my vantage point."

"A year older?"

"Well, when I was, well let me see, she was about eighteen years older than I, oh no, hell no, she was ten years older. So when I was eighteen, she was between twenty-six or twenty-eight, something like that."

"You mean that was when you had the affair?"

"Yes. Then when they got married, about two years later, she was close to thirty, and then one starts to look old. Secondly, also, she started to look older even when she was younger."

"How old was father then?"

"Father was forty-five years older than I."

"Sixty-five! So if you were twenty and she was thirty."

"No, he couldn't have been that old. There is something wrong. No, maybe that's not right."

"He was sixty-five?"

"That is something I would have to figure out correctly. That doesn't seem quite right."

"You said he was forty-five years old when you were born?"

"Yes, but I'm not so sure. No, wait a minute. No, let's see, he died in 1948 and he was seventy-six, and in 1948 I was thirty-eight. He was thirty-eight when I was born."

This was a way of arriving at reality. Forty-five referred to something else when he was *seven*. It indicated the confusion between mother and Eve.

"He was thirty-eight?"

"Yes."

"So he was fifty-eight years old and she was thirty?"

"Yes, and she was a very excellent dresser and well made up, you know, and all that, and after she got married she started to dress very simply and used no make-up and she was sliding into the thirties. This made the adjustment much easier for me."

"You mean now she could look more like your mother and less like your sweetheart?"

"Yes. In other words, there wasn't the outward obvious temptation."

Now the past had to be woven into the present.

"So when your father expressed his preference for Mary and told you to marry her, you married her?"

"Yes. It was around that time."

"And then you had trouble with your potency?"

"Quite possibly, quite possibly."

"Because you said your trouble with your potency really began after you were married."

"Oh, it began actually earlier."

"Really? How early do you mean?"

"Almost ever since I had *any* intercourse, very *frequently* I had a *mental block*."

He meant a physical inhibition. Calling it a "block" reduced his anxiety. This was a face-saving device, a narcissistic defense; i.e., a withdrawal from feelings at a baby-image level had itself become a source of anxiety. In another sense, castration anxiety was a warning of depression over object loss.

"What do you mean by a mental block?"

"Well, for some reason when the occasion was there I wasn't in the *mood*."

"What kind of block did you have? Do you mean you couldn't get an erection?"

"Yes, to put it very simply, and never as a constant thing, but it just occurred from time to time, just as in my marriage. Frequently there is no trouble at all from that point. From time to time, I just don't have the urge."

"What do you mean?"

"I had any amount of control I wanted. I could drag it out or not drag it out, and do more or less what I wanted. Only when the start was bad, it was impossible or nearly so."

"How about your wife? Was she concerned?"

"Mary? I don't know."

He laughed.

"Who else did you have in mind?"

"I really don't know. Any of the girls. Well, of course, she was, of course, because she took it as a rejection."

"How about your other girls? Did you have the same trouble with them?"

"No, at least to my knowledge it never bothered anybody."

"Except Mary?"

"Yes."

"With Eve it was all right?"

"That short time, yes."

"Was she mother's niece?"

"No, she was father's niece rather."

"He married his niece?"

"Yes. The whole damn thing is rather like Strindberg."

"A little on the incestuous side, huh?"

"Yes, which of course in addition I think flattered my ego very much and everything was going very well. *I was fully aware of the involvement.*"

He was really only partially aware of certain elements. The guilt and anguish over the necessity for renunciation were not conscious, nor was the loss of mother accepted.

"How do you mean?"

"I was aware *before* she married, I knew that she had quite an interest in father."

"How did you know?"

"She told me."

"She told you!"

"Yes."

"What did she tell you?"

"She told me she was in love with him but there was no hope that it would ever lead to anything."

"How long had she been in love with him?"

"From all I know, including from what she told me, I think easily since she was *sixteen years* old."

He must have been six or seven then! This showed how Eve and mother were equated. This probably was the reference point of the figure forty-five mentioned previously. This statement hid a complex. He was working a double front. At one level he had turned to father as a girl and away from the disappointing mother. At another level he had accepted Eve as a mother substitute. This allowed him to postpone the acceptance of mother's sickness and death.

"Before she had the affair with you?"

"Yes. That's when she told me."

"That's when she told you, when she was sixteen and you were six or seven, and father forty-five?"

"No, she told me when we had the affair."

"Oh, she told you when you had the affair?"

"Yes. It was somewhat obvious and I was *jealous of her relations* with my father."

"During your affair with her?"

"This was the only time we could talk."

"She told you while you were making love to her that she was in love with father?"

"Yes, in the intermissions, let's put it that way."

"She told you she was in love with father?"

"Yes, and had given up because there was no hope."

"So you felt there was hope for you?"

"Well then, as I said, uh, there was, then, in my intellectual frame of mind, I was very highly flattered."

"Because father was such a wonderful man?"

"Yes, no, also from a strictly snobbish point of view, on a strictly superficial snobbish level."

"How do you mean?"

"Here was a little boy, just eighteen, just graduated from high school and I was involved in this very complex thing that you only see on the stage, you know, and all that, you know."

The affair acted as a ready-made screen for his oedipal feelings, but had a severe traumatic effect nevertheless.

"In love with your beautiful cousin who was like a mamma to you and had dandled you on her knee and who was in love with your father? You were really mixing things up."

"Yes, at that point it was not *fearsome* at all *outwardly*. I don't think even *inwardly* because at that time I was at the point of *elation!*"

The elation signified mainly a successful denial of the loss of his mother.

"How do you mean?"

"Surely, because I had won her! It was when she married that it was pretty tough. At that time, even though I knew the victory was partly *by default*, it was still a victory. So, as I said, it had snob appeal. I think one can't overlook that in one's reaction either."

He was at this point calmly discussing a clinical problem. The affect was in the present situation. The therapist, therefore, returned to the present.

"Do you think this has had some effect on your relationship to Mary? You married her in a sense when father and brother approved?"

"Yes, the only thing that is contrary to the usual pattern is that while all my reactions were overt when I was young, they were subconscious when I was older."

"How do you mean?"

"At the point I married Mary, I had no awareness that the approval of my older brother and father had anything to do with it."

"Or that Mary was at all like Eve?"

"Yes. All that was deeply buried, while in the *original sin* it was out in the open."

This was a cryptic statement, meaning that he was aware of some of the oedipal elements when he was eighteen, although not of the connection between mother and Mary. He tried to appear indifferent but betrayed his tension by lighting a cigarette with his hands shaking.

"But tell me, didn't you think Mary was somewhat like Eve when she tried to suicide?"

"Yes! Of course it is difficult because these things are not noticeable to oneself because from the closeness the difference in personalities and intellectual interests and what have you are so strong that the common pattern for a closer view only comes out in *these discussions*. They don't come to mind by themselves because if you are in the situation you don't look at the pattern. You look at the very immediate things as they happen, the little details."

He had talked of his discussions previously.

"Tell me, did you have many discussions with father or your brothers?"

"On what?"

"About these problems and patterns?"

"No, well there was, like many people who grew up in this age and who have become much more relaxed in talking about all kinds of subject matters, sex and what not, there was still a little bit of reticence over being *too close* to father."

"You mean you were more that way with brother?"

"Yes. With father I could talk about my brother's girl friends and relationships not just from a joking point of view, but very much about the *complications* in my older brother's marriage, and we went into that in quite a bit of detail."

"He had complications in his marriage too?"

"Yes, but as far as one's own personal things, there was still a certain amount of reticence."

"You had to joke about them?"

"Yes."

"What kind of complications did your brother have?"

"Oh well, the one complication was that he married *a very young girl* who was *not mature for marriage* at that time, and he kind of *railroaded* her into *having a child* before she was ready at all."

This, of course, was one of his own fears and perhaps a fantasy in connection with Eve. At another level, he was the young girl himself.

"How much younger was she?"

"Oh, about the same difference as in my marriage, about thirteen or fourteen years."

"Thirteen or fourteen years?"

"Yes, this of course is where the pattern began. It runs closer between my oldest brother and my father and myself. My father's *first* wife was also quite a bit younger. She was twelve years younger."

"Your mother?"

This was a surprising bit of information about his self-fantasies.

"Yes. She also was quite a bit younger."

"So about the same difference between you and Mary?"

"Yes, yes."

"And your brother and his wife?"

"Yes, yes. And, uh, I think it took my sister-in-law quite some time to adjust to her marriage. She was always quite fond of my brother but he is, as I mentioned before, *a very difficult person to live with.* He is someone with whom it is very hard to establish *contact* for a great length of time, and of course she was very young and didn't know too many people. Well I think she had hardly any flirtations before to speak of, or anything. She came from a rather different background and there was quite a bit of adjustment necessary, which she has survived reasonably well, so that my father was always quite concerned about their relationship. We discussed it quite frequently. The other marriage was accompanied by more or less continuous joking because my father didn't much care for the wife of my middle brother even though he lived with them."

Actually he was talking about his affair with Eve, fantasies about his mother's and father's relations, his "affair" with father in terms of his identification with mother (the girl in him), and his brother too—condensation, reversal to the opposite, etc. The paragraph could be analyzed like a dream. In psychotherapy only the facets that are of immediate use at a superficial level can be developed.

"Why?"

"Oh, I think for rather good reasons. She's a rather superficial, society-type woman, clever and very loving on the outside you know, but nothing meant very much to her."

This also probably applied to his concept of mother.

He paused.

"This kind of rounds out that phase."

Now the interview could be pulled together.

"So in other words, Mary's father's death must have sort of reminded you somewhat of your father?"

"Yes, I think it brought a lot of these things out a bit. It turned out to be a very *traumatic experience* for her because she, as soon as he died, developed just terrible *guilt feelings*, just I think for the very fact that the man *never counted for anything* in the house and actually for very obvious reasons. He was a reasonably nice but a particularly *uninteresting* individual, and I think people don't face that when he died. She and her mother, both in different ways, had very *strong guilt feelings*. Mary nearly collapsed at the funeral Mass. I didn't know how I could support her to keep her from physical collapse, but I think the very fact that Mary was in such poor shape kept her mother going. I was in a position where I had to take bets with myself, which was better, that her mother's collapsing will keep Mary from collapsing, or the other way around. They just barely survived it. Mary, I think, has never been, or at least not any time she remembers too well, to a funeral."

In this situation there was a hidden reversal of things that happened at his mother's death, plus more. Actually he felt he never counted for anything and felt *uninteresting*.

"So how is she doing now?"

"Quite well, quite well. She calmed down after it was all over, but with relatives we haven't seen for years and never want to see again coming into the house and drinking our whiskey and that kind of thing. This to me seems like a barbarian tradition and of course her mother and sister-in-law go into the usual conversation of how nice he looked in the casket and sometimes I shudder at the language. I am not *overly sensitive* but when they literally speak of how nice the embalmers fixed him up, well!"

"Some fix?"

"Yes! It has an almost obscene character."

"What do you mean?"

"Oh, I just can visualize how they stuff things in to round him out a little here and there, you know. It's kind of a barbarian and vulture-like activity. They go into great details about that, how he would love the funeral and how he would have loved the way he looks!"

Now it was appropriate to make the references more personal.

"How was the funeral of your father?"

"We didn't have one."

"What do you mean?"

"As a matter of fact, I don't even know."

"You don't even know? But I thought you were there!"

"Yes, well the decision was there would be no ceremony and we just left it to the funeral home to do anything that was within the law, to just comply with the law."

"Well, what did they do?"

"Oh, I don't know, I just don't."

"You mean—I don't quite understand you?"

"There was no funeral."

"And you were there?"

"I don't know where his grave is, if any, or if he was cremated, I just don't know."

"And you've never asked your brothers?"

"I don't know whether they know."

"You never asked?"

"No."

"Why not?"

"Because I felt it was just entirely unnecessary because they didn't want a funeral, they didn't want any either."

"Why?"

"Because it didn't make any sense to me."

"And to your brothers?"

"All the brothers agreed."

The ambivalence toward his father led to hatred and denial of his death at the same time. The unresolved mourning and guilt were never worked out in an adult manner.

"All agreed?"

"I didn't make the arrangements so I don't know the details. We agreed that there wouldn't be any funeral or any grave or tombstone or anything like that."

"You mean you weren't curious as to whether they cremated him or buried him or threw him overboard?"

"No, the only decision was it has to be done in an established place within the legal requirements."

"Secretly?"

"Taken care of because *I personally never could see funerals of anyone.*"

This must refer to his mother too!

"What do you mean?"

"I, uh, don't know. But I think it was one of the few times that the three brothers were in full agreement."

"You mean you don't know who suggested it?"

"It might have been me. It doesn't seem odd to me at all. To me funerals, graves, tombstones are terribly odd."

"Did you feel that way when mother died?"

"Oh, yes. We never mentioned it. Actually I have no idea where my mother is buried. My brothers and I never paid any attention, visited her grave, or even thought about it. Of course my father did, but he was the old-school type, and he never tried to arouse any interest of that sort in us. So you see it was natural for me to feel this way."

"I'm just interested in your reasoning. What did Mary feel about it?"

"She was in agreement. I think my middle brother's wife was the only one opposed to it."

"What did she say?"

"She felt that there should be some, something, some ceremony or something."

"What did the undertaker say? You mean he never let you know where he was buried?"

"I didn't make the arrangements personally, as I said."

"Who made the arrangements?"

"I think my middle brother."

"You were never curious?"

"No, but I also wouldn't have any objection to asking."

"And you never wondered?"

"No. To me it is totally insignificant. I can remember my father. I don't need a grave. I don't need a tombstone. I don't need a funeral."

The trouble was that he couldn't forget.

"But nevertheless I wondered. But you remember your mother's funeral?"

"Well, she was buried. There was a funeral."

"You remember?"

"Yes. This I would say was about the first time but even then my opinions about funerals, graves and tombstones started to deteriorate very rapidly."

"But you were only a child."

"I was ten years old."

"Pretty young!"

"Yes, but I had a very strong impression that there was this gathering of completely disinterested people who came for a show."

He was referring to his own depersonalization and denial of affect.

"Did they talk about your mother?"

"Kind of, no, much less of that. Most of them just engaged in chitchat entirely."

"Where is she buried?"

"Somewhere, I don't know any more but in one of the Montgomery cemeteries. I never went back."

"And Eve?"

"Well, that I don't know either."

"Father never said?"

"Uh, no, I never asked him."

"Who told you she was dead?"

"I got a wire."

"From whom?"

"From father."

"He wired you telling that—?"

"Well, he didn't say it was suicide. That I learned later from my brother."

"Which one?"

"The middle one."

"The middle one?"

"Yes."

"How did she suicide?"

This was said in order to revive the old feelings.

"Jumped out of the window."

"At home?"

"Yes, and sleeping pills."

"Sleeping pills and jumping—both?"

"Yes. She took sleeping pills first and jumped is also the story as I remember it. I am reasonably *unsure* about it. Father several times did start to tell me about it. I would just listen but never egged him on to go into detail!"

"You didn't think father would want to be buried back in Montgomery. Nobody brought that up? He had never said?"

"I figured that he didn't give a damn about it."

"He didn't care?"

"No."

"It is all very interesting. I'll see you next week then?"

"I hope so."

"All right. Would you call early if you cannot come?"

"If not, I will call you. If I can't come, I will call. See you later."

It was now certain that he had never really given up the past. There had been no mourning, no reconciliation with reality and turning to new figures in a reality situation and as a man—only a reenactment of denied and repressed material in a modern setting and as an anxious and depressed boy.

The patient by now was chronically depressed and fearful and unable to deny it. For a while, he began to be involved in small accidents, such as cutting his hand, hitting his head while pruning a tree, and smashing in the front of his wife's car by backing his own into it. He complained of severe headaches and sleeplessness and took occasional doses of Seconal for this, prescribed by a physician to whom he had gone for a checkup. He was continually preoccupied by thoughts of aging and dying. This period lasted for about four months, during which time he was often absent, ostensibly because of colds or business trips. Around this time, his wife had been feeling very well but following a miscarriage she became depressed and he recovered his old poise. He related his fears of aging and dying to his father, whom he said denied aging actively and aggressively. He strongly disliked his own passive tendencies and for a while shifted the center of attention away from his love life to his work, where he said he had always selected fields of ambition where he couldn't fail and played with his career as he did with women. In both cases, he had never fully committed himself. He had shunned positions of management in just the same way that he had shunned fatherhood, and was now stuck at his present level where he felt professionally sterile. He had to be creative now or never, but had always felt he wasn't good enough to create anything worth while. When the therapist focused upon his fears of fatherhood, some interesting historical material emerged to the accompaniment of a marked increase in the frequency and severity of his migrainous headaches. These subsided as he began expressing more and more openly that he had always felt cheated, trapped and dammed up ever since Eve jilted him. He had always longed for an "intellectual" woman like Eve, and talked about two female professors he had almost married and who had defective children. Eve had wanted children badly but could not have them as father was "too old," and anyway did not dare to have any as she was his sister's daughter and the children would probably have been defective. He felt Mary's miscarriage meant his suspicions were correct; i.e., he could only father a defective child. He himself had secretly felt defective when he compared himself with his brothers. It was learned that his father's sister had also married a cousin and had had an idiot child. In spite of his fears and problems, he continued to have intercourse with his wife without trying to prevent conception. He brought out casually around the thirty-third interview that his potency had improved considerably. Around this time he made a slip and said, "Why didn't I want to have a burial for my *mother?*" (meaning his *father*). The material that appeared in connection with this slip revolved around Eve's character traits, which appeared remarkably similar to those of his mother. Both were nervous, apprehensive, deeply attached to father in an ambivalent manner, and phobic to the extent that they hated to leave home and tended to avoid people. The patient began to see how he had denied his mother's death in his attachment to Eve and how he had transferred the same cluster of affects grouped around both of them to Mary as well as himself. In this sense he had never buried the mother.

During the thirty-fifth interview, which occurred following the five-week summer vacation, he appeared changed in that he was more serious and pleasant in a less ingratiating way then formerly. He stated that he had had no headaches during the summer and was much less anxious, even though his wife was a month late in her period and probably pregnant. He remarked that his memories of the old days had "all loosened up." By this he meant his memories referring to Eve. Before, it had been a pat story. Now he remembered *feelings* as well as events. He realized that the kind of feelings he had for Eve were the same as those Mary wanted from him. He had also found himself frequently teary-eyed while driving along and thinking how much he had loved Eve, and he realized that his attachment to her had been the strongest feeling of his life. In an emotional way, without his old detachment, he talked of how he had really wanted and had had an idealized and sexualized son-mother relationship with all women, and how he derived a melancholy pleasure and excitement out of his realization that the relationships were all temporary. This material led in a number of directions. Eve and his oldest brother had had a "queer" relationship. He had told this brother about Eve and the brother had told him in turn how during the period when the patient was between seven and ten she had flirted with him and tried to have an affair but that he had walked out on her. This meant that she was on the rebound from the older brother. The older brother was tougher than he and able to run out on mother and not mind her fainting. The patient had never felt he had the exclusive rights to any girl, even Mary, and he had always had a longing for some kind of relationship that he felt could never be. The big shock of his life was that Eve and his father had not told him they were going to marry. He felt left out. He had kept his love for her secret for the ten years following their affair. The phrase "left out" went back into the past. Father and mother were very close and he never felt "included in" their intimacy. They went away on trips a lot and left him with a variety of domestics whom he despised. At the close of the interview, he remarked that his headaches were minimal to absent for the first time in twenty years. He connected this with his lessened tension and cutting down on his chain smoking of cigarettes. He also volunteered that his erections were so improved that his wife had stated he was a "new man." He felt that his opinion of Eve was now different from what it had been formerly. He described her *two* suicide attempts that forced his father to marry her. Like mother's fainting spells, they were dirty tricks.

The forty-second interview was the last one. By this time his wife was definitely pregnant again and he was anxiously concerned over her condition, claiming that he did not want *her* to be disappointed again. His ambivalence toward fatherhood, however, persisted. The interview went as follows.

"It took a long time to come here. I took a new route."

"A new route?"

"Yes. I'll start with a recent advance, as it were. You remember Mary had this accident and fell down the stairs. We discussed that the last time and following this, for the time being at least, I was aware the experience had really shaken her up. She's quite a bit more, she's out of that complete *lethargy* and *stupor* and not too *tense*, in other words *quite cheerful* now. When I see her in this more optimistic frame of mind, I wonder if this couldn't be the start to a more positive approach to her and our problems. It was very interesting—this being shaken up—there was the fear of her being badly *hurt*, the fear of her being *killed, dying*. It takes the fun out of giving oneself up to anyone, but nevertheless Monday night I was at a meeting and came home about ten-thirty in the evening and here she was with a reasonably high fever, 101° or something like that, and she had chills and was weakened by falling into this very *passive* pattern, not being feverishly incoherent but very demanding, wanting this and that, wanting to be *babied*, but being very rational about everything. She obviously *upset* me quite a bit and the fever went away completely overnight."

"Why do you think you were upset?"

"Why I was upset?"

"What do you think upset you, as you said, quite a bit?"

"Well, there is always in her this change of shall we call it vitality or something like that. There is always the chance, you have great hopes that there will be an upswing in her moods. This brought out the tense situation in which she was in. Just a slight fever and she could become very much *out of control*. So I talked a little bit about it with her the next day. She took it with very good grace, admitting that she knows she is never in *good control* of herself. The one thing I am at least pretty sure of by now is that at this present moment her problems are very strong and very severe, and just the patching up or even if there were a tremendous improvement of our personal relationship it *isn't enough*, in spite of the great improvement that has been achieved in our adjustment. It's a little bit of a vicious circle. It is hard to *to love* somebody who is on a very low level of *reciprocity*."

"How do you mean?"

He smiled ruefully.

"It is very hard to penetrate in any sense of the word."

"It is very hard to penetrate when you are fearful about loving or being loved. You said you didn't want to be hurt again because you came as close as you could ever come with Eve and look what happened."

"Yes. I would agree with you."

"Now I'm not putting it perhaps in your exact words. This is as close as I can get to it. How would you put it?"

The therapist wanted him to express it in his own words and hear himself say it—with more feeling. This could be used as a point of departure and review for the entire interview.

"Of course this pattern has existed. This pattern has brought me into marriage and regardless of what I do now this was still what got me into this marriage, that cannot be denied."

"What do you mean?"

"Father approved her and even when I start to realize these things, it is not enough. You have to do something about it. Let's put it on a more simplified basis. Regardless of how much I realize what the motivation was and what drove me into it and even understanding much better what her reasons and motivations were, the understanding doesn't change the fact that this is how it happened."

"Let's say the understanding does not change the past and it doesn't change the present, but it may change the future."

"In other words, I have said a number of things that showed there was some promise, some inherent promise here in the fact that she wanted me to be her husband. She wanted me to more or less change. She was ready and willing. She said carry me over the threshold in a figurative sense. Now we are married and I want to love you and be loved by you, and I said no. I said the same arrangement must continue, a marriage of convenience. Of course now the situation is, it isn't strong, but frequently I have the feeling of wanting to run away from the situation."

"What do you mean?"

"Well, there is this problem, that there is very little I can do regardless of how relaxed I get or how loving I get, and there is something she has to do on her own level too. What I don't know is whether I can do anything more than I'm doing."

"Do you mean in regard to penetration, intimacy or what?"

"I think it is the male function to penetrate, but at this point there is nothing to penetrate. In other words, if you have someone who is in a low mental state, you can't reach them."

"How do you mean?"

"She has at this point nothing, nothing to be penetrated."

This began to sound as if he had a definite aversion to the castrated female.

"What do you mean?"

"Well, if she is in a kind of state or lethargy or apathy, well, this is equivalent to there is nothing to penetrate. In other words, there is no reaction."

"You mean there is no way of getting in, emotionally?"

"Yes, other than physically, that is correct. This I think is the problem now to a really dangerous degree. It isn't just her reaction to me, it is to the entire outside world."

This had to be considered as a projection of his own feelings.

"You mean you are afraid that like Eve or like mamma she has given up?"

"Yes, she has *given up*, not just given up towards me."

"To the world—a different kind of suicide, or dying and going away?"

"Yes, well suicide is giving up the world. So I have the feeling I want to do something about it, yet *I am not enough for her!*"

This was a repetition of the oedipal situation.

"But this is what we talked about in connection with Eve. In what way are you not enough?"

"I know that if I change there is bound to be a change in her because she's got to live with me, but I can't predict what this change will be in her. We can say this, that if I change in my attitude then let's say the fear that I have concerning penetration might lessen to the point that I might dare to attempt to penetrate, and of course you know what I mean, not only the vagina but attempt to have an intimate relationship that means this is something more than a marriage of convenience. Then she has to change, and this may be painful for her, but at least it will make her feel she has some reason for returning and not giving up, or returning to the extent that she can see me as someone who can with her become a family. In other words, the turning point is one at which she is convinced that I can be a *father* as well as a husband and a boy."

"Do you think you are a father? You said Mary was probably pregnant."

"Actually the first effect has been really to scare the hell out of her rather than make her better, which is not too surprising really."

"Does it scare the hell out of you? Because I wonder if part of you still doesn't want this to happen."

"No, not really. The greatest source of my anxiety or anger and frustration is this penetration problem."

"As you said, the frustration you originally came to me for was a frustration over not being able to penetrate. You were occasionally physically impotent and then you found out that there was another kind of impotence, or an inability to penetrate into the heart, to communicate. It is as if you were really frustrated by not getting what you once got from Eve."

"This is very true, but one of the daily experiences that probably sets me back the most is strictly a reaction to when she is very *demanding, critical* and *unkind* in her judgment of people, and this is one of the things that throws me back yards or miles in our relationship, every time it comes up. It *shocks* me. It *frightens* me almost, even though I know that a lot of it is only gossip and defamation of people is one of the usual conversation topics, but it goes beyond that."

Here we might wonder if this were characteristic of his mother or himself.

"How do you mean?"

"Let me illustrate. One time when Mary was quite sick after her miscarriage, this good friend of ours came over and took care of Mary and brought her this and that. She *spoiled* her quite a bit, and when Mary felt better she sent a roast over to this friend and we kind of invited ourselves to their house for dinner. Mary was just about in the condition where she could go out to dinner and sit for maybe a half hour, and these friends, I think mainly for the reason they could hardly avoid it, also invited their sister and brother-in-law for dinner, and Mary was just *furious*, not that they had eaten our roast but for the lack of consideration when she was just up and wasn't up to company yet! She was just really up in arms about it and really very *angry* and very *unkind* about this friend of hers. This stuck in my mind for a very long time, and I was just really *shocked* about how *boxed in* her mind is that she completely forgot that *this woman* who had four kids and a big house to take care of without any help had come over almost every day and brought Mary things, made her

coffee and what not, and taken care of her own kids and everything."
Boxed in probably meant withdrawn and applied to himself.

"Like a good mother?"

"Yes, but Mary, when anything is wrong in some other family, will
rarely go over to see if she can help. She would never refuse but if
something goes on which interests her more she won't interrupt it.
She is really very *boxed in*."

It was apparent that he could only talk about himself indirectly.

"Maybe she *too* is afraid of being penetrated?"

"Oh, terribly so! This is just it! The usual term for that is having a
chip on your shoulder and this is to me very *frightening* and while I
understand it as a reaction, she didn't used to have it, it still upsets
me."

"You mean she has sort of an aggressive defense against being hurt?"

"Yes! For example, of late really *I* have been much more relaxed
and much more able if something comes up to not to just *freeze up*
and get *angry*, and I can cope more with her, but little incidents like
that *frighten* me."

Obviously he was fearful that he could not control his aggression.

"But you said Mary was willing to take in children and take care of
them, and delighted in having them."

"But she doesn't really."

"Did she have such a poor relationship *too* with her mother?"

"Yes, she is completely *boxed in* and it really *frightens* me."

"What do you mean by boxed in?"

"Well, completely *egocentric*. To me it appears almost pathological.
In the morning, for example, if I go into her room and she wants me
to do something, and I turn on the light before she is really awake, or
I turn on the light for some reason that has something to do with her
or both of us or me, and not just because I have forgotten or anything
like that, she has an almost *insane rage* reaction and immediately
shouts, 'Turn out the light!' I will say I have to get such-and-such
and can't get it. She will pull the covers over her eyes and gets
furious. These are things which are just terribly *frightening* to me
because they impress me as being on the borderline of *insanity*."

"Really? You mean you are afraid of her losing control?"

"It is a complete shutting off of the outside world, the real world,
as it were."

"As you said, the same thing was characteristic of your past. This
type of behavior in all the things that you described about Mary fits

your mother who was so emotional, and if we turn to Eve, we see that she too was full of uncontrolled feelings."

"This is right, but still I am frightened by it. The only thing is I feel like Atlas. With all my recognition of the past, I don't know how successful I will be in handling *my own problems* now."

"What do you mean?"

"I feel I have a terrible burden on my shoulders or, to put it less poetically, if I can adjust to her whims I will have to have more patience regardless of how much we get together in our sexual relations which, by the way, are good."

"Perhaps she may help you to solve your problems and you may help her to solve hers."

"The big question is can it be remedied? Has it gone too far?"

"What do you mean by too far? You implied once that a part of you was fearful of penetrating because of pregnancy and felt too little and too weak to carry such a load as a family, not as big a man as his father and his brothers who could do this, and enough like Atlas to be able to support a family. Yet the other part, the rational part, laughs and says I can do anything my brothers did, within reason."

"I think I better look for other examples."

"What do you mean?"

"Than my brothers."

"You mean you wouldn't want to support a family the way they did?"

"No, because the price was too high. Only one has children and the price he paid is too high."

"What do you mean? What price did he pay?"

"Well, his having a family, if I can interpret it right, was just as much of a counterreaction as my not having one. For him he was proving a point to repeat the story but not really getting rid of his own anxieties thereby. My oldest brother is at least in as bad shape as I am, or more so."

"How do you mean?"

"Oh, he is highly neurotic and had a nervous breakdown."

"He broke down? What happened?"

"Oh, he had what people refer to as a nervous breakdown, an inability to concentrate or do anything, and many other symptoms. He couldn't concentrate. He couldn't work."

"What happened to him?"

It was apparent that he feared the passive, feminine side of himself—the withdrawn, little-boy part still caught up by his need for and identification with emotional mother figures. It was necessary to explore his hopes, fears and fantasies of the future as expressed in terms of the brother.

"Oh, at that time he had a friend who was a physician in a state hospital, so he just went and lived in the house of that man whose wife was away on a trip. He was there almost as a private patient in a typical sanitarium, so he didn't have anything to do. He was fed and he could walk in the woods. This doctor was reasonably astute psychologically although not being a psychologist or a psychiatrist, and within three or four weeks he was rested enough and cheered up enough to go back to his wife."

This demonstrated what he really wanted from the therapist.

"Are you afraid then that this might happen to you?"

"No, I don't think so. I am stronger than my brother."

"No, but you said you felt like Atlas."

"No, when I said the Atlas thing, I really meant that I could do a lot about my own problems and I could do a lot about my relationships, but I cannot simply absorb somebody else's problems."

"Do you mean you feel you have enough to take care of your own self and are unable to take on the problems of a family in addition?"

"No, that is not what I mean. What I mean is that actually nobody, and certainly not me, can solve other people's problems. That's really all I meant. I can solve my problems. I can improve them. I can do something to solve the interrelationship problem, but I can't solve her problems."

"Why do you feel you have to solve her problems?"

"Because her problems are, well our relationships are mutual. It's really true!"

This implied that he was beginning to realize that his wife's problems were also his own.

"Do you mean your problems are mutual ones?"

"Let me put it this way. I made the remark before that the reasons which brought us together are irreversible. I can understand them better now and see them in a different light, but nevertheless these are the conditions under which it happened. Now I may be mistaken in this or not mistaken, but this is a point that is far from clear I think. I *picked* her out, *selected* her under conditions which for simplicity's sake I always used to call *being on the rebound.*"

"On the rebound from Eve?"

"Well both of us."

"And she was on the rebound from her cousin too?"

"Yes, but in either case, the individual, boy, girl friend or what have you, was nevertheless the last in a chain of events. It was some kind of a *rebound from life.* All right, the story is that it then turned out that what she wanted really wasn't to find a *haven from the tough realities of the world* like me, in other words the *playmate* situation, what she really wanted was to be a wife and mother. And this might be God damn well not true at all for me. I don't mean in a rational sense, but in a psychological sense."

"You may be right. This is the way part of you feels, but there is only one way of finding out. After all, she is pregnant."

"Her own problems existed before and went on and this pregnancy was just an outlet to pin me down!"

His little-boy fears made him feel trapped, boxed in, buried.

"How do you mean?"

"Well, this could be, let's face it."

"The only problem you can solve here is the one related to your fears of an intimate relation with any woman and your being on the rebound from old hurts. As you said, you became tired of playmates and always hiding from the tough realities of the world."

"There is a tendency for me to want to run away."

"But, as you know, although there are bad reactions and relationships, there are also good ones or you wouldn't have been attracted to her and wouldn't have selected her and stayed with her as long as you have. Okay? See you next week."

"Yes. I am reasonably sure. Next week I'll be on vacation with her. She can't go now."

"How long are you going to be on vacation? How many weeks?"

"Three weeks. We'll fly to Miami. By the way, *she* doesn't want to go on a plane and now *I* don't mind it too much. It seems she has taken over my old fears."

This showed how much their problems were mutual ones.

"So I'll see you next Friday and then won't see you for three visits."

"Yes."

"Good-by. Have a nice weekend."

"Thank you."

Following the forty-second interview, the patient was sent on a business trip and missed the following session. He then went on his vacation and upon his return he found that he had been assigned to a

new location in another state. He decided that as his symptoms were
minimal he would discontinue his therapy. A year later he wrote a
long message on a Christmas card, stating that his wife and child and
he were doing as well as could be expected. This meant that each of
them tended to have moderate depressive episodes and occasional violent quarrels, but he made no mention to symptoms of any kind other
than his "migrainous" headaches. These he stated had vanished. Because of his anxiety reactions to planes, thunderstorms, marriage and
children, we can classify this patient as one of the variants of anxiety
hysteria, although he came into therapy ostensibly because of his
wife's problems. Like the previous case, this one shows how much it is
necessary to realize that people who talk about other people's problems are talking about their own. Many times analysts are approached
by psychiatrists who wish to have cases supervised. This always turns
out to be indirect psychotherapy. This highlights the need for psychiatrists, therefore, to understand their own problems so that they
will not interfere with their therapeutic efforts. Such an understanding aids and permits a continual intensity of interest in clinical material with minimal intensity of personal disturbance.

Other characteristics besides the phobic fears that would classify
this patient as one near the hysterical pole were the obvious sexual
problems and emotional involvement, the proneness to trauma and
the oral intimacy problem. A theoretical discussion of anxiety hysteria
in some detail will be included in the following chapter. Here it will
be noted that the therapist did not directly analyze the meaning of
his fears or somatic symptoms. It would be merely an intellectual
exercise for him to realize that his fear of flying was a symbol of his
fear of sexual relations, that his fear of lightning was a fear of castration and the wrath of the father for his oedipal incestuous wishes.
Of course, the same thing applied to losing his mind or having his
feelings cut off. He was afraid of ultimately being abandoned and
unable to communicate feelingly either physically with his penis or
mentally with his mind. The shock he talked about concerning Mary
concerned Eve at one level and his mother at another. He was a
mother's boy from the start and constantly orbiting around her. Of
course, what had shocked him was the coincidence of the suicidal
attempts. He must have focused his oedipal guilt feelings on his
mother's death in the remote past and later on Eve's death. It is almost as if he had said at various times to himself. "If I had been a
better boy and hadn't run away, mama wouldn't have fainted (died)"
or "If I were a better man and hadn't withdrawn (run away), Mary

wouldn't have tried to die." He also felt guilty about his aggression and death wishes toward mother, Eve, Mary and father. The funeral arrangements or lack of them showed this clearly as concerned the father. His life was one perpetual rebound, with various traumas organizing and shaping his character around a childhood fantasy in which he was little Lord Fauntleroy who became "an empire unto himself." This type of narcissistic withdrawal is characteristic of any neurosis such as anxiety hysteria. In the case of the neuroses, there is only a partial withdrawal. Hysterics emote, feel intensely and become deeply involved, but there is a phony quality to their affects. When it is obvious, we call them histrionic. When it is more bizarre, we call them as-if characters or pseudoneurotic schizophrenics or borderline hysterical acting-outers. When narcissistic withdrawal is more complete and the regression involves a large segment of the personality, we call such cases psychotics. This is another way of considering the fact that different people tend to regress to different levels acutely, chronically or intermittently, and also tend to repeat themselves predictably.

Psychotherapy is artificially divided into symptomatic relief and character analysis. Any type of psychotherapy can produce transient symptom relief or change. The symptom relief produced through insight of the type furnished by sector psychotherapy, which stresses ego integration, is usually lasting and ultimately associated with adaptive character changes. These are always relative in extent, depth and duration of the pathological character traits, here and even in the longest psychoanalysis.

The discerning reader will have noticed by now one outstanding quality in all the many cases of anxiety hysteria described in this book. They all have been thwarted in solving their dependency-independency needs. The parent-child separation process, which should be a gradual one, has been interfered with by traumatic separations and a dispositional fixation at a passive phallic level. They are anchored in a past and in constant need of parental protectors from whom they can borrow controls that are missing or undeveloped in themselves. Their attitudes towards their protectors are ambivalent in part because of unsolved infantile ambivalent feelings and in part because of the discrepancy between their adult and infantile egos. This continually creates dissatisfactions, narcissistic wounds and complications. This all boils down to the neurotic need for more internalized controls and the completion of superego development.

The pathological mourning involved in this case was obvious. Eve allowed him to deny the loss of the mother, and Mary the loss of Eve.

One gets the impression, however, that the withdrawal process originated much earlier and was, as is usually the case, due to a chronic insufficiency in his relationship with his mother, i.e., a defective emotional climate. The acute losses thus acted as consolidating traumas that shaped character and destiny.

XVII

CONCLUSIONS

Pathological Mourning and Theory
Concerning Hysteria

The cases in this book have been mainly those called anxiety hysteria. In this final chapter, we will attempt to relate certain characteristics of this condition to the pathological mourning mentioned in Chapter II, and conclude with some general comments on psychotherapy.

Psychoanalysis teaches us that the anxiety in the previous cases was a warning connected with special traumatic past situations where denied affects associated with unmastered losses threatened to recur and to overwhelm the person. Instead of warning of a danger, such anxiety tends to be treated as a danger in its own right. It is usually handled by being displaced, distorted or converted into some kind of manifestation or symptom in a sphere of activity that disguises it and surrounds it with safeguards from recognition. Thus the various patients we have listened to complained about anxiety or concern over visiting, blushing, eating or working. A typical symptom symbolically expresses the forbidden longing and also the dreaded loss. A response like those of the patients we have heard could be justified only in terms of their childhood handicaps. Then they were helplessly dependent and their egos were too weak to cope with their own inner longings and the commands of their parents, i.e., what they felt they had to do and what they wanted to do. Anxiety hysteria is the prototype of the neuroses in general and can readily serve as a model for a discussion of all the neuroses. It frequently seems to be associated with a certain type of extremely de-

599

pendent child who needs to cling to its parents, and especially to the mother, because of feelings of extreme ambivalence. How does this ambivalence arise? Psychoanalytic observations and interviews such as we have listened to in the previous cases seem to show that although this syndrome appears to originate mainly around a crisis in the oedipal period of development, other sources are far deeper and extend back to acute and chronic deprivations and losses at the earliest levels of development. These losses vary in severity and are not always due to death, abandonment or even separation. This is mentioned because separations due to illness, accidents, vacations, etc., are as common as bumps on the head. Some losses are massive, sudden and obviously traumatic. Others are less severe but cumulative, chronic in occurrence and insidious in effect, for example, the mother who is deficient in empathy or ability to comprehend or communicate in terms of feelings, who never understands why her child cries or is happy or who does not allow her child to develop as a unique being rather than as an extension of herself. Chronic physical illness of either parent or child can also produce a chronic defective relationship.

What is important is the pathological reaction to these losses due to denial of a related group of affects, and a partial withdrawal from meaningful relationships that prevents a complete discharge and satisfaction of emotional needs. The denial is manifested as a detached lack of awareness of these needs. The withdrawal process is the main culprit. It is associated with a transfer of interests from the outside world of people and things to the self and the body, and the development of a whole series of regressive narcissistic sadomasochistic, anxiety- and depression-laden fantasies and reactions which need to be acted out. These are usually accompanied by some variety of masturbation. Whether or not pathological mourning is resolved or leads to further losses, regressions, narcissistic injuries and traumas of one kind or another is dependent upon the total emotional climate of the household, the response to the acting out and the persistent warmth, understanding and consistency of the parents or their substitutes. There is a qualitative and quantitative element in all losses and reactions to them which is characteristic in most syndromes. In cases of anxiety hysteria, for example, there is a history of great inconsistency in the handling of the child. Much petting, handling and exhibiting alternate with rigid feeding or sleeping schedules or sudden severe punishments or relative abandonment when another child appears. In any case, the child feels suddenly cut off from the mother and turns to an equally inconsistent father. The mourning involves a lost, idealized mother-child relation and a fighting interparental relationship. The child is usually used as a pawn in a rivalrous sadomasochistic parental game. Pathological mourning augments the normal oedipal relationships and prevents their solution. The sadomasochistic fantasy elements are often characterized by such sexualized themes as the femme fatale or vampire, the mater dolorosa, the Camillelike prostitute, the painfully virtuous nun, etc. There are male counterparts, of course. In any case, a relative lack of intimate relationships with persons, perpetual feelings of loneliness and inadequacy, are always present. The feelings can be summed up in the phrase "too little and too late." Denial of legitimate feelings of rage and grief is often encouraged by parents who cannot tolerate such feelings. This intensifies the pathology.

In adults, a neurosis becomes obvious when a person is required to take one of the new and ever larger steps toward independence and intimacy that occur throughout life and particularly when he has not successfully solved the problems and anxieties of the preceding stage. Of course, the same holds true of all kinds of mental illnesses. Most neuroses and many borderline states are variations of and developments upon the parent trunk of anxiety hysteria. This is probably the most common form of psychiatric illness, including the psychoses.

In its adult form, anxiety hysteria is often seen as a mixed obsessive-compulsive and hysterical neurosis. This neurosis is always found in association with various accentuated phobias. Phobias, conversions and dissociations or ego splits are symptoms and in various amounts exist in all types of mental illness. They are defenses against feeling and remembering rather than diseases. When they are especially prominent and associated with passive phallic fantasies concerning love, sex, rivalry, and strong if flighty feeling about people and things, we make a diagnosis of classical hysteria. Very early it was observed that anxiety hysterics appeared to have a "constitutionally" overdeveloped passive phallically derived pleasure in kinesthetic movements, such as walking or dancing, and it seemed then that neurotic inhibitions arose from the need for and failure of repression of castration anxiety associated with these pleasures. These were purely clinical observations, made especially in connection with cases of agoraphobia, which has often served as a model for the various phobic states. Actually, the differentiation of this phobia from others is a highly artificial and unnecessary one. Later, the role of castrative sadomasochistic fantasies developed around a defective relationship with the mother was underlined. Narcissistic withdrawal aspects were stressed later, as well as certain exhibitionistic

THE TACTICS OF PSYCHOTHERAPY

aspects. The case of the woman whose husband had deserted her is an example of the sadomasochistic aspects. Stronger than normal tendencies to form identifications with an aggressive mother, or substitute objects, were observed to be characteristic of these cases. The reasons for this were inadequately understood in the past, due to an unawareness of the importance of pathological mourning and narcissistic elements. Also noted early were the frequency of complaints of depersonalization and a sense of alienation from people, accompanied, interestingly enough, by dizzy spells and numbness in the extremities, especially the legs. This alienation is probably a part of the withdrawal process and the numbness a somatic equivalent based physiologically on hyperventilation. The former is also a connecting link with borderline states. It was also observed that in the analytic situation on the couch dizzy spells often appeared when oedipal memories and feelings were close to consciousness. The reasons for this have been quite unknown, but are possibly related to unnoticed hyperventilation effects and the emergence of sadomasochistic castration fantasies as well as alterations in consciousness due to the failure of narcissistic withdrawal defenses. In almost all cases of anxiety hysteria, the more easily revealed anxieties refer mainly to fantasies concerning the dreadful consequences of yielding to "sexual" intimacies and the need for protection from the consequence—abandonment by the parents. These physical sexual fantasies highlight a basically narcissistic problem in tolerating intimacies and close involvements at all levels. The dreadful part refers to the castration or mutilation loss component of the fantasy. This usually screens a sadomasochistic mother-child symbiosis. Some clinicians have listed such specific elements in anxiety hysteria as defective superego functioning, traumatic fixations due to witnessing adult sexual activities, and sadomasochistic childbirth fantasies. All of these are present, and can be considered as repercussions of pathological mourning. Various part aspects of this neurosis appear to have been emphasized at different times. In any neurosis all categories of object relationships appear affected simultaneously, some being more manifest at one time than others. Also, various patients specialize in one or more ways of expression of the basic problems. While males can be affected, anxiety hysteria seems to occur more openly and frequently in females. Biological and cultural factors lead males into counterphobic and homosexual acting-out pathways of symptom expression and accentuation.

For many years psychoanalytic clinical studies have shown that the tendency of the anxiety hysteric to regress orally with such ease is due in large part to a failure to have mastered many aspects of the earliest relations with the mother. Many important qualities commonly associated with persons fixated at an oral level, such as sadomasochism and the all-black or all-white thinking typical of the primary processes, are found transferred to a passive or phallic level. Other qualities such as accentuated envy, greed and intense jealousy in their personal relationships and their attitude toward possessions are largely oral in derivation. The longing for a baby in the male and, in the case of the female, feelings of having been deprived of a penis, are related also to an early defective mother relationship. An accentuated aggressive reaction to libidinal frustrations of all types always seems to be present. A dread of and longing for deep emotional and physical intimacies are frequently displaced to oral fantasies of devouring and being devoured. This may lead to anorexia or gluttony. Problems in connection with intimacy with persons and their reflection in the sphere of the body image, especially in terms of active and passive fears of penetration of the body cavities, appear to be partly oral in derivation. Other common qualities with some oral roots are the exaggerated passivity, a hostile dependency on others for self-esteem and a proneness for going to extremes. A marked tendency toward momentary suggestibility and compliance in personal relationships alternating with easy disappointment, lack of conviction, groundless disparagement and quick depreciation, object relations shot through with transient identifications, and difficulties with superego formation are other common features found in anxiety hysteria and are stressed in the literature. All these attitudes seem to bear a relationship to a defective and basically oral mother-child relationship. They suggest a primary fixation at a level of ego development where the ability for sharp perceptual differentiation of feeling states exists along with a relative weakness in the capacity for verbalization, abstract thought formation and the integration of complex feelings. An increase in the tendency to ambivalence and dissociation or ego splitting is a relative concept which cannot be easily separated from the inability to abstract, integrate or unite concepts. In the case of the previous patient (Chapter XVI), his early loss experiences with his mother and cousin explain to a large degree the increase in narcissism, withdrawal and deficiency of object relationships associated with the inevitable difficulties of his marriage and choice of a wife. A recognition of this inevitablity by the patient is of primary importance in diminishing neurotic guilt feelings and establishing a reconciliation with reality. This does not mean that hope for a change must be abandoned, but rather that active attempts to deal with reality must be made.

The problem of maintaining and losing control of aggressive re-actions to libidinal frustration was of paramount importance in all the cases we have considered. It can often be traced to fears, in the infan-tile world, of not being able to control the influx of and reaction to stimuli in all areas of relationships. Later, toilet problems, masturba-tion, sexual relationships between the parents, and many other prob-lems in control appear to take the center of the stage. The problem of the control of omnipotent and omnipresent aggressive and sexual fan-tasies in the adult case of anxiety hysteria shows to what a great extent denial and unmastered primitive thought processes have persisted. It is possible that infantile intellectual and perceptual precocity accom-panied by a weakness in the capacity for integration of stimuli would allow the stimuli accompanying the normal process of maturation and the inability to respond adequately to them to act as a trauma or nar-cissistic mortification. This is, relatively speaking, the opposite of the theory that considered the instinctual drives to be constitutionally ex-cessively strong. Another common way of describing this aspect of the problem is that the proneness of the neurotic personality to being traumatized is due to a constitutional or narcissistic sensitivity to libido change, but this application of clinical descriptive terminology is vague. At times separation from or loss of the mother even to the adult neurotic appears to be tantamount to ego disintegration. Repe-tition of the trauma of being abandoned is of primary importance in the genesis of the anxiety so frequently associated with all types of neurotic personalities. An understanding of the relationship of pathological mourning, and particularly the withdrawal aspects, is fundamental to an understanding of dissociative symptoms. In both young and old hysterics, anxieties over loss of control of aggressive wish-es and fears of being overwhelmed are commonly manifested in the form of separation anxiety in all spheres. There is a tendency in the adult to panic when frustrated at a sexual level. In the body-image sphere, inhibition or overcontrol of orgastic discharge may lead to per-petual unrest and hypersensitivity to sexual and aggressive stimuli from all sources as well as to the many physical concomitants associated with panic, and a conditionally developed unstable autonomic nervous sys-tem. Efforts to control sex and aggression may lead to an inhibition of the capacity to love and be loved, an ever-increasing and perpetual loneliness and hunger for personal contacts and a resentful over-dependence upon the whims of people.

In adult cases, the diffusion and confusion of the time perspective is striking. While consciously haunted by the passage of time, they paradoxically seem unaware of it. They usually remain juvenile in appearance, action, or thought. Secret intense masturbatory fantasies often lead to a confusion of fact and fantasy, a proneness for elaboration and exaggeration of current events, and a vividness of imagination. This is in large part connected with the persistence of the most primitive type of wishful thinking.

The emotionalism, penchant for histrionics, superficiality, lability and exaggerated nature of the feelings of the hysterical type of case have frequently been described, as well as the tendency for cyclic mood swings. The case of the lieutenant colonel in the WACs was a good illustration of these tendencies in the female. The men with the erythrophobia and food phobia illustrate the male approach. The infantile missing and mourned-for relationships and the narcissistic pathology were readily observable.

The heightened narcissism and certain interesting peculiarities of the body image of the hysterical type are well known. Most descriptions emphasize the flowing youthful and graceful movements, softness and bodily compliance which in most cultures are considered hyperfeminine and sexually provocative. Such qualities appear in both sexes very early in development and appear related to identifications with similar qualities in the mother, as well as constitutional factors. In the male they are usually considered effeminate or homosexual. There is an increase in the development of kinesthetic and equilibration sensitivity to responses, as well as specific disturbances in visual perceptual acuity and discrimination. Hypersensitivity to stimuli in these areas may be dispositional or traumatic in origin and responsible for the form taken by, as well as the appearance of, traumatic reactions. The relation of vision in the hysterical type to exhibitionistic and voyeuristic tendencies, primal-scene reactions and color shock on the Rorschach cards is well known. It is not only an indication of the need to modify instinct and sensory impressions, to defend against traumatic overstimulation, but a sign of screen hunger or trauma hunger and a fixation at an early ego level where the mouth-breast relation shared importance with the eye and the sight of the maternal face. The problems in connection with constricted visual fields appear related to the reappearance of or the regression to a primitive body ego level. Other less dramatic senses are often involved. From a psychopathological point of view, this type of phenomenon can be considered part of the withdrawal process.

It seems that the genital sexuality of some hysterics is infused with so much orality that it appears to be only an imitation of that of the adult. Frequently it has been found to have the aggressive if partial aim of devouring and destroying the dreaded but longed-for penetrating penis—a form of "angry yearning." Here the penis seems to represent an aggressive baby relating orally and sadistically to the mother's body. The origin of this type of behavior is frequently observed in the analyses of cases of hysterical frigidity where the genital sexual relation is found mixed with many unresolved oral-sadomasochistic drives and anxieties. In this sense an unresolved sadomasochistic relation with the breast and the mother has become a sadomasochistic relation with the penis and the father as well as later substitute persons and things. Other pregenital drives, of course, play some role in the formation of the hysterical personality. Of primary importance is the phallic-urethral component. This was demonstrated in the case of erythrophobia and the boy with the fear of homosexuality. The phallus-girl type of hysterical character is fairly common and the difficulties of the hysterical female with urination, castration fantasies and urinary penis and water-baby fantasies are well known in the psychoanalytic literature. The ambition and aggressions associated with urethral eroticism also appear to intensify the envy of and desire to displace the rival in the love relationship with either parent.

The narcissistic pathology of the hysteric is characterized by an intense dependency on others for self-esteem, a longing to receive love constantly and passively, feelings of grandiosity through identifications of either short- or long-term variety with rich, famous or powerful persons, a need to collect and manipulate admirers and intense feelings of inadequacy. The latter feelings intensify the need for masturbatory fantasies. These are a poor substitute for intimacies with persons.

The clinical picture in anxiety hysteria is characteristic from the point of view of the major point of fixation, the typical conflict situation, and the defenses, as well as the degree of pathology. The genitality may be largely colored by oral and phallic wishes, but it is often predominantly genital. The milder cases are concerned most of the time with persons in an holistic sense and the quality of their feelings is rich with shadings of emotion that show for all practical purposes the differentiation in range and tonal pattern of normal individuals. The characteristics of the genitality of the anxiety hysteric that give it a "pseudo" quality are the interest in perverse elements, especially oral and phallic, an accentuation of foreplay and an apprehension based upon fears of frustration and an eruption of sadomasochistic fantasies when close to the fulfillment of the sexual goal. These may be acted out by biting or scratching the partner during intercourse and orgasm—which is usually inhibited but not always absent, a kind of "angry yearning" once more. Because of castration or abandonment anxiety, there is in the female a defensive emphasis on the role of the clitoris in the sexual act to avoid sadomasochistic oral fantasies in connection with penetration fears. The confusion over the role of the pregenital elements in hysteria is compounded by the defensive use of pregenital material to avoid genital oedipal material and vice versa. There are additional complications when compulsive and obsessional elements are prominent.

A typical conflict is most easily understood in terms of an oedipal fixation; that is, the anxiety and depression are clinically found to be based on a feeling of the impossibility of breaking loose from an ambivalently loved object due either to an inability to transfer libido to a new object or to the conscious renunciation of a new love object because of guilt concerning abandoning the old object. The ambivalence toward the loved object is directly related to the angry yearning feelings of pathological mourning. The repressed yearning and anger at the faithless past love has usually been displaced to the husband or wife. The guilt can also be considered as part of the denied affect constellation associated with pathological mourning. There are other conflictual relationships. For instance, the guilt and dissatisfaction attached to the narcissistic masturbatory solution are due not only to the oedipal nature of the associated fantasies and the dread of the regressive, oral sadomasochistic elements, but above all to inner and outer pressures toward maturation. The envy and aggression of the anxiety hysteric and the ready tendency to depreciate what he or she is already getting and to exaggerate the pleasures of others are also important. A characteristic identification with the bad qualities of both parents tends to make any solution of their love life difficult. There is always a large variety of unsatisfied libidinal needs. Often transitory solutions of the conflictual demands oscillate between acting out of perverse regressive tendencies and the formation of neurotic symptoms in an early or late stage of development. Another common characteristic consists of oscillating between restricting and raging at the self or attacking parental figures.

The use of repression as one of the chief defenses in hysteria is usually considered as a demonstration of a fixation at a predominantly phallic-genital level, since repression is a more selective mechanism than denial and used mainly during the oedipal period of development. Actually, the difference between denial and repression in most cases is largely blurred. Legitimate losses, deprivations and grievances against the parents are internalized and converted into guilt feelings and depressive episodes that augment the guilt and depressive elements of the mourning reaction. This permits the maintenance of a tenuous narcissistic relation with the parents and binds excessive sadomasochism. Strong homosexual feelings, as well as anxiety, may lead to depersonalization reactions, as they did in the case of the organ player. In psychotherapy, an intense positive transference usually covers negative feelings which are generally difficult to express and at times to detect. A highly erotized transference often causes trouble and is often acted out on persons representing the therapist. Secondary gains are always prominent from the beginning to the end of treatment.

The strength of or lack of inhibition of the aggressive impulses of the anxiety hysteric are proverbial. They arouse great fears of retaliation as well as provoke environmental difficulties through all areas and levels of development. From a clinical point of view, the therapist should always be on guard for the more or less hidden aggressive components of the hysterical person's sexual relationships. In this sense, the anxiety hysteric talks about love and sex and leaves out the hate, or vice versa.

Alternation in masculine-active and feminine-passive polarities is often connected with the problem of whether a patient is concerned more with fears of castration or fears of loss of love. A review of the cases presented here will show that the word "onset" in the case of the adult anxiety hysteric is only a relative term.

The sadomasochistic fantasies of a hysterical mother may interfere with the nursing relationship of the baby with the breast and intensify splitting of the good and bad breast concepts of the developing ego. This highlights the difficulty of separating constitutional and dispositional factors. A striking personality difference between a mother and a nurse or mother substitute often exaggerates the initial ambivalence toward objects. These factors appeared to have some bearing in the last case presentation, in which the relationship with the mother and cousin was apparent and strikingly different.

The envy and increased sadomasochism of the hysterical personality usually accentuate certain dissatisfactions and anxieties present in the oedipal situation that normally drive the child toward maturation;

i.e., ordinarily the oedipal child feels physically small and inadequate in body and ability to perform as a sexual partner and feels driven to the parent of the same sex to obtain "know-how" conceived basically as an oral-anal introjection process. Normally this appears in the male as the fantasy, "By submitting to father, I take over his magic powers, bigness and role with mother." In the female it serves as a way of identifying with and sharing the mother's desired qualities for the sake of father. Instead of being pressured toward maturity by this push-pull relationship to the parents, the hysterical ambivalence creates a paralysis and a drive to postpone the solution of the oedipal conflict. It is extremely difficult to solve the problem of the biological components or concomitants of the exaggerated passivity and sadomasochism. The best available solution still remains to bring to light, in greater detail, the clinical material in each case reported. Tape recordings are useful for the study of such details. The need of a unifying theory like pathological mourning will then be readily apparent.

The use of recorded interviews is the most feasible way of convincing students of the practicality of a technique as well as a method of illustrating psychoanalytic theory. Sound movies, records and tapes are too expensive ever to become popular. However, it is probable that medical libraries of the future will contain tapes or records of illustrative therapeutic interviews, especially of cases of psychosomatic disease.

The love-hate-guilt sequence in hysterics is well disguised by regression and various displacements. Let us consider the case of agoraphobia in Chapter I. A defective relationship with the loss of her mother had led to defective relationships with her father, Mr. N, and her husband in terms of maturation and libidinal satisfactions. She had acted out forbidden oedipal incestuous masturbatory fantasies. Certain adult genital satisfactions were permitted, but the tender preliminary touching gestures were forbidden. This was not merely because they were tabooed by her adolescent superego represented, to a large degree, by the neighbors, but also because such gestures represented a painful and defective relationship with her parents. The bad mouth-breast-mother relationship had become a bad mouth-finger-genital-touching relationship. The anger was expressed more directly at the mother, and the husband was spared and accepted as the good and important person in her life. In many similar cases the husband or the mother-in-law bears the brunt of a woman's anger and it is necessary to evoke and resolve the repressed affects that relate to the mother.

Some phobic men, especially those with deep depressive and withdrawal tendencies, are unable to enjoy satisfactory feeling relationships with persons at all and end up having to relate to female genitals instead of to women, like the depressed and narcissistically withdrawn characters in the novels of Henry Miller. The primary defective relationship in such cases often appears to be especially intense and with both the father and the mother. The inability to complete maturational identifications with the father in his "good" aspects may show up in the male as a fear of a heart attack or a stroke, etc. It usually shows up in the retention of the pure sexless mother myth. All the phobic patients we listened to had defective parental relationships that did not allow them to grow up. All of them mourned their losses. Various aspects of the mourning constellation were present, and there were various degrees of denial, repression, withdrawal, acting out, etc. The erythrophobic man who was so concerned with his inadequate manhood and sexual life had an infantile attitude about sex and was unable to express how "mad" he was about his wife, mother and mother-in-law. The man with the food phobia also acted like an angry little boy. The maturational inadequacies were obvious. Psychosomatic complications are common in hysteria. The withdrawal and object-relationship defects, however, are deeper and more apparent in most cases of psychosomatic disease and the borderline states in the cases that were presented. The man with the peptic ulcer could not stand the intimacies of heterosexuality and marriage. The colitis case had a similar problem, although of less apparent emotional intensity. The loss of a basic trusting child-mother relationship was obvious in all these cases. It permeated all aspects of these patients' lives. Some cases are less obvious. At times a mild chronic failure in the relationship to the mother is brought to a focus and intensified by a traumatic separation due to illness or absence of some type. Reactive character traits can then sabotage each successive relationship and maturational stage. Maturation then acts like a photographic developer. It brings out, through contrast, the lack of psychosexual development; that is, it shows up weaknesses as well as strengths.

In these interviews we have been faced by patients who presented us with a great deal of material concerning their lives. This was for the most part quite conscious, although the relationship between various parts of the material was unconscious. In this sense these cases were dealt with from the point of view of a level of *observation* and a level of *clinical interpretation*. *Generalizations* were also made and the cases were discussed in terms of *clinical theory*. Little attention has been paid to psychoanalytic metapsychology and philosophy, as

many abstract concepts of psychoanalysis have little clinical usefulness. The usual resident and psychotherapist know little about
psychoanalytic interpretations and have a distorted picture of the kind
of clinical facts that are available to analysts. For this reason, the discussions have centered on psychoanalytic data concepts and interpretation, and it is taken for granted that the student is familiar with the
main body of psychoanalytic theory.

In these days of group activities and the cultivation of togetherness,
it should not be forgotten that group psychotherapeutic activities are
essentially concerned with covering up, role acting and understanding
only at a group level. This is not equivalent with understanding of the
self, body, symptoms and an understanding of the unconscious in
other than its more superficial and personal relationship aspects.

Psychotherapy is essentially a dual relationship between solitary
individuals. The therapist, like the patient, tends to be a solitary person withdrawn from the world and busily engaged in trying to understand one of the most complex organisms in all creation. Psychotherapy
attracts the solitary mind. Its understandings have been described by
Ziman (1960) as like mountain peaks discovered in the abstract world
of the intellect, which can be seen and their full magnificence enjoyed
only by making the long difficult journey oneself. The patient too is a
solitary person begging in one way or another to substitute understanding for the defect in his intimate relationships in both the past and the
present. Psychotherapy itself is essentially also a solitary relationship in
many aspects. Ideas begin in one mind and through understanding
spread outward. The struggle to create insight, understanding, and control is mainly a struggle of the therapist's will against the patient's weakness. This solitary aspect is of basic importance even though the neurotic may be at odds with the external world and the fact that if he is to
be effective in his response to psychotherapy he can never be completely
out of touch with the world of his contemporaries in age, occupation
and cultural level. This is why therapy on an outpatient basis tends
to be easier in the sense of being reality oriented than when conducted
in a hospital. Psychotherapy cannot sustain a continual passive attitude
on the part of either the patient or the therapist or therapy becomes
an artificial neurosis or at best a holding operation. The therapist,
however remote he may seem, is always bound closely to his theoretical
concepts and ideas. He comprehends the patient's ideas in his own
personal way and then returns them to the patient. Eventually, nothing
good or sound is thrown away—only personal vagaries and idiosyncrasies. It is in this way that the psychotherapy advances. As students and

practitioners of other methods of psychotherapy publish their methods in open detail, it may be increasingly possible to explain discrepancies and reconcile discordant results. The majority of schools of psychotherapy have some validity in their claims. Psychoanalysis, however, believes that such a validity is only a small part of the total body of knowledge in respect to both theory and practice. In practice, the psychoanalyst, regardless of whether he is doing psychoanalysis or psychotherapy, concentrates on making the unconscious conscious. The difficulties encountered in doing this have been formidable and have been related in detail by historians of the psychoanalytic movement. Acceptance of psychoanalysis as an integral part of our intellectual culture by the group or the individual is useless in respect to the treatment of the individual.

As Cottrell (1960b) has remarked, "Science is not an autonomous realm of knowledge governed by immutable rules but is a way of doing intellectual business. The truth value of a theory is not predetermined by the genius of its discoverer but depends upon the price other scientists will eventually put upon it." Psychoanalysts are well aware of the limitations of their science, but feel that the theories and technique of treatment that they do have to offer are the most holistic, rational and effective that now exist.

BIBLIOGRAPHY

Alexander, F. (1954), Psychoanalysis and Psychotherapy. *J. Am. Psychoanal. Assoc.*, 2:722-733.

Arlow, J. A. (1953), Masturbation and Symptom Formation. *J. Am. Psychoanal. Assoc.*, 1:45-58.

Arlow, J. A. (1963), The Supervisory Situation. *J. Am. Psychoanal. Assoc.*, 11:576-594.

Bellak, L. (1961), Free Association: Conceptual and Clinical Aspects. *Int. J. Psycho-Anal.*, 42:9-19.

Benedek, T. (1925), Notes from the Analysis of a Case of Ereuthophobia. *Int. J. Psycho-Anal.*, 6:430-439.

Bergler, E. (1944), A New Approach to the Therapy of Erythrophobia. *Psychoanal. Quart.*, 13:43-59.

Berman, L. (1943), Depersonalization and the Body Ego with Special Reference to the Genital Representation. *Psychoanal. Quart.*, 17:433-452.

Bettelheim, B. and Sylvester, E. (1949), Physical Symptoms in Emotionally Disturbed Children. *The Psychoanalytic Study of the Child*, 3/4:353-368. New York: International Universities Press.

Bibring, E. (1954), Psychoanalysis and the Dynamic Psychotherapies. *J. Am. Psychoanal. Assoc.*, 2:745-770.

Bing, J. F. and Marburg, R. O. (1962), Report of Panel on Narcissism. *J. Am. Psychoanal. Assoc.*, 10:593-609.

Bornstein, B. (1949), The Analysis of a Phobic Child. *The Psychoanalytic Study of the Child*, 3/4:181-226. New York: International Universities Press.

Bowlby, J. (1961), Childhood Mourning and its Implications for Psychiatry. *Am. J. Psychiatry*, 118:481-498.

Bowlby, J. (1963), Pathological Mourning and Childhood Mourning. *J. Am. Psychoanal. Assoc.*, 11:500-541.

Brenner, C. (1955), *An Elementary Textbook of Psychoanalysis*. New York: International Universities Press.

Christophel, H. (1936), Exhibitionism and Exhibitionists. *Int. J. Psycho-Anal.*, 17:321-345.

Cottrell, T. L. (1960a), Scientists Real or Imaginary? *The BBC Listener*, 64:291-292.

Cottrell, T. L. (1960b), Scientists: Solo or Concerted? *The BBC Listener*, 64:411-412.

Deutsch, F. (1939a), The Associative Anamnesis. *Psychoanal. Quart.*, 8:354-381.

Deutsch, F. (1939b), The Choice of Organ in Organ Neurosis. *Int. J. Psycho-Anal.*, 20:252-262.

Deutsch, F. (1952), The Art of Interviewing and Abstract Art. *Am. Imago*, 9:1-19.

Deutsch, F. (1953), Instinctual Drives and Intersensory Perceptions during the Analytic Procedure. In *Drives, Affects, Behavior*, pp. 216-228. Ed. by Rudolph Loewenstein. New York: International Universities Press.

Deutsch, F. (1954), Analytic Synesthesiology. *Int. J. Psycho-Anal.*, 34:293-301.

613

Deutsch, F., Kaufman, M. R. and Blumgart, H. L. (1940), Present Methods of Teaching. *Psychosomatic Med.*, 2:213-222.

Deutsch, F. and Murphy, W. F. (1955), *The Clinical Interview*. New York: International Universities Press.

Deutsch, H. (1929), On the Origin of Agoraphobia. *Int. J. Psycho-Anal.*, 10:51-69.

Deutsch, H. (1930), The Significance of Masochism in the Mental Life of Women. *Int. J. Psycho-Anal.*, 11:48-60.

Deutsch, H. (1937), Absence of Grief. *Psychoanal. Quart.*, 6:12-22.

Deutsch, H. (1942), Some Forms of Emotional Disturbance and their Relationship to Schizophrenia. *Psychoanal. Quart.*, 11:301-321.

Deutsch, H. (1951), *Psychoanalysis of the Neuroses*. Lectures 6, 7, 8, pp. 113-171. London: Hogarth Press.

Edel, L. (1961), The Biographer and Psychoanalysis. *Int. J. Psycho-Anal.*, 42:458-466.

Eidelberg, L. (1957), An Introduction to the Study of Narcissistic Mortification. *Psychiatric Quart.*, 31:657-668.

Eissler, K. R. (1943), Limitations to the Psychotherapy of Schizophrenia. *Psychiatry*, 6:381-391.

Eissler, K. R. (1953), Ego Structure and Analytic Technique. *J. Am. Psychoanal. Assoc.*, 1:104-143.

English, O. S. (1953), The Essentials of Psychotherapy as Viewed by the Psychoanalyst. A Panel Report. *J. Am. Psychoanal. Assoc.*, 1:550-561.

Erikson, E. (1959), Identity and the Life Cycle. *Psychological Issues*, 1 (1):18-166. New York: International Universities Press.

Fairbairn, W. R. D. (1946), Object Relationships and Dynamic Structure. *Int. J. Psycho-Anal.*, 27:30-37.

Federn, P. (1928), Narcissism in the Structure of the Ego. *Int. J. Psycho-Anal.*, 9:401-419.

Fenichel, O. (1928), The Dread of Being Eaten. *Collected Papers*, 1:158-159. New York: Norton, 1953.

Fenichel, O. (1931), Specific Forms of the Oedipus Complex. *Collected Papers*, 1:204-220. New York: Norton, 1953.

Fenichel, O. (1932), Outline of Clinical Psychoanalysis. *Psychoanal. Quart.*, 1:292-315.

Fenichel, O. (1937), The Concept of Trauma in Contemporary Psychoanalytical Theory. *Collected Papers*, 2:49-69. New York: Norton, 1954.

Fenichel, O. (1938), On Masturbation. *Collected Papers*, 2:81-88. New York: Norton, 1954.

Fenichel, O. (1939), The Counter-Phobic Attitude. *Collected Papers*, 2:163-173. New York: Norton, 1954.

Fenichel, O. (1944), Remarks on the Common Phobias. *Collected Papers*, 2:278-287. New York: Norton, 1954.

Fenichel, O. (1945), *The Psychoanalytic Theory of Neurosis*. New York: Norton.

Freud, A. (1936), The Ego and the Mechanisms of Defence. New York: International Universities Press, 1946.

Freud, A. (1960), A Discussion of Bowlby's Paper, Grief and Mourning in Infancy and Early Childhood. *The Psychoanalytic Study of the Child*, 15:53-62. New York: International Universities Press.

Freud, S. (1894), The Justification for Detaching from Neurasthenia a Particular Syndrome: The Anxiety-Neurosis. *Collected Papers*, 1:76-106. London: Hogarth Press, 1950.

Freud, S. (1895), Obsessions and Phobias: Their Psychical Mechanisms and their Aetiology. *Collected Papers*, 1:128-137. London: Hogarth Press, 1950.

Freud, S. (1896), The Aetiology of Hysteria. *Collected Papers*, 1:183-219. London: Hogarth Press, 1950.

Freud, S. (1899), Screen Memories. *Collected Papers*, 5:47-69. London: Hogarth Press, 1950.

Freud, S. (1908), Hysterical Fantasies and their Relation to Bisexuality. *Collected Papers*, 2:51-58. London: Hogarth Press, 1948.

Freud, S. (1909a), General Remarks on Hysterical Attacks. *Collected Papers*, 2:100-104. London: Hogarth Press, 1948.

Freud, S. (1909b), Analysis of a Phobia in a Five-Year-Old Boy. *Collected Papers*, 3:149-289. London: Hogarth Press, 1955.

Freud, S. (1914), On Narcissism: An Introduction. *Standard Edition*, 14:73-102. London: Hogarth Press, 1957.

Freud, S. (1924), The Passing of the Oedipus Complex. *Int. J. Psycho-Anal.*, 5:419-424.

Freud, S. (1926), Inhibitions, Symptoms and Anxiety. *Standard Edition*, 20:75-174. London: Hogarth Press, 1959.

Freud, S. (1937), Analysis Terminable and Interminable. *Collected Papers*, 5:316-357. London: Hogarth Press, 1950.

Freud, S. (1938), Splitting of the Ego in the Defensive Process. *Collected Papers*, 5:372-375. London: Hogarth Press, 1950.

Friedman, H. (1952), Perceptual Regression in Schizophrenia—an Hypothesis Suggested by the Use of the Rorschach Test. *J. Gen. Psychol.*, 81:63-98.

Fromm-Reichmann, F. (1943), Psychoanalytic Psychotherapy with Psychotics. *Psychiatry*, 6:277-279.

Fromm-Reichmann, F. (1950), *Principles of Intensive Pychotherapy*. Chicago: University of Chicago Press.

Fromm-Reichmann, F. (1954), Psychoanalysis and General Dynamic Conceptions of Theory and of Therapy—Differences and Similarities. *J. Am. Psychoanal. Assoc.*, 2:711-721.

Gero, G. (1936), The Construction of Depression. *Int. J. Psycho-Anal.*, 17:423-461.

Gill, M. M. (1954), Psychoanalysis and Exploratory Psychotherapy. *J. Am. Psychoanal. Assoc.*, 2:771-797.

Glover, E. (1929), The Screening Function of Traumatic Memories. *Int. J. Psycho-Anal.*, 10:90-93.

Glover, E. (1930), Grades of Ego Differentiation. *Int. J. Psycho-Anal.*, 11:1-11.

Glover, E. (1955), *The Technique of Psychoanalysis*, pp. 165-258. London: Baillère, Tindall and Cox.

Glover, E. (1960), Psychoanalysis and Psychotherapy. *Brit. J. Med. Psych.*, 33:73-82.

Greenacre, P. (1941), The Predisposition to Anxiety. *Psychoanal. Quart.*, 10:66-94.

Greenacre, P. (1949), A Contribution to the Study of Screen Memories. *The Psychoanalytic Study of the Child*, 3/4:73-84. New York: International Universities Press.

Greenacre, P. (1952), The Predisposition to Anxiety. *Trauma, Growth and Personality*, pp. 27-82. New York: Norton.

Greenson, R. R. (1958), On Screen Defenses, Screen Hunger and Screen Identity. *J. Am. Psychoanal. Assoc.*, 6:242-262.

Greenson, R. R. (1959), Phobia, Anxiety and Depression. *J. Am. Psychoanal. Assoc.*, 7:665-674.

Hartmann, H. and Kris, E. (1945), The Genetic Approach in Psychoanalysis. *The Psychoanalytic Study of the Child*, 1:11-30. New York: International Universities Press.

Henderson, W. F. and Smyth, G. Y. (1948), Phantom Limb. *J. Neurol., Neurosurg. and Psychiat.*, 11:88-112.

Hendrick, I. (1935), Ego Development and Certain Character Problems. *Psychoanal. Quart.*, 5:320-346.

Hendrick, I. (1942), Instinct and Ego during Infancy. *Psychoanal. Quart.*, 11:33-58.

Hendrick, I. (1951), Early Development of the Ego. *Psychoanal. Quart.*, 20:44-61.
Hoffer, W. (1950), Development of the Body Ego. *The Psychoanalytic Study of the Child*, 5:18-23. New York: International Universities Press.
Jacobson, E. (1943), Depression, the Oedipus Complex in the Development of Depressive Mechanisms. *Psychoanal. Quart.*, 12:541-560.
Jacobson, E. (1954), Transference Problems with Depressives. *J. Am. Psychoanal. Assoc.*, 2:595-606.
Jacobson, E. (1957), Denial and Repression. *J. Am. Psychoanal. Assoc.*, 5:61-92.
Katan, A. (1951), The Role of Displacement in Agoraphobia. *Int. J. Psycho-Anal.*, 32:41-50.
Knight, R. P. (1946), Psychotherapy of an Adolescent Catatonic Schizophrenic with Mutism. *Psychiatry*, 9:323-339.
Knight, R. P. (1949), A Critique of Present Status of the Therapies. *Cincinnati J. Med.*, 30:482-487.
Knight, R. P. (1953a), Management and Psychotherapy of the Borderline Schizophrenic Patient. *Bull. Menninger Clinic*, 17:139-150.
Knight, R. P. (1953b), Borderline States. *Bull. Menninger Clinic*, 17:1-12.
Kris, E. (1951), Some Comments and Observations on Early Autoerotic Activities. *The Psychoanalytic Study of the Child*, 6:93-116. New York: International Universities Press.
Kris, E. (1955), Recovery of Childhood Memories in Psychoanalysis. Meeting of the American Psychoanalytic Association, New York City, December 4.
Kris, E. (1956), The Personal Myth. *J. Am. Psychoanal. Assoc.*, 4:653-681.
La Forge, M. (1927), Scotomization in Schizophrenia. *Int. J. Psycho-Anal.*, 8:473-478.
Lampl-de Groot, J. (1950), On Masturbation and its Influence on General Development. *The Psychoanalytic Study of the Child*, 5:153-174. New York: International Universities Press.
Lewin, B. (1933), The Body as a Phallus. *Psychoanal. Quart.*, 2:24-47.
Lewin, B. (1935), Claustrophobia. *Psychoanal. Quart.*, 4:227-233.
Lewin, B. (1952), Phobic Symptoms and Dream Interpretation. *Psychoanal. Quart.*, 21:295-321.
Linn, L. (1953), The Role of Perception in the Mechanism of Denial. *J. Am. Psychoanal. Assoc.*, 1:690-705.
Loewenstein, R. M. (1950), Conflict and Autonomous Ego Development During the Phallic Phase. *The Psychoanalytic Study of the Child*, 5:47-52. New York: International Universities Press.
Loewenstein, R. M. (1963), Some Considerations on Free Association. *J. Am. Psychoanal. Assoc.*, 3:451-573.
Ludwig, A. O. (1954), Psychoanalysis and Psychotherapy—Dynamic Criteria for Treatment Choice. A Panel Report. *J. Am. Psychoanal. Assoc.*, 2:346-350.
Marmor, J. (1953), Orality in the Hysterical Personality. *J. Am. Psychoanal. Assoc.*, 1:656-671.
Murphy, W. F. (1952), Evaluation of Psychotherapy with Modified Rorschach Techniques. *Amer. J. Psychotherapy*, 6:471-483.
Murphy, W. F. (1953), Psychosomatic Disorders in the Service. *U. S. Armed Forces Med. J.*, 4:1003-1009.
Murphy, W. F. (1957), Some Clinical Aspects of the Body Ego. *Psychoanal. Rev.*, 44:462-477.
Murphy, W. F. (1958a), Character, Trauma and Sensory Perception. *Int. J. Psycho-Anal.*, 39:555-568.
Murphy, W. F. (1958b), A Comparison of Psychoanalysis with the Dynamic Psychotherapies. *J. Nerv. & Ment. Dis.*, 126:441-450.
Murphy, W. F. (1959), Ego Integration, Trauma and Insight. *Psychoanal. Quart.*, 28:514-532.

Murphy, W. F. (1961), A Note on Trauma and Loss. *J. Am. Psychoanal. Assoc.,* 9:519-532.

Murphy, W. F. and Chasen, M. (1956), Spasmodic Torticollis. *Psychoanal. Rev.,* 43:18-30.

Murphy, W. F. and Kligerman, S. (1950), The Associative Anamnesis in Teaching Insight Psychotherapy. *J. Nerv. & Ment. Dis.,* 11:2-8.

Murphy, W. F. and Weinreb, J. (1948), Problems in Teaching Short Term Psychotherapy. *J. Nerv. & Ment. Dis.,* 9:1-4.

Murray, J. M. (1961), On the Transformation of Narcissism into Ego Ideal. Meeting of the International Psychoanalytic Association, Edinburgh, Scotland.

Nunberg, H. (1955), *Principles of Psychoanalysis,* pp. 322-323. New York: International Universities Press.

Nunberg, H. (1961), *Problems of Therapy in Practice and Theory of Psychoanalysis,* 1:105-119. New York: International Universities Press.

Orr, O. W. (1954), Transference and Countertransference. *J. Am. Psychoanal. Assoc.,* 2:621-670.

Osmond, H. (1962), Letter in Amplification. *Med. Sci.,* 11:207-208.

Payne, S. M. (1946), Notes on Developments in the Theory and Practice of Psychoanalytic Technique. *Int. J. Psycho-Anal.,* 27:12-18.

Pfeffer, A. Z. (1959), A Procedure for Evaluating the Results of Psychoanalysis. *J. Am. Psychoanal. Assoc.,* 7:418-444.

Rado, S. (1933), Fear of Castration in Women. *Psychoanal. Quart.,* 2:425-475.

Rangell, L. (1954), Psychoanalysis and Dynamic Psychotherapy—Similarities and Differences. *J. Am. Psychoanal. Assoc.,* 2:734-744.

Rank, B. (1949), Children with Atypical Development. *Am. J. Orthopsychiatry,* 19:130-139.

Reich, A. (1951), The Discussions of 1912 on Masturbation and our Present-day Views. *The Psychoanalytic Study of the Child,* 6:80-94. New York: International Universities Press.

Reider, N. (1960), Percept as a Screen. *J. Am. Psychoanal. Assoc.,* 8-82-99.

Reznikoff, M. and Toomey, L. C. (1959), *Evaluation of Changes Associated with Psychiatric Treatment,* pp. 3-99. Springfield, Ill.: Charles C Thomas.

Rochlin, G. (1953), Loss and Restitution. *The Psychoanalytic Study of the Child,* 8:288-309. New York: International Universities Press.

Ruddick, B. (1961), Agoraphobia. *Int. J. Psycho-Anal.,* 42:537-543.

Schmideberg, M. (1933), Some Unconscious Mechanisms in Pathological Sexuality and their Relation to Normal Sexual Activity. *Int. J. Psycho-Anal.,* 14:225-260.

Schmideberg, M. (1947), The Treatment of Psychopaths and Borderline Patients. *Am. J. Psychotherapy,* 1:45-71.

Searl, N. (1929a), Danger Situations of the Immature Ego. *Int. J. Psycho-Anal.,* 10:432-435.

Searl, N. (1929b), The Flight to Reality. *Int. J. Psycho-Anal.,* 10:280-291.

Siegel, E. (1951), *Genetic Parallels in Perceptual Structuralization in Paranoid Schizophrenia: An Analysis by Means of the Rorschach Technique.* Dissertation, Clark University, Worcester, Massachusetts.

Spiegel, L. A. (1954), Acting Out and Defensive Instinctual Gratification. *J. Am. Psychoanal. Assoc.,* 2:107-119.

Spitz, R. A. (1945), Hospitalism. *The Psychoanalytic Study of the Child,* 1:53-74. New York: International Universities Press.

Spitz, R. A. (1946), Anaclitic Depression. *The Psychoanalytic Study of the Child,* 2:313-342. New York: International Universities Press.

Spitz, R. A. (1957), *No and Yes,* pp. 117-150. New York: International Universities Press.

Starcke, A. (1921), The Castration Complex. *Int. J. Psycho-Anal.*, 2:179-201.

Stengel, E. (1939), Studies on the Psychopathology of Compulsive Wandering. *Brit. J. Med. Psychol.*, 18:250-254.

Stone, L. (1951), Psychoanalysis and Brief Psychotherapy. *Psychoanal. Quart.*, 20:215-236.

Stone, L. (1954), The Widening Scope of Indications for Psychoanalysis. *J. Am. Psychoanal. Assoc.*, 2:567-594.

Szasz, T. S. (1954), A Psychoanalytic Theory of Phantom Body Parts and Phantom Pain. Meeting of the American Psychoanalytic Association, Detroit.

Szasz, T. S. (1955), The Ego, the Body and Pain. *J. Am. Psychoanal. Assoc.*, 3:177-200.

Waelder, R. (1925), The Psychoses: their Mechanisms and Accessibility to Influence. *Int. J. Psycho-Anal.*, 6:259-281.

Waelder, R. (1936), The Principle of Multiple Function. *Psychoanal. Quart.*, 5:45-62.

Waelder, R. (1962), Psychoanalysis, Scientific Method, and Philosophy. *J. Am. Psychoanal. Assoc.*, 10:617-636.

Wangh, M. (1959), Structural Determinants of Phobia. *J. Am. Psychoanal. Assoc.*, 7:675-695.

Weigert, E. (1954), The Importance of Flexibility in Psychoanalytic Technique. *J. Am. Psychoanal. Assoc.*, 2:702-710.

Weiss, E. (1933), A Recovery from the Fear of Blushing. *Psychoanal. Quart.*, 2:309-314.

Weiss, E. (1934), Bodily Pain and Mental Pain. *Int. J. Psycho-Anal.*, 15:1-6.

Weiss, E. (1935), Agoraphobia and its Relation to Hysterical Attacks and to Traumas. *Int. J. Psycho-Anal.*, 16:59-83.

Weiss, E. (1944), Clinical Aspects of Depression. *Psychoanal. Quart.*, 13:445-461.

Whitehorn, J. C. (1961), The Doctor's Image of Man. *N. E. J. Med.*, 265:302-309.

Wren-Lewis, J. (1960), Stuff and Science. *The BBC Listener*, 64:623-624.

Zetzel, E. R. (1953), The Traditional Psychoanalytic Technique and its Variations. *J. Am. Psychoanal. Assoc.*, 1:526-537.

Ziman, J. (1960), Science is Social. *The BBC Listener*, 64:251-252.

INDEX

619